AF342139

The Power of Color

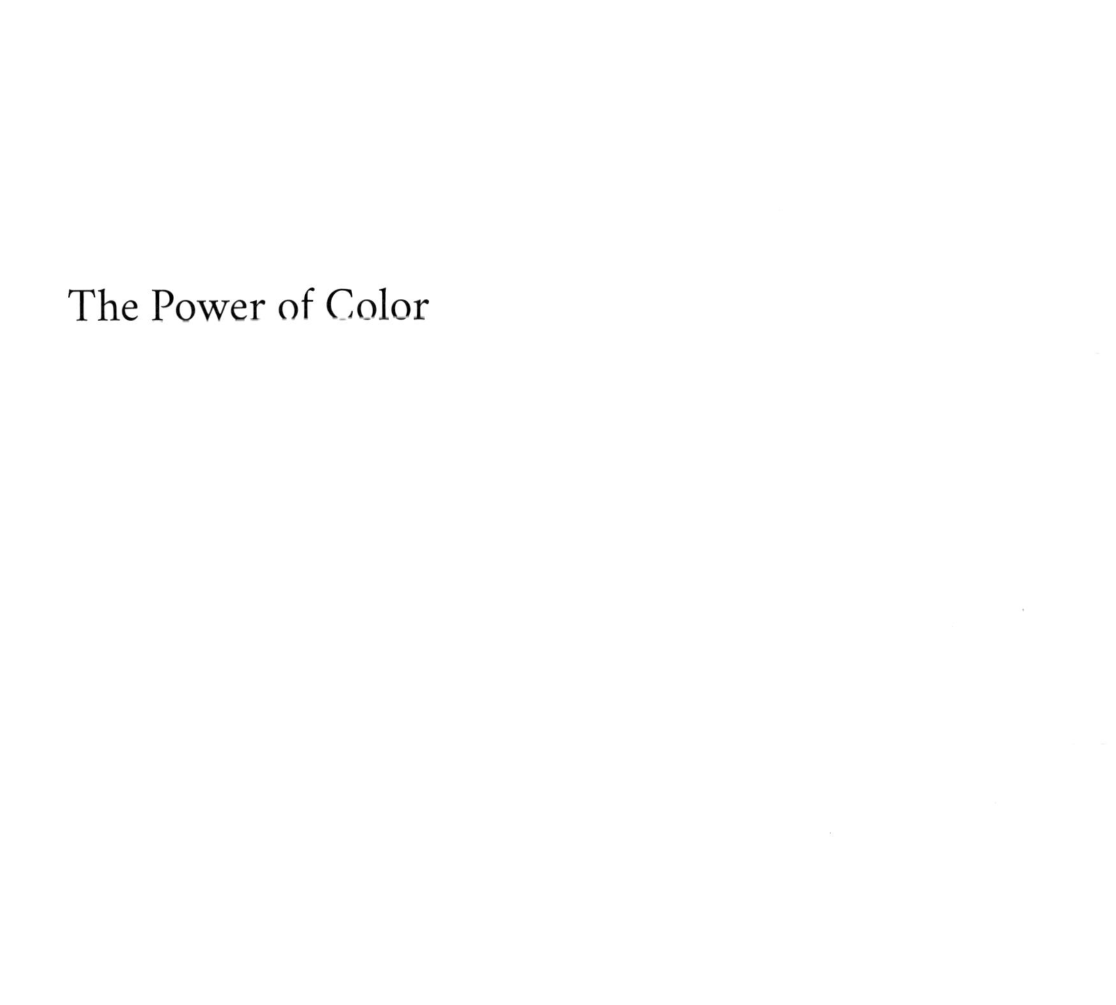

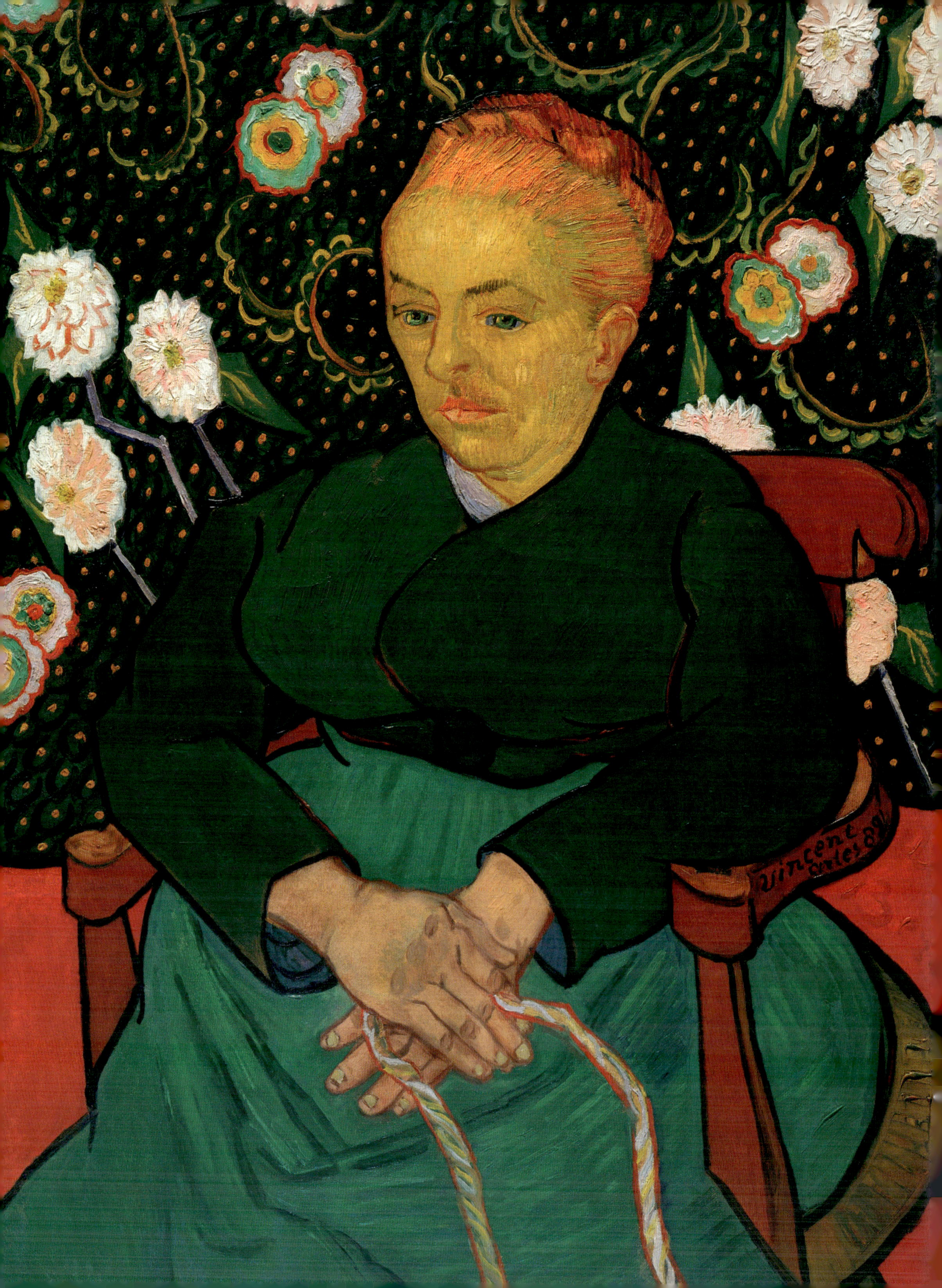

Vincent
arles 89

The Power of Color

Five Centuries of European Painting

Marcia B. Hall

Yale University Press   New Haven and London

Published with assistance from the Nancy Batson Nisbet Rash Publication Fund.

yalebooks.com/art

Designed by Leslie Fitch and Chris Crochetière
Set in Crimson and Source Sans Pro type by BW&A Books, Inc.
Printed in China by Regent Publishing Services Limited

Library of Congress Control Number: 2018946044
ISBN 978-0-300-23719-1

A catalogue record for this book is available from the British Library.

This paper meets the requirements of ANSI/NISO Z39.48-1992 (Permanence of Paper).

10 9 8 7 6 5 4 3 2 1

Cover illustrations: (front) Paul Gauguin, *Day of the God (Mahana No Atua)*, fig. 6.3 detail; (back) Sandro Botticelli, *Bardi Altarpiece*, fig. 1.32 detail
Frontispiece: Vincent van Gogh, *Le Berceuse (The Lullaby)*, fig. 6.7 detail

For my dear grandsons,
Benjamin Carter and Daniel Charles

Contents

Acknowledgments

This book has taken a scholarly lifetime to conceive, but its present form has been given shape in the past five years with the aid of Temple University and many generous people. A grant from Temple's Humanities and Arts Program Award defrayed the cost of images and permissions, and a sabbatical leave in 2016–17 provided me with the free time to write. I want to thank the students in my seminars in 2014, 2015, 2016, and 2017, who discussed the sources and literature and who eventually read chapters and commented on them. The library at the Center for Advanced Study in the Visual Arts, with the help of the wonderfully accommodating staff, served my research needs.

The writing has taken place over the past two years assisted crucially by many kind, smart people. I have appealed to conservation scientists and curators Barbara Berrie, Jill Dunkerton, Melanie Gifford, Micha Leeflang, Marika Spring, and Carl Strehlke shamelessly for help, as I have to those rare art historians who are knowledgeable about materials: Molly Faries, Andrea Kirsh, and Louisa Matthew. I have prevailed upon patient colleagues to read and advise me about chapters where their expertise is much greater than mine: Paul Barolsky, Therese Dolan, Estelle Lingo, Peter Lukehart, Gerald Silk, Larry Silver, William Wallace, and Robert Williams. Colleagues both at Temple and elsewhere have answered my questions, helped with images, and given me support: Costanza Barbieri, Tracy Cooper, Una d'Elia, Jill Luedke, Lorenzo Pericolo, and Ashley West. Friends and students—former and present—have listened and read and commented: Sarah Barton, Ellen Gayda, Laurie Glover, Gilles Heno-Coe, and Timothy Temple. I particularly want to thank four of my present graduate students at Temple who have worked as my research assistant, sharing their knowledge of bibliography and their digitizing and editorial skills: Bethany Farrell, Tiffany Hunt, Megan Reddick, and, in the proofs stage, Jessica Anders. Among my valued friends I count two editors, whose advice I particularly esteem, Gillian Malpass and Beatrice Rehl. I add my present editor, Amy Canonico, who has been a wonderfully helpful counselor in shaping the final form of this manuscript. Also at Yale I thank Raychel Rapazza, who can answer any question, and always with cheerful goodwill, and Patricia Fidler, who first expressed interest in this book.

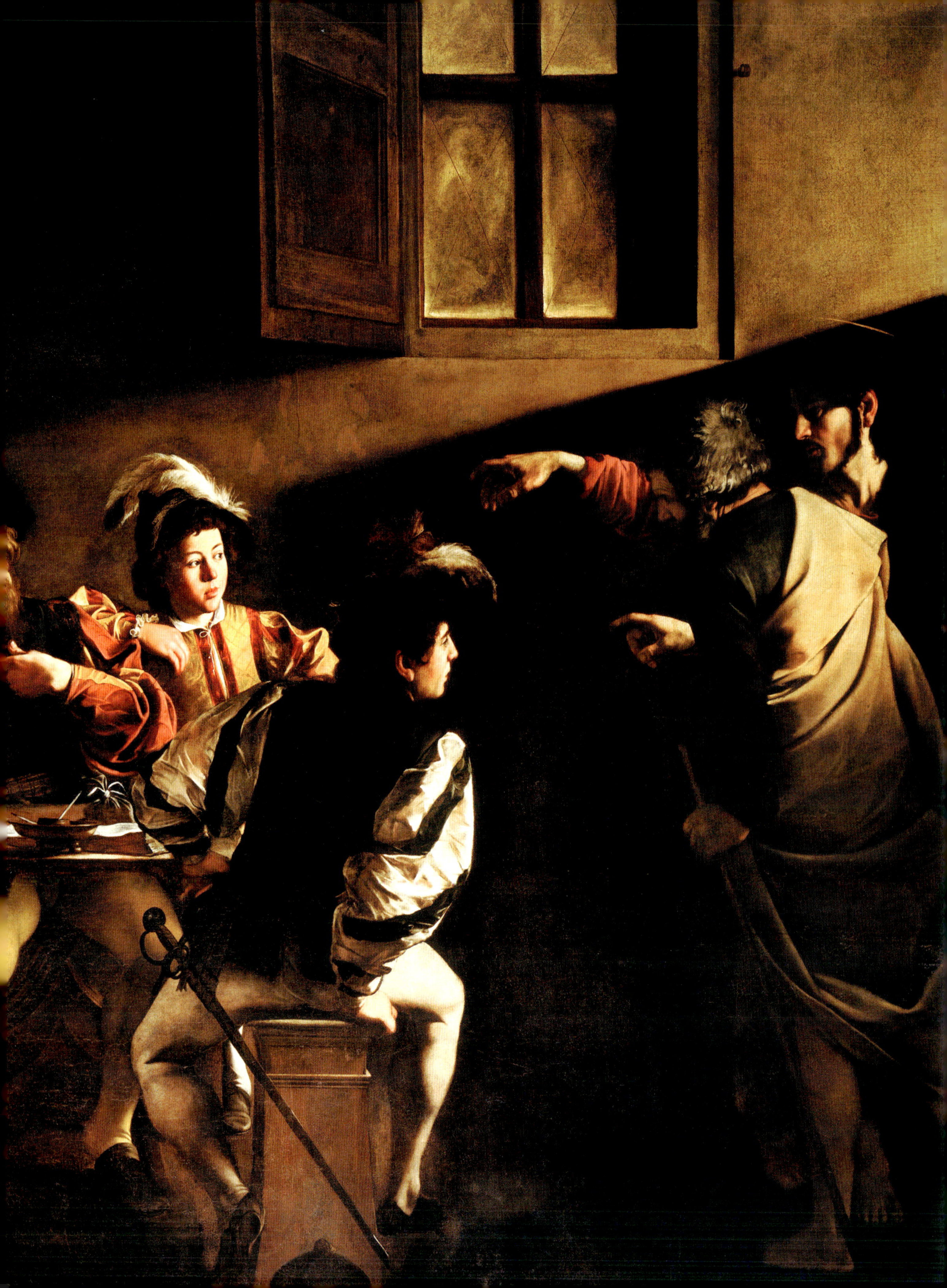

Introduction

Making, Materials, Marketing, Meaning

Contemporary artists often help us understand how their work is made by revealing their creative process. But this was not always the case, and it can be difficult to reconstruct how a painting was made centuries ago by just looking at it. Other painters could always use their experience to speculate, but it is only with the advent of scientific examination in the twentieth century that we can peep behind the surface and investigate the painter's process of creation. This book is about how pictures come to look the way they do, and what color can tell us about how painters used their materials; what those materials were; what influenced their choices of what to make and how to make it, such as who would buy it and for how much; and how all that affects what their pictures mean.

Numerous other influences have impacted the materials, making, marketing, and meaning of painting across the five centuries that I cover in this book: institutions designed to regulate artists, such as guilds and academies; ecclesiastical and state agencies with money to commission or buy outright; the demands of running a workshop; dealers. Harder to fix but just as real are traditional templates, codes of decorum, and the willingness of the culture to allow the artist's personal expression. These social and political factors loomed much larger before the present era, when artists answer first to themselves. Reconstructing the artists' world with all these variables helps us see their products with more appreciative eyes. Scientific studies, most often made in connection with paintings' conservation, can contribute to that reconstruction.

The role of conservation and the science associated with it has been expanding in the past generation. To the public in the United States, conservation has been a subject of mystery and low interest—although YouTube is helping to give it more prominence. The public in Italy has long been conservation-literate (there is a page in the daily newspaper in Florence dedicated to recent conservation news), but in the English-speaking world, only the most sensational, and often negative, stories catch public attention. The cleaning of Michelangelo's Sistine Chapel ceiling was such a story.

The restoration campaign created headlines in the 1980s when it was attacked for damaging the frescoes, whose color appeared to have been radically altered by the cleaning process. The contention was that the solvent, in use then for about twenty years, was removing more than the dirt, caused chiefly by centuries of burning candles and oil lamps in the chapel. One critic argued that Michelangelo had used a final layer (*l'ultima mano*) of glue mixed with carbon black to tone down the colors and to darken the shadows; this final layer, it was asserted, was removed in the restoration along with the accumulated dirt.[1] A painter adding such a layer had no precedents and no subsequent applications in the history of fresco painting.

The role of the scientist in conservation is clearly exemplified in the Sistine case. The grime on the ceiling was first analyzed chemically. Previous restoration campaigns were researched in the archives and the nature of previous interventions was studied. It was determined that varnish and glue had been used repeatedly to freshen the color and had then over time discolored. Restorers had strengthened the chiaroscuro where details had become obscure. The new solvent was tested, first in small patches, then on an entire fresco in the chapel, and it was found to remove the grime successfully.[2]

There are lessons to be drawn from this episode. We need to be better informed. We need to know both what standard artistic practice was at the time the work was created and what Michelangelo's personal style of coloring looked like. If these had been understood, the controversy would not have found legs. The problem for the restoration was that no one was prepared for what they found beneath the grime: Michelangelo's radical innovation of a new color mode. As will become clear in the chapters that follow, Michelangelo created a variant on fresco coloring that was designed to answer the demands of the site and the subject matter of the cycle. But he had given a clear hint of what was to come a few years earlier. He experimented with this color style in his easel painting, *The Doni Holy Family* (fig. o.1). The contrasts of large fields of brilliant color are not what we had come to expect from the era of Leonardo da Vinci and Raphael. But the color mode Michelangelo invented, which is called *cangiantismo* (from the Italian *cangiare*, "to change"), was not unprecedented. It had been described and used in the Quattrocento, just not on Michelangelo's scale. Successors copied it from him and continued to use it throughout the Cinquecento. Although there are still a few die-hards today who continue to reiterate the criticisms, the controversy has on the whole been resolved and the restoration accepted as what the Vatican claims:

the unveiling of Michelangelo's extraordinary, unexpected, original coloring.

The role of restoration was previously restricted to revealing the painting free of dirt and overzealous inpainting by previous restorers. Assessment of quality, authorship, and authenticity was the domain of an elite corps of self-styled connoisseurs who exercised their experience and judgment to solve these problems. An affidavit of authenticity from such an authority is still often an essential credential for selling a work of art at Christie's or Sotheby's. Today scientific studies can add crucial information, especially in judging the all-important questions of condition and quality, so connoisseurship, which has fallen into disfavor, is being replaced by science. Nothing of course will ever fully replace human judgment, but the contribution of scientific studies can augment it.

In order to assess the condition of a painting and to identify repaintings, the conservator needs to know a number of things, including what pigments were used. Information about pigments is of course of great interest to an art historian like me who is studying coloring, but the problem until recently was that the principal means of identifying a pigment was to remove a minute sample of the paint and analyze it under a microscope. Conservators were understandably reluctant to make holes in a Rembrandt or a Raphael, so sampling was done only on an as-needed basis. For the art historian—no more anxious to whittle away at the paint surface of an irreplaceable masterpiece than the conservator, of course—this could be frustrating. But recent nondestructive means of identifying pigments have come to the rescue.[3] Organic materials remain more elusive, but now we can know much more about which pigments have been used.

A WIDER APPLICATION OF CONSERVATION STUDIES

The results of scientific examinations of art are finding applications beyond the conservation laboratory. Although only the wealthiest institutions can support pure research not generated by the immediate practical needs associated with a restoration project, the contribution it can make to the history of art is being recognized. I have made use of studies conducted in conservation laboratories to tell us about painters' practices. The application of science to the study of art has burgeoned since the first use of x-ray in the late nineteenth century. Spin-offs

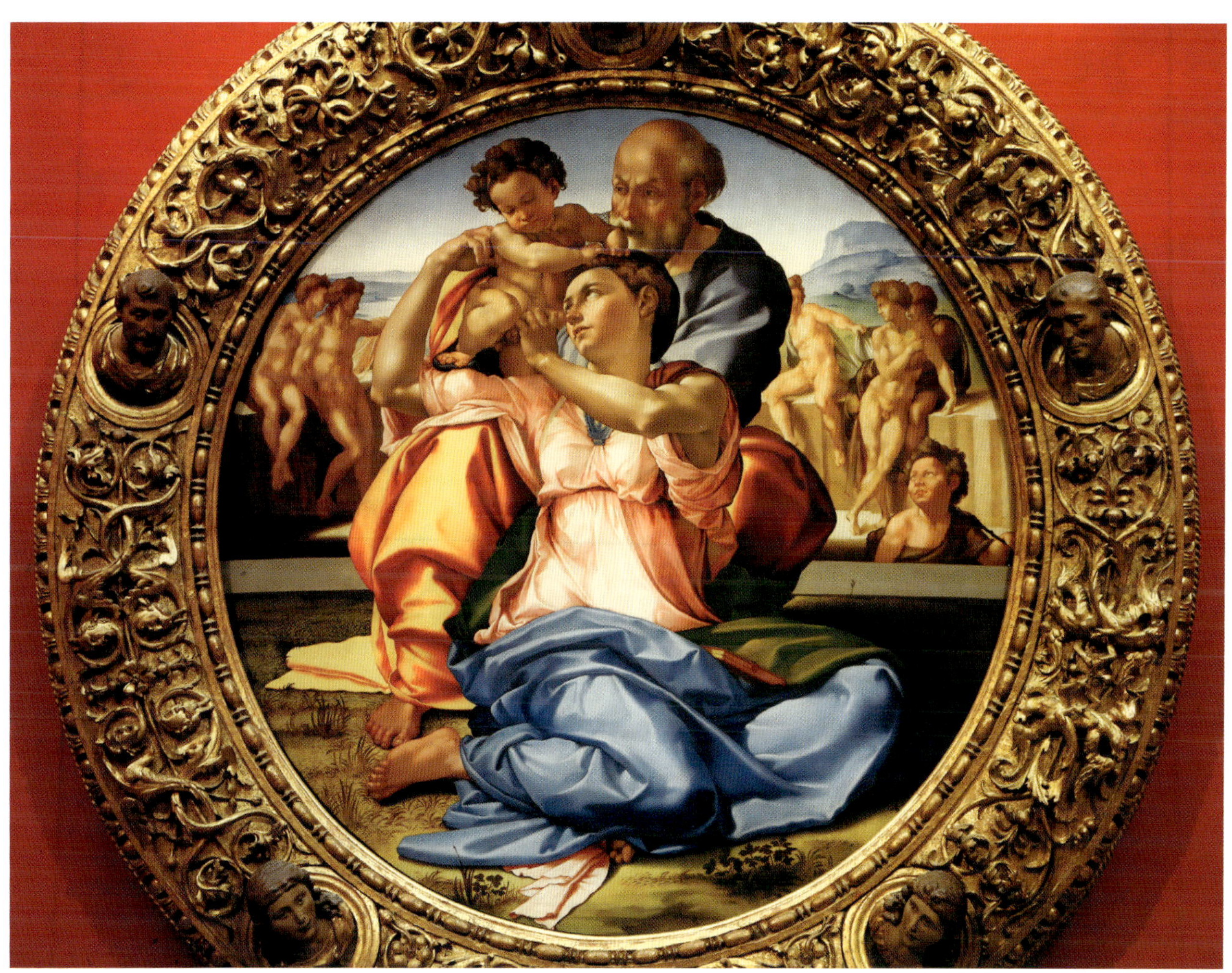

FIG. 0.1. Michelangelo, *The Doni Holy Family*, c. 1507. Oil and tempera on panel, 47½ in. (120 cm) diam. Uffizi, Florence.

of military and space age technologies since then have steadily added to the arsenal of investigative tools available to art scientists. Initially, conservation scientists published their findings only for other professionals, but at just about the same time I became interested in this literature, they went public. In 1977 the National Gallery in London published its first *Technical Bulletin,* designed to bring conservation information to the lay public, and other publications followed such as the *Bulletin* of the Hamilton Kerr Institute (1988–) and *Techné.* In 2013 the National Gallery of Art in Washington, D.C., produced its elegant journal *Facture* as part of an effort to increase conservation interest and literacy in the United States.

Now conservation science can identify not only the pigments, but also the layer structure, and with the help of infrared reflectography we can have images of the underdrawing, a stage in the preparation seen only briefly by the master and his workshop assistants before they concealed it beneath the paint. Of particular interest to us is the revelation of the priming, the tinted layer just below the paint, called *imprimatura.* The history of the tinted imprimatura has not been written before now because it could not be studied.[4] An invention of sixteenth-century painters, it was used in changing form until the mid-nineteenth century, when the Impressionists banished the tint and returned to painting on the white canvas. The imprimatura was a thin layer used to isolate the oil paint from the absorbent gesso or chalk preparation. Gradually it was discovered that it could be tinted and used as an expressive device to affect the painting's tonality, giving it a unity and creating an atmosphere.

Scholarly attention is being drawn increasingly to the role of replicas, variants, and copies. In the era of connoisseurship only the original was given high regard, despite the fact that in the past many collectors, including kings, princes, archdukes, archbishops, and the like, were often quite satisfied with a good copy. In Spain in the sixteenth century, when all things Italian were prized, a copy of a Titian was valued at more than three times that of a royal portrait by the esteemed Vincente Carducho, royal painter to the king. In fact, most collections were of copies rather than originals.[5] We are coming to recognize that replicas were an important part of the functioning of a workshop and were sanctioned by the master, whether or not he contributed to their execution. Scientific studies and creative use of new imaging technologies can reveal

unexpected insight into the workings of the workshop. We get hints from underdrawings hidden below the surface. When a cartoon was made (a full-scale drawing on paper), it was transferred to the support. Revisions in it suggest the hand of the master; perfunctory copying marks the work of an assistant.[6] The degree of freedom from the cartoon that the executant took can often be an index of his skill, his independence, and perhaps his status in the workshop. Of course it could also indicate that the master encouraged changes in replicas for variety or innovation.

The profession of conservation is coming to recognize that it has a place in a larger scheme. Sheila McTighe has made a plea to fellow scientists to expand the reach of what they call artistic practice. It should include such traditional art historical concerns as the painters' emulation of artistic forbears, the intellectual genesis of the paintings, painters' reflections on their craft, and the works' address to their audiences. "Scientific examinations shed light on these issues," she points out, "when they are in dialogue with other forms of research."[7]

Both art history and technical studies would benefit from a closer affiliation. It is the nature of scientific investigation to work on a case-by-case basis, and drawing broad conclusions is antithetical to scientific procedure. What is lacking in scientific studies is comparison across the centuries. As an art historian, for whom comparison is a fundamental methodology, I have no such scruples. I am undertaking here to give the long view. At the risk of oversimplifying and of being just plain wrong, I am attempting to pull threads through the fabric of these five centuries to see connections and identify innovation. What I hope emerges is an understanding of artistic practice and how it evolved, both at the individual and collective levels.

I have used the scientific literature whenever I can to reconstruct the painter's process. There are many more studies now than when I first embarked on this methodology in the 1970s. Then, there was not much known about the painters in the second half of the Quattrocento. That gap has been filled; now it is the second half of the Cinquecento in central Italy that needs attention. While the fifteenth, sixteenth, seventeenth, and nineteenth centuries are all about equally well studied, there is a huge lack of even basic information about painting in the eighteenth century. Those inequities are necessarily reflected here: whereas about one-third of my notes refer to technical studies in Chapters 1–3 and 5, in Chapter 4 that percentage is only about one-eighth.

COLOR

That said, this is not a book about conservation, or even about the scientific examination of paintings. As my title suggests, I am using the neglected but all-important lens of color to examine early modern paintings. Color is the yummy part of painting (*Color, mmmm,* as my students nicknamed this book), and the part that can be subversive, thus despised by the academicians, distrusted by stoics and ascetics, regarded as dangerously sensuous by rationalists. Tracing the reputation of color through these centuries is a fascinating roller-coaster ride. To us today, it is sometimes difficult to recognize how recently black and white still prevailed. It was the 1960s that saw the conversion to Technicolor in the movies, and in the same decade art historians converted to color slides. Educated in the 1950s and early 1960s, I remember that it was an extraordinary occasion when a color slide appeared on the screen. Art history books published before 1990 were illustrated almost entirely in black and white. Chromophobia in the academic world took the form of skepticism regarding whether we could access reliable knowledge of color. On the one hand, the modern reproduction process was disparaged. On the other hand, authorities offered sage admonitions regarding the possibility of knowing what the original color of a painting was. Now that most of the Old Master paintings in the world's museums have been cleaned and we no longer expect them to have a sedate patina of chiaroscuro from layers of dirty varnish, as our parents and grandparents did, we are seeing them more nearly as they were when they were painted. We are no longer so afraid of color. What this means, however, is that the study of color is still young, and discussion of color is still often omitted when paintings are analyzed. Better understanding of the materials of color and the procedures for using it can diminish that reluctance.

In my previous book *Color and Meaning* (1992), I developed some concepts for Renaissance painting that I am using here. In the fifteenth century the Cennini style of coloring used the pigments pure and added only white for modeling (modeling up). The Alberti style, seeking greater naturalism, used dark monochrome for the shadows and was more willing to mix pigments, at least by layering them (modeling down). For the early

sixteenth century I identified four modes of coloring that offered a choice to painters that had not existed before, such as the one Michelangelo invented and used on the Sistine ceiling.

Color and Meaning covered only the Renaissance. In this book, with its long trajectory, we need to cover a range of topics and track changes in technical procedures. I will examine developments in the making, materials, marketing, and meanings of paintings over five centuries, principally as they relate to color. *Making,* the first of the *M's,* includes techniques of preparing and painting. Before the nineteenth century, preparation was always laborious and required workshop assistance. Until commercially prepared canvases became available, the gesso had to be applied in multiple layers, each sanded and smoothed. Next came the priming (imprimatura), which could be white or off-white, or tinted. Whether rosy or gray, reddish brown or even darker, it affected the paint layers put down on top. The design was transferred to the support with the help of a *sinopia,* preliminary drawings, cartoons, and underdrawings, as appropriate. The application of paint moved from a meticulous process in egg tempera using small brushes and invisible strokes, to the spectrum of techniques made possible by oil, which could be varied in viscosity and in texture.[8] It could be applied pure in a single application, or layered, or physically mixed on the palette, or painted wet-in-wet, with small brushes or large. The training of the painter and the functioning of the workshop are crucial throughout our period until the mid-nineteenth century.

By *Materials* I mean the supports—wooden panel, canvas, or wall; the binders—egg, oil, or water; the pigments and dyes—mineral, earth, or organic; and the brushes, made from animal hair, which were initially made in the workshop. Cennini, writing around the end of the fourteenth century, prescribed the hair of the squirrel's tail (*vair*) or pig bristle as the only suitable brushes for use with the aqueous material of egg tempera.[9] Eventually, trained craftsmen carefully bound the bristles to the brushes and sold them in shops. A very cold winter in Siberia produced the long hair for the prized sable brush, useful particularly in watercolor, but they were also the brushes preferred by Gauguin, who declared: "When you use ordinary brushes, two neighboring colors mix. With sables, you obtain colors in juxtaposition."[10] Once the production of brushes moved to the factory, a range of shapes was offered and painters could select according to their needs. In order to obtain a broad stroke for a wash before the metal ferule was invented, for example, the painter would squeeze the bristles in his fingers to produce a fan shape.[11] Oil painting is the primary medium studied here, though we also consider fresco. Fresco is the procedure of painting a wall while the plaster is still damp, which was especially favored in central Italy, where the stable temperature and relative aridity promoted rapid drying. It was not a practical medium in the cold North, or in humid Venice, although Venetian patricians used it to decorate their villas on the terra firma, and Tiepolo was sought out in eighteenth-century Würzburg in Bavaria to fresco in a region where the medium had not been used in the past.

The availability of the materials and their cost always needs to be factored in, but they remained surprisingly stable until the Industrial Revolution of the nineteenth century. The buyers changed, however, and their tastes influenced what the painter painted. In *Marketing*, I am interested in the part of the distribution process that affects the product. The intended audience is always uppermost in the mind of the artist. Early in our period, especially in Italy, most paintings were commissioned, although scholars are increasingly aware that a lively trade took place in replicas sold from the shop, a practice that was more widespread in the Low Countries. In Catholic countries commissioning remained strong, as it did in France, where the state regulated culture. With the rise of the middle class, most paintings were bought on spec for domestic decoration, and this practice evolved until it was the norm by the mid-nineteenth century.

The fourth *M* is *Meaning*. There is little to be gained by studying the other three *M*'s if we do not ask what the painter in the end conveys to the viewer. While excessive speculation about the artists' intention can be suspect, the choices they make are an important objective clue to what they wished to impart, which can lift that discussion out of the realm of pure subjectivity.

The story this book tells is not just of changes in materials and their use, but also of the gradual liberation of artists from their role as menial manipulators of materials, subject to the oversight of a guild or a patron, to what we see today: artists as creative and independent commentators and critics of their culture in whatever visual language they choose.

SEEING COLOR

Most people understand the concept of warm and cool color: warm colors—red, orange, and yellow—advance; cool colors—blue, green, and purple—recede. There is in fact a hierarchy of allure with which painters work that includes temperature, but also value, intensity, and size of field. High value (whitish) attracts, low value (blackish) recedes. A more brilliant (intense, saturated) tone draws the eye before a more subdued one. A large patch will attract the eye, especially if it is high in value or intensity. Matisse, who understood the importance of quantity better than anyone, is quoted as saying: "1 cm^2 of any blue is not as blue as a square meter of the same blue."[12] Other factors can be used to draw the eye, such as uneven texture and visible brushstroke. The painter performs complex balancing acts in composing with color, manipulating a touch of brilliant red against a large field of cool blue, then introducing a dazzling *cangiante* combination (a shift from one hue to another in a modeling sequence, as in the *Doni Tondo*), which because it is unexpected is highly attractive. Any ravishingly beautiful combination of colors will draw the eye and stimulate a sensuous response (though individual viewers may respond differently). Painters understood this and often embraced the sensuous pull of colors. Some, however, resisted appealing to the senses with color: the seventeenth-century painters Poussin and Charles Le Brun come to mind.

Until recently, color needed to work hand in hand with perspective. In landscapes using aerial perspective, objects in the distance confirm optical experience by shifting toward grayish blue. The objects in the planes closest to us appear brighter and more saturated. A violation of those rules can be used to compress or disrupt space with expressive impact, as the Cinquecento painters Pontormo and Rosso understood and Matisse demonstrated.

Painters tried to record the effect of light on color, even long before the Impressionists. In the early Renaissance they were satisfied to depict relief (the illusion of volume) by manipulating value, but they became increasingly interested in fixing the direction of the light source, or sources, and imitating the illusion of a coherent and consistent lighting. Vermeer, by using harmonious colors, soft shadows, lack of focus, and diffused light, gives us a serene meditation on an ordered world (fig. 0.2). Caravaggio presents a different world with his sharply

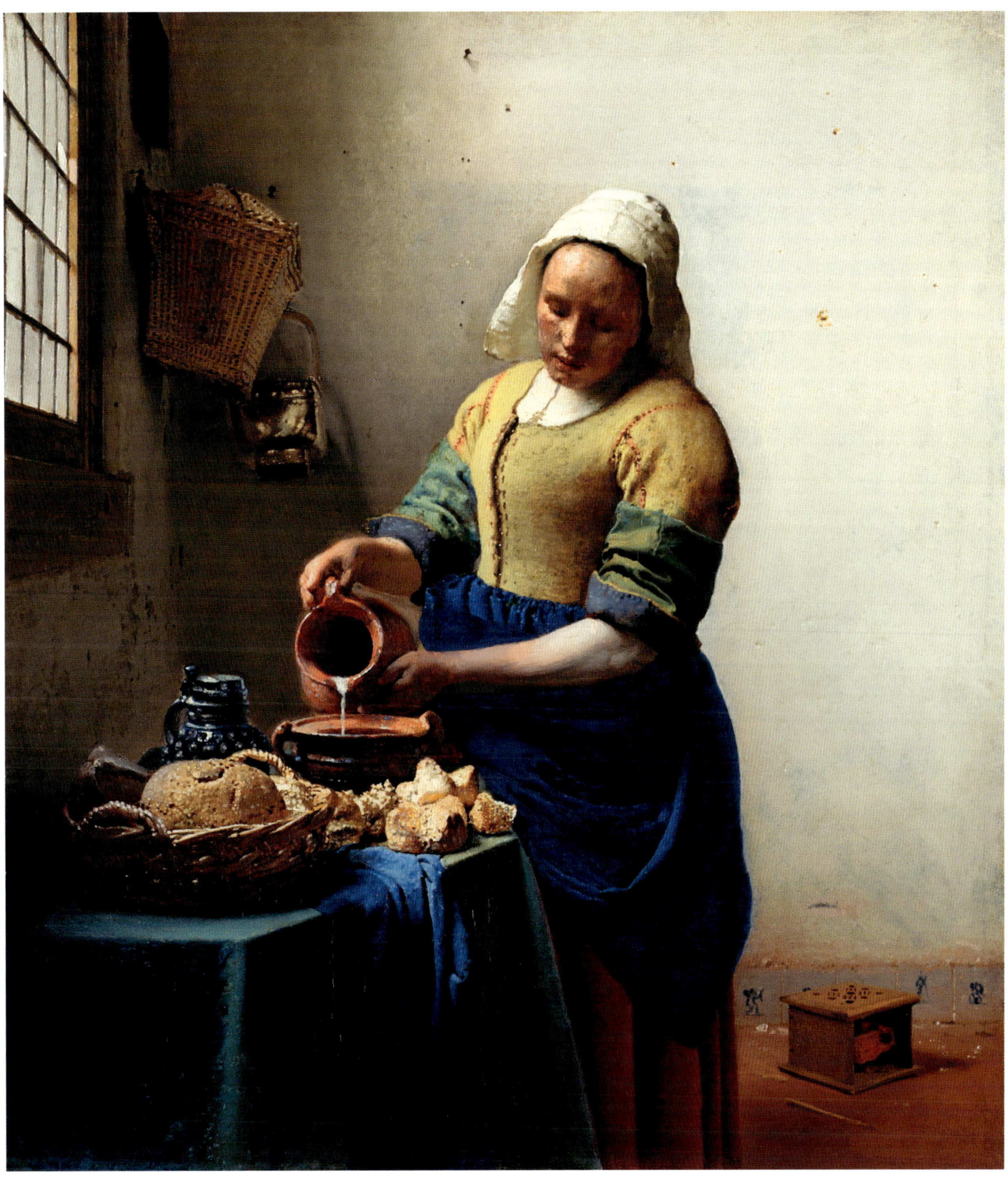

FIG. 0.2. Johannes Vermeer, *The Milkmaid*, c. 1660. Oil on canvas, 18 × 16¹⁄₈ in. (45.5 × 41 cm).
Rijksmuseum, Amsterdam.

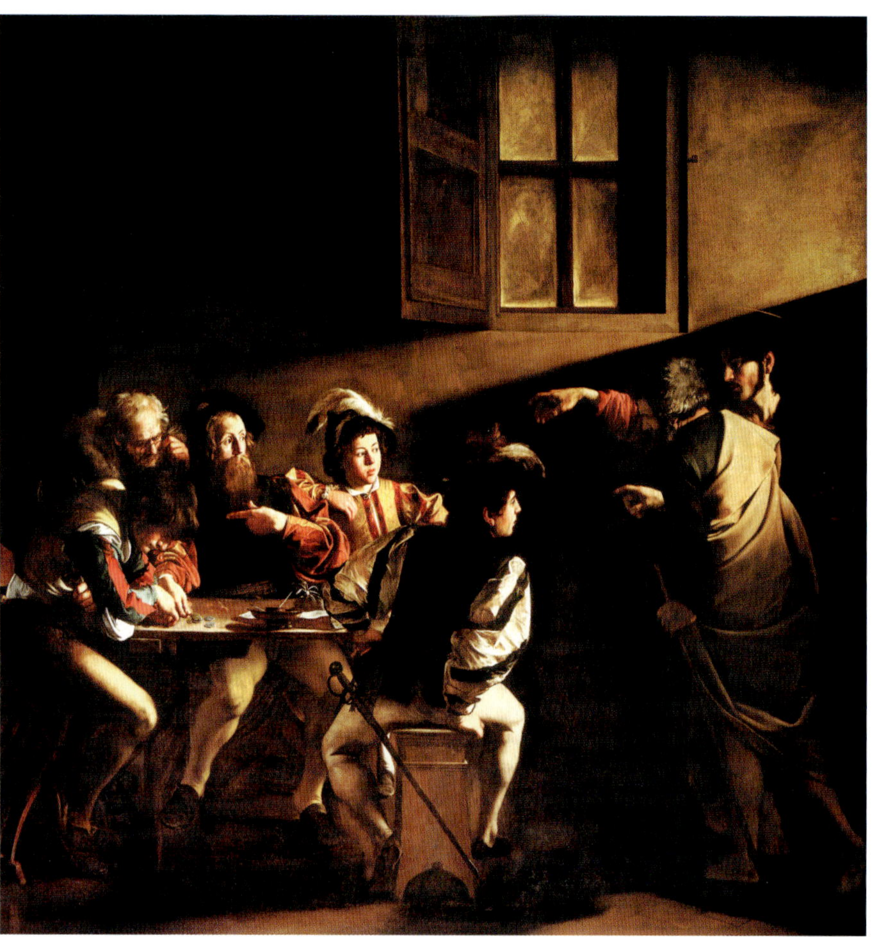

FIG. 0.3. Caravaggio, *Calling of Saint Matthew*, 1599–1600. Oil on canvas, 10 ft. 7 in. × 10 ft. 10 in. (322 × 340 cm). San Luigi dei Francesi, Rome.

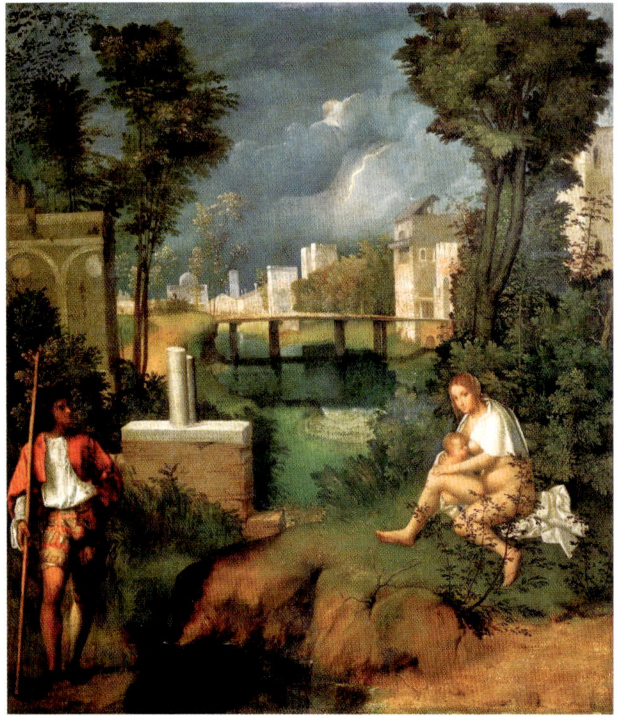

FIG. 0.4. Giorgione, *The Tempest*, c. 1508. Oil on canvas, 33 × 29 in. (83 × 73 cm). Gallerie dell'Accademia, Venice.

contrasted colors, hard edges, and dark, opaque shadows. His theatrically concealed light source suggests the presence of the supernatural invading the mundane (fig. 0.3).

Some painters depicted local color with conviction, such as Raphael or Poussin; others became enamored with capturing the accidents of light, such as weather conditions, reflections, and shiny or matte or translucent surfaces, such as Giorgione (fig. 0.4), or Van Goyen, or Monet's series on Rouen Cathedral. Some others, such as Cézanne, suppressed changes in lighting to achieve an effect of permanence. The difference is profound: whether we are shown what we know or what we see.

ORGANIZATION OF THE BOOK

Chapter 1 establishes the fifteenth century as a baseline against which we will chart changes in painting. It is a world in which artistic commissions were dominated by the Church—either by some part of the establishment or by patrons for ecclesiastical buildings—but where they would increasingly be shared with nobles for secular decorations. Civic institutions were important patrons as well. Authorized copies were available for the less affluent, or less confident, buyer, but their production was controlled by the large workshops as a secondary trade. Works were commissioned by contract between the patron and the painter, and these were very directive. The contract usually specified the subject, size, intended location, time-frame for completion, price, and payment schedule. Penalties for failure to deliver on time were sometimes spelled out; sometimes a preliminary drawing was attached; sometimes the model of an existing painting was specified, and on certain occasions the required placement of the figures. Sometimes provision was made for payment in advance for costly materials and their quality was described. Increasingly, as time went by, some of these decisions were left to the painters. By the mid-Cinquecento, painters were sometimes allowed to choose the subject.

Patrons of ecclesiastical works commissioned art both to express their piety and because it was a social obligation. Chapels provided a vault for family burials and their endowment paid for Masses the clergy were obligated to say for dead members of the family, to remit time in purgatory. As much as owning a conspicuous palace, commissioning the decorations for a family chapel ensured prestige. In Rome it was the pope who set the pace for artistic patronage, and the cardinals followed his

model. If the pope was ascetic, like the sixteenth-century Flemish Adrian VI or Pius V, the cardinals curtailed their expenditure on secular decorations and awaited a change in regime. If the pope was eager to leave his mark and enshrine his family name, like the Medici or Farnese, the cardinals took the opportunity to build and decorate their palaces and country villas.

This is the time when oil, the medium of choice throughout the period that will concern us, was first explored in Italy, replacing egg tempera there. The pigments did not change much until the revolution brought about by the invention of synthetic pigments in the nineteenth century. What did change was the way they were used. Fra Angelico's *Coronation of the Virgin* exemplifies the Quattrocento convention of using pigments in their pure, unmixed form (fig. 0.5). The blues are ultramarine, the red in the foreground on the blond saint is vermilion, the pinks are red lakes (perhaps somewhat faded with time), the gold is of course gold leaf. By the end of the century, colors were toned down with dark additives or were layered for more varied and complex effects.

The sixteenth century saw a significant rise in the status of artists. Chapter 2 reveals how artists expanded the possibilities of their materials and their own interpretive skills to fuel this rise. A polymath genius such as Leonardo da Vinci challenged the categorizing of artists as mere manual craftsmen, as did the poetic skill, social status, and artistic creativity of Michelangelo. Artists in Italy explored what was for them the new medium of oil and the new support of canvas, which had been used for portable works such as processional banners but was now employed for large-scale works such as altarpieces, to create an eloquent language of a scope not available before. The transparency of oil made it possible to underpaint with a tinted imprimatura, or priming layer, which would affect the colors put on top. Although its function was to prevent the oil in the paint layers from sinking into the ground, it could also function aesthetically to create a mood or unify the tonality. Canvas lent a texture to the surface, in contrast to the burnished surface of a wood panel; it could be as smooth as a linen handkerchief or as coarse as burlap. The consistency of the paint, thick or thin, could cover or expose that texture.

Regional differences distinguished Venetian from central Italian practice. Central Italy preferred wood supports and prepared the design meticulously, leaving little room for spontaneity. The Venetian Giorgione painted

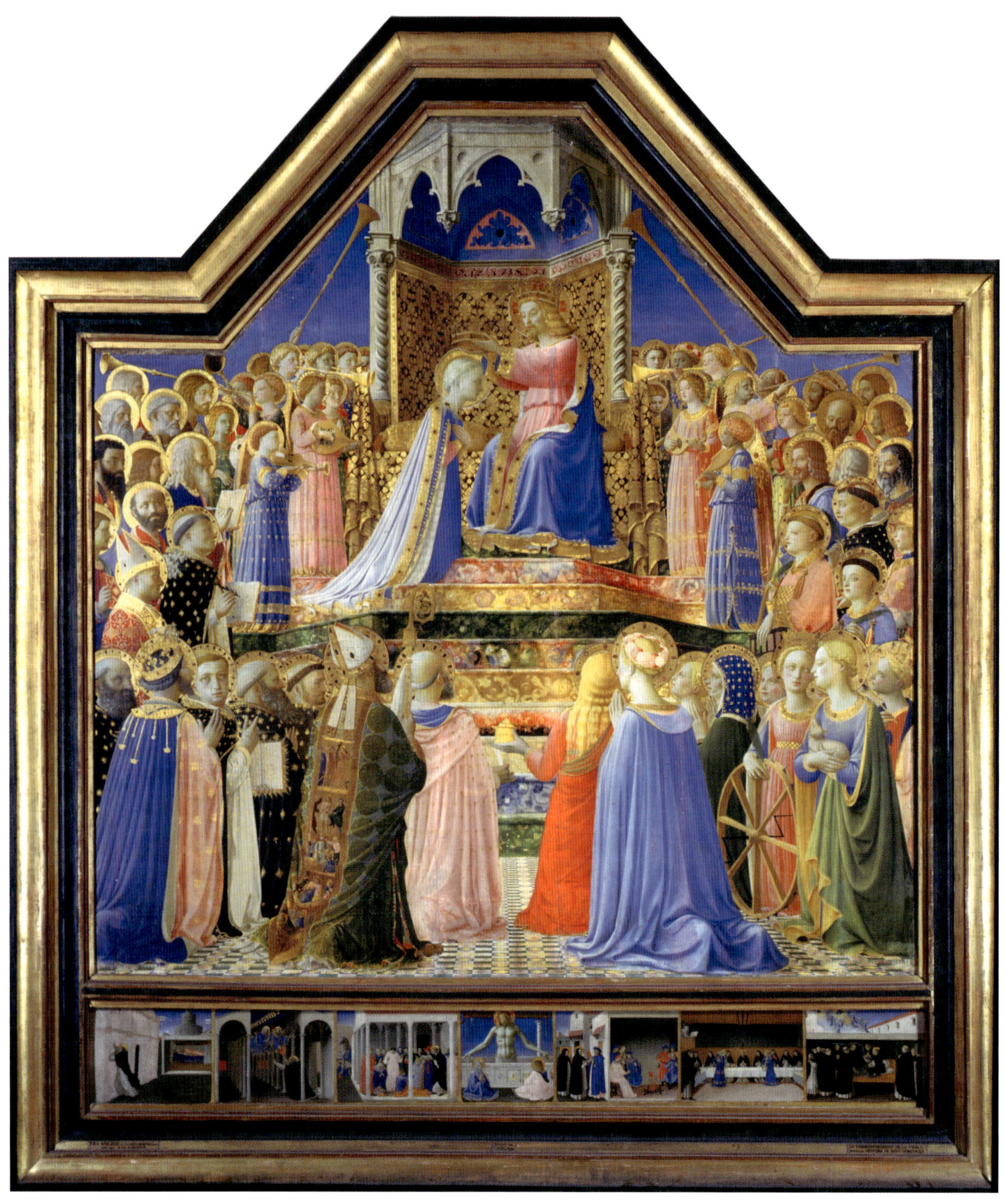

FIG. 0.5. Fra Angelico, *Coronation of the Virgin*, c. 1430–32. Tempera on panel, 82¼ × 81⅛ in. (209 × 206 cm). Louvre, Paris.

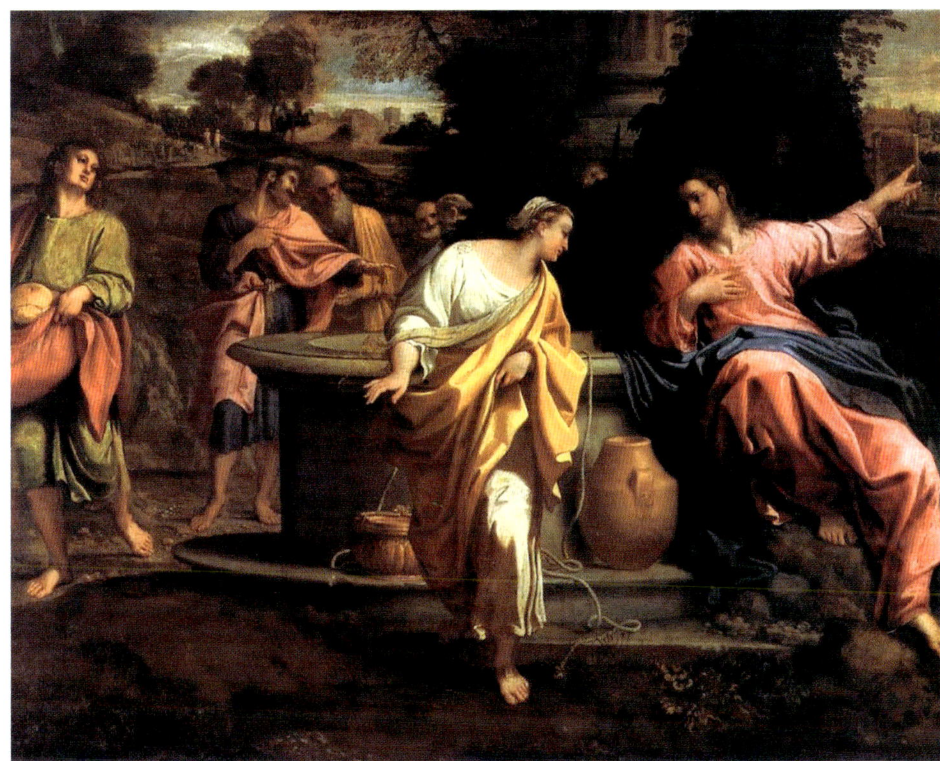

FIG. 0.6. Annibale Carracci, *Christ and the Samaritan Woman*, 1593–94. Oil on canvas, 67 × 88 ½ in. (170 × 225 cm). Pinacoteca di Brera, Milan.

The Tempest on canvas (see fig. 0.4). He was precocious in several ways: no one has been able to determine the source of the subject. It is unprecedented and unique, breaking with the custom of painting familiar, easily identifiable subjects. It is even possible that Giorgione chose the subject himself—a freedom not previously accorded to painters. Even more startling—at least from the perspective of a central Italian—he seems to have worked out the composition in the course of execution. Rather than projecting the placement of figures in advance, he painted the landscape meadow, then placed the nursing woman on top.[13]

Old rules no longer applied. Some daring masters such as Titian challenged the patrons to accept paintings as complete that they were accustomed to regarding as unfinished; these paintings with visible brushstrokes had more energy and eloquence than the conventional polished surface. The debate about how to regard sketchy facture would extend into the nineteenth century, when it was finally acknowledged that there is value to preserving the artist's creative process, and that something may be lost with traditional finish. Visible brushstroke provided the painter a personal calligraphy, a new rhetoric with which to express himself creatively. With it he could move away from the received template to generate a new interpretation or a fresh formulation, no longer pretending that the painting should fool the viewers into mistaking it for the real thing and instead inviting them to accept the materiality of the object.[14]

As demand for larger pictures and larger walls to be frescoed grew, painters developed expedient uses of the workshop, increasing the specialization. Painters also became more mobile; moving from one center to another meant they would hire freelancers for a project, rather than bring apprentices and assistants from home with them. This system proved advantageous to the masters, if not to the freelancers who could not count on work. Large numbers of painters from abroad migrated to Rome in search of training and the opportunity to study antiquity and the works of the modern masters, in particular Raphael and Michelangelo. What resulted was a breakdown in the workshop system, which precipitated the founding of academies where artists could receive instruction.

A range of coloring systems from which a painter could select was on offer in Rome in the early years of the century. Besides Leonardo's sfumato and Michelangelo's cangiantismo are *unione* and chiaroscuro, which endured well past the Renaissance. At the end of the century Annibale Carracci (fig. 0.6) practiced a version of unione, based on Raphael's use of color, and Caravaggio (see fig. 0.3) became the master of an extreme chiaroscuro dubbed tenebrist. These two manners divided the field at the beginning of the Seicento and were brought to the North by artists who had sojourned in Rome.

Scholars in the Netherlands have pioneered studies of the art market and have described a system that anticipated today's art market more than it resembled that of the Italian Renaissance. Chapter 3 explores the changes in painters' procedures and use of their materials that complemented these economic conditions. Most people recognize the constraints that the patronage system imposed, but we forget that the marketplace imposed a different kind of limit on the painters' freedom. Whereas the Renaissance artist knew in advance how much expensive ultramarine or gold or intricate brocade, or enriching layers of glaze the patron would pay for, the Dutch painter had to guess how much his unknown client would be willing to pay. Even eccentric artists in the Renaissance, such as Piero di Cosimo or, for that matter, Pontormo and Rosso, did not lack customers. But the headstrong genius Rembrandt could not sell enough to meet his expenses in this new market system, and others who were well known, such as Vermeer and Van Goyen, also lacked financial success. In a climate where demand was principally for small, secular domestic decorations, the artist needed to be an astute judge of what the market would bear. Efficient use of both labor and materials gained in importance and he (women artists were still rare) needed shortcuts that would save on both, but not result in a shoddy product. New methods for preparing the painting, new ways of using assistants, new ways of applying the paint, and new techniques of marketing all contributed to greater efficiency.

Regional schools continued to develop in the seventeenth century, and their products varied according to the local religion, form of government, and kinds of patronage. The Catholic cultures in the Netherlands, Italy, and Spain, for example, continued the patronage patterns of the Renaissance, granting artists lucrative ecclesiastical commissions not available in Protestant lands where the decoration of churches was forbidden. An international trade in pictures was promoted first in Antwerp, then in Amsterdam. Markets where clients could shop intensified competition, but dealers compensated by selling abroad at both the retail and the wholesale levels. Devotional pictures, produced by

assembly line, were shipped to Seville, then reshipped to the Americas.

Light became the fascination of seventeenth-century painters. The kind of dramatic chiaroscuro we see in Caravaggio was imitated. We associate it with the early work of Rembrandt, but he, like many others, migrated to a broader compositional chiaroscuro, creating areas of light and shade that corresponded to where the artist wanted to focus the viewer's attention. Vermeer's chiaroscuro, for example, does not dramatize as much as it creates a plausible ambience for the figure (see fig. 0.2). The role of color was to enhance this naturalism, so subdued tones replaced brilliant ones and muted earth pigments enjoyed favor. The medieval shibboleth that prohibited mixing or "corrupting" colorants finally crumbled. Aerial, or atmospheric, perspective, perfected to render atmosphere and distance convincingly, called for reducing not only the clarity of objects as they recede but rendering them increasingly bluish, in imitation of our perception.

Chapter 4 moves our story to France. From the mid-seventeenth century until the second half of the nineteenth century, the state regulated the production of art through control of education, exhibition, and patronage by the Académie Royale de Peinture et de Sculpture. Training was a state monopoly. Access to exhibition at the official Salon was determined by a jury chosen by the Académie, and the state purchased monumental works of history painting that it deemed worthy specimens of French culture. As those resources were inadequate to support them, painters had to make a living with works in the less prestigious genres, largely from portraits commissioned by the aristocracy. The academies in Florence and Rome were the model for the Académie, and the intention was to rival and surpass Italy as the cultural leader of Europe. The Prix de Rome was the pinnacle of achievement, a stipend to spend five years at the French Academy in Rome, awarded on the basis of a series of competitions. The Académie regarded color as subservient to drawing and dangerously sensuous, and advocated making symbolism the first priority in coloring, in keeping with its commitment to showing scenes of virtuous actions and teaching moral lessons with painting. All aspects of the painters' craft were codified so that they could be taught, leaving little opportunity for personal invention.

All this changed radically, however, with the death

of Louis XIV in 1715 and the rise of reactions, first the Rococo and then Neoclassicism. The grand style of Louis XIV and Le Brun was based on a severe classicism derived from Raphael and Poussin. The Rococo of Louis XV, under the direction of his mistress, Madame de Pompadour, turned to frothy renderings of erotic fantasies to decorate the boudoir and the bath. Chiaroscuro was replaced with pastel tones over a pale or rosy priming. Perspective was suppressed to push the figures into the intimate orbit of the viewer for his delectation. When this style was exported, as to Tiepolo's Venice, it served to glorify the families of the patrician patrons there and to decorate the palace of the bishop-prince, the ruler of Würzburg.

Reaction against Rococo frivolity first came with the realism of Chardin and Greuze. The middle class was prospering and replacing the aristocracy as the principal patron of art. They had little tolerance for Rococo fantasies and, like the Dutch burghers of the previous century, wanted small pictures to decorate the walls of their homes. Lofty acts of self-sacrifice by heroes, mythological and historical, might answer the needs of the Académie, but the buying public wanted scenes of upright people like themselves living virtuous lives. Chardin's sober householders, painted in a manner that lent them dignity and respectability, fit the bill. His coloring was as down-to-earth as his subjects, yet its subtle artistry lends it enormous appeal. Greuze often stepped over the line into a sentimentality that was better tolerated then than now, but he, like Chardin, gave the clients what they wanted. He had aspirations to recognition by the Académie as an esteemed history painter, but the gap between genre painting and history painting was unbridgeable, and he was ignominiously rejected in that role, despite his popularity with the public.

Neoclassicism suited the taste and aspirations of the Académie because it lent itself to the kind of ennobling subject of which it approved. But the Neoclassicists struggled to find a color style that matched their subject matter, and it was not until David returned from Rome with his assimilated version of Caravaggesque chiaroscuro that he fashioned a coloring consonant with his severe and consequential compositions. His elegant solution reinvented the grand manner, first in the service of the Republic and then for the monarchy of Napoleon.

The concept of the decorum of color was important in the eighteenth century, though never explicitly articulated. The requirement of the Augustan poet Horace that art, both painting and poetry, match nature was first revived in the Renaissance and frequently implemented thereafter. In the Rococo it was invoked as the basis for condemning fantastic creations and unnatural prettification. Horace's dictum as applied to color was definitively violated when Gauguin, followed by Van Gogh, first introduced nonrepresentational color.

An expanded repertory of materials and the continuing rise of a powerful new buying public combined to reconfigure the art scene in the nineteenth century, the subject of Chapter 5. The availability of synthetic pigments of bright yellows, greens, oranges, and purples, and cheaper brilliant blues transformed the palette. Brushes in new shapes made possible a new vocabulary of brushstroke. Manufactured pigments in tubes and commercially primed canvases released the painters from the confines of their studios, and these innovations meant that they needed no workshop assistants to prepare their materials. To be sure, commercially primed canvas and even paint in pigs' bladders had been available, especially in the large cities, for a long time, but now they were everywhere. As the state invested less and less in subsidizing art and the aristocracy declined, the taste of the middle class defined the market. Their preference for landscape and pictures related to their daily lives had little impact on the Académie, which upheld the Neoclassicism of Ingres and his followers (fig. 0.7), but the government recognized the necessity of supporting the artists independent of the Académie. Alternatives to the official Salon for exhibition began to appear, and dealers offered artists venues for their work to be seen and purchased. To be sure, official support did not extend to radical Realists such as Courbet (fig. 0.8), nor did it ever embrace the Impressionists. It favored a middle-of-the-road realism such as that of Gérôme. But by the last decade of the nineteenth century, Impressionists were being avidly collected in the United States and across Europe, and the art market had become international.

Underdrawings, chiaroscuro, continuous modeling, and polished finish all disappeared, together with subjects drawn from classical mythology and history. Though painters continued to use some traditional pigments alongside the new synthetics, there is a decisive shift in the look of paintings. The appeal of working directly on the white canvas was irresistible to most; the brownish, often murky, tonality that had so long

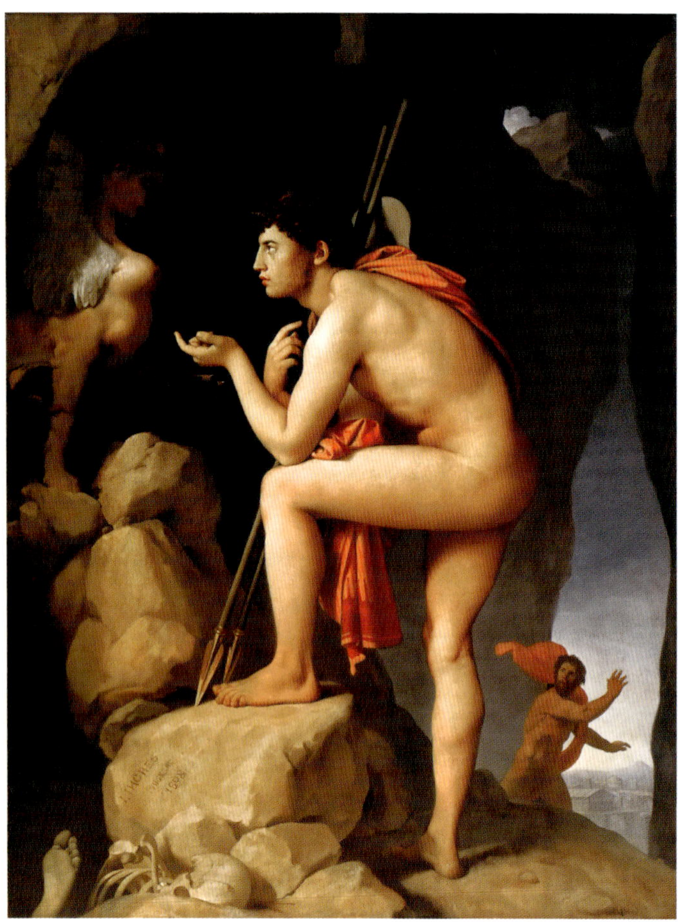

FIG. 0.7. Jean-Auguste-Dominique Ingres, *Oedipus and the Sphinx*, 1808. Oil on canvas, 74 1/2 × 56 3/4 in. (189 × 144 cm). Louvre, Paris.

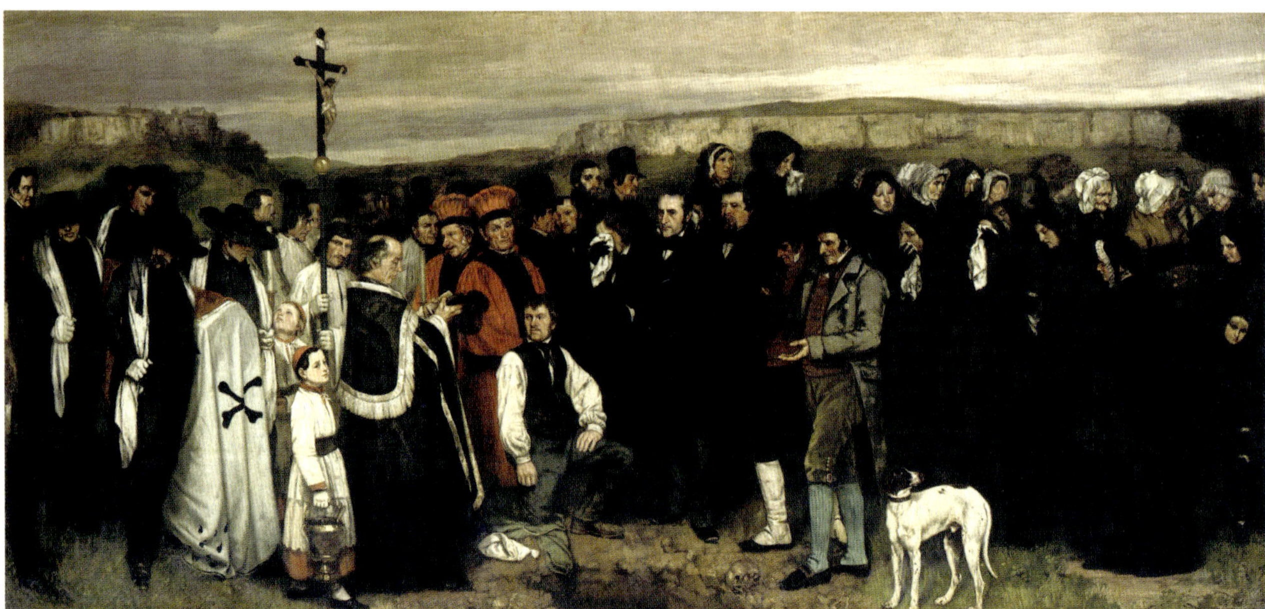

FIG. 0.8. Gustave Courbet, *Burial at Ornans*, 1849–50. Oil on canvas, 10 ft. 4 in. × 21 ft. 11 in. (315 × 668 cm). Musée d'Orsay, Paris.

prevailed was replaced by color that was not subdued by a tinted imprimatura. Contrived lighting, possible for indoor settings, gave way to accidents of sunlight or special conditions of weather. Besides landscape, the painters celebrated the excitement of urban life; the popular scenes of public entertainment in theaters or leisure in cafés, such as those of Degas and Seurat, were shown with the magic of gaslight.

Impressionism began to splinter as a movement in the 1880s and to be replaced by Post-Impressionism and Neo-Impressionism. Unlike their Impressionist predecessors, who had reveled in the sophistication of the newly industrialized Paris, the painters examined in Chapter 6 rebelled against the materialism of their urban culture and sought to represent spiritual values in their art rather than the fleeting and superficial image. Van Gogh fled Paris for the South of France, and Gauguin renounced decadent society and decamped to the French colony of Tahiti, where he celebrated the "primitive" with a palette of nonrepresentational colors. The triumph of color over drawing was accomplished in the twentieth-century movements of Fauvism, Die Brücke, and Der Blaue Reiter. Matisse, Kirchner, and Kandinsky found color, unleashed from its imitative function, to be the means to express their personal response to experience.

◆ ◆ ◆

My expertise is the Italian Renaissance, so that is my baseline here. The Renaissance is also the touchstone by which things were measured in the centuries that followed, by historians and artists alike. Renoir changed his style after he visited Italy in 1881; Cézanne referred to Michelangelo, Poussin, and Rubens to learn about structuring his pictures.[15] Rubens studied Titian, Veronese, Barocci, and Caravaggio in forming his style. Seurat knew the geometry of Piero della Francesca from copies at the École in his student days.[16] It is useful to be sufficiently familiar with the Renaissance to be able to compare what happened later. I have noted, for example, that with a few dramatic exceptions the materials remain much the same: the vermilion Fra Angelico used (see fig. 0.5) is the same bright red Monet chose for the flowers in *Bathers at La Grenouillère* (see fig. 5.10) four hundred and forty years later, and Angelico's ultramarine reappears in Michelangelo (see fig. 0.1), Carracci (see fig. 0.6), and Vermeer (see fig. 0.2), to be replaced with a synthetic version only in the nineteenth century.

The discipline of art history has turned away from the formal analysis of style and is chary nowadays of attempts to fathom artistic intent. I believe the study of technique can provide clues to meaning. Speaking of the "human values" embedded in the paintings of Monet and Cézanne, Richard Shiff wrote: "Painters such as Monet and Cézanne represented these values not only in their pictures, but inside their picture making, within their technical practice itself. The painters' techniques were largely determined by their concern for expressing such values—living them out, experiencing them. Form, or rather technique, could both represent and embody content."[17] The study of technique is the legitimate heir to formal analysis and a valuable index to the meaning of pictures.

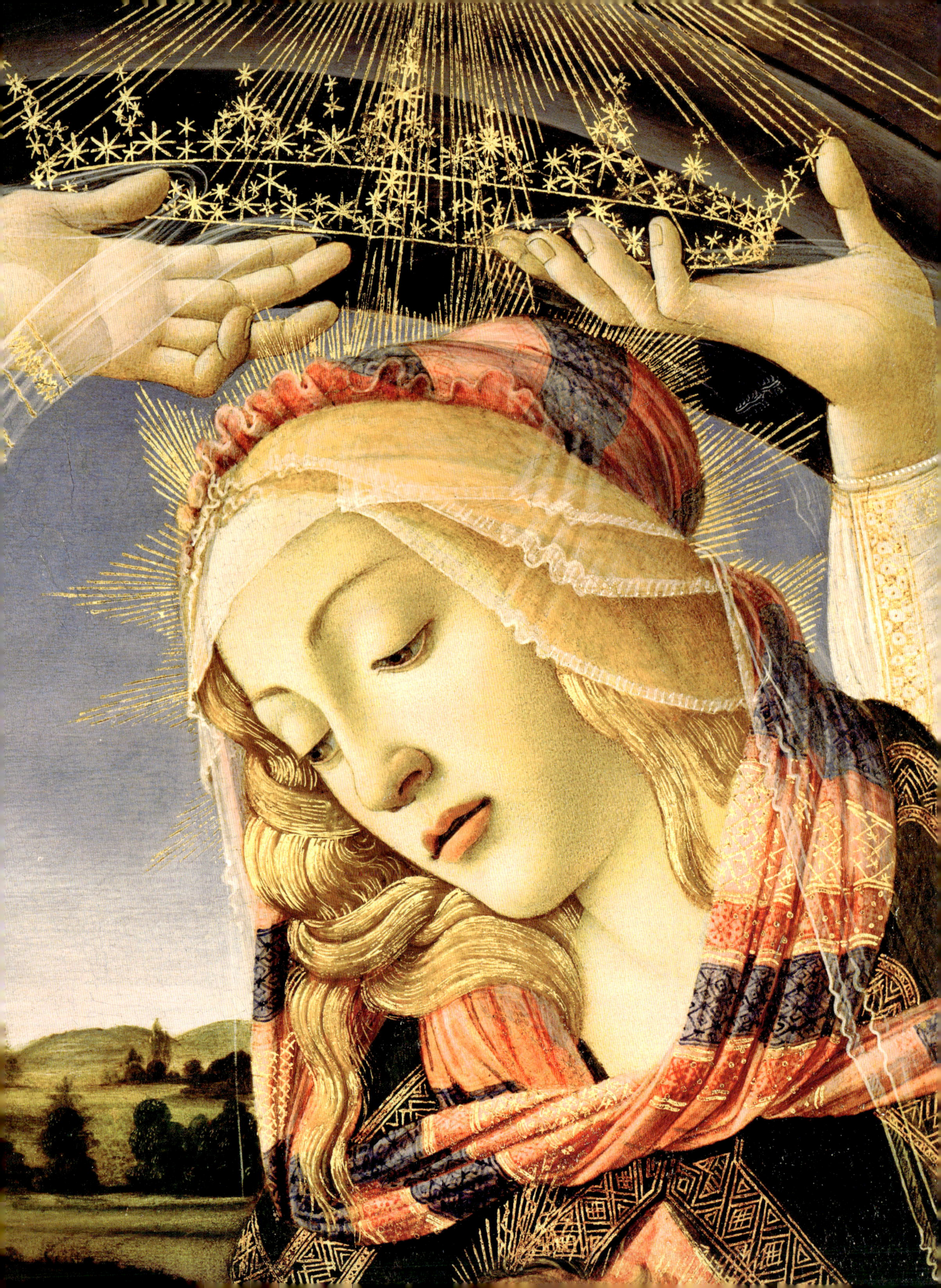

1   The Fifteenth Century

From Egg to Oil, from Gothic to Humanist Values

At the dawn of the Quattrocento, a Gothic coloring system matched the Christian culture. Abundant gold symbolized the celestial sphere; a white gesso ground enhanced the brilliance of the pigments bound in egg, which were used in their pure form to maximize their luminosity. As the humanist view gradually gained ground, Christian values were not displaced, but the focus shifted from the next world to this, and an aesthetic of naturalism took hold. We see gradually in the course of the century the painters moving away from the templates received from Byzantine icons and their iconography to their own inventions. They explored oil, dark modeling, cartoons, and underpainting alongside scientific perspective to mirror more closely this world in the painted world.

When a prominent Florentine in the 1410s desired to reduce the time he and his family members would spend in purgatory, he might commission an artist to decorate a family chapel, where the endowment he paid the church would purchase Masses to be said in perpetuity for his and his family's souls. Such a "good work" also accrued him status in the community. It worked in the same way as Jimmy Carter's or Bill and Melinda Gates's foundations today, which alleviate poverty and suffering in developing countries while garnering them prestige and respect. When Lorenzo Monaco was commissioned to paint the high altar for Santa Maria degli Angeli he must have felt deeply honored, for it was the main church of his Camaldolese order in Florence, where he was himself a monk (fig. 1.1). The patron commissioned him to paint the Coronation of the Virgin "for the soul of Zanobi di Ceccho della Frasca and his family," as the inscription along the base of the painting reads. It also tells us that it is "the work by Lorenzo di Giovanni, a monk of this order and his [associates]" in 1414.[1]

The painter is identified in this inscription, as he would not have been in medieval times. Nevertheless, the fifteenth-century painter was still in many ways working in a medieval artisan tradition. A contract between Don Lorenzo and his patron, della Frasca, would have stipulated what he would paint, what materials he would use and of what quality, the dimensions, and when it would be delivered and installed. An index of the scale of values is that a substantial percentage of the cost was in materials rather than the painter's skill. The contract for this piece has not survived, but we can deduce something

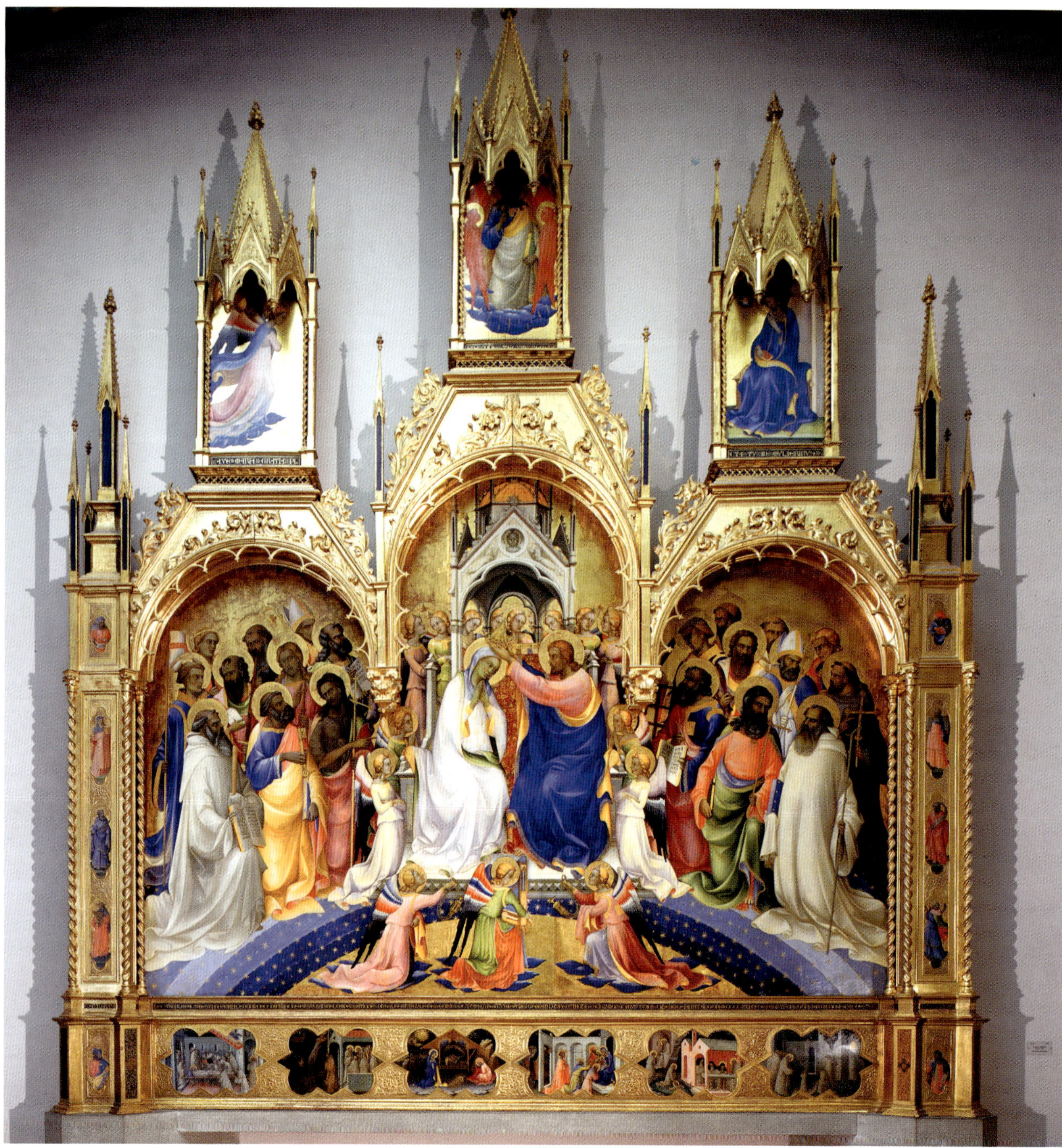

FIG. 1.1. Lorenzo Monaco, *Coronation of the Virgin*, 1414. Tempera on panel, 16 ft. 7 in. × 14 ft. 8 ¼ in. (506 × 447.5 cm). Uffizi, Florence.

about costs and procedures from the study of those that have.[2]

The work on an altarpiece began with the panel and its frame, prepared by a skilled carpenter and then gilded. For such a grand piece as this, measuring almost seventeen by fifteen feet, we can imagine that quite a lot of time and cost went into its preparation. Its ornate Gothic shape, with pinnacles capped by convex baldachins and

delicate finials, required skillful carving. This work would have been done by a woodworker and delivered to the painter. Analysis of contracts shows that on average the cost of the woodwork was between 15 and 30 percent of the total. Payment records for a lost work by Lorenzo Monaco of 1420 show that the woodwork cost 18 percent of the total.[3] The panel would then be gilded, perhaps in the carpenter's shop but more likely in Don Lorenzo's, by artisans trained in handling delicate gold leaf. The gold was virtually twenty-four karat and hammered into the thinnest possible sheets. These were manufactured by *battilori* (gold beaters) who ran their own shops and sold the gold leaves to painters and other artisans in stacks of a hundred. The source of the leaves available to Lorenzo and his fellow artists was the famed Florentine florin, which the gold worker would melt and then beat. The parts of the panel that were to be gilded were prepared with bole, a clay, usually red. The gesso under the bole would give a little, allowing punching and burnishing. The warm reddish tint the bole imparted to the gilded surface was sought and appreciated, but aging makes it sometimes show through more today than was intended. A skilled member of the workshop would stamp the haloes and other surface decoration into the gold with punches made and kept in the workshop, and he had to take great care not to break through the gold with the punch.[4] For this altar certainly a great many sheets of gold have been used. Contracts sometimes stipulate the quantity of gold and arrange for payment in advance; sometimes it was even provided by the patron. The payments for the gold leaf for Lorenzo's lost 1420 work amounted to 11 percent of the total.[5] Thus the woodwork and the gold together accounted for 29 percent of the cost of the commission.

PIGMENTS

The painter normally bought his pigments, which were mineral rocks and earths, manufactured compounds, or organics (from plants or certain insects) from apothecaries in raw form and had his workshop prepare them. This was a tedious, but very important part of what a *bottega* did, because the quality of the pigment depended upon the grind. If certain pigments were ground too fine they lost their tinting strength; others it was impossible to grind too much. How to handle each pigment was a closely guarded secret taught to the apprentices, which is why an apprentice's contract stipulated that he must remain in the service of his master until he matriculated into the guild and was ready to go out on his own. We are learning that pigments already ground were also sometimes available from the apothecary, so painters could ignore the warnings proffered in the contemporary how-to handbook of Cennino Cennini about adulteration, especially if they dealt regularly with one supplier.[6] In Venice there were even specialists called *vendecolori,*

who supplied artists and other craftsmen, as we will see.[7] When a patron was trying to choose a painter, a major criterion would have been the reputation for the quality of his colors as shown in works he had previously executed. One proviso found in some contracts is that the painting being contracted should be similar to and at least as good as a specific work cited. When Benozzo Gozzoli was commissioned to paint the *Madonna and Child Enthroned with Angels and Saints and Saint Zenobius* in 1461 (fig. 1.2), the contract stated: "First, in the middle of the said picture, the figure of Our Lady on the throne, in the manner and form and with the same decorations as the picture above the High Altar in San Marco, Florence," that is, the altarpiece by Gozzoli's deceased master, Fra Angelico.[8]

The most expensive pigment, ultramarine, was extracted from a semiprecious stone, lapis lazuli, that had to be imported from what is today Afghanistan. The laborious process of grinding, then washing and precipitating the pigment produced grades of blue of diminishing intensity with each washing. Because of its expense it was never sold already ground but rather was prepared in the workshop. The finest blue was reserved for the most important figures. Lorenzo drew the eye of the viewer to Christ by lavishing it on his robe, then used smaller patches on Peter and Matthew, and in the Annunciation on the pinnacles, especially in the Virgin's robe. Like gold, the quantity was sometimes specified in the contract, and the quality designated by the price or even supplied to the painter. Lorenzo's cost for blue for his 1420 work was 3.5 percent.[9] Other less expensive blues were available, but none had the same intensity or the purplish cast that was particularly prized. Often ultramarine would be underpainted with red to give it a more purplish tinge. Azurite was the second-best blue; derived also from a semiprecious stone, it was expensive but cheaper than ultramarine. If the patron did not wish or was not able to afford lapis, azurite (German blue, also called *azzuro di magna, azurro di Alamagna,* or *azurro tedesco*), which was slightly greenish, would be substituted. Cheaper blues could be provided by the dye indigo and by smalt, which is made from ground glass.[10]

The other strongest pigment on the palette was vermilion, an opaque fire-engine red derived from mercury. Together with gold and lapis, this primary triad centered and dominated the color schemes of early Quattrocento tempera paintings. In the *Coronation* we see vermilion on

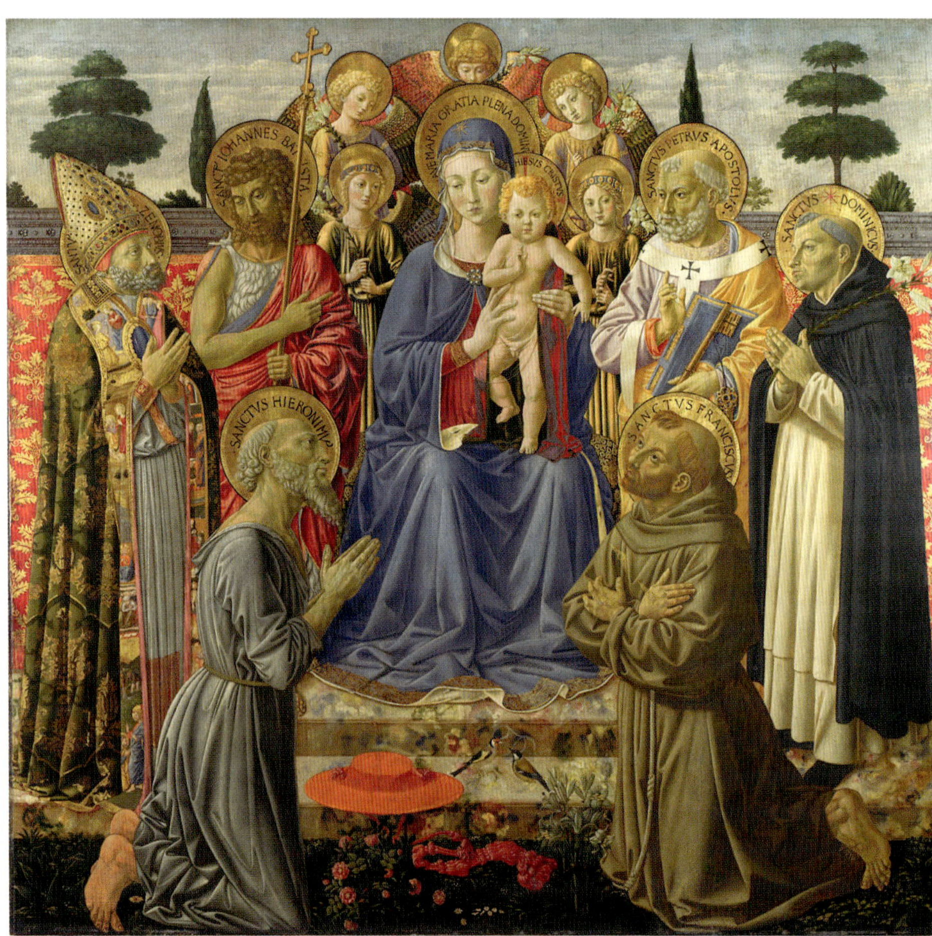

FIG. 1.2. Benozzo Gozzoli, *Madonna and Child Enthroned with Angels and Saints and Saint Zenobius*, 1461–62. Tempera on panel, 63¾ × 67 in. (162 × 170.3 cm). National Gallery, London.

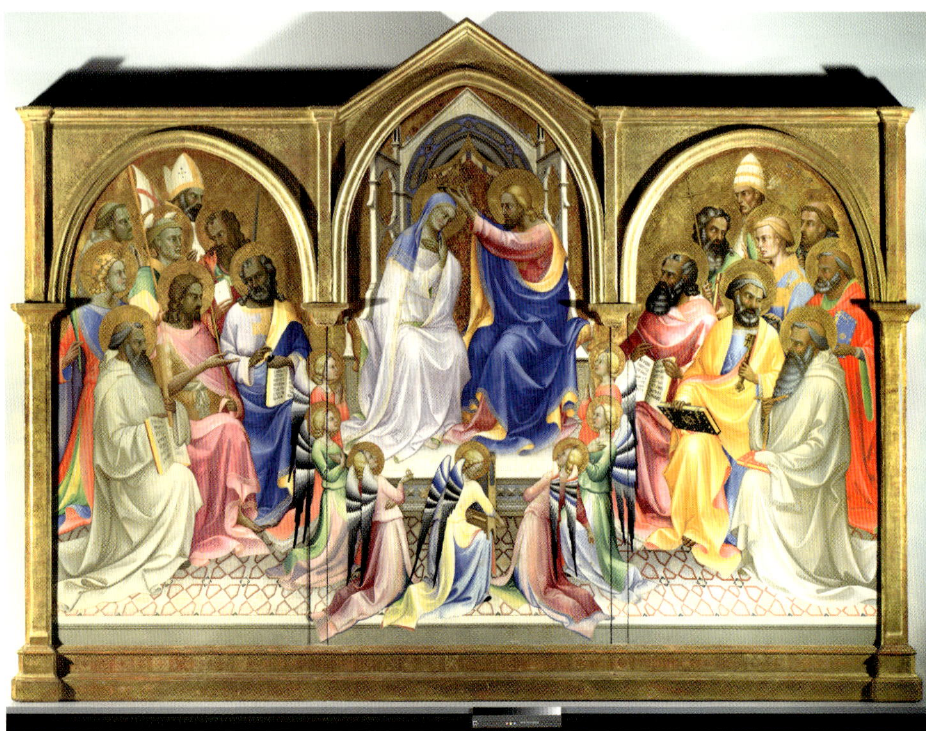

FIG. 1.3. Lorenzo Monaco, *Coronation of the Virgin*, 1407–9. Tempera on panel, 7 ft. 2¾ in. × 10 ft. 6½ in. (220.5 × 321.5 cm). National Gallery, London.

the central pinnacle in the mandorla and angels around the risen Christ; directly below on the cloth visible between Mary and Christ; and in the central angel below. The symmetry of these reds reveals the painter's strategy. We also note white-robed Camaldolese monks anchoring the outer edge on either side. This isochromatism, as John Shearman dubbed it—the deploying of a pigment so that it forms a pattern on the surface—is the principle of Don Lorenzo's and his contemporaries' color design.[11] It is made possible by the technique, described by Cennini, which uses pure pigments and models only with white.[12] The highly ornamental effect that results makes no pretense of naturalism; rather, it reflects the beauty of the celestial sphere that is represented here.

There is an earlier version of this *Coronation* in the National Gallery, London, that was made for another Camaldolese church (fig. 1.3). The saints have been changed and rearranged, but the placement of two monks clad in white as anchors at the outer edge is the same. What is surprising to discover is that the Virgin's robe was originally a deep mauvish pink, a fugitive lake pigment that has faded and is visible only under the microscope.[13] The white we see today—actually faded pink, now almost colorless—matches the color scheme in the later Uffizi version. The three white figures are misleadingly symmetrical but aesthetically satisfying. Don Lorenzo was lucky. Other paintings have suffered fading of red lakes that are far more disruptive to the color scheme.

Lake pigments are organic dyes that are precipitated onto a substrate. They were used in the fabric industry and could be had not only in reds, but also yellows. They are subject to fading in light, so much so that the yellows are almost never seen now except through the microscope. The pinkish drapery of the angel below Mary's feet in the Uffizi *Coronation* (see fig. 1.1) is one of these lake pigments.

Earth pigments are the least brilliant and least expensive. Dug from the earth, they could be found in a wide variety of colors: reds ranging from purplish to orangey to brown; yellow ochres, which move from mustard to brown; umbers and siennas; *terra verde*, "green earth," which was grayish, but could be surprisingly green. Earths would vary from one region to another, so the local supply could have a distinctive appearance. These earths are the backbone of fresco, in which, as we will see, most of the pigments derived from metals (lead, mercury, tin) could not be used.[14] Don Lorenzo used

a brownish ochre to shade Saint Peter's yellow robe, painted in canary lead-tin yellow, and another brown for John the Baptist's animal skin.

Missing from the Renaissance palette was a purple pigment, which had to be made by mixing blue and red, often lapis and red lake. The greens were the weakest pigments, and for foliage the most satisfactory was a mixture of blue and yellow, perhaps with a green, verdigris-containing glaze, which has the unfortunate tendency to turn brown over time in light. Some of the parched earth we see today in these paintings was originally a verdant green. Pietro Perugino's *Crucifixion with Saints* is an example (fig. 1.4).

Central to the aesthetic was the commitment to pure color. It was the craftsman's responsibility to use good materials, to prepare them to obtain the greatest possible brilliance, and to apply them undiluted and unmixed. Mixed color was considered "corrupted" and should only be used when no pigment existed, as in the cases of purple and foliage.[15]

Flesh was another of the colors that had of course to be mixed, usually developed from a combination of lead white and vermilion, with other tints added to indicate gender or age. Flesh was underpainted in a greenish tint that gave complementary shading, made up of a terra verde or a mixture that Cennini described as *verdaccio*, literally "dirty green."[16] Close scrutiny of many egg tempera paintings reveals this greenish tinge to the flesh, including the Uffizi *Coronation*. Often it is more apparent than one would wish, especially in the face of the Virgin, because the surface is abraded, perhaps vigorously scrubbed before organic solvents became available in the late nineteenth century, or because it was reverently touched or even kissed.

The number of pigments in ordinary use was about a dozen and a half, and the palette was further limited by the commitment to use them in their pure form. To introduce more variety, the painters sometimes used what Cennini describes as cangiante ("changing") colors. Instead of modeling up with white, the painter introduces a contrasting pigment for the light, or a hue shift, thereby creating a pleasingly ornamental effect. Because this cangiantismo is an artificial invention not found in nature, Cennini recommends it particularly for angels, to signify their supernatural character.[17] A lovely example can be seen at the left edge of the National Gallery version of the *Coronation* where a red drapery shifts to yellow. When

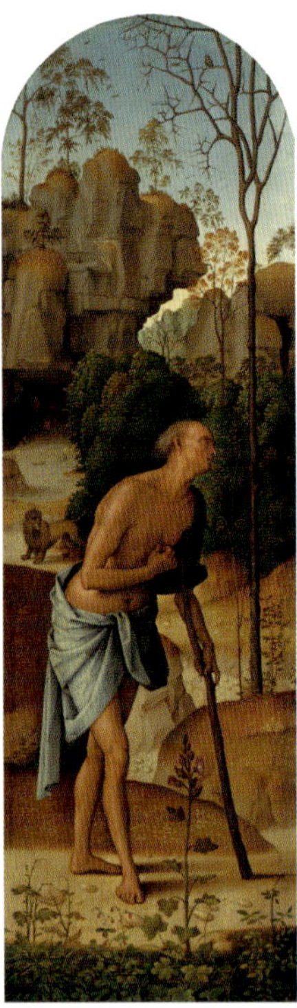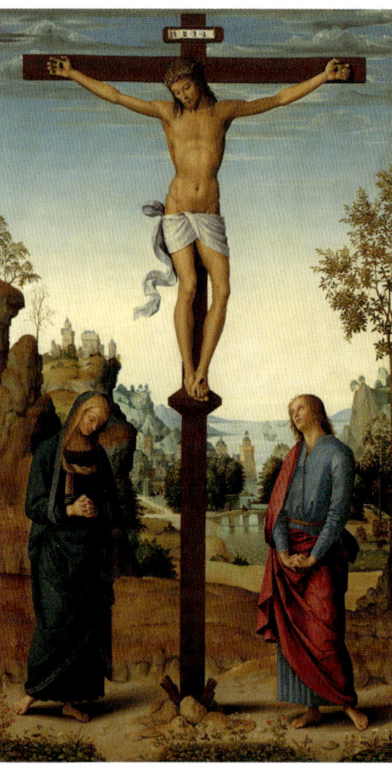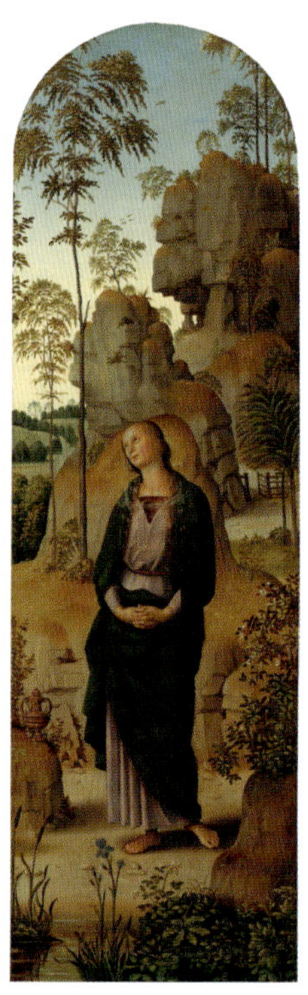

FIG. 1.4. Pietro Perugino, *Crucifixion with Saints*, c. 1482–85. Oil on panel transferred to canvas, 52 ¾ × 65 in. (134 × 165 cm). National Gallery of Art, Washington, D.C.

we look closely at several of these angels, we see that the highlights or shadows are in a contrasting color—for example, the white drapery of the angels flanking Mary and Christ shifts to a canary yellow, and the angel of the *Annunciation* shows a rainbow of tints from pink to green to blue.

CENNINI-STYLE VERSUS ALBERTI-STYLE COLORING

When he was ready to paint, Don Lorenzo would have taken a small amount of the powdered pigment and mixed it with egg yolk and some water. Cennini recommended using eggs of town chickens for flesh because the yolk was whiter than those of country or farm chickens.[18] It is not hard to imagine that the painter would have had to use a very small brush and short strokes to apply this sticky paint. Just like the egg on the breakfast plate, it dried almost immediately, so there was no blending possible. Shading was done by creating a network of hatching and cross-hatching. It is easy to see this hatching on the surface of egg tempera paintings if you can get close enough: note the individual strokes visible in Botticelli's face (see fig. 1.26).

Given how small the brush and how large the panel, it is evident that Don Lorenzo would have relied on his workshop for some of the execution. The predella (platform at the base) contains six narratives in quatrefoils

in small scale; these could have been assigned to one or more of the most advanced apprentices, as could the small saints on the frame and the pinnacles. These scenes could be worked at the same time that painting was proceeding on the main panel. Contracts often contain the stipulation that all the work should be by the master's hand (*da sua mano*). Michelle O'Malley has determined that what this means is that it must be done within the workshop and not subcontracted out.[19] Later in the century, contracts reveal some negotiating on this matter, as we will see.

Fra Angelico was another painter-monk in Florence, about a generation younger than Lorenzo Monaco. That quarter century difference meant that Angelico was a young painter in the 1420s, when great artistic events launched the Renaissance in Florence. In 1424 Lorenzo Ghiberti finished the first set of bronze doors for the Baptistery, which told the story of the life of Christ in quatrefoil panels of the same design as those of Andrea Pisano's doors of the 1340s. For his second doors, called the "Gates of Paradise," begun immediately after his first doors were completed, Ghiberti perhaps rebelled against the restriction of the Gothic shape that had been imposed on him, because for these Old Testament scenes he created large picture-shaped rectangles that allowed him to make use of his colleague Filippo Brunelleschi's newly

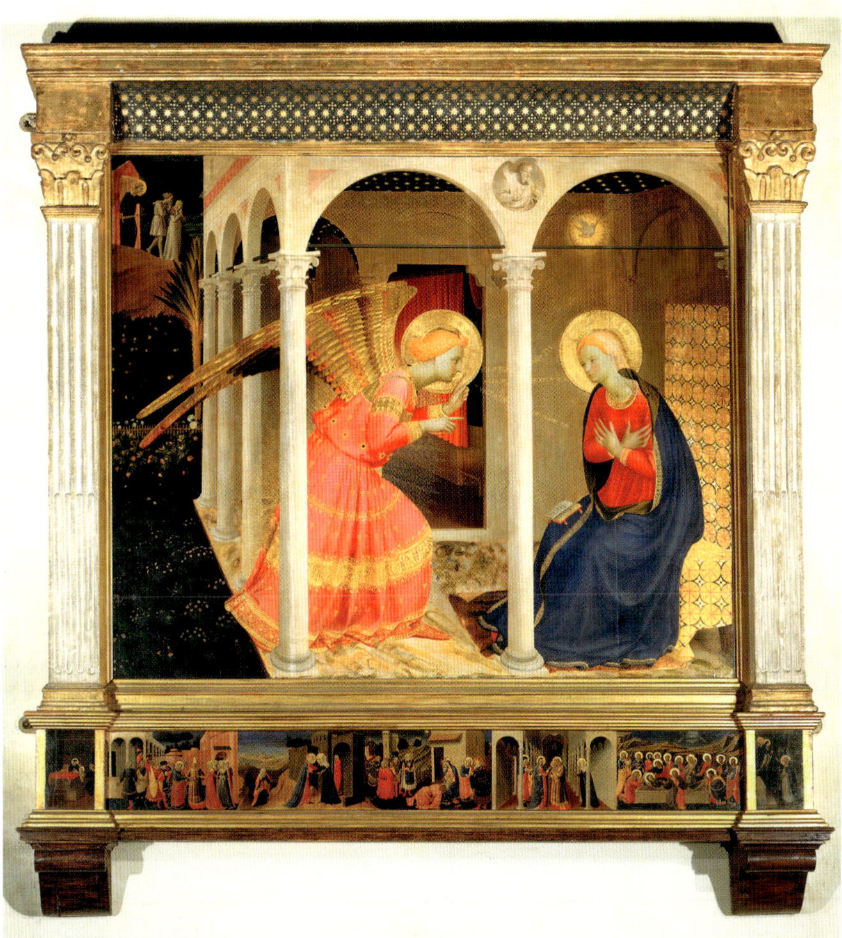

FIG. 1.5. Fra Angelico, *Annunciation*, c. 1432–34. Tempera on panel, 60 × 79 in. (150 × 180 cm). Museo Diocesano, Cortona.

demonstrated central-point perspective system. Masaccio and Masolino were using the new scientific perspective at the same time in their frescoes in the Brancacci Chapel to create the illusion of space recession. By the mid-1430s Leon Battista Alberti would be instructing artists in how to construct a perspective system with mathematical tools; he would also propose a new technique of modeling to replace the Cennini system. Alberti instructed painters to model up with gradients of white, as Cennini prescribed, but to use the pure color as the midtone and to model down to the shadow by adding black or a dark monochrome.[20] In this way they could achieve a closer approximation to what we see. By 1425 Don Lorenzo had passed on to his reward, but Fra Angelico was faced with having to decide whether to embrace modernity or cling to the medieval past. His choice was to adopt scientific perspective, but not Alberti's color.

We can understand his reasons. Because he was a friar, all his commissions were for ecclesiastical settings, and his sacred narratives could benefit from realistic settings. If he needed to show the Annunciation, he could use perspective to create a Renaissance loggia to make the setting convincing and contemporary (fig. 1.5). But how would he convey the supernatural dimension of this event without the gilded rays of divine light on which the dove of the Holy Spirit enters, or the dazzling golden embroidery behind Mary, or the wings of the angel Gabriel? Angelico practiced a decorum of coloring. Evidently he felt that gilded splendor had its place, and so, for example, when he frescoed the pope's chapel in the Vatican, he enriched it with brilliant ultramarine and gilding so that it sparkles like jewels. However, when he painted scenes from the life of Christ in the cells of fellow friars at San Marco, he abjured gold and blue, using only the most inexpensive earth pigments to decorate the walls of these men who had taken the vow of poverty. The painters who were younger than Angelico faced no such dilemma and gladly took up Alberti's recommendations for a more naturalistic coloring.

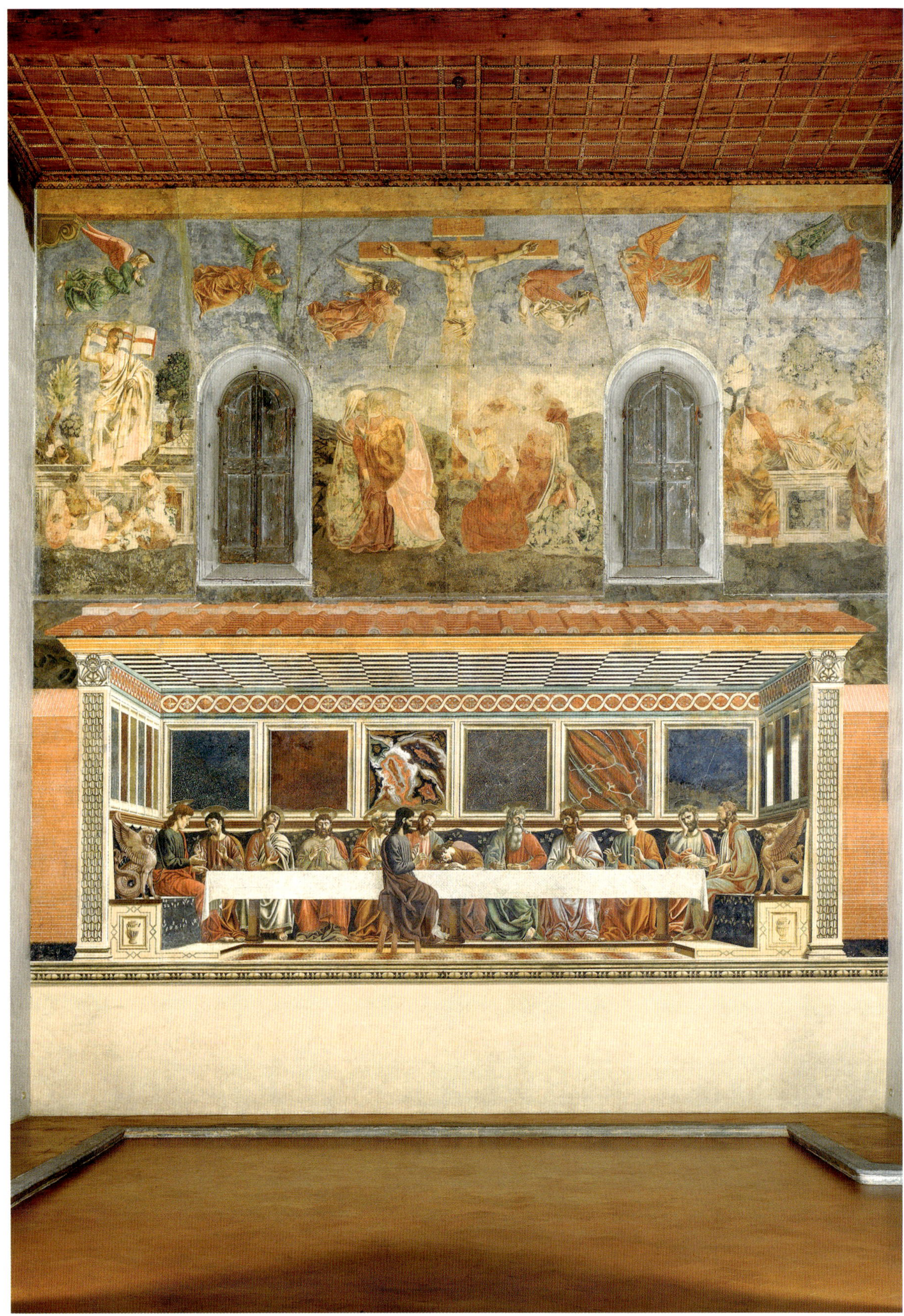

FIG. 1.6. Andrea del Castagno, *Sant'Apollonia* (*Last Supper and Resurrection*), c. 1450. Fresco, 32 ft. 2 in. × 14 ft. 9 in. (980 × 450 cm). Sant'Apollonia, Florence.

The other principal type of decoration was fresco, which was used especially in Tuscany and central Italy for wall decorations in palaces and churches. Andrea del Castagno was asked to cover the end wall of the refectory in Sant'Apollonia, a convent of cloistered Benedictine nuns. The subject the nuns requested was the usual decoration deemed most appropriate for the dining hall, the Last Supper (fig. 1.6). Above it, Castagno painted a Crucifixion flanked by the Resurrection and the Entombment. Because the nuns were strictly cloistered, these frescoes were hardly ever seen. At the time the convent was finally secularized in 1860, only the *Last Supper* was visible; the upper zone had been whitewashed. Although the *Last Supper* is well preserved, a leaky roof and seeping damp had damaged the upper zone in ways characteristic of fresco. When it became disfigured, the nuns had it covered over rather than try to repair it. Without the intrusion of moisture, fresco is remarkably durable because it becomes a part of the wall, so it is damaged only if the plaster of the wall deteriorates. By the time restoration was undertaken in 1953, drastic surgery was required. The plaster was so badly damaged that the only way to save the fresco was with the dramatic rescue process known as *strappo.*[21] The origin of the Italian term, meaning "to rip off," gives an idea of how this is done. A facing is attached to a portion of the fresco with a soluble adhesive, then it is pulled or torn off the wall, taking only the paint and the very thin layer of plaster to which it had bonded. It is then attached to a new support. These detached paintings may then be reinstalled in their original position, as was done in this case. On their new support they are insulated from the wall, but we can see the seams between the sections where it has been reassembled.

Castagno would have had his workshop prepare the wall with several layers of plaster, making the penultimate one, the *arriccio,* just rough enough so that the next layer will adhere. When he was ready to paint he would apply the *intonaco,* the final layer, on a patch just as large as he planned to paint that day, which is called a *giornata* (from *giorno,* meaning "day"). He would then apply ground pigment in water on the damp plaster. At the end of the day he would cut away any intonaco not used and bevel the edge so the next giornata could be inserted cleanly. As the plaster dries, the paint forms a chemical bond with the plaster. Once it has dried it cannot be altered except by painting over it *a secco* ("dry"), which in time will flake off.

Castagno needed to be quick and decisive, then, to be successful. The drying time varies with the region and the weather, but by the next morning it would be set. He had to know exactly what he wanted to paint, and he needed to be a good manager of a sizable workshop, so that the tasks of preparing the plaster and the paints would be done on schedule. He also needed helpers skilled enough to execute some of the painting. Less experienced apprentices might be assigned the sky or the landscape, more experienced ones the secondary figures. The master himself would probably paint the figure of Christ; if he was very rushed or had an assistant he trusted, he might paint only the head of Christ. There was no opportunity for retouching, so it had to be right the first time.

There were occasions, of course, when the painter would come back the next day and see a mistake that needed to be fixed. If he was very conscientious he could have the offending part chiseled out and re-plastered, rather than masking it with secco. Michelangelo found a halfway measure that worked quite well. The restorers called it *mezzo fresco* ("half fresco") when they discovered it in the Sistine Chapel. The painter would scrape away as much of the plaster as he could before it had entirely set, then mix in watery plaster and repaint the area.[22] Secco was necessary when an elaborate pattern such as a brocaded fabric was to be represented, and perhaps gilded. We see very little of such elaborations today because, being painted on top, they have fallen off. After Castagno, in the second half of the Quattrocento, as the taste for realistic detail and rich surfaces increased, so did secco elaboration. By the time Giorgio Vasari was writing in the mid-Cinquecento, these secco passages were showing damage. He scolded painters and warned them against secco, advocating for the disciplined use of only *buon fresco* ("true fresco").[23]

Castagno would of course need to have prepared his design for the wall before he began to paint. He would have worked it out in advance, but with the cost of paper being very high, he would not have made numerous experimental drawings. His guide when he started to paint would have been an underdrawing on the arriccio, usually in a cheap red earth called sinoper, hence this drawing is known as the sinopia. Once he applied

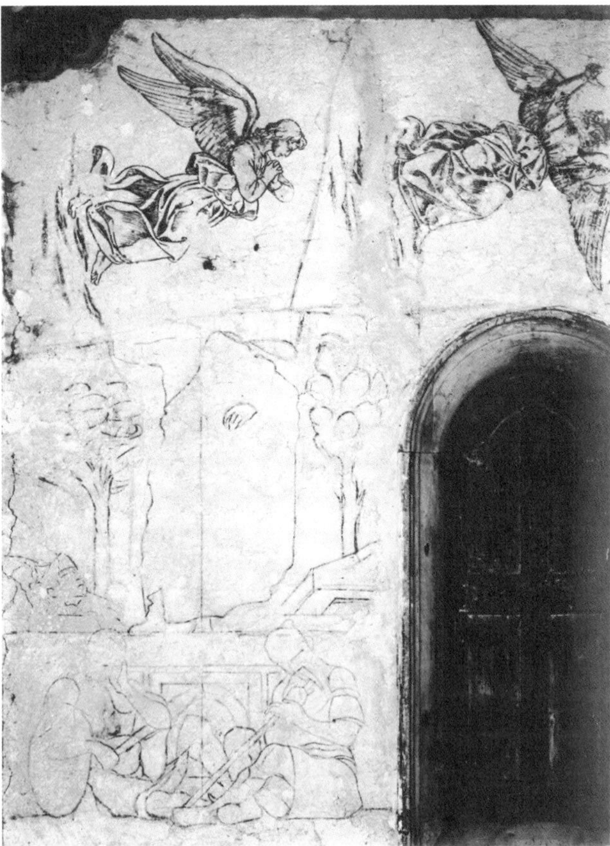

the intonaco, the sinopia would disappear and he would have to work from memory.[24] Normally these sinopie are never seen again by painter or beholder, but in the case where a strappo has been performed, the paint layer is separated from the arriccio and the sinopia becomes visible, giving us a glimpse of the working procedure (fig. 1.7).[25] A strange thing here is that the angels of the Resurrection in the upper left appear very clearly in detail and a tree and the sleeping soldiers are summarily outlined, whereas Christ is barely indicated. What could account for this variation in the level of finish in the sinopia? One explanation is that the apprentice who was assigned the angels was not as experienced as the one who would paint the soldiers, and perhaps Castagno himself was executing the Christ and needed only an indication of the figure's position because the details were in his mind or he could improvise.

The angels appear to have been transferred from a cartoon. Such full-scale drawings were only beginning to be used in fresco, although the technique was familiar from stained glass and other crafts. These cartoons were transferred onto the wall using the method known as pouncing; the outlines were pricked, then dusted with black carbon. The black dots (called *spolveri*) could then be gone over and connected with brushed sinoper, as was done here.[26] Cartoons will play an increasingly important part in our story as it develops.

In his *Last Supper*, Castagno has created a painted exposition of the central-point perspective system first demonstrated by Brunelleschi and then described by Alberti in 1435. Alberti belonged to a Florentine family that had long ago been exiled. He grew up in Genoa, then obtained a law degree in Bologna and went to Rome to work in the Curia. When Pope Eugenius took up residence in Florence in 1434, Alberti accompanied him.

In 1435 Alberti created his little book *On Painting* in the vernacular, which the painters themselves could read, and then the following year in Latin.[27] As a humanist, an architect, and a friend of the artists, he would dedicate his book *On Painting* to five of the leading artists in Florence. It was an attempt to help them elevate their status from craftsmen to intellectuals. Alberti described a system to give painters a mathematical means to create the illusion of space, replacing the empirical system that we see in Lorenzo's *Coronation*, where the figures are stacked on mysteriously rising ground and the arching star-studded blue band conveniently provides a place for the figures to stand. Castagno projects his boxlike room using orthogonals and a vanishing point at Christ's head, as Alberti directed. The geometrical precision and symmetry impose a pleasing order, giving the sense that everything is in its place. But the painter has played a trick on his viewer that maybe only a nun staring at it day after day while she ate her bread would have figured out. If she counted the architectural ornaments, instead of listening to the lesson being read by the abbess, she might recognize that it is twice as deep as it seems. Perhaps Castagno wanted to suggest that there is a mystical dimension to the scene that is not immediately visible. Certainly he wanted to show off his skill with the new perspective. To create the architecture the painter would have nailed a string with a weight attached and snapped it into the wet plaster, establishing straight lines. The same might be done to fix the vanishing point—nail holes, not visible from the ground, can sometimes still be seen in frescoes from a scaffold.

Castagno made surprising choices in his coloring. For the outdoor scenes of the upper zone we can see, despite the damage, that the tonality is light and bright, which would be considered normal for fresco. In the *Last Supper,* set in an interior, the coloring is much deeper and darker. It is as if the painter wanted to make this contrast convey the mood of hope that the *Resurrection,* which is the culmination of the story, conveys, while a sense of ominous brooding is present at the final meal the Apostles share with Jesus before he is betrayed. Judas, sitting across the table, is abruptly juxtaposed to Jesus, his dark hair and visage full of foreboding. He turns his head away into profile to avoid looking into Jesus's face. The draperies visible below the table seem carved out of stone, falling in heavy folds deeply incised with dark shadow. The colored marble panels on the rear wall heighten the drama, especially the one behind Peter, Judas, and Jesus.

The pigments are those that can be used in fresco, the earths. In the *Last Supper* there is no expensive blue.[28] The brilliant triad—gold, lapis, vermilion—is absent, as are the translucent pastels of the lakes. This is a palette suited to the monastic setting and budget. It is dominated by the red ochres, ranging from deep purplish to blood to orangey tones. Castagno has modeled these figures in some instances with strongly contrasting hue shifts (cangiante) and in others with the addition of dark monochrome, departing from the instruction of Cennini and following instead the advice of Alberti, whose modeling system was more naturalistic in its imitation of the behavior of colors in light. Cennini's system was, as we have seen, frankly artificial and otherworldly, and it created the further problem that a pigment such as yellow, which is intrinsically high in value, has only a limited range from light to dark, whereas blue can be lightened with white to a pale tint or, if used pure, would be a dark shade. Alberti's down- and up-modeling system allowed all the pigments to be lightened or darkened equally. Alberti's color system gave a measure of naturalism comparable to that of the perspective system.

THE NEW NATURALISM

In the same way that the humanists discovered that they could reconcile Christianity and the classical world, the painters found that naturalism was compatible with the Christian worldview. The celebration of this world that they read about in their antique literary sources need not be at odds with the Christian belief in God's good creation. As interest shifted from depicting the next world to this one, little by little the gold background of panel

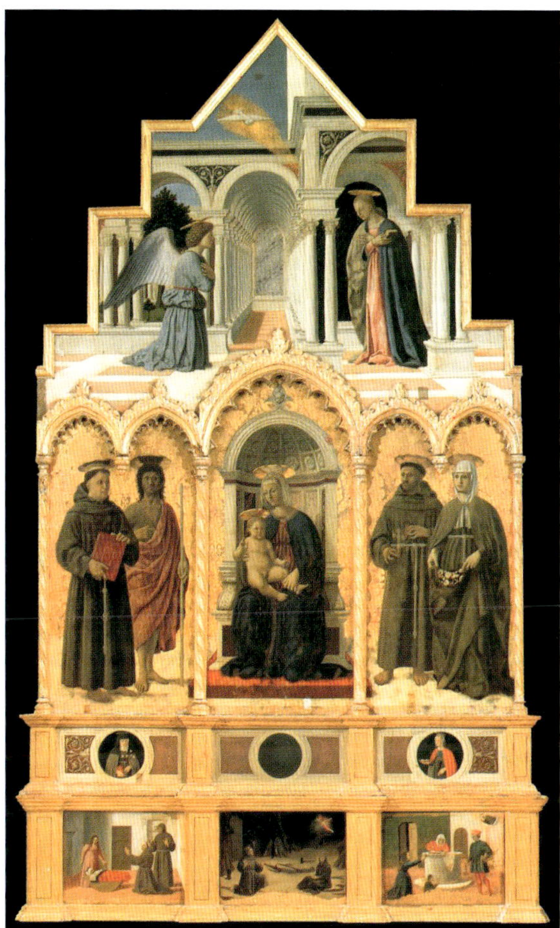

FIG. 1.8. Piero della Francesca, *Perugia Altarpiece,* c. 1470. Tempera (probably tempera grassa) on panel, 11 ft. 1 in. × 7 ft. 7 in. (338 × 230 cm). Galleria Nazionale dell'Umbria, Perugia.

paintings disappeared and was replaced with buildings and landscapes rendered with perspective. By the middle of the century in Florence, a gold ground looked old-fashioned. We can see Piero della Francesca chaffing at the requirement in the altarpiece he was commissioned to paint for a Perugian church in 1468 (fig. 1.8). If, as one scholar claims, he was called in to complete a work begun by another artist, it would explain its archaic form.[29] With tongue in cheek, surely, he painted reflections of the saints' pates on their haloes, which are depicted in perspective against the flat gold ground (fig. 1.9)! In the *Annunciation* that crowns the altarpiece, Piero showed off his command of perspective and his understanding of shadow and its role in the illusion of spatial recession: an ironic juxtaposition of the old Gothic ways and the new Renaissance. There were traditionalists among the patrons even in Florence, of course. Neri di Bicci was perfectly willing to accommodate their tastes up until his

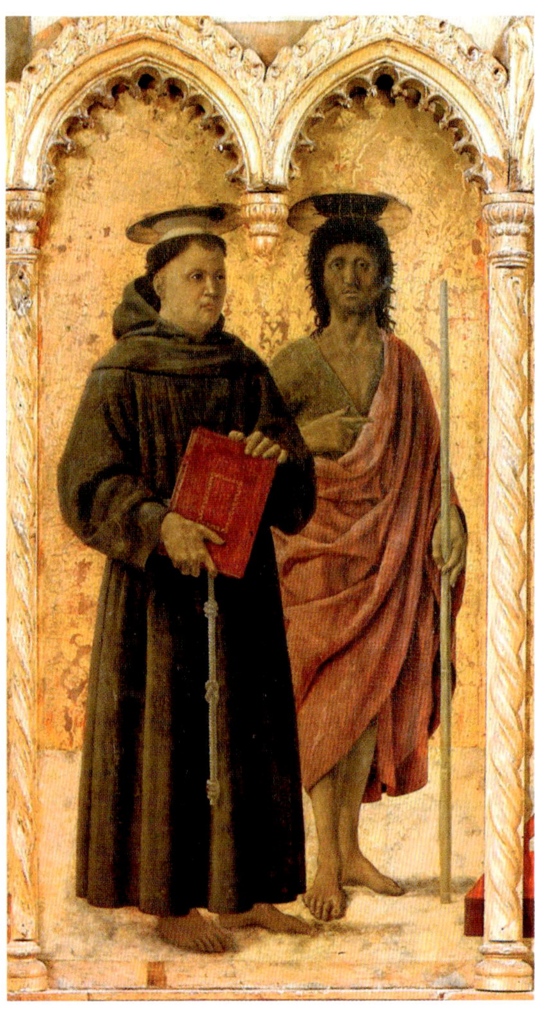

death in 1491 in his numerous altarpieces where, instead of landscape or architecture in the newfangled perspective, we find a gold ground.[30]

Alberti had advised painters not to use gold but to simulate it with yellow because they should show off their skill, which should be more valued than precious materials. With real gold the reflections were determined by the source of the light, flickering candles or lamps; with simulated gilding it was possible to control the reflection of light and make it consonant with the light source in the painting. Painting in this way would elevate the status of the painters, in Alberti's view. Within a year of Alberti's book, Fra Filippo Lippi took his advice and substituted yellow paint for gilding in his *Tarquinia Madonna,* dated 1437 (fig. 1.10). A few years later Domenico Veneziano, in his *Saint Lucy Altarpiece* (fig. 1.11), demonstrated his sensitivity to light: we see a beautiful brocaded cope worn by Saint Zenobius where the gilded pattern disappears into the folds, instead of being painted flat on top, as Lorenzo had done. The faux gilding picks up the light entering the church and the painting from the right.

In his color scheme, Domenico obeyed the spirit rather than the letter of Alberti's prescription. He has rejected the luminous Cennini-style palette, but he has judiciously avoided dark shadows and the overly wide range of values that the Alberti system can produce. He has toned down his colors, using pink lake as a leitmotif, together with shades of gray. Indeed a grayish tone threads its way through nearly all the colors, giving a pleasing unity. Only the Baptist's vermilion, echoed in Lucy's slippers, is allowed to remain undiluted. Of the painters working in the 1430s, when Alberti circulated his book, only Fra Angelico resisted and continued to use the medieval coloring system. Filippo Lippi was quick not only to abandon gilding in the *Tarquinia Madonna;* he toned down his coloring, even experimenting with substituting a grayish green with an orangey undertone for the Madonna's accustomed blue robe, and he pairs it with a mellow orangey color on her dress where we would expect vermilion.[31] He would repeat this dulcet tonality throughout his career. The masterful *Pitti Tondo,* with its complicated tripartite space, is bound together by his repetition of desaturated reds and blues, framed by the grays and tans of the architecture and furniture (fig. 1.12). He deftly chooses just the right intensity and size of field for the bedcover and curtains so as to draw attention to the mother in her bed, without letting her pop forward

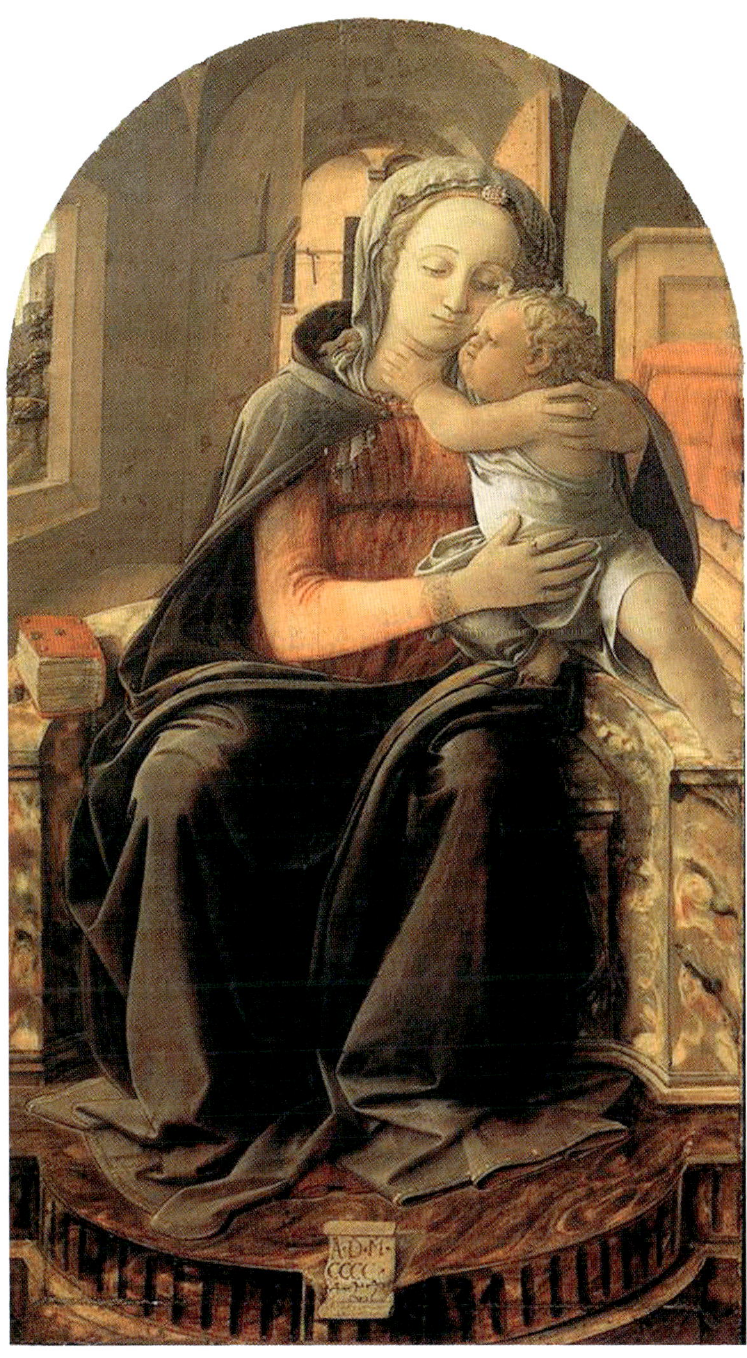

FIG. 1.10. Filippo Lippi, *Tarquinia Madonna*, 1437. Tempera on panel, 59½ × 26 in. (151 × 66 cm). Galleria Nazionale d'Arte Antica, Rome.

and disrupt the carefully calculated recession. There is virtually no gold, no ultramarine, no bright-red vermilion color here. We are presented with a plausible rendering of a Renaissance palace and a stylish Florentine mother who might well live in it. We are persuaded of the Virgin and Child's special status not by any supernatural paraphernalia, but only by the perfection of the Virgin's beauty and the ideal proportions of their setting.

The harsh effect that Alberti's down-modeling with blackish shadows produced can be seen in Benozzo Gozzoli's *Madonna and Child Enthroned with Angels and Saints and Saint Zenobius* (see fig. 1.2). Fra Angelico's principal assistant and follower, Gozzoli was quick to convert to Alberti's down-modeling once his master was dead. The contract of 1461 mentioned earlier stipulated not only that Angelico's work serve as a model. It laid a further burden on the painter by designating the eight saints who must be included, and also, with exceptional stringency, their position in the composition. This meant that Gozzoli had to balance Saint Francis in his dun-colored

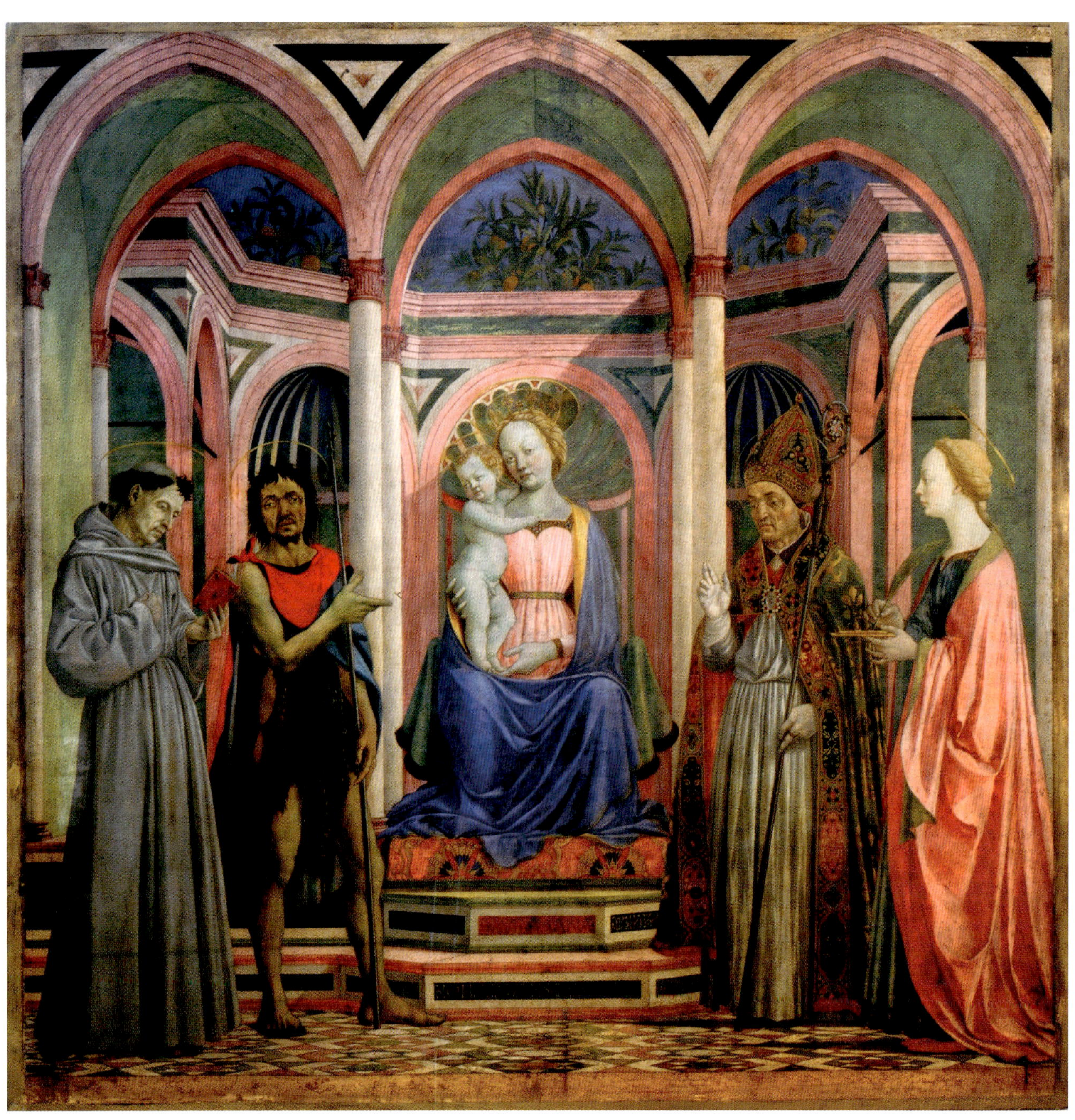

FIG. 1.11. Domenico Veneziano, *Saint Lucy Altarpiece*, c. 1445–47. Tempera on panel, 82 ¼ × 85 in. (209 × 216 cm). Uffizi, Florence.

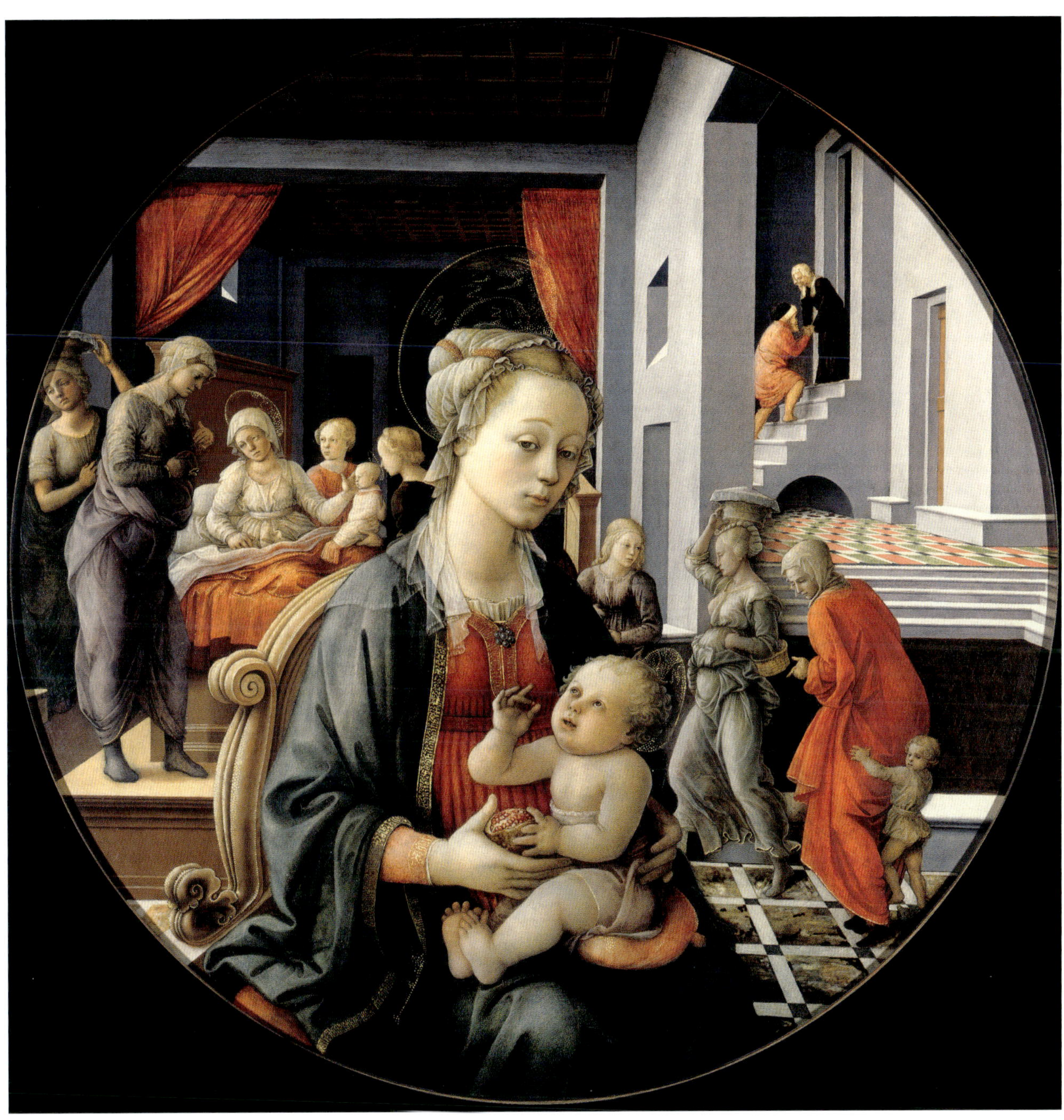

FIG. 1.12. Filippo Lippi, *Pitti Tondo,* 1452. Oil on panel, 53 in. (135 cm) diam. Palazzo Pitti, Florence.

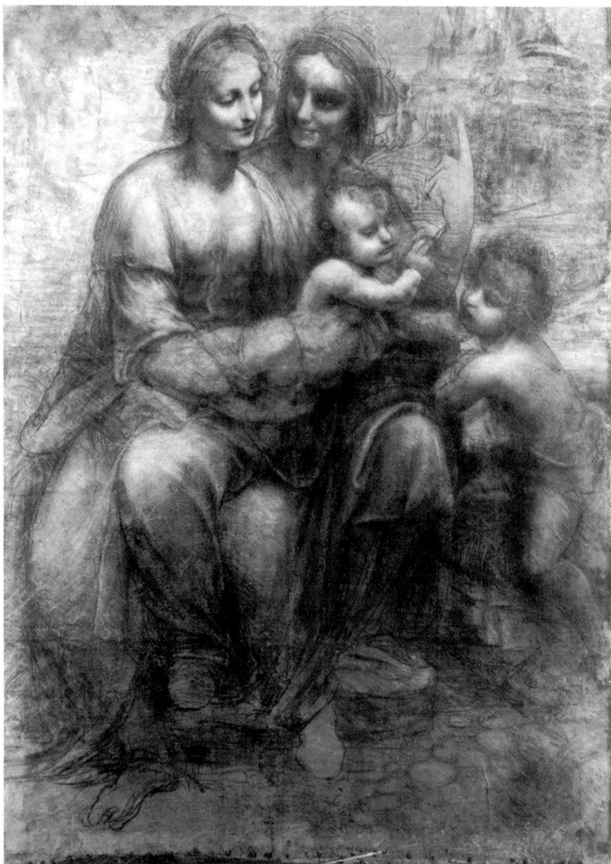

FIG. 1.13. Leonardo da Vinci, *Madonna and Child with Saint Anne*, c. 1499–1500. Charcoal and white chalk on paper, 55¾ × 41¼ in. (141.5 × 104.5 cm). National Gallery, London.

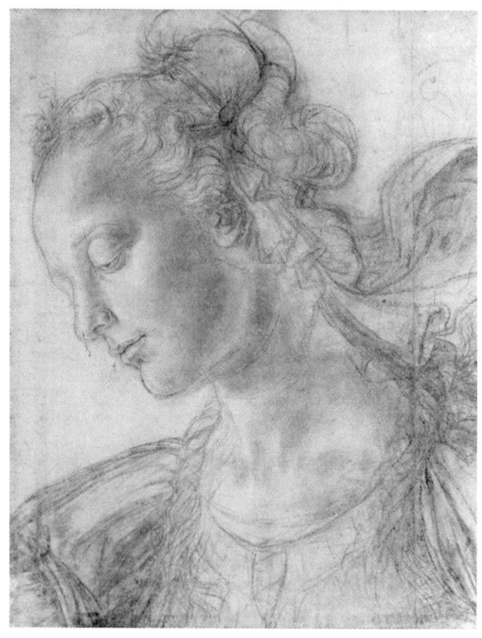

FIG 1.14. Andrea del Verrocchio, *Cartoon of a Head*, n.d. Black chalk and wash on paper, 16 × 13 in. (40.8 × 32.8 cm). Christ Church, Oxford.

habit with Saint Jerome, who as a cardinal was conventionally depicted in a bright-red robe. His solution was to show Jerome in his desert garb, neutral gray. These are the kinds of problems with which the fifteenth-century painter, working within the conventions of costume and the specifications of a contract, had to deal. Gozzoli has elected to conform to the new taste for more naturalistic color by reducing the intensity of his pigments, even the Madonna's blue, and by modeling his draperies down with dark monochrome in the Albertian manner. His scene is a plausible rendering of a gathering of saints and angels in a terrestrial garden, though it might be judged also a little pedestrian and mundane.

PREPARING TO PAINT: THE CARTOON

At the very beginning of the sixteenth century, Leonardo returned to Florence, after an absence of nearly twenty years when he was working at the Sforza court in Milan. Soon thereafter he put on public display a cartoon he had been working on. It is now lost, but a later version

has survived (fig. 1.13). It could be said that its exhibition changed the course of Florentine painting, but since cartoons had been in use since the 1440s, we need to investigate why this was a revolutionary artistic event.

Until printing increased the supply, paper was too expensive to be used much for experimental drawing. Artists drew on the wall they were going to plaster and paint, or on wax tablets and other reusable surfaces. Even so, by the 1440s some or most painters were preparing their frescoes with cartoons. We have seen that Castagno had used cartoons in Sant'Apollonia, and there is evidence that Paolo Uccello, Domenico Veneziano, and Piero della Francesca were all early users of cartoons for their frescoes. Indeed, because fresco must be executed quickly before the plaster dries, preparatory drawings that could be transferred at the time of painting were useful and, as compositions became more intricate, they became almost indispensable. In fact, almost as interesting as who used cartoons is who did not. Neither Fra Angelico nor Fra Filippo Lippi, already mature professionals in the 1430s, used cartoons.[32] Lippi even painted his frescoes in Prato and Spoleto in the 1460s without cartoons, which means that his pupil, Sandro Botticelli, and his son, Filippino, did not have the practice instilled in them in their workshop training. They were the exceptions in their generation.[33]

For panel painting, the adoption of cartoons took longer, but by the 1460s they were beginning to appear. The Pollaiuolo brothers were trained by Castagno, so it was logical that they would adopt the practice,[34] as well as Alesso Baldovinetti, who had assisted Domenico Veneziano.[35] It was Andrea del Verrocchio, who trained several of the most important painters in the last quarter century, who made the practice standard.

Verrocchio, in the tradition of the Florentine workshop, as advocated by Cennini, taught his pupils to draw by making precise copies of drawings. His large workshop produced paintings, sculptures, and goldsmiths' work. He was a superb draftsman, so his pupils learned from the best. Vasari praised his heads of women, made with a graceful manner and elaborate hair arrangements, which Leonardo imitated.[36] An example is the pricked drawing in Verrocchio's *Cartoon of a Head* (fig. 1.14). The medium of black chalk came to be preferred over pen or silverpoint at about this time because it enabled the artist to create the light and shade without hatching or sharp contour, and with a softness that is similar to what the oil medium allows. The chalk is smudged or stumped, creating tonal values that can be directly transcribed into the underpainting.[37] The painters who received this training went on to incorporate the use of cartoons in their practice. Domenico Ghirlandaio, who was kept busy as a frescoist, would have found cartoons an integral part of the preparation process also for panels. We have pricked cartoons surviving for panel paintings by Lorenzo di Credi and by Leonardo. Filippino, though he depended less on cartoons for his panels, used them for his frescoes. Perugino in particular learned to appreciate their usefulness in keeping a record of designs, which could be modified and reused.

These large and successful workshops were necessarily organized for efficiency. Filippino, for example, like his contemporaries, had many projects in hand at the same time. When he died in 1504, at the age of forty-seven, an inventory of one of his two workshops showed that at least thirty-two pictures were in various states of finish, as well as pieces of marble and stucco, carved

frames, wooden book covers, and chests and other pieces of furniture, all to be painted.[38] The cartoon was the culmination of the preparation process, which went through laborious stages of different kinds of drawing. The painter's conception would first be recorded in a compositional sketch, which would then need to be worked up in figure studies, often using studio apprentices as models. Individual studies had to be assembled in a more polished compositional study, with necessary revisions incorporated. A cartoon of the entire picture could be so large as to be unwieldy, so it might never be made; instead, partial cartoons could be pieced together. Figure studies could be squared for transfer—that is, a grid drawn over them that would allow an assistant to enlarge them to the full scale. These partial cartoons would be transferred to the painting surface, either by pricking the outlines and rubbing black chalk through the holes (*spolvero*), or by incision onto the damp plaster or the gesso. An underdrawing would then be made, connecting the dots or tracing the incised lines with a brush and liquid paint, indicating the modeling in summary fashion.

Leonardo of course learned to make pricked cartoons in Verrocchio's workshop, but when in 1481 he received a commission to paint an altarpiece for a Florentine church of the Adoration of the Magi, he rejected what he had been taught and instead worked out his design on the panel (fig. 1.15).[39] After drawing the perspective construction at the top, he drew the figures freehand with a dry graphic medium, reworking the contours to find the exact definition. He then reinforced it with black watercolor. Over this underdrawing he created undermodeling with a brush and blue watercolor, probably indigo. On top of this he applied a white lead layer diluted with a lot of medium to fix the underlying layers. To introduce sfumato or effects of chiaroscuro, he applied a mixture of lead white with umber, irregularly blending it with his fingers. This was clearly an experimental approach, but it may have been created to compensate for the inadequacy of working with piecemeal cartoons. With his method he could see the whole composition, anticipating the practice of making full-scale cartoons that would develop early in the next century. His choices reflect his consuming interest in light and graded shadow, which he would study empirically in his notebooks over the succeeding decades. This painting was left uncompleted when he departed the next year for Milan, but it conveniently reveals his working method.

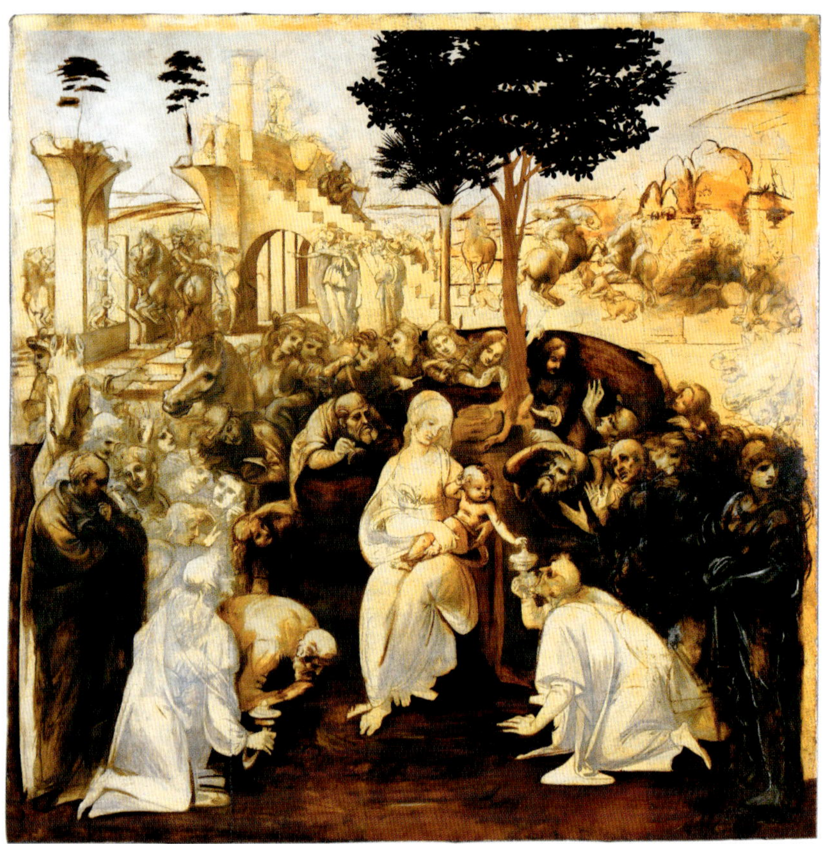

What remains to be done is the coloring. It is evident that it would have been a very different interpretation of the subject from the usual Florentine treatment, such as Botticelli's for Santa Maria Novella of around 1475 (fig. 1.16), or Ghirlandaio's (fig. 1.17). This was to be a very dark and pensive meditation on the epiphany of the Son of God, not the celebration with a cortege of exotic kings that the Florentines were accustomed to seeing. Translucent oils put down on top of this very dark underpainting could not result in anything but a very dark picture. To lighten it he would have had to mask the darks already applied with lead white or other opaque pigments. Leonardo had his own agenda, which was to explore chiaroscuro across the composition, not one figure at a time, as the method of preparing piecemeal cartoons favored. Quite unlike Jan van Eyck and the Flemish models, he did not want to focus on minute details, but to envelop his figures in atmosphere and shadow that would conceal insignificant detail. The precise rendering for which the Flemish painters found oil so useful, as we shall see, was the antithesis of Leonardo's reason for using it, which was to soften edges and fuse forms—his famous sfumato, or smoky tone.

This ambition is not yet realized in the unfinished *Adoration,* but it became increasingly apparent as his painting style developed, as for example in the *Madonna of the Rocks* in Paris. For some of his pictures he did use cartoons, especially, and understandably, for his portraits. Certainly he made many preparatory drawings. Leonardo preferred to work very slowly and erratically, taking time out to make his scientific observations and record them. He failed to deliver to his patrons many of the paintings commissioned of him because he kept working on them and never considered them finished.[40] This erratic working method is why he needed to avoid fresco and invent a new medium for the mural of the *Last Supper,* and later for the *Battle of Anghiari.* In both, involving oil in at least the first case, his experiments failed.

After Leonardo left Milan and returned to Florence, he worked out a design for what would become the *Madonna and Child with Saint Anne* in a full-scale cartoon. The one that survives and is seen in London—in charcoal and black and white chalk on eight sheets of paper glued together—is a later version of the original drawing, but it can give us an idea of what it was that captured the attention of the Florentines who, according to Vasari, lined up for two days to see it and marvel.

There is no record of a cartoon ever having been put on public display before, so Leonardo's decision to exhibit it suggests that he knew just how novel it would appear to the painters especially. His reason for going to the work and expense of making a full cartoon is apparent when one views it. It has a unity of tone and chiaroscuro that is unprecedented in the works of his Florentine contemporaries. Their piecemeal approach resulted in works that are satisfactory in design and composition, to be sure, but additive in effect. The figures often fail to conceal that they have been studied separately and then juxtaposed. Color may serve to focus the eye on the major figures, but the even lighting gives equal importance to everything.

The pieced cartoon suited the Quattrocento aesthetic. Central-point perspective encouraged an arrangement of figures parallel to the picture plane, with the vanishing point set near the center, and architecture and figures diminished according to the mathematical formula. One often finds a kind of isocephaly, in which each figure, developed with interesting and varied detail, has been lined up in the foreground. Perugino's *Marriage of the Virgin* (Caen, Musée des Beaux-Arts) is a characteristic example, as are his frescoes of Famous Men (fig. 1.18). Often background details of landscape or architecture will have the same degree of detail and color intensity as those in the foreground, diffusing the focus and scattering the viewer's attention across the whole picture. This strategy gives richness and may prolong viewer attention, which is important in devotional works that will be seen year in, year out, but it sacrifices drama. In Leonardo's cartoon the uneven light reinforces his dense composition of overlapped figures. He has concentrated his attention on the modeling of the faces, stumping the chalk to give them softly graduated shading. One can see how much he has learned and retained from Verrocchio (see fig. 1.14). Here as there, he indicates the hair with loose, undefining strokes; he has even left Anne's pointing gesture unfinished, to be worked out at a later stage, but the carefully observed light gives volume to the figures. What results is an intensity, a concentration of attention among the actors that makes one feel as though they are physically present in a new way.

It is easy to understand why the next generation would begin to create full cartoons, even if it meant having to cut them up into manageable pieces to use them

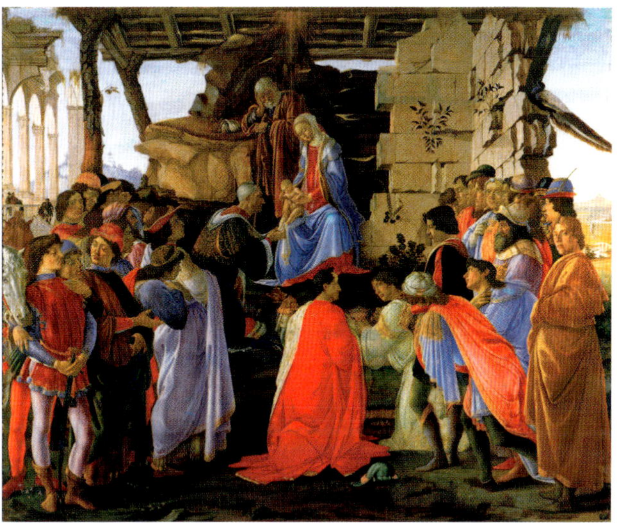

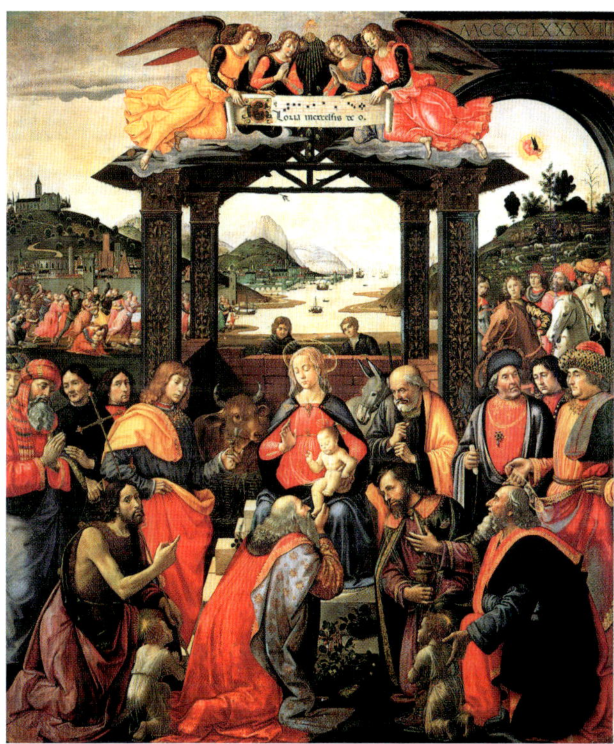

FIG. 1.16. Sandro Botticelli, *Adoration of the Magi*, c. 1475. Tempera on panel, 43 ¾ × 52 ¾ in. (111 × 134 cm). Uffizi, Florence.

FIG. 1.17. Domenico Ghirlandaio, *Adoration of the Magi*, 1485. Tempera on panel, 9 ft. 4 in. × 8 ft. (285 × 243 cm). Ospedale degli Innocenti, Florence.

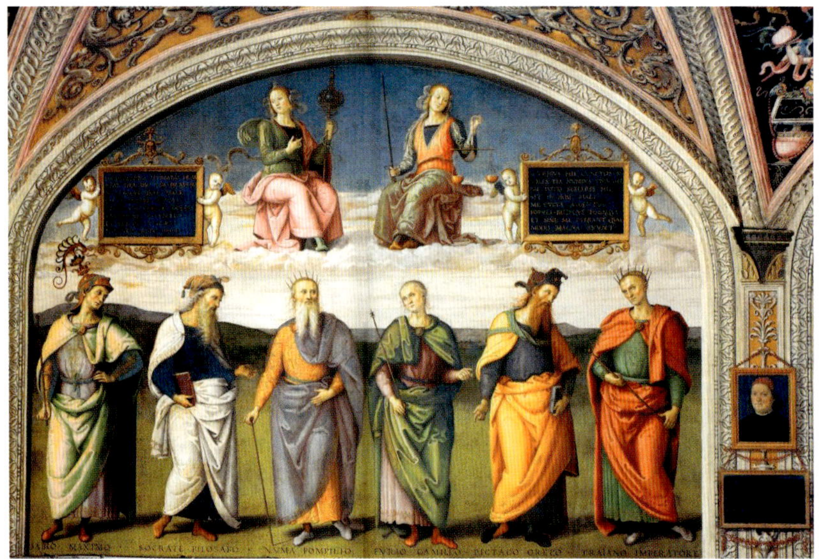

FIG. 1.18. Pietro Perugino, *Famous Men,* 1497–1500. Fresco, 9 ft. 7 ¼ in. × 13 ft. 8 ½ in. (293 × 418 cm). Collegio di Cambio, Perugia.

in painting. Almost immediately, in 1503, the Signoria, in commissioning Leonardo and Michelangelo to paint battles commemorating Florentine victories in the Sala del Consiglio, apparently required full cartoons, for there are payments recording the process.[41] It is fortunate that they did, because that was all that came of the project, and those cartoons for the *Battle of Anghiari* and the *Battle of Cascina* were studied and copied until they fell apart. To overcome the problem of the cartoon being too big to handle, the master would sometimes have them cut up and used as needed, or would have substitute cartoons made by copying the portion needed for the day's work.[42] In the sixteenth century, cartoons became collector's items, so painters might preserve them intact to be gifted or sold. Raphael, when he was too busy to execute a painting for a distinguished client, might send him a cartoon as recompense.[43]

OIL

The Albertian system of modeling was not as aesthetically successful as Cennini's—adding black can produce murky color. It was not widely adopted in the manner he prescribed, but it prodded the painters toward greater naturalism. A greater spur was probably contact with Flemish oil paintings. Both the Albertian and the Netherlandish systems favored verisimilitude and a darker palette, but where Alberti's system could become dingy and cheerless, oil could produce a unique luminosity.

The transition from tempera to oil as the preferred medium in Italy was a process, not the event Vasari reconstructed. Cennini had recommended using oil for certain specific purposes, so it was not unknown, but it was not until the last third of the Quattrocento that Florentine painters began painting with it, usually in combination with egg tempera, and it was not until the Cinquecento that oil replaced tempera.[44] Italians could have been inspired to learn the technique by meeting visiting painters from the North, but it was primarily by seeing the paintings that had been imported. The Medici in particular collected them: Paula Nuttall catalogued thirty-three works by Netherlandish artists in the Medici collections and thirty-one in other patrician collections, mostly anonymous. One of the few identified by artist was a tiny Jan van Eyck, *Saint Jerome in His Study,* listed in Piero de' Medici's inventory of 1456–63.[45] Florentine painters would have had ample opportunity to study it and other examples.

A few Flemish painters had traveled to Italy. There is some evidence that Petrus Christus, the principal painter in Bruges after Van Eyck's death in 1441, visited Milan; certainly his works were collected in Italy—there is one identified in the Medici collection. Rogier van der Weyden is known to have worked for the duke of Ferrara and perhaps to have traveled to Rome for the Jubilee in 1450. Cosimo Tura in Ferrara, in his *Allegory* from the late 1450s, shows the systematic use of glazes in oil in the Netherlandish manner, which strongly suggests a firsthand knowledge (fig. 1.19). It is a showpiece of faux gilding, jewels, and ornaments—fabulous fish-dragons with ruby eyes and pearl teeth—and deep, rich coloring.

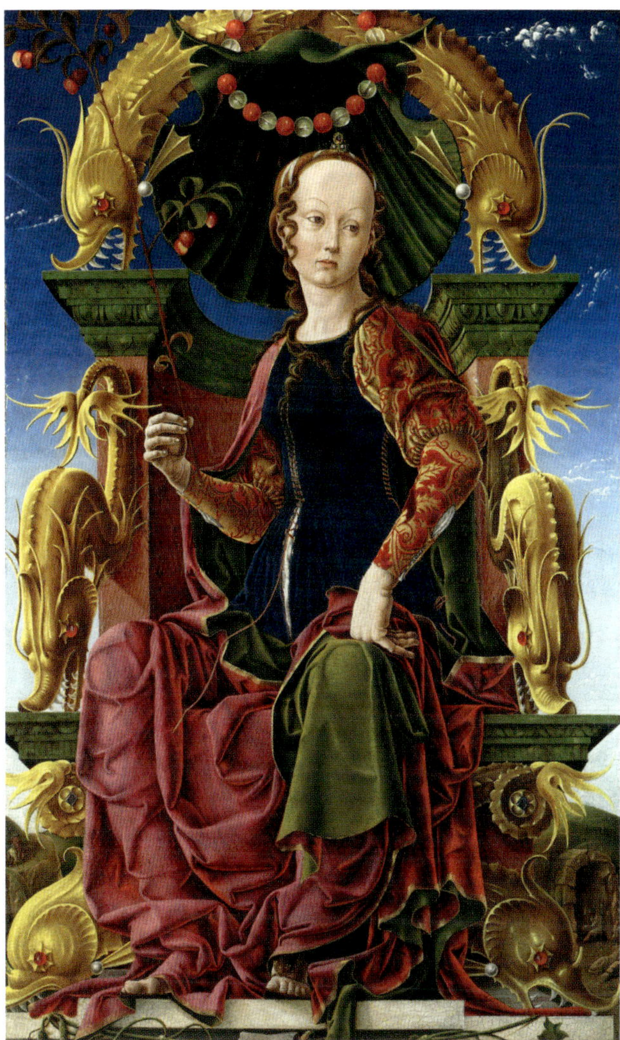

How he learned it we don't know. Perhaps Rogier stopped in Ferrara on his way to Rome, or a member of his shop delivered a painting to the duke.[46]

We do know that a neighboring duke, Federigo da Montefeltro, imported Justus van Gent, who worked at his court in Urbino from 1473. The duke was evidently interested in oil painting, for he already had in his employ Piero della Francesca, who must have converted to oils in the mid-1450s. Piero's early *Baptism of Christ* (London, National Gallery) is an exemplary tempera painting, with green underpaint in the flesh and hatched brushstrokes. By the time he finished the central panel of his *Madonna* for the Confraternity of the Misericordia (Sansepolcro) in 1454, he must have been painting in oil, to judge by the wide drying cracks, which one does not find in tempera.[47] By 1466 he was known as a painter in

oil, for he was contracted to paint a banner in oil that year.[48] When Justus arrived in Urbino, Piero was already working there, so the two court painters must have had interesting exchanges.

Jan van Eyck had perfected the use of oil glazing in transparent layers. Unlike the oil technique developed in sixteenth-century Italy, where broad effects were sought, Van Eyck used very small brushes to create intricate detail. The dazzling luminosity of jewels and the texture of everything, from soft fur and hair to metallic candlesticks and gleaming fabrics and brocades, commanded the attention of Italian painters. Painting in tempera, with its matte surface, they could not begin to capture effects like these, nor could they achieve the depth of color. Van Eyck's technique depended on the transparency of oil and on layering. Consensus on his modeling technique has not been reached; it is hoped that the present study of the huge and complex Ghent Altarpiece will yield new understanding. In the Washington *Annunciation*, he used three layers, with some black in the lower two layers and then pure, deep saturated color in the final glaze. Other studies have found only a trace of black in the deepest shadows.[49] The white he used was the ground, and probably a white imprimatura, which would shine through the light areas and would be selectively masked by the glaze used for the shadows. A reflection might be rendered with just a touch of opaque lead white. Robert Campin, his predecessor, and Rogier van der Weyden, one of his successors, used egg tempera layers under their oil layers, but Van Eyck did not.[50] This describes the principles of the Eyckian technique. In practice it was more intricate.

The *Annunciation* has suffered damage from an eighteenth-century transfer to canvas, but it has been conserved and recently meticulously studied at the National Gallery in Washington, D.C. (fig. 1.20).[51] Van Eyck prepared his composition on a white ground with a detailed black underdrawing using a brush and a liquid material, probably water-based, as was common practice. There are no redrawings, which suggests he may have worked from a preliminary drawing. For the perspective he incised lines into the ground with a straightedge. These lines do not converge perfectly; the perspective is the kind of empirical system used in Italy until Alberti— it is not until Albrecht Dürer that we find anyone in the North making a scientific study of perspective. The viewer's position was fixed by the reflections, in the same

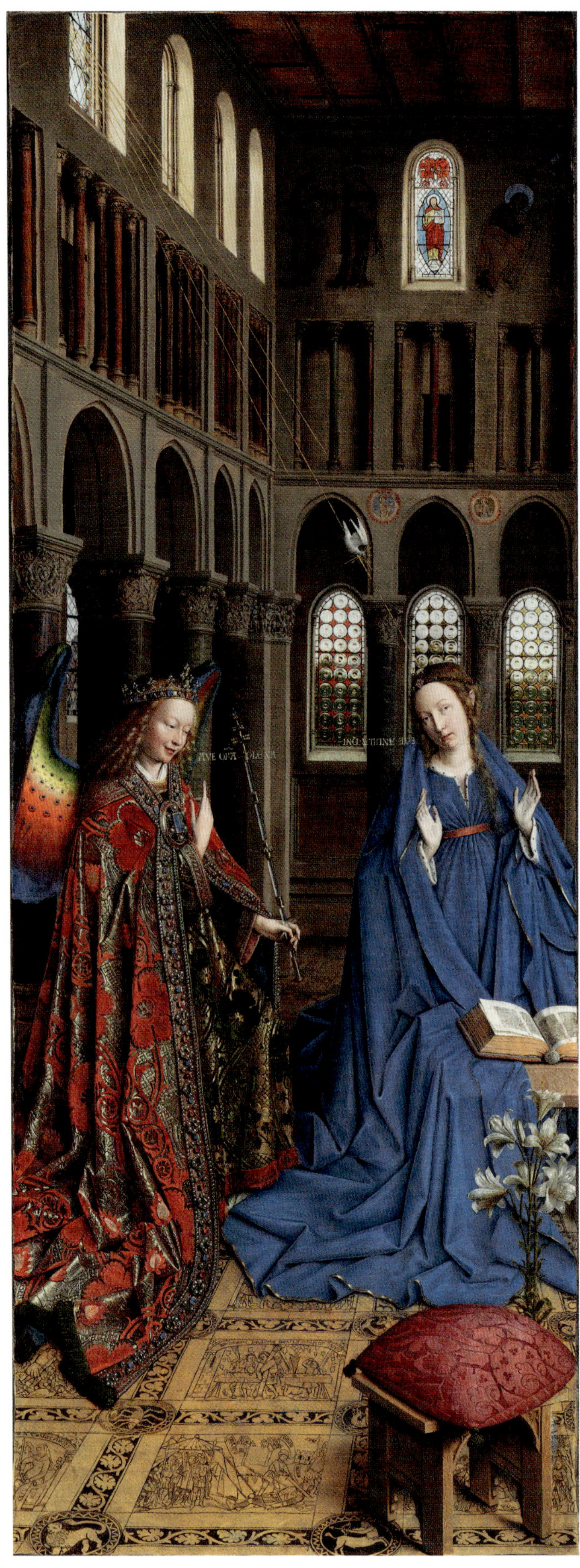

FIG. 1.20. Jan van Eyck, *Annunciation*, c. 1434–36. Oil on panel transferred to canvas, 35 1/2 × 13 1/2 in. (90.25 × 34 cm). National Gallery of Art, Washington, D.C.

way that the placement of the vanishing point fixes the viewer's position in the Italian central-point perspective system.

For light areas, he normally reserved the area and painted directly on the reflective white ground. The dove, however, was added in the last stage of painting and was painted on top of the background. As a final step, the lines he had incised for the heavenly rays he then filled with the only real gold in the painting, which is otherwise replete with faux gilding on the figures.

There are no special secrets to his oil medium that explain his technical brilliance, nor are his pigments exceptional, though they are of the highest quality. He used the best ultramarine and did not underpaint it here with azurite, as he sometimes did. The two underlayers in the Virgin's blue drapery are ultramarine, but with admixtures and of a coarser grind than that of the final glaze, originally sapphire blue but now degraded, producing an unintended light blue. He used vermilion for his opaque reds, glazed with expensive deep-red lake derived from insects such as kermes. Green passages are glazed with a transparent copper green. The use of such precious materials suggests that it may have been intended for a very important patron and a location such as the ducal chapel of the Chartreuse de Champmol.

The intricacy of Van Eyck's technique was not easy to discover from visual examination, however, and some Florentines trying to imitate it got it wrong. It was exacting and time-consuming work because each layer needed to dry before the next glaze could be applied. Some of Van Eyck's followers abridged the process, further misleading would-be imitators. White was used for modeling by painters of the next generation, for example.[52] Justus van Gent had certainly abandoned the slow buildup of layers when he painted the very large altarpiece of the *Communion of the Apostles* (1474) at the court of Urbino. Its poor condition suggests that he did not allow sufficient drying time before painting the next layer.

Antonio Filarete, who was a sculptor and architect, gave the first description in Italian of the process of Flemish oil technique in his treatise compiled in 1460–64. He admits to understanding the process only partially. He describes glazing and emphasizes the importance of letting it dry between layers, but he instructs the painter to "prepare the shadows with the tint you prefer, and then when all is dry give a thin coat of the colour which is to clothe the preparation, and round the form more

completely, heightening with white or any other tint that will harmonise with that which you have given to the object." These instructions sound more like tempera practice than Flemish, and rather than clarifying may have added to the misunderstandings.[53]

TEMPERA GRASSA IN FLORENCE

In Florence the first attempt to emulate Flemish oil painting took place very soon after Filarete's treatise, in an altarpiece of 1467–68 by the Pollaiuolo brothers, principally by Antonio (fig. 1.21). The chapel for the cardinal of Portugal was made as a memorial to the young cardinal who had died in Florence in 1459 on his way to Austria, where Pope Pius II had appointed him papal legate.[54] The cardinal was the brother-in-law and cousin of the king of Portugal, so no expense was spared on this gem of a chapel. For the altarpiece the executors felt it appropriate to have it painted in a manner that the cardinal would have known in his native land, where painting practice was derived from the Flemish. The patrons therefore went to the trouble of importing oak boards to make the panel because it was the support used in Flanders, not the poplar universally used in Italy.[55] The sumptuous garments of the three saints, especially the jewel-encrusted robe of Saint Vincent, are more familiar in Flemish than in Florentine paintings. The medium is oil, although there are traces of tempera in underlayers.

Here we have a demonstration of how difficult it can be to copy technique with nothing more reliable to go on than visual observation. This can serve as a warning to art historians trying to reconstruct how something was painted without the aid of scientific analysis. Pollaiuolo got it wrong. The shadows of the velvet cloak of Saint James and the robe of Saint Vincent have been modeled down in what he must have thought was the way the Flemish modeled. What we see is not the deep tones penetrated by light but a dark, murky color. The Pollaiuolo brothers continued to explore oil, but with their imperfect understanding of the technique. In the later *Martyrdom of Saint Sebastian* (London, National Gallery, 1475), the paint does not appear to have been built up layer by layer, as in the Flemish technique, but to have been laid down in a single thick application, which led to drying cracks and raised, bubbling paint.[56]

Pollaiuolo and other early experimenters with oil in Florence often combined it with tempera. They had perfected the painting of flesh with their egg-bound

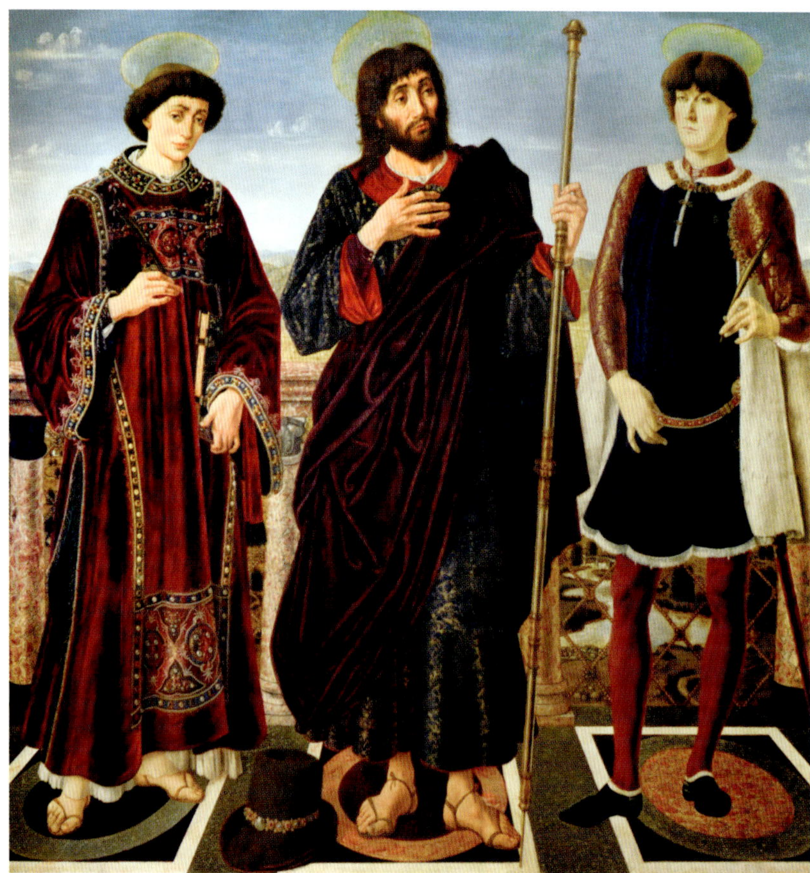

FIG. 1.21. Antonio del Pollaiuolo, *Three Saints*, 1467–68. Tempera grassa on panel, 76 ¾ × 70 ½ in. (179 × 172 cm). Uffizi, Florence.

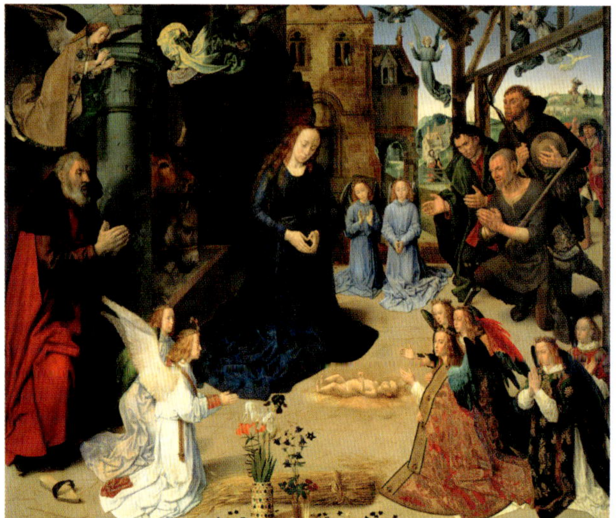

FIG. 1.22. Hugo van der Goes, *Portinari Altarpiece*, delivered 1483. Oil on panel, 8 ft. 4 in. × 10 ft. (253 × 305 cm). Uffizi, Florence.

greenish underpaint and seemed disinclined to give it up. They sometimes used tempera as their first layer and then glazed in oil over it. A favorite compromise used by painters in the later Quattrocento is what the Italians call *tempera grassa* ("fat tempera"), in which some oil is added to egg tempera to increase the saturation of the color. The typical hatching brushwork of tempera was retained, but deeper and richer color could be achieved. In paintings of mixed media, tempera grassa tends to be used in dark colors, while light colors are in tempera. Even those painters who continued to paint primarily in tempera such as Botticelli and Ghirlandaio have been found to have tried out all the combinations.[57]

The arrival of the Portinari Altarpiece in Florence in 1483 to adorn the altar of one of the major churches had a demonstrable impact (fig. 1.22). Commissioned by the agent of the Medici bank in Bruges, Tommaso Portinari, the huge triptych was much more accessible than pictures in private possession. The most frequently cited is Ghirlandaio's response in his *Adoration of the Shepherds* for the Sassetti Chapel, where his unidealized shepherds are unprecedented, but other painters were equally if more subtly affected. Painters could also encounter Flemish works when they traveled in Italy. It is thought that Perugino saw the Sforza triptych by the workshop of Rogier van der Weyden when he visited Pesaro to paint two portraits of Costanzo Sforza. Rogier's city descending a hill could be the source of the city in the background of Perugino's *Crucifixion with Saints,* where the meticulous detail of the landscape and the symbolic flowers in the foreground are certainly inspired by Flemish painting (see fig. 1.4). The flowering plants, which are precise enough to allow identification, are strikingly like those running along the border in the Portinari Altarpiece.[58]

Other Netherlandish paintings were collected in Florence and known to painters. Bishop Pagagnotti had a small triptych by Hans Memling (fig. 1.23), which he must have made available to painters, because a detail of the watermill in the background shows up in works by Filippino Lippi (fig. 1.24, upper right) and Fra Bartolomeo.[59] This is among the most traceable instances of Florentines imitating Flemish models, but there are many others, some more suggested than explicit.

Filippino, as the son of Filippo Lippi, was beginning his training in his father's workshop alongside the older Botticelli in 1469 when his father died. How much he might have learned about oil from his father is uncertain, although there are hints that Filippo was impressed with Flemish painting as early as the 1430s and 1440s (recall his faux gilding in the *Tarquinia Madonna;* see fig. 1.10). Botticelli, though he felt it necessary to experiment, clearly preferred the tempera technique in which he was trained, but Filippino was enamored of the deep colors and the meticulous detail of Flemish painting, as is evident in the faux gilding and rendering of jewels and metalwork in his *Four Saints* (fig. 1.24). It appears to be painted in tempera grassa. The medium has not been established by testing, but we can see hatched brushwork. The deep shadows of the draperies are probably reinforced with dark paint, rather than glazed in multiple layers.

After 1460 the oil medium must have been the buzz in the workshops, yet some of the painters trained earlier were not enticed. Their attitude seems to have been: It's an option, which has advantages in certain situations, but there is no reason to abandon the egg tempera technique that I have perfected. This may characterize the response of the generation born around 1440, including Cosimo Rosselli, Botticelli, and Ghirlandaio. Together

with Perugino, these were the painters chosen to fresco the newly rebuilt papal chapel at the Vatican under the patronage of Sixtus IV, and were therefore regarded as the cream of the crop. That they were all accomplished frescoists may help account for their reluctance to embrace oil, because the technique and palette of tempera and fresco have much more in common than do oil and fresco.

In this period when a major upheaval in materials was taking place, I would like to look more closely at Sandro Botticelli as an example of his generation. He zigged and zagged among the various alternatives, employing pure tempera and then at times tempera grassa; in other instances he used oil-based glazes over egg tempera underpaints, and he sometimes painted certain portions in tempera and others in oil. His late *Mystic Nativity* (London, National Gallery, 1500) is entirely in oil.[60] He matched his technique to the project, so that it has been difficult to trace a development in his color style, contributing to difficulties in establishing a chronology of his undated works. From his training with Fra Filippo Lippi he would have inherited his master's relatively subdued coloring. His *Adoration of the Magi* in the Uffizi, a small altarpiece dated 1475–76, looks very much like a painting in the tradition of tempera (see fig. 1.16). The vermilion drapery of the second magus at the center anchors the color scheme, and its brilliant red is a leitmotif throughout the panel, echoed in the Virgin's robe and in flanking figures. Whites are prominent, together with slightly paled blues, so the red, blue, white triad, combined with an absence of dark shadows, creates a festive air.

He adjusted his coloring and probably his medium not only to the subject but perhaps also to the viewing conditions. We do not know anything about the original site of the *Primavera* (fig. 1.25) and the later *Birth of Venus.* If the latter was, as we usually assume, commissioned about a decade later as a pendant to the *Primavera,* then perhaps different lighting helps account for the darker background in the *Primavera* and the very light-filled atmosphere of the *Birth of Venus.* In any case, it's appropriate that the colors of the apparition of Venus, blown in from the sea by the zephyrs to the shore, should be pale and almost without shadow. Everything about the way Botticelli has chosen to paint her suggests a remote, otherworldly realm: the receding shore, the unmodulated sky, and the inverted V-shaped waves are all highly stylized. Venus herself is contoured with a dark line that

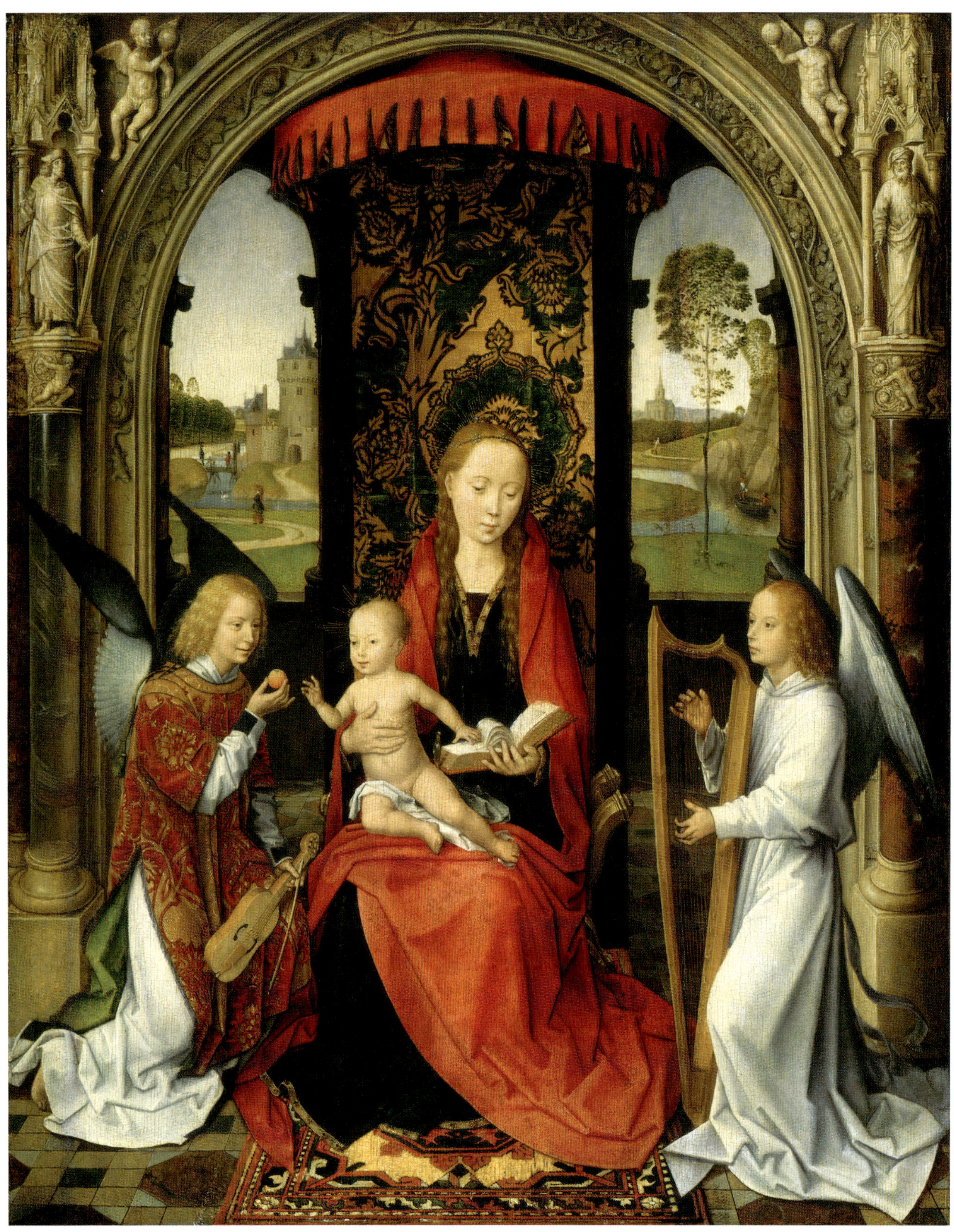

FIG. 1.23. Hans Memling, *Pagagnotti Triptych*, after 1479. Oil on panel, 22 ¾ × 18 ¼ in. (57.5 × 46.5 cm). National Gallery of Art, Washington, D.C.

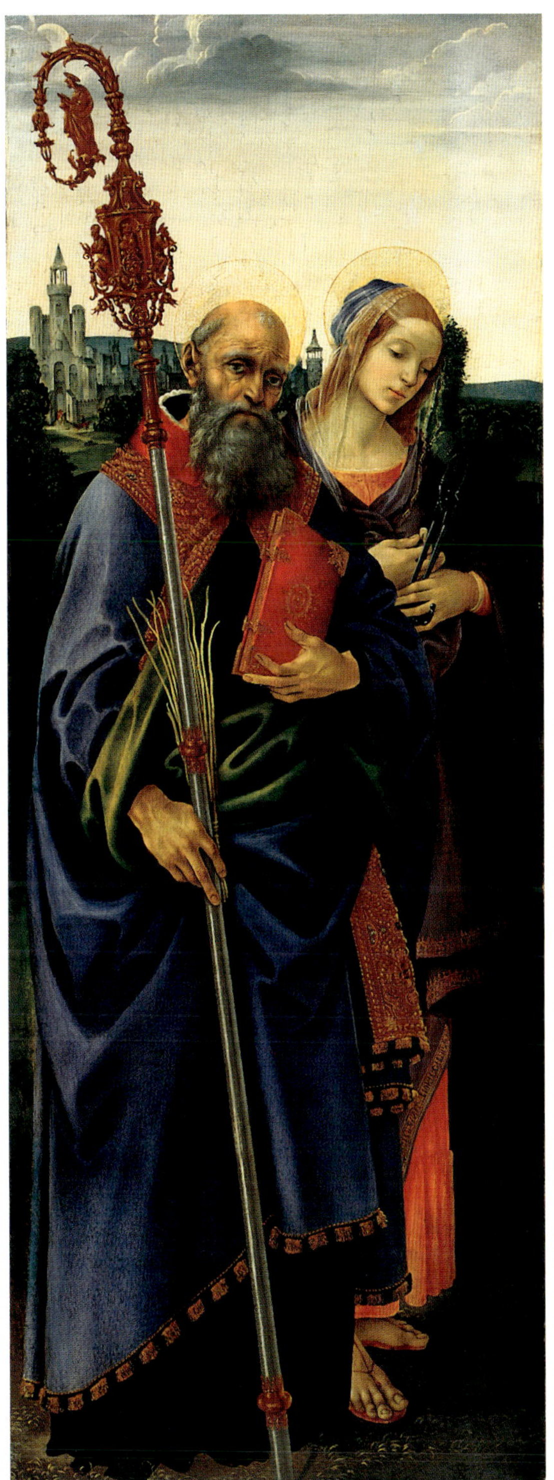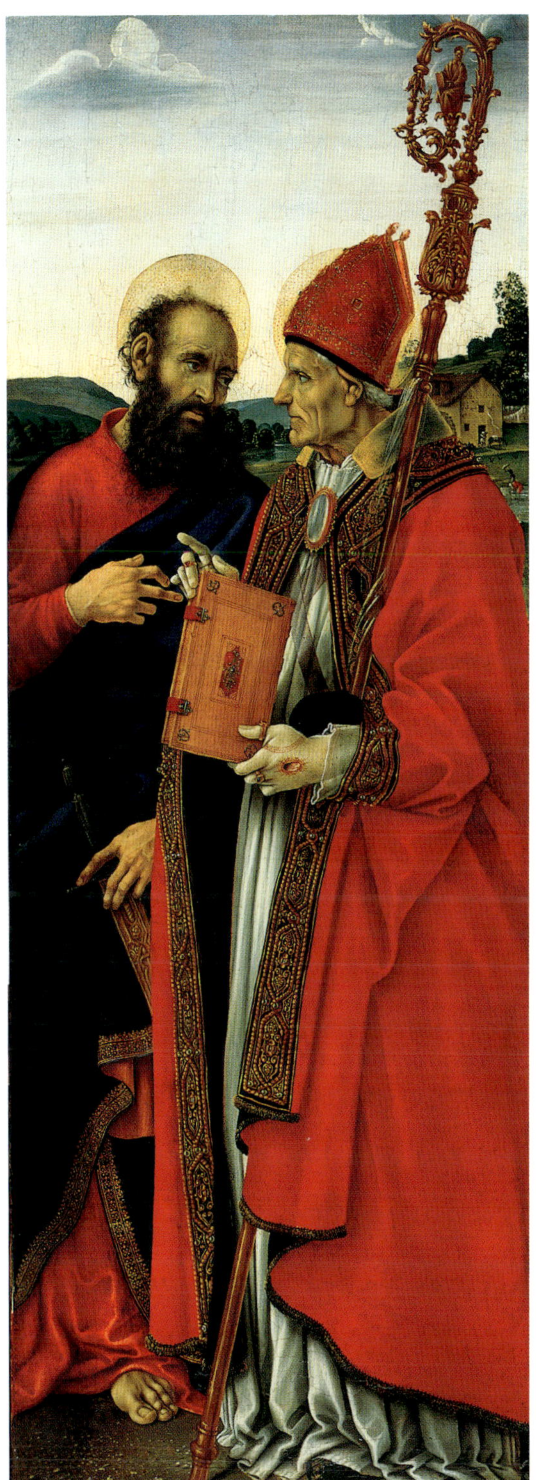

FIG. 1.24. Filippino Lippi, *Four Saints*, c. 1483. Tempera (probably tempera grassa) on panel, 62 × 47 in. (157.5 × 119.5 cm). Norton Simon Museum, Pasadena.

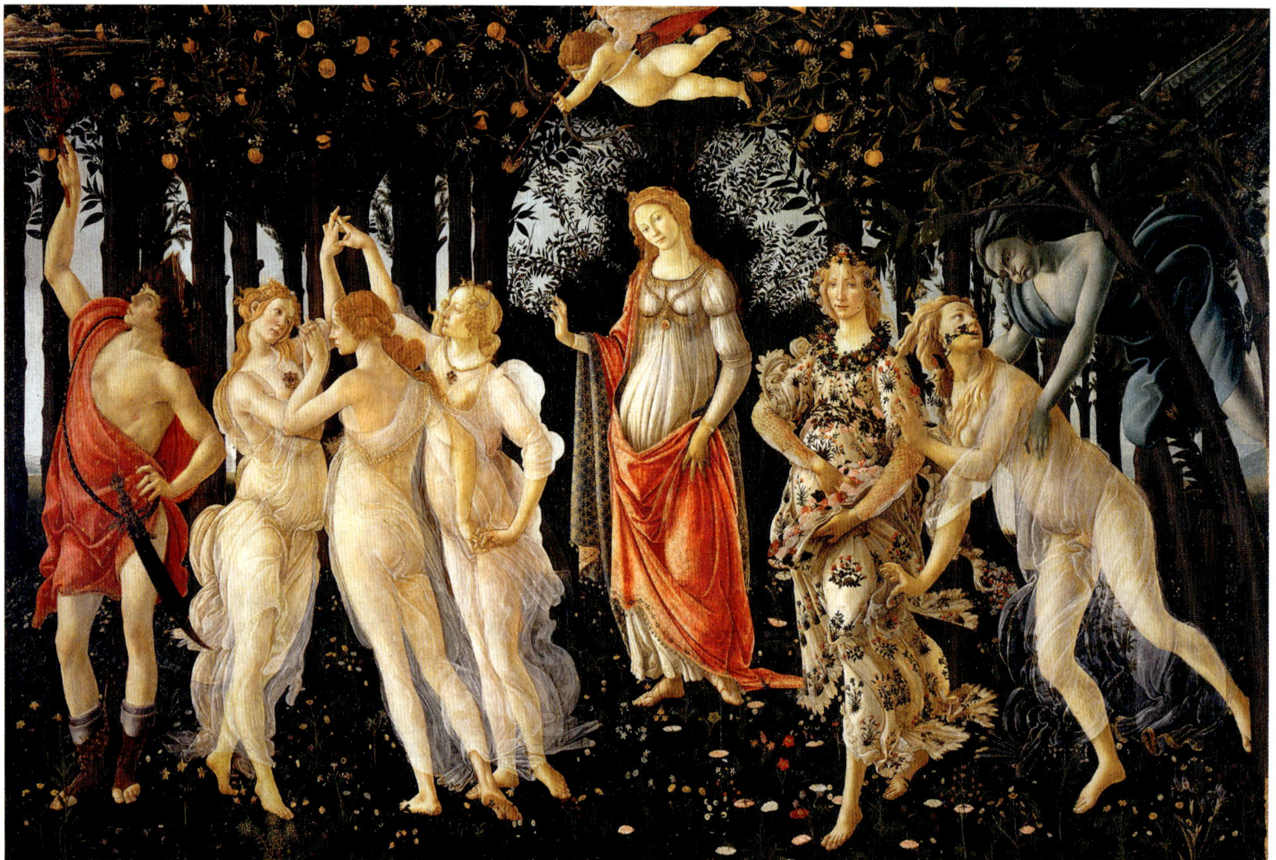

emphasizes the geometrical shapes of which she is composed, such as her neck and face, and flattens her form. Her flowing hair is actually gilded, and there are touches of gilding throughout the vegetation and on the edge of the shell. The coloring is that of tempera, but in the cool tonality of Fra Filippo, not the brilliant, saturated tones of Don Lorenzo. Some of the colors are underpainted in a pale gray, and the flesh is underpainted with the green traditional in tempera.

For the deeper-toned *Primavera,* which is not on canvas like the *Birth of Venus* but on panel, the medium is tempera grassa.[61] This allowed the painter to create the dark grove that serves as the backdrop and sets off the splendid flesh and gossamer draperies. He did not use a single imprimatura across the panel, but primed the foliage area with black and the flesh with white. If the central figure represents Persephone, goddess of spring, just emerged from the underworld, as Jonathan Kline has convincingly proposed, then the dark screen suggests effectively the threshold of Hades, while the nymphs and graces with their warm flesh and diaphanous whitish

drapery belong to the world above that welcomes her back.[62] These are techniques not found in the pendant. In the *Birth of Venus,* Botticelli did not need the effects that could be achieved with oil. He actually preferred the hard edges of tempera rather than the softened blending that oil allows. The linearity lends an abstracting quality that suits his mythological subject. He exploited the inherent linearity of tempera in the same way when he wanted to show the otherworldliness of the *Madonna of the Magnificat* (fig. 1.26), where the Virgin is surrounded by angels in the celestial sphere and, as in the *Birth of Venus,* everything—hair, brocade, and garment edges— is tinged with gold.

Botticelli did not use pure oil until the late *Mystic Nativity* of 1500—at least no other instance has yet been found—but at about the same time, when he painted two panels with the story of Saint Zenobius, he returned to egg tempera, using oil only for specific purposes.[63] He showed familiarity with both linseed and walnut oil, but chose to make use of the brilliant, high-value properties of the tempera palette. If these panels were created to celebrate a marriage, as has been suggested, perhaps he thought that the light and brilliant tonality characteristic of tempera would be more suitable than the darker tones so ably rendered with oil.

Ghirlandaio also steered away from oil, although like Botticelli he used it with specific pigments and occasionally tempera grassa.[64] As the premier frescoist in Florence in the 1480s and 1490s, until his death in 1494, he must have found that tempera, with its direct application and hatched modeling like that used in fresco, was more to his liking and suited to his talents. Even its bright coloring suited him, to judge from the *Adoration of the Magi*, the important altarpiece for the Ospedale degli Innocenti, where vermilion draperies dominate and, joined with vivid yellows and oranges, convey the mood of celebration (see fig. 1.17).

Verrocchio was another of the generation of Botticelli, Ghirlandaio, and Rosselli. He was himself principally a sculptor, but his workshop was one of the largest and most productive in Florence, and he had as his assistants some of the most important painters of the next generation. Like the other established masters in the 1470s he did not take up oil in his paintings, but he would likely have used it in his metalwork, and he allowed his assistants to try it out.[65] When he assigned Leonardo the landscape in the background of the *Baptism of Christ*, which Verrocchio himself was executing in tempera, Leonardo painted it in oil (fig. 1.27). Lorenzo di Credi, also from his workshop, became one of the earliest and best of the painters to take up oil. Perugino, who also worked in Verrocchio's workshop, became the painter who practiced the oil technique in a manner closest to the Flemish.

Pietro Perugino was a prolific painter who operated workshops in both Perugia and Florence.[66] He was chosen by Pope Sixtus IV to paint the altarpiece in the newly rebuilt Sistine Chapel in 1481. He was in demand, and around 1500 his reputation was very high. He was famously called the best painter in Italy in 1500 by Agostino Chigi, the Sienese banker to Pope Julius II and patron of the Villa Farnesina, who said: "No other masters are worth so much."[67] It is no wonder that the promising young Raphael chose to join his workshop around that time. Even Vasari, who didn't like him, saying he would do anything for money, also remarked that his paintings were so highly valued that many were bought in France, Spain, Germany, and other countries.[68]

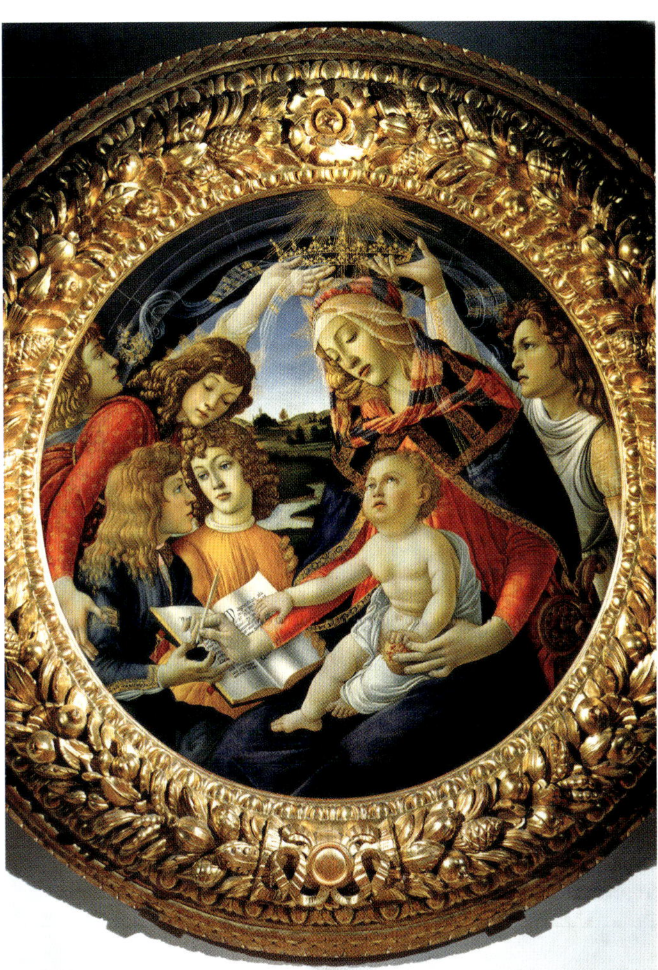

FIG. 1.26. Sandro Botticelli, *Madonna of the Magnificat*, 1481. Tempera on panel, 46 × 47 in. (118 × 119 cm). Uffizi, Florence.

It is not yet clear when Perugino converted from tempera to oil or how he learned it, but it was probably in the early 1480s at the latest. Unlike many of his colleagues, he was not using tempera grassa, nor did he use dark monochrome to reinforce his shadows. In those paintings that have been analyzed dating from the end of the 1490s, such as the altarpiece for the Certosa at Pavia (London, National Gallery), it was found that he layered in a manner very like his Northern colleagues, using an opaque underpaint and glazing with transparent pigments.[69] He must have begun by experimenting: Vasari says that three of his panels had darkened and cracked because the underlying layers had not dried before he applied the next. There was not much local experience he could draw upon.

It is in the mid-1490s that Perugino's coloring jells, perhaps as a result of his sojourn in 1494 to Venice, where

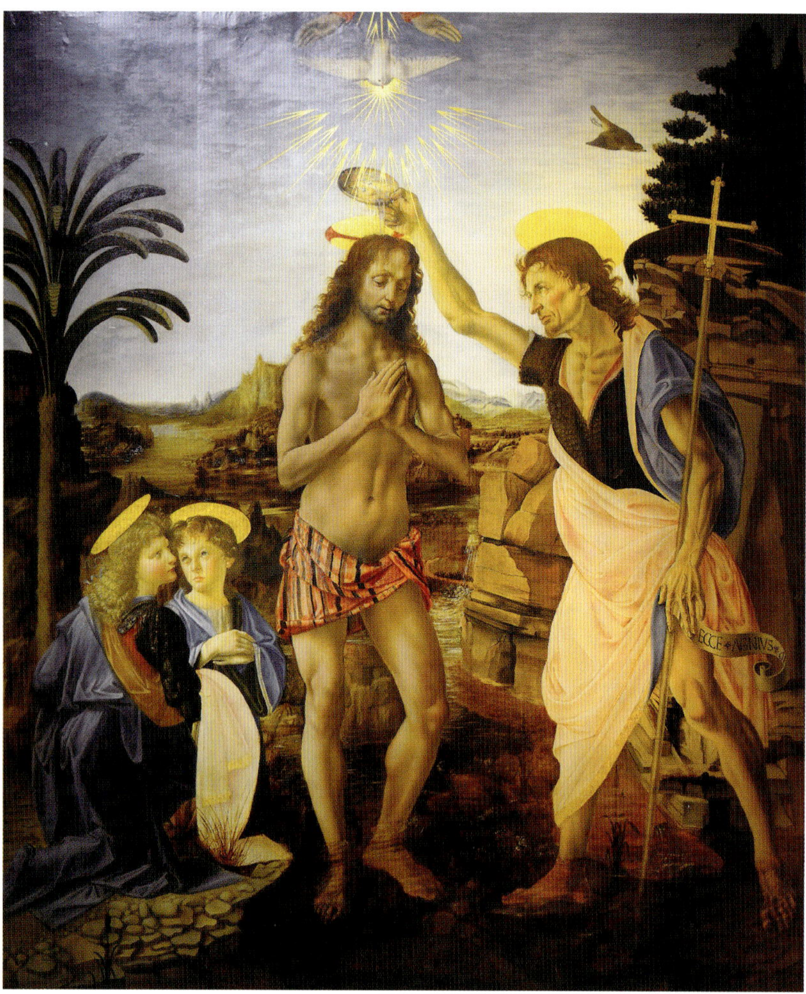

FIG. 1.27. Andrea del Verrocchio (distant landscape by Leonardo da Vinci), *Baptism of Christ*, 1472–79. Oil on panel, 70 × 59 in. (177 × 151 cm). Uffizi, Florence.

he was commissioned to paint a piece for the Sala di Consiglio that was never executed. It may be, as Craig Smyth proposed, that on this trip he learned the technique being practiced by Giovanni Bellini and brought it back to Florence.[70] On his return he painted the *Lamentation* for Santa Chiara, in a style that is unmistakably influenced by the Flemish (fig. 1.28).[71] He obtained in this work the deep and resonant colors of Flemish layering. In a raking light the shadows are thick and slightly raised, and it appears that there is little or no white in his modeling. Its coloring, as much as its focused composition, conveys the mournful spirit of the friends who have gathered around the dead body of Christ. He is laid out at the center on a white cloth, an altar cloth that doubles as the shroud. This solitary white draws the eye to it and sets off the dark but richly varied tones around it.

At about the same time, Perugino painted his *Vision of Saint Bernard* (fig. 1.29). The saint looks up to find the Virgin standing before him. There is no suggestion

that this is an apparition; she is as vividly present as the painter can make her. He conveys the sweetness of the event with his soft, fused colors: the muted red and blue of the Virgin's draperies, the dark surround created by the grand loggia. Here again Perugino makes astute use of white, dictated of course by the monk's habit but exploited to make it a focal point that balances the Virgin, who faces the light entering from the right. We see Perugino's exceptional skill in creating vibrant greens, which had eluded Quattrocento painters, though not their Netherlandish colleagues. Verdigris does not work well in egg, but when bound in oil it can produce tones like these, which the painter has deployed around the protagonists. It was largely from this master that Raphael learned both how to paint in oil and how to color.[72]

These painters would transfer the cartoons on the imprimatura, a layer of paint made up primarily of white lead, on top of the gesso preparation to isolate the ground

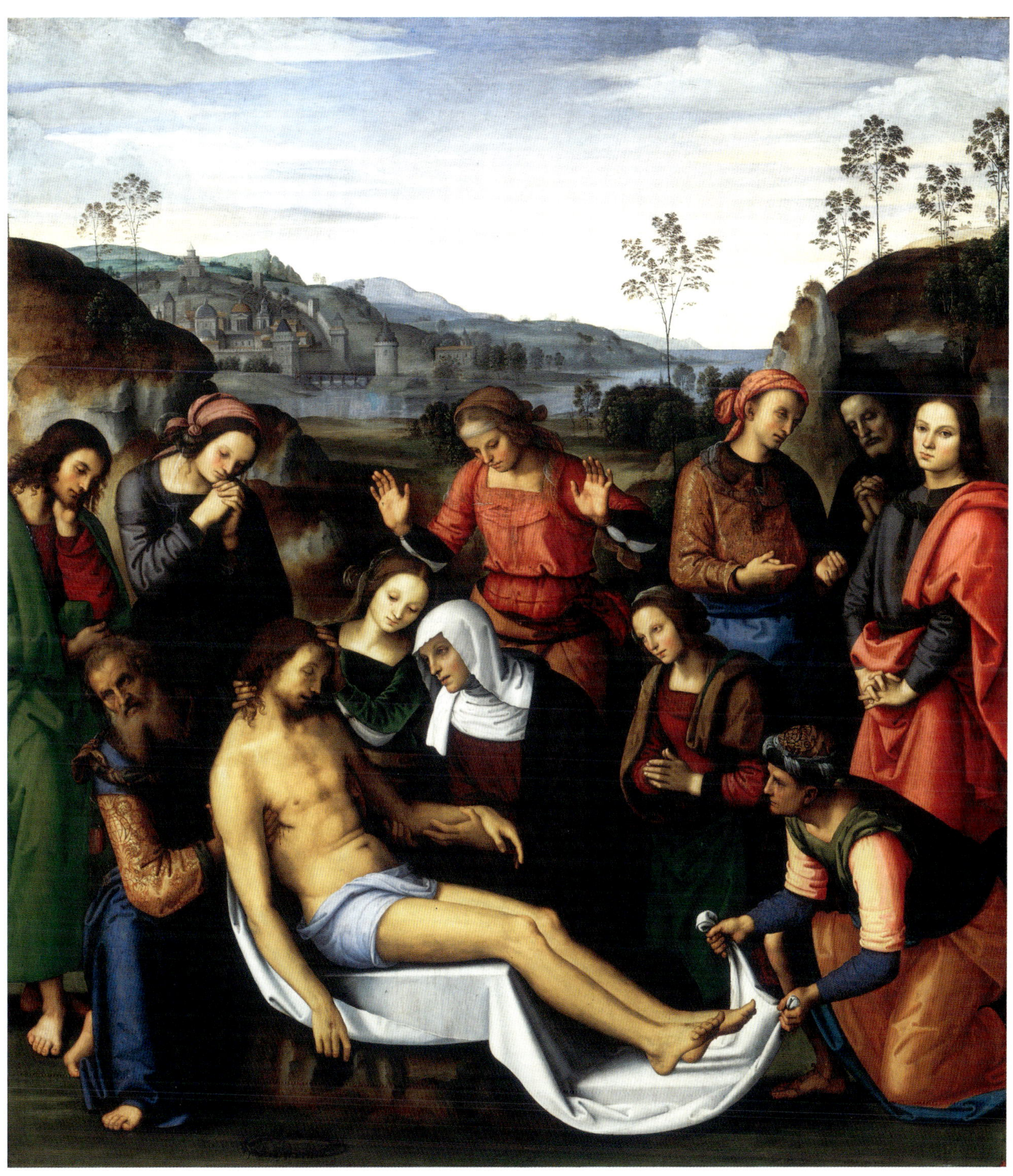

FIG. 1.28. Pietro Perugino, *Lamentation*, 1494. Oil on panel, 66 × 69 in. (168 × 176 cm). Uffizi, Florence.

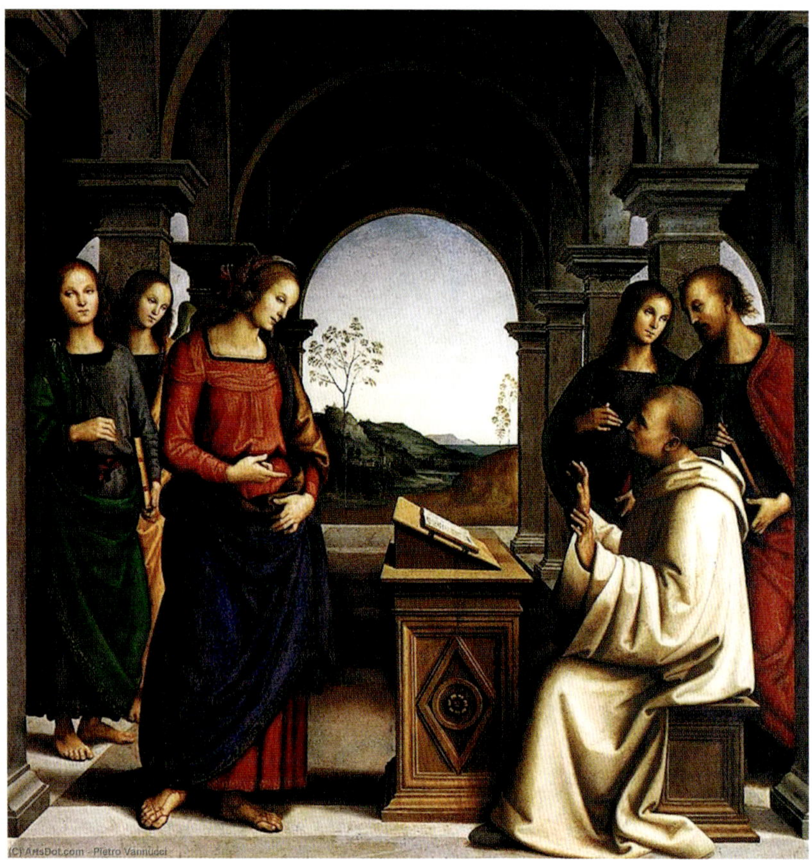

FIG. 1.29. Pietro Perugino, *Vision of Saint Bernard*, 1493. Oil on panel, 68 × 67 in. (173 × 170 cm). Alte Pinakothek, Munich.

and prevent it from absorbing oil from the layers of paint above. Perugino used a slightly yellowish imprimatura, perhaps to cut down the brilliance of the gesso ground.[73] Without this priming the oil paint would become lean and matte in appearance. Because the gesso ground did not absorb egg, no such priming was needed in tempera. It would become an important innovative technique in the Cinquecento, as we will see in Chapter 2.

VENICE

Renaissance painting in Venice is renowned today for its coloring, and in the Renaissance, Venice was famous as a source of coloring materials. Through the port, lapis lazuli arrived from the East and azurite from Germany, as well as many other colorants. Venice was a center of numerous crafts, such as mosaic, maiolica, dyed fabrics, and of course glass. Beginning in the 1490s there appeared specialist shops that sold coloring materials to the various craftsmen, called vendecolori. Painters alone would not have generated enough business to make such specialization possible, which is probably why vendecolori have not been found in other cities, but the craftsmen

in Venice constituted a critical mass. Such shops would have become places for artisans to meet and exchange information and where painters might have been encouraged to try materials used in other crafts. Pigments based on dyes, such as the lakes and indigo, formed an important part of their palettes, as we have seen. Because of this abundance, Venetian painters experimented with colors more than their less advantaged colleagues. That said, the materials that have been found by laboratory examination so far are not very different from those used in central Italy or in earlier tempera painting. Rather than novel pigments, it was the combinations these artists invented that give Venetian color such vibrancy. Giovanni Bellini was obviously fascinated with trying to find new combinations that would allow him to simulate effects of light, and when he moved to oil, the possibilities of glazing with contrasting colors.

Vasari's version of how the Early Netherlandish manner of painting in oil arrived in Italy, through the arrival in the mid-1470s of the peripatetic painter from Sicily, Antonello da Messina, has long been discredited because the dates don't work; but it looks more and more

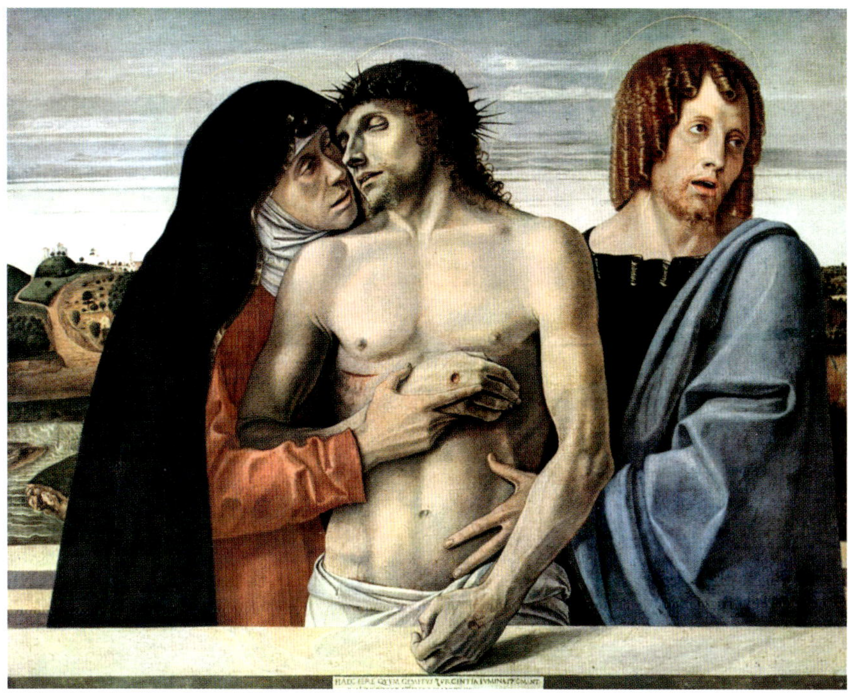

FIG. 1.30. Giovanni Bellini, *Pietà*, 1467–70. Tempera on panel, 33 ¾ × 42 in. (86 × 107 cm). Pinacoteca di Brera, Milan.

as though even his premise that Venice was the nexus from which knowledge of oil spread to other centers is wrong. We have already seen that Ferrara and Urbino were engaged in the practice as early as the 1450s, and that in Florence in the 1460s the Pollaiuolo brothers were using oil, even though their understanding of Flemish technique was flawed. Nevertheless Bellini was probably the first painter in Italy to adopt a technique very like the Flemish. He used it consistently for over forty years, and taught it to the great Venetians of the Cinquecento, Giorgione and Titian.

Bellini was born in 1430, so he is the rare painter (together with Perugino) who was trained in tempera painting and practiced it for years before moving to oil. As we are learning was true of everyone, his conversion was a process and not a sudden transformation. He was using oil alongside tempera already in the 1450s, but he was not yet exploiting it for its optical qualities by glazing, and his handling of it was not yet substantially different from his handling of tempera.[74] He did not adopt the Flemish technique of modeling and glazing until the early 1470s. His Pesaro Altarpiece (Pesaro, Musei Civici, c. 1473–75) was executed entirely in oil in the Flemish manner.[75] There were many Flemish paintings being imported into Venice, so he would have had the opportunity to study their technique firsthand.[76]

Bellini's tempera works create miracles of light and atmosphere in a medium not very well suited to it. Always meticulous, he made underdrawings even when they would be concealed by his opaque paint. His crisp edges are contoured, but these contours do not flatten his image, as they do Botticelli's, because of his strong modeling. His coloring was always subdued. In his deeply moving *Pietà*, the Virgin's robe is not the expected lapis but blackish, in keeping with her profound grief, and likewise the blue of John's robe is paled, its pigment possibly not even ultramarine but azurite or even a dye like indigo (fig. 1.30). A piece like this was made for private devotion and for close viewing. It is only at very close range that we see the trail of blood running from the wound in Christ's hand up his arm, clotted halfway to the elbow—a scrupulously conceived detail revealing the painter's thoughtful meditation on how blood would have flowed with his arms raised on the cross.

We do not know what the catalyst was that propelled Bellini to choose to paint in oil. We used to think it was a response to the arrival in Venice of Antonello da Messina, who was an accomplished practitioner of the Flemish technique. However, most scholars date the beginning of the Pesaro Altarpiece to 1472 or 1473, so that even though it apparently took a long time to complete, it was well advanced before Antonello's arrival in 1475. Antonello may have learned Flemish technique firsthand from a painter in Italy or abroad; certainly his altarpiece for

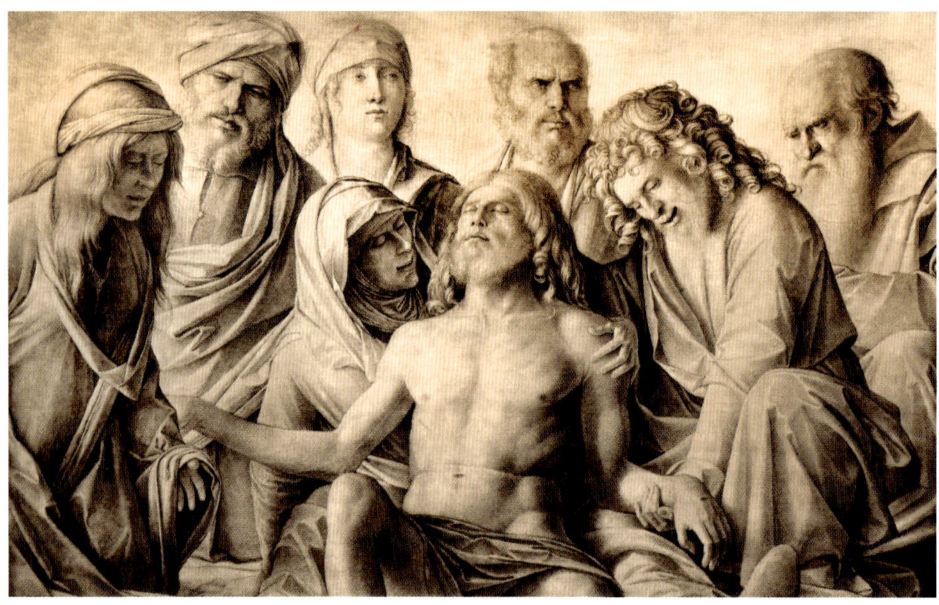

FIG. 1.31. Giovanni Bellini, *Pietà* (underdrawing), late 1480s. Tempera on panel, 29 × 46½ in. (74 × 118 cm). Uffizi, Florence.

San Cassiano in Venice, or what survives of it after the fire in the church (Vienna, Kunsthistorisches Museum), is a showpiece of transparency and reflection and finely wrought detail, but whether Bellini learned anything new in terms of technique from it is now moot.

Bellini seems to have varied his technique, working sometimes in a very efficient and straightforward manner, and at other times experimenting in a leisurely way, applying his colors in complex structures, mixing several pigments together in one layer, then glazing in a contrasting color. In such cases as the Pesaro Altarpiece, we sense him feeling his way to find the effect he wants. In some passages we find multiple layers. He does not work with formulas; his skies are painted in a dozen different ways. In his next major altarpiece after the Pesaro, the very large panel for San Giobbe of about 1478–80 (Venice, Accademia), after making an extensive underdrawing on the gesso ground, he applied an imprimatura of tempera grassa, probably because with the addition of tempera it would dry more quickly than pure oil. His paint layers are simpler than for the Pesaro Altarpiece.[77] And the color range is more restricted—for example, the only blue used is ultramarine. There are some areas painted in tempera, such as Saint Sebastian's loincloth, and we can only guess at the reasons. Perhaps he wanted to differentiate its texture from the Virgin's veil, which is in oil; but the knot is impasto, not possible to achieve with tempera, so it must be painted in oil. Tempera was used for some details of the architecture, where speed of drying might have been the reason. Altogether, the handling

is more broad and the technique simpler, suggesting that it was executed with more dispatch and conviction than the protracted process of the Pesaro piece.

What is distinctive about Bellini's working method is that he made very detailed underdrawings on his support—more detailed than in his Florentine contemporaries' works—with the same precision as one finds in Northern painting. His paintings with these underdrawings generally were executed at least partially in oil, so there may be a connection between his adoption of the Flemish oil technique and a Northern type of underdrawing.[78] There exists an extraordinary *Pietà* dated now to the late 1480s that gives a clear idea of what his preparatory drawing looks like (fig. 1.31). Considered for a long time to be a finished work in grisaille, most scholars now recognize that this is the kind of underdrawing, with its careful study of chiaroscuro, that he made in preparing to paint. It has been suggested that under thin glazes such underdrawing would show through.[79]

Bellini's practice differed from the Florentines' cartoons made piecemeal. Like Leonardo's in his *Saint Anne* cartoon, Bellini's allowed his study of light to determine the composition. Unlike the Florentines, he appears to have used the underdrawing rather than a cartoon. Where a cartoon was made, it's likely that a member of the workshop made it, perhaps from the underdrawing, so that the workshop would have a copy, or so that the assistant could make and sell a copy.[80]

Bellini never allowed himself to become old-fashioned. He continually revised and updated his style,

even late in his long life. By the 1490s he was beginning
to experiment with softer forms and contours and a more
spontaneous procedure. He ultimately abandoned the
elaborate underdrawing and moved toward more dia-
grammatic outlines, anticipating, or paralleling, what his
younger colleagues, Giorgione, Sebastiano, and Titian,
would do.[81]

THE CHANGE OF TASTE IN COLOR

We have seen how different Don Lorenzo's or Fra
Angelico's paintings look from Pollaiuolo's. In Florence,
when taste shifted to a deeper tonality, which came with
the fashion of Netherlandish oil, the painters began mixing oil with their tempera and found they needed to use
different pigments. The vermilion/lapis/lead-tin yellow
triad that worked so well in tempera no longer pleased.
The pigments available didn't change dramatically, but
some behave differently in oil. Ultramarine, the jewel
of the tempera palette, which artists had avoided diluting with any additive, was found to dry eccentrically
in oil and to darken. It behaves best with a little lead
white added, which aids the drying, but also reduces
the intensity.

In Venice too the conversion to oil brought a shift in
the palette. Paul Hills has described the ways Giovanni
Bellini adjusted his color for oil, away from the brilliant
blues, reds, and especially yellows, toward browns.[82]
Bellini evidently enjoyed experimenting, trying to exploit
the luminosity of his medium. Where he could simply
have used a brown earth, instead he created a mixture:
white lead, carbon black, a little ochre, a few particles
of vermilion. The earth alone would be flat and opaque,
whereas his complex mixture scintillates.[83]

The adjustments the Florentines made were different
but they accomplished the same rebalancing, conforming to new tastes. Perhaps because in Florence the conventions of color for the apparel of saints were more
fixed than in Venice, the painters did not invent whole
costumes, as Bellini might do, but instead shifted to a
different pigment of the same hue. The Virgin's accustomed lapis, now toned down and diluted with white,
was paired with delicate, transparent red or pinkish lakes
instead of vermilion, as we see in Perugino's Virgins
painted after the turn of the century—for example, the
Marriage of the Virgin (Caen, Musée des Beaux-Arts, 1500–
1504) or the *Assumption of the Virgin* (Florence, Santissima
Annunziata, 1504–7). (The reds are often more pinkish

today than they were originally because red lake fades.)
Sometimes the Madonna's red is of a deeper, browner
tonality, seemingly based on a red earth. Because the blue
had been deprived of some of its intensity it is not often
underpainted with red anymore, and azurite appears as
its undercoat, also for reasons of economy.

Saint Peter's traditional uniform of yellow over blue
could be particularly disruptive to the balance of a composition because the high-value yellow leaps forward
and attracts the eye. Bellini had been among the first to
make use of the arsenic pigments orpiment and realgar,
which had been missing from the palette, although as
trade documents show, they had continued to be available.[84] Cennini had warned against using them because
they were highly poisonous.[85] Why the painters of the late
Quattrocento decided to ignore this warning we do not
know. The pigments provided a gold orange that filled a
hole in the spectrum of pigments. They have been found
in the Pesaro Altarpiece. In the San Zaccaria Altarpiece
(Venice, San Zaccaria, 1505), the robe of Peter, who stands
in front of the light entering from low on the left, takes
on a deep-orange cast.

Botticelli's Bardi Altarpiece is more somber in its
coloring than we might expect (fig. 1.32). The pigments
have not been analyzed, and it is rash to guess, but the
reds on the three figures are similar, composed to create a triangle of deep tones, which appear to be closer to
red ochres than vermilion or red lakes. The white lilies,
flesh, and Child's drapery, and the light-brown marble,
set off against the hedge of dark-green foliage, combine to
relieve the dark without undermining the intended mood
of melancholy.

Filippino continued to delight in saturated color even
as he incorporated some deeper tones. In his splendid
Four Saints (see fig. 1.24) lapis and vermilion still dominate, but Saint Apollonia, tucked behind, wears a purple
robe shimmering between blue and plum highlights,
which strikes the eye as a new discovery. It is a stronger and deeper version of his father's favorite grayish
mauve, which Fra Filippo used repeatedly on draperies—
for example, on the Madonna in the San Lorenzo
Annunciation and the saint at the left in the Barbadori
Altarpiece (Paris, Louvre). There was no purple pigment, as we have seen, so the hue rarely appears. When
Filippino introduces it on the robe of Saint Zenobius
in his altarpiece for the Signoria, it has the force of
novelty (fig. 1.33). All these Florentine painters of the

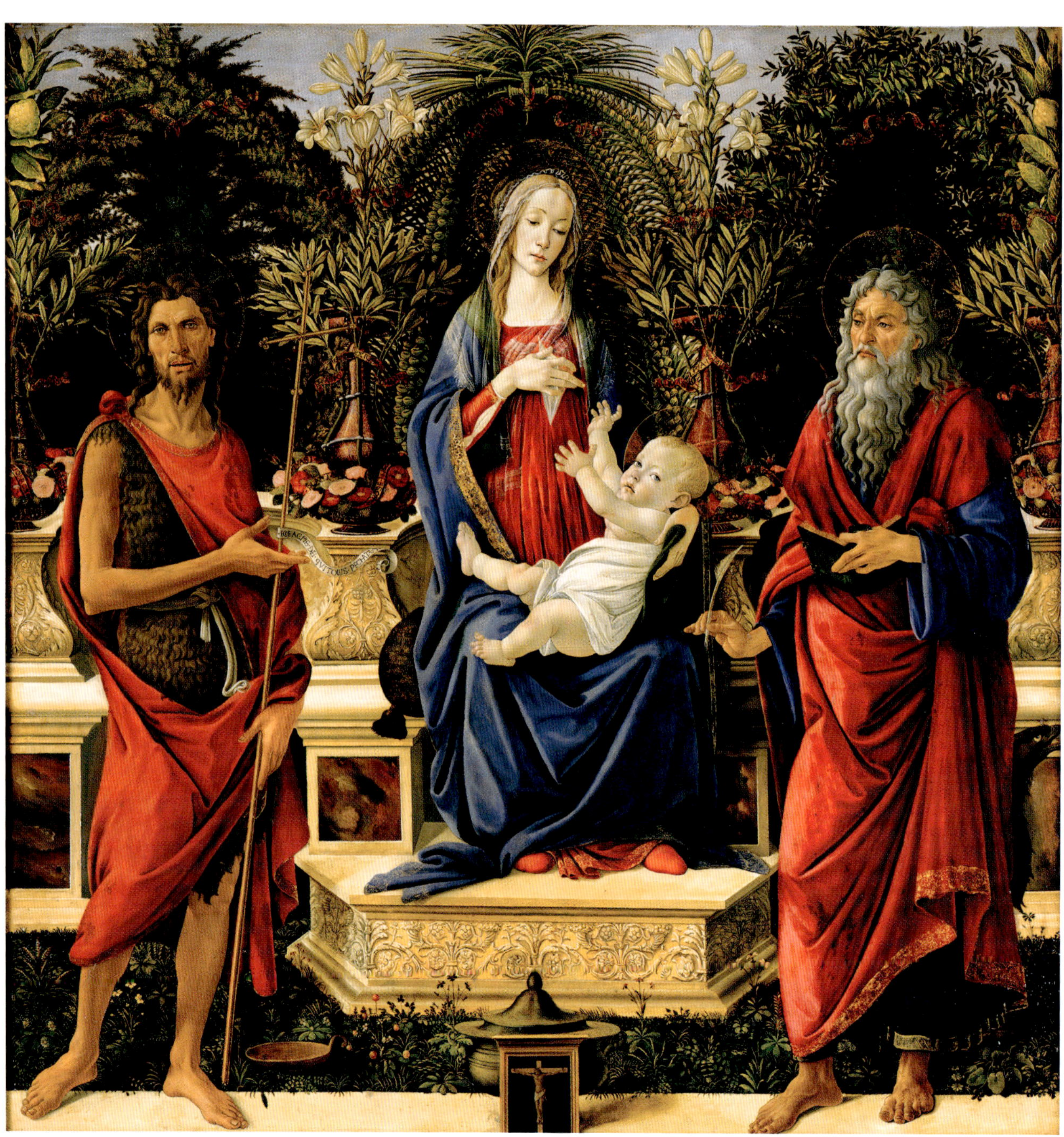

FIG. 1.32. Sandro Botticelli, *Bardi Altarpiece*, 1484–85. Tempera on panel, 72 ¾ × 70 ¾ in. (185 × 180 cm). Gemäldegalerie, Berlin.

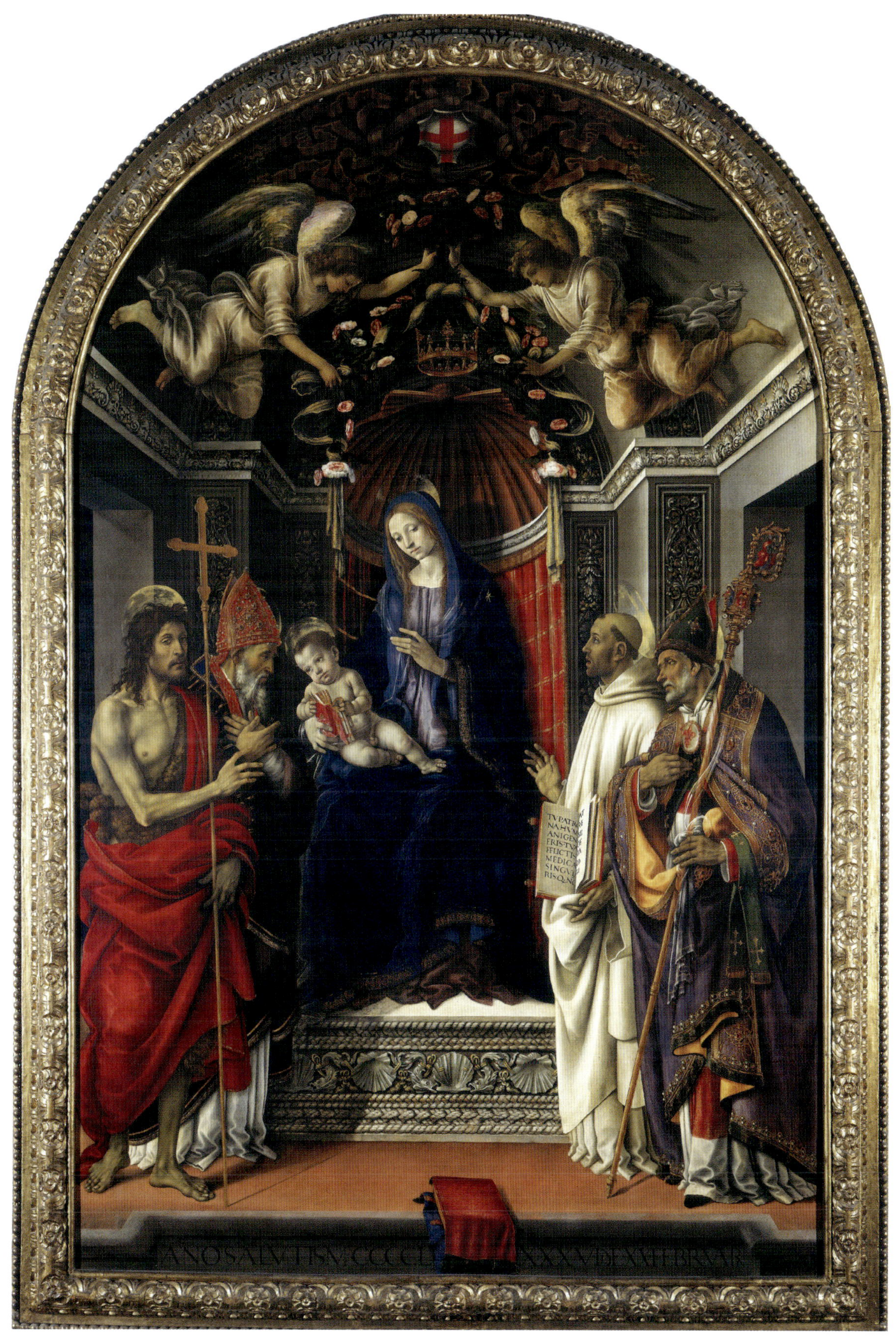

FIG. 1.33. Filippino Lippi, *Saint Zenobius Altarpiece*, 1485–86. Tempera (probably tempera grassa) on panel, 11 ft. 7 in. × 8 ft. 4½ in. (355 × 255 cm). Uffizi, Florence.

late Quattrocento have moved in their coloring toward deeper, less brilliant tones, in keeping with the taste for greater naturalism and away from the vibrant, artificial Cennini system of pure color.

THE WORKSHOP AND MARKETING

Perugino, Ghirlandaio, Botticelli, and Filippino Lippi were the most prominent and successful painters in Florence in the last quarter of the century. There were others who were not in such demand among the patricians. Cosimo Rosselli was at the peak of his career, it turned out, when he worked alongside Perugino, Ghirlandaio, and Botticelli on the frescoes in the Sistine Chapel in the early 1480s. Vasari made a kind of object lesson of him, perhaps trying to explain how he came to be included in this distinguished company. Vasari tells his story with verve:

> It is said that the Pope had offered a prize, which was to be given to the man who, in the judgment of the Pontiff himself [Sixtus IV], should turn out to have done the best work in these pictures. The scenes finished, therefore, His Holiness went to see them; and each of the painters had done his utmost to merit the said prize and honour. Cosimo [Rosselli], feeling himself weak in invention and draughtsmanship, had sought to conceal his shortcomings by covering his work with the finest ultramarine blues and other lively colours, and had illuminated his scenes with a plentiful amount of gold, so that there was no tree, or plant, or drapery, or cloud, that was not thus illuminated; for he was convinced that the Pope, like a man who knew little of that art, must therefore give him the prize of victory. When the day arrived on which the works of all were to be unveiled, that of Cosimo was seen with the rest, and was scorned and ridiculed with much laughter and jeering by all the other craftsmen, who all mocked him instead of having compassion on him.

But, as Vasari says, "the scorners turned out to be the scorned," because,

> as Cosimo had foreseen, those colours at the first glance so dazzled the eyes of the Pope, who had little knowledge of such things, although he took no little delight in them, that he judged the work of Cosimo to be much better than that of the others. And so, causing the prize to be given to him, he bade all the others cover their pictures with the best blues that could be found, and to pick them out with gold, to the end that they might be similar to those of Cosimo in colouring and in richness. Whereupon the poor painters, in despair at having to satisfy the small intelligence of the Holy Father, set themselves to spoil all the good work that they had done; and Cosimo laughed at the men who had just been laughing at his methods.[86]

Vasari is commenting on a taste that by the 1480s he knows to be old-fashioned. The equation in the appreciation of the painter's skill versus the value of the materials had, by the time of the Sistine frescoes, reversed from early in the century, as Michael Baxandall pointed out long ago.[87] By Vasari's time, those who didn't understand the proper priorities had unrefined taste. Vasari is perhaps also trying to explain Cosimo's subsequent failure to win commissions from the elite who patronized the other three. Back in Florence, rather than clients who were known for their patronage of the arts, Rosselli worked chiefly for confraternities, where the selection of a painter was apt to be made by men with little experience, working as a committee, a system that favors the lowest common denominator, as Michelle O'Malley has pointed out.[88] The big four—Botticelli, Filippino Lippi, Ghirlandaio, and Perugino—received higher prices on average than the second-rank painters such as Rosselli and Neri di Bicci, who catered to a lower class of clients.[89] These painters filled a niche, serving less sophisticated and more conservative clients, but ones who still wanted altarpieces with their personal choice of iconography and saints.

Perugino was enormously successful around the turn of the century in part because he had invented an innovative production technique. By reusing cartoons, he was able to produce works of consistently high quality at the same time that he could delegate work to assistants. He might reuse only peripheral figures, as Verrocchio had done, or main figures, or even the whole composition. The *Assumption of the Virgin* that he painted for Santissima Annunziata in 1507 (Florence, Accademia) was in fact a somewhat simplified adaptation of the *Ascension of Christ* that he had painted for San Pietro in

1496–1500. Vasari claimed that he had been ridiculed for this repetition and that it put an end to his career in Florence, but O'Malley shows that his success continued unabated in Perugia.[90] What had previously been acceptable became evidence in advanced Florence of a lack of invention, a quality increasingly valued in the sixteenth century and beyond.

We used to think that the artists of the first rank sold only on commission, but in recent years we have come to recognize that they engaged in selling a second line of products aimed at a less elite clientele. These are the works that in the tradition of connoisseurship were relegated to the category of "workshop" and were not considered a significant part of the artist's output. We have begun to ask how they came to be produced and marketed, and we are recognizing that at least by the later Quattrocento, masters began granting a certain leeway to members of the workshop. Assistants must have been permitted to make use of cartoons or even to make their own variants and to sell them from the workshop. This had the advantage of keeping the master's works in the public eye. It was also a way for assistants to increase their income and expand their experience. The assistants could keep themselves busy during periods of slack demand. The works of the second line were most typically private devotional works, "Madonnine," but Botticelli's *Venus*, extracted from the large *Birth of Venus*, seems also to have been a popular work to be replicated. Several versions survive (Turin, Berlin), and in his Life of Botticelli, Vasari speaks of female nudes in a number of Florentine houses—"*case*" not "*palazzi*," which implies that the clientele was not the patricians.[91] Recognizing this "on spec" production helps account for the works that can be associated with the style of a master, but which are not of the finest quality. The practice makes sense as a measure to keep the business profitable and the flow of income sufficient to sustain a large number of assistants.

The workshop of Pseudo Pier Francesco Fiorentino—or "Lippi and Pesellino Imitator," as he is more accurately called—bears witness to the sizable market that existed. He had a stock of cartoons of Fra Filippo Lippi and figures of Francesco Pesellino from which his shop produced variants of their panels, principally Madonna and Child devotional panels. These panels began to appear around 1460, and production continued into the 1490s, so they were executed for the most part after the deaths of the masters (Pesellino died in 1457; Lippi died in 1469). Since technical evidence indicates that Lippi did not use cartoons for his figures, Megan Holmes surmises that the cartoons were made from tracings either in Lippi's shop or from the altarpieces in situ.[92] This lucrative practice—some 160 paintings have survived—appears to have benefitted only the imitator rather than the inventors.

The back-door trade was not limited to Florence, or even to Italy, as we shall see. It was probably practiced in any large workshop. Giovanni Bellini must have had a lively trade in his specialty, Madonna and Child paintings for private devotional use, because there are large numbers surviving, with some—although his compositions—clearly not executed by his hand. Like Perugino, he was a good businessman who was adept at multiplying his production by extracting and reusing figures, or adjusting a pose or varying the setting. He must have kept cartoons and albums of drawings that could be called upon to create a new version, much as Titian did later. We find a reversal of what we expect to be normal practice, in which the master painted the central and principal figure in his *Madonna and Child with Saints Paul and George*, which was certainly a commission (fig. 1.34). Here Bellini had an assistant replicate the central figures from the masterful *Madonna of the Trees* (Venice, Accademia, c. 1487), but he himself painted the flanking figures, perhaps because there was no usable cartoon available.[93]

Besides the apprentices, assistants, and collaborators who made up the workshop, there were also "externals" available for situations of heavy demand, at least in Florence. Some were even specialists: for example, Bartolomeo di Giovanni operated his own shop and was called upon by Ghirlandaio and Botticelli to execute his specialty, small-scale figures, such as the predella of an altarpiece, which was less important and most easily delegated. Ghirlandaio used him for the predella of his *Adoration of the Magi* (see fig. 1.17, but without the predella), but also for the scene of the Massacre of the Innocents in the background.[94]

By the late Quattrocento, contracts sometimes stipulated what work the master himself was responsible for—for example, painting the figures, or designing the figures and painting their heads. We can infer from

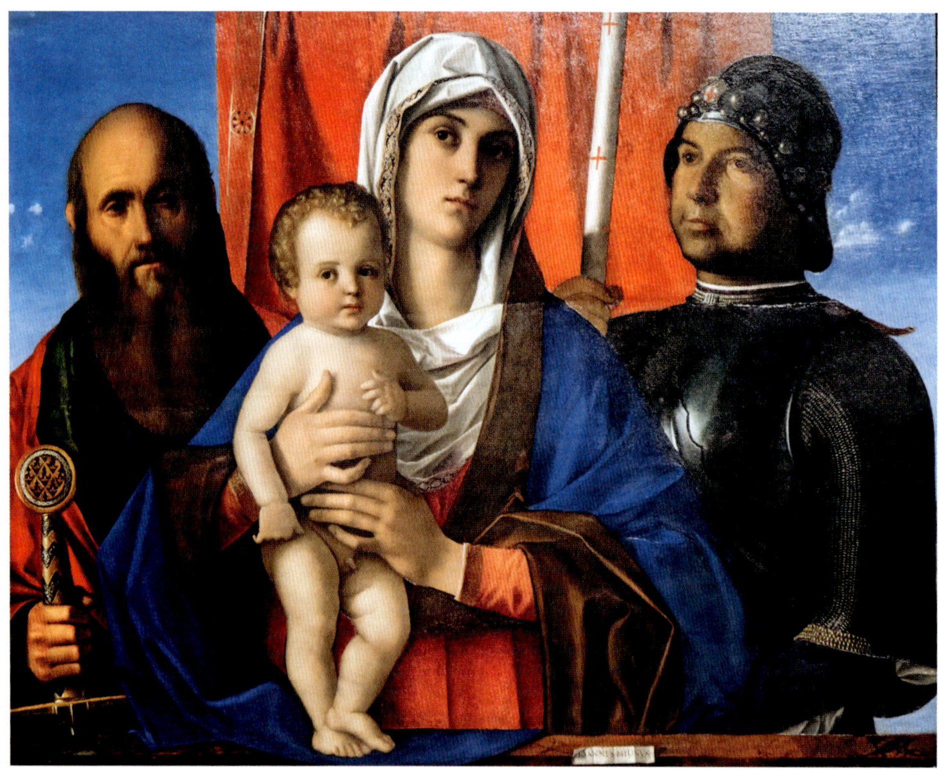

FIG. 1.34. Giovanni Bellini, *Madonna and Child with Saints Paul and George*, 1490–1500. Oil on canvas, 25 1/2 × 34 1/2 in. (65 × 88 cm). Gallerie dell'Accademia, Venice.

such arrangements, as O'Malley points out, that it was understood between client and painter that the workshop would be heavily involved in the execution.[95]

CONCLUSION

Over the course of the fifteenth century, changes to materials and the use of color would pave the way for the artists' turn toward naturalism. The medieval coloring system described by Cennino Cennini of modeling from pure color in the darks up with added gradients of white to the lights was replaced by humanist Leon Battista Alberti, who recommended modeling both up with white and down from the pure color with dark monochrome for greater naturalism. Imported Flemish oil paintings also prompted changing tastes, demonstrating a system of layering that painters in Florence attempted to imitate beginning in the 1460s, and even earlier in other locations.

As we have seen, in the course of the century, taste moved toward increasing naturalism, away from otherworldly luminosity to a plausible depiction of this world. The medieval prejudice against mixed color as "corrupted" gave way to an appreciation of how it can give a nuanced simulation of the fall of light. Although the pigments themselves did not change, painters' preferences

and the way they employed them did. With the introduction of oil, gold grounds were replaced first with solid blue skies and then increasingly with graduated tones streaked with clouds, modulation made much easier with the fluid oil medium. Modeling became more subtle, sometimes by the addition of dark additives, but with oil, deep, rich tones could be obtained by layering without risk of dirtying the color. Colors could be toned down, eliminating or limiting the unnatural pure pigment by layering or mixing, and with oil, translucent shadows could be achieved that had not been possible with matte, opaque tempera. Many painters, not willing to give up egg tempera entirely, combined it creatively with oil to create tempera grassa, the distinctive medium of the late Quattrocento.

The cartoon was the century's other major innovation. Following the invention of the printing press, paper became more plentiful, and artists developed procedures by which drawings could be gradually refined through sketches, to figure studies, to compositional studies, to cartoons. They could work up more complex compositions and insert intricate inventions of poses, of perspectival settings, and of ornaments, which could then be transferred to the prepared support, even by trained assistants.[96]

The cartoon enabled the efficient use of members of the workshop, who could be deployed more readily on tasks appropriate to their level of skill and experience. This of course was the traditional modus operandi of the artisan's workshop, but the change that was taking place was a refinement in the differentiation of tasks. Because they could take on more work, larger workshops appeared and some, like Verrocchio's, worked in a wide range of materials. These larger botteghe made it easier for masters to take jobs in different centers and work there for extended periods of time without having to give up their home base or take the whole shop with them. Verrocchio, for example, undertook the large project of the equestrian bronze statue of Bartolomeo Colleoni in Venice, where he resided for twenty-six months, until his death in 1488.[97] Unlike Donatello, who, when he took on a similar project in Padua in the early 1440s, gave up his Florentine shop, Verrocchio was able to turn over the management of his to Lorenzo di Credi and keep it operational. Such an arrangement anticipates the development in the sixteenth century of the peripatetic workshop, in which artists such as Giorgio Vasari or Francesco Salviati would take on a job and hire assistants from the local pool of talent for the duration of the job.

The widespread use of the cartoon also made possible innovations in marketing. Assistants could be trusted with transferring and executing a cartoon as a replica or a variant and could sell it ready-made to a customer who didn't want, or couldn't afford, to commission it. In this way the workshop assistants were kept busy and perhaps could earn some extra money on the side.

Finally, the cartoon facilitated naturalism. At first painters used partial cartoons and pieced them together. The problem was that they never saw the whole composition at once and the additive look, characteristic of Quattrocento style, resulted. When, as the century drew to a close, some painters began to give up the piecemeal cartoon, a new kind of narrative and aesthetic unity emerged: it was the unity of visualizing a scene at a single moment in time with a single light source. Giovanni Bellini and Leonardo da Vinci demonstrated how the whole painting could be drawn and its pattern of light and shade studied. With oil, the contours could be softened so that forms blended and flowed into one another. With these innovations it was a short step to the dramatic narratives and the harmonious inventions of the High Renaissance.

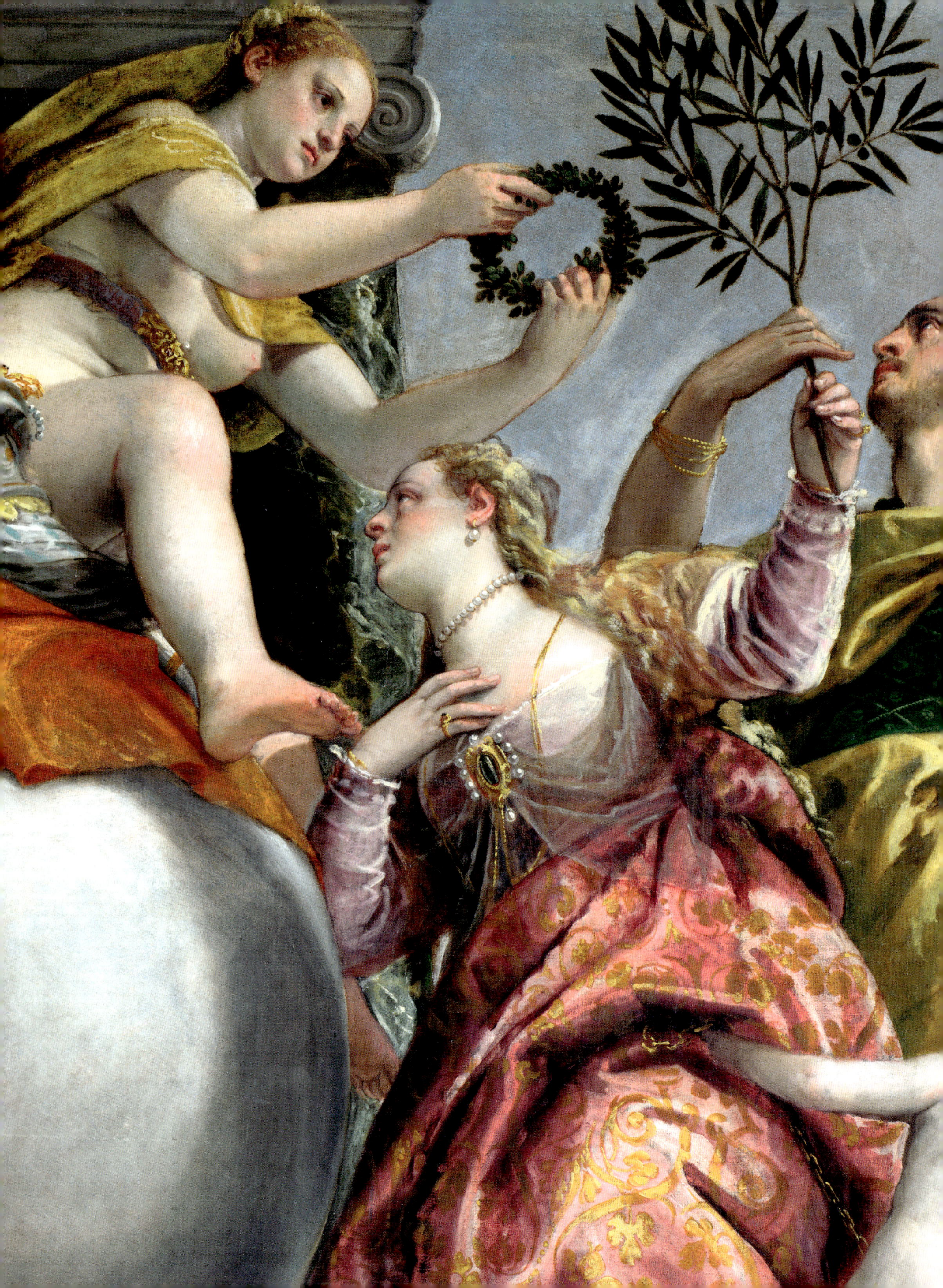

2 The Sixteenth Century

New Techniques for New Levels of Expression

By 1500 painters had for the most part settled on oil as their medium of choice, enabling them to move further away from the received template and closer to a personal version of their subject, first by exploring its transparency and then its variable texture. We know that compared to egg, oil is translucent. While it is true that egg can be thinned with water to drape the Madonna's head in exquisitely delicate diaphanous veils or wrap Botticelli's Graces in enticingly sensuous see-through raiment, it is the nature of egg to cover and of oil to be permeable to light (see fig. 1.26). This translucency made possible the use of a tinted imprimatura, which had both aesthetic and practical consequences.

The education of the artist changed in the sixteenth century. The traditional workshop system broke down and gave way eventually to academies. Many artists no longer remained in a local workshop for all their training, but instead traveled to Rome to study the ancient monuments and modern masters. When a painter came to Rome in the early Cinquecento, he was offered a choice of color styles, more distinct from one another than ever before. By the second decade, he could select from among four distinct modes developed by Leonardo, Raphael, Sebastiano del Piombo, and Michelangelo. All these modes except Michelangelo's exploited the transparency of oil by selective use of priming, or tinted imprimatura. Because it is the first layer, colored imprimatura provided the basic tonality and determined the mood of the painting.

SFUMATO, UNIONE, CHIAROSCURO, CANGIANTISMO

Leonardo's sfumato (smoky) mode is characterized by muted color, even monochrome, with edges softened as if seen through smoke (see fig. 1.15). Leonardo's technique of undermodeling (a monochrome version of the light and darks) may be seen as the precursor of a middle-toned imprimatura, lending a darker, unifying tonality to all the colors placed on top. Raphael invented the unione mode to preserve the gentle fusion of tones achieved by Leonardo, but to reintroduce the beauty of color.[1] For his harmonious unity of colors he reduced the contrast of light and shade as well as the saturation of his tones by using a pale imprimatura. The chiaroscuro mode as practiced by Sebastiano del Piombo and late Raphael introduced a dark imprimatura. It opened up the range of value between the lights and the darks and used brilliant saturated color in the mid-tone for dramatic effect. By the end of the century, Tintoretto and Caravaggio would develop a dark imprimatura for stunningly dramatic effects. Michelangelo adapted from Trecento and Quattrocento practice the technique of modeling by shifting from one hue to another (cangiantismo), but by enlarging the scale and putting it at center stage he turned it into a mode. Because colors in nature do not shift, cangiante colors are artificial and highly ornamental. Unlike the other modes, cangiantismo is high in value and takes advantage of the inherent brilliance of the pigments; it therefore uses the white of the support without tinted imprimatura.

In the past, our young painter would have learned his master's style; then when he went out on his own he might vary it according to his needs, borrowing occasionally from his peers. Now he could choose his color style, even changing and adapting it as needed. If he arrived in Rome after September 1513, and if he was lucky, he might meet up with any one of these masters of the trade. To be sure, the aging Leonardo was hiding inside the Vatican at the Villa Belvedere, working principally on alchemy and rarely seen, and Michelangelo was holed up in his studio working on the *Moses* for Pope Julius's tomb, but both Sebastiano and Raphael were at work there.[2] Perhaps our young painter could trail along in the entourage of fifty artists who were said to accompany Raphael to the Vatican every morning. We will see how these modes were taken up and developed, combined, used selectively in fresco, and even hybridized by the painters in central Italy in the course of the century.

THE UNIONE MODE AND THE TINTED IMPRIMATURA
By the time Raphael painted the devotional tondo of the Madonna and Child with Saint John in Rome (the picture known as the *Alba Madonna*) for an unknown patron, he had mastered the coloring system we now call unione, of which it is perhaps the ultimate exemplar (fig. 2.1).[3] Unione, as the name implies, is the mode that sought coloristic consonance. With a palette limited to blues, greens, red, and brownish tones to set off the chain of flesh tones descending from center to left, the painter links the figures to one another and to their landscape: the blue of the Virgin's robe, echoed in paler tone in the sky and in the distant hills; the delicate greens picked up in her turban; John's sheepskin balanced at the right with the tree trunk and then reverberating in the

greenish-brown ground and the buildings behind. We recall that ultramarine was the crown jewel of the early Quattrocento palette, and that the painters learned that in oil it needed to be diluted with lead white. Nowhere before has it been so successfully harmonized with the surrounding tones as here, where the painter makes a virtue of its paled, diluted form. The Virgin's red robe has likewise been toned down to blend with the flesh tones adjacent. Yet despite the studied reduction in the saturation and value range, Raphael gives us more color than Leonardo had allowed. He has learned from Leonardo's sfumato but made his own adjustments in favor of unione. It is as though he recognized both the virtue and the shortcoming of sfumato: he reintroduces beautiful color without sacrificing the appealing softness of sfumato.

Raphael departed here from his former procedure found in his Florentine pictures of applying an off-white imprimatura, which rendered the colors laid on top bright and lively.[4] Here, surprisingly, he introduced a granular yellow imprimatura, which contributed to the more muted and harmonious tonality.[5] Clearly he was seeking an alternative to his own earlier practice, which derived from the early Renaissance and had been used by Van Eyck and his followers to enhance the jewel-like sparkle of their colors, and he also did not want the murkiness of Leonardo's dark underpaint.

Antonio da Correggio's use of a pinkish imprimatura is an easier to understand choice of priming because its effect is readily visible. The warm glow of flesh that permeates Correggio's pictures, whether devotional or mythological, and the sensuous blending of tones make his pictures unique. Correggio painted his *Madonna of the Basket* in the 1520s (fig. 2.2). Born in 1489, he had by then discovered his mature style. In his teens he was one of the very first painters to explore a darkish priming, learned presumably from Leonardo, but he soon recognized that his particular talent lay in adapting Leonardo's sfumato without its component of dark monochrome, to create sweetly blended contours and gentle transitions. The tonality he made his own was based in a soft gray and flesh, enhanced by an undertone of what conservators have described in this picture as "a light pinkish gray priming."[6] Working independent of Raphael, as far as we know, he arrived at a similar coloristic solution, his own version of unione.

If we compare it with a Quattrocento treatment in

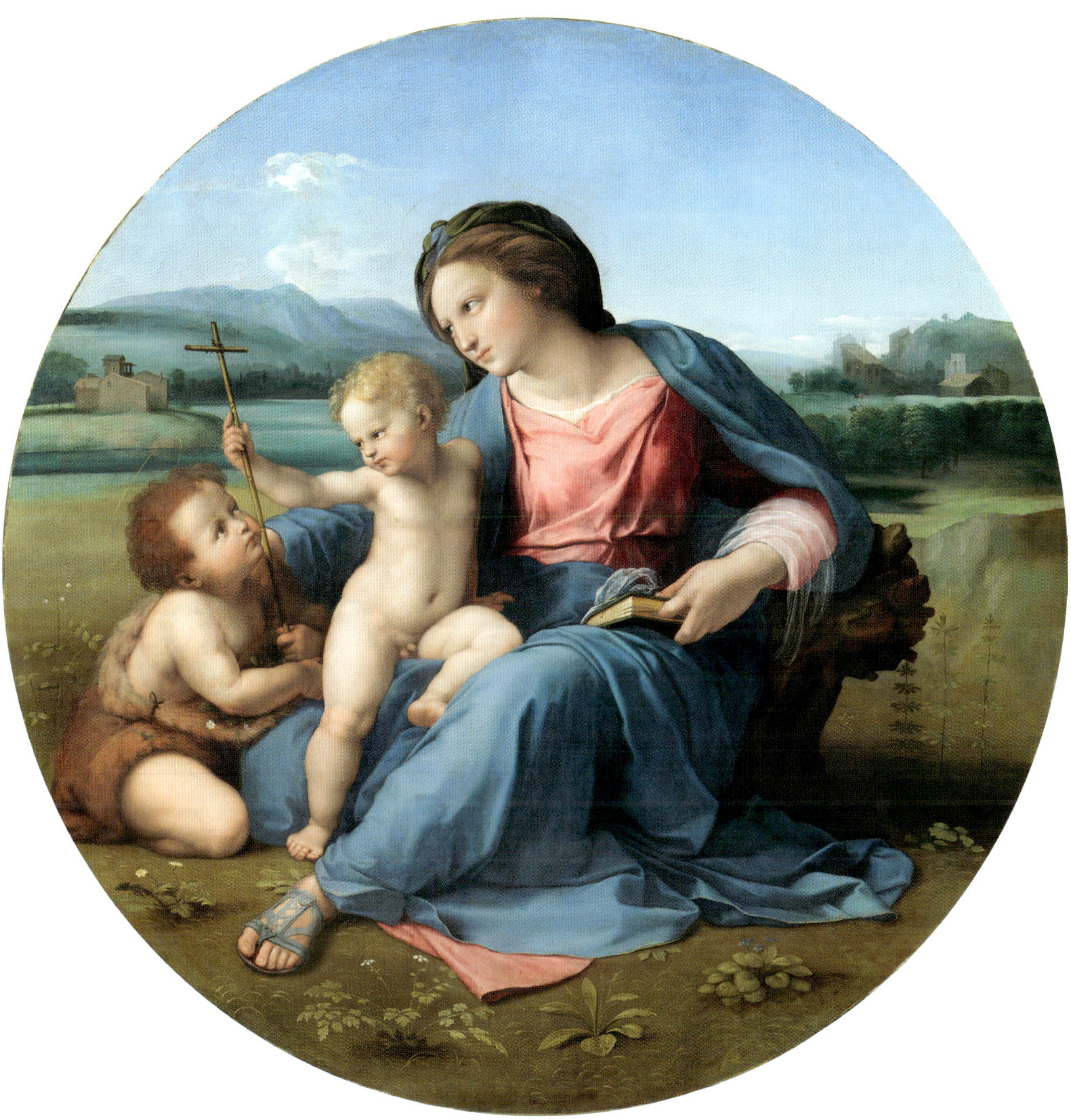

tempera of a similar half-length devotional Madonna and Child by Verrocchio, dated c. 1476–78 (fig. 2.3), we see how Correggio has exploited the qualities of his medium to soften and blend. Verrocchio's modeling looks harsh, his drapery folds pleated. As arresting as the Virgin's prayerful adoration of her infant is, the tender intimacy of Correggio is lacking. This is of course due to the difference in pose, and intimacy was clearly not Verrocchio's intent; his formal and more distanced arrangement with angels present is well served by his more severe and more hard-edged style. He seeks contrast and clarity, as he made clear when he chose to fill the corners with curtains sharply demarcated against the sky.

Correggio's tender portrayal is equally well served by his close interweaving of mother and child, both of them

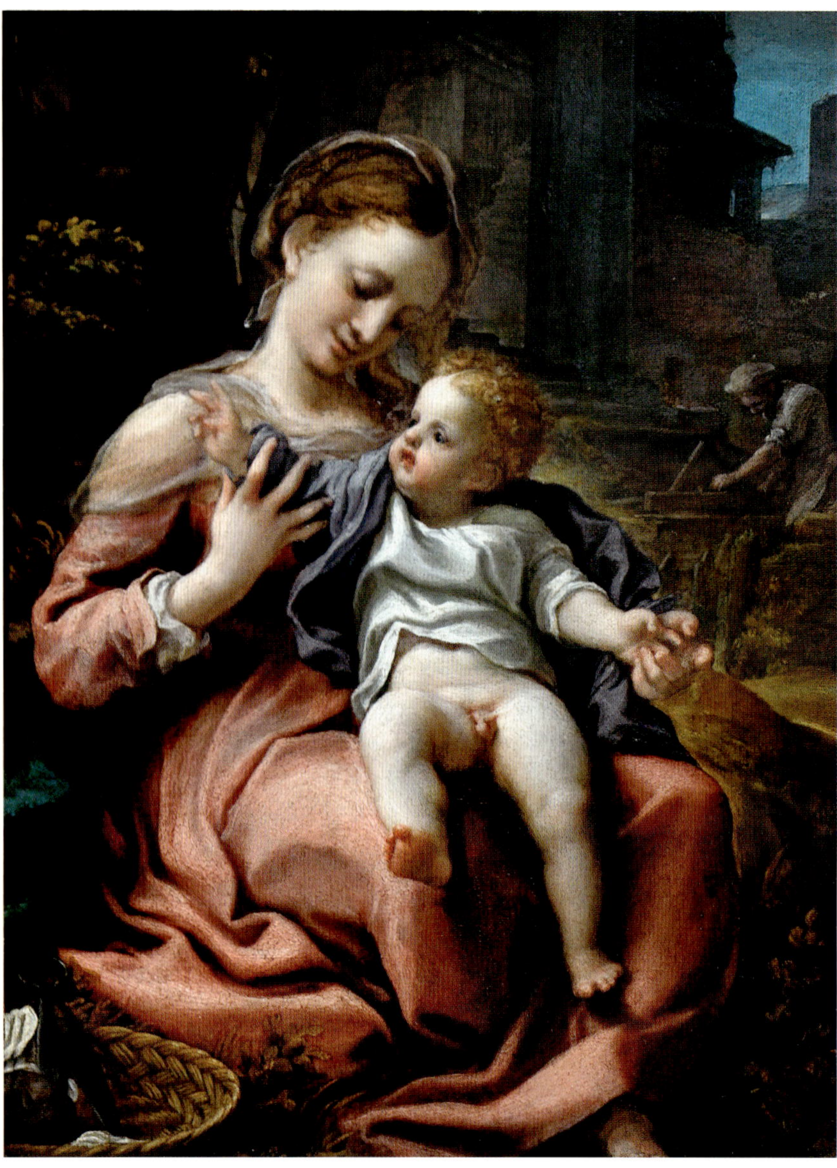

FIG. 2.2. Correggio, *Madonna of the Basket*, c. 1524. Oil on panel, 13 ¼ × 9 ¾ in. (33.7 × 25 cm). National Gallery, London.

intent on unveiling the breast the child eagerly seeks. So too is his close unity of colors, their contrasts reduced because they are desaturated, their values pulled together as if seen through a softening haze. From below the visible surface, that grayish-pink undertone infuses the whole color scheme. A rare grayish pigment, stibnite, has been found in a number of his paintings.[7] He may have sought this unusual material to create the special grayish tonality that marks his coloring. Viewers of Correggio's little picture are not encouraged to assume a devotional attitude, as they are before Verrocchio's; rather they are invited to feel the poignant love that binds Correggio's mother and child together.

Harmony, serenity, perhaps even comfort and reassurance are the feelings we take away from our encounter with Correggio. Raphael in his early career sought much the same effect. The series of Madonna and Child devotional panels he executed during his Florentine sojourn between 1504 and 1508 are variations on a theme, and he was experimenting not only with setting, pose, and composition, but also with color. These pictures are remarkably consistent, however, in achieving a new gentle blending of tones and in rejecting the sharper contrasts both of hue and of value that mark his predecessors' pictures, even Perugino's, who was also working in oil and was a master of coloring. The cartoon Raphael prepared for *La Belle Jardinière* in black chalk (fig. 2.4), stumped to convey the shadows, reveals his careful study of Leonardo's cartoon. Like Leonardo he is studying here the chiaroscuro of the whole composition, and the

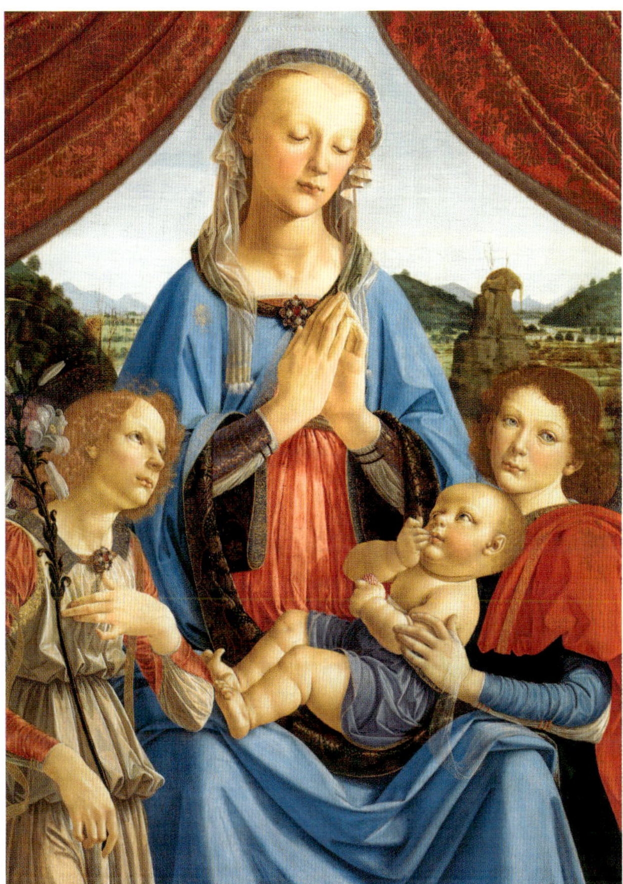

FIG. 2.3. Andrea del Verrocchio, *Madonna and Child*, c. 1476–78. Tempera on panel, 38 × 27 ¾ in. (96.5 × 70.5 cm). National Gallery, London.

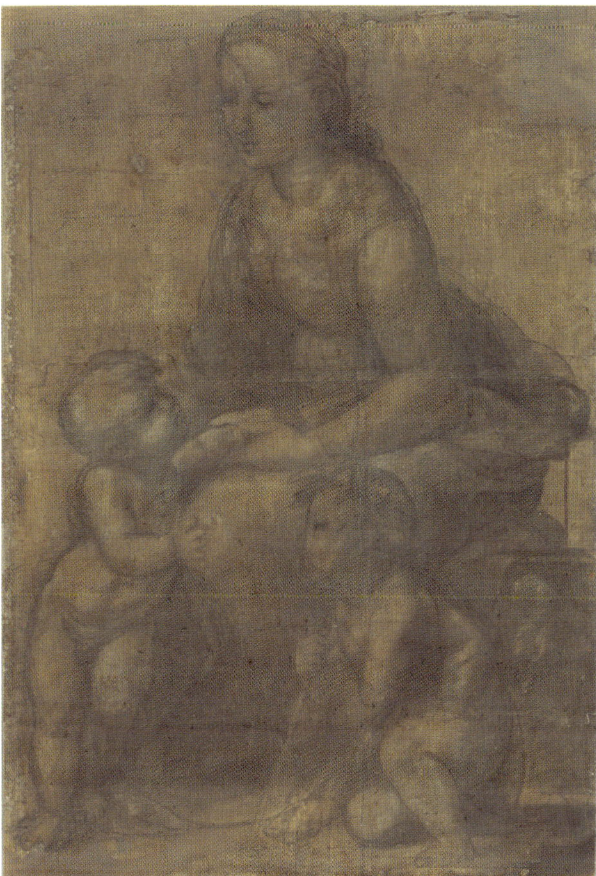

FIG. 2.4. Raphael, *La Belle Jardinière* (cartoon), c. 1507. Black and white chalk on paper, 36 ¹⁵⁄₁₆ × 26 ³⁄₈ in. (93.7 × 67 cm). National Gallery of Art, Washington, D.C.

additive effect of Perugino's design has been put behind him. Clearly there is a new hierarchy of priorities operating here: the effect of the whole is more important than any individual hue. The trend that Michael Baxandall found initiated in the second half of the fifteenth century has here reached its culmination: the skill of the painter is valued more than the materials themselves.[8]

RAPHAEL IN THE STANZE

It was the frescoes that Raphael was executing in the Vatican at the same time as the *Alba Madonna* that assured his position in Rome. Current research indicates that he was hired one room at a time and that there were competitors surrounding him. This was Pope Julius's modus operandi: he would hire multiple artists and put them all to work simultaneously, then choose the one he preferred. The others were left to languish. In the case of the Stanza della Segnatura, Raphael replaced Il Sodoma, who had planned and executed part of the ceiling, while Perugino worked on the ceiling of the adjacent room, the

Stanza dell'Incendio, where Raphael would eventually fresco the walls.

The Stanza della Segnatura was the first of the rooms that Raphael was commissioned to paint in a series that would be continued after Julius's death in 1513 by his successor, Pope Leo X. The Segnatura has been identified as Julius's library, where his 218 volumes were housed, divided into four large groups: Philosophy, Theology, the Arts, and Jurisprudence. (The remaining principal field of the world of knowledge in the Renaissance, Medicine, did not concern the pope.) The decorations were accordingly conceived to reflect both the divisions of the disciplines and their unity. The theme of the ceiling is the convergence of the four forms of inspiration in a single truth. The traditional iconography of libraries was to represent a collection of famous men, often depicted with their books, and indeed, that is the kernel of Raphael's scheme here. At the center of the *Disputà*, for example, representing Theology, are the four doctors of the Church, each with his books, titles plainly legible, around him. Plato

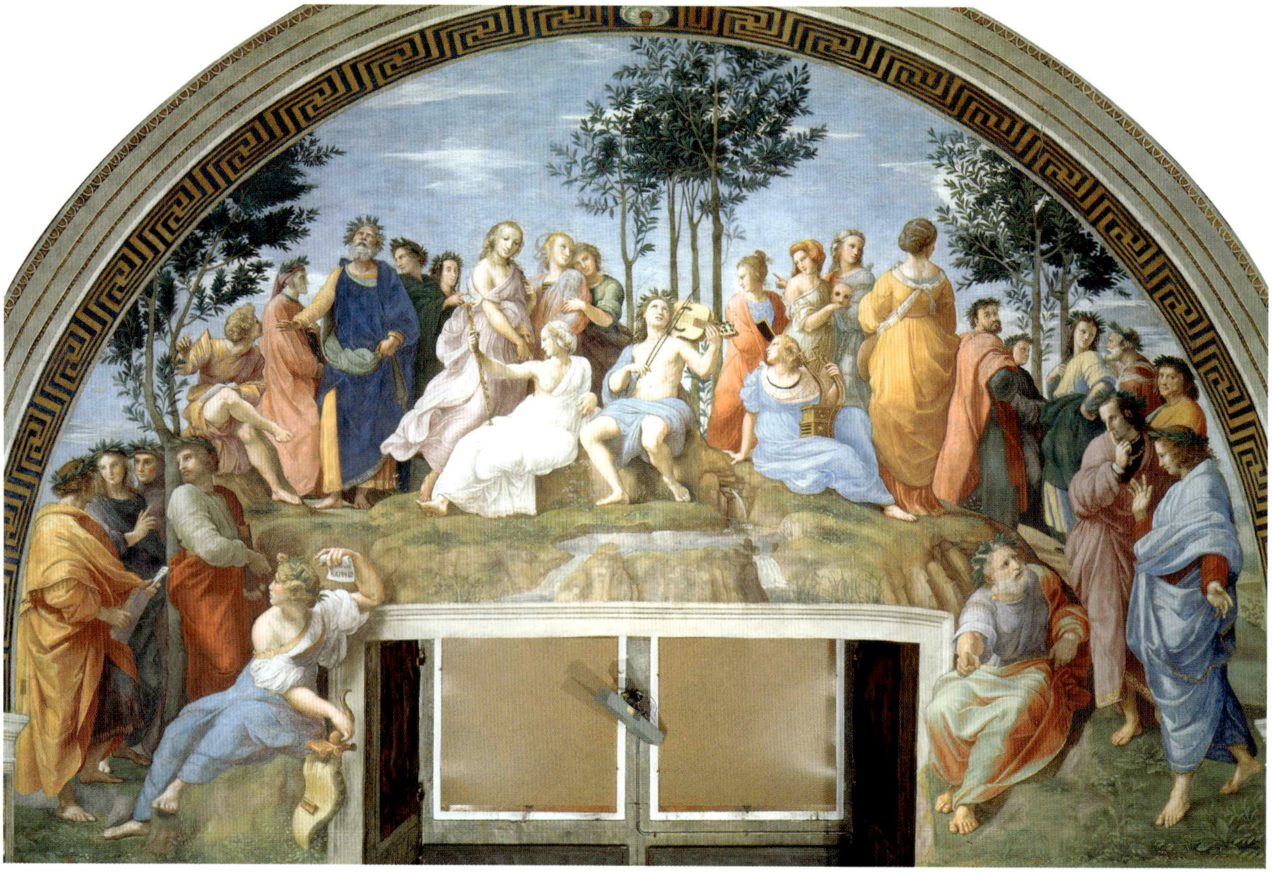

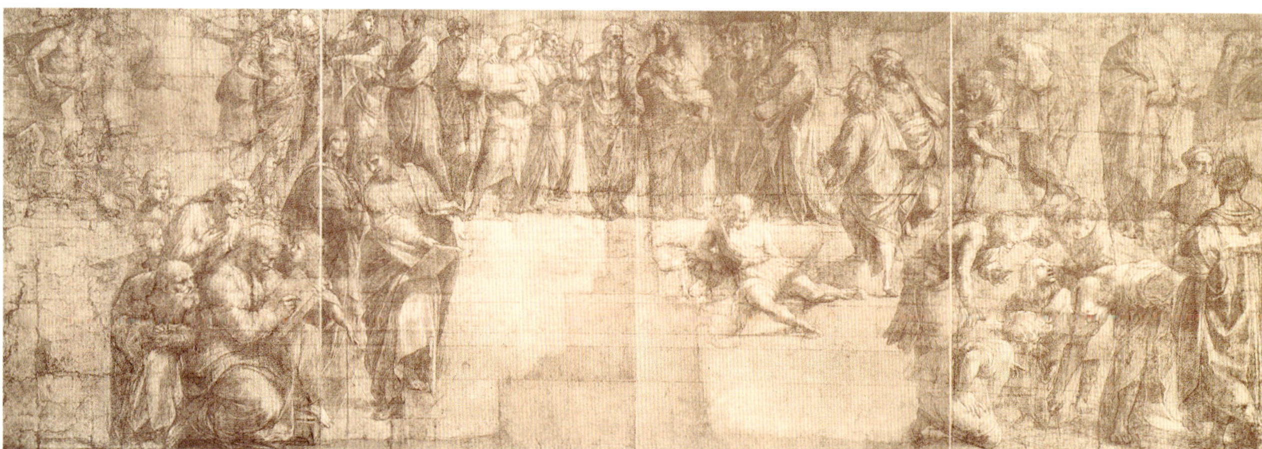

FIG. 2.5. Raphael, *Parnassus*, 1511. Fresco, 21 ft. 11 ¾ in. (670 cm) wide. Stanza della Segnatura, Vatican, Rome.

FIG. 2.6. Raphael, *The School of Athens* (cartoon), c. 1508. Charcoal, black chalk, white heightening on paper pricked for transfer, 9 ft. 6 in. × 26 ft. 3 in. (280 × 800 cm). Pinacoteca Ambrosiana, Milan.

and Aristotle, books in hand, are the focal point of the fresco dedicated to Philosophy, the *School of Athens.*

The way Raphael redesigned the traditional scheme was illustrated by Ernst Gombrich in a brilliant visual comparison of Perugino's illustrious men for the Cambio, created less than a decade before work was begun in the Segnatura (see fig. 1.18).[9] Perugino's figures stand in an orderly file, each embodying the virtue symbolically represented on the cloud over his head. They are separated compositionally with no overlapping, and each is distinguished coloristically. Raphael transformed this traditional lineup into a dramatic interaction among the actors, who are engaged in speaking or demonstrating or listening. History becomes a dialogue, a lively interchange shared eagerly among participants who pass on their learning. The humanist passion for unearthing and reconstructing the history of ideas is captured by Raphael's dramatization.

In his coloring, Raphael found a style that expressed the essence of the message. The generous humanist concept of the unity of all knowledge, pagan or Christian, secular or religious, expressed in different languages but bearing witness to a single truth, is given visible expression in the colors, which although composed of distinct hues are woven together in a harmonious and interactive flow (fig. 2.5). It is the look of all the colors participating with one another that distinguishes the Segnatura frescoes and the unione mode. The eye moves from one figure to the next effortlessly, with those in groups or sequences harmoniously related because the brilliance of their drapery is rendered at the same level. In technical terms, the colors are similar in value and in saturation. The use of a full cartoon, of the kind that has survived for the *School of Athens* (fig. 2.6), made possible the preparation of the pattern of light and shade and of tonality across the whole composition that both the unione and chiaroscuro mode depend upon. This overall unified and dramatized rendering sets these Cinquecento works apart from the more staccato compositions of the Quattrocento, such as Perugino's. As was discussed in Chapter 1, cartoons in the Quattrocento were not made for the whole composition typically but for individual figures. It has been suggested that the *School of Athens* cartoon was installed temporarily on a wall of the Segnatura and that substitute cartoons were made for the individual parts, keeping the vision of the whole before the eyes of everyone working on the fresco. With the full-scale

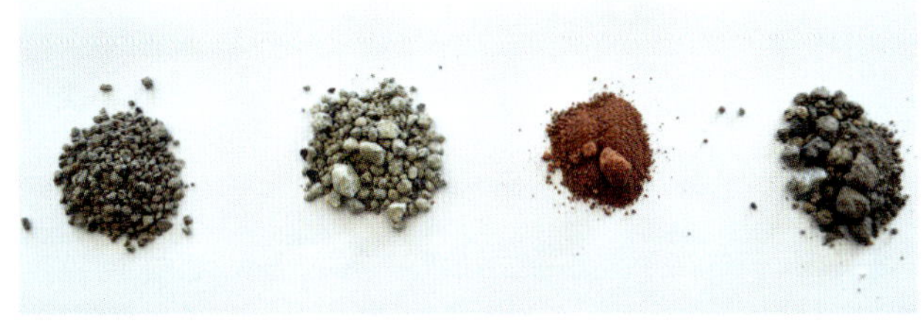

cartoon, Raphael could entrust with confidence the execution of sections of this large wall—it measures more than twenty-six feet at the base—to his assistants.

No one has explained how Raphael achieved the effect of unione in these frescoes. I would like to propose the hypothesis that, as in the case of his use of priming, Raphael was introducing a new procedure here. The practice of preparing the wall for fresco was not identical in Florence and Rome, as Michelangelo learned to his chagrin in the Sistine when his plaster began to mold a couple of months after he frescoed it. He was advised to change the mixture to compensate for the damper climate of Rome and to add more *pozzolana* to the mix.[10] Pozzolana, a volcanic ash available locally and not used in Florence, has a tint, either brownish, grayish, or even purplish. Samples show the range of tints found in pozzolana (fig. 2.7). Normally, Roman frescoists, in order to mask the color of the pozzolana, applied a white layer over the intonaco (the final layer of plaster), which was called *intonachino.* There are two documented instances in which this intonachino was omitted in Roman frescoes of this period. Sebastiano del Piombo made use of the purplish cast of his intonaco when he painted his *Polyphemus* at the Villa Farnesina for Agostino Chigi,[11] and at almost the same moment Raphael used the grayish tinge of the intonaco in his *Isaiah* fresco in Sant'Agostino.[12] (We will come back to Sebastiano, who plays an important part in this story.) Looking at the Segnatura frescoes, we need to account for their unprecedented color. Is the extraordinary unione of the Segnatura frescoes the result of a similar omission of intonachino, in order to make use of the de-saturating effect of a slightly brownish intonaco, a tint lent by the pozzolana? This would adjust the tonality of his fresco in a way analogous to a tinted imprimatura in oil painting. The watercolors applied on top would be neutralized and pulled together into an overall concord such as what we see.

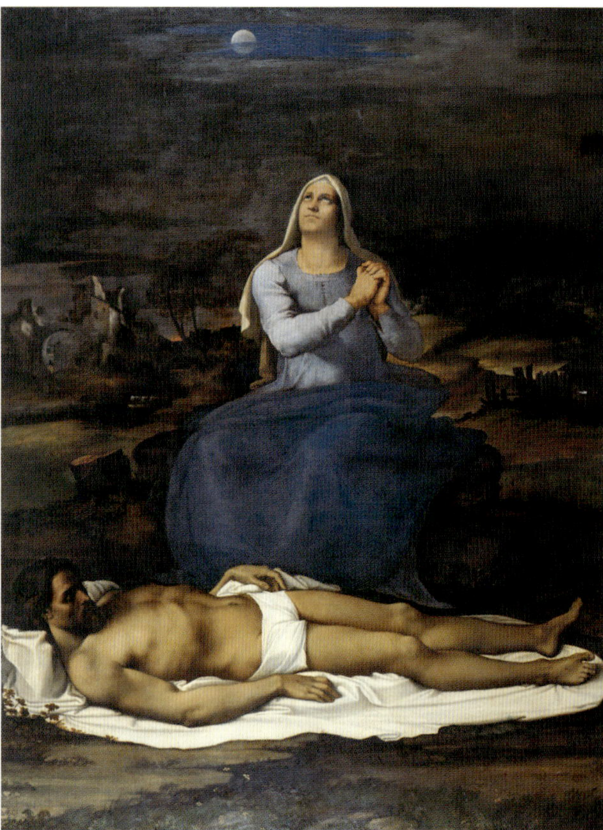

FIG. 2.8. Sebastiano del Piombo, *Pietà*, c. 1515. Oil on panel,
8 ft. 6¼ in. × 7 ft. 4½ in. (260 × 225 cm). Museo Civico, Viterbo.

Julius, even though preoccupied with wars and claiming no particular intellectual authority, must have recognized that Raphael had achieved a unique marriage of
content with form, for he hired him to carry on with the
next room, the Stanza di Eliodoro.

THE CHIAROSCURO MODE

The subjects for the Eliodoro were of a different order,
and Raphael must have felt they called for a different
mode of coloring. These are historical moments, chosen to highlight achievements of the living pope whose
portrait was included in each scene, and they required
an intensification of drama. Contrast, especially of light
and shade, conveys the violent expulsion of the thief
Heliodorus, who would rob the temple treasury. In the
Mass at Bolsena, sharply contrasted primary colors, set off
with black, distinguish the contemporary Swiss Guards
on the right from the anonymous original witnesses
to the miracle of the bleeding host, who are rendered
in soft sfumatesque pastels on the left. Black shadows,
which are nowhere to be seen in the Segnatura, are substituted here for the gentler transitions seen there. Did

Raphael make use of a darker pozzolana here to facilitate
his chiaroscuro?

The acme of his accomplishment in this new chiaroscuro mode would not be seen by Julius, for the
Liberation of Peter from Prison was painted after his death
in February 1513. (So also was *Pope Leo I Repulsing Attila
the Hun*, in which Leo X stands in for his fifth-century
namesake, Leo I.) The savvy Raphael, recognizing how
difficult it is to see the subtle color effects he had created in his *Parnassus* in the Segnatura, limited his palette
essentially to four colors for his fresco in a similar position above the window here, and relied on sharp contrast
of light and shadow to tell the story. An eerie moonlight
sets off the guards at the left. A grid of bars daringly
scores the central scene, where an angel in a blaze of
golden light invades the blackish cell where Peter sleeps.

Raphael had begun to substitute the chiaroscuro
mode for unione in some of the oil paintings at this
time, although he continued to use unione and a lightly
tinted imprimatura in his altarpieces, notably the *Sistine
Madonna* and the *Saint Cecilia Altarpiece*.[13] As we will see,
most of his works after 1515 employ a dark priming and
the chiaroscuro mode. Who invented the chiaroscuro
mode is still an unsettled question, whether Raphael or
Sebastiano del Piombo, but the weight of evidence favors
Sebastiano. By 1515 Sebastiano had created his nocturne,
the *Pietà*, unmistakably in the chiaroscuro mode and
using a tinted imprimatura (fig. 2.8).[14] Sebastiano was
probably the most technically innovative painter of the
Cinquecento. Even before he departed Venice for Rome
in 1511, in his *Salome with the Head of John the Baptist* he
was working with a very pale gray priming.[15] In his
early years in Rome he famously used drawings supplied by Michelangelo, which he combined with his own
strong sense for the power of color. According to Vasari,
Michelangelo supplied a cartoon for his *Pietà*.[16] Although
Michelangelo's *disegno* of the principal figures is powerful indeed, the *colorire* of the landscape setting, eerie and
mysterious, creates an atmosphere of melancholy that
conveys the Virgin's emotions even better than her gesture and face.

A few years later, in 1517 in his *Raising of Lazarus*
(fig. 2.9), for the notorious competition with Raphael's
Transfiguration, Sebastiano again made use of sketches
by Michelangelo. His manner has become more Roman
and more Michelangelesque, with monumentally sculptural figures, especially the commanding Christ. His

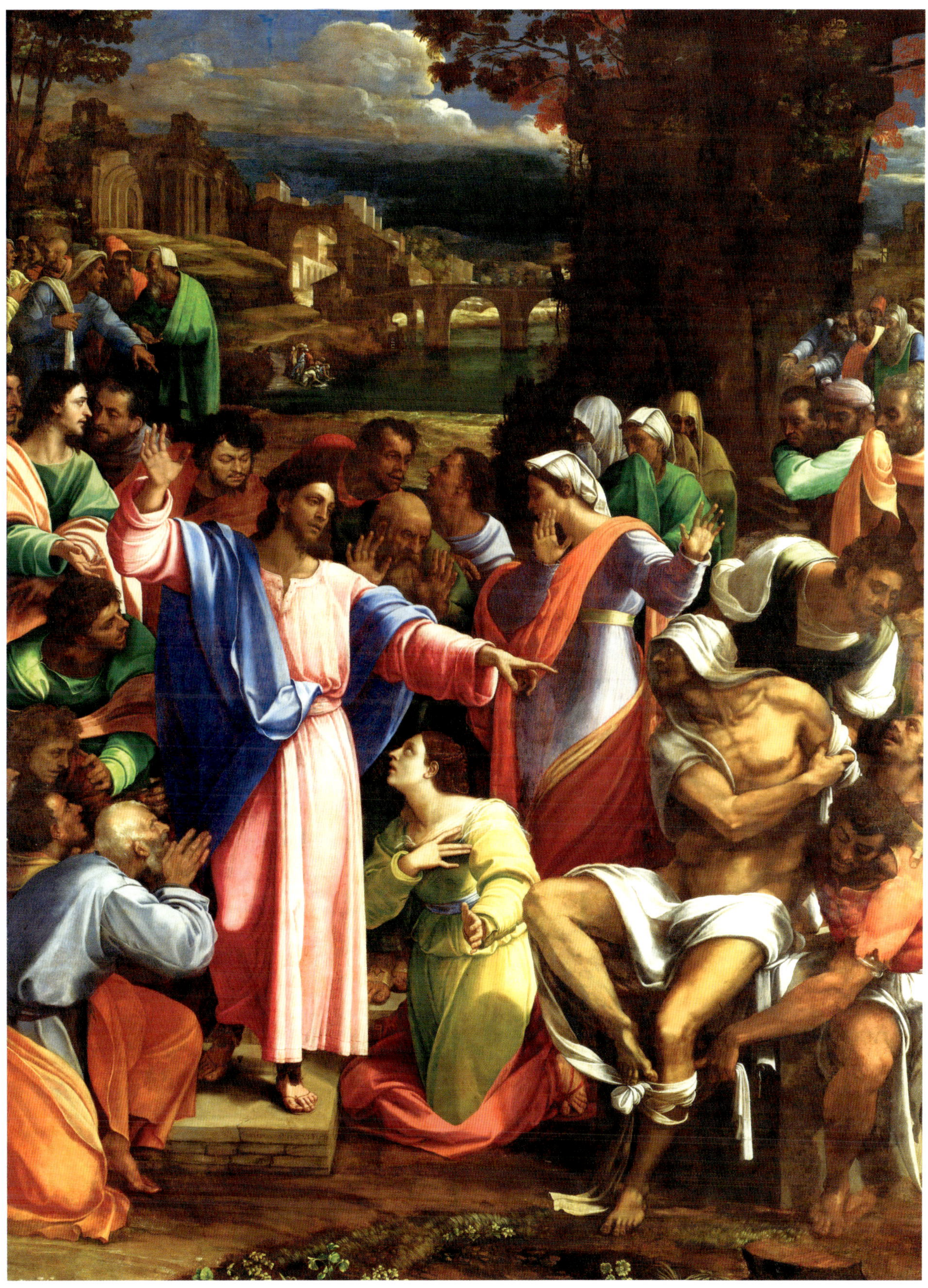

FIG. 2.9. Sebastiano del Piombo, *Raising of Lazarus*, 1517–19. Oil on panel transferred to canvas, 12 ft. 6 in. × 9 ft. 6 in. (381 × 289.5 cm). National Gallery, London.

coloring has changed too, but it is no less impressive. Conservator Jill Dunkerton reminds us that this huge panel has suffered greatly, but we can nonetheless see that Sebastiano, the foreigner from the Veneto, intended to create a showpiece of Venetian coloring, throwing down the gauntlet to Rome and the divine Raphael.[17] His technique is complex, making full use of Venetian-style glazing, adapted to Roman taste, but this is clearly a painting in what we would come to designate the chiaroscuro mode. He laid down an imprimatura of light to mid-brownish gray color, still light enough for lines of black underdrawing to be clearly visible to the painter. He underpainted every drapery with a contrasting color, sometimes mixtures, sometimes multiple layers, then used translucent glazes in contrasting colors. He is striving for richer and more complex effects and, as we will see, Raphael's late style adopted a similar layering procedure. This darker and more dramatic picture reflects the taste for chiaroscuro that was taking hold of Rome in the second half of the 1510s.

In his coloring of Christ we can see a vestige of the reverence for lapis lazuli as a precious material that had prevailed in the Quattrocento. In the mantle and robe of Christ, Sebastiano used pure, unadulterated ultramarine in the shadow and added white lead for the highlights.[18] The contrast with Raphael's use of ultramarine in the *Alba Madonna* tells us something about the difference between the unione and the chiaroscuro modes and about the evolution of taste in Rome. Raphael, we saw, had willingly sacrificed the brilliance of the blue for tonal unity; Sebastiano treasured the intensity of the pigment and the high contrast it contributes to his color scheme. Raphael would adopt a similar palette of high contrast and saturated colors in this half decade, culminating in his final *Transfiguration.*

MICHELANGELO AND THE MODE OF CANGIANTISMO

At the same time that Raphael was beginning his frescoes in the Segnatura, across the way in the Vatican Palace, Michelangelo had begun work in the Sistine Chapel. His task was to paint the vault, which had been damaged when structural problems caused a crack running the whole length to open in 1504. The chapel had to be closed for six months while repairs were made and tie rods were installed to stabilize the vault. The blue sky with gold stars that had completed the decoration commissioned by Sixtus IV in the 1480s had to be repainted.[19] Julius decided

not simply to repair or repeat what had been there, but to replace it with an altogether new decoration.[20]

The coloring style Michelangelo chose was not that of his contemporaries, either Raphael or Pinturicchio or Perugino or his friend Sebastiano, although it was an elaboration of the Quattrocento device of cangiantismo, which all of these painters used in small passages for variety or ornamental effect (fig. 2.10). Cangianti passages can be found in Raphael's Segnatura (see fig. 2.5), and Perugino used the device liberally in his vault fresco in the Incendio and in his *Famous Men:* note the two figures standing at the right (see fig. 1.18). Michelangelo took this familiar technique and amplified it. What had in the past been a peripheral ornament became in his hands a new mode of coloring, in which its anti-naturalism became the signal of supernatural content. Instead of creating shadows with a darker monochrome, Michelangelo went back to the Cennini style of modeling up with white, or he created modeling by juxtaposing hues of graded value—that is, with cangiantismo.

Michelangelo had experimented with cangiantismo already in Florence in his panel painting of the Holy Family, the *Doni Tondo* (see fig. 0.1). There he put on display the sculptor's rejection of Leonardo's fuzzy-edged sfumato, creating figures as if hewn in marble and crisply contoured. His distaste for the softening effect possible with oil is made apparent in his solid colors, which, in the manner of egg tempera, shift boldly rather than transitioning seamlessly. His remark, made much later—to Sebastiano del Piombo, who had prepared the wall of the Sistine for the *Last Judgment* with his personal formula for oil mural—that oil painting is for old ladies and lazy people, did not refer only to painting in oil on the wall, it seems.[21] He never painted in oil again, and when paintings were required of him, he managed to find a surrogate to do the actual painting after his cartoon.[22]

Michelangelo's coloring can be called a new mode because not only does it make use of cangianti passages on a scale never before conceived, but also because it does not imitate sfumato or undertake to create the musical harmonies of unione, nor does it employ the dramatic dark shadows of chiaroscuro. Like the Quattrocento up-modeled fresco style from which it is derived, it utilizes the whiteness of the plaster to create high values and whitened highlights, with pure color or a shift of hue to create the shadows. Because Michelangelo's coloring depends upon the white plaster,

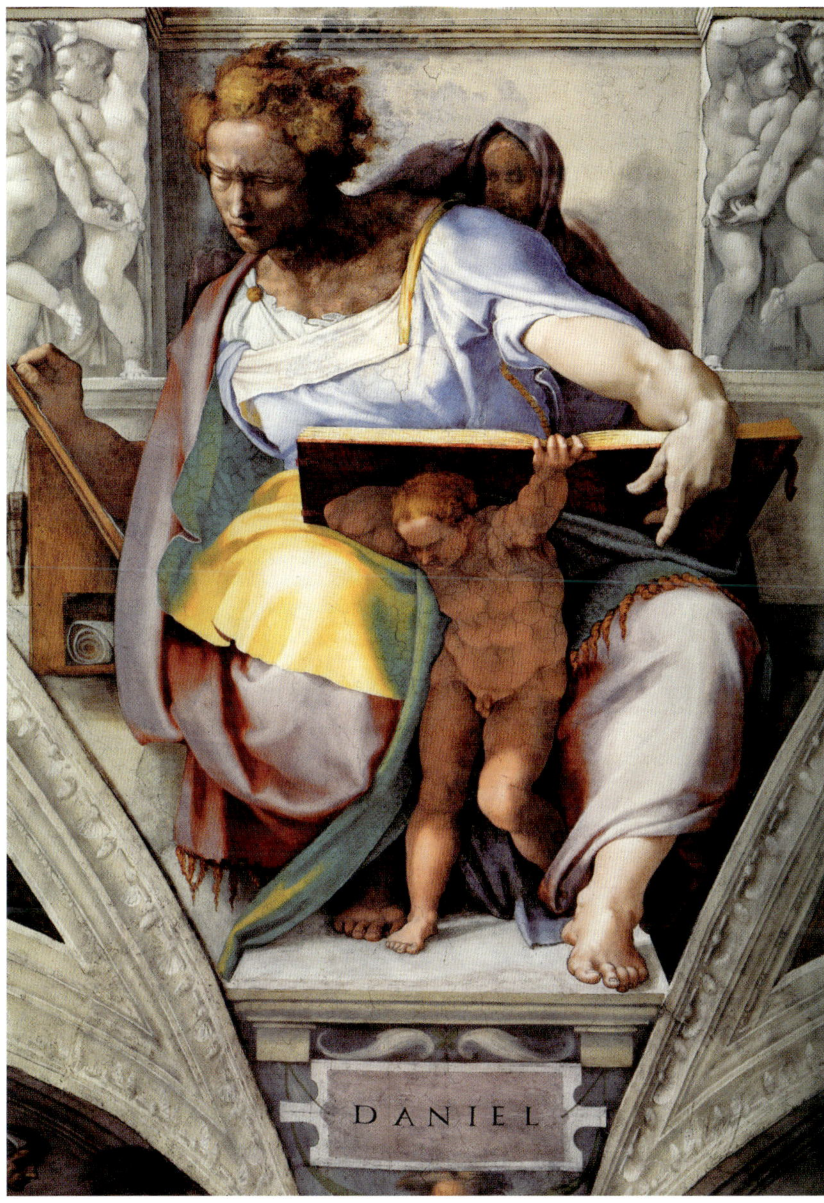

FIG. 2.10. Michelangelo, *Prophet Daniel*, 1508–12. Fresco. Sistine Chapel, Vatican, Rome.

he used intonachino, unlike Raphael who, I contend, preferred the dulling or neutralizing effect imparted to the plaster by the tint of the pozzolana.[23] Naturally, not every drapery shifts in hue; the mode of cangiantismo is marked not only by the prominence of cangianti but also by the blond tonality achieved by up-modeling and the brilliance of the colors.

Why did Michelangelo depart from the coloring of his contemporaries? As Venetian critics make clear, there were many who did not appreciate his fantastic inventions.[24] We need to think about the special conditions of his project: the spine of the Sistine vault is more than sixty feet above the head of the viewer and not brilliantly lit, so legibility was a problem, as the painter discovered

after he had completed the first of the Genesis panels, the *Deluge.* He never thereafter attempted a similar deep space, but arranged his figures in the foreground in a frieze or relief-like arrangement at the surface. He recognized that a high-value tonality with large planes of color made the desired impact. There are small-scale cangiante passages in the *Deluge,* but they are too delicate to project to the viewer on the floor. It is in the Delphic Sibyl adjacent to the first bay that he enlarged his cangianti drapery to monumental scale for the first time. At this point it is fair to say that he has invented a new coloring system, a mode distinct from what is being practiced by his contemporaries.

A second reason that Michelangelo may have sought

a new mode of coloring for the Sistine is the subject. Taking place as his scenes do on the ceiling, their position invokes the heavenly realm, and the last half of the Genesis scenes take place in the heavens. The exalted theological content seems to require a level of abstraction to match and convey it. Raphael was Michelangelo's nearest model and rival. The unione coloring system he had evolved derived from Leonardo and Perugino, but moved beyond them toward an idealized mode that represented a plausible but perfected reality. The accidents and imperfections of nature have been excised, leaving only the essential. There is an element of abstraction in Raphael's distilling process, but what we see does not violate the laws of nature, as Michelangelo's does. Raphael is most often concerned with representing the divine present in this world, thus his color system is well chosen. The space inhabited by his divine figures is subtly transformed and perfected by their presence.

Certainly Raphael's coloring could have been made to work on the Sistine vault, but Michelangelo was not an artist who imitated his peers. The system he invented made use of artifice and ornament to separate the realm of his images from the world we know and suggest their exalted content as no other could.

LATE RAPHAEL

During these years Raphael had become the most important person on the Roman artistic scene. He was a good administrator and he was always gracious, a far easier person to work with than the prickly Michelangelo. Pope Leo piled diverse tasks on him, including making him Bramante's successor as the architect of Saint Peter's. In order to fulfill his obligations, he had to invent the new organization for an efficient and productive workshop that is described below. In fact, his pupils, especially Giulio Romano and Perino del Vaga, as well as Giorgio Vasari, later imitated the methods he shaped, and they transformed artistic production.

After 1515 he developed his painting technique for efficiency and consistency. The pale imprimatura of his Florentine period and his early years in Rome gradually became darker, accommodating his increasing preference for chiaroscuro rather than the look of unione.

The next operation was to transfer a drawing onto the support from a full-scale cartoon. Such underdrawings are visible in infrared reflectogram, such as one for the *Holy Family of Francis I* (fig. 2.11). None of Raphael's

cartoons from this period has survived, but we know that one existed for the *Saint Michael* because Raphael made a gift of it to a would-be patron, Alfonso d'Este, for whom he did not have time to make a commissioned painting.[25] A cartoon has been preserved for the *Stoning of Saint Stephen,* which was probably commissioned of Raphael by Gian Matteo Giberti after he was named *commendatore* of Santo Stefano in Genoa in 1519 (fig. 2.12). Raphael died before the painting was delivered and Giulio Romano executed it, but the cartoon may have been made while he was alive and certainly reflects the practice of his workshop.[26] More than thirteen and a half feet tall, the cartoon shows the chiaroscuro composition in charcoal and black chalk. It would have been based upon a *modello,* which in turn was built from preceding compositional sketches and figure studies. The modello would be squared so that its transfer to the panel was a mechanical process that any number of assistants in the workshop could be entrusted with. Raphael would have supervised the entire preparatory process and normally would have been involved in making figure studies and fixing the composition. There are masterful figure studies in red and black chalk surviving for his last painting, the *Transfiguration,* that give us an idea of this intense stage of preparation.[27] Although he relied heavily on his workshop and entrusted assistants with particular tasks, there was no place for their personal style. He wanted every piece that left his studio to bear the marks of a Raphael. As had been true in the Quattrocento, the best assistant was the one who had best assimilated the master's style and could simulate it.

Raphael's technique truly distinguished itself in the final paint layers that he applied in two different colors. With a top layer thin enough to allow the lower layer to peek through, he could create a vibrancy of color. The tonality was not that of pure pigments, but he was not using physical mixtures. It strikes the eye as fresh, something newly invented, which stands out in just the right degree from the dark background. He put a pink layer under a thin layer of glaze of lapis or green, for instance, which could create a cangiante effect. On the sleeve of the *Madonna della Perla* (1519–20), the pink underlayer is modulated into blue-tinged shadow (fig. 2.13). In this way he avoids the harshness of blackish shadow in this highlighted area, and the tones merge into one another. To what extent Raphael permitted his most-skilled assistants to execute these final layers is not knowable, but whoever

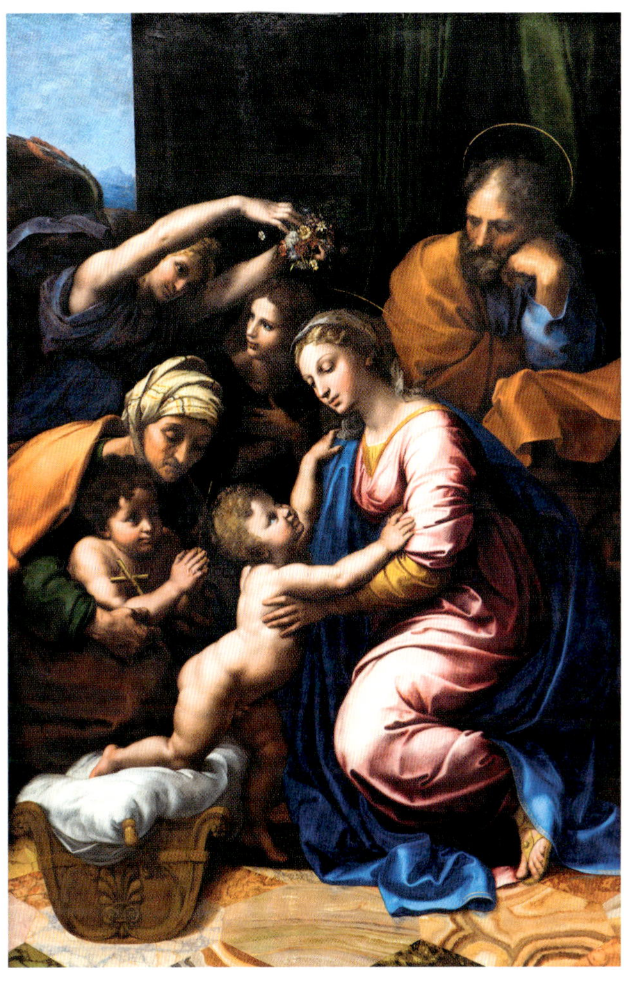

FIG. 2.11. Raphael, *Holy Family of Francis I,* 1518. Oil on panel transferred to canvas, 81 × 55 in. (207 × 140 cm). Louvre, Paris.

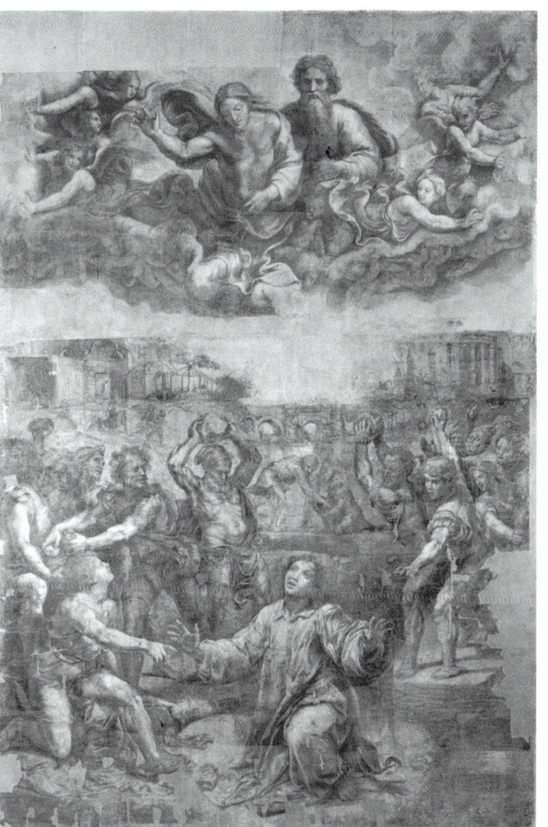

FIG. 2.12. Raphael and Giulio Romano, *Stoning of Saint Stephen* (cartoon), c. 1520–21. Charcoal and black chalk on paper, 13 ft. 7¼ in. × 9 ft. 4¼ in. (412 × 285 cm). Musei Vaticani, Rome.

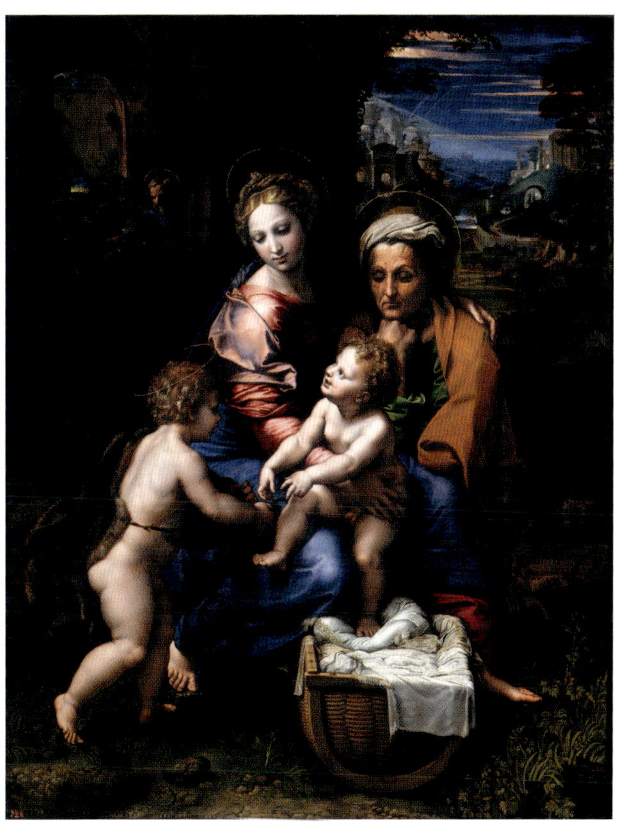

FIG. 2.13. Raphael, *Madonna della Perla,* c. 1519–20. Oil on panel, 58 × 45⅔ in. (147 × 116 cm). Prado, Madrid.

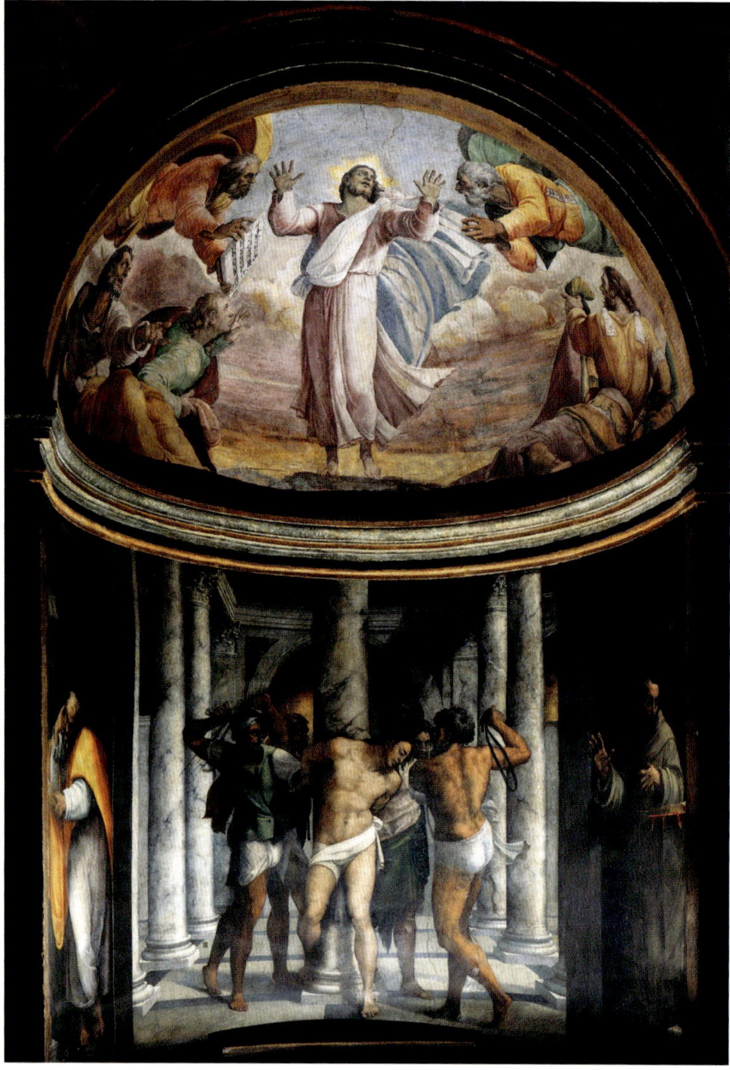

FIG. 2.14. Sebastiano del Piombo, *Flagellation*, 1516–24. Oil mural. Borgherini Chapel, San Pietro in Montorio, Rome.

painted them, they bear the stamp of Raphael and not the assistant's hand.

This cangiantismo is very different from Michelangelo's. Michelangelo juxtaposed large fields of contrasted color for a more sedate and grandiose effect. The two artists had different purposes and different tasks. Michelangelo sought to command the eye of his distant viewer and impress him with the authority of his biblical hero. Raphael sought to entice his with the tender, delicate femininity of his Virgin.

Just how distinctive and demanding Raphael's painting technique was is revealed by the fact that even his prize pupil and most accomplished successor, Giulio Romano, did not follow it once Raphael had died and he was working on his own. Giulio abbreviated the process, giving up the two-layered structure and using thicker

paints of physical mixtures and fewer hues.[28] The opaque, blackish, and sometimes muddy tonality we associate with him is the result.

SEBASTIANO VERSUS THE RAPHAEL WORKSHOP

Since 1516 Michelangelo had been in Florence, sent off there by Pope Leo, who was perhaps a little scared of him, to work on a project that would bring further glory to the Medici: to create a richly sculpted façade for the church of San Lorenzo, the Medici family parish. Michelangelo threw himself into the project, only to have the commission canceled by the pope in what must have been a disappointment on the scale of his loss of Pope Julius's tomb a little more than a decade earlier. While Michelangelo was absent, Sebastiano became his surrogate in Rome, constantly exchanging letters and keeping him informed of all that was going on. If a patron in Rome wanted a work by Michelangelo, the most he could hope for was that Michelangelo would supply drawings to Sebastiano, who would then execute the painting, as he had done in the cases of the *Pietà* and the *Raising of Lazarus.* This was the understanding Pierfrancesco Borgherini had with respect to his chapel and the *Flagellation* (fig. 2.14), and indeed Michelangelo did send Sebastiano drawings for it.

Sebastiano, although he was close enough to Michelangelo to use his drawings in his paintings, did not follow Michelangelo in coloring. In fact, he moved in the opposite direction from cangiantismo with his chiaroscuro. He even pioneered the chiaroscuro wall painting in his *Flagellation,* where he abandoned fresco and substituted oil. The painting forms the altarpiece of the Borgherini Chapel, which took him eight years to complete, beginning in 1516. Work was suspended for two years while he labored over the *Raising of Lazarus.* When he returned to work on the chapel, sometime after May 1519, he executed the fresco in the lunette, a Transfiguration, that scholars take to be his response to Raphael's last altarpiece. Then finally in the late summer of 1521 he was ready to begin executing the altar wall, the *Flagellation* flanked by Saint Peter and Saint Francis.[29] The delay may well have been prolonged by his experiments with the new technique he was introducing. Recognizing that fresco, because it is watercolor over white plaster, is necessarily high in value and not suitable for somber events, he sought to create the same drama in fresco that he had achieved in his easel paintings by using the same medium of oil. His image of Christ on the concave wall surrounded by his torturers envelops the worshipper with its mood of pathos and suffering nobly endured. The deep, resonant blackish tones of oil-bound darks could never have been accomplished with fresco. Sebastiano painted the first successful oil mural—succeeding not only where the great Leonardo had failed, but perhaps also Raphael and his workshop in their experiments in the Sala di Costantino.[30]

Modes of coloring were one expression of the rivalry and competition that were central to the lives of artists working in Rome in these years.[31] The contest over the commission to decorate the Sala di Costantino can give us insight into this combative arena. When Raphael died in April 1520, the Sala di Costantino had been barely begun. How much, if any, had already been

painted is unknown, but there ensued a scramble in which Sebastiano sought to wrest the commission from the heirs of Raphael, Giulio Romano and Gianfrancesco Penni. Six days after Raphael's death, Sebastiano wrote to Michelangelo, asking him to support his bid to take over the Sala di Costantino. Michelangelo was reluctant and made only a half-hearted attempt on Sebastiano's behalf. Sebastiano reported that the word on the street was that Raphael's workshop—which Sebastiano disparagingly referred to as the *garzoni* ("shop boys")—intended to paint it in oil. In fact, two trial figures in oil were executed and were eventually incorporated into the final scheme, the allegories of *Comity* and *Justice* (fig. 2.15). Whether they were done under the oversight of Raphael himself before his death is unknown, but it does seem possible. By this time Sebastiano must have been convinced that his own experiment with oil mural, still kept secret even from Michelangelo, was going to succeed, so he must have been doubly eager to have the opportunity to display his skill at the center of the Vatican. When it became clear that he would not secure the commission, he urged Michelangelo to obtain it for himself, hoping no doubt to work beside the great master. Sebastiano continued to badger Michelangelo in his letters, implying that this commission would restore the prestige he had lost with the withdrawal of the San Lorenzo contract. He makes clear with his language how high feelings were running in this contentious situation. He writes to Michelangelo that he "wants to carry out your vendettas and mine in one fell swoop, and to give those malign people to understand that there are other demigods besides Raphael of Urbino and his garzoni."[32] In the end, the workshop persuaded Pope Leo that they had Raphael's drawings, and they painted the Sala in buon fresco.[33]

What Giulio and Penni intended to create was an alternative mode of coloring in fresco to Michelangelo's cangiantismo. In place of his high saturation and high-value color, they produced coloring that was naturalistic and serious without being somber. There is a smoky gray tonality that suggests atmosphere, in contrast to the airless brilliance of the Sistine vault. The initial experiment with oil mural in the two allegorical figures, which are very dark, suggests they were searching for an innovative facture that would correspond more closely to the look of easel paintings in oil, one that would provide a plausible naturalism for the historical narratives of the emperor Constantine. Their rejection of the oil experiment was

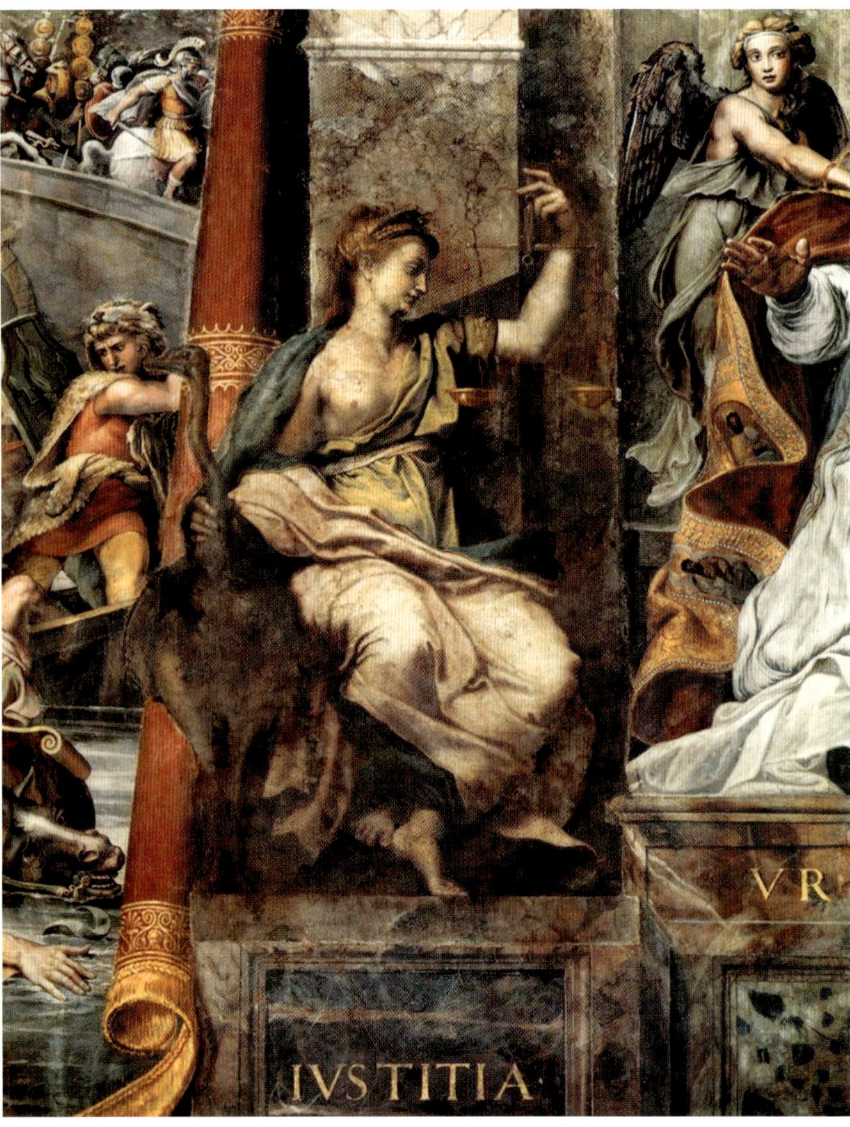

FIG. 2.15. Raphael's workshop, *Pope Clement VII* (fresco) and *Justice* (oil), 1520–24. Sala di Costantino, Vatican, Rome.

based, I assume, on the decision that it would make the room too dark.[34]

The tug-of-war here is of a kind that could not have occurred in Quattrocento Florence. Certainly there was a competitive environment in Florence with rival workshops vying for business. In Rome, however, the choices patrons made were based less on practical matters such as the bottega's reputation for speed, efficiency, cost, and the quality of materials used, and more on style. Painters in Rome felt freer to experiment. In fresco they could choose among three options: an oil mural executed in deep and somber tones, a light-toned traditional fresco, or Michelangelo's anti-naturalistic cangiantismo, with its brilliant and ornamental look. The modes offered clear aesthetic choices, allowing the patron to express his particular taste.

RESPONSES TO MICHELANGELO AND HIS CANGIANTISMO

The painting usually gathered under the rubric of mannerism is distinctive in its coloring. It owes much to Michelangelo's cangiantismo, especially in the medium of fresco. Easel paintings, especially altarpieces, remain more conservative in their coloring and frequently pay homage to Raphael, as, for example, in Perino del Vaga's *Nativity* (Washington, D.C., National Gallery of Art, 1534). There is a moment of experimentation early on in Florence in the 1520s, however, when Jacopo Pontormo and Rosso Fiorentino ("Red the Florentine," nicknamed for his red hair) take up cangiantismo, creating some of the most daring, surprising, and memorable altarpieces of the Cinquecento.

We often note the idiosyncratic proportions and perspective of Pontormo's and Rosso's pictures, but we note

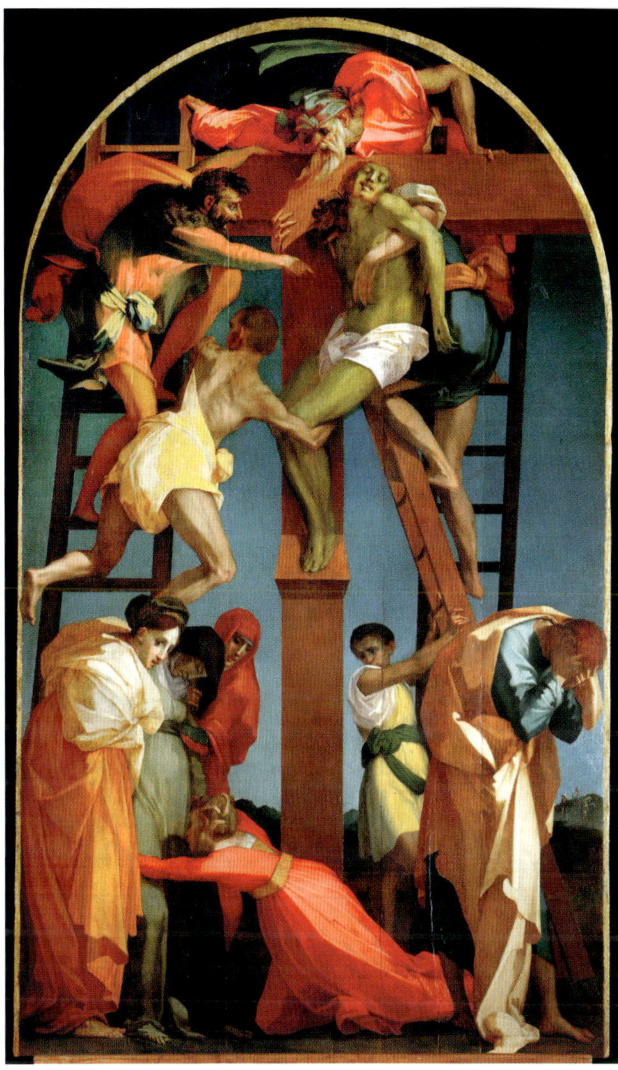

FIG. 2.16. Rosso Fiorentino, *Deposition*, 1521. Oil on panel, 11 ft. 2¼ in. × 6 ft. 7 in. (341 × 201 cm). Pinacoteca, Volterra.

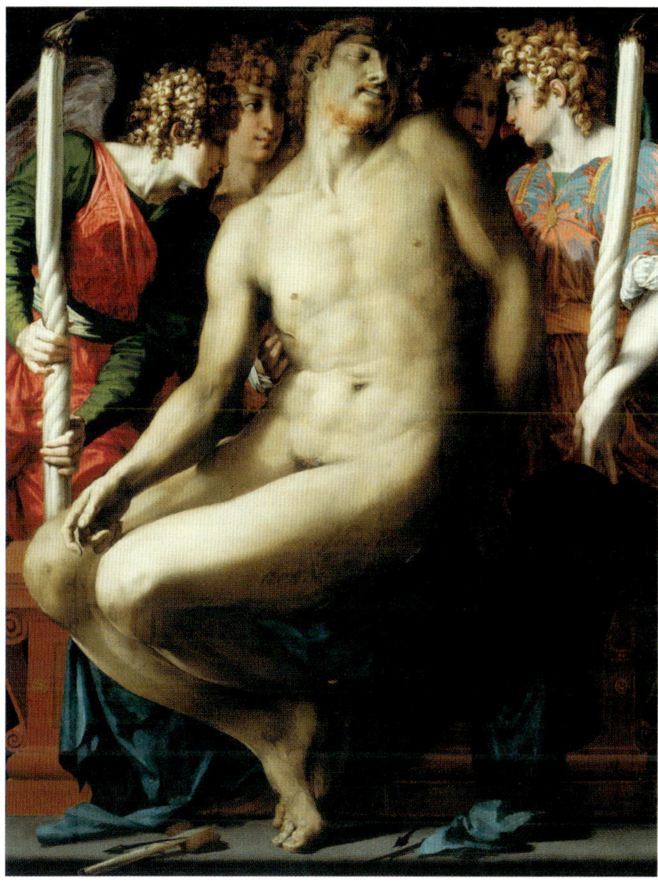

FIG. 2.17. Rosso Fiorentino, *Dead Christ in the Tomb*, c. 1524–27. Oil on panel, 52½ × 41 in. (133.3 × 104.1 cm). Museum of Fine Arts, Boston.

less often the source of their eccentric coloring. These painters experimented with cangiantismo in panels for palace decoration (for example, Pontormo's Joseph series for the Borgherini family) and in altarpieces. The earliest such experiment is Rosso's *Deposition* in Volterra (fig. 2.16).

Against an unnaturally brilliant blue sky and a grid of ladders and cross, men struggle to lower Christ's body. Excited reds encircle it. At the lower right, John, bent with grief, is the target of a theatrical beam of white light that also reaches to the shoulder of one of the supporting Maries. What is striking is that none of the colors is modeled down in the shadows. The coloring is the artificial mode of Michelangelo, with a few ornamental cangiante passages, such as the turban of the old man leaning over the top of the cross, or the drapery of the one at the left who screams and points helplessly.

It was indeed an experiment, for in his next altarpiece, the *Marriage of the Virgin* (Florence, San Lorenzo), commissioned by Carlo Ginori, Rosso has abandoned the blond tonality in favor of a dark, Leonardo-derived background out of which brightly colored passages sparkle, with limited cangiantismo. Rosso was the pupil of Andrea del Sarto, and it is from him that he would have learned to use a dark imprimatura.[35] In what is perhaps Rosso's masterpiece, the startling *Dead Christ in the Tomb,* created after he had departed Florence for Rome, the scene takes place within the tomb, where the dark background was required (fig. 2.17). The darkness is overcome, literally and figuratively, by the Easter dawn light entering as the stone is rolled away. One angel adds dazzle with a cangiante passage of orange shifting to pale blue in his drapery. Such a cangiante does not necessarily

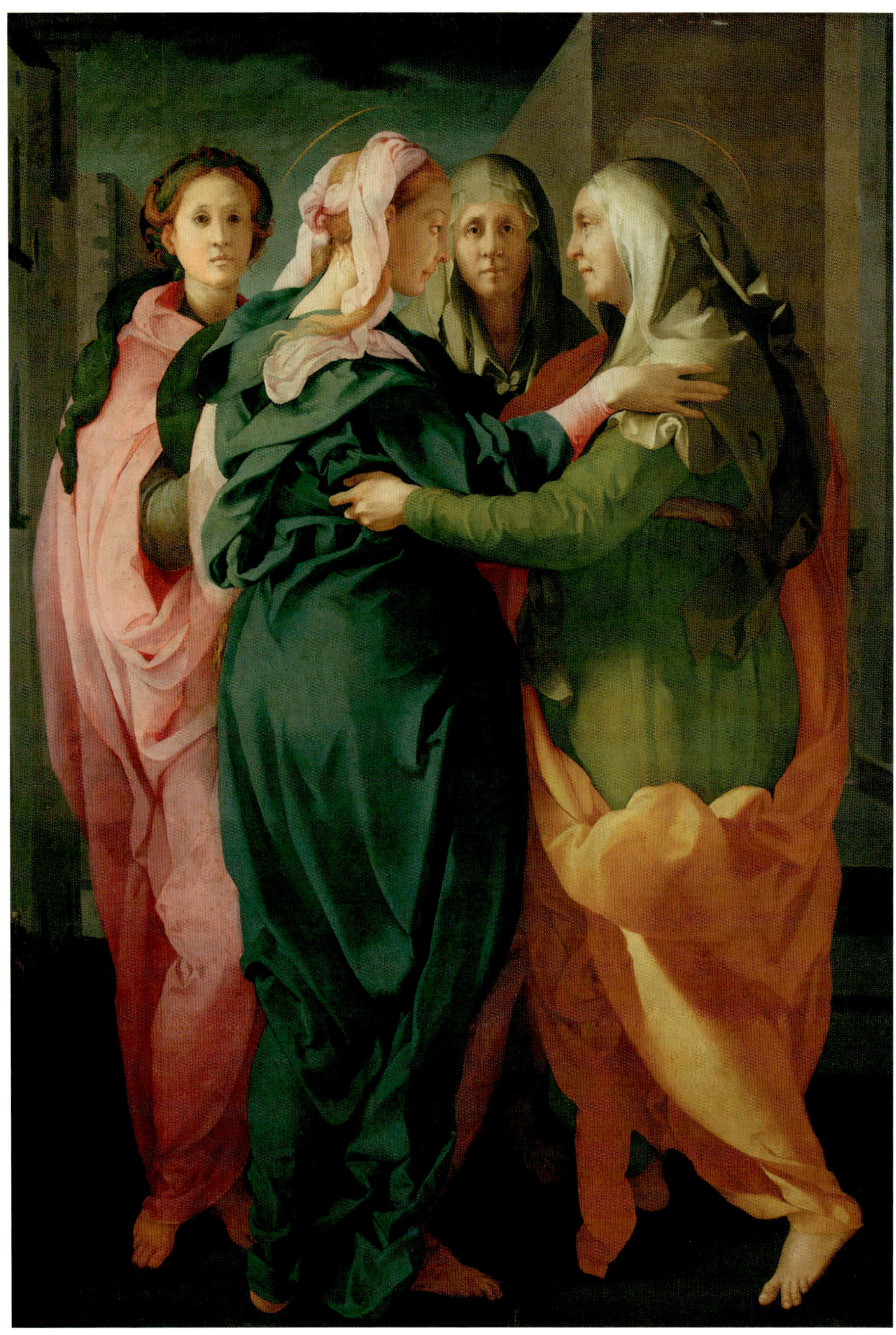

FIG. 2.18. Pontormo, *Visitation*, c. 1528. Oil on panel, 79 1/2 × 61 3/8 in. (202 × 156 cm). Pieve di San Michele Arcangelo, Carmignano.

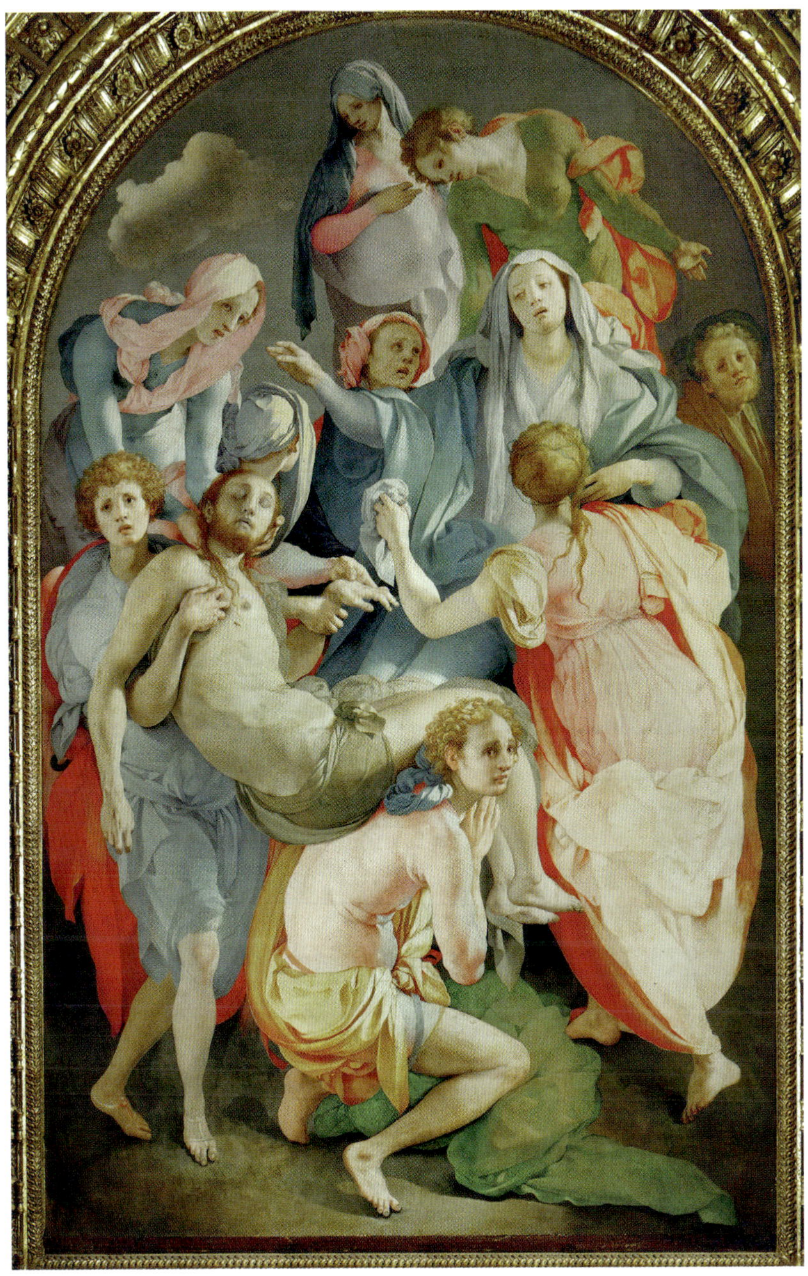

derive from Michelangelo, of course, nor does the label "cangiantismo" mode fit altogether comfortably here, but neither does "sfumato," "unione," or perhaps even "chiaroscuro," though the last is the closest match.

What we see in the wake of the Sistine vault is experimentation and artists combining modes in novel ways, sometimes creating new hybrids. Pontormo's altarpieces fit the categories even less well than Rosso's: the mysterious *Visitation* (fig. 2.18) and fascinating *Entombment* merit a close look. The *Visitation* disconcerts us with the appearance of two women (presumably serving women) who look out at us, giving them importance not merited

by their anonymity, at the same time that they each eerily echo the features of the protagonists. It is as if we see Mary and Elizabeth simultaneously in profile and in full face. The groups' resemblance to the antique Three Graces—plus one—deepens the mystery, and the disparity of scale between the women and the men at the left adds further to our discomfiture. But the coloring is equally outlandish. The very large fields of color with minimal modeling recall the Sistine, and so does the bold hue shift in Elizabeth's drapery.

The *Entombment* (fig. 2.19) shares with *The Visitation* a blond palette. In his life of Pontormo, Vasari remarked of this picture that it is "painted without shadows," by which he meant that there is no dark monochrome added to the shadow, as is also the case in Rosso's Volterra *Deposition* and the *Visitation*. Vasari, from his perspective writing at mid-century, found such a return to early Quattrocento practice anomalous. These panels are all painted without a dark imprimatura. Is there a tinted priming at all? We would like to know, but there are no technical examinations yet. Pontormo's *Entombment* is the altarpiece of the Capponi Chapel, which also contains by him a stained-glass window and a fresco of the *Annunciation*. What Pontormo achieves here is a consonance of coloring among the three works in the chapel. This could explain his choice here, but it does not account for it in the enigmatic *Visitation*. Seemingly dissatisfied with the classicism and idealized color that his predecessors, Raphael and Andrea del Sarto, used as vehicles to suggest the supernatural, Pontormo turned to the anti-naturalism of cangiantismo. Enhanced by his eerily elongated bodies and compressed or inflated space, the colors propel these scenes out of the sphere of the mundane to an otherworldly reality. We might ask: For a subject of grief, why did he not choose chiaroscuro, the mode that best expresses a dark mood? Closer examination of the interpretation the painter is giving us may reveal the reason for his choice. We are told that originally there was a lunette above the wall opposite the altar, now destroyed, of God the Father with arms extended to lament his son.[36] The mother raises her hand in a gesture of farewell. The subject then is the lamentation of earthly Mother and heavenly Father, and the portent of coming resurrection. The coloring, calling attention to itself with its unexpected ornamental quality, startling cangianti, and transcendent beauty, points to the mystery half concealed here.

AFTER RAPHAEL AND THE SISTINE

What we see in the coloring of the painters in Rome who succeeded Michelangelo and Raphael is a kind of artistic schizophrenia. For their frescoes they adapted the coloring style of Michelangelo, and for their easel paintings a chiaroscuro that derived from Raphael's late Roman works. An example is Michelangelo's close follower Daniele da Volterra. It is no surprise to find him embracing cangiantismo for his frescoes. What is surprising is that for his oil altarpieces he preferred chiaroscuro. Perhaps for these painters, aware of their position as

epigones, this was a way to pay homage to each of the giants. It was also a practical solution. Cangiantismo, with its blond tonality, was suited to decorate large rooms, in particular palace walls. As we noted earlier, blackish walls do not make cheerful surroundings. The fantastic quality of cangiantismo suited the hyperbole and playful humor that Perino del Vaga and Francesco Salviati introduced to leaven the dynastic extravaganzas they were required to create for the Medici, the Farnese, and the would-be pope, Cardinal Ricci.

Perino's assignment for the frescoes in the Sala Paolina was to celebrate his patron, Pope Paul III (Alessandro Farnese), in two interlocked narratives. One identified him with Alexander the Great, his natal name, the other with Saint Paul, his papal name. Perino was wise enough to understand that the only way to make such a conceit palatable was with humor. He contrasts Michelangelesque sculptures in faux bronze for the Deeds of Alexander with Raphaelesque unione, enlivened with delicate cangiante touches, for the life of Saint Paul. The enormous faux bronze reliefs become mock-heroic when Perino stuffs them with oversized Michelangelesque figures in serpentine poses (fig. 2.20). The spiritual heroics of Saint Paul, such as his martyrdom by beheading, he renders in small roundels, which are trivialized by the swirl of pastel ornaments that surround and even overlap them (fig. 2.21). Even here in the reclining nudes, Perino seems intent upon combining the two great masters by sweetening and feminizing, in a Raphaelesque manner, figures that derive their initial inspiration from the doughty Ignudi of the Sistine vault. The sophistication and wit of these conceits relieves what could have been unbearable pomposity.

Vasari and Salviati were childhood friends. They met in Florence in 1523, according to Vasari's account in his life of Salviati. In the 1530s they were both in Rome, and Vasari reported that there was nothing of importance that they did not copy. When the pope left town, they gained admission to the Vatican and "remained there from morning to night with nothing to eat but a morsel of bread, and where they were almost benumbed with cold." During these years their coloring styles in easel paintings followed the current taste for a kind of chiaroscuro, a dark background setting off brighter colors. When in 1538 Salviati painted his *Visitation* fresco in the Oratorio di San Giovanni Decollato, however, he followed Raphael in the early Stanze, with some

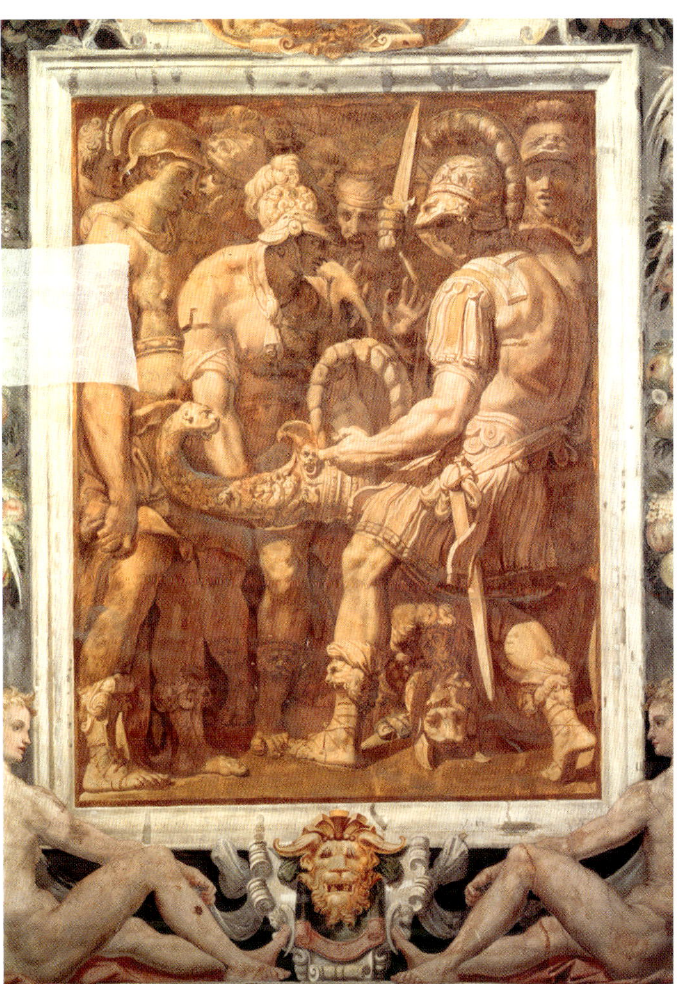

FIG. 2.20. Perino del Vaga, assisted by Pellegrino Tibaldi, *Alexander Cutting the Gordian Knot*, 1542–47. Fresco. Sala Paolina, Castel Sant'Angelo, Rome.

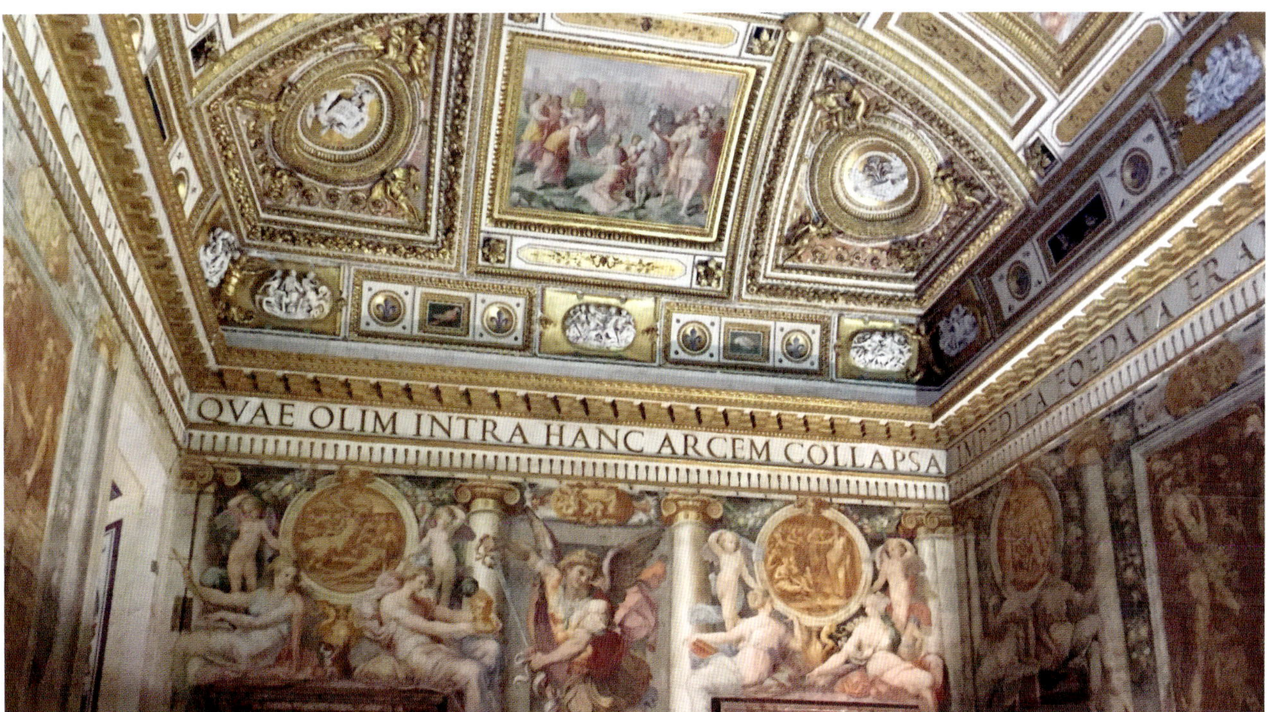

FIG. 2.21. Perino del Vaga, *The Muses Erato and Thalia and the Blinding of Elymas*, roundel at right, 1542–47. Fresco. Sala Paolina, Castel Sant'Angelo, Rome.

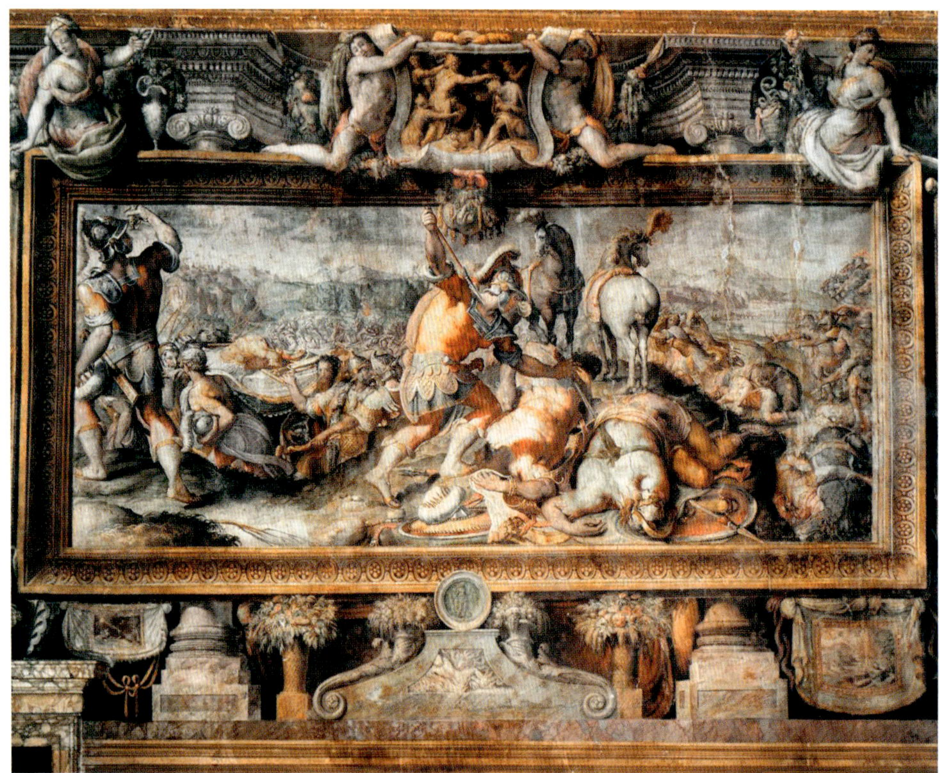

FIG. 2.22. Francesco Salviati, *Death of Saul*, c. 1553. Fresco. Sala Grande, Palazzo Ricci-Sacchetti, Rome.

added ornamental flourishes in poses and in cangianti. Hereafter, however, he exploited cangiantismo in his fresco cycles, first in Florence for Duke Cosimo's Sala dell'Udienza, and then in Rome, where he replaced Perino after his death in 1547 as the favorite of the Farnese and the papal court. Cosimo, the duke called back to Florence from exile, saw himself as reincarnated in the Roman hero Camillus returning home in triumph. To celebrate Cosimo's military and political successes Salviati employed a style simulating Roman sculptural relief, and to enhance the effect of relief he avoided deep shadow with scintillating cangianti and kept the viewer's eye on the surface.

In Rome, for Cardinal Ricci's *Salone*, he painted a very eccentric version of the life of King David. The long walls challenged him to unify them not only compositionally but also coloristically. In the *Death of Saul* he avoided chaotic variety by using bright cangiante passages in orange shifting to yellow for the major figures, the fallen Saul and the triumphant Jonathan, depicted twice, while muting the other colors and keeping them in the range of gray (fig. 2.22). This description fits his frescoes of the Fasti Farnese in the Farnese Palace as well. His limited palette in these large fields, which virtually eliminates blues and greens, does not seem at all

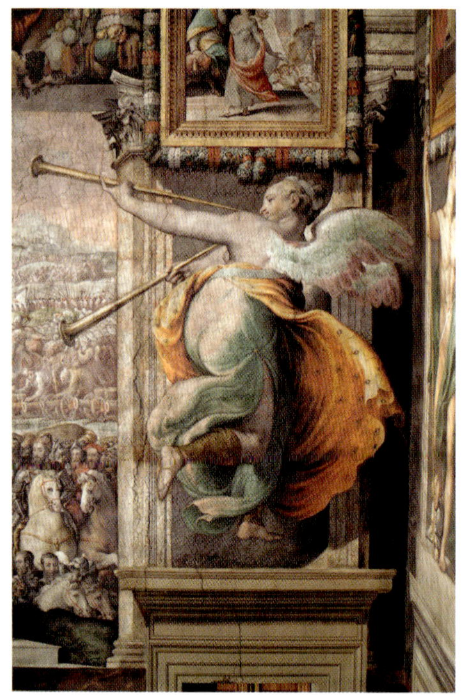

FIG. 2.23. Francesco Salviati, *Trumpeting Allegory*, 1553–63. Fresco. Palazzo Farnese, Rome.

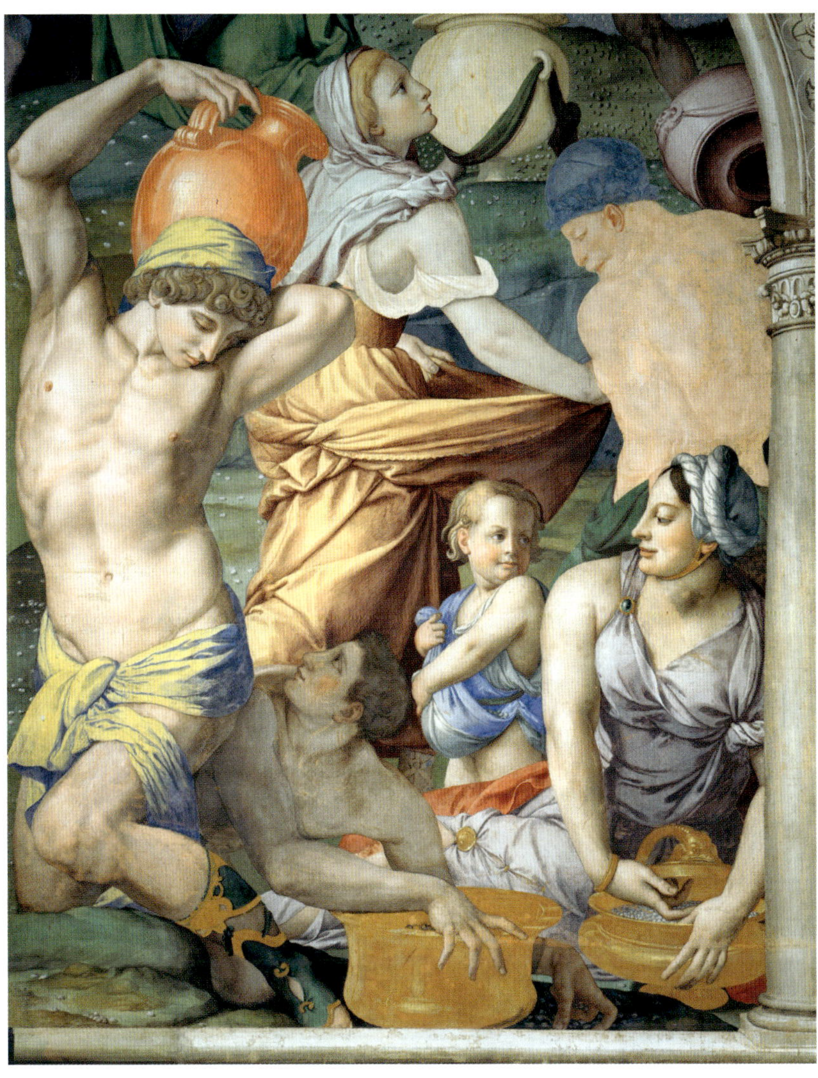

FIG. 2.24. Bronzino, *Gathering Manna*, 1540–42. Fresco. Chapel of Eleonora, Palazzo Vecchio, Florence.

impoverished, and the huge expanse is tied successfully together by the repetition of shades of orange and gold. In compartments on the sides, such as the one depicting a Trumpeting Allegory (fig. 2.23), he admits a wider range of tones, as he would also do in the smaller fields in the chapel of the pope in the Cancelleria. Salviati also applied the cangiantismo mode to his easel paintings, often minimizing the dark background preferred by his contemporaries. His coloring may seem far removed from Michelangelo's large passages of unmodeled cangianti, but we need to remember that Salviati's scenes were not on a vault sixty feet from the viewer's eyes. His is cangiantismo executed on a smaller and more delicate scale. Particularly notable is the absence of down-modeling with dark monochrome.

Agnolo Bronzino, working in Florence, shared with his Roman contemporaries a divided mind when it came to coloring. In his frescoes he imitated Michelangelo, but in his panel paintings his model was Raphael. The tiny Chapel of Eleonora in the Palazzo Vecchio is a showcase of up-modeled cangiantismo, where there is scarcely a drapery that is not conspicuously shifting in hue (fig. 2.24). But for the original altarpiece of the *Pietà*, now in Besançon, Bronzino rejected the prevailing taste for chiaroscuro, avoiding blackened shadows and filling his sky with a luminous lapis (fig. 2.25). The effect is closer to Raphael's unione—to his *Saint Cecilia* altarpiece (Bologna, Pinacoteca), for example—but he may also have been seeking a consonance between the tonality of the walls and the altar such as his master Pontormo had achieved in the Capponi Chapel (see fig. 2.19), to which Bronzino is evidently indebted for elements of his composition.

The schizophrenia of Rome and Florence did not apply to Giulio Romano. He steered a career of great success as a frescoist in Mantua from 1524 until his death in 1546, but he did not embrace Michelangelo's

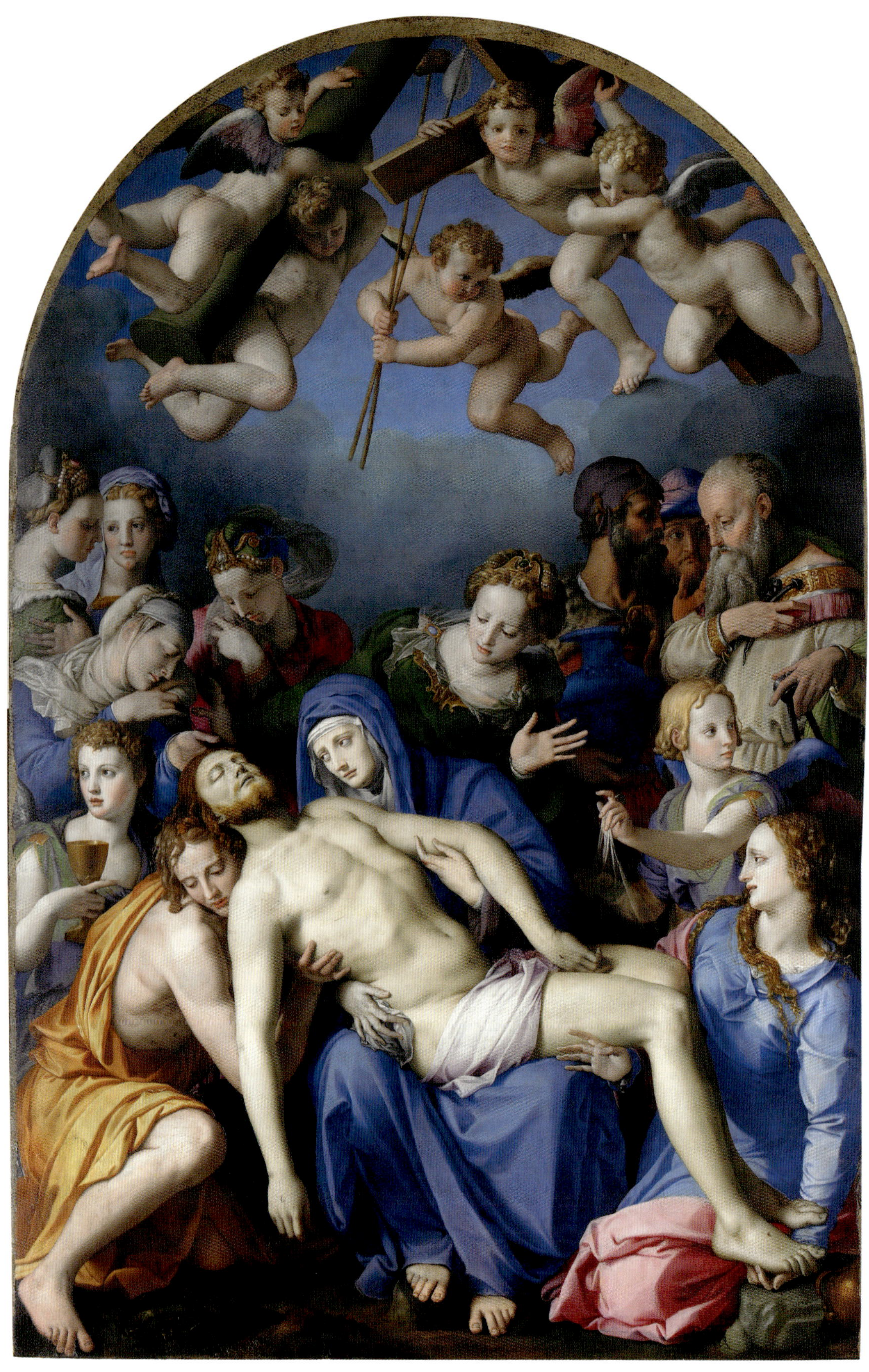

FIG. 2.25. Bronzino, *Pietà*, 1543–45. Oil on panel, 8 ft. 9½ in. × 5 ft. 8 in. (268 × 173 cm). Musée des Beaux-Arts, Besançon.

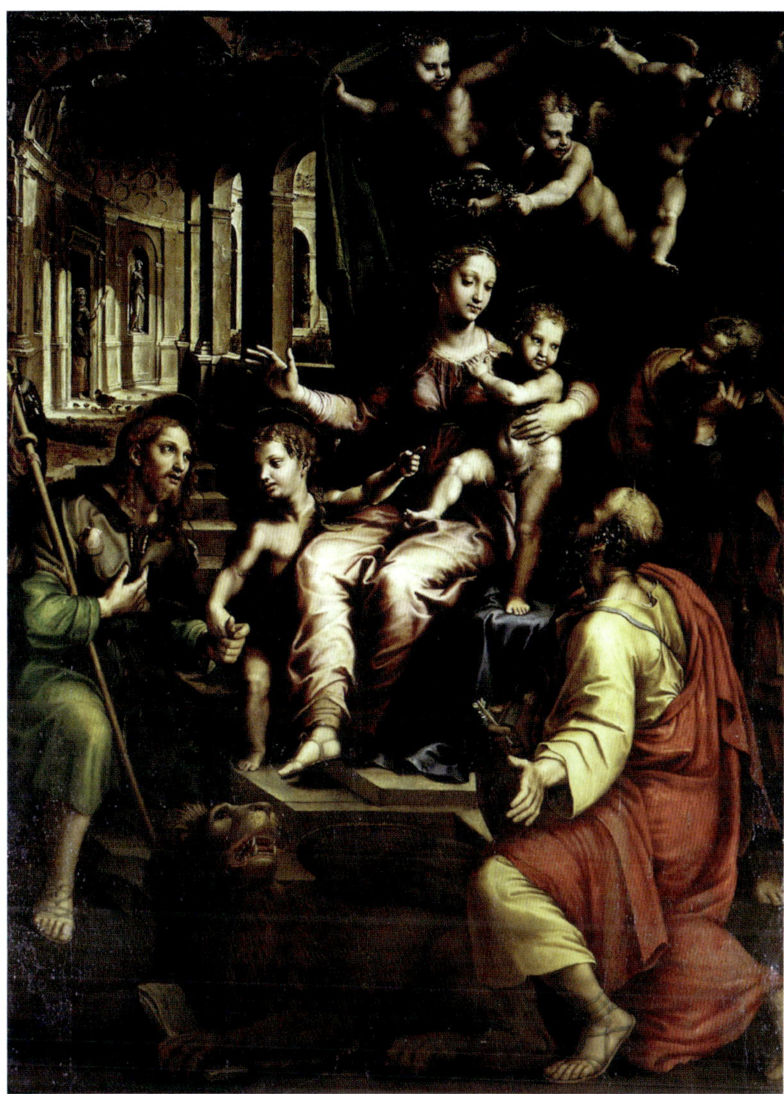

cangiantismo. For his patron, Federico Gonzaga, he was called upon to create extravaganzas similar to those invented by Perino and Salviati, but he chose to remain close to the orbit of his mentor, Raphael. Giulio had always loved chiaroscuro. The pieces Raphael assigned to him in the busy years, such as the portrait of Doña de Requesens y Enriquez de Cardona-Anglesona (Paris, Louvre, 1518), reveal his predilection. After Raphael's death, whatever Giulio painted in Rome has an inky background with saturated colors jumping out. Particularly characteristic is his use of black in the shadows, creating a harsh contrast that Raphael had avoided. With his extreme chiaroscuro he was able to introduce drama even in such a staid and inherently static subject as the *sacra conversazione,* as in his Madonna and Child with Saints, known as the *Fugger Altarpiece,* where a brightly lit

glimpse into a reconstructed Roman ruin (the Market of Trajan) heightens the effect of the dark behind the figure group (fig. 2.26).[37]

Giulio covered the walls of Gonzaga's pleasure palace, the Palazzo Te, with extraordinary and often fantastic frescoes, which allowed him to exercise his considerable imagination. He and his patron were compatible, sharing a sometimes bawdy sense of humor. There is a range of color styles on display at the Palazzo Te, where the plan was to unfurl one fantastic conceit after another for the delectation of the guests as they moved from one room to the next. The color style varies according to the subject. In the *Sala dei Giganti,* the most flamboyant of the decorations, Giulio has the walls appear to collapse and crush the titans. Everything is exaggerated, the modeling and especially the scale of the titans who parody

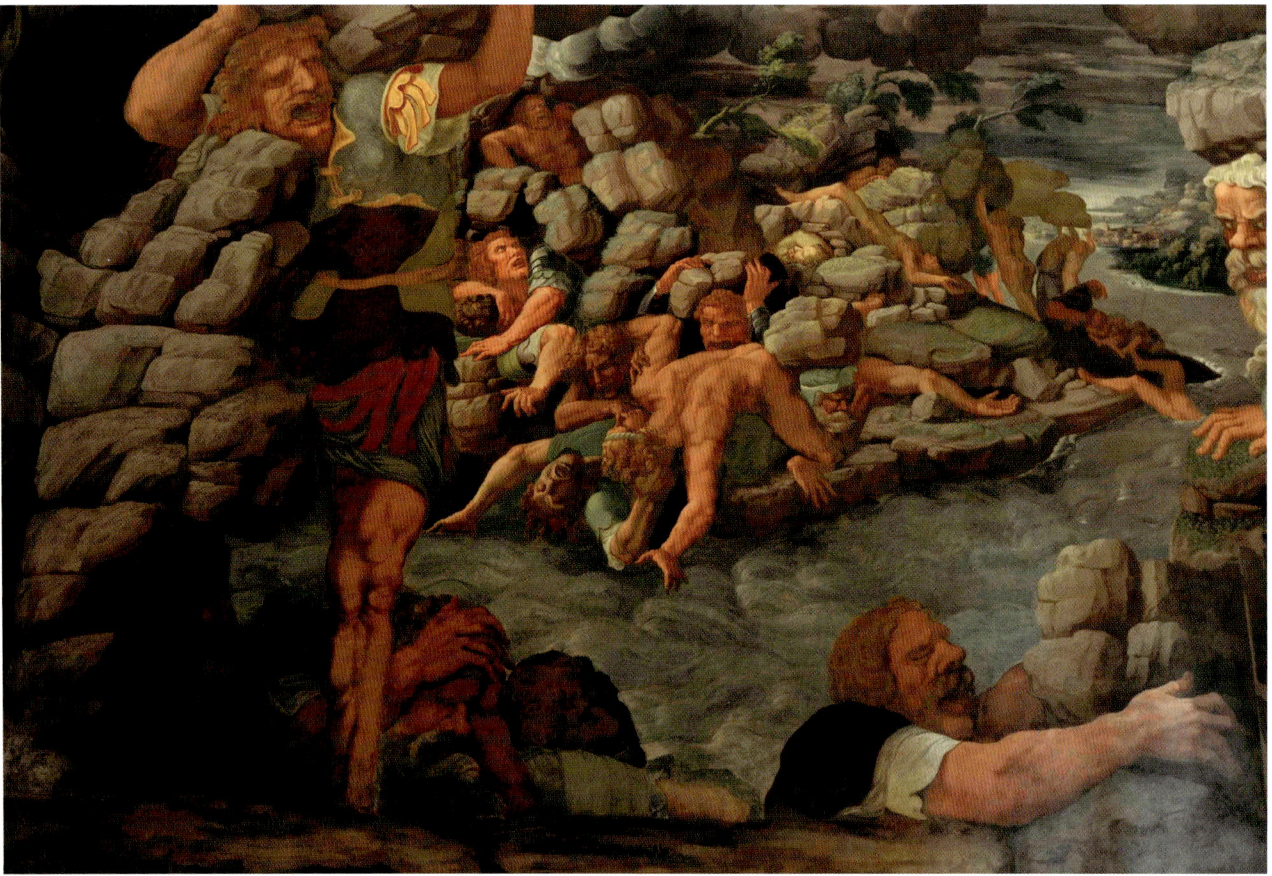

Michelangelo (fig. 2.27). Even the doors are frescoed so that the illusion of cataclysm is uninterrupted. Nowhere, however, either here or in the other rooms, is the coloring Michelangelesque. Giulio remained true to Raphael and developed his own coloring from the Sala di Costantino. Its muted hues and grayish-beige undertone can be seen in the room dedicated to the story of Cupid and Psyche. Interestingly, in the vault, Giulio depicted a night sky for the final triumph of Psyche when the gods receive her. For this he needed chiaroscuro exceeding what is possible in fresco, so he took up a version of Sebastiano's oil mural.[38]

Michelangelo's legacy was a mode of coloring that was found satisfactory to most of the frescoists working in his wake. It was still very much in use in the 1570s, for example, in the Passion cycle in the oratory of the Gonfalone, where some seven painters must have agreed in advance to employ it. It also solved a problem that had plagued artists since the introduction of down-modeling in the Quattrocento. Painters who found that mixing their colors and adding dark monochrome in the shadows gave them the desired increase in naturalism also found that this technique did not work well in fresco. As thinking about modes matured and was incorporated into practice, the viability of employing different modes for different mediums gradually took hold.

The modes opened choices to the painter that had never been available before. In choosing to match a mode to a mood or a medium, or to mix modes, he distinguished himself not just in terms of his superior craftsmanship but intellectually. The traditional system of training apprentices in the workshop assured proper training in the craft and assured continuity, but it did not foster creativity. As long as it was in place, artists traded freedom to express themselves for a measure of job security. In the course of the sixteenth century the workshop system broke down and was eventually replaced by academic training for artists, which not incidentally accorded them higher social status. The transition from one system to the other was not smooth or painless or quick.

In the course of the sixteenth century, the training of painters evolved from the apprentice system as described by Cennino Cennini at the beginning of the fifteenth century to something more like the modern system of paying for instruction. As happens today, artists who were not yet equipped to earn their livelihood undertook to obtain as much experience on their own as possible, to avoid having to pay for it. In the medieval system Cennini described, a boy was indentured to a master for around seven years, during which he would be taught the trade and given room and board in exchange for service.[39] The youngest apprentices swept the floor and carried the firewood, and with instruction, they learned to grind the pigments. They were taught drawing, first on erasable wax tablets, and then as they gained proficiency, in pen, metalpoint, and chalk on paper. They were taught to draw from the model. From time to time they were called upon to model a pose for the other apprentices or even for the master.[40] Especially for fresco, where drying time was a factor, they were indispensable in preparing the plaster, mixing the pigments, and transferring the design to the wall. Normally when the apprentice reached the age of seventeen, he could matriculate in the guild and work on his own or work as a paid associate in a workshop. By the end of the century a successful painter like Giovanni Bellini or Pietro Perugino might have a large bottega with a number of such paid affiliates. Raphael would have come into Perugino's workshop on this basis around 1500, when he reached the age of matriculation.

Raphael went on to set up his own shop, of course, and by the time he had worked in Rome for a few years, he was in such demand that he needed a small army of assistants whom he employed on his multiple projects. An expert manager, as Perugino also was, Raphael organized his workshop in a revolutionary way as a collaborative team. Rather than the assembly line arrangement typical of the Quattrocento, in which assistants were required to reproduce the master's drawings, he allowed them to develop his invention or *concetto* according to their own particular talents. He might correct these drawings, and another assistant might be assigned the task of developing the next stage of the design so that the end product was distinctly a "Raphael," but there was not the danger that he would repeat himself as Perugino had done and—a further advantage—the pupils were given leeway to develop their own styles.[41] After his death, his pupils Giulio Romano (in Mantua) and Perino del Vaga (in Genoa and then in Rome) went on to establish their own shops along similar lines.

Raphael's system certainly had advantages in efficiency, and he certainly trained excellent masters using it, but it contributed in the long run to the breakdown of the traditional workshop system and the deterioration of conditions for young artists. As Rome became increasingly a mecca for young artists, many came with rudimentary or no prior training with a master. They competed for jobs while at the same time scrambling to educate themselves, making drawings after the Raphaels and Michelangelos and the myriad of antique fragments around them. Giovanni Battista Armenini, when he wrote *On the True Precepts of the Art of Painting* (1587), described the vicious cycle he and others had confronted when he arrived in Rome around 1550 as an eager young painter. Masters who wanted as much work for the money as they could get paid their assistants by the job or by the day "as though they were wretched peasants," or even "by the span."[42] The result was that speed took precedence over quality, as the young artist quickly learned. Vasari, describing the early career of Raphael in Florence, in which he shed his provincial past and taught himself by studying Leonardo and Michelangelo, created the model of the first self-fashioned artist. In the new system, artists who no longer depended upon a single master for their training were freed to fashion their own artistic identities; however, living in poverty, working without guidance, and scrambling for hack jobs for their daily bread, they had little opportunity to do so.

Throughout our period, until well into the nineteenth century, the norm was that painters were trained in a master's studio. They were taught traditional practices with oversight until they were deemed ready to go out on their own. Just how standardized the process was varied with time and place, as was its success in readying them for the marketplace. Where guilds were in control, a glut of artists could be avoided. Without guild control, as in late Renaissance Rome and in nineteenth-century Paris, the situation for would-be painters could become perilous.

Looking closely at the period described by Armenini, we see that after Raphael's student Perino del Vaga died in 1547, there were very few workshops operating on a continuous basis in Rome. Michelangelo kept no students, and by 1549 he was finished with painting the

Pauline Chapel and was devoting himself to oversee-ing the building of Saint Peter's. Francesco Salviati, who took Perino's place as the favorite painter of the papacy, traveled back and forth between his native Florence and Rome, and he was absent altogether in 1556–58, work-ing in France. He received the major commissions, such as the decoration of Cardinal Ricci's newly acquired palace and the Cappella del Pallio in the Palazzo della Cancelleria, but he did not maintain a Roman workshop where he trained apprentices or employed assistants on a sustained basis.

We can get a sense of how the workshop was operat-ing at this time by looking closely at the assistants hired by Salviati during his busy years at mid-century. He hired a large number of local assistants, but he had not trained them. For Cardinal Ricci's palace, he himself painted only in the principal room, the Salone with the story of David (see fig. 2.22). For the ten adjacent rooms the car-dinal required to be painted, he gave carte blanche to his trusted collaborators, Poncio Jacquio and Marc Duval. He also picked up painters who were available—for example, Pellegrino Tibaldi, who had assisted Perino del Vaga in the Castel Sant'Angelo until his death, and Domenico Zaga. At the Cappella del Pallio the busy master himself executed the altar in oil and the frescoes in the lunettes, but above the second register he limited his involvement to supplying designs, and we do not find his hand.

Nicole Dacos has identified the work of two Span-iards, Roviale Spagnuolo and Gaspar Becerra, there.[43] Vasari also listed them as collaborators in his decora-tion of the Sala dei Cento Giorni in 1546, and Dacos has also found Becerra's hand in the Della Rovere Chapel of Daniele da Volterra. So for these large-scale projects there was a corps of freelance assistants, many of whom were foreigners, who moved from job to job and master to master. They could not be expected to acquire the style of each new master. Evidently the patrons toler-ated a wider disparity of style than had previously been acceptable.

The situation described by Armenini was one in which the traditional workshop system had broken down. From the point of view of the artist, it was dire: many painters had to abandon their career. For the mas-ter, the new situation created new challenges and new possibilities. Patrons wanted larger and larger spaces covered, and sometimes, as in the case of Cardinal Alessandro Farnese, they wanted it done with great speed. Vasari executed the large Sala dei Cento Giorni in the hundred days specified by the patron by exploiting the labor market. He had to assemble a workshop quickly in Rome, so he used what must have been a group of painters who had worked together before to execute the entire upper zone. Filling it with copious ornaments, they created a coherent design, but one that is quite distinct from the lower zone. Here Vasari himself took charge of the important histories showing the deeds of Pope Paul III, making use of those painters who were able to work in his style and follow his designs.

These masters, Perino, Salviati, and Vasari, exer-cised less control and oversight than their predecessors had, but unlike Raphael, they took all the credit. Their assistants, even though they were mature artists, never achieved independent status or the prestige to be hired as masters themselves. Of the assistants working for Perino, Salviati, and Vasari, only Pellegrino Tibaldi, who was born in 1527 (making him twenty-one or so when he was working for Salviati), became a master with commissions of his own, and he achieved this position by moving back home to Bologna, away from the killing competition of Rome.[44]

As a result, painters had to rely on educating them-selves.[45] Federico Zuccaro, who would later found the Roman Academy, made a series of drawings showing his brother Taddeo suffering as an apprentice under an abu-sive master and having to train himself by copying the works of Raphael, Michelangelo, the façade decorations of Polidoro da Caravaggio, and the antique ruins every-where around.

In the seventeenth century in Rome, the conditions described by Armenini in the late sixteenth century continued to prevail. Patrizia Cavazzini, who worked from court records, describes part-time painters who declared that their careers were painting, but worked as soldiers, paint-grinders, or something else. Some had other vocations such as notary before learning drawing and becoming painters. Their options were to pay to join a studio and learn from a master, or they could attempt to teach themselves by copying the art around them, as Taddeo Zuccaro had done. These studios or schools seem to have been focused on copying much more than on theory. There was a surprising mobility from one school to another, so it was not a question of learning the style of the master, as it had been in the workshop. Even apprentices (usually called *servi*, or servants,

significantly) moved around.[46] An apprentice might be
required to do the work of a household servant such as
making beds, housecleaning, grocery shopping, tending
the fire, and carrying water.[47] When the shop boy moved
up to become an assistant he was entitled to some pay,
but it was usually held until he left the master's service.
Permission might be given him to sell independently
and keep the profit.

In seventeenth-century Rome there were art dealers
—such as a certain Pellegrino Peri, who had a shop where
he sold his pictures—who contracted with foreign painters upon their arrival in the city to paint for him, both
copies and original work. The terms were a kind of in-
denturing, but they gave the painter a job and a start. He
lived with the dealer and worked on the premises, as in
the old-fashioned master/pupil system. The best of them
broke free after a year or so and went out successfully on
their own. Peri also lent them money, sometimes to their
regret.[48] Giovanni Benedetto Castiglione, who came from
Genoa, was quickly identified as a talented painter by
Peri, who therefore tried to keep him out of sight by urg-
ing him to paint upstairs. The sage Castiglione, however,
insisted on staying in the shop, where he presumably
hoped to be noticed by potential clients.

The creation of academies was intended to provide an
alternative and more dignified manner of training artists and preparing them for careers. They appeared first
in Florence, then in Rome and Bologna, and eventually
in France. When in 1563 Vasari persuaded Duke Cosimo
to sponsor the Accademia del Disegno in Florence, he
was fulfilling a lifelong ambition to raise the status of
the artists to that of the poets, and artistic practice to
that of a liberal art. It has been shown that subsequently
the Accademia became a useful tool by which the state
controlled the arts, but this was not the intention at the
outset, nor was it the purpose of the Roman Accademia
di San Luca.[49] In Rome the motivation was to replace
the broken workshop system and to provide training
of artists.[50] The Carracci too recognized the need for
professional instruction and instituted their Accademia
degli Incamminati in Bologna in 1582. The opportunity
to draw from the model virtually disappeared when the
traditional workshop dissolved; it was too expensive for
young artists to undertake on their own. It was the principal benefit the academies would offer.[51]

In addition to drawing from the model, the academies offered instruction in perspective, anatomy, and
other essentials, and once Federico Zuccaro took charge
in the Roman Accademia, lectures in theory became an
important offering. The French would imitate the Roman
Accademia di San Luca when they founded their own
Académie Royale in the mid-seventeenth century, but
because it was immediately commandeered to serve the
monarch and the state, the training of French artists was
closely controlled, a story we will pick up in Chapter 4.

The plight of artists described here is the story of
the underclass and especially immigrants to Rome. In
seventeenth-century Rome, the papal court and the cardinals continued to spend lavishly and large workshops
such as Bernini's flourished, but those working in them
were no longer dependent solely on a master for their
training, which was augmented and professionalized by
the Accademia. In Venice, the presence of a guild controlled many aspects of training, production, and sale so
that the traditional workshop, often family based, continued to function.[52] There in the sixteenth century the use
of canvas largely replaced wood supports. Especially in
the hands of Titian, its use would open up the new world
of textured surface.

TITIAN AND OPEN BRUSHWORK

We have seen that early in the Cinquecento, painters
began allowing the tinted priming to show through
the translucent oil layers to unify the tonality of their
painting. It took longer for them to avail themselves of
another of the qualities of oil, its capacity to create a textured surface, and to make use of the expressive power
of impasto. A perfectly smooth surface had always been
one of the marks of good craftsmanship, so it was not
an easy transition for artists or patrons to learn to value
texture, but the use of canvas as a support helped ease the
way. Canvas was pioneered in Venice, where because it
was a shipbuilding center and a port, varying weights and
weaves for sails were available in abundance. Cheaper,
less heavy than wood, and easier to transport because it
can be rolled, canvas had practical advantages over panel.

Canvas had been used in the Quattrocento, particularly when weight was a matter of concern—for example,
for banners to be carried in processions. The early users
of oil on canvas prepared it as they did a panel, with layers of gesso to create a perfectly smooth surface. Only
slowly did they test the possibility of allowing the texture
of the weave to show through. Once oil painters discovered that all they needed to do was apply an isolating

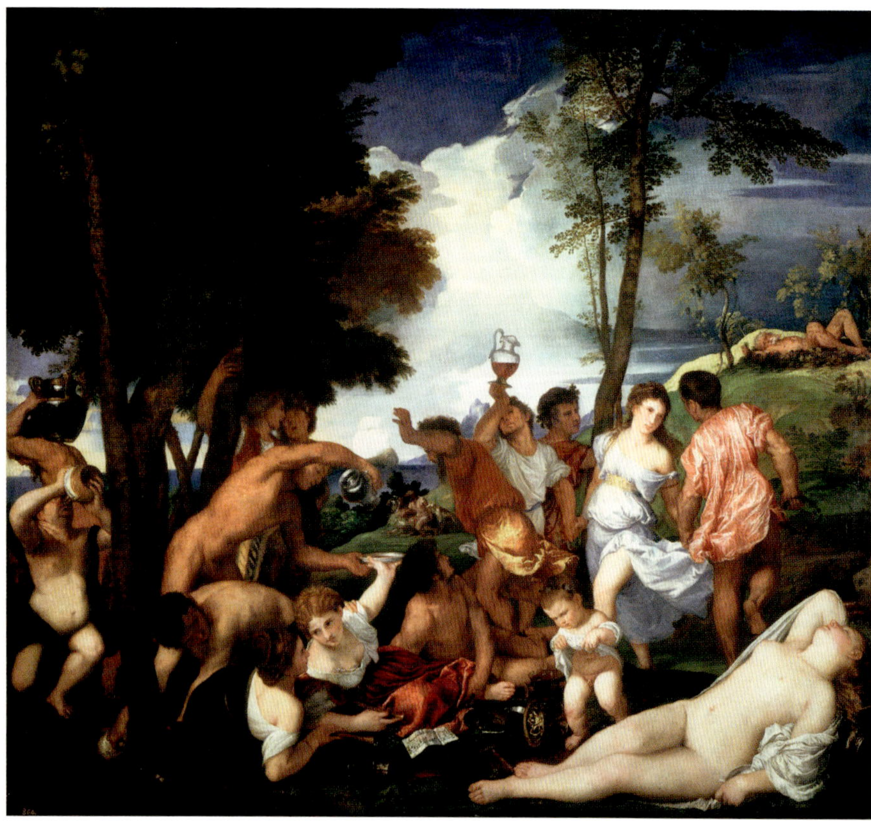

layer between the canvas and the paint, the combination of oil on canvas won the field and would eventually replace all other supports.[53]

It was Titian who was most important in exploring the texture that oil paint could offer. His paintings before 1540 that have been studied in the laboratory were found to have a gesso preparation. It was not necessarily thick enough to fill in the interstices of the weave but just to cover the tops of the threads, so the texture of the fabric was not suppressed, only diminished.[54] Most often Titian primed his canvas with lead white and some black, giving the imprimatura a light-gray appearance. He experimented with various tints, but he became less consistent in this practice toward 1530, and by the mid-1540s he was painting directly on the gesso, as he would choose to do increasingly in his later career. Only after he had been painting on canvas for decades and had begun to appreciate the advantage of exploiting the weave did he try out the effect of mixing thin and thick paint side by side.

In the preparation of the design, Venetian practice diverged from that of central Italy. It used to be thought that Giorgione, and following him Titian, dispensed with a careful preparation and at most sketched only rough outlines before beginning to paint. Recent research has revealed fine brush underdrawings in early sixteenth-century works on both panel and canvas by Giovanni Bellini, Cima da Conegliano, Sebastiano, and even Giorgione, but we know that Giorgione allowed himself a great deal of freedom in the process of painting, as we saw in his exquisite little canvas *The Tempest* (see fig. 0.4), where he painted the woman on top of the already-painted landscape.[55] A central Italian painter would have planned it out and left space reserved for the figure.

It now appears Titian only brushed in major figures with broad, fluid lines in black paint. He did not work entirely freehand, to be sure; nevertheless, his procedure is more improvised than his contemporaries', and it is certainly a far cry from Raphael's regular practice of transferring a detailed cartoon. This was Titian's first step in his long career that would eventually lead him to an innovation that would open a new dimension of expression.

Using only a rough underdrawing, he made changes as he went along. He would develop the composition in the painting process, repainting with additional layers to make corrections or canceling an area by painting it out. Frequently he made changes to reposition a head to increase the interaction between figures. Rather than

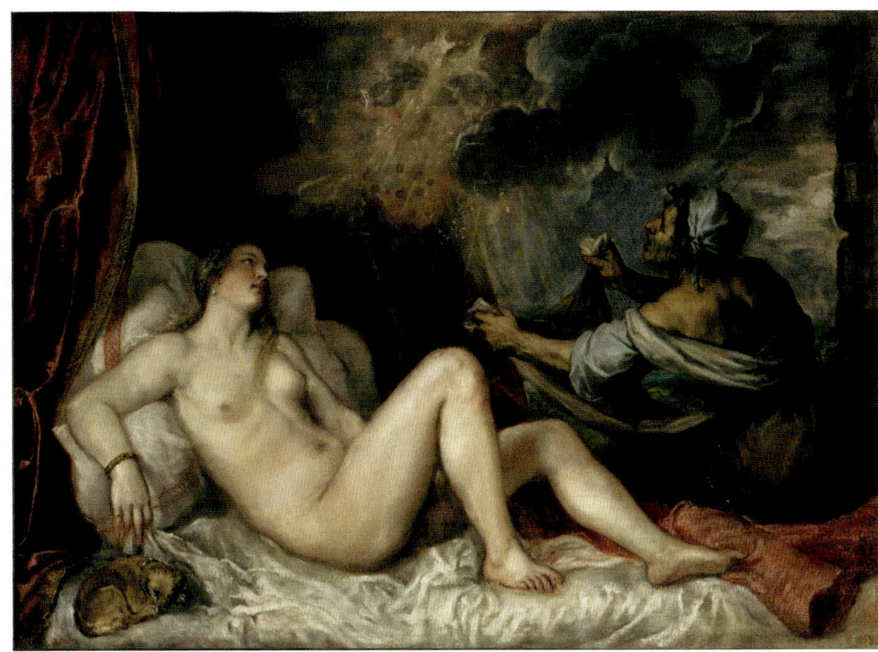

reserving an area for a figure, he might paint the figure on top of the landscape, as Giorgione had done.[56] His spontaneous approach made it difficult to delegate to the workshop, as Raphael learned to do. Titian's assistants in his early and mature period were largely limited to preparing his materials and making replicas.

Titian experimented in these years with impasto and the direction of his brushstroke, which is occasionally visible. He developed a keen awareness of which areas required fine finish because they were prominent and could be seen at close range and in good light, and which areas could be given more summary treatment. For example, he lavished attention on details in the *Bacchanal of the Andrians* for the Camerino of Duke Alfonso d'Este (fig. 2.28), but left the distant God the Father at the summit of his great *Assunta* in the Frari in bold impasto. His treatment of flesh is literally sensuous, appealing to the sense of touch, as Roger de Piles said was true of Rubens.[57] (Rubens made careful study of Titian and of Veronese.)

In 1545 Titian sojourned in Rome and made pictures for the Farnese, including *Danaë and the Shower of Gold* for the chancellor, Alessandro. After returning home to Venice he seems to have decided to cast his lot with the emperor rather than the pope. He visited Charles V in Augsburg, made his portrait, and one of his son Prince Philip, soon to become king of Spain. Titian then initiated a bold undertaking. He created

another version of the Danaë (fig. 2.29) and sent it as a gift to Philip, a maneuver that resulted in the agreement to make a further six mythological paintings known as *poesie*. Philip did not determine the subjects, or even the timetable. Titian was granted the extraordinary freedom to choose the subjects and to dispatch the pictures on his own schedule. In keeping with the boldness of the gesture, he pushed beyond his previous boundaries to work with an unprecedented spontaneity. Techniques he had previously used in selective passages he now applied to the entire painting. He had explored unblended brushstroke experimentally in his portrait of his friend Pietro Aretino (Florence, Pitti). Aretino reportedly liked the portrait, but significantly he felt the need to explain away the rough texture, saying if the painter had been paid more he would have given it a more finished appearance.[58] In his portrait of Philip, he rendered the armor in excruciating detail. But for the lovely Danaë imprisoned in her tower, he contrasted long, languid strokes on her flesh with the way he painted her wizened warden. The old woman, who greedily holds up her apron in the hope of capturing some of the treasure, is treated with rapid impasto blobs—*macchie*, as Vasari called them. The sheet beneath the Danaë is rendered with agitated impasto strokes that express her eagerness, set beside passages where the canvas shows through thin paint.

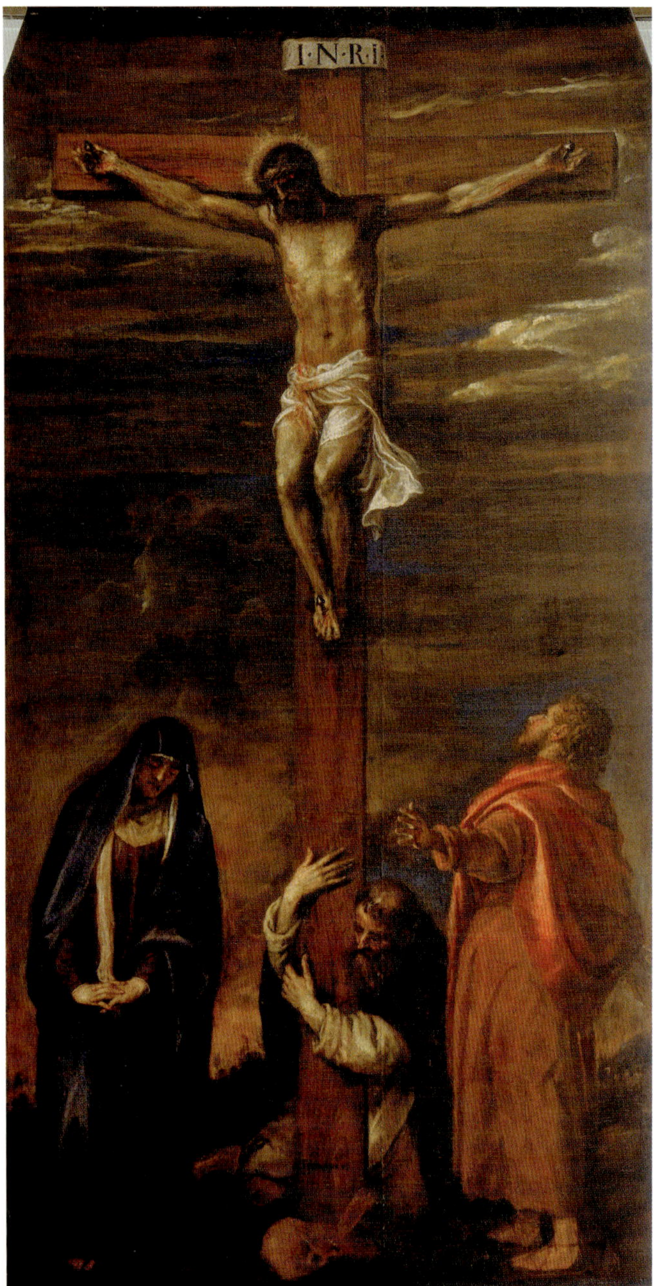

FIG 2.30. Titian, *Crucifixion*, 1558. Oil on canvas, 12 ft. 2 in. × 6 ft. 6 in. (371 × 197 cm). San Domenico, Ancona.

Coarse canvas of the sort Titian grew to prefer in his later years allows the brush to bounce slightly across the tops of the threads. The color of underlying layers can remain visible in the gaps. When a brushstroke is laid with a quick, light touch over a layer that is already dry, especially with a stiff paint containing lead white, the fresh paint may be slightly repelled by the underlying layer. Again the color beneath may show through. We are calling this "open brushwork," and with its apparent unfinish, it opens an invitation to the viewer to engage as never before.[59]

The sensuous Danaë and her open-mouthed acceptance of Jupiter's penetration of her sanctum entice the viewer to a new level of emotional participation. Titian has recognized that the traditional smooth finish keeps the viewer at a remove. The perfect poise of a well-designed contrapposto figure invites admiration but not empathy. His second Danaë has lost the composure of her more demure sister. She has discarded the drape, which opens a dark triangle between her legs that the painter daubed suggestively with dark, unblended strokes. The daring technique is well matched to the unexampled titillation he explores here.

Several years passed before Titian came to terms with how he might apply his new technique to a religious work. In the Ancona *Crucifixion* he has used rough texture to incite the worshippers to spiritual emotion (fig. 2.30). They are urged to engage with the unrestrained grief of the actors. Mary here has lost her grace and equanimity, Dominic clutches the cross, John throws open his arms in anguish. The brooding sky sets off the lonely figure of Christ, whose face, concealed in shadow, must be completed by the beholder. Titian has understood that his own feeling is transmitted in his brushstroke, creating a new kind of bond with the beholder.

In paintings prepared with a full-scale cartoon to which the hands of various assistants have contributed, the creator's imaginative idea is transcribed and refined into a cerebrated distillate. The perfection of the design is what is sought. Titian, bypassing the process of preparatory drawing, transcribed his idea directly onto the canvas with his brushstroke. His idea is recorded in the stroke with vigor and feeling, and viewers respond with their own emotion to that energy.

Titian was ahead of his time with his discovery of open brushwork and the appeal of unfinish, but the ground had been prepared by the increasing freedom that painters exercised in their handling. Note, for example, the broad brushwork in the drapery of Rosso's *Dead Christ in the Tomb* (see fig. 2.17). As the painters' status rose, collectors became interested in their process of conception: cartoons and drawings began to be collected. Increasingly collectors could appreciate how the painter's imagined idea is conveyed directly to the viewer in the sketch or the apparently unfinished work. Vasari was able to appreciate the power of the sketch, but he held conflicting ideas. He remarked of Giulio Romano that often his drawings were much better than his paintings, because they were made when he was fired up with the idea.[60] But at the same time he took Titian to task for his *pittura di macchia* ("blobs").

Titian's contemporaries were as reluctant to accept "imperfection" in painting as they were in sculpture: They replaced missing limbs of Roman statues such as the Laocoön. They were both intrigued and bewildered by Michelangelo's *non finito.* For example, the Medici duke inherited sculptures of the four slaves (Florence, Accademia), left in various stages of unfinish in Michelangelo's workshop because he had decided against using them on the tomb of Pope Julius. Unwilling to display them inside the palaces, the grand duke decided to incorporate them into a fantastic grotto in the Boboli Gardens, designed by Bernardo Buontalenti, where their rough condition would seem consonant with this evocation of an anomaly of nature, with its cave-like walls and stalactite ceiling.

Marco Boschini in the next century understood that, up close, Titian's (and Tintoretto's) paintings are a mass of blobs, but when the viewer moves back and sees them from an appropriate distance, the chaos resolves into a coherent image. This movement that the spectator makes engages him as a participant with the painter in the creative act.[61] Titian discovered that forms painted with impasto, paint raised on the surface, seem closest to the viewer's eye, so he could create space by making the distant objects smooth and untextured. This kind of unfinish would grow in popularity as time went by. Collectors in the seventeenth century increasingly sought to buy rough sketches because they appreciated the intimate glimpse of the artist's process that they provide. We will return to the aesthetic of the sketch with Delacroix and the Impressionists.

Titian, like Rembrandt, who in his later years would learn much from him, abandoned the facture of finish and the perfected poise of the classical model. A figure off-balance or overwhelmed with grief, in becoming vulnerable, invites our empathy. See, for example, his precariously balanced Europa on the back of the abducting Jupiter/Bull (Boston, Gardner Museum); or Saint Margaret (Madrid, Prado), whose disheveled garments express her terror of the dragon at her feet; or Andromeda (London, Wallace Collection), whose pose Titian reworked throughout the process of painting, only

finally achieving the poignant veering curve away from the monster in the sea that unbalances her.[62] Perfection, he seems to say, distances and excludes the beholder. A rough-textured painting can express more and engage the viewer better than the perfectly finished one.

VERONESE AND BROKEN COLOR

A remark attributed to both Titian and Degas—"It is the business of the painter to use Venetian red [a dull earth pigment] and make it look like vermilion"—distills the genius of Veronese. We can account for his genius with science only up to a point; some of it is inspired intuition, his innate sense for color harmony.

Paolo Veronese, as his name implies, was not a native of Venice but moved there from Verona in 1553. He arrived, with his own style fully formed and distinct from Titian's and Tintoretto's, to execute a state commission of ceilings for the Ducal Palace. By this time Titian was famous internationally and would be the first choice for any Venetian commission, but these ceilings were to be done in fresco, a medium Titian no longer practiced and one in which Veronese had considerable experience. He would become the favorite of patrons who preferred his joyous creations and his high-value palette over Tintoretto's blackish chiaroscuro. Today, Veronese is often dismissed as a lighthearted decorative painter. Perhaps he does not show enough angst for our taste— Van Gogh, Caravaggio, Rembrandt are the Old Masters preferred in these days—but this is to seriously underrate him.

Veronese's ill-deserved reputation for frivolity and superficiality may be encouraged by a misunderstanding of the transcription of the notorious hearing before the Inquisition in 1573. Called before them to answer questions about his *Last Supper,* recently installed in the refectory of Santi Giovanni e Paolo, Veronese responded that he had included a dwarf and a German soldier because he was trying to fill up the space. His answers might sound flippant, but he was honestly giving voice to the dilemma of the painter commissioned to fill a canvas measuring more than eighteen feet high by forty-two feet long, when the scripture accounts for only thirteen participants. The fault lay with the patron, not the painter. Veronese was renowned by this time for his paintings of banquets— he had made four for refectories before this one. He captured a party atmosphere better than anyone. His strength was in celebratory subjects rather than somber ones, and his coloring style was ideally suited to them. The patron of the refectory where they wanted a Last Supper, the Dominican friar Andrea de' Buoni, should have understood that the premonition of the Passion, which needs to be a part of the subject, was not easy to convey with Veronese's radiant style. Eventually the case was settled and all parties were satisfied with a compromise: the title was changed to *Feast in the House of Levi.*

In light of our contemporary appraisal of Veronese, it is interesting to read that Théophile Gautier wrote in 1860 that Veronese was the greatest colorist who ever lived.[63] In curious contrast, the seventeenth-century French academician Roger de Piles remarked: "He does not show any great intelligence of the claro obscuro in his dispositions. He did not understand it as a principle of his art."[64]

Both these critics, one approving, the other censuring, were responding to what we now know was Veronese's distinctive practice. The examination of his paintings in the laboratory has revealed that he used a very pale tinted imprimatura and occasionally painted directly on the gesso. Even when Tintoretto and Bassano were using dark primings, Veronese adhered to his choice of a lead-white priming, to which he might add a touch of carbon and a little ochre.[65] The nineteenth-century critic Gautier appreciated Veronese's practice because it corresponded to the way painters of his day, precursors to the Impressionists, were beginning to paint, in rebellion against the academic tradition represented by de Piles, which promoted tinted imprimatura, or by Gautier's time a monotone underpainting. Veronese did indeed avoid dark shadows, both those that can be assisted by colored imprimatura and those achieved with chiaroscuro by the addition of dark monochrome.

He modeled his draperies with a darker consonant color. In the *Dream of Saint Helena,* for example, her mustard-yellow skirt is shaded with the same red lake that is used in the overdress. In the *Allegory of Love, Happy Union,* the man's bright-yellow drapery is shaded in a deep bluish green, which echoes the verdigris of his sleeve just above (fig. 2.31).[66] These examples of his shading are a clue to the way he composed with color. He created a rich tone made up of several related pigments, then he colored an adjacent figure by picking up one of the components and combined new related pigments. The two colors he has created are akin but distinct, and richly harmonious. Because his color is so vibrant, it is tempting to think that he is working like an early Quattrocento Cennini-style artist using pure, fully saturated pigments, but he is not. This is the magic referred to by Titian/ Degas: he makes an incandescent effect by the way he arranges standard materials. This use of contrasting color for modeling might seem to be related to cangiant-ismo, but its purpose is the opposite. Cangiante colors shift to hues that contrast and thereby call attention to their disparity. They are not inimical pairings, to be sure, but they are artificially combined, not combinations you see in nature. Veronese models with a contrasting but friendly color, which looks natural. The eye does not see them as vibrant reverberations, enhancing one another, though indeed they are.

Critics praise Veronese's treatment of textures, especially textiles. There is no more stunning display of heavy brocades, filmy veils, shiny satins, fur, and velvet to be found in paint. Only Titian equaled his handling of flesh, but a distinction can be drawn between their ways of handling it. Titian painted his nudes to move the viewer's emotion; Veronese evokes admiration for his nudes just as he commands our awe in his handling of fabrics. In fact he appeals not so much to the emotions as to the senses. In his *Temptation of Saint Anthony* (Caen, Musée des Beaux-Arts), he played off the rippling muscles and tawny skin of the satyr against the pearly-white flesh of the demonic temptress. He insists on the sense of touch: the woman presses her long, curved nails delicately into the palm of the hand Anthony raises to protect himself. Veronese often evokes the sense of hearing by including orchestras and choirs in his pictures. One of his delightful inventions shows Venus covering the ears of Adonis, asleep on her lap, to prevent his hounds, impatient for the hunt, from rousing him with their barking (fig. 2.32). Touch is everywhere in Veronese's pictures, religious or mythological, and its sensuousness is enhanced by his coloring. At the center of his masterpiece, the *Mystical Marriage of Saint Catherine* (Venice, Accademia), the Christ Child reaches to grasp Catherine's finger as the boy beside her tenderly lifts her hand to touch the Child's body. In his *Mars, Venus, and Cupid,* a cascade of touches begins with Mars caressing Venus, who in turn tousles Cupid's soft curls as the boy reaches up in alarm to grasp his mother's wrist, and the puppy jumps eagerly on him (fig. 2.33). The chain of gestures is linked together with strokes of gold, beginning on Mars's helmet and armor, moving over and down

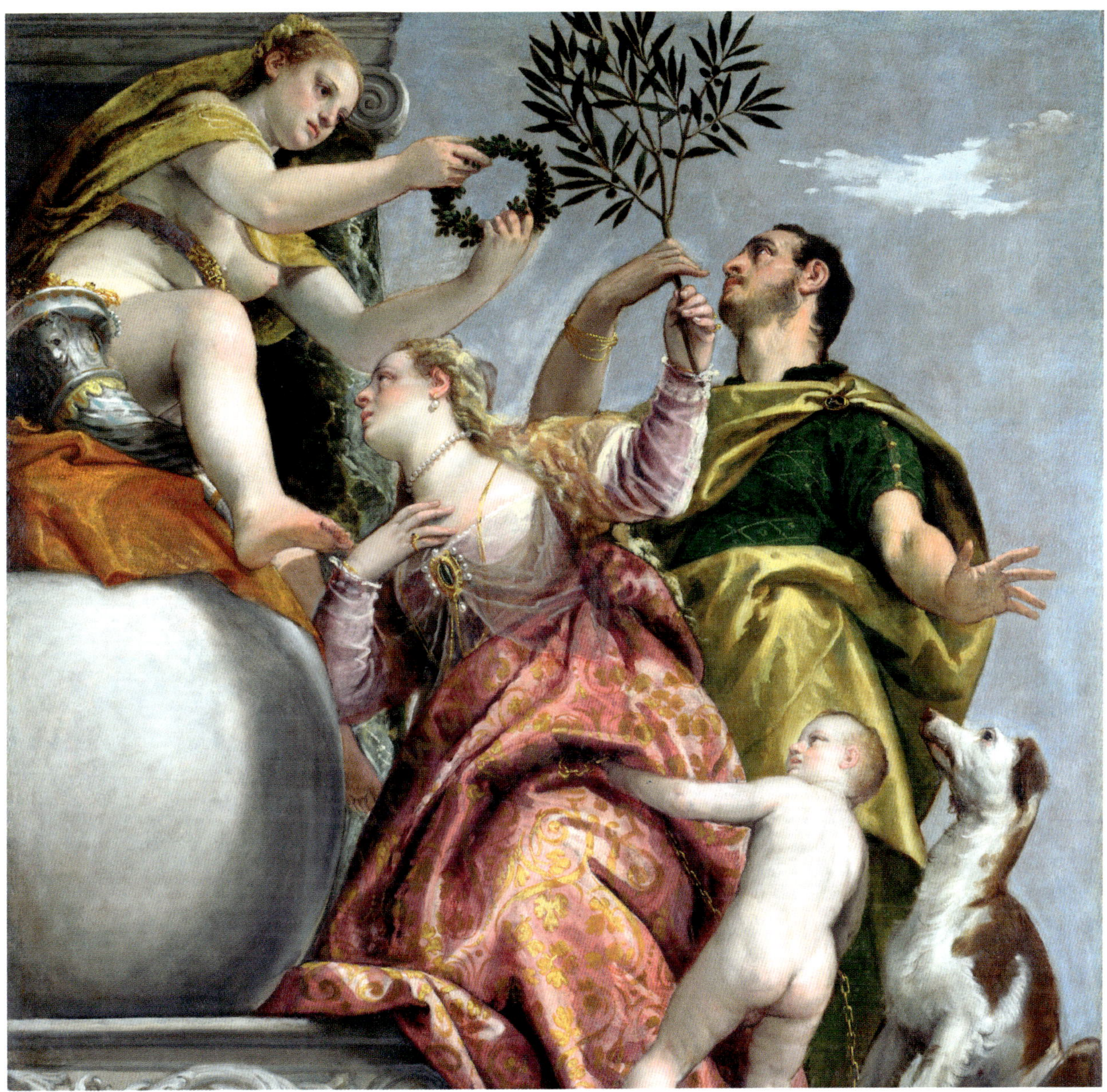

FIG. 2.31. Veronese, *Allegory of Love, Happy Union*, c. 1575. Oil on canvas, 73 ¾ × 73 ½ in. (187.4 × 186.7 cm). National Gallery, London.

to Venus's hair and garments, descending finally to the spotted puppy. None of the golden tones is identical, but they relate visually and are echoed in the sky behind.

Philippe de Champaigne, in lecturing on Titian's *Entombment* (Paris, Louvre) before the Académie Royale in the 1660s, called attention to his use of broken color in the red shades on the Virgin's blue robe.[67] It was the Académie that gave the name "broken color" to Veronese's color and considered him its exemplary practitioner. An understanding of what is meant by "broken color" has only recently come into focus. There seems to be no sixteenth-century term, and no equivalent Italian

term, but one finds seventeenth-century references in English, Dutch, and German.[68] Vasari showed an appreciation for the kind of harmony being discussed here when he criticized its absence as "when the colours are laid on brightly and vividly in a disagreeable disharmony so that they are tinted and loaded with body."[69] None of the theorists in the sixteenth century discusses Veronese's color. Armenini does not mention him at all, and Raffaeolo Borghini's short biography lists a number of works but does not comment. Giovanni Paolo Lomazzo merely remarks that "he displayed his supreme art of coloring" in *The Marriage at Cana*.[70]

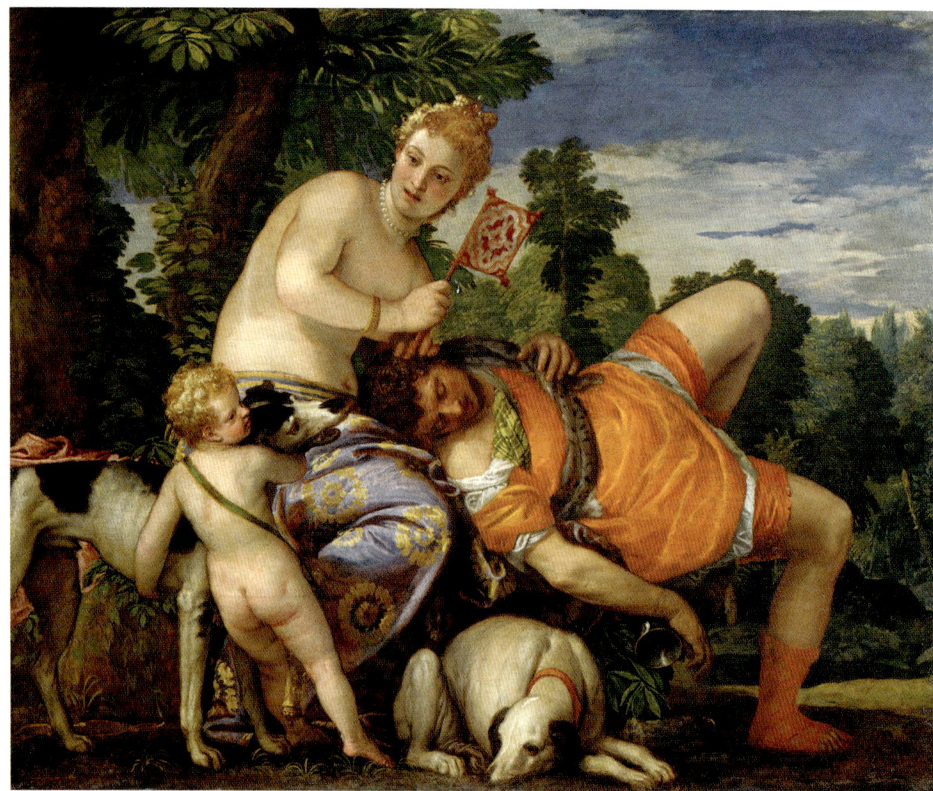

It is likely that the origin of *couleur rompue* (literally, "broken color") refers to the old concept of (cor)rupted color—that is, mixed—creating a color that falls between the hues. The various writers at the Académie, where the term acquired its definitive meaning slowly, experienced difficulty sorting out whether it should be used for the judicious juxtaposition of tones to achieve an effect of unity (union) through optical mixing, as De Piles argued in describing Veronese, or whether it should be reserved for physical mixtures, as André Félibien contended in his dictionary entry of 1676–90:

> Colours are broken when they are not used all pure and simple, but when one mixes two or more together to weaken or subdue one that is too vivid; such as to diminish the vividness of lake one blends in a bit of terre verte; or when taking away the brilliance of ver-milion one blends in a brown-red, either while mixing the paints on the palette or while working on the canvas after applying them there. If a drapery that is of a bright yellow is shaded with a dark lake one says that this drapery is *yellow broken by red*. It is yet better said that it is *yellow shaded with lake*, if the two colours are separate, because the word "broken" is only used

accurately when the colour is not pure but mixed with another one. And finally a broken colour, among painters, is one that is extinguished, and of which one diminishes the force; which serves well to create the union and the agreement which ought to exist among all those [colours] that compose a painting. Titian, Paul Veronese and the other Lombards have all made happy use of them.[71]

Certainly what Félibien described matches what cross sections reveal of Veronese's structures. Veronese excelled at glazing one color on top of another to create a third. His structures are deceptively simple, as we have seen: a mixture of two opaque pigments glazed with a third, judiciously chosen to maintain clarity. De Piles went beyond Félibien to describe an effect more difficult to analyze. What de Piles admired beside his mixtures and layering was Veronese's artistry in the placement of colors in relationship.

Ultimately what was recognized as couleur rompue by the academicians was an effect that could be achieved by several techniques. Titian and Tintoretto, in the view of the Académie, also achieved it, but if we accept the nar-rower and more manageable definition of Félibien, that

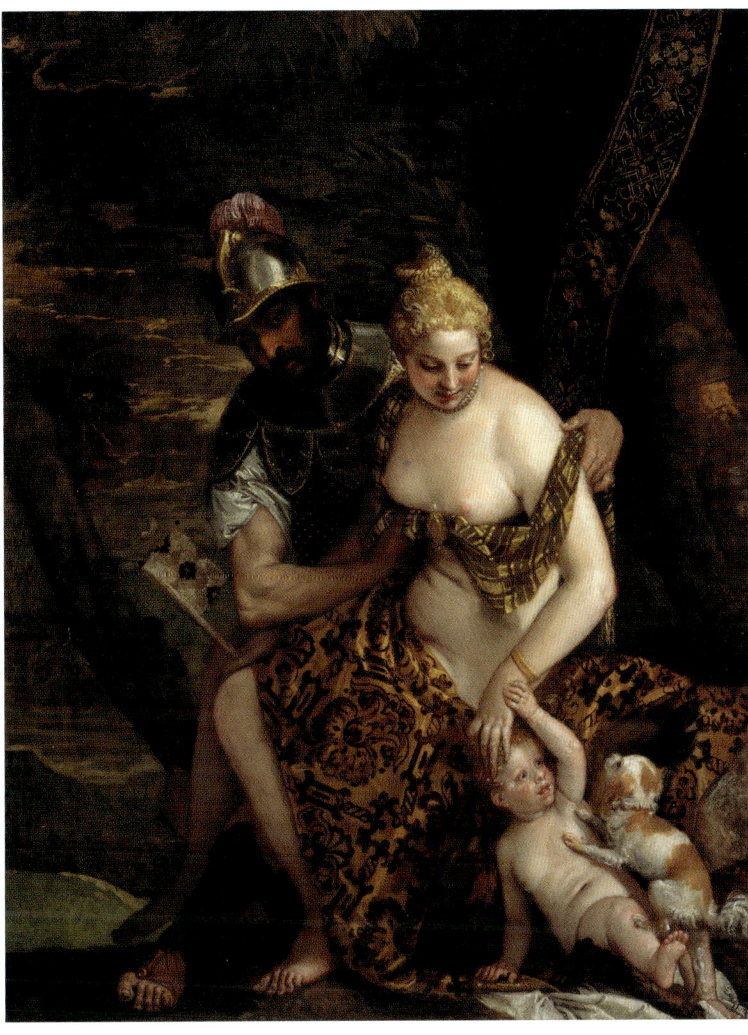

FIG. 2.33. Veronese, *Mars, Venus, and Cupid*, c. 1580. Oil on canvas, 65 × 49 ⅘ in. (165.2 × 126.5 cm). National Galleries of Scotland, Edinburgh.

broken color is a technique of mixing and layering, then only Veronese's practice fits the definition. In Dutch landscape painting of the next century, the technique was an essential addition to the painters' repertory.

It is clear that what Veronese was doing, and what Félibien is describing, is unique in Cinquecento practice, and the academicians were right to try to isolate it and describe it. The practice would have a rich life in the succeeding century, particularly, of course, in France.

BAROCCI

The Council of Trent in its decree on sacred images (1563) had endorsed images in churches that appealed to the emotions of the viewers but avoided any taint of the lascivious. Federico Barocci developed a style that could perfectly answer these requirements, so that his altarpieces were in demand for Counter-Reformation churches in Rome and throughout central Italy.[72] Working in Urbino, Raphael's natal city, he studied early

Raphael and adapted from him and from Correggio a pale-gray imprimatura. At a time when a dark palette was being used widely, he introduced clear, clean colors, softened with a sfumato derived from Leonardo and Correggio in what could be called a revival of the unione mode. His contemporaries spoke of the *vaghezza*, meaning "loveliness," of his coloring. The description suggests its particular appeal: he created images that had a sensuous allure, without crossing the line into the sensual or the erotic, much as Correggio had done.[73] The viewer was drawn in to participate empathetically, an approach that would be cultivated in Baroque religious images.

Barocci's coloring more than anyone else's poses the question of whether it should be defined as cangiantismo or broken color. His shifting hues are unquestionably ornamental, yet he is committed to plausible naturalism. His use of a light imprimatura resembles Veronese's, but his coloring is more frankly decorative. In fact Rubens

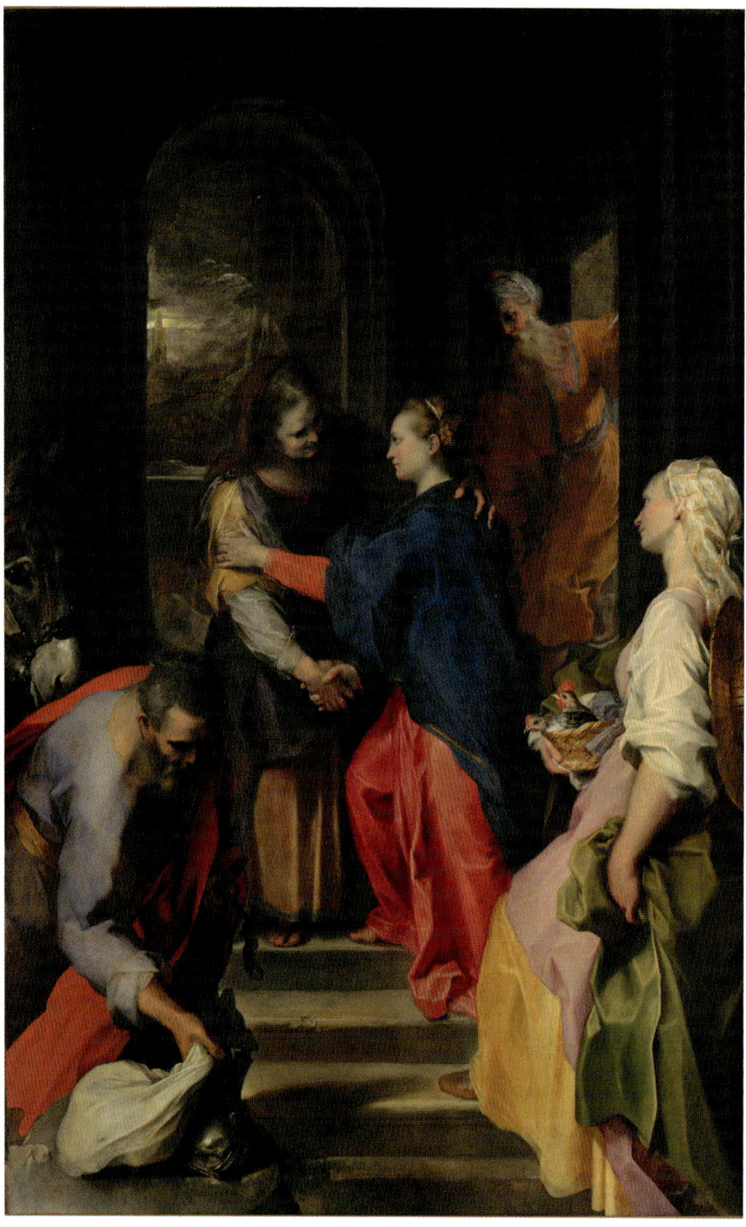

studied Barocci during his sojourn in Italy in the first decade of the new century. Barocci had made two altarpieces, the *Visitation* and the *Presentation of the Virgin*, for Santa Maria in Vallicella (the Chiesa Nuova), the church of Filippo Neri's Theatine Order, where Rubens would eventually contribute the high altarpiece. Barocci put aside the artificial and self-consciously graceful postures his contemporary painters were striving for. Modeling a religious ardor for the viewer, the actors in his pictures give themselves over to their emotions. In the sweetened atmosphere they seem to radiate generosity and goodwill. Barocci painted without restricting contours so that one form blends with another and

energy flows freely. Neri was particularly fond of the *Visitation*, and he would sit and meditate in front of it for hours (fig. 2.34). For him it emanated a spiritual energy that conveyed him to an ecstatic state and caused him to swoon. According to the testimony at his canonization trial, he was found passed out in front of the painting on several occasions.[74]

Barocci suffered from a chronic illness and was able to work only a few hours a day. He was notoriously slow to produce, and his patrons learned to exercise patience. He would make multiple preparatory studies for each painting, beginning with studies from the model in charcoal or pastel. Next, according to the critic Giovanni Bellori, who seems to have been well informed, he made clay or wax figurines from these drawings; then he clothed them, and then he would drape the live model and make a small monochrome cartoon in gouache or oil. Along the way he made lighting studies, perspective studies, nature studies, and color studies, often using pastels and sometimes oil sketches. These oil sketches were not common practice, but some seventeenth-century painters such as Rubens followed Barocci's example. Finally he would move to a full-sized cartoon, which would be incised on the prepared canvas. He had a large workshop to assist at various stages. By the time he reached the cartoon, the picture was so meticulously prepared that he could rely on assistants for much of the work.[75]

Barocci's single-handed revival of the unione mode of early Raphael and Correggio was noted by the Carracci in Bologna, who were seeking alternatives to the depleted *maniera* of central Italy. They too returned to drawing from the model to revitalize postures and gestures and eliminate the artificiality of late maniera, and to a light imprimatura, in strong contrast to the chiaroscuro of Tintoretto and then Caravaggio.

DARK IMPRIMATURA, TINTORETTO, AND CARAVAGGIO

Both Tintoretto and Caravaggio were technically inventive, developing the dark imprimatura that Sebastiano del Piombo and Giulio Romano (on the basis of his work alongside Raphael) had explored earlier in the century. For both Tintoretto and Caravaggio, the dark priming allowed an expressive spontaneity and greater efficiency, and for both of them these were interlocked. Tintoretto created excitement with his quick, unblended brushstrokes that could convey a sense of rapid movement, where carefully studied execution would have frozen the action. He sought to convey more an impression than a calculated effect. An air of premeditation was something Caravaggio also sought to avoid.

Tintoretto found that a dark priming could contribute not only to the theatrical effects he sought, but was also economical in terms of materials and his time. His clients, primarily artisans and confraternities, sought him out because he gave them good value for their money. He often let the ground show through and serve as a middle ground. When he was painting very large canvases, as he often did, the dark priming saved on pigment and labor.[76] In contrast to our expectation of Venetian painters and to the image of spontaneity Tintoretto staged of his

procedure, he prepared his compositions carefully, drawing from wax figurines, which he could place or hang in a stage-like box.[77] He could experiment with the lighting, adjusting it until he found what he wanted. He was not the first or the only artist in the Cinquecento to use such figurines: both Barocci and El Greco are recorded as having used them. Michelangelo had relied on them to study the poses of the more than four hundred figures in the *Last Judgment*, for instance, but Tintoretto is the most famous.[78] Once these drawings were squared and transferred to the canvas, he could turn over the execution to his workshop. His imprimatura varied from dark reddish brown to dirty browns to almost black. Although Joyce Plesters and Lorenzo Lazzarini's speculation that he used his palette scrapings for his priming has now been denied, it suggests how arbitrary and varied his choices seem to be. Sometimes only part of the canvas was undercoated with dark, while another part where the composition was to be brightly illuminated would not be primed.[79]

Tintoretto only moved to a dark imprimatura in the 1560s, and even then he was never consistent, preferring always to experiment. His coloring in the 1550s and earlier, for example *Susanna and the Elders,* is built on a warm brown ground, exploiting the contrast between nude Susanna's luminescent flesh, affirming her innocence, and the dark foliage behind her, the pool, and the hedge, which screens the peeping elders (fig. 2.35).[80] Their bald heads at either end rhyme and are connected also by the repeated reddish drapery, which by fading in intensity dramatically speeds the recession. Susanna is surrounded with glittering objects—pearls, her comb, the silver vessel that holds her oil—that catch the light, as do her jewelry and golden braids, enhancing her sensuousness. Such a picture can rival any in Titian's poesie for erotic appeal.

The painter moved away from such languor to tenser compositions in the 1560s, where his abbreviated application of paint creates something that is more energized and drier and certainly less dependent on delectable coloring. Now the contrasting patterns of light and shade already visible in *Susanna* take control and manage the viewer's attention. The enormous *Crucifixion* for San Rocco is dominated in its tonality by the dark sky that dampens the colors (fig. 2.36). Painted in indigo, it has faded to a gray brown, but the composition coheres because of the chiaroscuro.[81] A triangle of light points inward to the cross and an aureole of light emanates

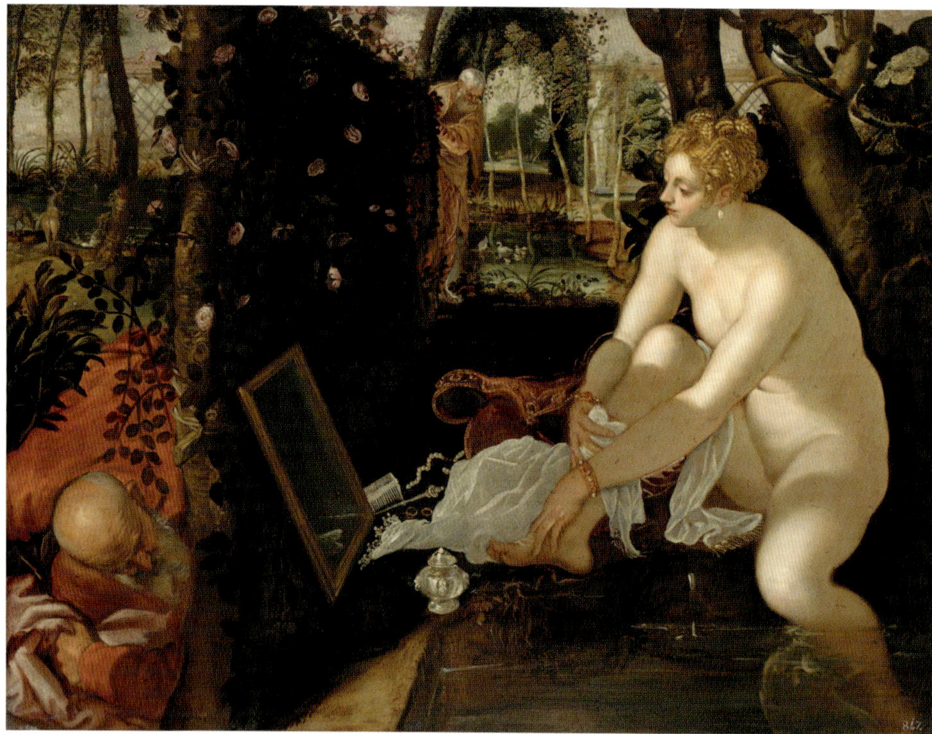

from Christ; around it are, rhythmically arrayed, the sundry groups. Nothing is drawn to our attention by means of color so much as by light and dark. His imprimatura could become even darker in the 1580s and 1590s, and hue was less and less important even as the tension intensified. Only Caravaggio matched him in arresting dramatic effect by the time he painted his final *Institution of the Eucharist* (fig. 2.37). As translucent angels swirl

around a flaming candelabra, Tintoretto invoked all his powers to make manifest the miracle of the transubstantiation of the host.

Caravaggio's technique was designed to capture the expression of emotion, often intense emotion. His method of work was, as far as we now know, unique. He would pose the model before him and, working on the dark primed canvas, paint directly on it. There is no

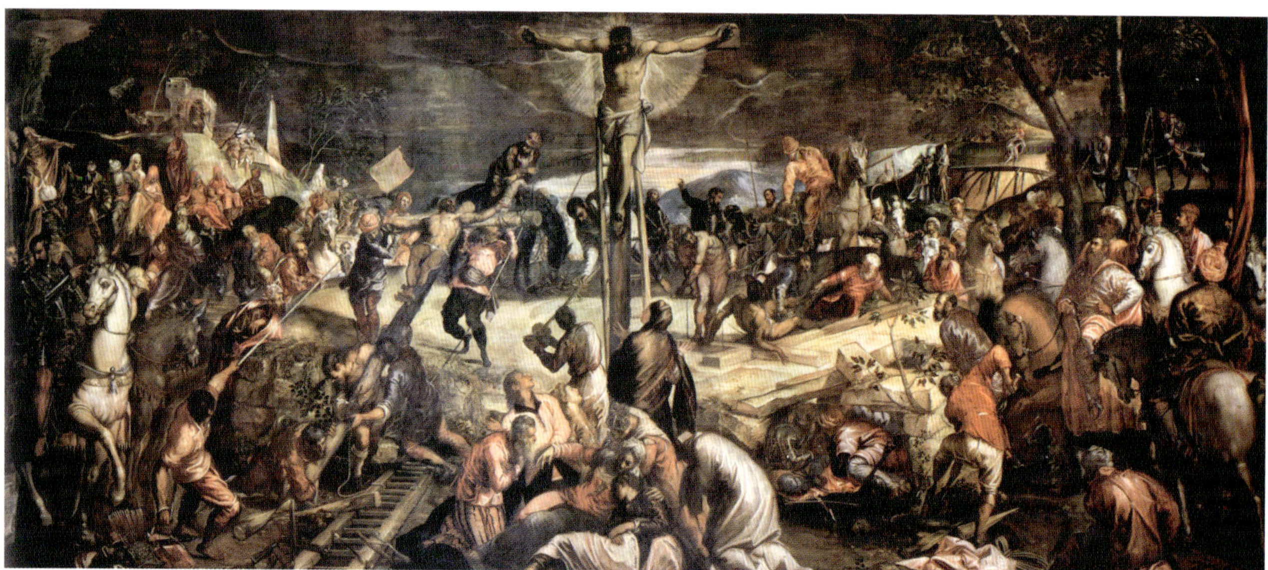

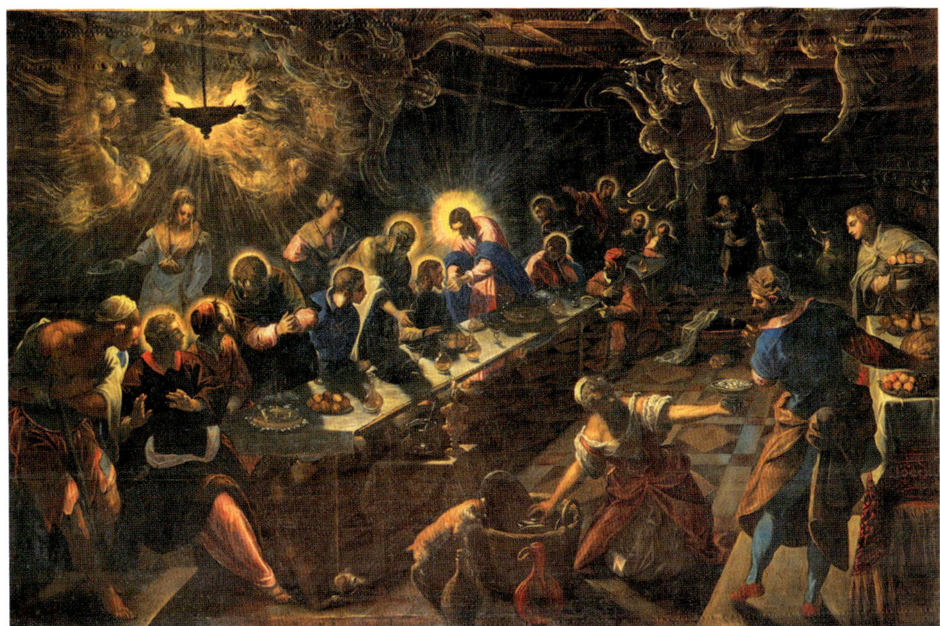

surviving evidence that he made preparatory drawings. Small incisions in the wet paint indicated the position of the sitter, so that when they returned after taking a break he could arrange the sitter exactly as he had been positioned. Presumably he felt that he could capture expression more convincingly than if he worked from preliminary studies, where there is always the danger of overworking and losing the unconstrained directness that he sought. Rapid execution with very little reworking helped him capture often startlingly convincing expressions. By preparing the canvas in advance with the dark priming, he could accelerate his execution. He rarely added background or even middle ground, allowing the priming to serve. The dark ground serves to remove his scene from a specific setting, effacing historical period and bringing a moment from the past into the present.

This is not to say that Caravaggio did not make corrections. In his early half-length paintings of figures such as the *Boy Bitten by a Lizard* (London, National Gallery) or the subtly seductive *Bacchus* (Florence, Uffizi), we see him studying facial expression. In this he is the opposite to Tintoretto, who regularly turned heads and concealed faces. Tintoretto's expression is conveyed more in body language and gesture than in studied faces, which would have slowed the action. With Caravaggio we are sometimes invited to prolonged contemplation by certain ambiguities, secondary figures who seem to be puzzled by what they are witnessing, such as the groom holding

the horse in the *Conversion of Saul* (Rome, Santa Maria del Popolo), or the innkeeper in either version of the *Supper at Emmaus* (London, National Gallery; Milan, Brera). There is no painter before Caravaggio as concerned with facial expression.

His ability to convey extremes of emotion is no less compelling, and he did not shrink from the distortion that suffering can invoke. Saint Andrew is shown at such a moment (fig. 2.38). According to the story, he never ceased preaching and proselytizing while he hung on the cross for an excruciating two days until his final moment, when Caravaggio depicts him. Everything works together to insinuate Andrew's fortitude, which is so poignantly absent from his body, face, and posture. The dark priming sets the tone out of which soldiers and onlookers partially emerge. The pained woman at the left has no more of the ideal or heroic about her than does the emaciated saint. Caravaggio had originally painted her with her hand over her painfully disfiguring goiter, but then repainted it with her hand at her side, reinforcing the downward pull of Andrew's sagging body.

Caravaggio introduced a new kind of sacred image in Counter-Reformation Italy, shorn of transcendence and depicting sacred persons as desacralized. In his *Calling of Saint Matthew* (see fig. 0.3), for example, the only suggestion of divine presence is the light entering at the right and the gesture of Jesus evoking that of Michelangelo's God creating Adam on the Sistine ceiling. The setting

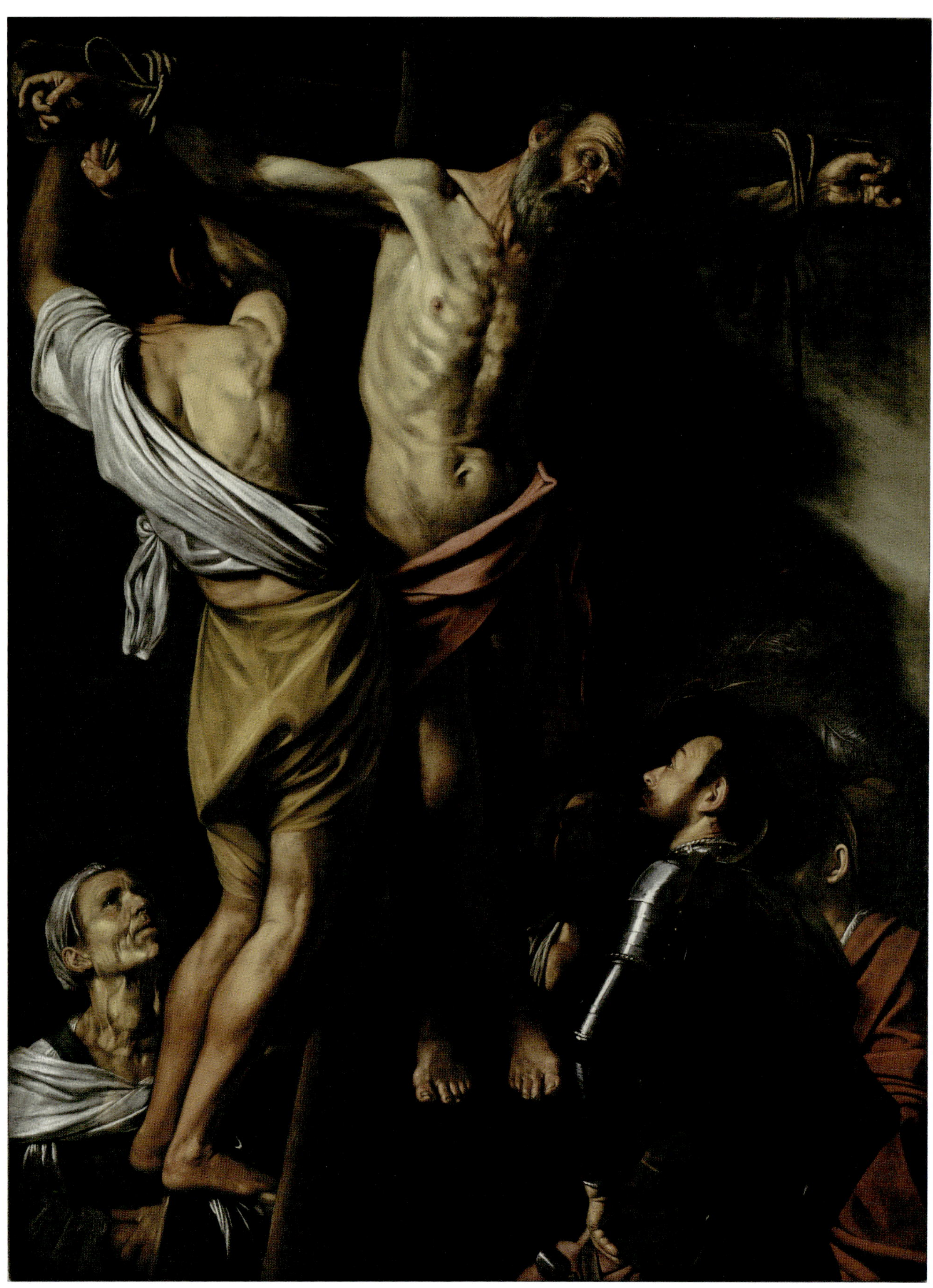

FIG. 2.38. Caravaggio, *Martyrdom of Saint Andrew*, 1606–7. Oil on canvas, 79 11/16 × 60 1/16 in. (202.5 × 152.7 cm). Cleveland Museum of Art.

has no hint of lofty classical architecture, but is rather an ordinary street in which Matthew is seated at a table collecting taxes. The man counting the money is so intent on his task he is unaware of Jesus's gesture calling him. Caravaggio, drawing upon the Antwerp tradition of "dirty feet and filthy fingernails" identified by Koenraad Jonckheere, painted Matthew's thumb with which he holds the coin rimmed with dirt, signifying his sinful humanity.[82]

Caravaggio's colors often seem brighter than they actually are. As Janis Bell showed, it is their placement that makes them seem vivid.[83] According to Bellori, Caravaggio called vermilion and bright blue "poison."[84]

CONCLUSION

Sixteenth-century painters explored the potential of oil. They began with experiments in tinted imprimatura and the creation or expansion of the modes in coloring, sfumato, unione, chiaroscuro, and cangiantismo. Sfumato cannot be said to have survived as a mode in its own right, but the soft edges associated with it often informed later coloring styles when sensuousness was desired; it was also often built into unione. Michelangelo's mode proved to be well suited to the hyperbole and artifice of maniera, especially in fresco, but as a mode of coloring it did not survive into the Seicento. Unione, on the other hand, became the defining mode of coloring for classicism, and the revivals of classicism instituted by the Carracci and the Académie Royale depended upon it. Chiaroscuro, achieved with a dark imprimatura, became the indispensable means to manipulate light and to create drama right up until the mid-nineteenth century, when the Impressionists definitively discarded it.

The changes in materials and the range of ways they were used in the Cinquecento sent out waves that, by affecting what the painter could do, ultimately helped to elevate his status in society. The painter could now create a mood, or give expression to his interpretation of a subject; the painter using egg or even tempera grassa was much more circumscribed. Sensuous flesh, such as we see in Correggio, now became a part of the painter's repertory and thus opened the whole realm of classical mythology as a subject for secular decoration. As memorable and appealing as Botticelli's *Birth of Venus* is, it is more an intellectual puzzle than an appeal to our sense of touch. Compare Botticelli's Venus with Correggio's in *Venus, Cupid, and Mercury* (fig. 2.39): the

airless atmosphere of Botticelli gives way in Correggio to a moisture-laden mist that softens contours and eases transitions. Correggio's soft modeling brings the flesh to life in all its alluring roundness, and the viewer's senses are aroused. Linear contour, so important to Botticelli in creating his lyrical, abstract rhythm, has vanished. Texture is difficult to imitate in egg tempera, but oil, with its variable viscosity, enables the painter to distinguish flesh, feathery wing, hard, shiny metal, hair, lush vegetation, satiny fabric, and conditions of weather and light. Giorgione makes us feel the shimmering stillness of the impending thunderstorm in his *Tempest* (see fig. 0.4). Titian can re-create the carefree spirit of a summer day with scudding clouds passing randomly overhead and diffused light, as he did in the *Bacchanal of the Andrians* (see fig. 2.28).

These new expressive possibilities distanced the painter further from his medieval role as artisan, a process begun in the Quattrocento but still far from completed in the early Cinquecento. The breakdown of the traditional system of training apprentices in the workshop, though creating a chaotic and painful period of transition, ultimately contributed to liberating the artists to do what the literary artist does—to express mood and construe his subjects. The goal of equality with the poet first articulated by Alberti in *On Painting* was achieved at least symbolically with the founding of the Accademia del Disegno in Florence in 1563.

Evidence is abundant of the struggle for status that artists were engaged in from Alberti on. It was the attitudes and habits of patrons that needed to change. Michelangelo, who was particularly conscious that his family connections distinguished him from others in his trade, once remarked with disdain that he had never run a shop, like those who made parade banners and painted *cassone* (bridal chests): he had only worked on commissions of popes, civic governments, and members of the elite.[85] An important motivation for Vasari to write his *Lives* was to insist on the status of the artist as the equal of the poets. He took to task abusive patrons and praised the liberality of others.

Conditions changed very slowly, but they changed first in Italy. When El Greco moved from Italy to Spain, he was dismayed to find himself required to submit to treatment that, after his decade in Venice and Rome, he regarded as medieval.[86] Artists in major centers such as Rome, Venice, or Florence, if they were fortunate, were

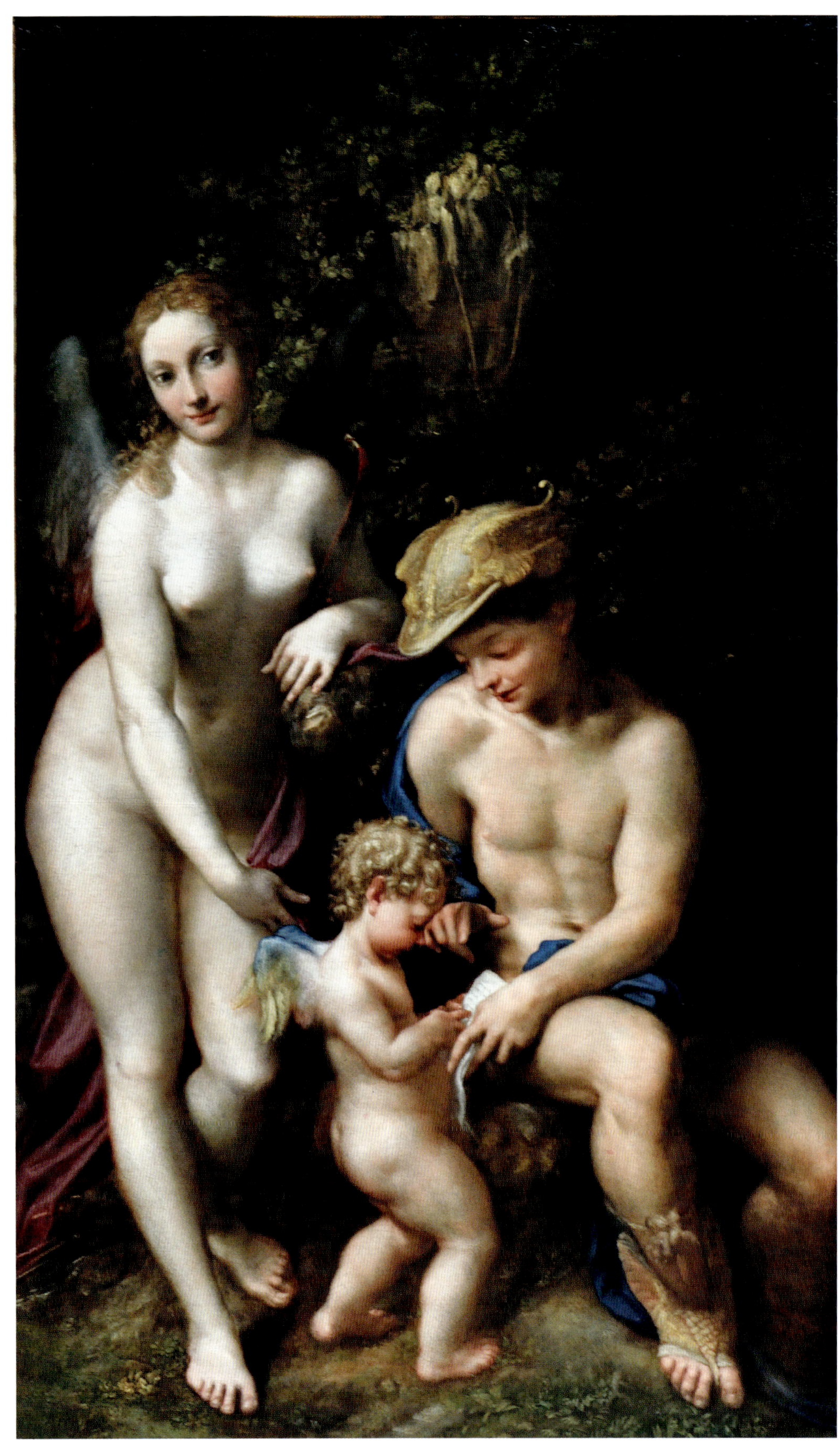

FIG. 2.39. Correggio, *Venus, Cupid, and Mercury,* c. 1525. Oil on canvas, 61¼ × 36 in. (155.6 × 91.4 cm). National Gallery, London.

increasingly entrusted by patrons with interpreting their subjects and, little by little, even with selecting the subject themselves. Collectors eager to acquire the work of a particular painter would sometimes suggest that they would accept any picture the master would send them. Even as early as the beginning of the Cinquecento the very demanding Isabella d'Este, marchesa of Mantua, instructed her agent that if Leonardo was pleased to make a picture for her studiolo, then she would leave the subject and the schedule to him to decide.[87] As the artist's training shifted from workshop to academy, the elevation of his status was codified.

As the century progressed, creative painters were increasingly willing to discard time-honored requirements such as a smooth and polished surface. Titian discovered that oil could be textured to create an agitated surface, with thick impasto played off against paint so thin the canvas showed through, and that with visible brushstroke he could create excitement and solicit the emotional participation of the viewer. Willingness to violate another prohibition, the one against the physical mixture of pigments, opened up a new realm of coloristic freedom. This "corrupted" or broken color could yield a brilliant ornamental palette, as Veronese revealed, or, as we shall see, a more naturalistic one, which allowed landscapists in the seventeenth century to shift away from idealized mythologies to recording the look of the world around them.

In central Italy the battle lines were drawn between the Carracci, revivalists of early Raphael and Correggio, with their pale priming, and the advocates of a theatrical tenebrism in the manner of Caravaggio. The rivalry between these two schools would dominate the scene in the opening decades of the seventeenth century.

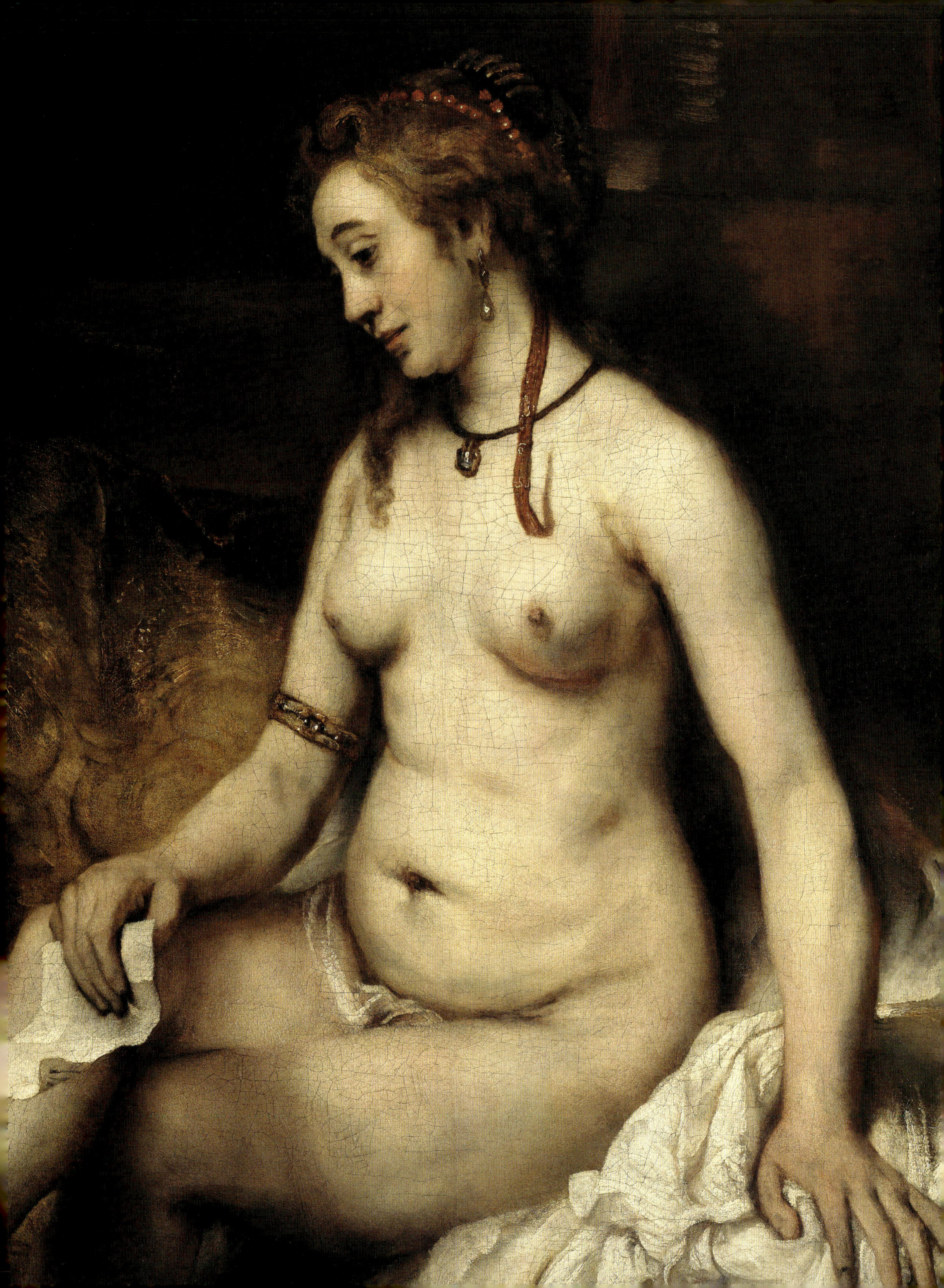

3 The Seventeenth Century

The Economics of Art

With the seventeenth century we enter a new era in which the market could make or break an artist. It was always true that a painter who chose to run a shop needed to be a good businessman, but now a new clientele and new economic conditions controlled the artist more than ever before. We will discuss *making*, especially as *marketing* affected it. A new competitive market system took definitive shape in seventeenth-century Holland and spread to Flanders, France, and even Italy, in which art dealers began to play a role as intermediaries. Painters needed to create as efficiently as possible to support themselves. They served a new middle-class clientele who wanted paintings to decorate their homes. These were clients, not necessarily educated in the humanist tradition, who cared more for a recognizable portrayal of their own lives and surroundings than for re-creations of classical myths, and they had limited resources to spend on art. For the painter, the cost of materials and the amount of time it took to execute a work loomed now as significant factors. Scrutinizing the career of Rembrandt reveals that many factors were now operating in favor of the artist's autonomy, but others also circumscribed it.

Rembrandt is among the first and is certainly the most famous artist ever to declare bankruptcy. We have seen that when the workshop and training system broke down in Rome, young artists had to scramble to subsist. And we read about patrons in the Renaissance who were slow to pay artists in their employ—especially, it seems, court artists, who worked at the pleasure of their lords and had to wait until everyone else was paid. Andrea Mantegna wrote to the Marquis Ludovico Gonzaga in 1478 itemizing what he had not received that he had been promised: "It is five years since your Lordship promised to pay me with that property, which I do not reckon a good sign. I hoped that in that time your Excellency would have paid me with the said possession, that is the 800 ducats, as your Excellency promised; and I still had hope that you would help me build the house as was promised."[1] Eventually, however, Mantegna owned his home in the center of Mantua.

Michelangelo complained about his patrons, especially the heirs of Julius II who persecuted him about the money he had been paid in advance to purchase marble for the tomb of the pope, but we know now that he was quite a rich man. His lifetime income and his worth at his death were unheard-of for an artist.[2] The disasters that befell Rembrandt were hardly possible in the conditions under which artists worked in the Renaissance, but few if any of his predecessors could afford to be as independent and as unbending in their standards as Rembrandt. Even when he was in bankruptcy, for example, he continued to use his pigments lavishly, and he charged more for his paintings than his peers. Nevertheless his financial difficulties were not just the result of his unwillingness to compromise, but were tied to new market conditions that made him and his fellow artists vulnerable to financial woes as never before. The social and artistic freedom painters now enjoyed came at a price.

The export of goods by land and sea had been pioneered in the North in the sixteenth century, but this trade was still largely contained within the European continent. When the Age of Discovery opened up global markets, the new Dutch Republic established its economy based on the export and import of goods carried on the ships of the Dutch East India Company to the far corners of the world. A new class of merchants enjoyed unprecedented prosperity, and they desired to spend some of their profits on paintings to decorate their homes.[3]

Artists supplied this market largely with paintings made on spec. Working in an economy subject to the cycles of boom and bust that are characteristic of capitalism, many established painters suffered economic hardships.[4] Vermeer's widow had to plead for time to pay the debt left by her husband, whose assets were insufficient to sustain her and their eleven children.[5] Despite Jan van Goyen's successful career as a landscape artist, when he died in 1656 he left a staggering debt of 18,000 guilders, forcing his widow to spend her last years in the almshouse.[6]

Examining Rembrandt's well-studied career sheds light on the new conditions under which painters were working. After completing his apprenticeship in his hometown of Leiden, Rembrandt went to Amsterdam to study for an additional six months with Pieter Lastman. Lastman had spent several years in Italy at the beginning of the new century and became familiar with Caravaggio's distinctive manner. Rembrandt learned chiaroscuro from Lastman, but he quickly adapted it and created his own distinctive version of tenebrism. In *Judas Returning the Silver* he used a light neutral gray, unlike Caravaggio's black (fig. 3.1). He contrasted patches of light and dark to achieve his dramatic effect, silhouetting his figures against the gray with graduated shades

full of subtle color, ranging from coffee to amber to gold, without the abrupt contrast of Caravaggio. Unlike Caravaggio, whose figures are held close to the picture plane and set off against a dark background, Rembrandt's nuanced tones allow him to create layers of receding space. At the age of twenty-three, he has found the unique golden tonality that would characterize his pictures for the next two decades. He had already come to the attention in 1631 of Constantijn Huygens, the artistic advisor to Prince Frederik Hendrik of Orange, who praised his *Judas* extravagantly and at length.[7]

Ever the shrewd businessman, Rembrandt recognized that opportunities were much greater in the burgeoning commercial center of Amsterdam, so he moved there in 1632. He set up his own studio and took students, who paid a hefty 100 guilders to work with him. He was prospering, selling his paintings through the dealer Hendrick van Uylenburgh, who procured portrait commissions for him and whose cousin Saskia he married in 1634. He was also making portraits for patrons in The Hague.[8] He bought a house in a fashionable district of Amsterdam for 13,000 guilders, but it slowly became evident that it was more than he could afford. When Saskia died in 1642 she left a will, normal for the times, leaving her husband her estate, unless he remarried, at which time he was obliged to turn over half to their son Titus. Rembrandt made a number of professional and financial mistakes in the 1640s. He stopped making payments on the house, and he turned away commissions for portraits, a bad move because portraits garnered new clients and kept a painter before the eyes of the elite class.

With a personality that inclined him to take risks and defy conventions, both artistic and financial, Rembrandt was vulnerable in a way that artists in the past, working for landed patrons or prelates or ecclesiastical institutions, had never been. In hard times the first to feel the effect are always the producers of luxury goods, as when war cuts off imports and curbs trade and the economy retracts. Rembrandt was teetering on the brink of financial disaster when the Anglo-Dutch War broke out in 1652. Reduced demand for pictures and tight cash were sufficient to push him over the edge. Unable to repay the loan on his house, he borrowed money from friends and acquaintances, which he was then unable to repay. The only recourse was to declare bankruptcy.[9]

Problems in his personal life were exacerbated by his financial crisis. Since 1649 he had been living with

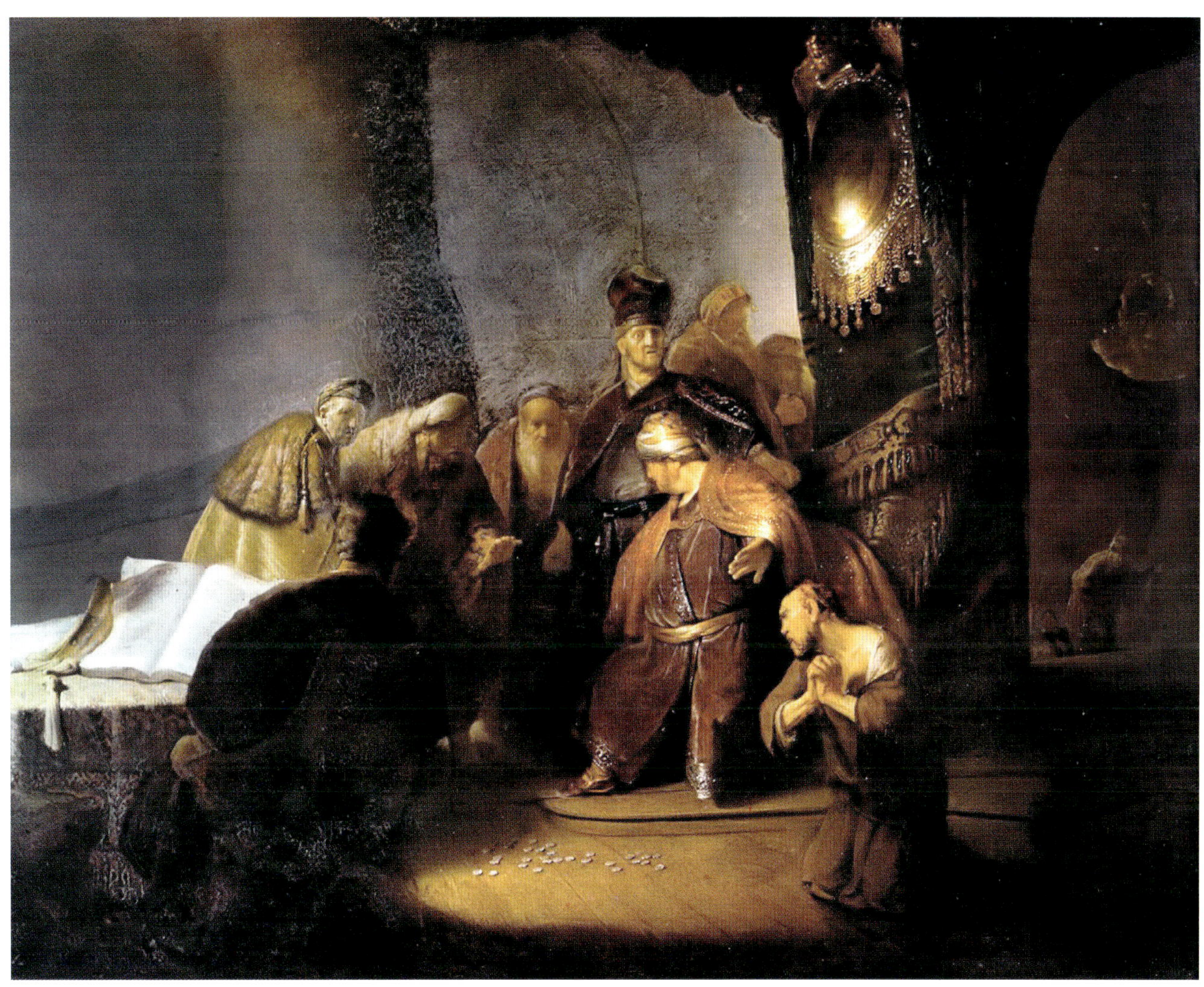

FIG. 3.1. Rembrandt, *Judas Returning the Silver,* 1629. Oil on panel, 31 × 40 ¼ in.
(79 × 102.3 cm). Private collection, London.

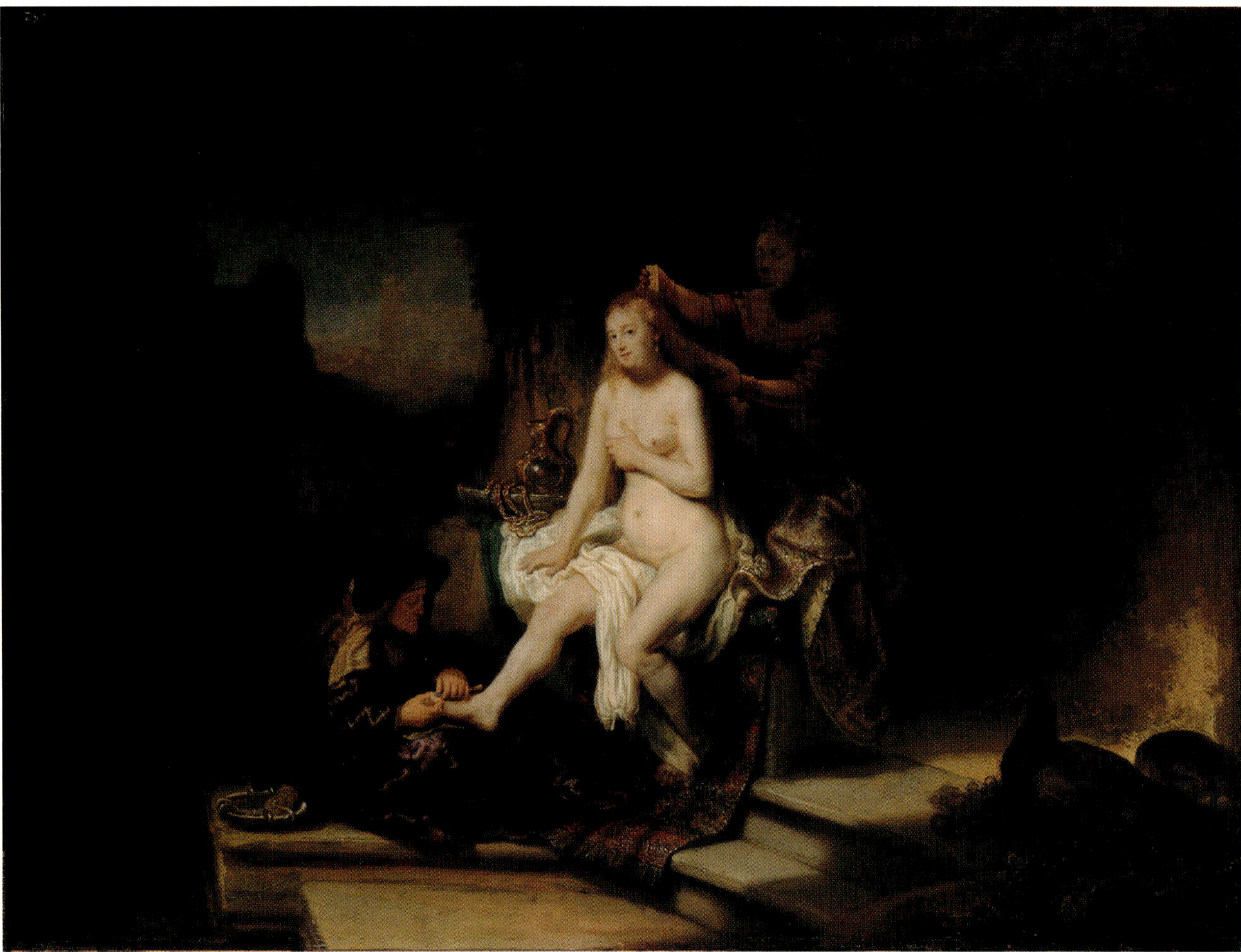

FIG. 3.2. Rembrandt, *Toilette of Bathsheba*, 1643. Oil on panel, 22½ × 30 in. (57.2 × 76.5 cm). Metropolitan Museum of Art, New York.

Hendrickje Stoffels. When she became pregnant in 1654, she was called before the council of the Reformed Church and forced to admit that "she had lived with the painter Rembrandt like a whore," for which sin she was barred from the Lord's Supper. Rembrandt could not marry her because he could not afford to give over to his son Titus the portion of his estate required by Saskia's will. He was helpless to rescue Hendrickje from her ignominious and painful situation.

How these hardships affected his art can be seen by comparing two paintings of Bathsheba, the first made in 1643, when he was enjoying the height of his popularity (*Toilette of Bathsheba,* fig. 3.2). One has no difficulty seeing how this lovely lady caught the eye of King David. She looks at us and covers herself, conscious of her beautiful body, while two servants groom her for her encounter with the king. She is surrounded by rich fabrics and gilded objects and her smooth flesh shimmers. Whereas

Caravaggio did not explore translucency, Rembrandt became adept at drawing attention by creating a beautiful passage that is resplendent without being brilliant, either in the sense of being brilliantly colored or ostentatious. In a passage like this we can see the dark coming through and giving texture to the cloth.

Between this *Bathsheba* and the second version of 1654 (*Bathsheba at Her Bath,* fig. 3.3), Rembrandt had lost his place as one of the most popular painters in Amsterdam. A new style, influenced by Anthony van Dyck's elegant portraits, was preferred, but Rembrandt, unwilling to follow fashion, continued on his path toward an ever less refined and smooth manner, probing the secret thoughts of his subject. In the second *Bathsheba,* he used Hendrickje as his model and changed the moment: he shows her reading the letter from King David. In this later, more profound version, what we see is not her excited preparations but her quiet resignation, her humble acquiescence to the

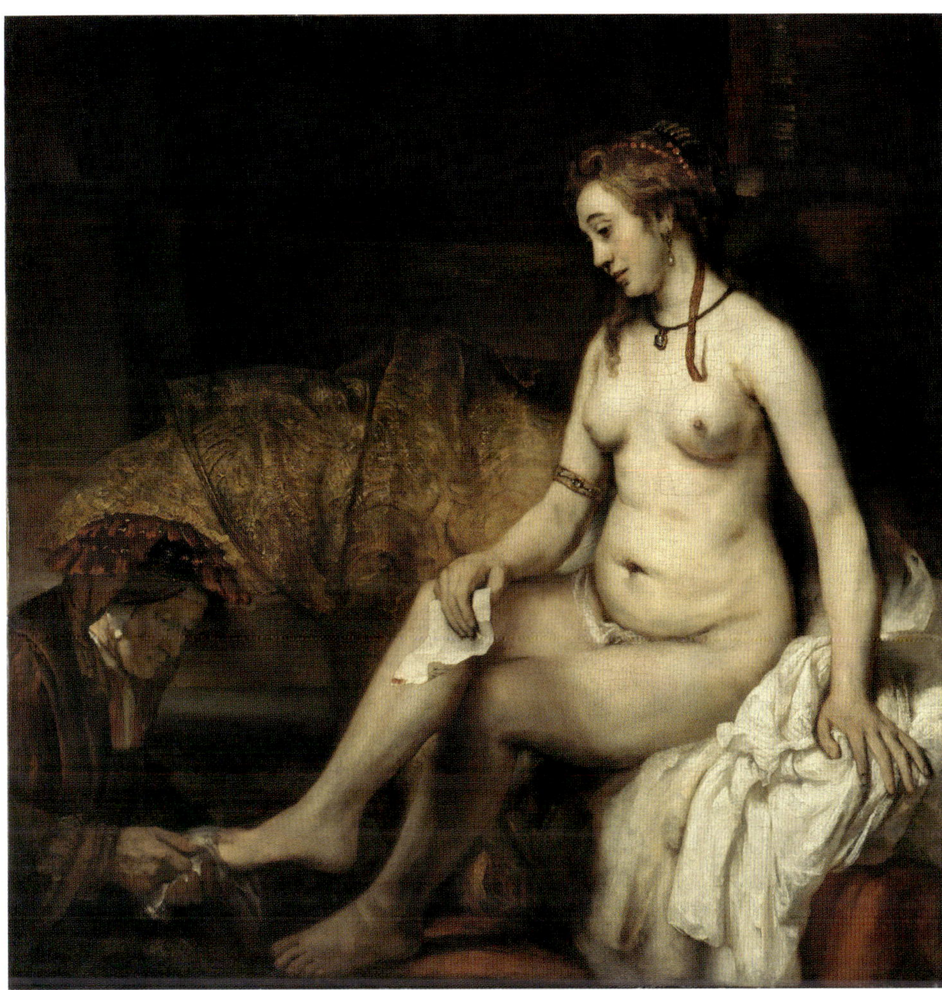

FIG. 3.3. Rembrandt, *Bathsheba at Her Bath*, 1654. Oil on canvas, 56 × 56 in. (142 × 142 cm). Louvre, Paris.

will of the king. She is older: her skin is mottled, it has lost its sheen. The painter's interpretation finds resonance between Hendrickje's predicament and Bathsheba's. There is nothing outwardly heroic in her; her beauty is hidden and inner, rather than striking and sensual. Look at her large hands and feet. They are blunt in shape and roughly painted, not posed elegantly with self-conscious grace. It is in fact the absence of self-consciousness that distinguishes her. Rembrandt's handling of the paint, with its fluctuating contours rather than defined shapes, mirrors Bathsheba's conflicted thoughts. She is flattered certainly by David's attention; at the same time she grieves over Uriah, her husband whom David has sent to his death on the front line of battle. She would resist David perhaps, but she knows she cannot.

An image like this reveals why Rembrandt was no longer the favorite of the elite of Amsterdam. They treasured Italian Renaissance paintings above all else. The most prestigious collectors of the day owned primarily if not exclusively Italian paintings, with perhaps a few

Rubens and Van Dycks.[10] Rembrandt's homely Bathsheba is no goddess or creature imaginatively re-created as in the Italian mode, but real flesh, inhabited by a conscience and by consciousness of her vulnerability. This Bathsheba is not nude; there is a tinge of the naked in her, as if she is on the verge of shame, but it isn't Eve's shame, it is the awareness of being flawed and imperfect. Kenneth Clark called Rembrandt "anti-classical," correctly I think.[11]

Certainly his second version of *David Playing the Harp for King Saul* displays the unorthodox technique and iconography that put his patrons at odds with him (fig. 3.4). Antonio Ruffo, a wealthy and important collector in Messina, wrote through intermediaries to complain that the painting of *Alexander* (now in Glasgow) that Rembrandt had shipped to him was pieced together from four scraps of canvas and so badly sewn together he felt it would come apart and ruin the painting. Ruffo hinted that he believed Rembrandt had begun the piece as a head and then enlarged it with the added strips,

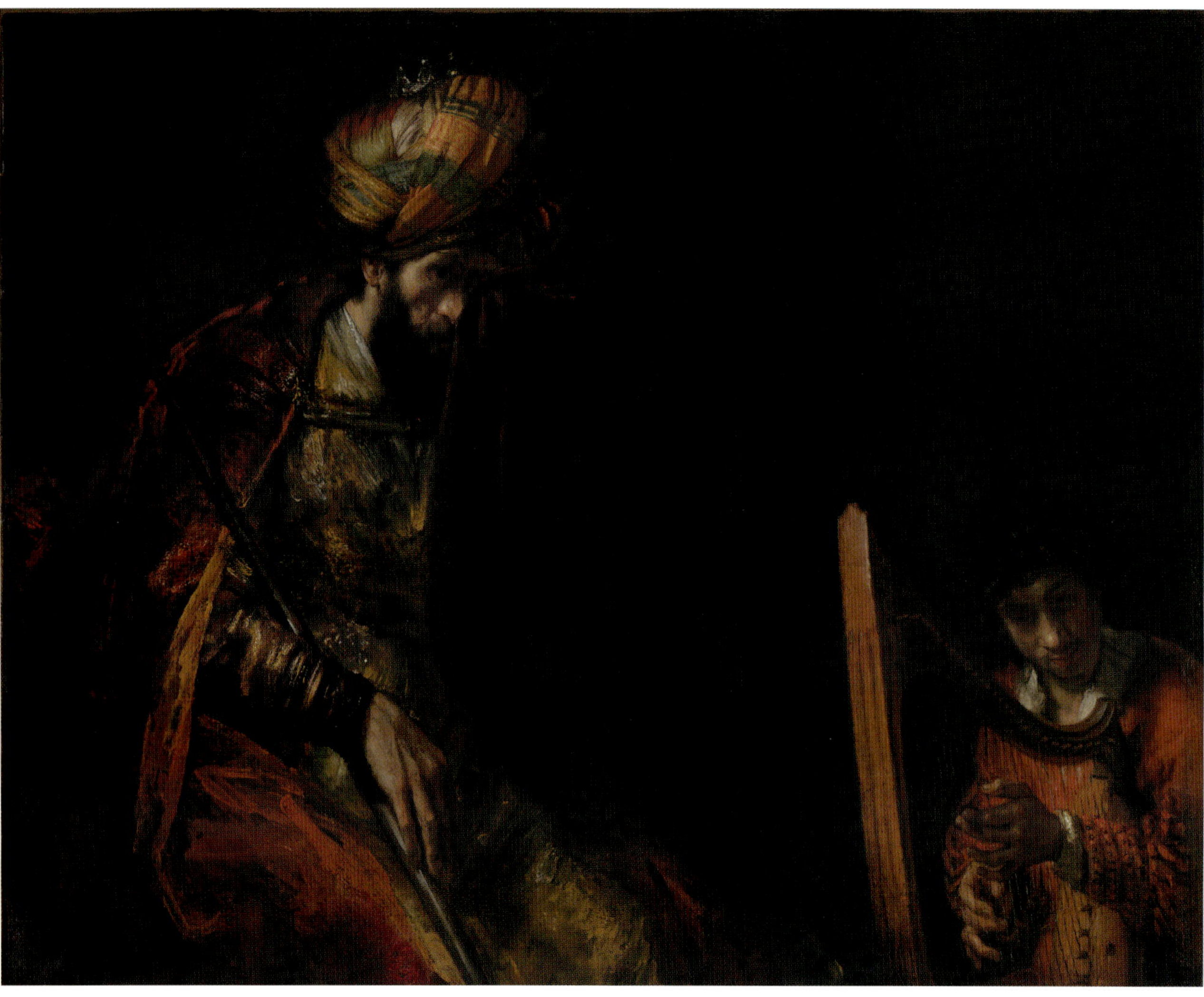

and declared that he should only pay for a head.[12] The painter apparently frequently pieced his support. When his *David Playing the Harp* was cleaned, it was found to be on no fewer than fifteen pieces of canvas![13] The painter knew that his thick application of paint would conceal the seams. Rembrandt's choice of moment is unique: when this story was depicted, which was rare, Saul was shown, morose and wary, holding the javelin he is about to hurl at David, or he is in the act of attacking David, as in the version by Il Guercino (*Saul Attacking David,* fig. 3.5). Rembrandt's own earlier version shows Saul as an august monarch, tense and suspicious, lording it over the humble boy with his harp. In the painting from the mid-1650s he slows the story down and deepens the feeling, showing Saul so moved by the music that he wipes a tear from his eye with the curtain. David, so often the

Apollo-like beautiful boy, is shoved down into the corner, and unflattering shadows mottle his face. Saul is no beauty either, but the regal display of sumptuous color in his attire with its enticing tactility draws us to him. Rembrandt is showing us that, contrary to the classical tradition but like the late Titian, people don't have to be beautiful to be appealing or to evoke compassion. The arrangement of the figures, leaving an expressive void at the center between Saul and David, defied the rules of classical composition as much as the figure types and the facture.

Ruffo's complaint about Rembrandt's prices was not without basis. Ruffo pointed out that the 250 guilders he was offering to pay, a reduction by half from what the painter had invoiced, was already four times the going rate in Italy of 62.5 guilders for a head, which is what

Guercino charged. Rembrandt had always charged much more than his contemporaries, which may have been regarded as an index of excellence by his patrons in his heyday, but served as an impediment to sales when fashion moved on.

Rembrandt's coloring, based as it was on subtly varied tones of brown, ranging through every tint from gold to cinnamon to chestnut and mahogany to chocolate, with touches of red but virtually no blue—certainly not brilliant and expensive ultramarine—would not have attracted collectors any more than did his unconventional subjects and pasty surfaces. Having perfected the smooth, or "fine," style in his early work—capturing detail, texture, and form with incredible realism, as in *Judas Returning the Silver* (see fig. 3.1)—in mid-career he increasingly moved toward the rough style, just at the time when the smooth or "fine style" was gaining favor among connoisseurs. Inspired by the open brushwork of late Titian, he left his brushstrokes unblended. He piled on his pigment in thick impasto, then scraped it back in places to show color underneath. This is a part of his facture in his late *Return of the Prodigal Son*, where the technique is bolder, freer, and more unorthodox than ever (see fig. 3.23). Paint was applied with the palette knife. A glance at the ladies and gentlemen portrayed by Rembrandt's successful rivals working in the manner of Van Dyck, Jacob van Loo, or Govaert Flinck, in their satin dresses and classical settings, suggests that these patrons did not prefer images of biblical penitence and compassion for their walls (see Flinck, *Portrait of Susanna van Baerle*, fig. 3.6).

So not only did the painter now have to deal with the vagaries of the economy, he also was subject to changes

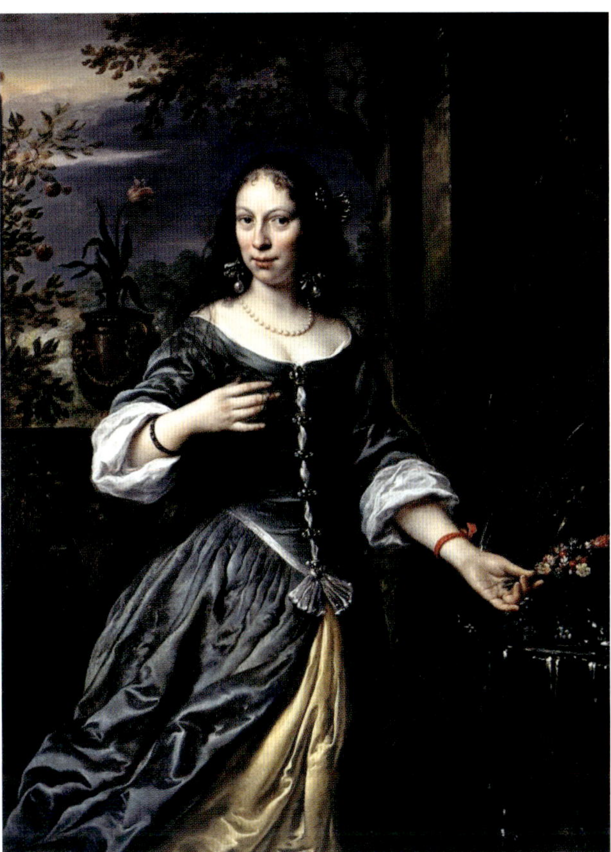

FIG. 3.6. Govert Flinck, *Portrait of Susanna van Baerle*, 1655. Oil on canvas, 54 ⅜ × 40 ⅞ in. (138 × 104 cm). Gemäldegalerie Alte Meister, Kassel.

in taste and fashion. Amsterdam had become the auction center of Europe, and the important paintings were sold there. The elite client, now with a far wider market of works available, including prestigious paintings of the past and from abroad, perceived his social status as being reflected in what he collected, not just what he commissioned. The painter was no longer competing only with his peers on the local scene, but with the whole history of art, at least since the Renaissance. If he wished autonomy from the tyranny of the patron, as Rembrandt did, he needed to appeal to that other market, the new class of merchants who bought what they liked for domestic decoration. Rembrandt's high prices and his unwillingness to economize on his materials meant that his appeal to this clientele was limited, setting him apart from his contemporaries in this as in so many other things. Most of his peers were all too aware that the margin of profit was slim, and that to make a living they needed to be good businessmen, producing works at the lowest possible cost in labor and materials.

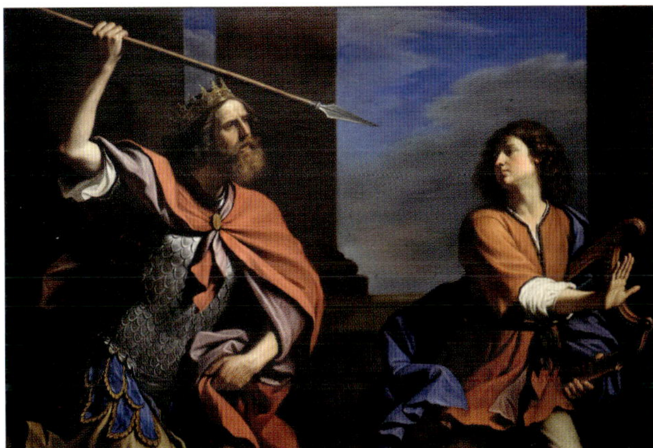

FIG. 3.5. Il Guercino, *Saul Attacking David*, 1646. Oil on canvas, 57 ⅞ × 86 ⅝ in. (147 × 220 cm). Galleria Nazionale d'Arte Antica, Rome.

EFFICIENCY

In the painter's ideal world, one commission would follow another in smooth succession, but as any contractor knows, the flow of work is erratic. There are times when there are not enough hours of daylight to keep up with the demand, and slow times when assistants are being paid to do nothing. In the painter's workshop, to keep them busy and to increase the income, it made sense to have them produce replicas that could be sold directly to a client, either from the shop or at a market or fair.

We have seen that cartoons, especially when they were reused in whole or in part, were another way that central Italian masters used both labor and creative inventions economically. Although serial production was very limited in Italy, it was another story in sixteenth-century Antwerp, where the export of pictures became the lifeblood of the artists' community. The city became the capital of art sales in Europe, and most of it was the export of on-spec production. The markets reached from Portugal to the Baltic. Statistics for exports in the years 1543 to 1545 show that of a total of 130 shipments, 24 percent went to Iberia, 24 percent to Germany, 18 percent to England, and 9 percent to Italy. (The remaining 25 percent is grouped as "Other.") Some of those pictures were sent to Seville, where they were reshipped to New Spain.[14]

Assembly line production was not the only way the Antwerp painters answered demand. They developed methods for streamlining workshop production, centered on underdrawing directly on the support, in which the master made such efficient use of assistants that he needed to do very little of the actual painting, and yet could produce a work of high quality in his style. Such works might be commissioned altarpieces custom-made for the patron, but on designs that could be altered, recombined, and reused for far-flung clients who neither knew nor cared about the replication.

An example of this long-distance commissioning and of the workshop procedure to produce a major altarpiece under these conditions is the *Reinhold Altarpiece;* in 1516 Joos van Cleve in Antwerp was commissioned to paint this work for the chapel of the Brotherhood of Saint Reinhold, in the Church of Our Lady in the Polish port of Danzig (Gdansk). The interior is an elaborately carved Life of Christ by Jan de Molder and his Antwerp workshop (fig. 3.7), which can be concealed by Van Cleve's painted wings showing the Passion of Christ (fig. 3.8). The Brotherhood was one of six in the city, made up

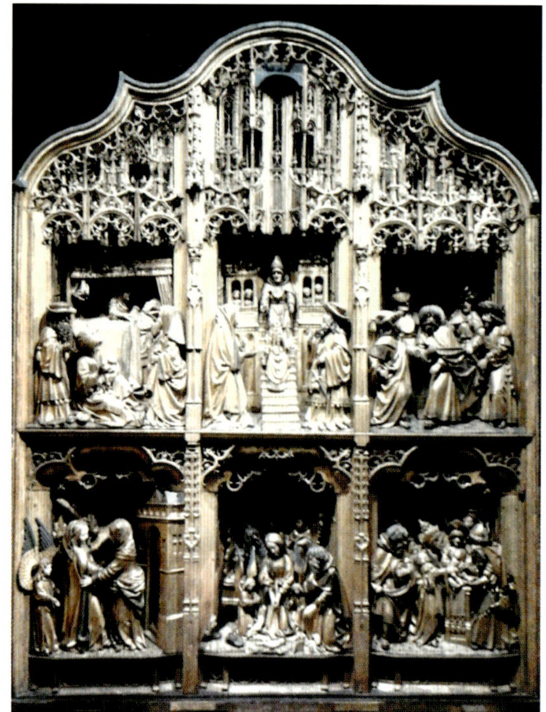

FIG. 3.7. Jan de Molder and workshop, *Reinhold Altarpiece,* sculpted interior with scenes of the life of Christ, 1516. Wood, 76 ⅜ × 62 ¼ in. (194 × 158 cm). National Museum, Warsaw.

of merchants from various Flemish cities with which Danzig had a brisk trade, and some of which had competing chapels in the same church. The patrons may have used an agent for the commission, who supplied de Molder and Van Cleve with details about the iconographical and material requirements and who took care of the payment.[15]

On the outside of the wings we see Van Cleve's painted images of Saint John the Baptist on the left and Saint Reinhold (a self-portrait of the painter) on the right. The interior wings are painted with eight scenes from the life and Passion of Christ: the *Presentation in the Temple,* the *Baptism of Christ,* the *Last Supper,* the *Agony in the Garden,* and below, *Ecce Homo, Christ before Pilate, Christ Carrying the Cross,* and the *Crucifixion.* Very detailed underdrawings in the altarpiece have been discovered with infrared reflectography (IRR), which give us the chance to learn something of how Van Cleve allocated work within his workshop for efficiency (fig. 3.9).[16] These remarkable images may have been based on cartoons that Van Cleve and his shop had made, or they could have been worked up by someone in the workshop using a liquid medium, presumably ink.

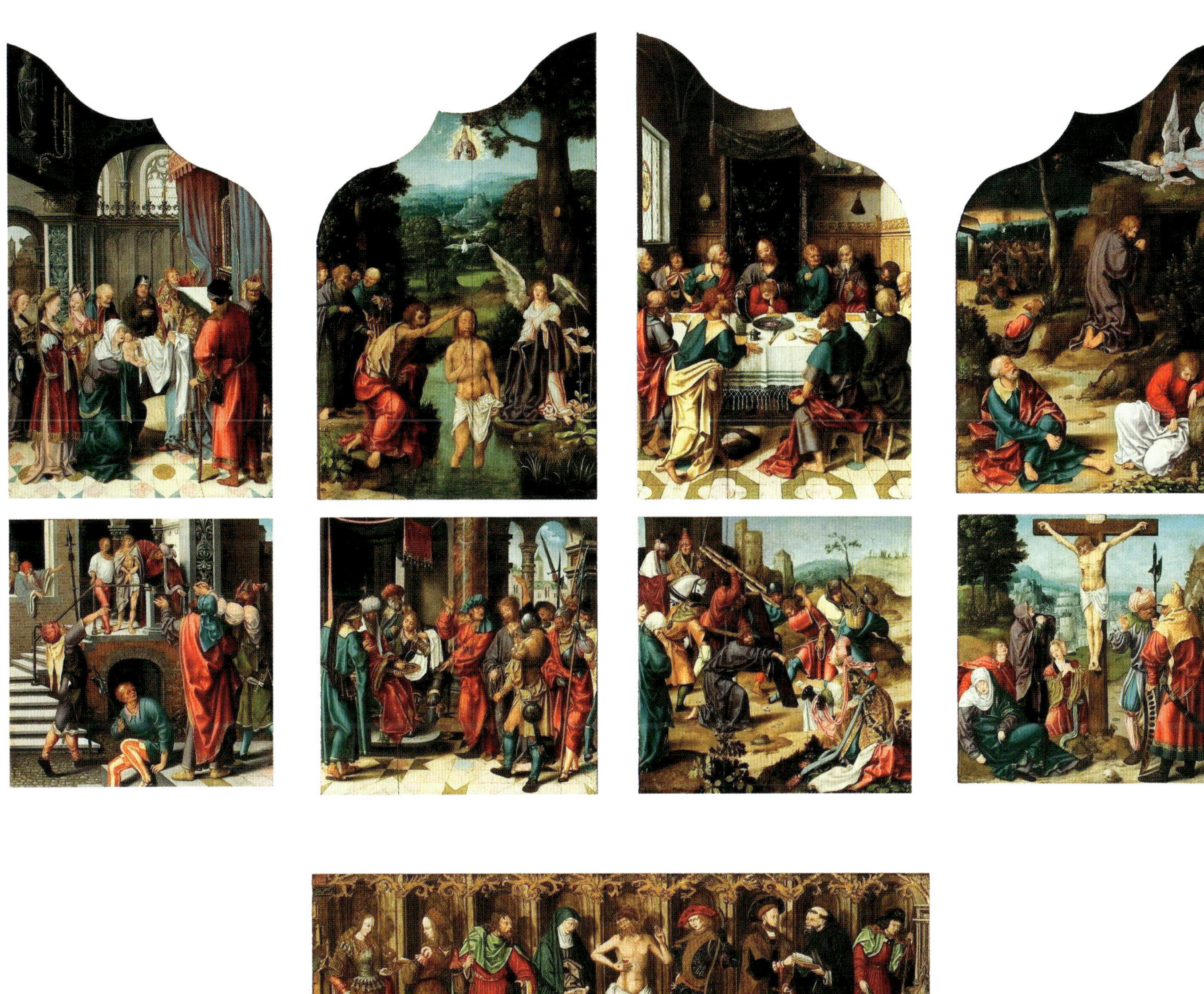

FIG. 3.8. Joos van Cleve and workshop, *Reinhold Altarpiece*, 1516. Oil on
panel, 8 ft. 4 ⅜ in. × 10 ft. 3 ¼ in. (255 × 313 cm). National Museum, Warsaw.

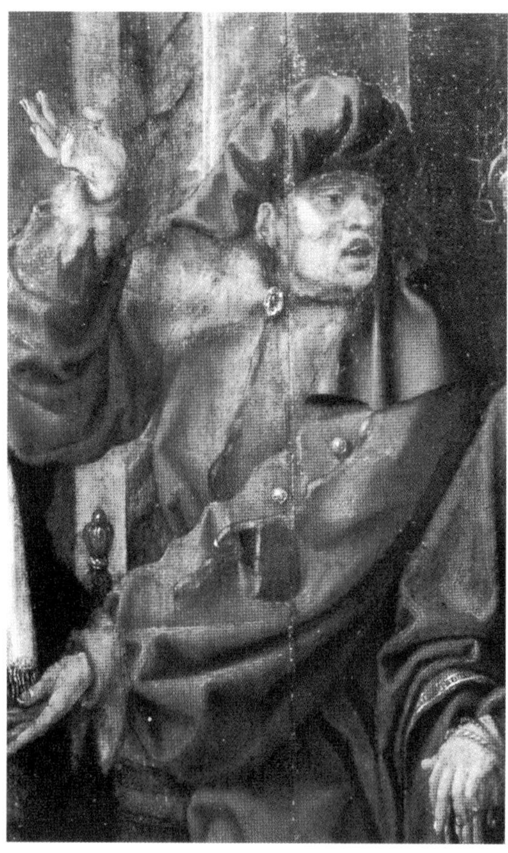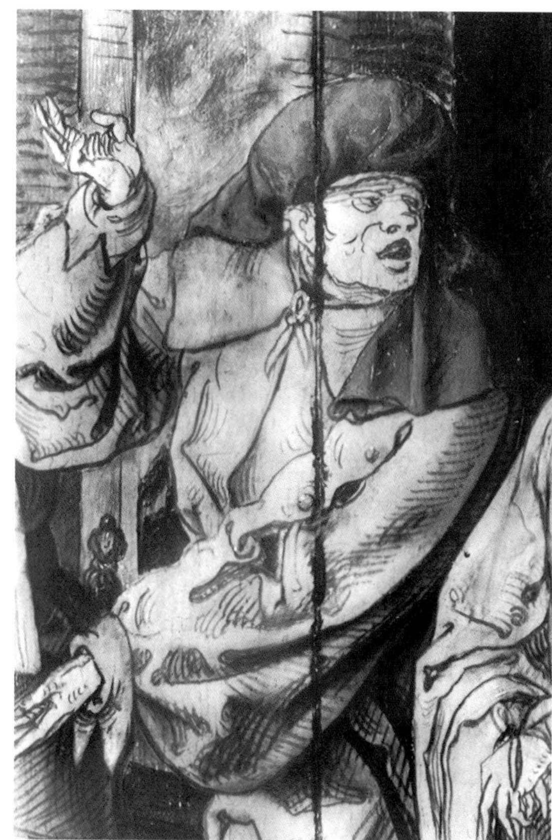

The underdrawing might have functioned as a form of presentation drawing to show to the commissioner, but in any case it made the subsequent painting process more efficient. Its detail would have obviated the need for changes in the course of painting—to be avoided because they would lengthen the drying time. Color notations and inscriptions have been found, perhaps to be used as a guide to assistants in the execution, or as part of the planning process to determine the distribution of major pigments and to estimate the quantity that would be required. Very thin, transparent application of paint allowing the underdrawing to show through meant that any assistant in the workshop was able to execute the painting in the style of the master.

Like the central Italian use of cartoons, the underdrawing allowed the master to busy himself with invention rather than execution. In Antwerp, where export was so important, such a procedure allowed for quick and cheap production of altarpieces. The master himself might intervene in the final stage: this painting shows elaboration both in color and in details that seem to have been made by the master himself, probably in response to the commissioner's wishes. In Italy, where the clientele

was much more localized, recognizable replication was not expedient. Part of the patron's performance of commissioning a family chapel in an Italian church was, after all, his display of fashionable taste in a unique work of art and devotion, and exported works did not travel far enough to guarantee that the replication would not be discovered.

GUILDS AND DEALERS

Throughout the Middle Ages, the guilds had made it their business to control supply and to guarantee quality. Having the right number of painters available in a community to answer the demand, but not so many that prices would fall below a living wage, was traditionally a guild concern, until the boom in Antwerp made such oversight unnecessary there. Besides limiting the number of apprentices and the immigration of artists, the guilds made membership expensive and sometimes required a masterwork as a prerequisite to matriculation, and they controlled the conditions under which a master who had trained elsewhere might practice. Control of the supply of artists worked much more successfully in the North than in Italy. We have seen how, beginning in the middle of the sixteenth century, especially in Rome, there was a glut of painters—many of whom came from abroad, either from other parts of the Italian peninsula or from the North or Iberia—that caused hardship there and undermined the system of production. The Antwerp guild was forced by the rapid expansion of the art market to take a pragmatic approach to controlling distribution. The presence of many art dealers who were not members simply made control impossible. The guild did continue to control the production process to help maintain reputations and support demand—for example, by inspecting sculptures prior to export and attaching its seal as a guarantee of quality.

Fifteenth-century Bruges, the home of Jan van Eyck and Hans Memling, had been the center of the export trade until its river silted up, when that center shifted to Antwerp.[17] But the protectionist guild contributed to Bruges's loss to Antwerp by actively discouraging the sale of uncommissioned works and placing a ban on foreign painters. Antwerp responded to the surge in demand for luxury goods all across Europe by catering to this new kind of client, men and women of the urban middle and upper classes. They differed from the traditional clients of the moneyed elite, who had always been surrounded by pictures, and they needed more guidance, which in Antwerp could be provided by the dealers.

Dealers served both the low end of the market and the high end. We begin to find paintings showing collectors in their galleries and dealers in theirs. The Antwerp gallery represented by a follower of Frans Francken the Younger shows well-dressed gentlemen admiring both art and natural wonders as well as musical instruments in an elegant setting (fig. 3.10). The painting in the foreground shows musical instruments and pictures being destroyed by donkey-headed men, recalling the outbreaks of iconoclasm that had occurred in the late sixteenth century. By the time this was painted, Antwerp dealers were concentrating their attention on paintings.[18]

An important marketing tactic that functioned very successfully and would be copied in the next century in Holland was the institution of a year-round gallery where clients could come and buy a readymade; or survey the offerings before deciding which painter to commission; or select a semi-finished work and have it customized by adding their own portrait or coat of arms to a diptych of the Virgin and Child, or their own and their wife's name saints to an altarpiece.

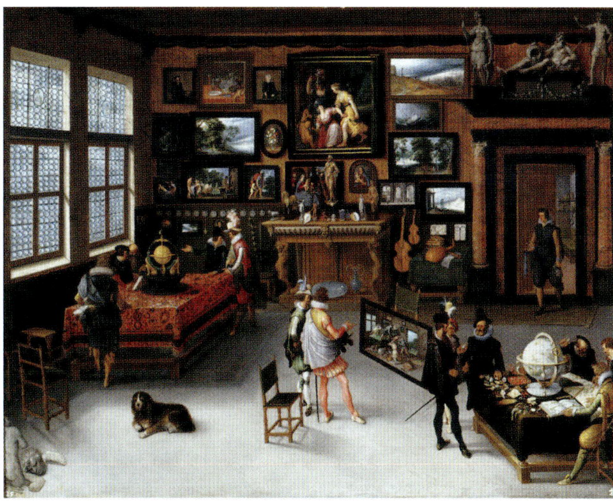

FIG. 3.10. Adriaen van Stalbemt, *Gallery Picture* (*The Sciences and the Arts*), c. 1650. Oil on panel, 35 ⅜ × 46 in. (89.9 × 117 cm). Prado, Madrid.

Italians seem to have retained a preference for the tradition of working on commission, with on spec production a minor sideline. It is certainly a fact that there was nothing in Italy like the export trade and marketing that was developed by dealers in Antwerp, such as Van Cleve's large-scale altarpiece for a specific chapel in faraway Danzig. In Venice the laws protected the painters from dealers by permitting only painters to sell works of art. It has been suggested, however, that in the long run these laws, like those in Bruges, hurt rather than helped the painters. In both cities, which did not see a rise in population, local demand eventually stagnated.[19]

MARKETING IN HOLLAND VERSUS ITALY

This more practical and commercial approach was typical of the North, in contrast to Italy, where marketing, like the artists' training, was uncontrolled. In central Italy from the fifteenth century on, there is no perceptible influence of the guilds on supply, demand, or production. The success of Antwerp and Holland contrasts with the chaos rampant in the Italian markets, particularly in Rome. In Italy, anyone who wanted to could declare himself an artist and work independently as long as he could make a living at it.[20] We have seen that young artists, many of whom came from abroad, lived from hand to mouth, picking up work on any project that might be available, scrambling for instruction they could not really afford to pay for, working second jobs, including selling pictures, and thus never receiving proper training. There may have been more high-end commissions available in Rome than in most places because of the demand of the popes and cardinals, but those commissions went to the upper tier of painters with established workshops. Those high-end botteghe did not serve the market of those who wanted readymades: Madonnas or copies of miraculous images or copies of works by famous painters. The Roman market, which was not controlled as it was in the North by any institution, was haphazard. Merchants might even commission works from well-known painters and then resell them immediately.[21] There were dealers, most of whom were foreigners, who served this market from their own shops, as in the case of the successful dealer Pellegrino Peri, who came to Rome from Genoa, and who was described in Chapter 2.[22] If pictures were exported, it was most likely done through one of these foreign dealers.

Marketing and production in the Northern Netherlands began to change with the formation of the Protestant Dutch Republic in 1581. Up until this point, the centers of artistic production had been in the Southern Netherlands, particularly Flanders. We have seen that the prosperity that marked the Dutch Golden Age brought about a rapid expansion in the market for luxury goods, in particular for paintings.[23] In Protestant areas, the Church as the principal client gave way to middle- and upper-middle-class customers who wanted not paintings of Virgins, but landscapes and genre scenes for the walls of their homes. It has been estimated that in the Dutch Republic the number of painters may have increased as much as fourfold between 1600 and 1619, doubled again between 1619 and 1639, and increased another 50 percent

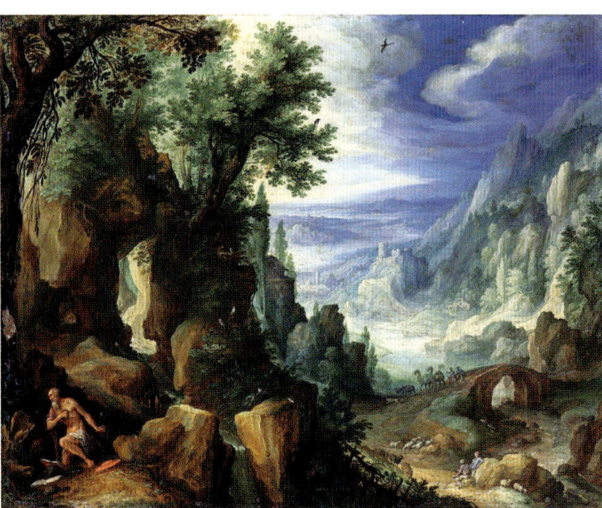

FIG. 3.11. Paul Bril, *Landscape with Saint Jerome and Rocky Crag*, 1592. Oil on copper on panel, 10⅛ × 12⅞ in. (25.75 × 32.8 cm). Mauritshuis, The Hague.

in the next two decades.[24] Travelers and documents attest to this new taste for paintings. The French schoolmaster Jean-Nicolas de Parival, who lived in Leiden for twenty years, wrote in the 1660s: "I do not believe that so many good painters can be found anywhere else; also the houses are filled with very beautiful paintings and no one is so poor as not to wish to be well provided with them."[25] A mass market such as we saw in Antwerp in the sixteenth century developed, but based now on local consumption rather than on export.

Guilds had barely existed in the fifteenth and sixteenth centuries in the Northern Netherlands, where production was not of a quantity or quality comparable to that of the South. The tremendous surge in Golden Age demand coincided with the expansion of the role of guilds, which then played an important role in promoting painting and stimulating demand. For a public that was not sophisticated about art, the showrooms set up by the guilds, where they controlled the pricing, provided a guarantee of quality.

LANDSCAPE PAINTING

Landscape was not an established genre in Italy until the late Cinquecento. Many of the painters who practiced it were actually immigrants from Flanders, where it was a flourishing genre.[26] The most successful was Paul Bril, who was born in Antwerp and heir to the tradition of Joachim Patinir (see *Landscape with Saint Jerome and Rocky Crag,* fig. 3.11). Bril moved to Rome in the 1580s, worked for popes Gregory XIII, Sixtus V, and Clement VIII in the Vatican, as well as many other prominent Roman families, and created the classicizing landscape that was critical to Claude Lorrain in the creation of his own classical landscape.[27]

Some Flemish landscape painters also went to the Northern Netherlands beginning in the 1580s, fleeing the turmoil of the Spanish invasion and religious suppression. Roelandt Savery is an example. He was brought as a boy by his family from Flanders to Utrecht, where they took refuge from the violence and anarchy of the pillaging Spanish troops. His older brother Jacob established himself as a painter and etcher in the already prosperous but artistically underdeveloped Northern Netherlands. When his brother died in 1603, Roelandt traveled to the court of Rudolf II in Prague, where he worked until the death of the emperor in 1612, when he returned and eventually settled again in Utrecht. His landscapes, derived

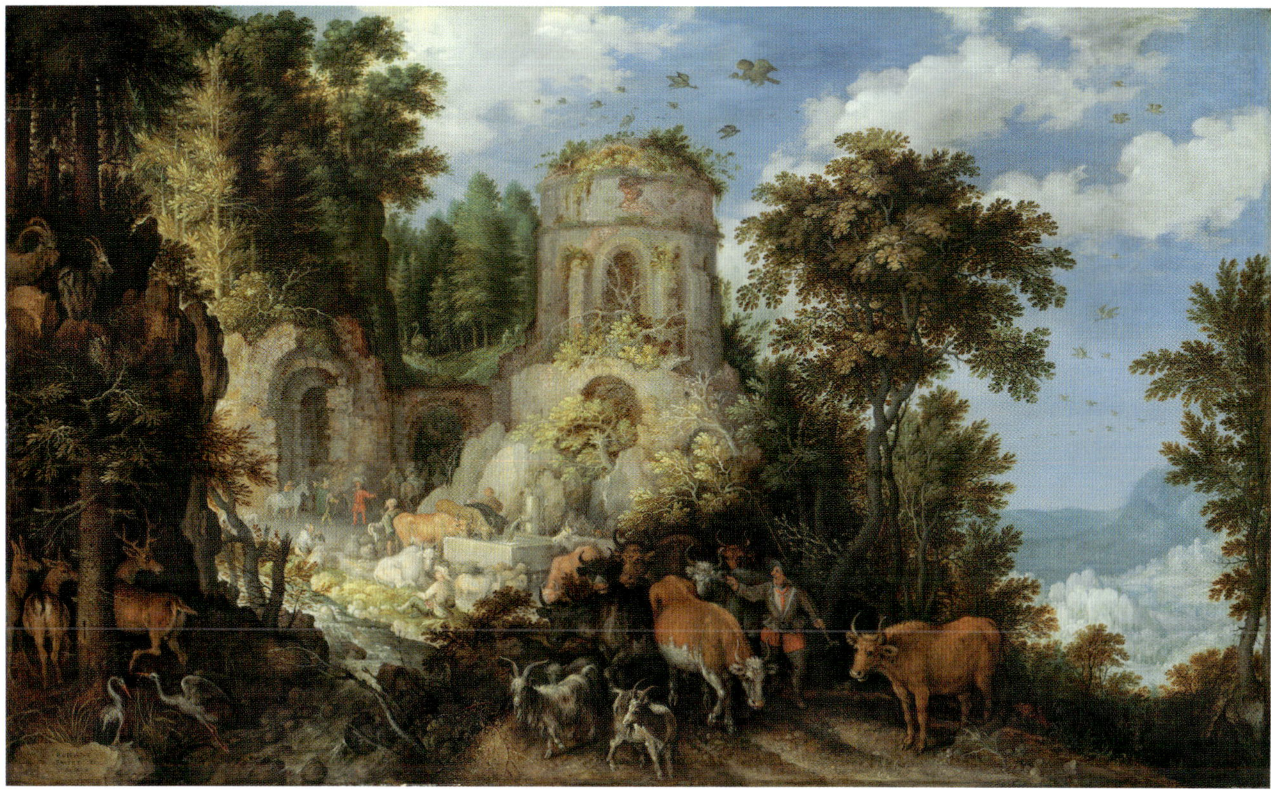

FIG. 3.12. Roelandt Savery, *Landscape with the Flight into Egypt*, 1624. Oil on panel, 21 ⅜ × 36 in. (54.3 × 91.5 cm). National Gallery of Art, Washington, D.C.

from the Patinir tradition of the worldview panorama like Bril's, found favor among Dutch clients, and he sold his pictures at good enough prices until his death in 1639.

His *Landscape with the Flight into Egypt* is an exemplary sample (fig. 3.12). In a dramatic mountain pass below a romantically ruined classical temple, a watering trough has attracted all manner of animals, which Savery had studied and drawn at the emperor's zoo when he had worked for Rudolf II.[28] In the bustle it is easy to miss the Holy Family passing through the gate, though three shepherds have removed their caps, sensing the holy presence. The scene is a splendid, brightly colored, imaginary invention, painted in the conventional manner of Flemish landscape with three zones, moving from brown foreground to a green middle ground to blue background. It was a complicated process of preparation and execution, involving planning in underdrawings, then painting a light-colored ground over a base color for each of the three areas. Next, each zone was worked up with harmonizing colors, letting the underpaint show through. An area of the foreground was reserved for the animals and figures to be painted after the landscape. This zoned underpaint allowed Savery to use a light tan in

the middle ground to attract attention to the mysterious light, breaking through and illuminating the area around the Holy Family.[29]

When a generation of native Dutch painters grew up with the Flemish example before them, they wanted to represent their country as it was, reflecting their pride in the newly established Dutch Republic.[30] Savery's picturesque mountains bear no resemblance to flat Holland, where there are no classical ruins, as the Romans built nothing more elaborate than a rough military outpost. In the late 1620s several painters in Haarlem initiated a new style that brought to life in paint the Dutch countryside. Jan van Goyen and his contemporaries rejected both the fantasy and the elaborate preparation of Savery and his Flemish colleagues, choosing instead a thin application of muted colors that evoke the distinctive look of the Dutch landscape. In his *View of Dordrecht,* where more than two-thirds of the canvas is devoted to sky, we see the town, dominated by the church, across an expanse of river dotted with boats of all kinds (fig. 3.13). It is seemingly uncomposed, casual in its arrangement. The unstudied feeling of the execution enhances the sense of a transient moment, but one that is full of movement and drama.

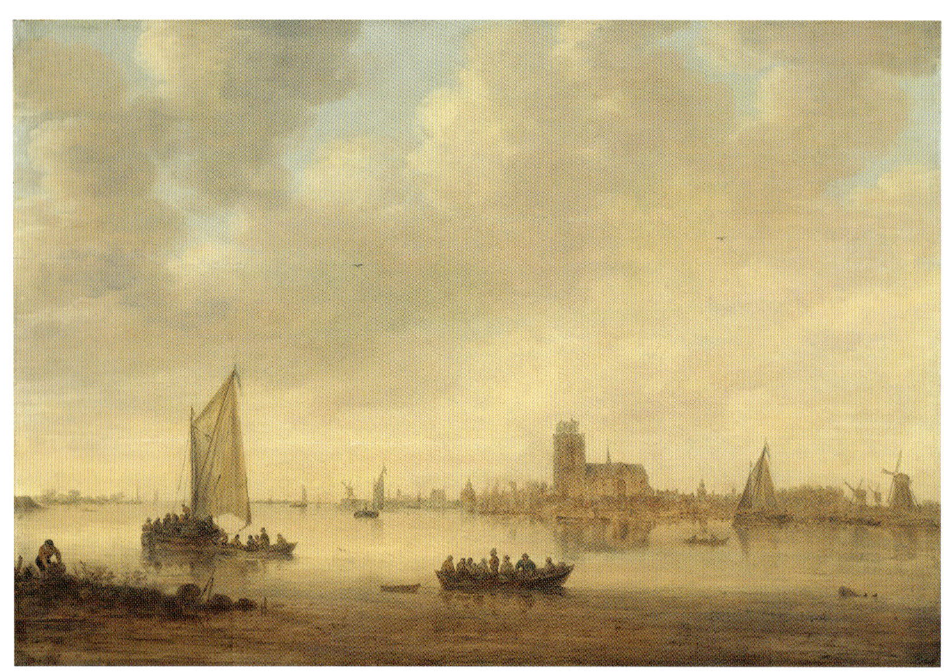

FIG. 3.13. Jan van Goyen, *View of Dordrecht*, 1644. Oil on panel, 25 1/2 × 37 3/4 in. (64.75 × 95.9 cm). National Gallery of Art, Washington, D.C.

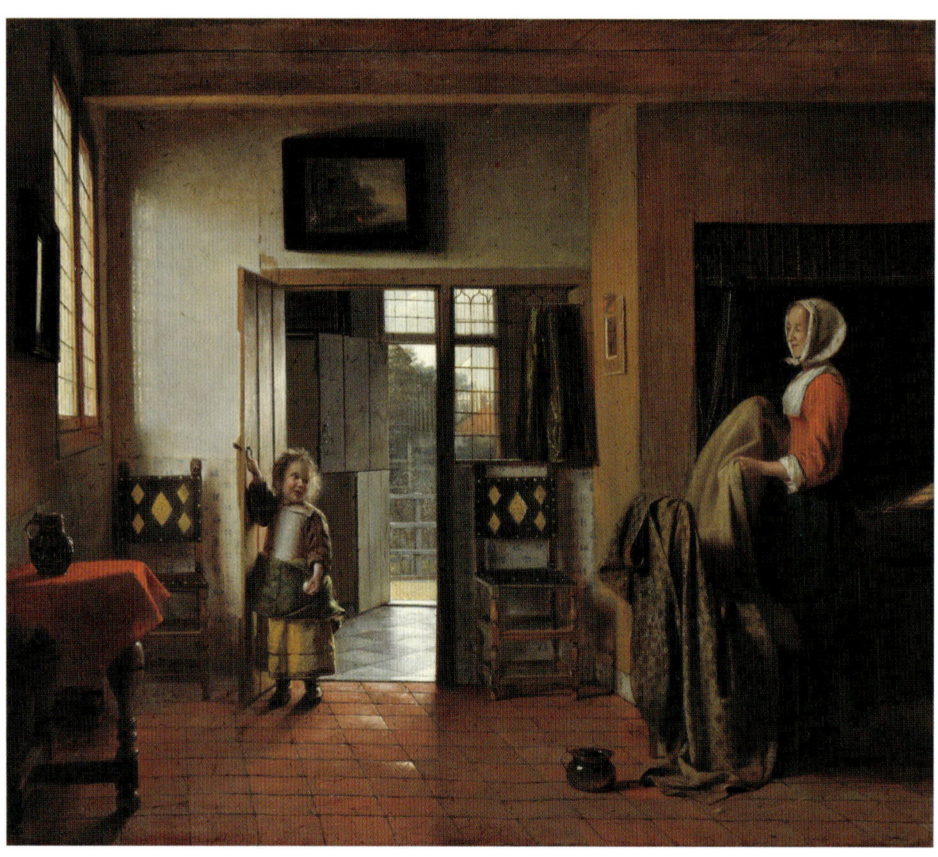

FIG. 3.14. Pieter de Hooch, *The Bedroom*, 1658–60. Oil on canvas, 28 3/4 × 32 1/2 in. (73 × 82.6 cm). National Gallery of Art, Washington, D.C.

The cloudy sky gives the painter the means to manipulate light and shade so as to create both spatial recession and the threat of an impending storm. In the dark foreground a boat is crowded with dark figures silhouetted against a patch of sunlight that streams through the clouds. The water rapidly shifts to a middle tone that serves to set off the dark boat with sails that rise to contrast with the whitish clouds. The town is convincingly depicted on the distant shore in middle tones, low in contrast. The Flemish zones of light and dark have been subtly adapted to render the look of Dutch landscape.

For such works, celebrating the commonplace, artists needed a more efficient working procedure to produce pictures at prices accessible and attractive to a public not yet accustomed to collecting art. Van Goyen and his contemporaries, the "tonal painters," as they have been called, created a facture that was economical both in terms of materials and time. They applied a quick sketch to thinly applied ground with minimal layers on top, and Van Goyen further shortened the working time by painting wet-into-wet. The materials used were earths and other low-cost pigments, such as smalt for the sky, suitable to the muted tonality being sought; ultramarine is virtually never found in his works.[31] The effect is often, as here, almost monochrome, with water and sky a similar grayish brown. Clouds create patches of light, and where blue sky shines through, it is a paled blue. The mood has been called melancholy, but I find it serene, reflecting an acceptance of the way things are in this world and humankind's place in it.

These landscapists were not like their Flemish predecessors, who worked from their imaginations, nor were they like the plein-air painters of nineteenth-century France—though they would influence them. They rarely painted out-of-doors. They obtained their lifelike scenes by sketching on-site, using sketchbooks and often chalk. They then developed these sketches in the studio, not hesitating to move things about, selecting, eliminating, and rearranging to achieve a pleasing composition. They differed too from their contemporaries to the south, the great Poussin and Claude, who tamed the Italian countryside and disciplined nature to fit the needs of the pattern of their compositions.

This new approach suited the Dutch temperament and culture. Dutch Protestants were practical people. Following Calvin, they did not much believe in human heroes. The panoply of Catholic saints and martyrs was rejected, and they believed that the deity should not be imaged. On the other hand, Calvin *promoted* representing the world around us, as the celebration of God's creation. The Calvinists had removed all sacred images and whitewashed their churches, so there was not much call for altarpieces, except in regions that had remained Catholic.

Some clients turned to the serene domestic interiors of Pieter de Hooch or Jan Vermeer as more accessible subjects for contemplation than the exploits of pagan gods and goddesses (see de Hooch's *The Bedroom*, fig. 3.14, for example). There were also lively scenes of country peasants and tavern life by such painters as Adriaan Brouwer and Jan Steen for those who enjoyed a little low life and bawdy humor.[32] But landscape came to be greatly favored by the buying public who purchased paintings created on spec by the artist from his shop, in markets or fairs, or from dealers.[33]

Van Goyen produced more than twelve hundred works, so it is clear that he worked rapidly. His paintings appear frequently in inventories of the period and his average price is among the lowest, if not the lowest, during the period he was working, 1626 to 1650.[34] Even with this level of sales, when he died in 1656 he was in debt.

Jacob van Ruisdael, who is generally regarded as the greatest of the Dutch landscapists, did significantly better than Van Goyen in the marketplace. His paintings sold for more than twice as much.[35] Probably in 1650 Ruisdael traveled to the eastern border with Germany, where the flat coastal fields give way to a hilly forested area. Around the mid-1650s he moved from Haarlem to Amsterdam, where the taste was moving toward more fantastic, or at least imaginary, landscape, and Ruisdael gravitated in that direction from his earlier, more realistic style, as in *Forest Scene* (fig. 3.15). Although Ruisdael's landscapes are often described as dramatic, what he presents is not like later Romantic renderings of the Sublime. Rather than pinnacle experiences, they record what you could expect to see on a walk when you come upon a random arrangement of natural elements that somehow speaks to you. The drama may be in the tension the sky creates with rapidly shifting clouds, the possibility of a storm approaching, or in the shivering trees, or in the impenetrable darkness of the woods before you. The treatment of color tells the story. Nature is described in tones of brown and deep green; the sky is a pallid gray blue, sometimes overcast with wispy clouds, but often animated with fast-moving cumulus heaps

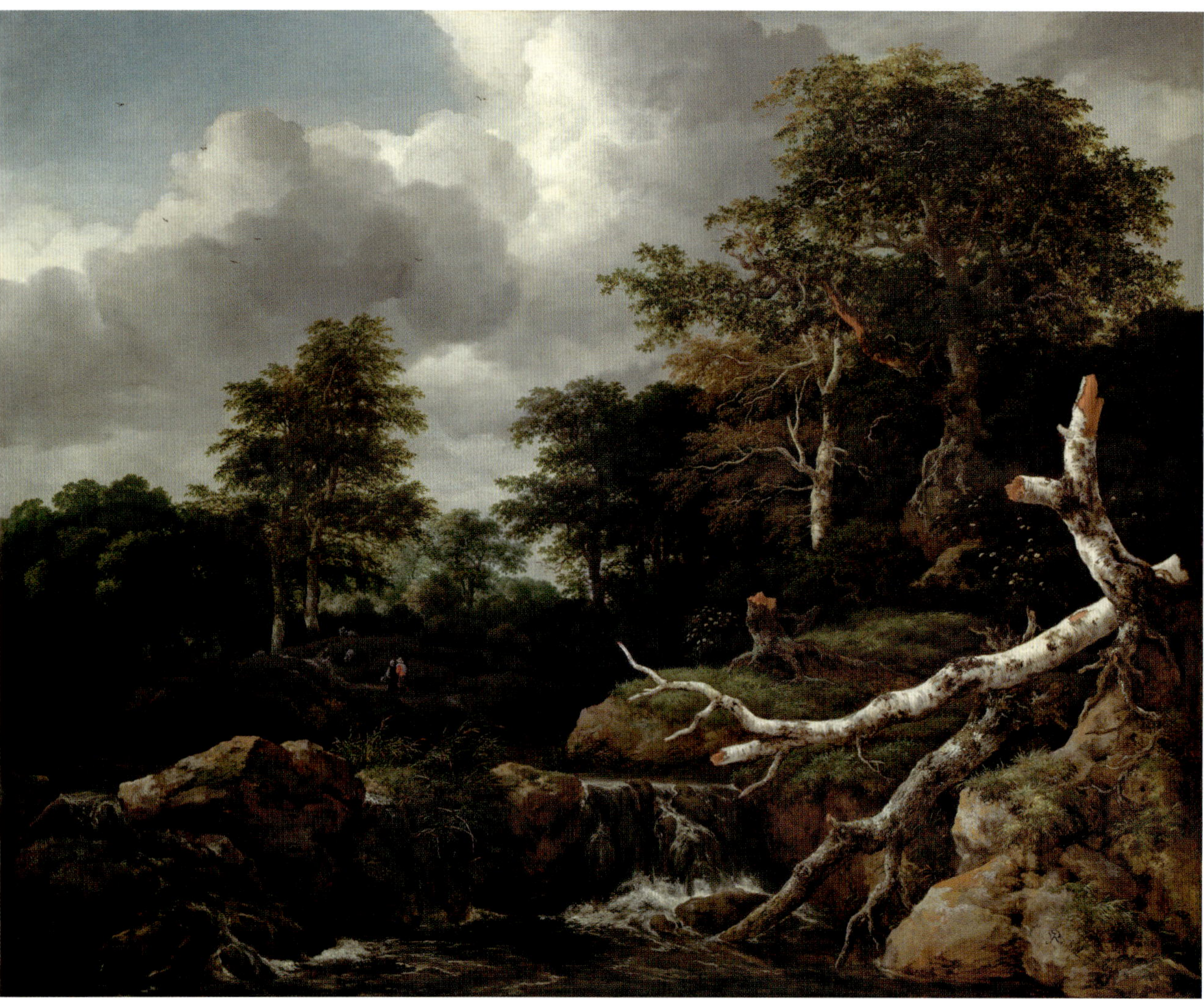

FIG. 3.15. Jacob van Ruisdael, *Forest Scene*, c. 1655. Oil on canvas, 41 9/16 × 48 9/16 in. (105.5 × 123.4 cm). National Gallery of Art, Washington, D.C.

that darken to a stormy center. They cast shadows that mottle the ground with patches of light and dark, useful in indicating receding space. Except for snowscapes, it is not possible to determine the season from the foliage. Ruisdael's landscapes are inhabited, but the individuals are not significant. They are minute compared to the scale of figures in Italian or Italianate landscapes. They are part of the ordered scheme of nature—even when it looks wild—but not because of their impact upon it. Like many of his contemporaries, Ruisdael had the figures added in by assistants, almost as an afterthought. A traveler may wear a red cloak, but it will make a very small spot of animation and will likely be painted with a muted earth pigment. The bright, intense pigments preferred in Italy and by the Flemish such as Savery are eschewed in favor of subtle lifelike mixtures, based in earth tones.

There is much debate among scholars as to whether any—or how much—symbolism should be found in landscapes such as these. John Walford makes the most convincing case, taking a middle course between the extremes of those scholars who see symbols everywhere and those who deny any allegorical meaning.[36] In Ruisdael, the wildness of nature remains; it is even sought and encouraged. When he finds a heroic tree he makes space for it, subordinates those around it, giving rein to its rebellious shape, directing the light to it. Flashes of white in the fallen beech or the standing one behind it here make the deep dark of the wood more foreboding. It is hard to miss the presence of a church spire on just about every horizon, and blasted or fallen trees like this one suggest the transience of life, while their heroic arboreal counterparts may bring to mind the courage required to carry on.

That the Dutch focused on light and dark to measure space is indicated by the discussion in seventeenth-century Dutch art theory of specialized words, *"houding"* and *"reddering."* Ulrike Kern discussed them as describing the practice of arranging colors and tones in a spatial relationship.[37] Whereas houding, which will be discussed later in this chapter, refers to restricting light as a means of unifying effects, reddering creates the illusion of space by alternating bands of light and shade, a derivative of the Flemish three-color zones of landscape. We saw how Van Goyen employed this system in his *View of Dordrecht*, rationalizing it by his use of a broken cloud cover (see fig. 3.13). It could also serve to order the space of interiors. Another look at de Hooch's *The Bedroom* reveals how the painter used light and shade in alternation to lead the viewer's eye through the recession of rooms (see fig. 3.14). Color contributes, diminishing in intensity and value as it moves back from red tiles to gray to yellow beige, until it reaches the dull green of the distant garden. Laterally, too, the carefully studied variations in value measure the distance across the room, from darker below the window; to reflective light in the middle, where reinforcing light enters from behind; to the right side, where the light weakens and the woman casts a deep shadow behind her. The methodical sequence of spaces and the clarity of the position of each element convey the sense of a tranquil, well-ordered domestic realm.

Water is everywhere in Dutch landscape and sea-scapes, as it is in this land that was largely reclaimed from the sea. Restrained by manmade dikes, water is a constant threatening presence, its malignant force acknowledged in scenes of storm and shipwreck and flood, on the one hand. On the other hand, it is also acknowledged as the source of Dutch wealth and plenty. Harbors filled with trading ships bear witness to the seas as the source of Dutch prosperity, and the power of water domesticated and harnessed is seen in canals that glide through the fields. Between 1612 and 1635, merchants invested in a project using windmills to drain the marshy bogs and inland lakes north of Amsterdam and Haarlem, increasing the size of the region by one-third, providing rich, arable soil for farming and pasture, and bringing a rich profit to the investors.[38] Then, through the collaboration of private investors and municipalities, the whole of Holland was crisscrossed with canals to provide reliable horse-drawn transportation between communities.[39]

For the Dutch, landscape and seascape reminded them, even if unconsciously, of their achievement in wresting this land from the sea and making it prosperous and politically preeminent. For Claude and Poussin, French painters working in Rome, landscape had no such political significance. They set out to raise the genre, which was held in the lowest esteem both in Italy and later by the French Académie Royale. Like the Italians Annibale Carracci and Domenichino, they placed mythological subjects and stories from ancient history in classicized settings, intending to give them the same moral seriousness as other, more elevated genres. They imposed the same order on their landscapes as we find in religious or mythological scenes.

Claude perfected the imaginary pastoral scene, framed with classical temples, or the harbor at sunset with ships gently riding the waves, peopled with small figures embarking or debarking. He re-created subjects from biblical history, such as the *Embarkation of the Queen of Sheba* (fig. 3.16); or ancient history, such as *Cleopatra Landing at Tarsus;* or from literature, such as *Odysseus Departing for Ithaca.* The real subject, however, is the evocation of luminous atmosphere. Often facing into the sun, Claude was a master of atmospheric perspective and of space receding toward the horizon. He painted with multiple layers in order to achieve the effect of mist.[40] His materials and the way he used them point up how different his clients and their expectations were from the contemporary Dutch. The Dutch landscapists who were looking for the least expensive materials with which to obtain the effects they wanted used smalt for their skies, as we have seen. Claude used costly ultramarine quite freely in his skies and draperies, but then mixed it with smalt, reducing the intensity of the color and the drying time.[41] His friend Joachim von Sandrart worked alongside Claude when he was in Rome and described how they would paint together in Rome on-site. Claude's canvases were too large to tote around, so he must have been making sketches, which he worked up in the studio. Sandrart reported that when they first met, Claude was studying a scene and mixing colors on-site, which he would then apply in the studio.[42]

Poussin did not take up landscape until the late 1640s, when Claude's pictures were already in demand among illustrious Roman patrons—popes, princes, cardinals, ambassadors, and French and foreign nobility. These pictures are much larger and grander than their Dutch counterparts, designed as they were for palatial settings. Poussin, like Claude, sought to ennoble the genre

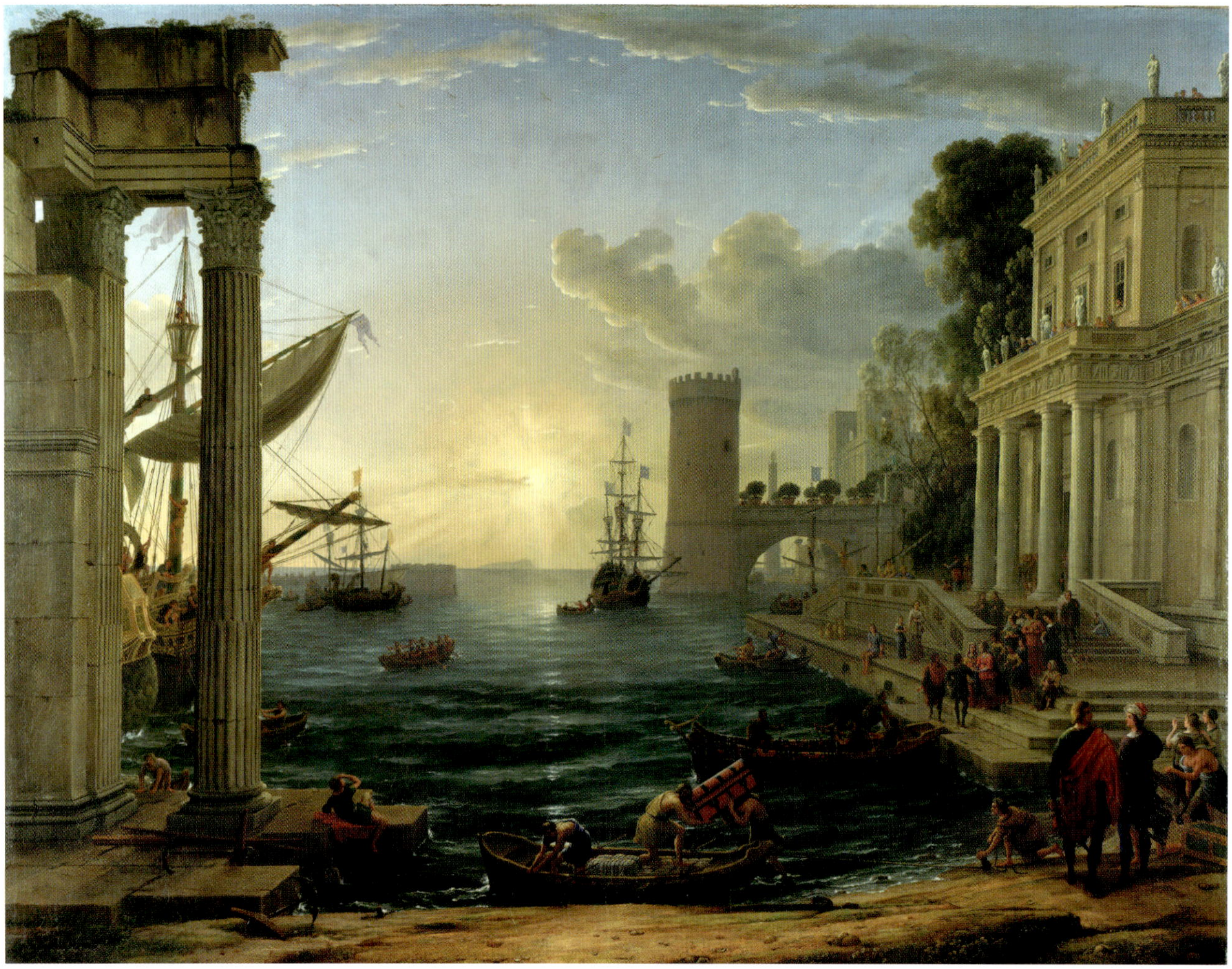

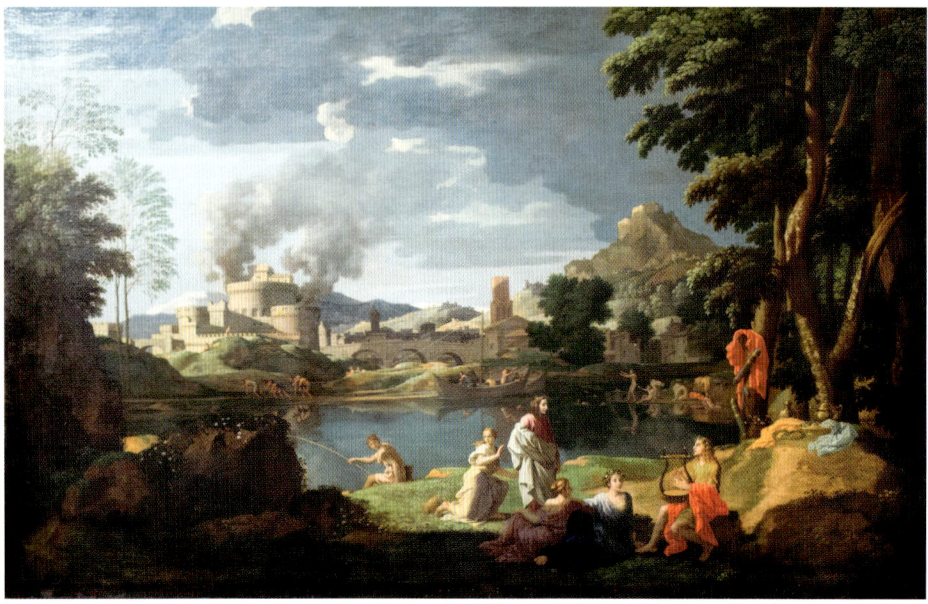

FIG. 3.16. Claude Lorrain, *Embarkation of the Queen of Sheba,* 1648. Oil on canvas, 58 ¾ × 77 ⅜ in. (149.1 × 196.7 cm). National Gallery, London.

FIG. 3.17. Nicolas Poussin, *Orpheus and Eurydice,* 1648. Oil on canvas, 48 ⅞ × 78 ¾ in. (124 × 200 cm). Louvre, Paris.

of landscape by idealizing and classicizing it. The rustic naturalism of the Dutch countryside has been tamed and manicured to provide a suitable setting for exalted subjects such as Orpheus and Eurydice (fig. 3.17). Orpheus is carefully picked out with color, the other figures subordinated with pale, neutralized tones. The perfected balance of landscape is echoed in the dignified poise of the figures, even Eurydice at the moment of being fatally struck by a serpent. The Dutch took nature as their subject more to express their symbiotic relationship to it than to demonstrate their dominance over it. Where figures appear, they are small and anonymous, workers or travelers moving through the landscape of which they are integrated parts.

MARKETING OUTSIDE HOLLAND

Conditions of marketing and commissioning were different in areas that had remained Catholic and monarchical such as Italy, Flanders, and France. There were large and lucrative ecclesiastical commissions as well as state-sponsored projects of the courts. Poussin, as a Frenchman living in Italy, did not benefit as much as Rubens, but he had a group of sponsors who kept him busy with commissions. Rubens's patronage resembled more the traditional Renaissance Italian system than the open market of his Dutch Protestant peers.

Flanders was under the rule of the archduke, appointed by the Spanish king, whose court was based in Brussels. Rubens's parents were members of the urban patrician class, a class that at this time in Antwerp aspired to the lifestyle of the gentry and the nobility. Upon his mother's death in 1608, which brought Rubens back from his eight-year sojourn in Italy, he had everything he needed for a successful career: talent, experience, a substantial inheritance, and ready access to patronage. Rubens went about quickly remedying the one defect in his credentials. Painting was not a highly regarded occupation and working for one's living was not appropriate to his aristocratic class, whose members lived on profits derived from real estate. He sent away to Genoa for copies of a court judgment that had been passed down in 1590, which rejected the claim of the guild that to sell pictures a painter had to have studied with a master for the requisite years. One Giovanni Paggi had claimed that because he was of noble birth and self-taught, he was exempt from the requirements imposed by the guild on artisans. The court upheld his

claim, declaring that painting was one of the seven liberal arts and was noble itself. This is what Rubens needed to consolidate his position in Antwerp society.[43] With three sources of income—his court appointment, his real estate dealings, and the sale of his paintings—Rubens had large amounts of money at his disposal. He could ask high prices, like Rembrandt, and he got them. His social success was assured in 1624 when the ruling Spanish monarch, Philip IV, ennobled him, making him not just a member of the urban elite, but a nobleman.

Rubens set about controlling another lucrative stream of income. He recognized that the sale of prints of his works, if of high quality, could enhance his image. He learned from his most enterprising sixteenth-century predecessors, in particular Raphael and Albrecht Dürer. Within a little more than a quarter century of the invention of printmaking in the 1470s, a few painters had divined how they could use prints to promote themselves. Dürer was a skilled woodcutter and engraver, or at least he employed highly skilled craftsmen, so his prints, especially his *Life of the Virgin* and the *Passions,* appealed not only to collectors but also to a broad audience as devotional images. They were widely disseminated and were admired across the Italian peninsula as well as the North. Raphael, too, was quick to see the commercial potential and entered into collaboration with the engraver Marcantonio Raimondi, to whom he supplied designs. The entrepreneur Il Baviera was responsible for the business side of the Raphael print enterprise and for marketing the editions. These were not in the proper sense yet reproductive prints, as David Landau and Peter Parshall have insisted, because they were prints of preparatory drawings or designs made expressly to be engraved, such as the superb *Massacre of the Innocents.*[44] Nevertheless, Raphael was in control of what was disseminated under his name, and his work became known across Europe. By the mid-sixteenth century there were collectors amassing prints. Some of them were certainly members of the elite, but some certainly were not. The sale of prints, often in shops or fairs and markets, paved the way for the large-scale collecting of both prints and paintings that developed in the seventeenth century, and for the democratization of the art market.

Rubens was angered by unauthorized prints of his works, which he considered inferior in quality. In 1619 he obtained a privilege, or copyright, entitling him to publish copies of his works in the Netherlands as well as

France. He incorporated accomplished engravers into his workshop and collaborated with them. He encouraged them to imitate the brushstroke and surface quality of his paintings, thereby producing prints that captured some of the élan of his paintings.

This workshop included other specialists, such as Frans Snyders, whom Rubens often called upon to contribute animals and still-life elements to his paintings. The precocious Anthony van Dyck got his training with Rubens, who identified him as "the best of my pupils." He was specifically named in the contract for the ceiling of the Jesuit church as one of the disciples who was permitted to execute Rubens's designs. Rubens greatly valued the contribution of his workshop. Given his huge number of commissions and the scale of some of them, he could not possibly have executed them alone. In fact it is clear that he didn't think his role was primarily to paint, but rather to invent. As will be discussed, Rubens did not ask a higher price for paintings executed by his hand than for those invented by him, executed by his shop, and retouched by him.

FACTURE

The competitive market of the new century required efficient production, and technical innovations made it possible. Where painters had relied in the past on careful preparatory drawings, now they attacked the painting surface directly and were often more willing to revise and repaint. If anything characterizes seventeenth-century painting, however, it is its diversity—there are exceptions to every rule one tries to frame. Interest in capturing effects of light is a universal concern, to be sure, but the means vary. Thus undermodeling in neutral tones, perfected by Rubens, called at the time "dead coloring," allowed painters to design on the support. Poussin, however, continued to make meticulous preparatory designs for each of his canvases and had no use for spontaneity. Italian painters generally prepared their supports with a reddish imprimatura, as did Poussin, but Rubens and Van Dyck and others used a light-gray tint. Particularly in Italy, aerial perspective was perfected as an extension of traditional perspective; in Holland what is referred to by the peculiar term "houding" also encompasses surface texturing. Behind all these innovative practices lies a new attitude toward color in which the mixed tone is preferred to the pure, and the artist seeks verisimilitude rather than sheer chromatic allure.

TINTED IMPRIMATURA AND DEAD COLORING

By 1630, in Holland at least, it was normal practice for a painter to buy his support already primed. In Leiden, for instance, documents record that the authorized preparer had died and that painters were forced to travel some distances to buy their primed canvases and panels, so a certain Dirck de Lorm petitioned the guild to take over the trade.[45] The availability of pre-primed supports in other locations is still being studied. If they were available, it was only in major artistic centers.

The tint of the priming seems to have varied with locality: Van Dyck, who worked in such widely separated cities as Antwerp, Genoa, and London, was found to have used whatever priming was standard locally.[46] Poussin also varied his priming with his location. During his first stay in Rome (1624–40) he used a brown ground of chalk and brown earth pigments, which was consistent with what was being used by painters in Italy at the time. When he moved back to Paris briefly in 1640–42, he adopted the practice current then in France of covering a reddish ground with a second layer of gray. Then upon his return to Rome and for the rest of his career there, he continued to prepare his canvas with the double ground of red ochre and gray to give warmth to the flesh in his figured compositions, except when he painted landscapes (which he took up only after about 1650), where he reverted to the brown ground for their cooler tones. He may have been exceptional in not buying pre-primed canvases. Most painters, if they used a second priming, applied it in their workshops. The fact that available material was decisive in Poussin's choice of grounds is indicated by the fact that he used red pigments of a different chemical makeup in Paris and Rome.[47]

His red ground did not always serve him well over time. Its purpose was not only to smooth the texture of the rough canvas but also to impart a warm tonality to the gray layer. This gray provided a middle tone that could be left thinly painted. However, abrasion or the iron oxide in the red has sometimes increased the reddish effect, particularly in faces.[48] Nineteenth-century critics believed that Poussin's red ground had ruined many of his pictures. Indeed in some cases the effect has been disastrous—for example, in the *Crucifixion* at the Wadsworth Athenaeum, Hartford, where the dark ground, chosen to enhance the drama, has overwhelmed the colors and made the space and forms difficult to read (fig. 3.18).[49]

In the course of the sixteenth century, painters had worked out their personal approach to the newly invented tinted imprimatura, which could act as a middle ground.[50] The preoccupation of the painters in the seventeenth century with the organization of light and shadow—that leitmotif of the Baroque period—led them to focus on variations in tonality. A new invention, the dead coloring, as this monochrome sketch was often called at the time, was as crucial an innovation in the seventeenth century as tinted imprimatura had been in the sixteenth.[51] The name, although it meant the color of a corpse, must also have referred to the flat look, the matte surface, resulting from the absorption of the oil medium by the earth pigments. We need to distinguish between "tinted imprimatura" and "dead color." In contemporary sources "dead color" is used for both. We will continue to use "tinted imprimatura" for colored underpaint and limit "dead color" to the monochrome sketch.

Rubens has provided us with a rare example of dead coloring in his unfinished *Henry IV in the Battle of Paris* (fig. 3.19). He apparently had his assistants work up the battling figures in the upper right, then he outlined the soldiers in the foreground on the beige imprimatura. The white highlighting is easier to see in reproduction than the areas of gray and brown wash. Sketching like this was a rapid and economical way to envision and elaborate compositions, and it aided the painter in creating a number of optical effects that cannot be

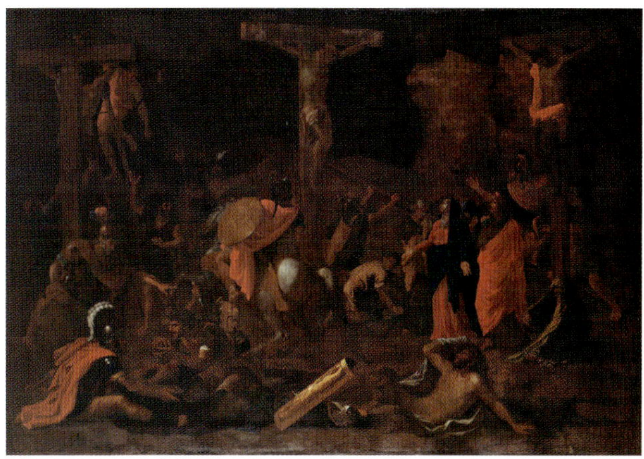

FIG. 3.18. Nicolas Poussin, *Crucifixion*, 1644–46. Oil on canvas, 58 1/2 × 86 in. (148.6 × 218.4 cm). Wadsworth Atheneum Museum of Art, Hartford, Conn.

achieved by direct painting with color.[52] In this procedure the painter was working out the tonal organization, the pattern of light and shadow. This sketch replaced the detailed underdrawing, such as we saw in Van Cleve (see fig. 3.9), or cartoons, such as we found in use in central Italy (see Raphael's *La Belle Jardinière* [fig. 2.4], *School of Athens* [fig. 2.6], and, with Giulio Romano, *Stoning of Saint Stephen* [fig. 2.12]). It incorporated not just modeling in the preparatory stage, as in underdrawing, but importantly, the disposition of light and shade across the composition.

The final painting could be as thick or as thin, as strictly adhering to the dead coloring or as revising,

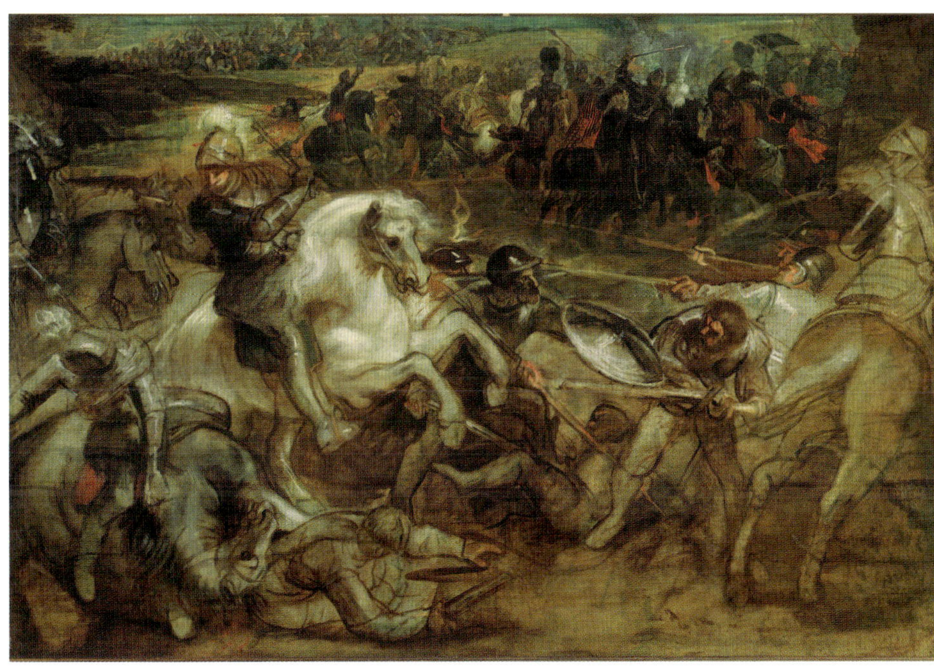

FIG. 3.19. Peter Paul Rubens, *Henry IV in the Battle of Paris*, 1624–26. Oil on canvas, 5 ft. 8 1/2 in. × 8 ft. 6 1/3 in. (174 × 260 cm). Rubenshuis, Antwerp.

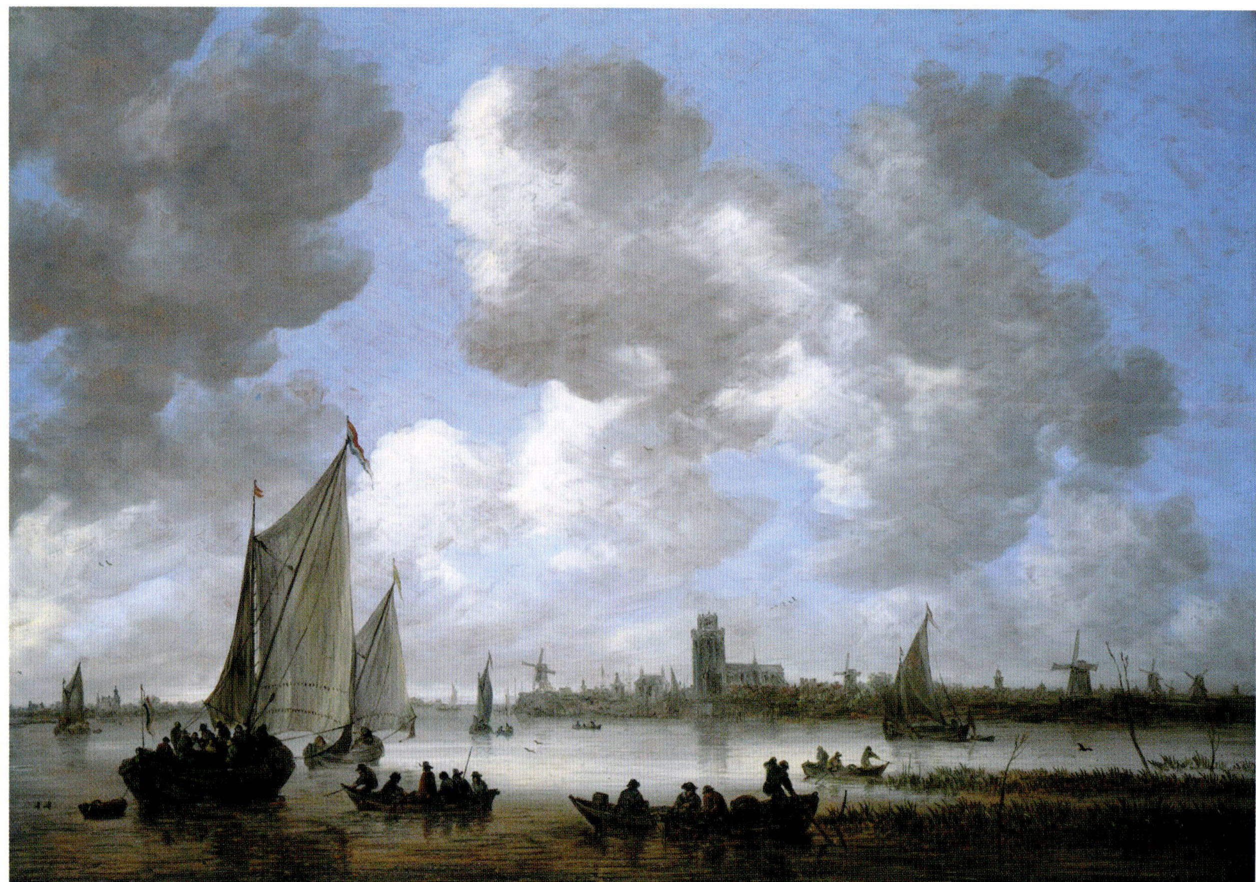

as the painter wished. The dead coloring allowed the painter to envision the final product as he worked and to adjust and revise as he went along. It sometimes merely mapped out areas in tone, but sometimes, at least for Rembrandt, it was "a provisionally completed whole," in Ernst van der Wetering's words.[53]

The dead color was a great aid in composing and executing complex compositions, but it was time-consuming, adding an extra stage to the preparation. Dutch landscapists, therefore, for whom efficiency was essential, often omitted the dead coloring stage. Van Goyen began by using it, then by the early 1630s, as he developed his direct manner of painting, he omitted it.[54] If he was working from a sketch he might not make a monochrome sketch (dead color), but put down a few pre-liminary notations in white chalk, then allow the warm brownish tone of the ground with which he prepared the panel to show through in many parts of his final painting (see fig. 3.13). As the darkest of the paints, it served as the shadow into which he swirled mid-tones and highlights wet-into-wet, completing paintings such as this in one

sitting. The grain of the oak panel might create ripples in the water.[55] In his later work, such as another view of Dordrecht dated 1651 (fig. 3.20), he sometimes used a deeper and more expensive smalt for his skies that could look very much like the ultramarine that Ruisdael was using, but the foreground was executed with the same rapid, sketchy strokes in almost monochrome tones of ochre and brown as his earlier works.

Underpaintings or monochrome sketches could be used as a record of a design and also to show to clients. Such must have been the case for those painters in Italy who stocked dead-colored paintings that could be dis-played to potential customers, to be worked up only if a buyer came along who wanted one.[56] For them it was a marketing strategy, creating a product between a ready-made and a commissioned work, which conserved both time and materials until the sale was contracted. There are few examples of dead coloring to be seen today, prob-ably because those that were left in a painter's studio or dealer's shop were finished by the lucky finder, who could sell them as originals.

Leonardo can be said to have invented the ancestor of dead coloring, visible in his unfinished *Adoration of the Magi* (see fig. 1.15). Andrea del Sarto is one of the few painters to have followed him in actually undermodeling. We can see in his unfinished *Sacrifice of Isaac* in Cleveland that the flesh of Isaac and the angel are not just primed in a light brown but modeled (fig. 3.21). What is surprising is to discover that the working up of the painting was far more systematic in the seventeenth century than in the sixteenth, at least in Holland. Sarto has left the donkey in the right middle ground entirely unpainted, but has nearly finished Abraham's drapery. The recommendation of the Dutch art theorist and painter Gerard de Lairesse to work from back to front no doubt reflects the workshop practice of at least some seventeenth-century artists: Rembrandt has been found to have worked very systematically from back to front, as did Van Goyen,[57] and there is evidence that Rubens did as well.[58] Although there are certain similarities in the procedures of painters working in Holland, Flanders, Italy, and France, there are also important differences that we will be discussing.

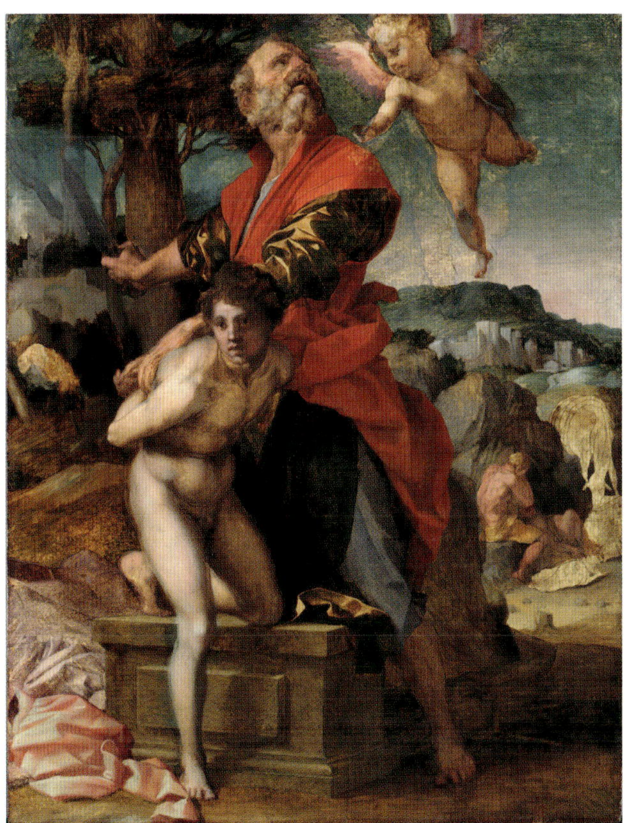

FIG. 3.21. Andrea del Sarto, *Sacrifice of Isaac*, c. 1527. Oil on panel, 81⅞ × 67⅝₁₆ in. (208 × 171 cm). Cleveland Museum of Art.

HOUDING, AERIAL PERSPECTIVE

A major concern of the seventeenth-century painter was to create the illusion of recession and the separation of the things in the picture, for which various devices were invented. We discussed reddering for creating the illusion of space in Van Goyen's landscape and de Hooch's interior. The Dutch had another word for their way of separating but unifying things in a painting, "houding." It is an elusive concept, related to, but distinct from, aerial perspective, sometimes elided by the theorist with reddering.[59] One should have the sense of being able to walk through the space in the picture, they said. One Dutch theorist explains that if houding is lacking, then "things appear entangled in one another, packed together, or falling towards us in a tumble."[60]

This is an important concept because it points to what they were trying to achieve, the opposite of the painters of the maniera, such as Pontormo or Rosso, who compressed space and filled the picture surface with ornamental forms (see figs. 2.16–19). In fact no one in the Renaissance was as interested in the continuous recession from foreground to horizon as seventeenth-century painters were. Vasari makes this clear when he talks about perspective as an "adornment."[61] Renaissance painters were focused on the figures, which they arranged with great attention to their poses and their interactions, but the background, either landscape or architecture, was an afterthought. That Raphael conceived the figural composition of *The School of Athens* separately from its grand antique architectural setting is evident from his cartoon, which shows only the figures (see fig. 2.6). Even in Venetian painting, figures are placed more in front of the field or background than in it.

The painters of the smooth or "fine style," such as Gerard Dou and the young Rembrandt, had perfected numerous painterly tricks to represent reality convincingly, in particular, control of gradation of color, as in Rembrandt's *Judas Returning the Silver* (see fig. 3.1). Poussin, as we shall see, was a master of aerial perspective, the system of manipulating tone to simulate the influence of the atmosphere on the visibility of the object receding into the distance, but houding, especially for Rembrandt, involved more.

Together with light and shade, color and texture, surface played an important role in producing houding. Rembrandt would have been aware of Vasari's description of Titian's late style, his *pittura di macchie*, or blobs,

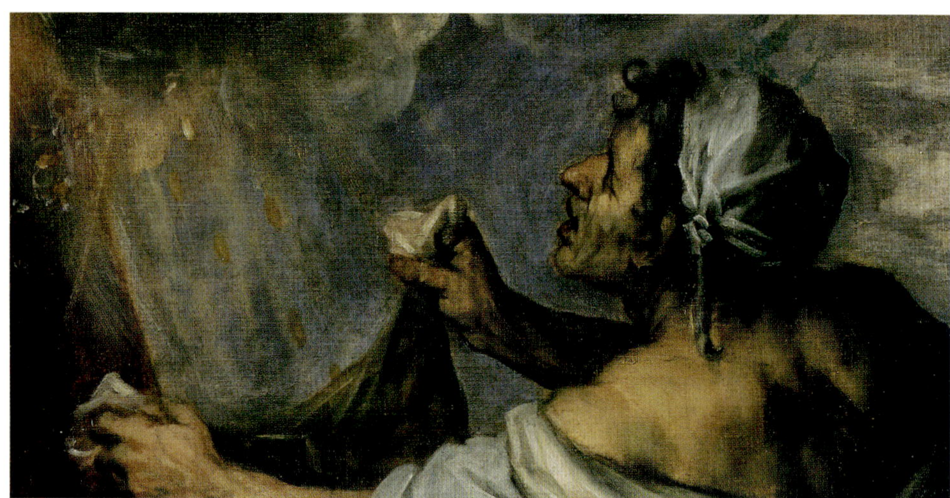

FIG. 3.22. Titian, *Danaë and the Shower of Gold* (detail; see fig 2.29).

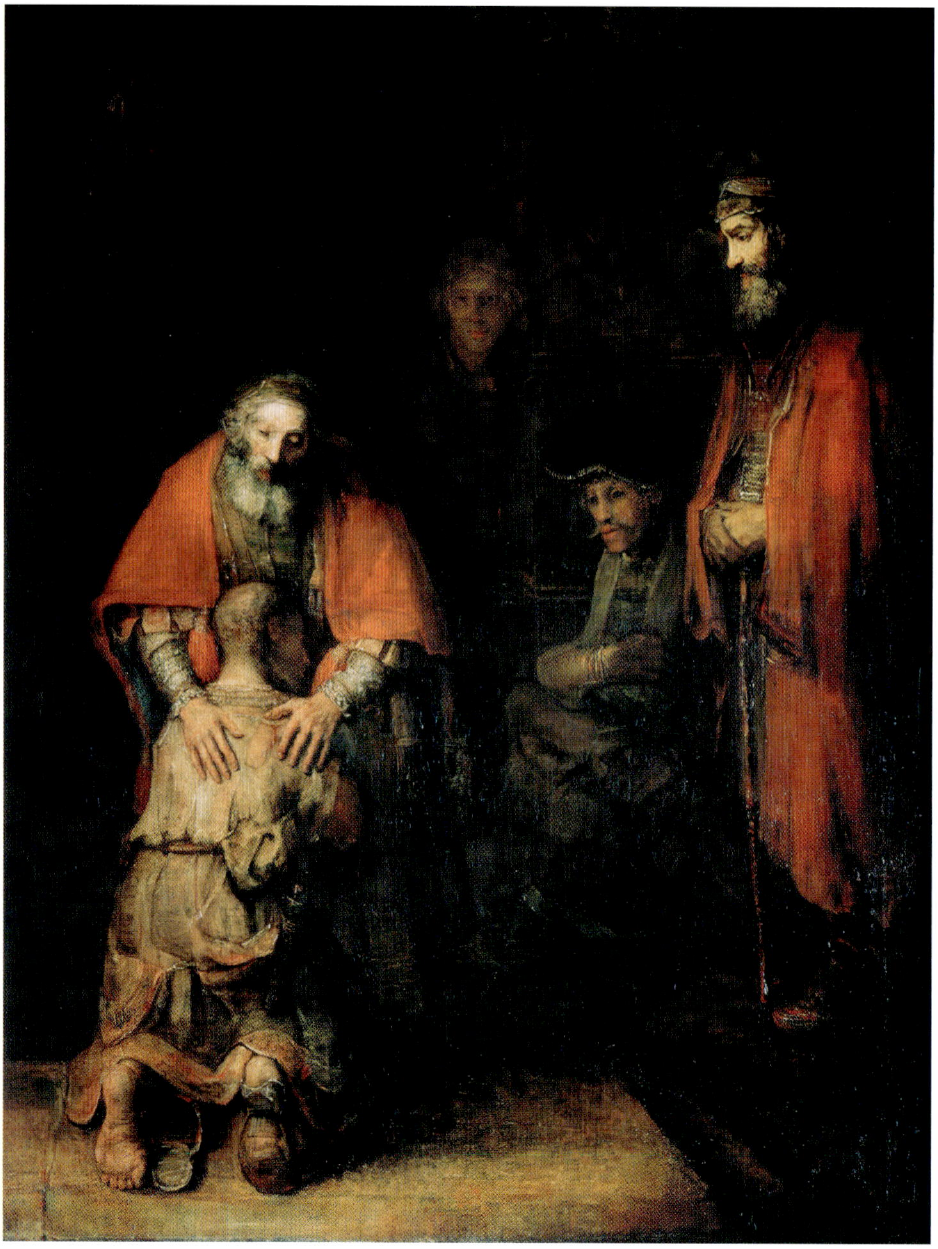

FIG. 3.23. Rembrandt, *Return of the Prodigal Son*, c. 1668. Oil on canvas, 8 ft. 7 1/8 in. × 6 ft. 8 3/4 in. (262 × 205 cm). Hermitage, Saint Petersburg.

which was quoted almost word for word in 1604 by Karel van Mander. Recall the open brushwork of his second *Danaë* (fig. 3.22; see fig. 2.29). Vasari had emphasized that Titian's pictures "cannot be looked at from close quarters, but from a distance they appear perfect." It was said that Rembrandt did not want his pictures viewed up close and would tug viewers away, saying, "The smell will bother you." Vasari also warned young painters not to try to paint this way until late in life, advice that Rembrandt followed. Like Titian, Rembrandt did not prepare with preliminary drawings but worked directly on the canvas, making corrections as he went along. It was understood in Rembrandt's circle—quite possibly the discovery originated with him—that a rough texture makes things appear close, and smooth surfaces recede.[62]

The "rough style" that he adopted in his maturity, and refused to abandon despite the turn of fashion against it, enabled him to create houding, a convincing sense of space, with the texture of his paint. He used thick impasto, such as we see in the *Return of the Prodigal Son,* where the paint seems sometimes to be applied with the palette knife (fig. 3.23). Bright red pushes the father forward and draws us to him, but the thick paint on his sleeves presses him on our attention. The older brother at the right echoes his red in a more subdued tone, towering over his bent father, his hands folded, unwelcoming. This vigorous brushstroke is at odds with the quiet stillness of that long, compassionate embrace that is the center of the scene (fig. 3.24). It is only with this application of the paint that the artist conveys the tumultuous and profound feeling. There is no movement. We see only the back of the kneeling son. The father's face is serene, his eyes half closed and unfocused, yet in the gesture of those hands drawing his son into him, the story of forgiveness is told, a forgiveness that for Rembrandt channeled the forgiveness of the Lord for frail and erring humanity.

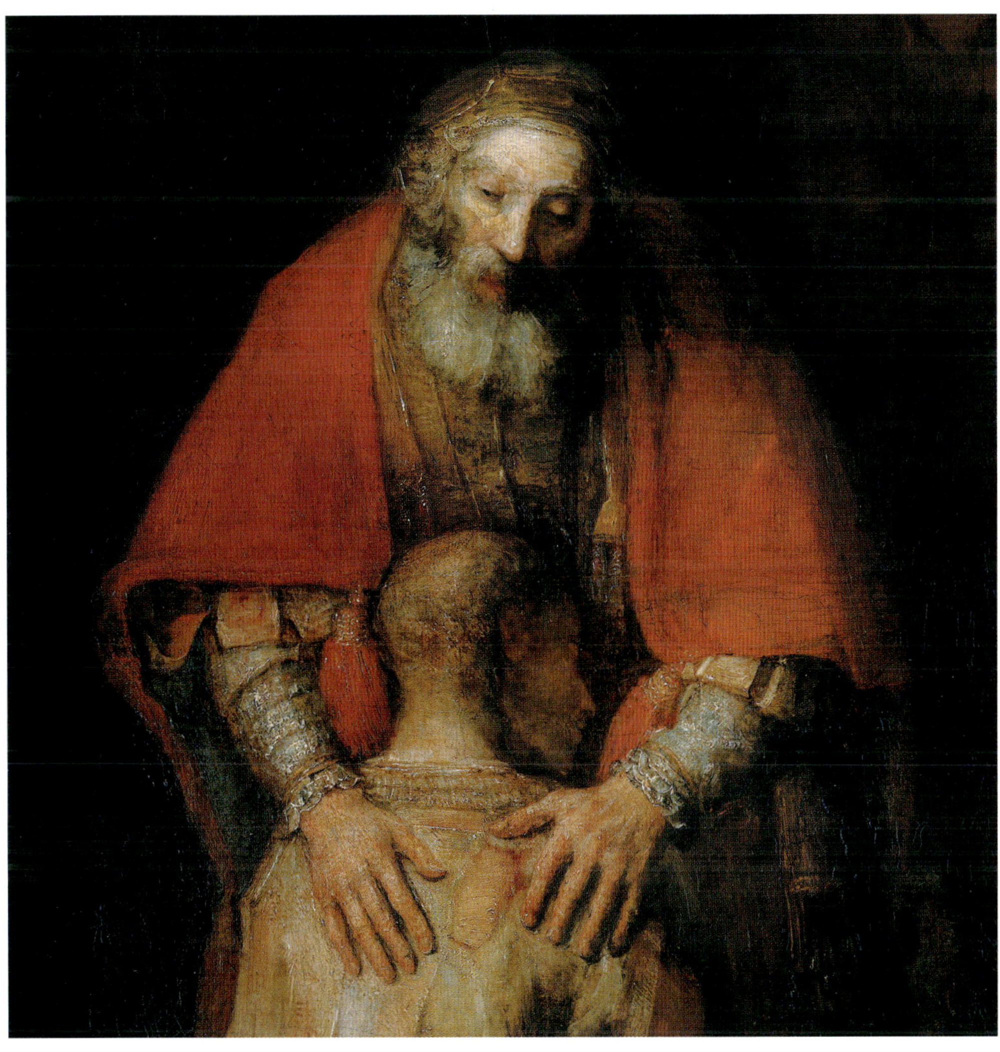

FIG. 3.24. Rembrandt, *Return of the Prodigal Son* (detail; see fig. 3.23).

Rembrandt used a limited palette, concentrated in browns and gold tones. He painted typically with mixtures of two to four pigments.[63] We have seen that Renaissance painters preferred to keep their colors pure and unmixed, creating novel and subtle effects by layering or glazing one pigment over another. In fact we moderns have become so accustomed to mixing we forget what a novelty it was when it first appeared.

The medieval prejudice against corrupting color only finally broke down in the seventeenth century, and then it resulted from the pursuit of naturalistic effects of light and atmosphere. When landscape entered the repertoire as a genre, painters needed to imitate flickering light. Small brushstrokes of indeterminate color could replicate nuanced conditions of weather far better than large fields of color glazed over with a contrasting tone, which works well when modeling drapery. Painters preferred to mix pigments, producing a "broken," or tertiary, color.

The concept of broken color enters the workshop vernacular at this time, and we have seen that it was discussed and defined later in the Académie Royale, particularly in relation to Veronese. "Corrupt" derives from the Latin root meaning "to break"—*"rumpere"*—which suggests the origin of the term in English and in French (couleur rompue). As is often the case, the treatises lagged behind practice: the concept of breaking color appeared in Holland only in the second half of the century.[64] In 1675 Joachim von Sandrart recommended that painters use broken or lighter colors for the distance, so that they would be less distinguishable, and "whole" colors up closer—in other words, to create aerial perspective. He regarded unbroken color as unpleasant, harsh, and piercing. Broken color was essential for houding because patches of pure color cannot properly recede.[65]

Certainly the intention of Dutch landscapists such as Van Goyen, who were striving to portray the countryside in particular conditions of weather and light, was to "break" the pigments and to create tones that matched what they observed in nature. Rembrandt too was searching for gradations to depict recession or shifts in the source of light. The dead coloring, or brownish underpaint, also served to produce a degradation of chromatic values.

POUSSIN

Anthony Blunt remarked that "Few artists of Poussin's importance had so little natural talent or such unsatisfactory training."[66] During Poussin's long residence in Rome—interrupted for only a two-year sojourn back in Paris (1640–42)—he had ample opportunity to study classical antique sculpture and the masters of Renaissance art, and this was his principal training. He had spent about a decade in Paris before his departure for Rome in 1624 by way of Venice. Titian was Poussin's model in his early Italian career, but by about 1633 he had discovered that Raphael's adaptation of classical antiquity better suited his purpose. The commissions and subjects that were available to him as a foreigner were not the lucrative altarpieces for Roman churches but were mythological pictures for learned private patrons. For them he chose themes of love especially, often selected from Ovid's *Metamorphoses.* Blunt argued convincingly that syncretism and comparative religion were subjects of great interest in Poussin's Roman circle, and that Poussin intended his mythological paintings to convey symbolic meanings to suit that interest. The themes he selected of metamorphosis never treat the transformation of a human into an animal or an insect (such as Circe or Arachne) but always into plants or flowers, allegorizing death and regeneration.[67]

The painter had access to and was much taken with Titian's "Este Bacchanals," which were then in the Aldobrandini collection in Rome. He even made a copy, which still exists, of the *Feast of the Gods,* originally painted by Giovanni Bellini but then modernized by Titian, and motifs from the other bacchanals can be found in his mythological paintings.[68] For instance, the sleeping nymph in *Midas and Bacchus* (fig. 3.25) is borrowed from Titian's *Bacchanal of the Andrians* (see fig. 2.28). Poussin has adopted Titian's open and closed background and his rich but muted coloring and gendered flesh tones. But even with Ovid as his source and Titian as his model, Poussin's figures are not alluring and sensuous, but refined and abstracted so as to allude to allegorical meaning. For this purpose the idealizing style of Raphael was a better model.

Poussin revived the Cinquecento practice associated particularly with Tintoretto, but used also by Barocci and the Carracci, of arranging figurines on a stage in a box.[69] The wax or clay figures, about four and three-quarter inches tall, could be dressed in fabric to allow the study

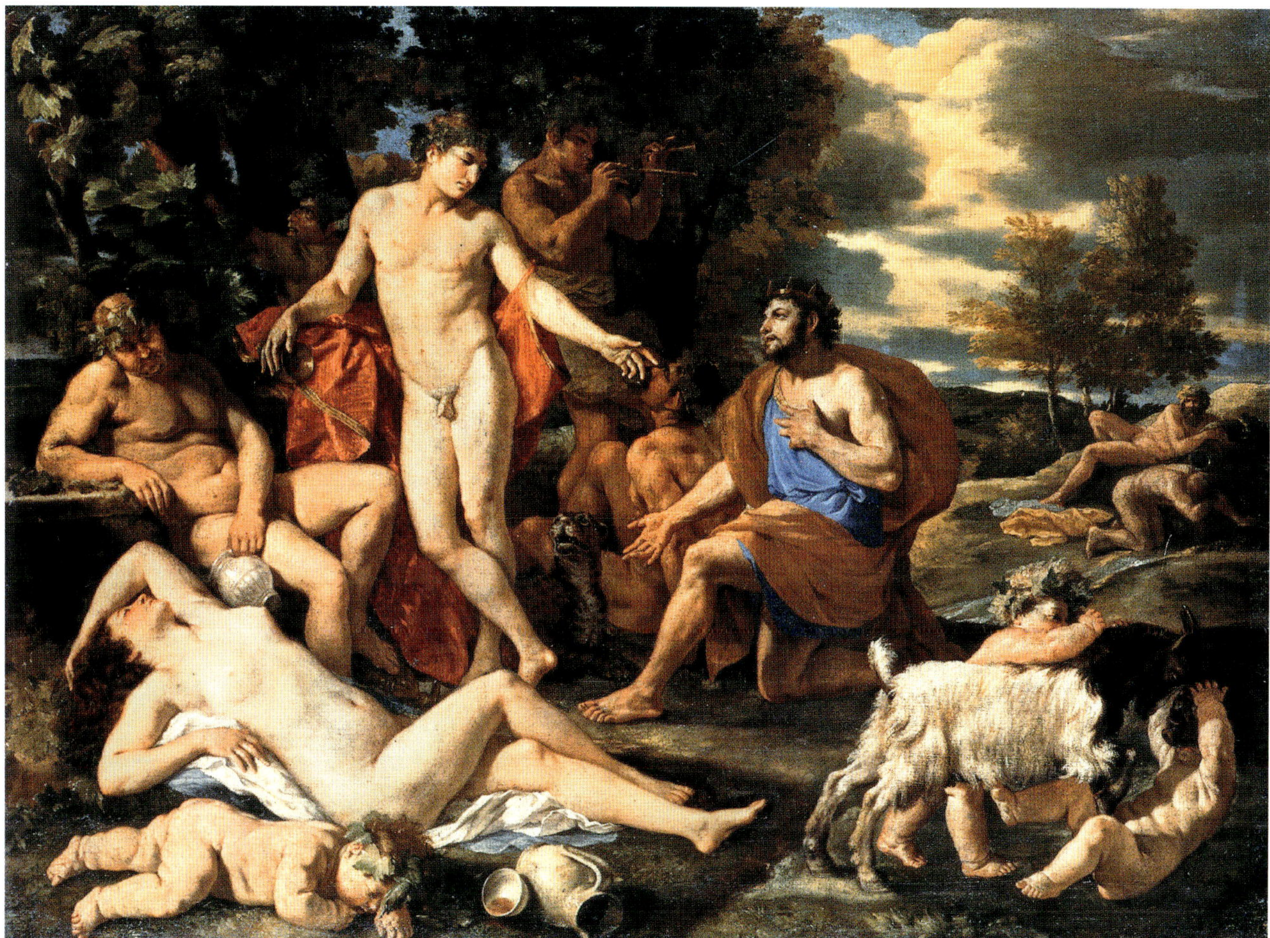

FIG. 3.25. Nicolas Poussin, *Midas and Bacchus,* 1629–30. Oil on canvas, 38 ¾ × 60 ⅕ in. (98 × 153 cm). Alte Pinakothek, Munich.

of drapery folds. The artist then manipulated the light until he found the effect he wanted.[70] Tintoretto would make only rapid sketches of single figures to enlarge and then transfer to the canvas. He would then paint quickly and thinly to preserve a look of spontaneity. Poussin, for whom "spontaneous" was not a part of his mental vocabulary, studied his compositions in multiple preparatory drawings, honing and perfecting. In drawings for the *Holy Family on the Steps* we see him adding and substituting figures, playing with the architecture and the setting, the arrangement of the still life on the steps, and the low viewpoint, all essential to the majesty of the final painting (fig. 3.26). The lighting, studied in surviving and lost pen-and-wash drawings, was calculated to convey the symbolic hierarchy. Only the Virgin and Child face fully into it; John as the mediator between the Old and New Testaments is strongly illuminated but turns into the shadow. Elizabeth and even more so Joseph, as personages of the pre-Christian era, are deeply shadowed.[71]

What houding was to the Dutch painters, aerial perspective was to Poussin. Although he was not interested in the kind of tonal modeling that could be achieved with dead coloring, he was interested in the power of light to create the illusion of space, and for this he drew his inspiration from the Italian tradition of perspective. Lighting in conjunction with perspective creates the space of Poussin's pictures. He utilized both central-point and aerial perspectives. In the *Holy Family on the Steps* a reverentially low viewpoint replaces the Renaissance throne or supernatural elevation. Each element of the architecture is projected to a vanishing point just to the left of the Virgin's feet, a point that was actually indented in the paint film.[72] The regal Virgin holds her son up as if to present him to the world, and he reaches out both to receive the fruit offered by the infant Baptist and in blessing. The figures are seated on a staircase that continues to rise behind them. The perspective of these steps was laboriously worked out in central-point perspective, with the viewer's eye level at the step where we see Elizabeth and Mary's feet.[73]

The view from below obviates the need for a landscape receding toward the horizon, which is usually seen in paintings of Poussin's mature period. For these he practiced aerial perspective, so named by Leonardo to describe the way objects in the distance change in their appearance. Leonardo's writings were newly elaborated in the early Seicento by Matteo Zaccolini, who translated and interpreted Leonardo's treatise in his own four-volume treatise on color and perspective (1618–22). According to Giovanni Bellori, Zaccolini was a friend of Poussin's patron Cassiano dal Pozzo, who acquired the treatise for the Barberini Library.[74] Zaccolini showed that colors diminish in a systematic way toward a bluish tone at the horizon. He created a color scale, based on Leonardo's, and diagrammed at what relative distance each hue appears bluish. Shadowed parts of colored objects seem to appear bluish before illuminated parts.[75] His system was far more nuanced than the three-zone

system practiced by Flemish landscapists such as Savery (see fig. 3.12). Because it was now understood that each hue transmutes at a different rate and shadows alter before illuminated areas, the abrupt shifts of the zoned system were avoided. Poussin adapted these ideas from Zaccolini, together with study of the projection of shadows, and applied them, creating a system that was copied by his French peers and became part of the official art of the Académie Royale, which endured well into the nineteenth century.

His Parisian patron Jean Pointel is said to have requested a painting of "several women, in which you can see different beauties" in 1648. Poussin decided on the Old Testament subject of Eliezer and Rebecca at the well, the story in which Abraham sends his servant, Eliezer, to Mesopotamia to find a wife for his son, Isaac (fig. 3.27). He finds Rebecca—"who was very pleasing to look at," as we are told in Genesis 29:18—with other women drawing water. She gives him water for himself and his camels, and Eliezer takes this to be a sign from Yahweh and gives

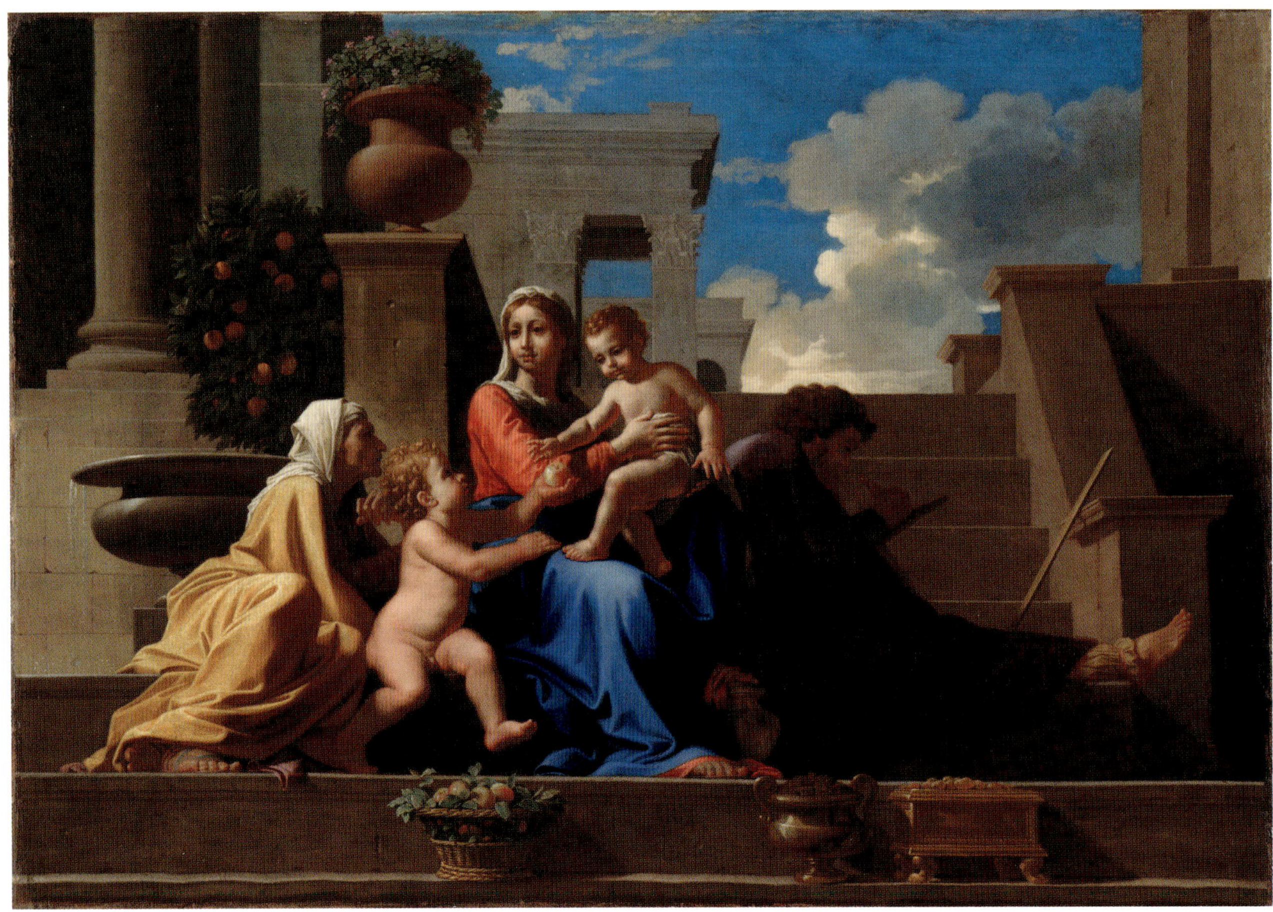

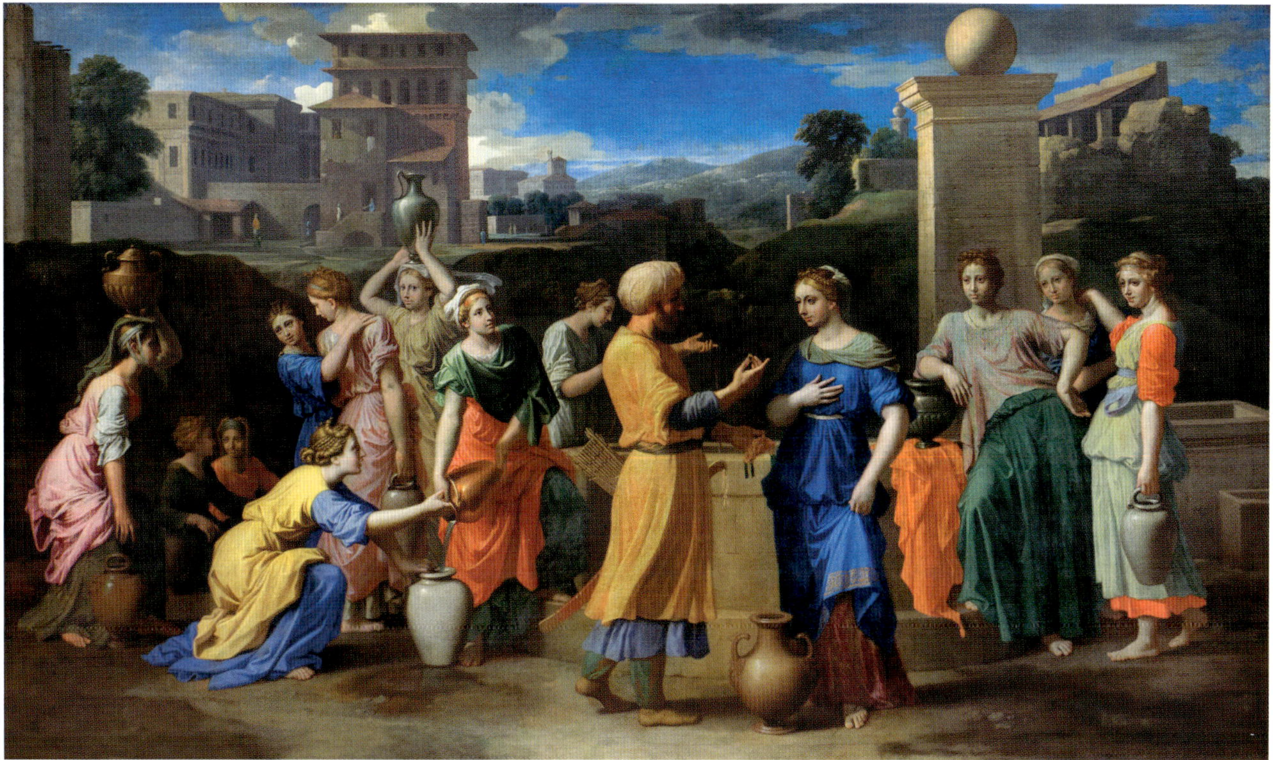

FIG. 3.27. Nicolas Poussin, *Eliezer and Rebecca at the Well*, 1648. Oil on canvas, 46 1/2 × 78 1/3 in. (118 × 199 cm). Louvre, Paris.

her the bracelets and gold ring with which Abraham entrusted him. Poussin's composition is calculated with mathematical precision. He places Eliezer in the exact center on the vertical axis, and his hand offering the ring is on the horizontal axis. We are intended to be reminded of the composition of the Annunciation, the New Testament counterpart to this divine election. Rounded jugs repeat across the picture, establishing its rhythm and echoing the feminine curves of the maidens. The coloring is equally calculated, but subtle and complex in its balance. The principals are given the largest fields of pure color: Eliezer as the only man is unique in his orangey gold, while Rebecca's ultramarine blue is echoed in smaller and paler fields on the draperies of two of her companions. The protagonists are framed with two strong reds, which are prevented from becoming too prominent by moving into shadow. The surrounding figures are swathed in more muted tones, but they retain enough strength to be attractive—some even in cangiantismo—to answer the patron's request for beautiful women.

Poussin usually set his scenes against deeply and continuously receding space, usually landscapes. Here, for example, there is a convincing recession from foreground to the horizon, unlike most Renaissance pictures where we see an abrupt shift from frontal stage to background, with the middle ground absent. Note, for example, how small the figures are in the distance of Raphael's *Madonna di Foligno* (fig. 3.28). Poussin has absorbed Zaccolini's instructions on how to reduce the intensity of color, sharpness of forms, and gradual shift of distant tones toward blue.[76] Note the muted tones and softened contours of the women in the second tier, especially the one with the urn on her head.

Poussin increasingly adopted Raphael's planar and symmetrical organization of space, emulating antique relief, introducing a solemnity that indicates the loftiness of meaning. He abjured Titian's jubilant playfulness and spontaneity along with his oblique lines of recession and the open/closed composition that he had previously preferred. The solemn, almost ritualized compositions he invents along Raphaelesque lines have a gravity in keeping with their veiled content. Poussin found a manner— divergent from those of his "Baroque" contemporaries such as Bernini or Il Guercino or Rubens—that, while expressing the emotions of the actors, avoided soliciting the emotions of the viewers and appealed instead to their intellect. In the 1630s and 1640s he moved his coloring

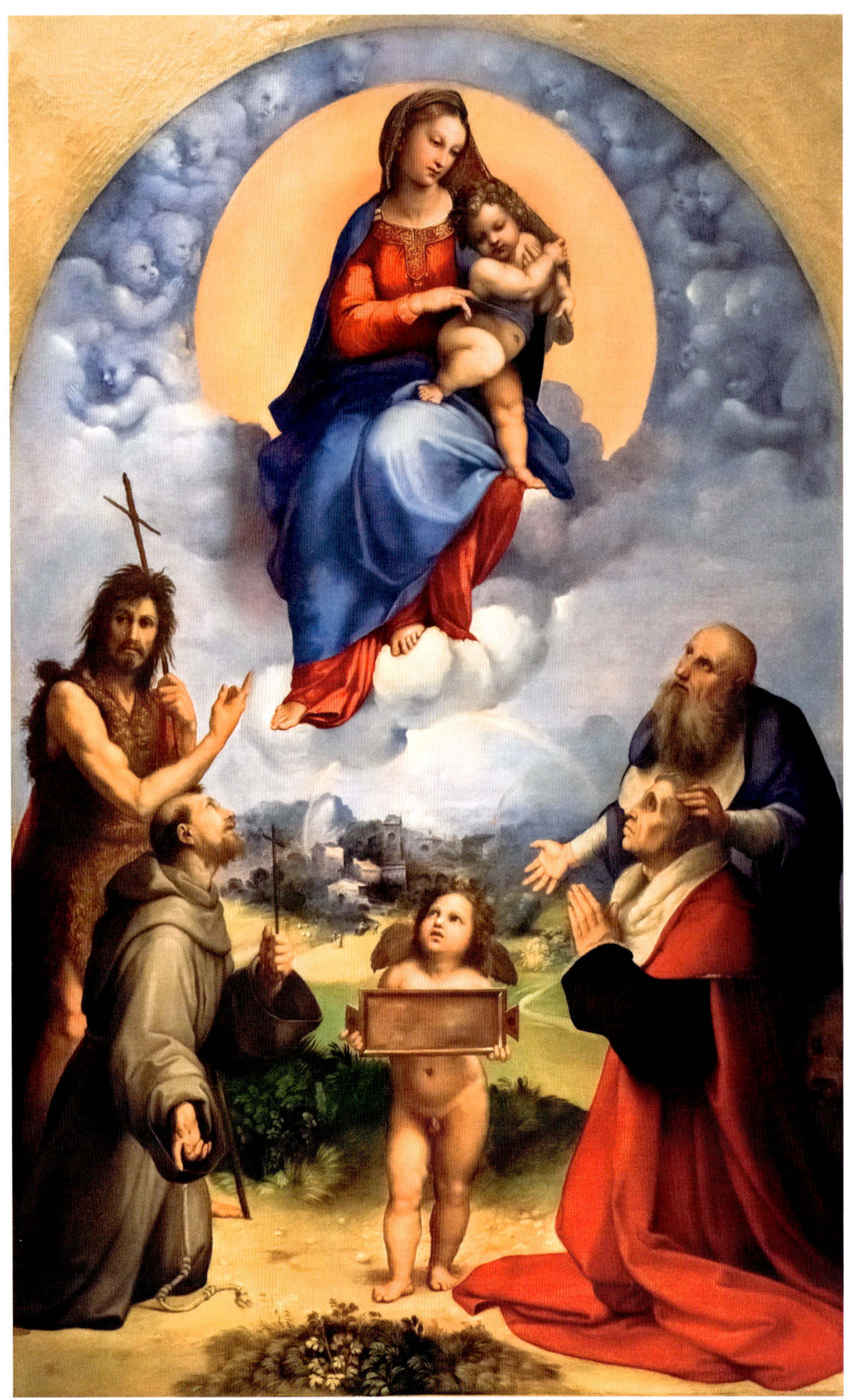

FIG. 3.28. Raphael, *Madonna di Foligno* (detail), 1511–12. Oil on panel
transferred to canvas. Musei Vaticani, Rome.

away from luscious toward ratiocinated, just as his lighting developed from dramatizing to clarifying. He chose his colors with deliberation to reinforce the planarity and symmetry of his composition. In contrast to contemporary practice, he preferred pure, brilliant colors unmixed and not covered with translucent glazes.[77] Working in the manner of Raphael and making use of a smooth and polished surface, he avoided the textured brushstroke that Titian had invented and that many of his contemporaries imitated. The color scheme of the *Holy Family* is severely restricted to the primaries. It is focused on the Virgin: brilliant ultramarine and vermilion with a touch of white in her veil. Elizabeth's gold completes the primary triad, and Joseph's purplish robe all but disappears in the shadow. Ultramarine appears again in the sky with white clouds that reinforce the flesh tones of the children. All other colors are akin to the brownish tonality of the architecture.

Poussin did not use dead coloring, apparently, but he underpainted his flesh tones selectively, using a light gray under highlighted areas and a darker gray under shadowed areas. In order to convey differences in age and gender he varied the gray—for example, using a greenish gray under the shadows of Mary's hands and a dark brown gray under the shadows of Elizabeth's face. By varying the thickness of the upper layers he could make as much use of underlying layers as he needed.[78]

He was a deliberate and prudent painter. He did not search for the composition on the canvas, and he did not paint by inspiration. For architecture he incised lines in the wet paint. He reflected long on the disposition and placement of figures in his compositions. He wrote to a client in 1647: "I have found the conception of the idea. . . . The subject is the Passage of the Israelites through the Red Sea. The composition will comprise twenty-seven figures."[79]

RUBENS

Rubens's approach was very different, but it was as appropriate to his desired effect as Poussin's was to his. Rubens, as a Flemish Catholic, worked in a state ruled by a royal court. His patrons were quite different from his Protestant republican contemporaries in the Northern Netherlands and from Poussin working as a Frenchman in Rome. The aristocratic friends of Rubens's parents welcomed him into their circle, even if being a painter was not a high station. Like Poussin, but unlike

Rembrandt, he traveled extensively in Italy, and also to Spain. As a diplomat he was sent to Paris in 1622 and to Madrid in 1628–29. Even before his departure from Antwerp in 1600, for what turned out to be an eight-year sojourn in Italy, he was introduced to the Archdukes Albert and Isabella, rulers of the Spanish Netherlands, who provided him with letters of introduction.

He stayed first in Venice, where he absorbed the lessons of Titian, Tintoretto, and Veronese, which would influence him deeply as he formed his own style. The duke of Mantua, Vincenzo Gonzaga, was charmed by the debonair Rubens, employed him to paint family portraits and altarpieces, and sent him on a diplomatic mission carrying gifts to the court of Philip III of Spain. There, Rubens studied the extensive collection of Raphaels and Titians, and upon his return to Italy he visited Rome and Florence as well. He was working in Genoa in 1608 when he learned that his mother was ill. He returned home, but she had died by the time he reached Antwerp. He established himself there and married Isabella Brandt, the daughter of an important municipal official, and within a few months he was nominated to the post of court painter to the archdukes in Brussels.

Rubens brought back with him much that he had learned in Italy. For the rest of his career he would make oil sketches to prepare his paintings and to show the client what the finished work would look like. He must have learned this procedure in Italy, perhaps from Federico Barocci, for Rubens's oil sketch still survives for his altarpiece for the Chiesa Nuova in Rome, where Barocci had also contributed two altarpieces.[80] Soon after Rubens's return, the mayor of Antwerp, Nicolaas Rockox, commissioned him to make the *Samson and Delilah* now in London (fig. 3.29).[81] His second and more finished oil sketch is about twenty inches square and closely resembled the final version, and although the background is only sketchily painted, it was more than sufficient to convey the idea to the patron. A very rough preliminary sketch also exists, where Rubens was working up his idea (figs. 3.30, 3.31). By the time of the later sketch he had opted for a more poignant, quiescent sleeping Samson in place of the violent giant of the first sketch. On one known occasion Rubens made alternative designs in the form of oil sketches between which the patron might choose.[82] As he became busier he would turn over sketches like this to be executed by his workshop.

That he used oil sketches instead of chalk or pen

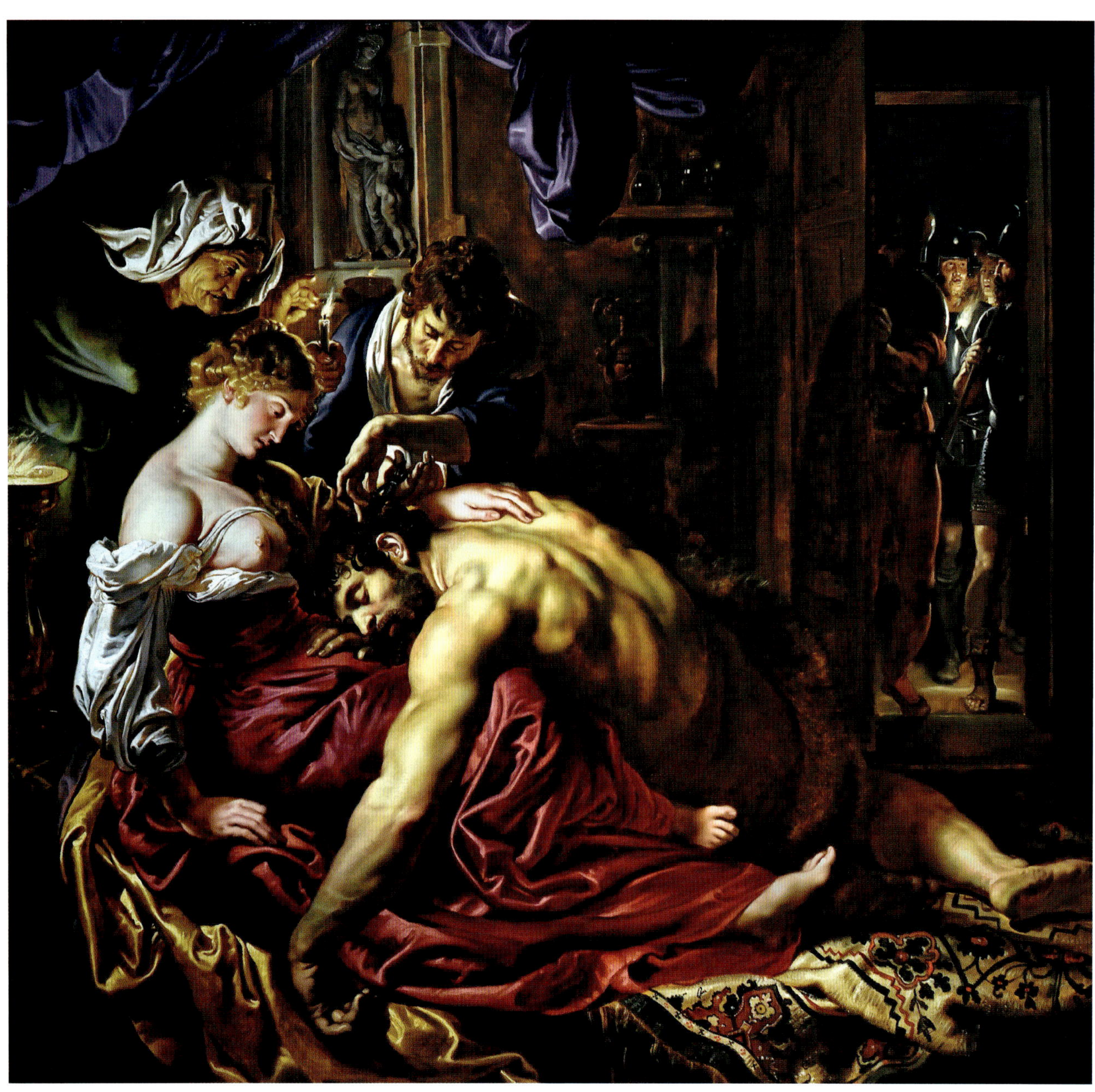

FIG. 3.29. Peter Paul Rubens, *Samson and Delilah*, c. 1609–10. Oil on panel,
72 ⅘ × 80 ¾ in. (185 × 205 cm). National Gallery, London.

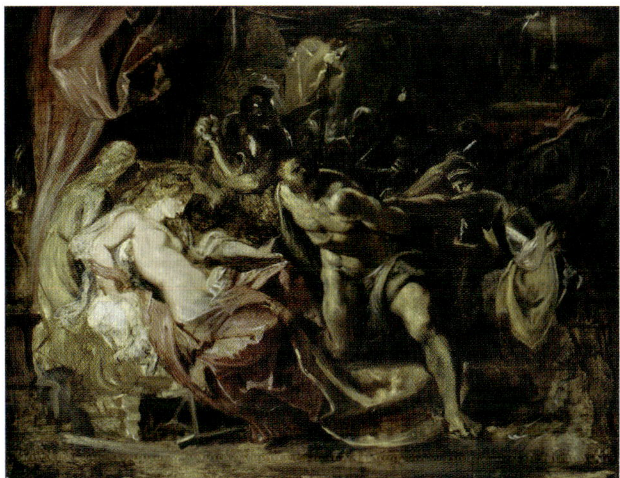

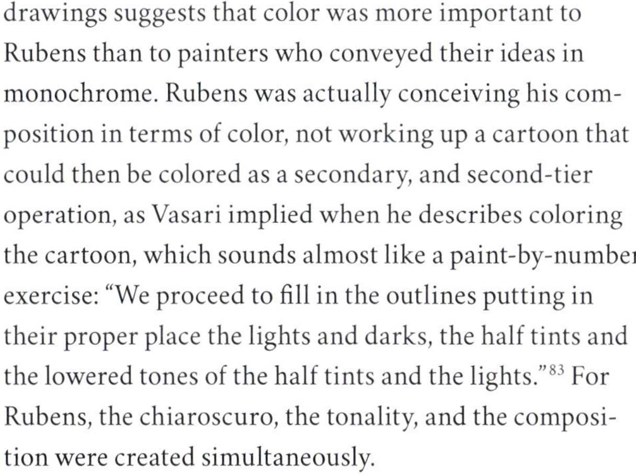

FIG. 3.30. Peter Paul Rubens, *Samson and Delilah* (sketch), 1609–10. Oil on panel, 19¾ × 26⅛ in. (50.4 × 66.4 cm). Art Institute of Chicago.

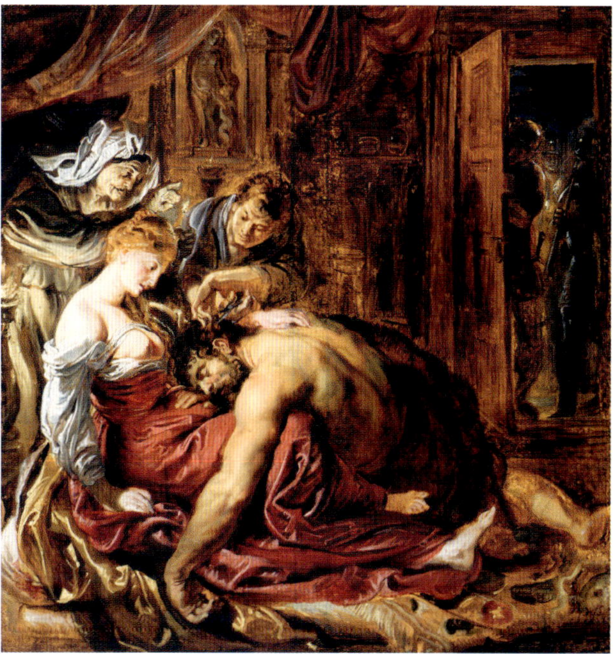

FIG. 3.31. Peter Paul Rubens, *Samson and Delilah* (sketch), c. 1609. Oil on panel, 19⅞ × 20½ in. (50.5 × 52.1 cm). Cincinnati Art Museum.

drawings suggests that color was more important to Rubens than to painters who conveyed their ideas in monochrome. Rubens was actually conceiving his composition in terms of color, not working up a cartoon that could then be colored as a secondary, and second-tier operation, as Vasari implied when he describes coloring the cartoon, which sounds almost like a paint-by-number exercise: "We proceed to fill in the outlines putting in their proper place the lights and darks, the half tints and the lowered tones of the half tints and the lights."[83] For Rubens, the chiaroscuro, the tonality, and the composition were created simultaneously.

Also from Italy, Rubens brought Caravaggesque chiaroscuro. He had been so impressed with the painter that when the altarpiece the *Death of the Virgin* was rejected by the church for which it was commissioned, Santa Maria della Scala in Rome, he steered his patron, Vincenzo Gonzaga, to acquire it for his spectacular collection in Mantua, and he himself made a copy of it. In *Samson and Delilah,* interior light sources of the kind Caravaggio introduced create strong contrasts of light and shade. An oil lamp at the left lights Delilah's and Samson's upper bodies, the maid holds a candle to guide the barber, and the soldiers who hover at the door are ominously illuminated by the torch one of them holds. These kinds of startling effects that Caravaggio invented

were widely imitated in the following decade all over Europe. As successful as Rubens is at painting in this mode, he would soon abandon it for what would become his signature sunny atmosphere.

Preliminary to the oil sketch, Rubens, who was a master draftsman and loved to draw, sometimes worked out his composition and lighting in drawings. He would then transfer the drawing to the small panel for the oil sketch, using a brush and a translucent red brown. The colors were indicated with cheaper versions of the pigments to be used in the final painting, as here, for example, red earths were substituted for the crimson lakes and vermilion of Delilah's satiny robe. Like his Dutch contemporaries, Rubens worked from back to front, leaving space reserved for the figures.[84]

The oil sketch was particularly useful to Rubens for his large-scale projects, where he would use his well-trained workshop to execute his designs and then he would retouch as needed. For his tapestry projects such as the *Life of Constantine,* the oil sketch served as their model for cartoons on paper, which were delivered to the weavers.[85] The public must have developed respect for these sketches very quickly, and the works must have become collectors' items within a decade; in 1620, when the Jesuit fathers in Antwerp commissioned him to paint the ceiling of their new church with thirty-nine panels

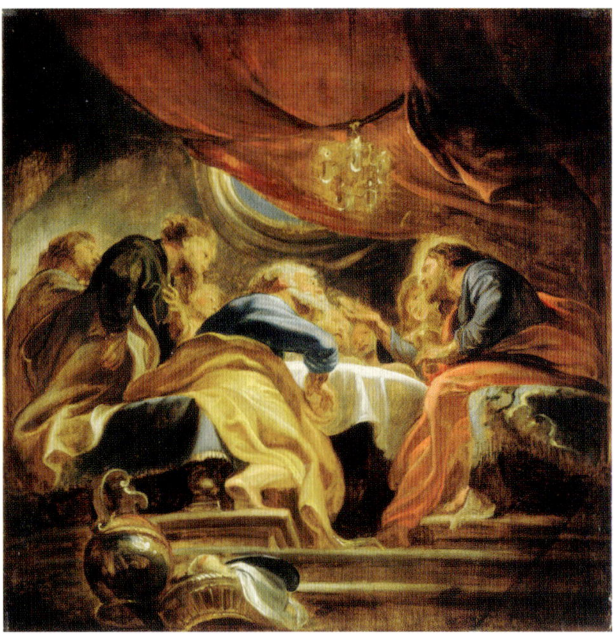

FIG. 3.32. Peter Paul Rubens, *Last Supper* (sketch), 1620–21. Oil on panel, 17¼ × 17⅜ in. (43.8 × 44.1 cm). Seattle Art Museum.

(destroyed by fire in 1718), the contract required that he was to make the oil sketches, but that the panels could be executed by his workshop. Most interesting is the offer they made: either the Jesuits would keep the sketches or, if Rubens wanted them, he would paint an additional altarpiece for one of the side chapels. Rubens evidently treasured his sketches as a resource on which he could draw in the future, so he opted to make the altarpiece. The *Last Supper,* seen from below like many of these compositions, looks up to an oculus, which is the source of illumination (fig. 3.32). The steeply foreshortened figures did not need to be drawn in careful detail, and they were colored in cheaper pigments than the vermilion, crimson lake, and ultramarine blue that were probably used in the final paintings.[86]

By 1621 Rubens was in great demand. He was given the most prestigious commission he would ever receive from the queen of France, Marie de' Medici, to make twenty-four canvases celebrating her life to decorate the gallery at her Luxembourg Palace. For this huge undertaking he was paid 20,00 crowns. Only Rubens would have been able to manage it, and he did it with astonishing speed. As he said of himself in seeking another large and prestigious commission: "I confess that I am, by natural instinct, better fitted to execute very large works than small curiosities. . . . My talent is such that no undertaking, however vast in size or diversified in subject, has ever

surpassed my courage."[87] The first nine pieces were ready to be taken to Paris in May of 1623, only fifteen months after the contract had been signed.

The contract specified that Rubens was to paint all the figures himself, and that the queen reserved the right to have figures that did not please her retouched or altered after delivery of the paintings. This left Rubens free to have everything except the principal figures executed by his workshop, from oil sketches of the kind worked out for the *Samson and Delilah* and the Jesuit church ceiling. The sketch for the *Arrival in Marseilles* shows that he worked out the entire composition, to which only minor changes such as the orientation of the bridge of the ship were later made (fig 3.33). The subject, like most in the series, has little intrinsic drama or action, but with his characteristic ingenuity, Rubens fills the foreground with sea creatures, in particular three succulent mermaids who flash their voluptuous flesh, rejoicing over the arrival of the queen on French soil (fig. 3.34). Their exuberance is so over the top that it makes us smile, adding a light note. The hyperbole introduced throughout the cycle of the sometimes mundane events saves it from pomposity. One suspects that Rubens reached back to his Italian experience and recalled Giulio Romano's work in the Gonzaga's Palazzo Te in Mantua (see fig. 2.27) and perhaps Perino del Vaga's decorations of the life of Pope Paul III in the Castel Sant'Angelo, where similar deflating humor was used (see figs. 2.20, 2.21).

For large commissions he certainly used the procedure of supplying the design to his workshop for execution—perhaps augmented with detailed drawing— and then retouching with his own hand. There were times, however, when he chose to paint himself, as in the *Judgment of Paris* in London (fig. 3.35). We can see how greatly he enjoyed engaging with both its sensuous display and the subtle psychology of the actors. The great goddesses of Olympus display their charms to the bewildered mortal, Paris. The victor, Venus, points diffidently to herself; Juno bristles in offense. No oil sketch survives and multiple pentimenti reveal that he had not worked out the composition fully before he began to paint. One can see with the naked eye the putto between Venus and Juno that he painted out, for instance, and numerous adjustments can be observed in the x-ray (fig. 3.36).[88]

Rubens here displays the full powers of his brush and his imagination. A filmy haze washes over the landscape; turbulent clouds and shivering trees express the

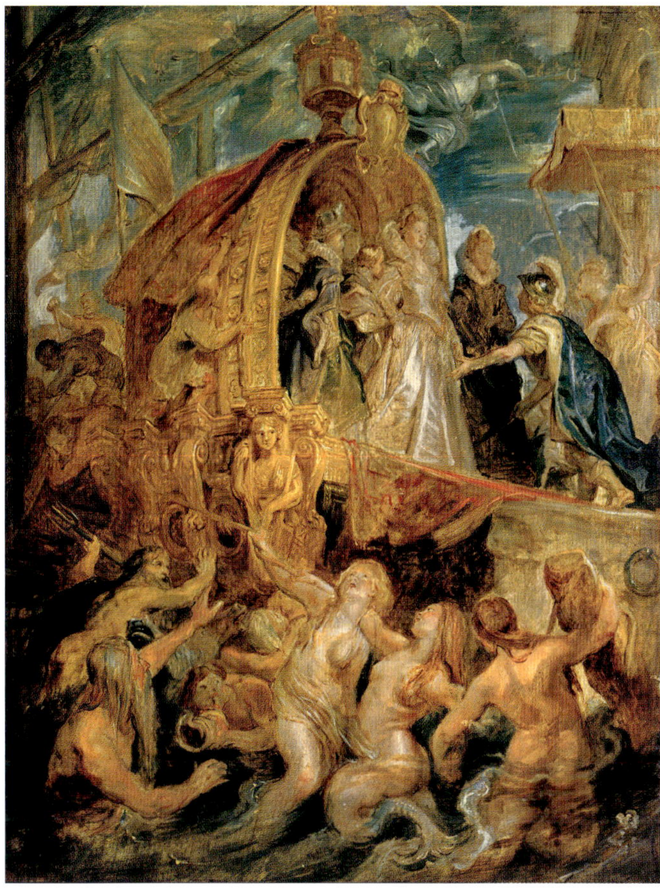

FIG. 3.33. Peter Paul Rubens, *Arrival in Marseilles* (sketch), 1622–25. Oil on panel, 25 1/5 × 19 3/4 in. (64 × 50 cm). Alte Pinakothek, Munich.

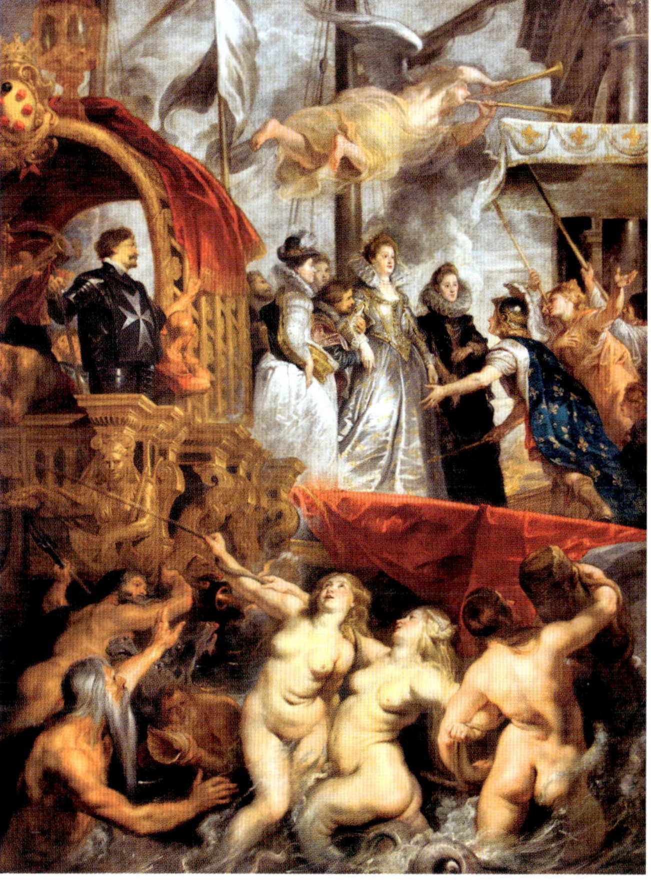

FIG. 3.34. Peter Paul Rubens, *Arrival in Marseilles*, 1621–25. Oil on canvas, 12 ft. 11 1/8 in. × 9 ft. 8 1/8 in. (394 × 295 cm). Louvre, Paris.

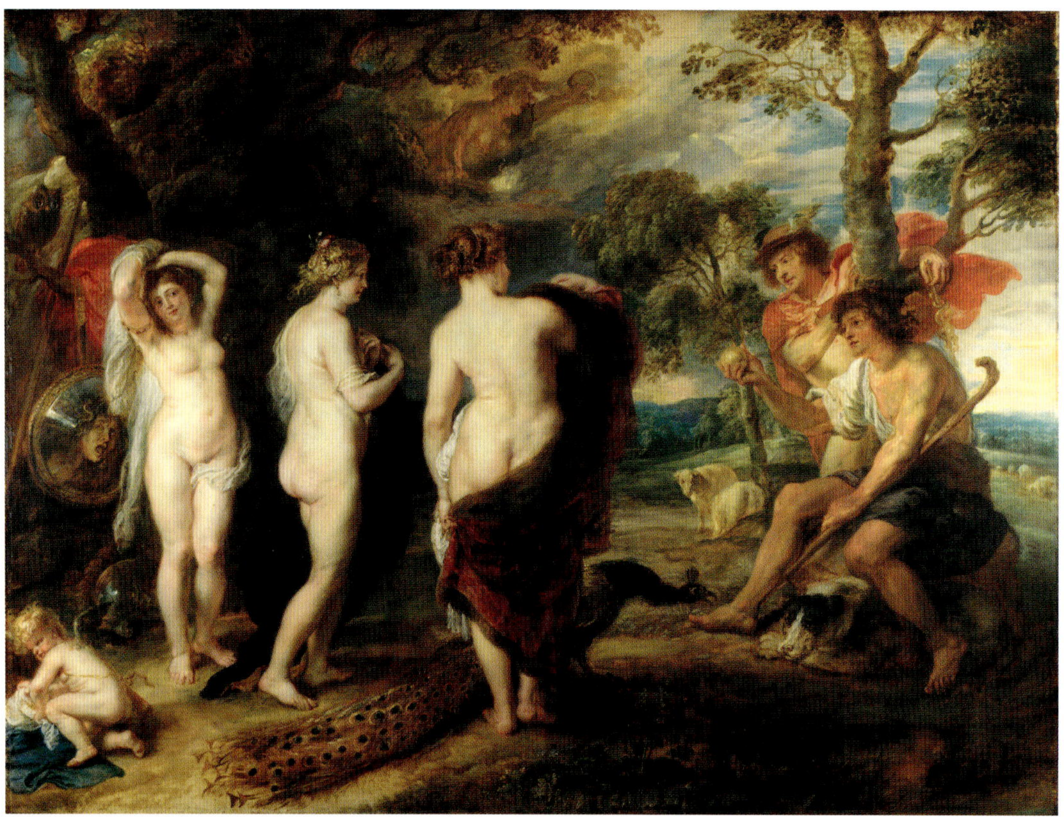

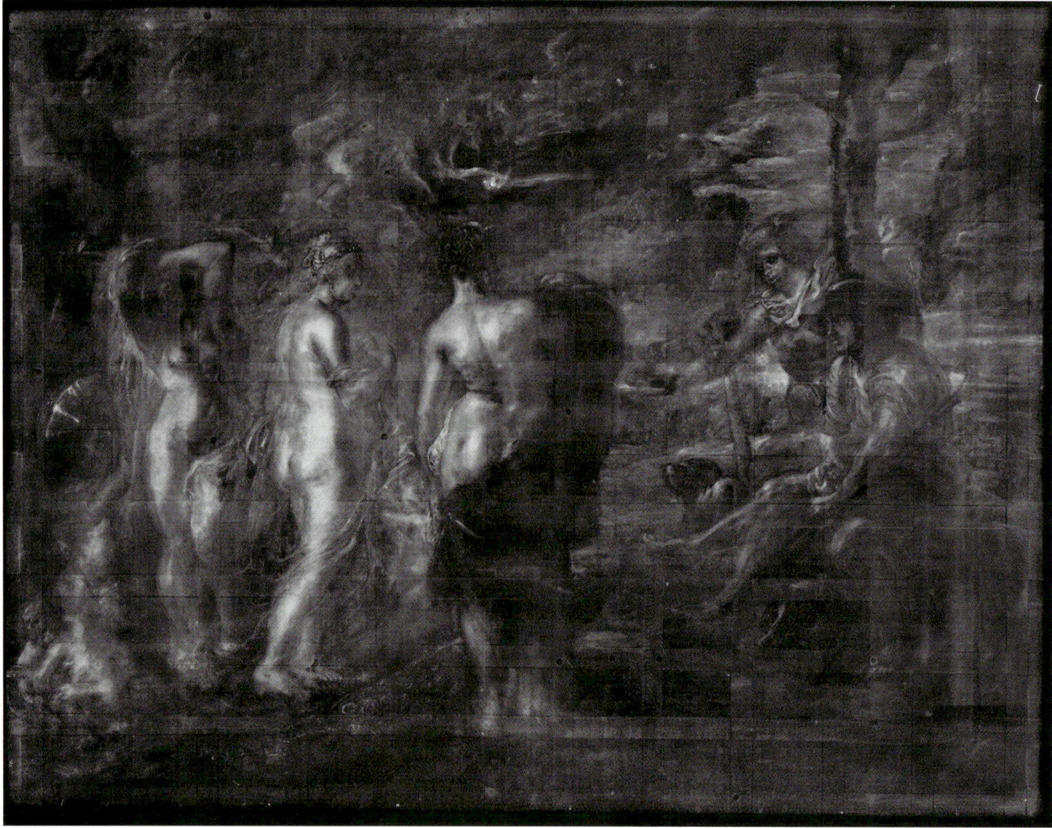

FIG. 3.35. Peter Paul Rubens, *Judgment of Paris*, c. 1632–35. Oil on panel, 57 × 76 ¼ in. (144.6 × 193.75 cm). National Gallery, London.

FIG. 3.36. Peter Paul Rubens, *Judgment of Paris* (x-ray; see fig. 3.35).

turmoil within the bedazzled Paris. Colors weave their way across the panel and bind it together: the red of Mercury's cloak echoes in Minerva's gown, which she has hung over a branch at the left, and then is deepened into a regal purple on Juno's robe at the center. Muted blue, established in Venus's garment that Cupid is bundling up in the lower left, is carried across in the peacock's tail and neck and reverberates in the distant hills and patches of sky. But it's the glowing flesh of the goddesses that dominates the scheme. Much of what surrounds them is a rich brown that sets them off. The luscious sheen of their skin with rosy touches and bluish shadows is what engages the viewer. Paris is dark skinned and ruddy and his head is in shadow. Color is brilliantly handled to express the hierarchy of interest, but it is not brilliant in itself. A generation after Rubens's death, this painting came into the hands of some unidentified owner who had it repainted to bring it more in line with the official dogma of the French Académie. As we will see in the next chapter, it exemplifies the positions of the respective sides, the protagonists of Poussin versus Rubens, in what came to be called the quarrel of the Poussinistes and Rubénistes.

ORIGINALITY

It is interesting that in the case of the *Judgment of Paris,* Rubens preserved the design by allowing a studio assistant to make a copy in slightly reduced format, which he archived for future reference, taking the place of the oil sketches used for large compositions.[89] For those large compositions, he would do more or less retouching himself, depending on the importance of the client. Rubens was notified that he needed to deliver the remaining canvases of the Marie de Medici cycle at the beginning of February 1625. On January 10 he wrote to a friend: "I must resolve to take my hands off my pictures; for otherwise there will be no time for the colors to dry or for the journey from Antwerp to Paris." He had calculated in an earlier letter that fifteen days should be allowed for the journey because the roads were so bad.[90] This means that he had to allow at least ten days for drying before rolling the canvases for transport. He went on to say that this would not inconvenience him, "for I should have had to retouch the entire work anyway in its destined place (I mean in the gallery itself)."[91]

For Rubens, what was essential in calling a work an original by him was the invention, not the execution. We saw this attitude developing among patrons such as Alessandro Farnese in Rome in the middle of the Cinquecento, when he ordered the decoration of the large Salone in the Palazzo della Cancelleria to be completed in one hundred days. It was well understood then, as it was in Rubens's time, that a large *équip* was required for these monumental projects. What emerges in the seventeenth century is a market of connoisseurs who cared greatly that a work be authentic, and sometimes demanded assurance of it. As we enter the modern world of markets, when paintings began to be made to display in collectors' galleries rather than to decorate private homes or chapels for salvific purpose, the issues of quality and autograph take center stage.[92] Certainly the commissioned painting had always been a symbol of status, but the collector now expects to be judged as a connoisseur by his peers. With what he buys, he puts on display his good taste and his judgment. The remarks about Rubens's *Lion Hunt,* which was rejected, give the flavor of the discourse.[93]

Rubens had painted it on the order of Sir Dudley Carleton, British ambassador to the Netherlands, for Lord Henry Danvers. What Rubens was not told was that Danvers intended to make a gift of it to the prince of Wales. Danvers, in sending it back, complained in a letter to Carleton that "the peece [was] scarce touched by his own hand, and the postures so forced, as the Prince will not admit it into his gallerye."[94] Rubens had declared to William Trumbull in a previous letter of January 26, 1621, when he was consigning the painting: "It has been gone over by my hand not lightly, but touched and retouched everywhere equally."[95] The connoisseur is so sure of his judgment that he is willing to contradict the word of the painter himself.

A paradox has developed in seventeenth-century connoisseurship, which is at odds with accepted workshop participation, as Anna Tummers points out.[96] How much value should be attributed to the painter's own hand? Rubens remarked to Lord Carleton: "If I had done the entire work with my own hand, it would be well worth twice as much."[97] Even as Rubens asserts that this retouched painting is autograph, at the same time he declares that if he had painted every stroke, it would be worth twice as much. In earlier correspondence, when he was negotiating with Carleton to exchange paintings in his studio for a collection of antique marbles, he had put values on works that not only reflect his assessments but also reveal the paradox again. Works and copies that have been begun by pupils, then worked on by the master, do not differ much in price from those by the master's own hand.[98]

This conundrum continues until the nineteenth century, when the categories we use today in attribution were definitively formulated. Museums, auctions, and dealers today separate paintings into autograph, painter and workshop, workshop, after, and even further refinements. But such categories clearly did not operate in Rubens's thinking, nor were they generally accepted in this period. There is ambiguity that remains unresolved at this point over the relative value of the artist's intellect (the invention or conception) and his hand.

CONCLUSION

The new market for art that began taking shape in the North in the sixteenth century became the norm in the seventeenth. Anonymous customers, who varied in their tastes, wealth, education, and experience with art, replaced the identifiable and known patron of the past. This market was both secularized and domesticated, which meant that artists needed to specialize in new genres, such as landscape or domestic interiors or portraits, and find new subjects to please this new clientele.

In this climate where artists and clients did not know one another, dealers as middlemen became increasingly important. A scruffy lot in Rome in the Cinquecento and still in the Seicento, dealers had acquired a higher status in the North already in the sixteenth century. In seventeenth-century Holland, dealers were taken into the system and began to be professionalized. They were often required to become members of the guild and were thereby restricted by its rules. Some low-end dealers employed artists to work for them, making copies or work by the dozen, but there were dealers at the high end of the market who represented major painters.[99] Rembrandt moved into the house of Hendrick van Uylenburgh, who represented him and with whom he collaborated. Rubens sold through dealers in Paris and other centers, besides selling directly from his studio. Dealers would grow in importance in the next century, until they virtually assumed the vacated role of the patron-protector in the nineteenth century.

What we see developing more strikingly than ever before is a bi-level market. On the one hand, there were the wealthy connoisseurs, descendants of the privileged aristocrats who were brought up surrounded by art and were accustomed to the process of commissioning and buying; on the other hand, there were the newly prosperous merchants who aspired to a certain level of luxury, which included decorating their homes with pictures, but whose taste ran to the familiar and accessible. It should be no surprise then to find greater diversity than ever before among painters fashioning themselves to satisfy this varied market. A Rubens could borrow from the Italian tradition to serve his patrons, who more closely resembled those of the Renaissance tradition. He employed a large workshop, chose subjects drawing upon the antique, and indulged in extravagant exuberance and hyperbole to flatter the erudition of these patrons. Rembrandt targeted a clientele of middle-class burghers with aspirations to a gentrified lifestyle. For them he made portraits and moody renderings of familiar biblical stories executed on a scale commensurate with their domestic settings. Poussin, working largely for learned clients in Italy but also in Paris, imbued his severe and serious renderings of classical myth or biblical story with moral and philosophical messages. Van Goyen and de Hooch and the "little Dutchmen" catered to the newest class of clients for whom scenes of their countryside and tidy homes confirmed a patriotic pride in their newly shaped republic and newly won prosperity, or celebrated rural daily life.

The universal concern with light and naturalistic spatial recession led painters to perfect techniques such as aerial perspective and broken color, or to experiment with rough textures. Many of the prohibitions that had survived largely intact through the Renaissance, such as mixing pigments and leaving the surface rough and unfinished, crumbled, casualties of the search for convincing naturalism.

The painter needed now to pay close attention to issues of cost if he was going to survive in this highly competitive market. New techniques and procedures, such as dead coloring, broken color, and the oil sketch, provided means of producing works in which the workshop could contribute efficiently while maintaining a level of quality that would satisfy the critical connoisseur. Concern for cost led most painters to economize on their materials by painting more thinly, as Van Goyen did, or underpainting expensive pigments with cheaper ones, such as azurite or smalt under ultramarine, or red earth under lake or vermilion. Even Rubens painted his oil sketches thinly and substituted smalt for more costly blues that would be used in the final painting.[100]

Sometimes the dead-colored underpainting or the oil sketch was shown to the prospective client, in preference to keeping on-hand pictures already finished with expensive materials in the hope of selling them. Rembrandt, on the other hand, in keeping with his contrarian disposition, showed no interest in efficiency or economy, even when he was broke. He never skimped on materials, and in this respect he was as uncompromising as he was regarding current taste and fashion.

Even in Catholic regions it was no longer just the altarpiece that was the most prestigious commission. It was now large-scale decorations for heads of state, continuing and expanding along the lines laid down in the projects of Cinquecento princes and popes such as Farnese in Italy to cover the walls of their palaces with scenes aggrandizing the person and family of the patron. Rubens's Marie de Medici series and his ceiling of the Banqueting Hall at Whitehall in London look forward to Louis XIV's takeover of the artistic establishment to serve his state and personal propaganda in France in the later seventeenth century, as described in the next chapter.

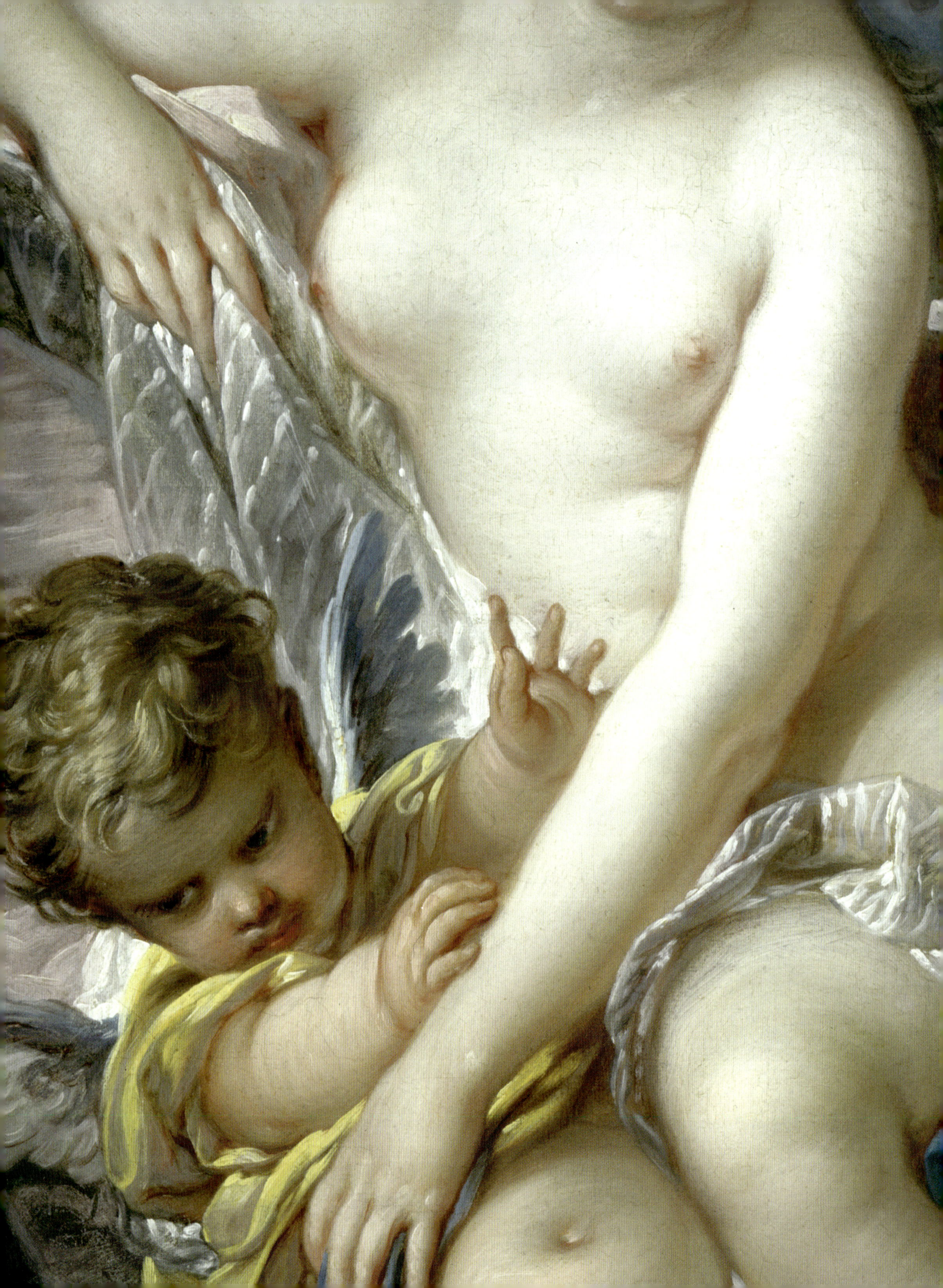

4 The Eighteenth Century

The Politics of Art

The eighteenth century sees the definitive politicization of art, which would ultimately come to play a role in the wrenching events of the French Revolution. Louis XIV's takeover of the art establishment in the service of the state, beginning around 1660, laid the foundation for what followed. Crucial to Louis's program was the revival of the antique notion that art must conform to a certain decorum, memorably articulated by Horace and given new life in the Renaissance by Baldassare Castiglione in his famous book *The Courtier.* Castiglione's description of the qualities necessary to the courtier were of great interest at the palace of Versailles, where Louis gathered the nobility and imposed rigid rules of etiquette, and the concept of the appropriate, the proper, and the suitable provided the guideline not only for behavior but also for art.

There was a hierarchy of artistic genres, each of which had its own rules of decorum: the appropriate way to paint a history painting differed from what was suitable in a portrait or a landscape. There could be said to be a decorum of color as well. Poussin provided the reliable model for how to color history painting, and the purpose of coloring in serious painting, according to

the founding director of the Académie, Charles Le Brun, was symbolic.

THE ACADÉMIE

When Le Brun and a group of painters protected by the monarch founded the Académie Royale de Peinture et de Sculpture in 1648 it was a declaration of independence from the medieval guild, la Maîtrise, which had recently moved to reestablish its eroded authority.[1] Since the guild's inception in 1391, artists with royal commissions had been granted *lettres de brevet* (patent letters) exempting them from guild dues and other restrictions. As the number of *brevetaires* and those noblemen empowered to grant them grew, there evolved a two-tiered system that undermined the power of the Maîtrise.[2] Following the precedent of the Italian academies in Florence and Rome, Le Brun and his cohort separated artists from craftsmen. In rejecting the control of the guild, the academicians identified themselves as learned practitioners of another liberal art such as poetry or music. It is an index of how slowly France had been moving out of the Middle Ages that the French trailed the central Italians in setting up an academy by more than three-quarters of a century.[3]

Closing that gap, drawing abreast of the Italians, and indeed surging past them would become the goal of Le Brun's Académie and of the royal bureaucracy.

The French royal interest in an academy on the Italian model may have extended back to the 1620s. At that time Simon Vouet, who had been living and painting in Rome since 1612 as a *pensionnaire* (one receiving a stipend) of King Louis XIII, was elected *principe* of the Accademia di San Luca, the first Frenchman to obtain its highest office. From 1624–27 he served very effectively, instituting needed reforms of its teaching program and charitable function and resolving its financial crisis.[4] During the 1620s the French contingent in Rome, which was numerous, raised more alms for the Accademia than any other national group. Vouet's leadership was cut short after two and a half years when he was called back to Paris.[5] Vouet returned home and continued his very successful career, converting from his Caravaggesque style to a classicizing manner informed by the Carracci. The dark chiaroscuro he had preferred gives way to a sunny palette of clear, harmonious colors (fig. 4.1).[6] He was made First Painter to the King and worked for the leading patrons, including

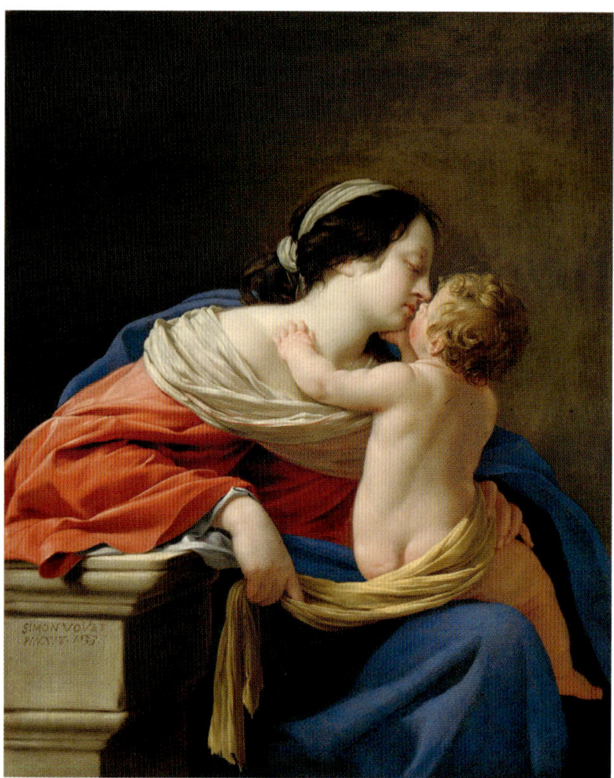

FIG. 4.1. Simon Vouet, *Madonna and Child*, 1633. Oil on canvas, 43 ⁷⁄₁₆ × 35 ³⁄₁₆ in. (110.3 × 89.4 cm). National Gallery of Art, Washington, D.C.

Louis XIII and his minister, Richelieu, until his death in 1649. Peter Lukehart has argued that in summoning Vouet back to France, Richelieu, on behalf of Louis, had intended that Vouet would establish in Paris an academy with Rome as the prototype.[7] In the end, the younger Le Brun and colleagues of his generation undertook the project; ironically, it may seem, Vouet opposed and attempted to thwart it by establishing an ill-fated rival. There is no doubt that it was the Roman Accademia that served as the model for the French, which copied it in providing instruction in drawing and lectures on art theory. The all-important difference was that the Académie Royale became an arm of the state, which financed it and directed its commissions to glorify the monarch and the monarchy. In that sense, it had more in common with the Accademia del Disegno in Florence, which was directed by the *luogotenente* of the grand duke.

It was Cardinal Richelieu as minister to Louis XIII who launched the campaign in the early 1640s to establish the cultural supremacy of France. Poussin, the exemplar of classicism, was ordered back to Paris from Rome as First Painter to the King in 1640 to model the new aesthetic. Poussin and Vouet were commissioned to make altarpieces for a royal chapel where the Gothic architecture was masked under a cloak of classicism. It was intended to showcase the preferred style in both its architecture and paintings.[8] The government thus established a decorum of style to which artists who wished to receive royal commissions were obliged to conform. Some argue that the styles of Vouet and Poussin were incompatible, and that enmity festered, particularly on Vouet's part, mostly over being displaced. Certainly their styles derived from opposing factions in Italy, and the classicism Poussin evolved after the 1630s was well matched to the preferences that would emerge in the Académie Royale.

Jean-Baptiste Colbert, as minister to Louis XIV, invoked the newly formed Académie to continue and expand on Richelieu's program. Louis declared that he would not replace the all-powerful Cardinal Mazarin as prime minister after he died in 1661. This is said to be the moment of his famous pronouncement to Parlement: *"L'état c'est moi"* ("I am the state"). With Colbert in charge, they set out to usurp Italian primacy in the arts, both by acquisition and in production. Colbert wrote in a letter of 1669: "We must make sure to have in France everything of beauty in Italy."[9] In the early decades of the sixteenth century François I had inaugurated the acquisition of Italian Renaissance art and artists. He had persuaded Andrea del Sarto to visit Paris; he hired Rosso Fiorentino and enticed Francesco Primaticcio away from the duke of Mantua to decorate Fontainebleau; and Benvenuto Cellini came to the court in 1540 and made his famous *Saltcellar* for François. The king had also tried to acquire a work from Michelangelo unsuccessfully, and—most memorably—he had lured Leonardo da Vinci to his service, where Leonardo had died in 1519, leaving his three masterpieces: the *Madonna of the Rocks, Mona Lisa,* and *Madonna and Child with Saint Anne,* which passed into the royal collection and are now exhibited at the Louvre.[10] François launched a program, which Colbert and Louis XIV would vigorously pursue, of obtaining originals, or at least casts, of the greatest statues of antiquity. For this they deemed that France needed a resident presence in Rome, which could be provided by a second French Academy located there, founded in 1666.[11]

By 1664 Colbert had been made minister of fine arts; as vice-protector of the Académie he became, in effect, its supervisor. The artist Le Brun was its director. To further the education of French artists in the achievement of Italian art of the recent past and of antiquity, the prestigious Prix de Rome was inaugurated, a stipend to study at the French Academy (Académie Française de Rome). Typically it was a fellowship of three to five years, and there were awards made to painters, sculptors, and architects—and eventually in the nineteenth century, for historical landscape painting. Its director was well situated to help acquire any work, especially antiquities, that might come up for sale, and its students of sculpture could be enlisted to make copies or casts of antique masterpieces that were then returned to France to decorate Louis XIV's palace and gardens at Versailles.

The program of the Académie Royale was centered on the instruction of drawing, over which the state maintained a monopoly. Students were taught to draw first from other drawings and prints, then from casts, and finally from the model. Providing live models was so expensive that individual artists could not afford it, so the service provided by the state was welcomed. The Académie did not provide other instruction, which continued on the old model of the student seeking training in the atelier of a master, with whom he lived, and who judged his progress and managed his trajectory toward a professional career.

The other function the Académie undertook was also based upon the Roman example of providing lectures on theory, especially those provided by Federico Zuccaro.[12] Recognizing the need to develop a language of criticism for discussing art, Le Brun called upon senior academicians to make presentations on such matters as invention, proportion, perspective, color, expression, and composition, and to lead the discussion that followed. Of the artists chosen for study in these *Conférences,* only one was not Italian: Poussin. Le Brun delivered the first of these on Poussin's *Israelites Gathering Manna,* followed by Sébastien Bourdon on *Christ Healing the Blind.*[13] Poussin's lifelong residence in Rome qualified him to represent Italian art in the modern manner for the academicians, but he was also a point of pride in sharing their heritage. Poussin was the conduit through which Renaissance artistic values and principles were channeled and thus the exemplar for academic classicism. The king acquired as many of his paintings as he could, thereby establishing the extraordinary collection that can be seen at the Louvre today.

The Prix de Rome was awarded each year (with occasional lacunae) to the painter of the most distinguished history painting, which was considered the queen of the genres because it was the most difficult. The next genre in the hierarchy was portraiture, followed in order by landscape, genre painting, animal painting, and still life. History paintings were expected to be large, multi-figured, and appropriate to hang in a public place. Subjects could be historical, mythological, religious, or literary, but they should convey seriousness, dignity, and a high moral message and they should demonstrate the prowess of French painting. The style appropriate to history painting derived from the idealized classicism of the Italian Renaissance as it had been refined and modernized by Poussin. Jean-Baptiste Corneille won the Prix de Rome in 1668. On his return from Rome he was admitted to the Académie Royale in January 1675 on the basis of his reception piece, *Hercules Punishing Busiris* (fig. 4.2).[14] The esoteric subject was not imposed on him: he chose it, possibly because Louis was associated with Hercules, as he was with Alexander.[15] Busiris is the Egyptian pharaoh who has captured Hercules and is going to sacrifice him to the gods. Hercules breaks his chains and slays Busiris and his son. The violence and melodrama make it a suitable picture for a public site intending to inspire courage and moral fortitude, but it is not a picture one

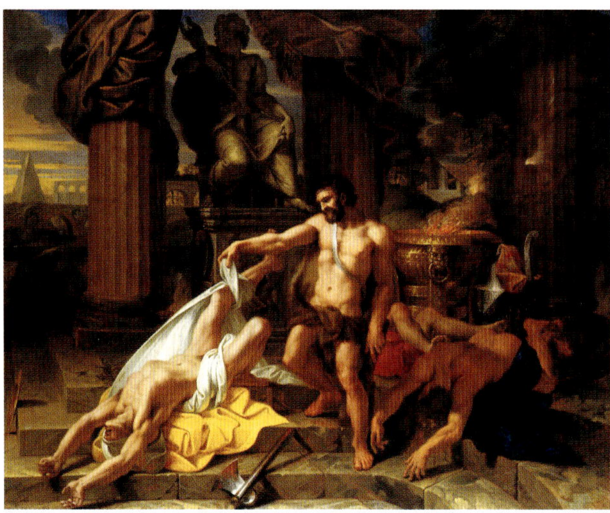

FIG. 4.2. Jean-Baptiste Corneille, *Hercules Punishing Busiris,* 1675. Oil on canvas, 55 ¾ × 71 in. (141.5 × 180.5 cm). École nationale supérieure des Beaux-Arts, Paris.

would want to hang in the dining room of one's private residence. Reinforcing the theatrics of the grand style is the chiaroscuro, a stage-like lighting that falls on the protagonists and plunges the surroundings into gloom. Yellow and white drapery and flesh focus the viewer's attention, while neutral browns set them off. The French grand style shares with the Italian Baroque a taste for grandiosity, but it is more distanced and the emotional temperature is cooler.

The Académie in Paris was the center of artistic education. Provincial branches were set up, but if an artist was going to succeed he had to go to Paris to enter the studio of a member of the Académie. Like everything else in Louis's France, the system was centralized and focused on the capital, precluding alternatives and diversity. The training was keyed to a system of competitions for which the masters groomed their students. The senior academicians who made up the juries to award the prizes knew and agreed on the criteria. The masters of the ateliers knew what the juries were looking for. They could train their students to pass the tests and they could make judicious decisions about when the students were ready to enter a competition. The lack of freedom, so abhorred today, that defined this system was essential to achieving the goal of defining the rules of art, which were then inculcated, preparing the winners to take on state commissions.

LE BRUN AND THE RULES OF ART

Colbert and Louis understood art to have one primary purpose: to enhance the prestige of the monarchy and aggrandize the image of the king. The artists of the Académie were put to work under the direction of Le Brun in creating not only paintings and sculptures, but also tapestries, furniture, and ornaments of all kinds. In much the same way that Louis assembled the entire court at Versailles and kept the courtiers captive under his surveillance, engaging in elaborate rituals that left no time for hatching conspiracies, so the artistic establishment was pressed into full-time service of the king, leaving no one free to serve his rivals. Le Brun came to Louis's attention because Nicolas Fouquet, the minister of finance, had engaged him from 1658 to 1661, together with the architect Louis Le Vau and the landscape architect André Le Nôtre, to create the extravagant decorations of his Château de Vaux-le-Vicomte. Fouquet bought up three villages to acquire the land he needed, then put the villagers to work, with all eighteen thousand, it is said, maintaining it. He was such a bad judge of human nature that he invited Louis and the court to a great fête to admire it when it was ready. It seems not to have occurred to him that Louis might see this as a challenge to his position, or that he might be roused to jealousy. Fouquet was arrested, charged with misappropriation of funds, and spent the remaining nineteen years of his life moldering in prison, but Louis was inspired. He hired Le Brun, Le Vau, and Le Nôtre and set out to transform his father's hunting lodge outside Paris in Versailles into what was surely the most sumptuous palace that had been seen since antiquity. For nearly three decades Le Brun dedicated his considerable powers to glorifying the Sun King and his residences.

Later in 1661 Louis called Le Brun to Fontainebleau, where he was in residence, gave him an apartment in the palace, and charged him to paint any subject of his choice from the life of Alexander the Great. It was understood of course that the young conqueror Alexander represented the young King Louis. Le Brun chose Alexander in the Tent of Darius, or as it was called in the seventeenth century, *The Queen of Persia at the Feet of Alexander.* Le Brun's interpretation does not put at the center Alexander's display of friendship for Hephaestion, as was usual in the sixteenth century (for example, in Veronese's famous version now in London), but focuses instead on Alexander's mastering and denying the immediate passion aroused

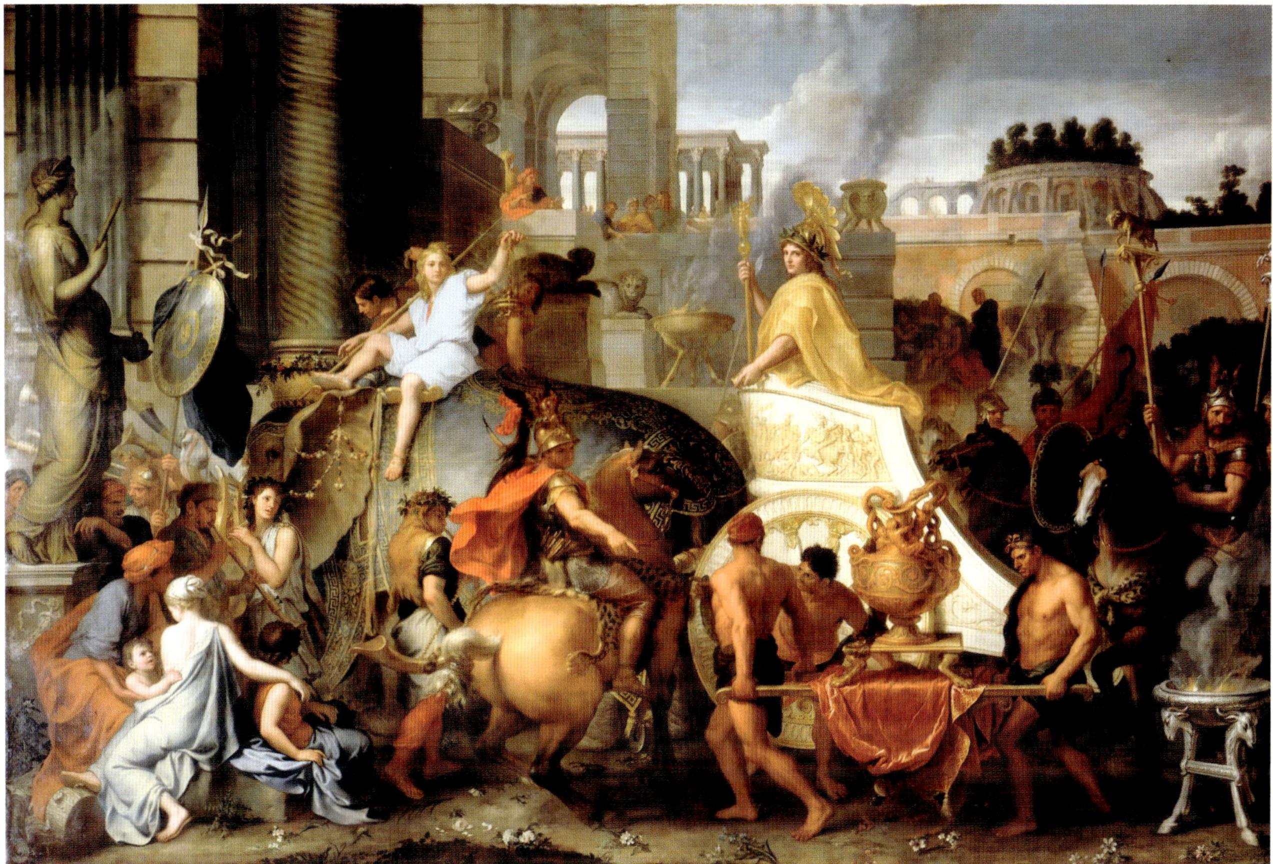

FIG. 4.3. Charles Le Brun, *Alexander Entering Babylon*, c. 1665. Oil on canvas, 14 ft. 23¼ in. × 23 ft. 6 in. (450 × 707 cm). Louvre, Paris.

in him by the sight of the beautiful Persian princess, Darius's daughter. The moral is, as Donald Posner put it, "Virtue not for its own sake, but as the duty of a gallant monarch."[16] Louis was pleased with the painting and he ordered that the series be continued with four more huge canvases created before the end of the 1660s. *Alexander Entering Babylon* (fig. 4.3) was one of two that were shown to Gian Lorenzo Bernini when he visited the Gobelins Manufactory, where the furnishings for Versailles were produced, in 1665. It shows Alexander riding in a silver and gilt chariot drawn by elephants—Le Brun had the opportunity to study elephants from life in the menagerie at Versailles designed by Le Vau for Louis and completed in 1664. The painting measures nearly fifteen by twenty-three feet, yet we know it was painted rapidly because it and the *Passage of the Granicus* were completed after the *Tent of Darius,* which was begun in the late autumn of 1661.

André Félibien used *The Queen of Persia at the Feet of Alexander* as the subject of a booklet to demonstrate Le Brun's use of what he calls "friendly colors" to unify a

composition. Charles-Alphonse Defresnoy had used the term to describe the practice of the Venetians, in particular Veronese, for colors that participate in one another and are mixed together.[17] This is the most detailed explication of what the Académie meant by "couleur rompue." Félibien makes clear that Le Brun has achieved a facsimile of Raphael's unione (*"union"* in French). All the colors "communicate" with one another—for example, Alexander's purple and gold cloak links to the violet purple mantle of Darius's wife, kneeling at his feet. The colors are broken, or mixed, to create these links and harmonies.[18]

Although very little is known about Le Brun's materials and working procedure and there is no information about his workshop, the speed with which he worked tells us that he relied heavily on his assistants. Like his model, Poussin, he did extensive research in books to assure that his depiction would be authentic, both in terms of the setting and of the protocols and customs of the Alexandrian Greeks, as they were then conceived. We see the attention given to the material culture in *Alexander Entering*

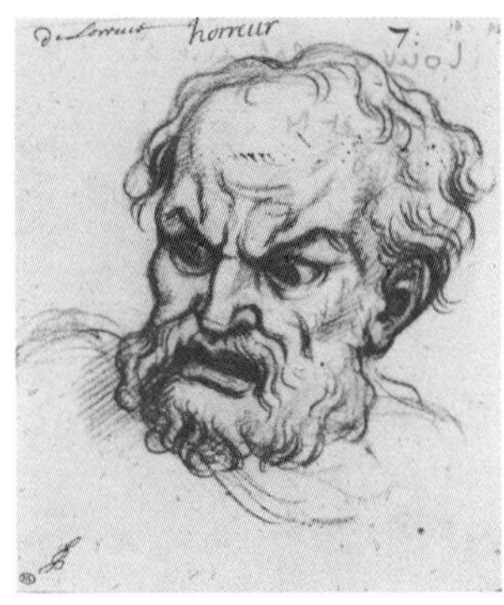

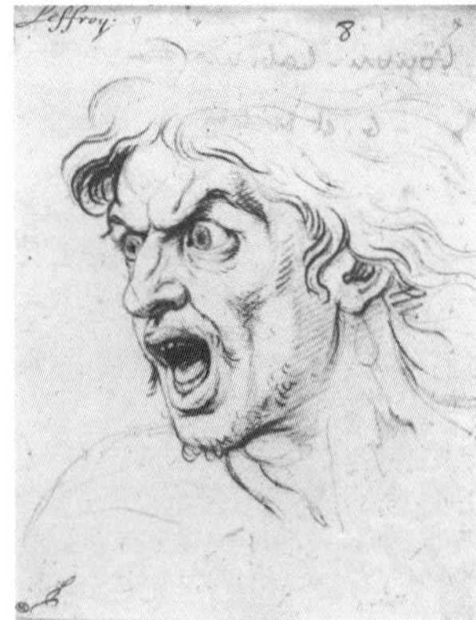

FIG. 4.4. Charles Le Brun, *Passions of the Soul (Horror and Dread)*, 1698. Black chalk on paper, 10 × 7 ¹⁴⁄₁₆ in. (25.2 × 20 cm). Louvre, Paris.

Babylon: the armor, the silver incense burners mounted on rams' heads, the chariot. He even distinguished between Greek and Asian horses. We know from surviving drawings that he made compositional sketches in ink with wash, redrawn often in pencil or chalk and then reinforced with black ink. He then created meticulous studies of figures, often making nude studies of figures that would later be clothed, as Raphael had done. Like Rubens, he poured his creativity into the invention and the preparation of the composition, freeing himself from execution, which could be left to assistants. Like Rubens, he would retouch the final painting.[19]

Le Brun's finish is unlike Rubens's, however. There is none of the bravura brushstroke that dazzles the eye in a Rubens. Rather it is smooth, cool, and impersonal, more like Poussin's, the model of academic classicism. His use of color follows the same pattern. It describes materials accurately but does not dwell on textures or surfaces. Even when the materials depicted are opulent, as they are in the *Alexander Entering Babylon,* they do not dazzle or delight as they do in Venetian painting. The appeal is made through the intellect—"See how accurately reconstructed this is"—and not the senses or the emotions.

The mission of the Académie can be summed up in Le Brun's intention to create a system for representing the emotions that could be taught. Taking as his point of departure René Descartes's *Passions of the Soul* (Les passions de l'ame, 1649), in which the philosopher undertook to describe the inner workings of the emotions, Le Brun sought to describe the outward manifestations. He studied faces, locating the points of expression for each emotion, and just how they looked when they were experiencing anger or despair, tranquility or surprise. He gave a Conférence on the subject and wrote a treatise illustrated with his drawings. He wanted to create a code by which the viewer will invariably recognize the emotion expressed (see, for example, *Passions of the Soul [Horror and Dread],* fig. 4.4). The code could even become a convention. It is an intellectual process, not intended to stir the same emotion in the viewer, but to be identified without uncertainty or ambiguity. As Jacqueline Lichtenstein put it, Le Brun's drawings "distinguish only the passions represented in a painting, not the passions provoked by it."[20] This was just another aspect of the program to create a set of rules that could be taught to Académie students, who did not, after all, have a native tradition of classical art to draw upon, and who came from diverse backgrounds. In order to create a national style, the Académie needed to have a system that would put all students on common ground, so that for projects under Le Brun's direction an army of painters could work side by side, and the result would have coherence and could be identified as a French style. There was of course ample precedent in Cinquecento Rome, where Vasari, Perino del Vaga, and Salviati, as well as Taddeo Zuccaro, among others, used a large workshop to execute their designs. The difference is that the French were more interested in a seamless, uniform execution.

The five Alexander paintings served as a prelude to what would become Le Brun's life work, managing the decoration of Versailles and providing Louis with suitably extravagant ornaments to express his personal glory and that of his absolute monarchy. The supreme expression is the Hall of Mirrors, the nearly three-hundred-foot-long wing overlooking the gardens connecting the apartment of the king with the apartment of the queen (fig. 4.5). Its construction was begun in 1678. It was lined with 357 mirrors, which were among the most expensive materials available and were the monopoly of Venice, where the glass industry had invented a tin-mercury

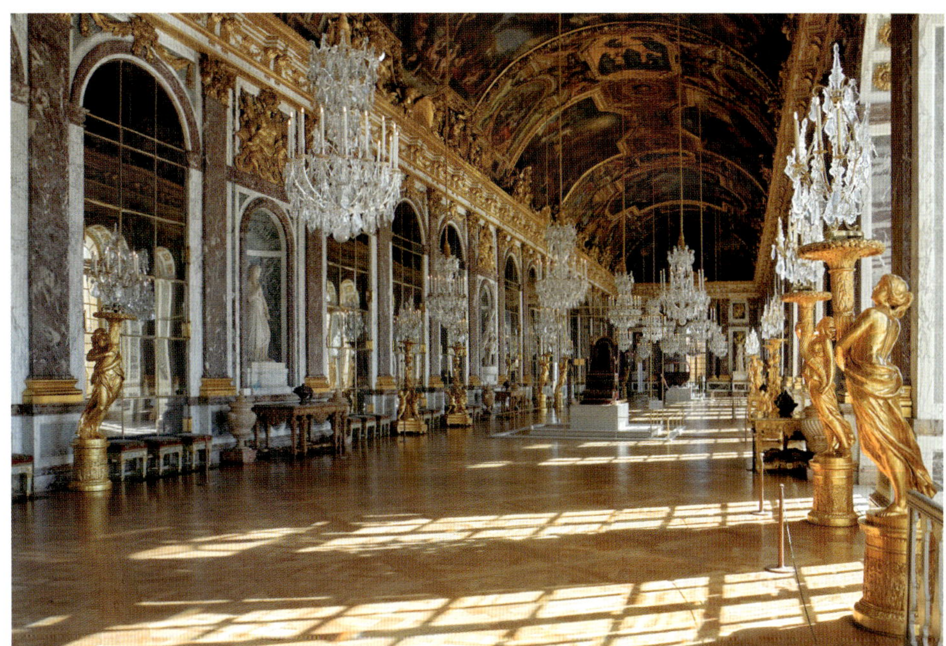

amalgam as coating. To acquire what was needed for this specular display, Colbert enticed workers to come from Venice and make the panels in France.[21] The gallery was furnished with tables and chairs of solid silver executed under the direction of Le Brun (but in 1689 these were melted on the order of Louis to pay for the war of the League of Augsburg, along with many others of his ornaments in precious metal). Le Brun painted the ceiling in 1681–84 with scenes celebrating the greatest achievements of Louis's first seventeen years of reign. Abandoning the discreet allegorization of the king that he had hitherto employed, as in the *Triumph of Alexander* series, Le Brun presents Louis as himself, robed at the same time in antique armor and the French royal robe of state: *The King Governs Alone* (fig. 4.6). With brazenness that today we find appalling, Louis is shown as the embodiment of the French state. The model is certainly such Renaissance ceilings as the Sala Regia, the reception room of the pope, and the Sala Paolina in the Castel Sant'Angelo, another papal reception room, celebrating the deeds of Pope Paul III Farnese. But where those rooms use chaste white stucco for framing, the same stuccos are entirely gilded at Versailles.[22] For these scenes Le Brun makes use of pagan deities such as Minerva, who represents both wisdom and war, advising and upholding the king. For all its grandiloquence, Le Brun nevertheless chooses the traditional classical format, showing these colossal ceilings as if the spectator is viewing them

head-on as an easel painting, rather than using the more modern and fashionable *di sotto in sù* ("seen from below"), the viewpoint in vogue in Baroque Rome and used by Rubens in his Whitehall ceiling, for example.[23] This stylistic conservatism, adhering to the classical tradition, is characteristic of Le Brun; in this case it lends a dignity and a seriousness that the more spectacular illusionism, with its affecting brio, might jeopardize.

Le Brun believed that color should be symbolic. In the same way that he invented a grammar of facial expressions, which the viewer could recognize as representing specific emotions, colors carried and should carry specific and identifiable meanings. Of course they must create a pleasing aesthetic effect, but they were not selected or utilized for their power to move the emotions or to persuade. The messages of the program were delivered seriously and as factual; they were not conceived as hyperbolic rhetoric. The extravagant claims being made on Louis's behalf were to be taken as rational statements. They were not leavened with humor like Rubens's Medici series, based on Italian Renaissance example.

After the death of Colbert in the 1680s, Le Brun began to lose his authority. The year before his own death in 1690 he observed the melting of his ornaments of gold and silver for Versailles to raise money for the war, a symptom and a symbol of the passing of his power in tandem with Louis XIV's. The Académie veered from the path that had been set. The opponent of *Poussinisme,*

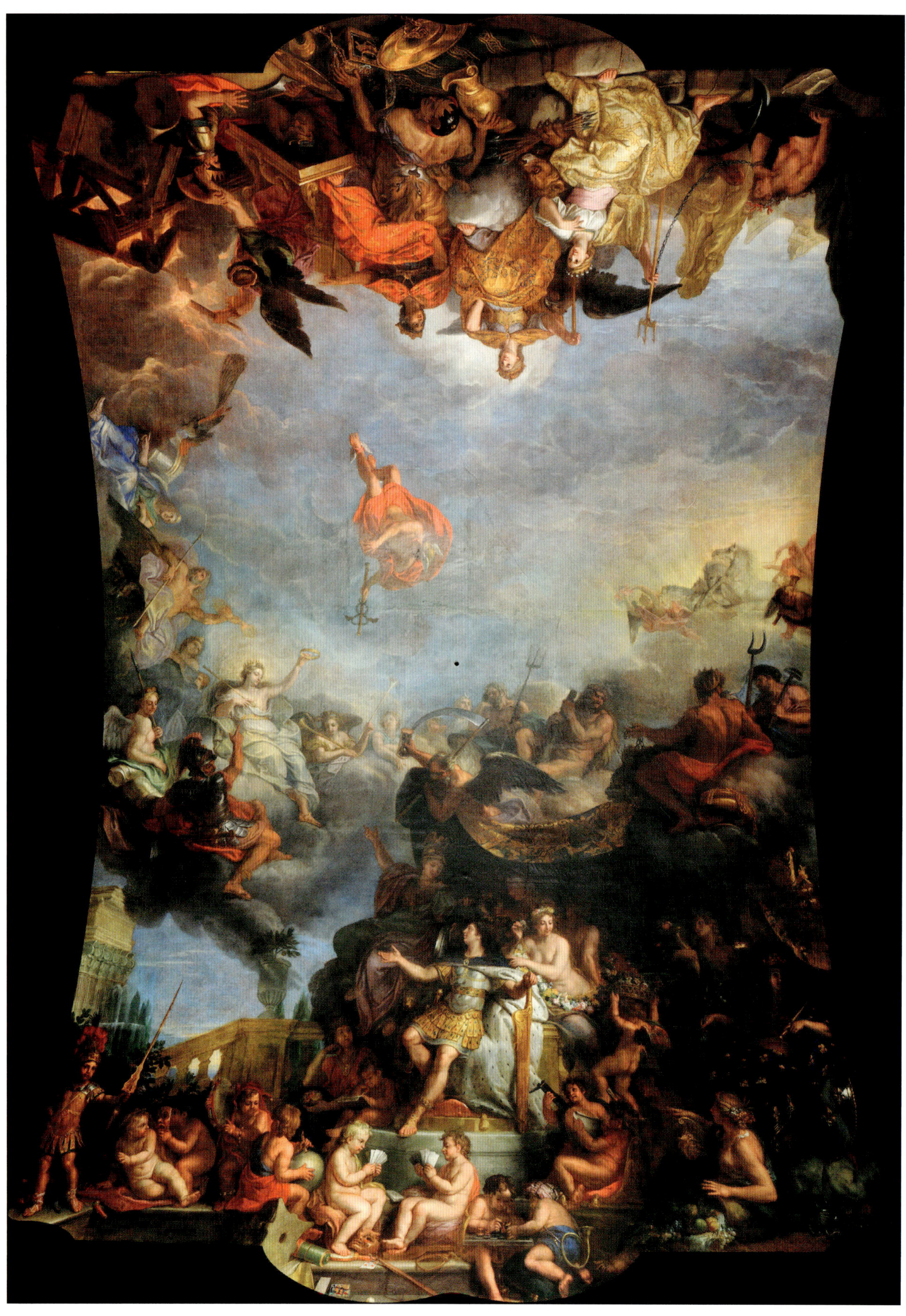

FIG. 4.6. Charles Le Brun, *The King Governs Alone*, 1681–84. Oil on canvas, 26 ft. 4 in. × 16 ft. 4 in. (800 × 500 cm). Château de Versailles.

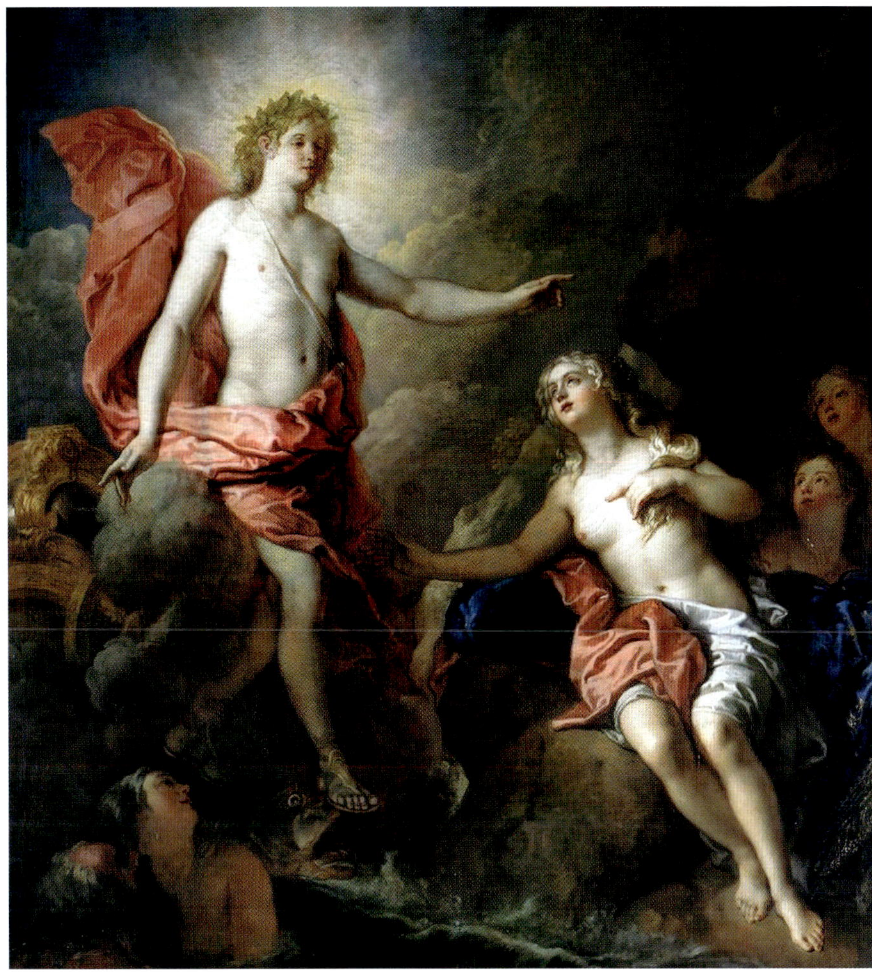

Roger de Piles, was admitted as a member, even though he was not a painter, and his influence surged and came to dominate in the eighteenth century. He challenged the established position that line is superior to color and reason is to be privileged over emotion.

In fact as soon as Colbert died, the Rubénistes began their ascendancy. There was apostasy even among Le Brun's own followers. A painter who had been a student of Le Brun and had been successful as one of his assistants, Charles de La Fosse, was accepted into the Académie in 1673. Yet he fell increasingly under the spell of Rubens. In 1687 he was commissioned to paint *Apollo and Thetis* to go over the mantle in the king's bedchamber at the Grand Trianon (fig. 4.7). Apollo is seen descending from his chariot of the sun and is welcomed home by the adoring Thetis for a good night's repose. Certainly Louis is to be identified with the sun god as always, but Thetis here is a more voluptuous maiden than any Le Brun had painted. Rubens's influence is visible not only in the address to the viewer's emotions, but also in the sensuous textures of flesh, fabric, and hair, and in the sumptuous coloring.[24]

What the Académie had been seeking in the Conférences was to analyze and classify the elements of painting. Roger de Piles's famous "Tables"—in which he ranked fifty-six of the greatest painters in four categories, composition, drawing, color, and expression, and awarded them a score of zero to eighteen points—is both the summa and reductio ad absurdum of such a quest. His highest marks went to Raphael and Rubens, but Rubens scored so well only because de Piles was his champion in the infamous Poussinistes–Rubénistes quarrel.[25]

DISEGNO-COLORE, POUSSINISTES-RUBÉNISTES

Jean-Antoine Watteau was among the first to benefit from Roger de Piles's attack in the 1690s upon the hegemony of drawing and the denigration of color, which Le Brun's Académie had preached. The debate initiated in the sixteenth century over the superiority of line or color (the *disegno–colore* debate) centered around the allegation

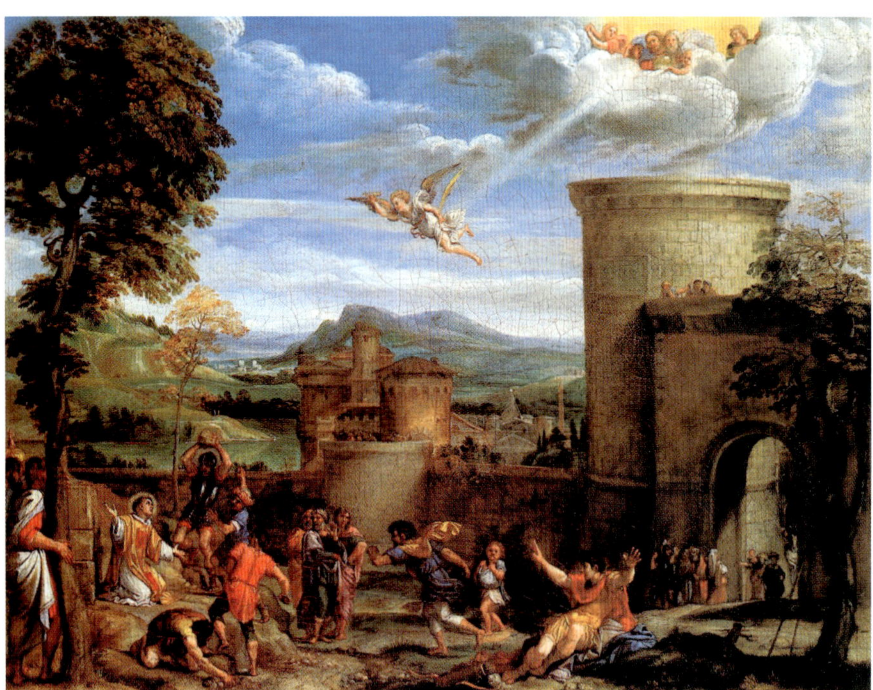

FIG. 4.8. Annibale Carracci, *Martyrdom of Saint Stephen*, 1603. Oil on canvas, 20 × 26 ⅜ in. (51 × 67 cm). Louvre, Paris.

that disegno records the essential and colore the mere accidents or contingencies of vision. Giorgio Vasari, as the champion of central Italian art, of course considered drawing more important than coloring, because it was where central Italian painters excelled—they invested their best efforts in perfecting the drawn cartoon, after all. The Venetian critics Paolo Pino and Ludovico Dolce responded, predictably, by proclaiming the superiority of coloring, in which their painters excelled. Giorgione and Titian worked with only rough sketches and improvised with the brush and pigment, creating miracles of naturalistic imitation.

Vasari's Aristotelian definition of "disegno," which opened the debate, tells the story. Drawing, he says, is an activity of the intellect acquiring knowledge of a universal kind from the past accumulated experience of individual objects.[26] Through experience, the painter learns what the idea of a thing is and can therefore discard whatever is deficient in the particular thing under study. The emphasis upon intellect stakes out the terrain: drawing is a function of a rational process. By definition, color is an accident of inferior matter.[27] Color records temporary, ephemeral conditions, such as weather, light, reflections, occlusions—mere appearance. A glance back at Titian's *Bacchanal of the Andrians* (see fig. 2.28) reminds us of the Venetian genius in capturing the look of clouds passing overhead, or the way a stand of trees casts some

figures in the shadow and puts others in dappled light; or the textures of glass, fabrics, supple female flesh, and muscled male skin. Contrast this with Bronzino's *Pietà* in the museum at Besançon (see fig. 2.25). Drawn line and hard contour convey us to a realm of abstract ideas, making clear that we must work out the ratiocinated meaning but (apparently) not be distracted by the exquisite marble-like figures.

Vasari distrusts the Venetians' dependence upon flawed natural appearance and asserts the perfection of Michelangelo and Raphael, remarking that Titian doesn't know how to draw. Ludovico Dolce responds that to be convincing a painter must be able to imitate the softness of flesh and the glint of armor as well as the sheen of fabric and the gloom of night.[28] But in this discourse, color ends up being only the means to verisimilitude, whereas drawing is capable of capturing the essence of things and depicting the ideal. Drawing appeals to the higher capacity of reason, color to the senses and the emotions. This hierarchical distinction is at the root of the denigration of color and the distrust it often engendered in later times.

Le Brun, with his commitment to making painting intellectually respectable, insisted on the Vasarian view that drawing was the proper, primary concern of the painter; the design contained the significance of the painting because it addressed the reason of the viewer. It is not surprising then to find that he regarded the

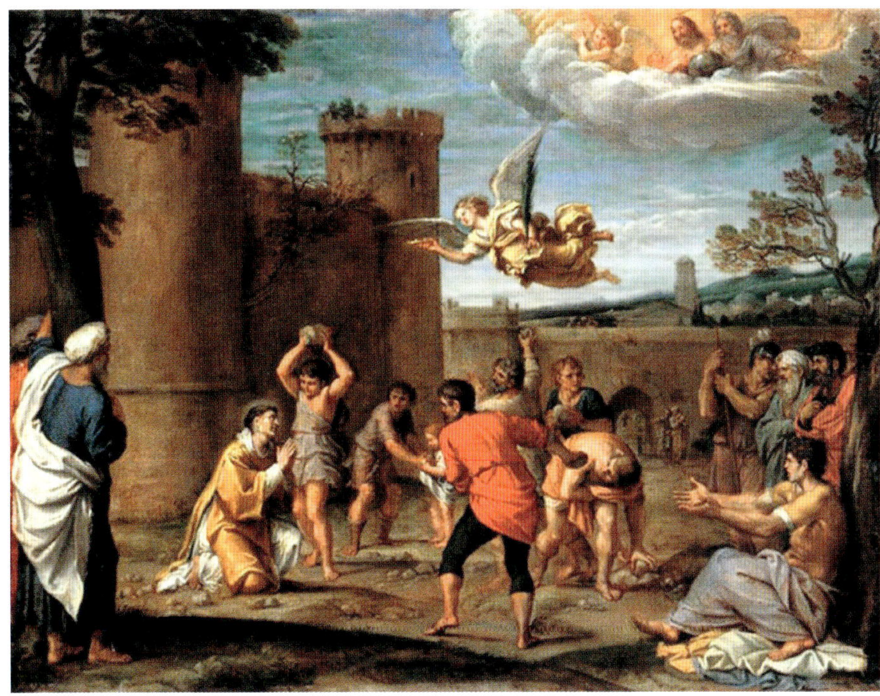

FIG. 4.9. Annibale Carracci, *Stoning of Saint Stephen*, c. 1603–4. Oil on copper, 16 1/8 × 20 7/8 in. (41 × 53 cm). Louvre, Paris.

importance of coloring to lie in its symbolism, but there was apparently not complete agreement on that point among the academicians. The discussion held in front of Carracci's oil on copper *Martyrdom of Saint Stephen* (fig. 4.8) and another version by the same painter, called the *Stoning of Saint Stephen* (fig. 4.9), demonstrates the academic method of discourse and a range of opinion on how color was used by Renaissance painters. Sébastien Bourdon's discourse of June 2, 1668, is recorded only in notes made later, but it is a rare case in which we have a record of the discussion following the presentation. Bourdon claimed that Carracci's colors were symbolic: the angel clad in white represented the purity of the celestial spirits. The red and the yellow on the drapery of Saint Paul, seated with arms raised, each had particular symbolism, the red representing the animosity with which he caused the blood of Christians to flow, the yellow, which is associated with the light, implying his future conversion. Bourdon found a mystical dimension in the colors of each of the figures. But when the academicians turned their attention to the second version of the subject and compared the two, they noted that the corresponding figures were dressed in different colors. This lack of uniformity led them to formulate the rule that in purely allegorical subjects the painter can observe the symbolism of colors, but in pictures of historical subjects they must ignore them and concern themselves only with

the "economy and sweet union" of the colors.[29] As is usually the case with strict theoretical formulations, practice tended to be governed by practical considerations.

In the back and forth debate that continued over several years, Le Brun made clear his position in discussions of Poussin. A Conférence presented by Jean Nocret in December 1670 on Poussin's *Ecstasy of Saint Paul* described Poussin's coloring approvingly but without reference to any symbolism. Le Brun took the podium a month later to discuss the same work. The entire picture, he proclaimed, was a "mute theology" in which the least detail, even of coloring, "hid so many mysteries." He made clear that it was his intention to correct Nocret and to insist upon the coherent intellectual nature of coloring.[30]

Later in 1671 Gabriel Blanchard, who upheld the superiority of the Venetians over the central Italians and even of Zeuxis over Apelles, launched an attack on the Académie's position on color. The next year Le Brun, reasserting the primacy of *dessin*, attempted to squelch the debate with the following statement:

> It must be considered that colour in painting cannot produce any hue or tint that does not derive from the actual material which supports the colour, for one would not know how to make a green with a red pigment, nor blue with a yellow. For this reason it

must be said that colour depends entirely on matter, and, as a result, is less noble than design, which comes directly from the spirit.[31]

Blanchard's pro-color position was taken up in a series of pamphlets by Roger de Piles, who, although he was not a member of the Académie, had been following the argument. It was de Piles, we remember, a strong advocate of Rubens, who advised the Duc de Richelieu to buy Rubens's paintings, such as the *Judgment of Paris* (see fig. 3.35). The resulting quarrel pitted the Poussinistes against the Rubénistes, a quarrel that threatened to undermine the rationalist premise of academic theory, and temporarily succeeded.

De Piles's strategy in defending color was to claim that it's as much a rational process as drawing. He first asserted that color is indispensable because it is what makes things visible: "Nature is only imitable as far as she is visible and she is only visible, as she is coloured."[32] He then distinguished between the material of the painter's color, the pigments, and the mixture that the painter creates to imitate nature. Pigments are not the equivalent of colors that we observe in nature. The challenge to the painter is to translate what is viewed into a convincing simulacrum. His trump card was to take the argument used to justify dessin and apply it to couleur: the painter must correct the colors of nature, he argued, just as he must correct its form with his drawing.[33]

Coloring requires the painter not only to go beyond imitation and to compensate for the inadequacies of nature, but also to create a harmonious ensemble that is both pleasing and affecting. The ensemble depends on the deployment of the chiaroscuro, not merely to model figures and objects and to assure that they are properly distanced, but to attract the eye and agreeably deceive it. The painter's task is to compose his colors with an eye to their harmonious interactions. De Piles has at last made the case for the engagement of the intellect in the facture of picture-making, beyond the creation of a design. At the same time, he elevated the status of coloring and subversively underscored "appeal to the emotions" as a desirable attribute of painting.

The issue of appeal to the emotions had come to the fore in the Counter-Reformation. Protestants and puritans and moral purists distrusted emotion and therefore color, whereas the Catholic Church advocated it. At the same time that the Calvinists rejected images and whitewashed their places of worship, the Catholic Counter-Reformation embraced heartrending martyrdoms of saints and explosive visionary events using the means of paint, and especially color, to make the invisible visible and the miraculous plausible. The decree on images promulgated by the Council of Trent in the final session in December 1563 and published in 1564, in response to the attacks by Protestants, affirmed the utility of images in the education of the faithful and, in the words of the decree, as a means "to move the emotions" of the viewer.

In the nineteenth century the debate took a political turn. The opposition of Jean-Auguste-Dominique Ingres as the proponent of line, versus Eugène Delacroix as the champion of color, was actually about the perception in the popular mind of the alignment of Delacroix and the Romantics with the radical left, the Socialists, and Ingres and the Neoclassicists with the political right, the reaction. A famous cartoon shows the two as warring medieval jousters. Entitled "République des arts," and published in the *Journal pour Rire* on July 28, 1849, it makes the politics explicit in the inscription on the hem of Ingres's horse's skirt, which punningly reads, "Rubens is a Red" (meaning Socialist).[34] Color was associated with anti-establishment partisans, and those holding power regarded it with wary caution. In fact, though it is never overt, the seventeenth-century debate was political, and probably also chauvinist: the academician representing the establishment aligned against the outsiders, the supporters of Rubens—who was Flemish, not even French. The power of color to subvert rationality would be further celebrated in the twentieth century.

Rubens, who had never had a following in the Académie, was a prime influence on Watteau, the rising star of the new generation. In place of heavy-handed political allegories of the type Le Brun was called upon to produce, patrons were increasingly enjoying the kind of small, delicately painted scenes of love at which Watteau excelled.

WATTEAU

Jean-Antoine Watteau, like Rubens, was born in Flanders. When he moved to Paris soon after the turn of the century he was a member of the community of Flemish artists who lived and worked on the fringe, selling small genre paintings in the Flemish and Dutch tradition at the fair at Saint-Germain. He must be the most famous painter to have begun his career as one of those talents exploited by wholesalers. His friend and early biographer Edme-François Gersaint gives us this picture of the seamy side of painting production:

> In those days, many small portraits and subjects of devotion were wholesaled to the merchants in the provinces, who bought them by the dozen or even the gross. The painter for whom [Watteau] had just begun to work was the one most in demand for this kind of painting, in which he maintained a considerable turnover. He had as many as a dozen miserable pupils whom he used like manual laborers. The only talent that he required of his apprentices was for quick execution. Each one had a job. Some did skies; others did heads; this one painted draperies; that one dabbed in the highlights. Finally the picture found itself finished when it had passed through the hands of the last one.[35]

Watteau was adept at speedy execution. His prodigious talent and imagination were discovered soon enough. After two apprenticeships, in 1709 he applied and came in second in the competition for the Prix de Rome; when he applied again in 1712 he was instead awarded provisional membership in the Académie. By 1717 he was accepted in the Académie Royale, which created a special category, the *fêtes galantes,* for his gently sensual scenes of aristocrats gamboling in fantasy parklands. The old guard would not accept them as history painting, to be sure, but they had to recognize that this painter and this new genre belonged within the fold of the establishment.

Watteau's new genre mirrored the change of taste and mood that marked the turn of the century. In Le Brun's time, Watteau would not have had a chance, as Thomas Gaehtgens has remarked, but the Sun King and his regime were in decline.[36] Watteau wittily shows in one of his pictures Louis's portrait being packed away in a crate. The commitment to high moral seriousness in art passed to England, where Lord Shaftesbury articulated his call for paintings of civic virtue, while Paris turned to these subtle scenes of flirtation and seduction so brilliantly depicted by Watteau. His elegant ladies and courtiers dressed in pastel satins are seen at such a distance that their features can't be distinguished and their expressions remain ambiguous.[37] Rubens's Garden of Love is filled now with wispy, laconic idlers in an imaginary landscape, where cupids fly about, where

trees and mountains are ethereal, and cares and commitments have been shed before entering. Colors are desaturated as if seen through the film of distance, and Watteau's feathery brushstroke breaks up the surface so that figures seem as insubstantial as they are petite and far away. This ingratiating color is often underlain with a rosy ground on top of the conventional red ochre, or sometimes with only a white imprimatura, as in the *Pilgrimage to Cythera* (fig. 4.10).[38] He studied groups of figures separately in rough sketches, then combined them, correcting the scale as necessary, so that the composing took place on his canvas using a fluid drawing, in bright red, probably lake, which was probably intended to show through the upper layers of paint.[39] This procedure, so different from the academic, helps account for the casual appearance of his composition, and for the knots of figures in haphazard but pleasing relationship to one another.

Watteau was clearly on the side of Rubens in the Poussinistes–Rubénistes quarrel, which was not so much about color versus line as it was about reason versus feeling. Scrutiny of Rubens's paintings reveals that they are on the whole not brightly colored. In fact Poussin used more bright color—carefully modulated to establish the spatial recession, to be sure—than Rubens. What distinguished Rubens's manner was his loose brushwork, derived like Rembrandt's from Titian, to engage the feelings of the viewer. It is interesting to study the way a Rubens was revised and repainted after his death to make it conform to academic taste. Roger de Piles had recommended to Duke Richelieu that he acquire Rubens's *Judgment of Paris,* discussed in Chapter 3, for his collection (see fig. 3.35). When the duke was forced to dispose of many of his paintings and it came on the market, it did not meet the Académie's standards of decorum and was in part repainted by an unknown hand and shorn of the lighthearted humor Rubens had invested it with. Rubens had had a studio copy made to preserve his design. By comparing this unchanged copy in Dresden (fig. 4.11) with the altered original we can see what revisions were made and, in the process, get a sense of how the Académie viewed Rubens. In particular the figure of Paris, son of the king of Troy, had to be made more dignified. The academicians implicitly criticized Rubens for the moment he chose: Paris is shown gazing and indecisive, rather than at the pinnacle of the narrative when he awards the apple to Venus. As a result, his gesture

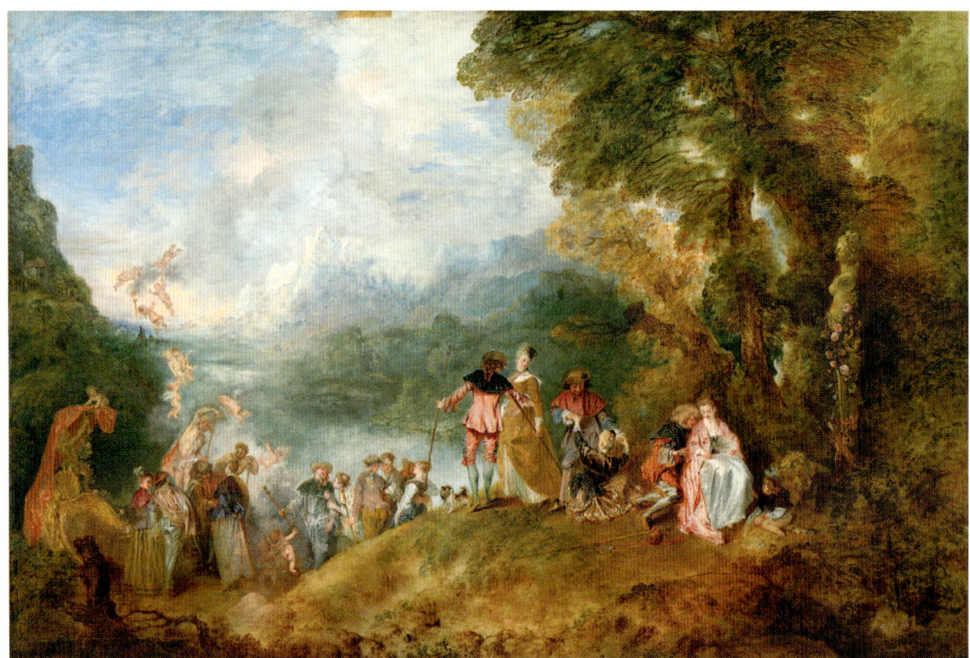

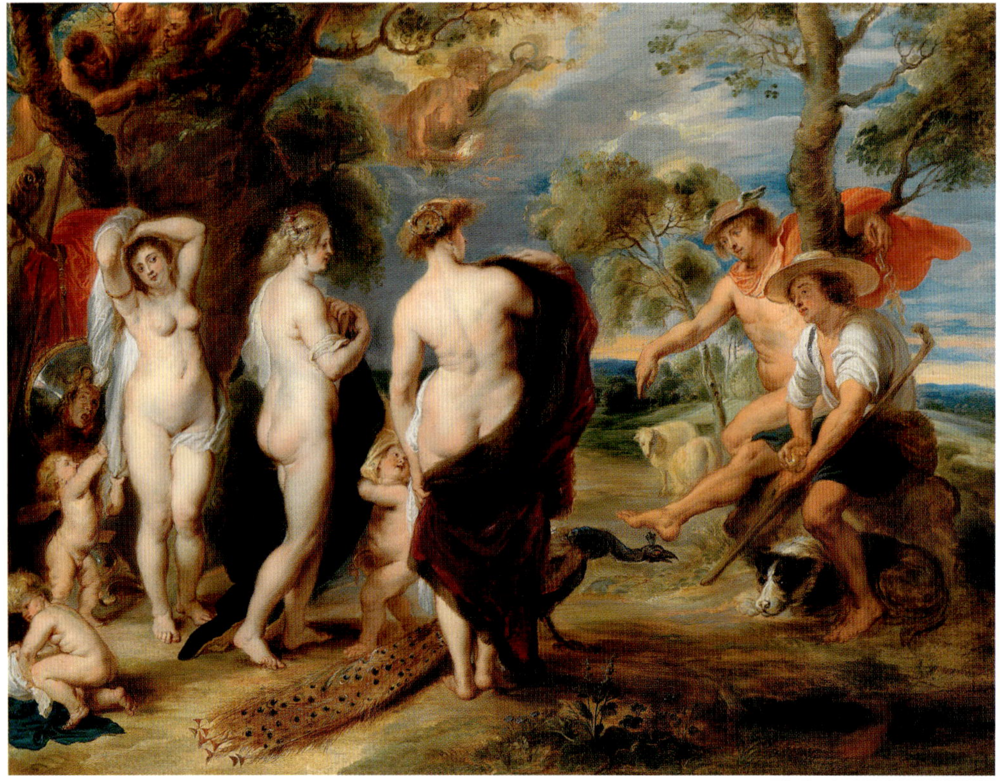

was revised.[40] Also Paris has been "improved" in costume and in posture.[41] Rubens originally portrayed him not as the famously handsome son of King Priam, but as a shepherd-boy dolt who is dazzled by the goddesses dropping their drapery for his perusal, a response that the viewer shares. His awkwardly extended leg has been lowered to the ground, and he has been ennobled with a

straw hat and a muscular torso. The satyr-voyeurs who excitedly discuss the merits of the disrobing women have been removed, probably because they were discomfiting reminders to the male viewer of the sexual connotations of what he was admiring. Interestingly, Rubens's color remained unaltered. What was not acceptable to the Académie was the appeal to the viewer to participate in the emotions of Paris, and the way the brushstroke invites that participation.

In the Rococo, Watteau's successors, chief among them François Boucher, would celebrate the dethroning of reason with the exuberate crowning of the erotic in lush, sensuous coloring.

THE ROCOCO

The eighteenth century is the time when art entered the public domain and viewing it became a leisure activity of the middle class. Opportunities for artists to exhibit their work to the public were limited for the academicians, who worked in private, more so than for the denizens of shops, which were open to the streets and the public. In the Netherlands and Flanders, of course, dealers served all levels of the market. Even in Italy there were occasional public exhibitions of art—for example, on certain saints' days in Rome when works in private collections were put on display at several churches. At the Pantheon an annual juried show was sponsored. Diego Velázquez even participated in 1650 when he was in town, displaying his portrait of his servant *Juan de Pareja* (New York, Metropolitan Museum) to great acclaim. In Venice beginning in the last quarter of the seventeenth century, the Scuola di San Rocco sponsored temporary exhibitions of the works of young artists. In France, markets such as the one at Saint-Germain served the low end, serviced largely by Dutch and Flemish dealers, but before the Salon was instituted artists at the high end had very little access to the public. What was different in Paris was that when the polite public was offered an opportunity to view the work of the academicians, or on a rare occasion, some portion of the royal collection, it was always officially sponsored and controlled.[42] In the early years of the Académie there had been irregular intermittent exhibitions of the work of members to the public; beginning in 1667 there were seven such exhibitions by the end of the century, then another in 1704, which was the last until 1725.

The democratization and the politicization of art are reflected in developments in its display to the public, leading to the establishment of public art museums all across Europe from the eighteenth century on. The year 1737 was serendipitous. In 1737 Anna Maria Luisa de' Medici, the last of the family who had ruled Florence since the sixteenth century, willed all the Medici possessions to the Tuscan state, provided nothing should ever leave Florence. This paved the way for the opening of the Uffizi Gallery to the public twenty-two years later. In 1737 in Paris the Académie opened to the public the first Salon in the Louvre where members displayed their new work. It would be fifty-six years before the first exhibition of art, confiscated by the Revolution from the royal and aristocratic collections, was displayed in the Musée de Louvre, but over the course of that half-century the French public learned to take responsibility for their national culture and to discourse about it.[43] Beginning with that first Salon, what had been the exclusive province of the rich became a place where the classes met and debated values, giving voice to their differing views of the proper function of art.

The public that packed the Salon was at the start a heterogeneous and unruly crowd who, as Thomas Crow has demonstrated, were not on the whole collectors of art.[44] At the beginning there were few with any command of a language of aesthetic criticism. Creating such a language among the artists had been a goal of the Conférences sponsored by Le Brun in the early Académie. Yet the very availability of the art that the Salon offered the public spawned critics who publicized their judgments, whether considered or not, and engendered debate. The public, having been invited in, thus found a voice. As the century wore on, art criticism became increasingly sophisticated and increasingly able to reflect the political and social views of the critics. Perhaps because de Piles had developed and publicized discussion of color, the critical language of color was more highly developed from the start, and color was a frequent topic of critics. Denis Diderot, editor of and contributor to the *Encyclopédie*, became the chief spokesman of a group of critics who opposed the art of the court and the establishment, and their first target was the ultrarefined and elitist painting of the Rococo, sponsored particularly by Louis XV's mistress, Madame de Pompadour.

At court there was resentment at the rise of Jeanne-Antoinette Poisson from the bourgeoisie, first to the king's official mistress and then to his trusted friend and advisor. The future Marquise de Pompadour made up in beauty what she lacked in noble lineage, except in the eyes of the court. Despite her tact, her charm, and her beauty, no one believed that this arriviste would hold the king's attention for long. In that view the courtiers were much mistaken. Pompadour imbibed the elaborate rituals of the court and responded to the backbiting that was endemic there with kindness and generosity. Even

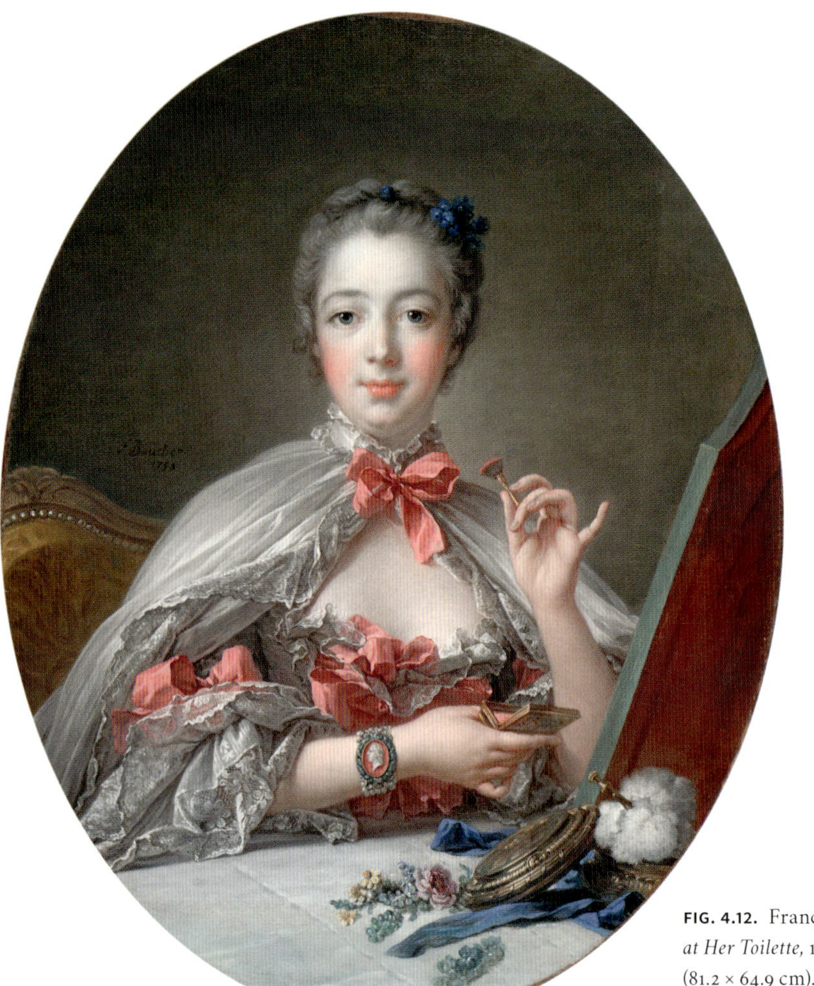

when the physical side of her relationship with the king subsided, she nonetheless maintained her position of authority and it was her taste that ruled. The Rococo is generally regarded as a flight from the politics and propaganda that had motivated the academic art of Le Brun and Louis XIV, but there is an undeniable political message embedded in the painting that Madame de Pompadour patronized and that her favorite painter, François Boucher, practiced, and it did not escape the attention of the early critics of the Salon. Though no one dared directly criticize the king's favorite, the critics deplored the feminization of taste, particularly the passion for pink.

Madame de Pompadour had her portrait made again and again by the leading painters—Boucher, Jean-Marc Nattier, Maurice Quentin de la Tour, François-Hubert Drouais—in her exquisite satin taffeta gowns with her powdered and brightly rouged cheeks. The most intriguing is Boucher's *Madame de Pompadour at Her Toilette,*

showing her with brush in hand, applying her makeup (fig. 4.12). Because the modern viewer probably believes that the purpose of makeup is to conceal flaws and disappear from view, not flaunt its presence, we are puzzled and have overlooked the political message embedded here. As Melissa Hyde has shown, cosmetics were the privilege of the aristocrats; when the king's favorite had herself painted in the act of painting her face, she and her painter were making a statement about the status she had achieved and the power that she wielded.[45]

Madame de Pompadour commissioned the pair of paintings of the rising and the setting of the sun for her château at Bellevue, where eventually the tapestries based on them adorned the king's bedroom. In the *Rising of the Sun*, Apollo reluctantly parts from the adoring Thetis, his sea goddess, to take the reins of the chariot of the sun from her, as amorini push the clouds of night away. In the *Setting of the Sun*, the god eagerly descends from his chariot to join his lover as the blanket of darkness

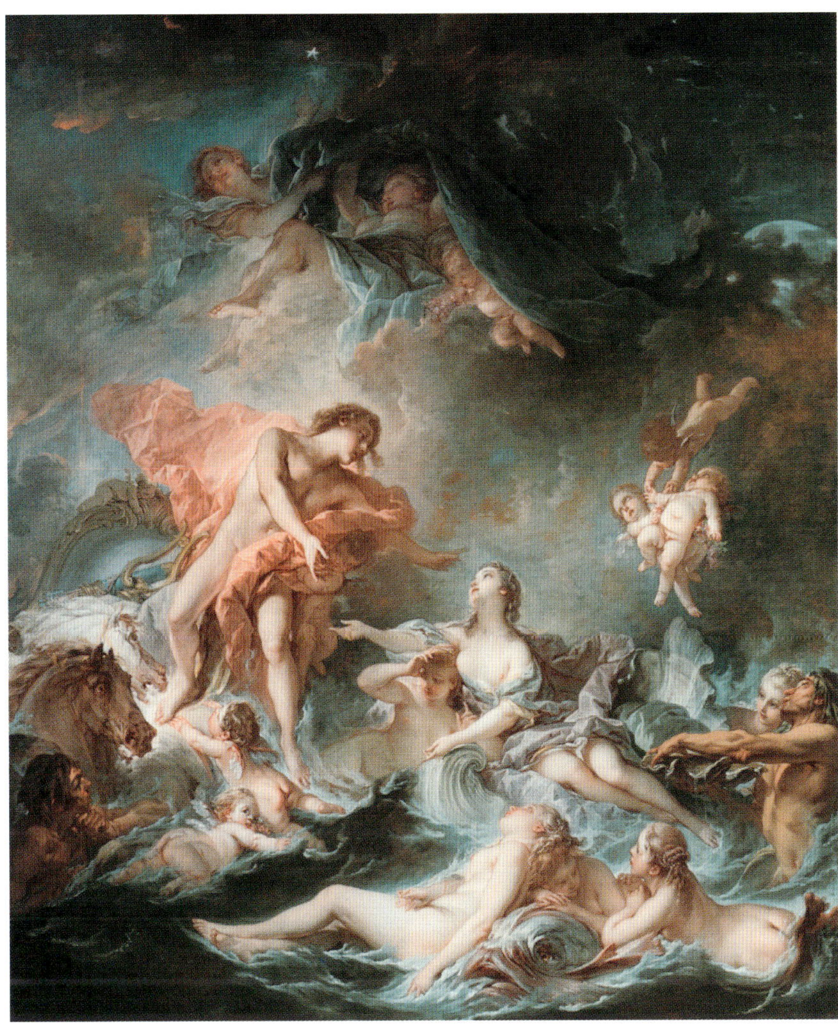

FIG. 4.13. François Boucher, *Setting of the Sun*, 1752. Oil on canvas, 10 ft. 5 in. × 8 ft. 6 in. (318 × 261 cm). Wallace Collection, London.

closes around them (fig. 4.13). She will give him comfort and repose—and more—after his wearying day of work. De La Fosse's version looks stiff and staged in comparison (see fig. 4.7). Boucher is a genius at imagining a world in the sky, where the mundane laws of nature are suspended, and making it a convincing alternative and improved reality.

Following upon the brief career of Watteau, Boucher expanded the *style galant* to focus on the loves of the Olympians. Like Watteau and Rubens, his mythologies take place in a realm remote from the here and now. Central-point perspective, that consummate tool of naturalism, gives way to clouds, airy but substantial enough to support graceful nudes, or water of a similarly improbable density. We might imagine that such charmingly erotic images as these would have been enjoyed in privacy, but on the contrary the Apollo and Thetis pair were exhibited as a centerpiece in the Salon of 1753. These paintings belonged by definition to the noblest genre, that

of history painting, but in the critics' view they degraded it by substituting frivolous eroticism for its proper stately seriousness. The covert reason for the attacks of critics was the association of the king and the upstart Pompadour with Apollo and his lover.

It was above all the cosmetic coloring that drew the fire. In his coloring, Boucher rejected the time-honored convention of classicism, the imitation of nature. His palette instead centered on pale blue, pearly white, and rose, the tints of makeup, and it was that chimerical rose that most provoked, with one critic saying, "Everything is rose-colored and lasts no longer than the rose."[46] His seductive rosy flesh was especially deplored, with another critic writing, "In fact in fairyland, his use of color might be very beautiful. That rosy flesh can only be for fairies."[47] One critic made explicit the gendering of color: "His color is never male, it is rarely true to life, and is almost always too bright," meaning, I think, that it is lacking in chiaroscuro.[48]

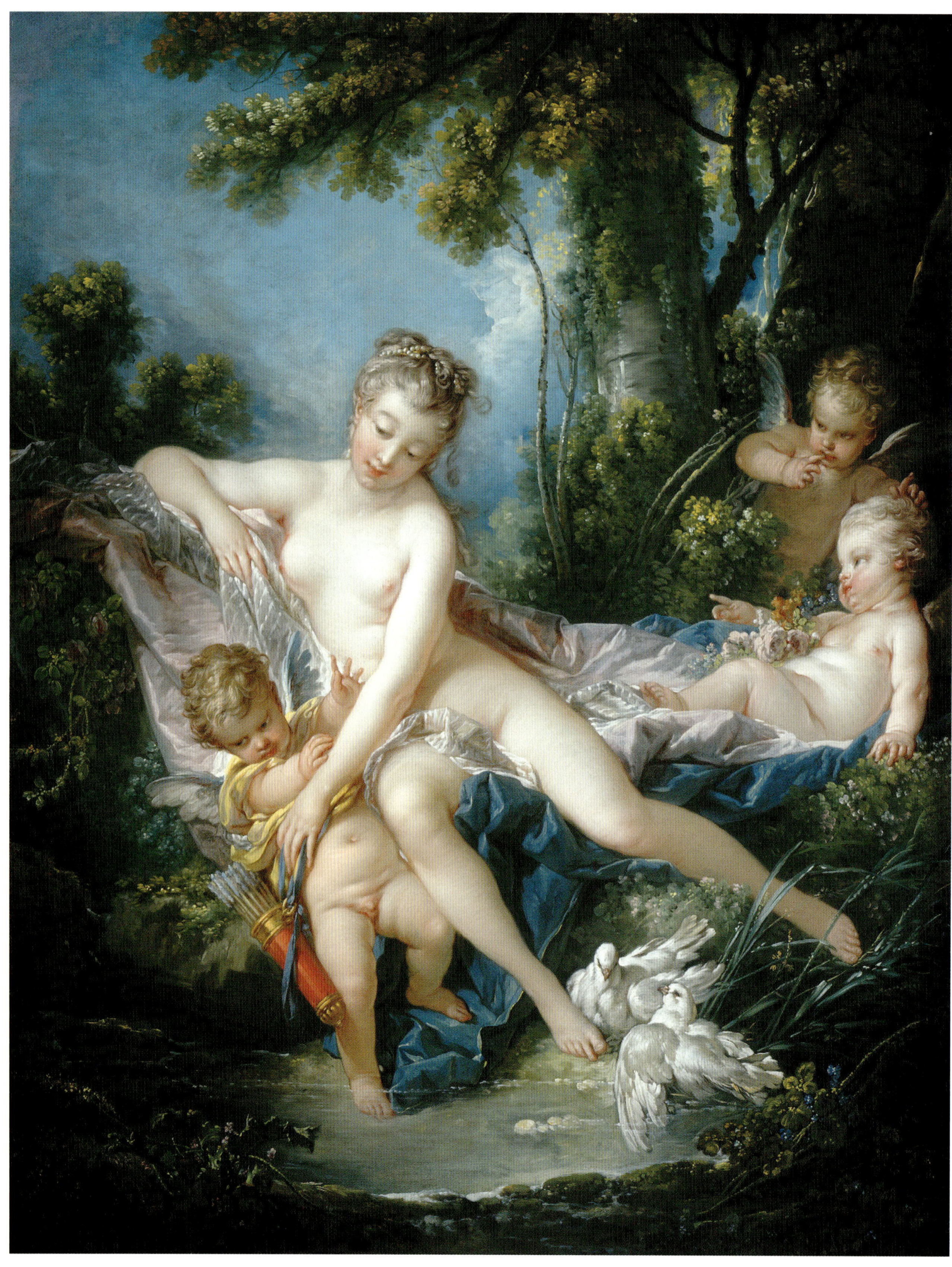

FIG. 4.14. François Boucher, *The Bath of Venus,* 1751. Oil on canvas, 42 1/8 × 33 3/8 in. (107 × 84.8 cm). National Gallery of Art, Washington, D.C.

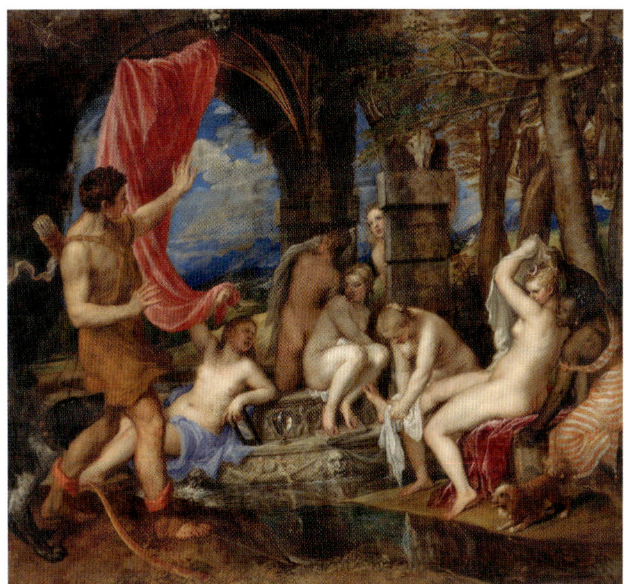

In the new, less rigidly formal regime of Louis XV, courtiers were flocking back to Paris, away from the tedium of Versailles and its court etiquette. For the *hôtels* they built they preferred small canvases that would fit the overdoors or walls of intimate, delicately gilded salons. Boucher devised a style that leavened Rubens but retained his lighthearted appeal. He painted his exquisite *The Bath of Venus* (fig. 4.14), also for Pompadour's Château de Bellevue, together with its pendant, *The Toilette of Venus* (New York, Metropolitan Museum of Art), appropriately enough for the *appartement des bains*.[49] It gives a privileged glimpse of the petite goddess dabbling in the water with a rebellious baby Cupid under her protective arm. Rococo was opposed to perspectival spatial constructions because they distance viewers, placing them on the other side of a pane of glass or a doorway, as it were. The space of these pictures is made as close and as inviolable as possible, giving over the image for the exclusive delectation of the viewer. Here access to Venus's bower is screened behind with delicate foliage, feathery and imprecise.[50] The only precedent for an Olympian observed bathing is Titian's very different *Diana and Actaeon*, and the contrast is informative (fig. 4.15).[51] The goddess Diana reacts with regal rage at the intrusion of the mortal Actaeon. Titian's Diana is heroically active, masculine even in her vehemence. Boucher's Venus, engaging in an intimate feminine ritual, is passive, innocent, and vulnerable, charmingly unaware of the voyeur.

Titian's architecture and woods that surround Diana, as well as his emphatic coloring, reflect her dark anger and predict the controlling act she is about to undertake, condemning the hunter to a cruel death in the jaws of his own hounds. Boucher's delicate, powdery tints remind us of the boudoir or the nursery.

Diderot sniped at Boucher throughout the 1750s, but after Boucher's protectress, Madame de Pompadour, died in 1764 he went after him with a bludgeon. He believed that painting should be morally grounded: "Boucher is completely unaware of this, he's always morally defective." In his commentary on the Salon of 1765 he attacked Boucher's personal morality: "Nothing but beauty spots, rouge, gew-gaws, frivolous women, libidinous satyrs, bastard infants of Bacchus and Silenus . . . the degradation of taste, colour, composition, characterization, expression, drawing . . . the imagination of a man who spends his time with prostitutes of the lowest grade."[52] In contrast, Diderot championed Jean-Baptiste Greuze, who "is always honest and crowds gather in front of his paintings." Although Diderot proclaimed that Boucher should be "out of the Salon, out of the Salon," King Louis did not agree; in that year Boucher was made First Painter to the King.[53] The opposition to official art deepened in the next generation leading up to the Revolution, led by Diderot's endorsement of Greuze and Jean-Baptiste-Siméon Chardin, painters who appealed to the taste of the rising bourgeoisie.

GREUZE AND CHARDIN

Diderot's taste was governed more by politics than by aesthetics, and today the case in favor of Greuze is a hard sell. His most appreciated painting, the *Village Bride*, shows a domestic narrative depicting the betrothal of the daughter of a rural family with a brood of children (fig. 4.16). The bride stands at center, her arm looped through the groom's as he receives the dowry from her aging father. A younger sister weeps quietly as she clings to the bride, while an older one looks on with mixed feelings from behind their father. The burly notary shuffles his papers; Maman holds onto her precious daughter. An unconcerned baby sister feeds the family of chicks from her apron, portending the brood the young couple would produce. Greuze has carefully rendered the emotions of each so as to appeal to middle-class visitors to the Salon of 1761, who could identify with the actors and appreciate the simple, familiar ritual of love. The virtues of family,

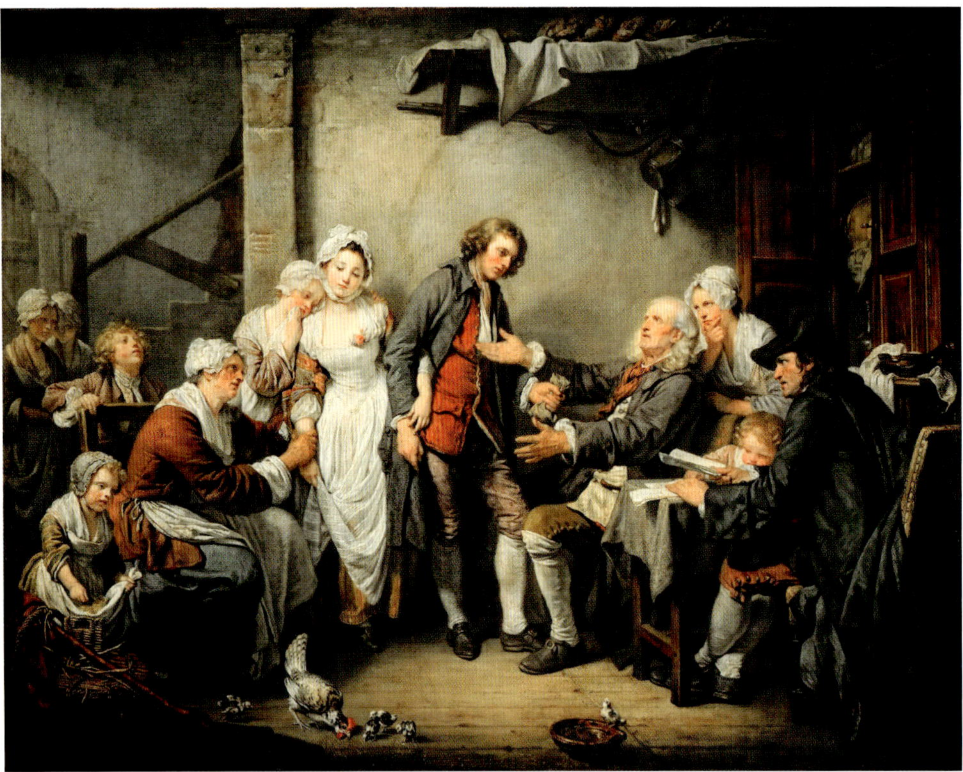

FIG. 4.16. Jean-Baptiste Greuze, *The Village Bride*, 1761. Oil on canvas, 36 × 46½ in. (91.4 × 118.1 cm). Louvre, Paris.

devotion, and hard work celebrated here contrast sharply with Boucher's fantasies. Greuze makes his point with his choice of color: not a hint of makeup or powdered pastel, but earthy colors of browns and grays, with white, the color of innocence, picking out the bride. The large family points to the purpose of love and marriage as procreation, not recreation.

Greuze was part of the revival of Dutch genre painting, which began to be felt in the second and third decades of the century. It offered a democratic art that set itself against that of the Académie and the court.[54] Greuze took up the anecdotal character of Dutch genre painting but enlarged it, literally, in the sense that the measurement of the *Village Bride* is more like three by four feet than the petite pictures on which it's modeled. He intended his enlargement to be also in significance and the depth of feeling it elicits. Indeed, critics proclaimed themselves deeply moved by its honesty: "The graceful suppleness of a pretty waist which is the work of nature not of art is painted with a delicacy beyond all praise. . . . His brush can ennoble the rustic genre without altering its essential truth."[55]

Greuze intended to challenge the criteria for the category of history painting in order to modernize it. In his genre paintings he imitated antique and Renaissance

sculptures, and he wished to arouse the participation of the viewer just as history painting did.[56] Diderot, who supported him, found official painting as practiced by Boucher and Jean-Honoré Fragonard to be superficial as well as lascivious. He made an opposition between fantasy and truth to nature, calling the former mannered and false, declaring they were the same thing. Diderot was uneasy with sexual seductiveness, which he claimed could compromise aesthetic judgment: "It seems to me I have seen enough tits and buttocks; these seductive objects interfere with the soul's emotions by throwing the senses into confusion."[57] Greuze's *Village Bride,* on the other hand, "is full of wit and delicacy. His choice of subject is a proof of *sensibilité* and good conduct."[58] According to the critic Étienne La Font de Saint-Yenne, the senses, to which Boucher and his color made appeal, were opposed to the soul.[59]

The sentimentality that we object to in Greuze's paintings was exactly what Diderot promoted. He recognized that the new viewers for art brought into being by the Salons wanted paintings that would touch their emotions and confirm the moral values they tried to live by. Like Le Brun, Diderot believed art should be morally uplifting. Unlike Le Brun, he believed that it should appeal to the emotions, not just reason. The Académie,

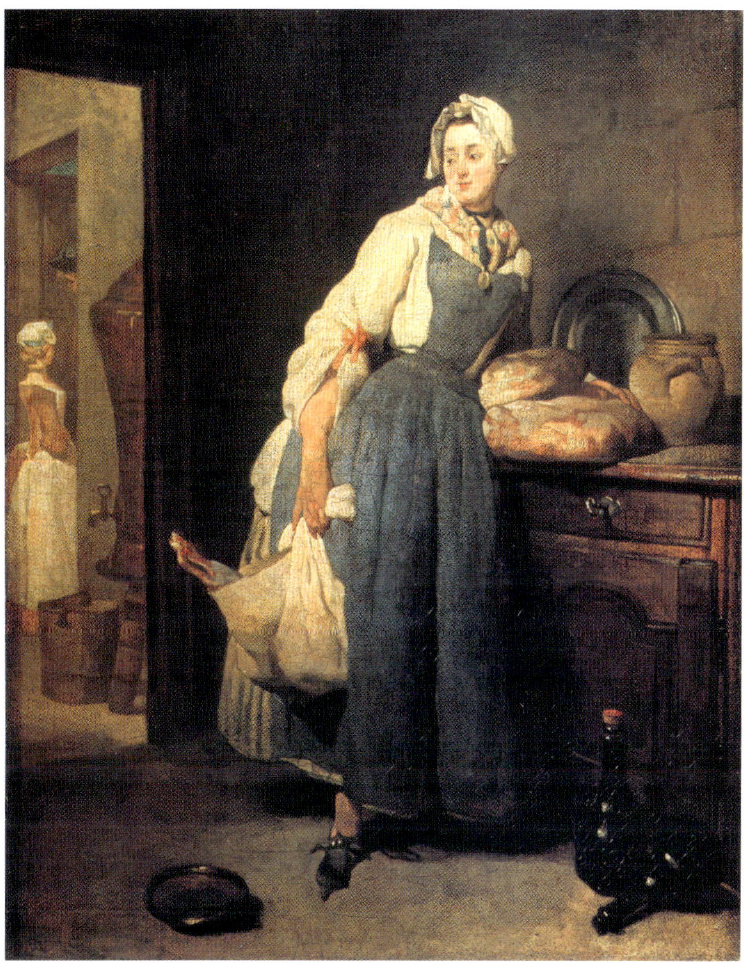

however, was impervious to attempts to undermine its traditional teachings, and under the superintendent, the Comte d'Angiviller, it moved decisively against efforts to found alternative salons or offer artists opportunities to exhibit outside their domain.[60]

Chardin was another successful painter working, at least initially, outside the circle of court patronage. Even though he was not trained in the academic manner and began his career in the lowly genre of still life, he was accepted into the Académie in 1728. He was appointed to numerous posts, including hanging the Salon of 1761. In 1757 Louis XV granted him coveted quarters and a studio in the Louvre. He respected the Académie but, drawing no doubt on his own unorthodox experience, he attacked the system of drawing from copies and casts instead of from nature.

Chardin, like Greuze, connected to the tradition of Dutch genre painting, and like his Dutch predecessors he made small, unpretentious pictures, which he sold to bourgeois clients. These pictures usually depict a single

figure often going about daily household chores, such as the servant returning from the market exhibited at the Salon of 1739 (fig. 4.17).[61] She is laying the bread down and holds a bag in her other hand with a joint of meat protruding, but like so many of Chardin's figures she seems distracted or lost in her thoughts. She rises above the mundane task she is engaged in and takes on a dignity above her station. As in Dutch domestic scenes, she is surrounded by the furnishings of an orderly pantry, surroundings that convey the sense of a well-run household. Chardin's facture and his colors show a similar restraint. Working on the conventional double ground of red under brownish gray, he mixes his colors so as to mute their intensity. There is no more virtuosic display in the way he paints than in his subjects, and his austerity of both making and materials is a proper match to those subjects.

Although his pictures give the impression of having been meticulously worked, in fact he worked rapidly. We have no drawings, so we assume that he sketched directly on the ground with chalk. He worked up the composition

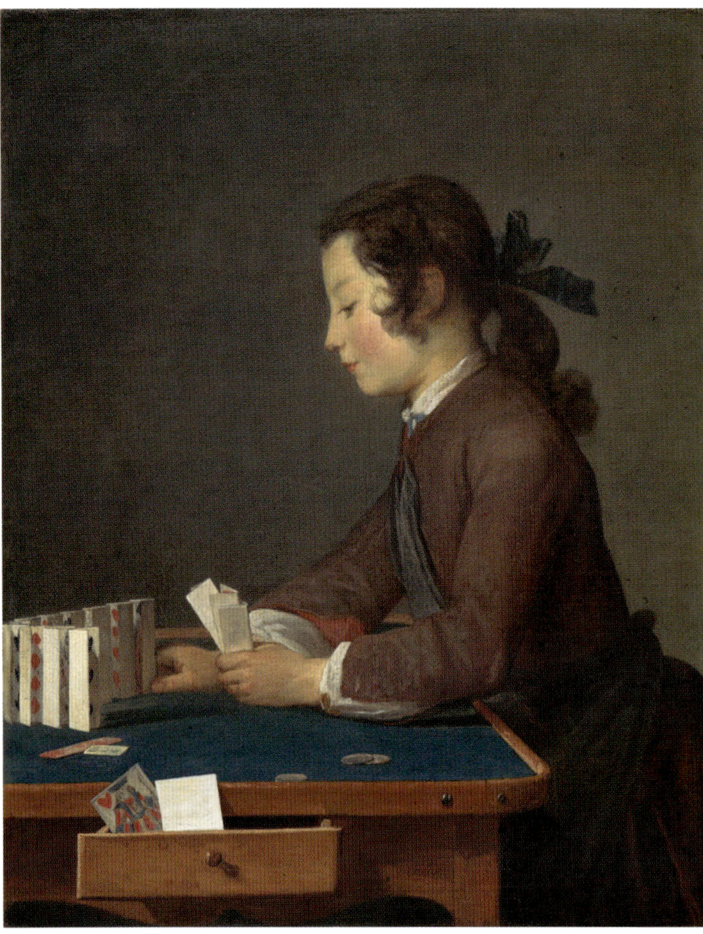

in brownish monochrome, refining and modifying as he went along, but his drawing is uncertain and there are corrections to the contour lines in nearly all his paintings. To recover the light passages, he wiped the brown tone out with a rag dipped in solvent. In order to tone down his whites he added chalk, which absorbs oil and increases the transparency of lead white and makes it more pasty. He used pure lead white for brilliant highlights and opaque passages.[62]

Unusual subjects treated in an unusual manner by Chardin are his children, who gain new dignity and seriousness at his hand (fig. 4.18). Children in art were generally either miniature adults, doll-like mannequins displaying good behavior, or else raucous ruffians creating havoc, displaying the results of poor discipline and courting the moral censure of the viewer. A new regard for children and their upbringing had begun to appear in the late seventeenth century, most famously in the work of John Locke, whose *Some Thoughts Concerning Education* (1693, translated into French in 1695) argued for a more humane education that would develop virtue. There were

even advocates for making education enjoyable. The bishop of Cambria, François de Salignac de la Mothe-Fénelon, who was the mentor of Louis XIV's grandson and advocated the education of girls, wrote in 1687: "Let's make studies enjoyable; let's conceal it under the appearance of freedom and pleasure; let's sometimes allow children to interrupt their studies with small spurts of amusement; they need these distractions to relax their minds."[63] The *House of Cards,* a picture Chardin typically created in multiple versions and replicas, shows a boy of ten or eleven absorbed in arranging cards (see fig. 4.18).[64] He is not playing cards, but building a construction. He is a well-dressed, middle-class lad remarkable for his poise and his assurance. Both boy and table are parallel to the plane, but the open drawer and subtle oblique lines such as the bend of his elbow and the V made by the standing cards prevent the serene scene from being dull. Color works in the same understated way, hardly noticed but masterfully controlled. The boy's jacket and hair harmonize with the neutral brownish background. The deep blue of the felt on the table is darkened in the ribbon that

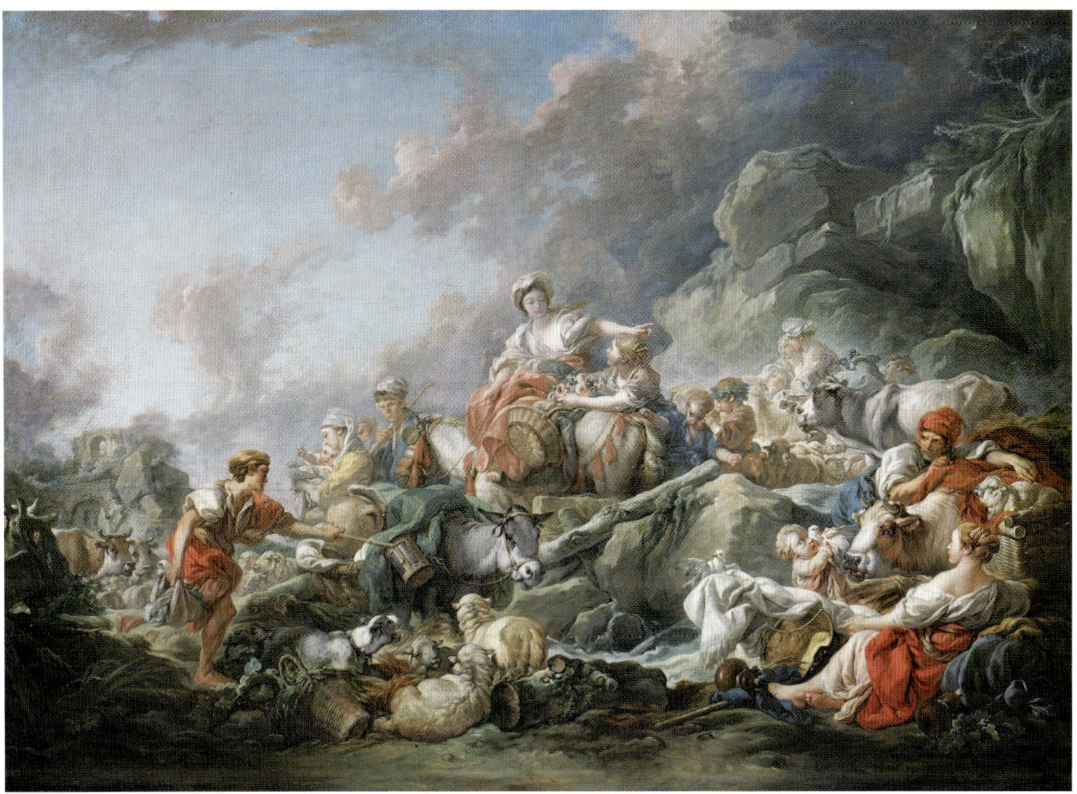

FIG. 4.19. François Boucher, *Return from the Market*, 1767. Oil on canvas, 6 ft. 10 in. × 9 ft. 6 in. (190.5 × 209.6 cm). Museum of Fine Arts, Boston.

holds back his hair and is repeated in the cards. Muted red on the lining of his jacket relates to the hearts and diamonds on the cards. That is all, except for the crucial whites, varied in tone and texture, and the play of shadows. The whole is neither commanding nor artificial, a trivial moment given gravity by its perfect harmony.

In the artistic politics of seventeenth-century France, Chardin and Greuze played an important role, providing for the increasingly well-defined class of wealthy bourgeoisie who had a taste for painting an alternative to the hedonistic art of Madame de Pompadour and her favorite painters. Comparison of Chardin's *Servant Returning from Market* (see fig. 4.17) with a version by Boucher (fig. 4.19) puts their separate worlds in juxtaposition.[65] Boucher's painting is large. Lightly clad figures are jumbled together with benign and adorable farm animals, all set against a majestic expanse of blue sky and rosy clouds. The coloring is as remote from nature as is the composition, a pastel escape from grubby reality. For Chardin, the naturalistic coloring of the *Servant Returning from Market* offered an opportunity to view daily life as having significance: while she performs her domestic chores responsibly, she sees beyond them. She is as tidily dressed as her pantry is orderly. The blue of her dress is echoed in the shadow of the corner behind her, subtly conveying a sense of harmony with her surroundings.

VENICE

The political situation in Venice was very different from France. The declining Venetian state was not sponsoring art, so it was left to the principal families, both ancient and new, who had the means to decorate their *palazzi* with glorifications of themselves and their lineage. The other source of patronage was the churches, which required both altarpieces and ceiling decorations. Giovanni Battista Tiepolo evolved a fresh and airy manner that was lauded at the same time that it puzzled and engaged the viewer in sophisticated visual play.

Tiepolo was the eighteenth-century Rubens, but his work was shaped by the traditions of Venice instead of Flanders. Like Rubens, he received commissions from the patrician elite for large-scale projects—in his case, chiefly for frescoes—and so he depended upon a large and well-trained workshop to execute his designs. Like his Renaissance predecessors in Venice, that workshop was comprised largely of family members, in particular his son Domenico. Like Rubens, he was a master of the oil sketch, and his were prized as Rubens's were by collectors. Tiepolo was also a master of bravura brushwork, which he learned at least in part from his study of Rubens.

Although in Renaissance Venice, fresco was not favored because all the walls are footed in water, Venetians then and in Tiepolo's time wanted fresco in their villas on the terra firma. Tiepolo's approach to the medium revised the traditional technique, particularly so that he could treat light, and with it color, in a way completely unlike his predecessors. The sixteenth-century frescoists had unified their pictures by simulating a consistent source of light, but Tiepolo, in accordance with his and his contemporaries' interest in theatrical effects and deep spatial recession, sought something more than mere plausible consistency.

Many of his commissions were for ceilings, in both churches and residences. He was particularly, almost uniquely, sensitive to the natural lighting. Svetlana Alpers and Michael Baxandall's study of the ceiling fresco of Santa Maria dei Gesuiti showing the *Institution of the Rosary* has demonstrated how Tiepolo took into account the changes in light that occur in the course of a day. Such consideration required that he adjust his cast shadows, fudging them in a way that is not perceived unless scrutinized analytically, but creating a more convincing illusion throughout the day.[66]

In his first commissions he had not yet discovered his light. His tenebrist pictures were heavily modeled, his figures muscled like Tintoretto's. His faces too were made expressive with strong modeling. Then he discovered Paolo Veronese as his exemplar. Tiepolo took from Veronese not only his bland, expressionless faces and his blond palette, but also his theatrical presentation. The early *Crucifixion* in Burano shows a mannerist-like packing of figures, but with Veronese (see figs. 2.31–2.33) as his guide, he adopted a logical, stage-like arrangement in space and let body language and the overall distribution of light and color convey the drama. His contemporaries recognized his art as *paolesca* and appreciated the evocation of the great Venetian past.[67]

His genius was for engagingly inventive composition, exploiting the Rococo taste for asymmetry, and making brilliant use of the expressive void. No one has surpassed Tiepolo's use of negative space. There is a deceptive simplicity to his designs; his forms are often difficult to make

out at first, and we have to work to read them. He was a master at "making strange," at defamiliarizing, a device that was especially effective with his sophisticated audience when he began with a familiar picture of Veronese.[68] Familiarity on the part of viewers is assumed, as is the skill to decipher the conundrums of complex images, and viewers are meant to feel flattered by the assumption and elated by their success in disentangling the image.

For his ceilings he had to take into effect the curvature of the vault and often a long viewing distance. At the Treppenhaus in the Würzburg Residenz (1751–53), where he frescoed the grand stairway with the Four Continents, he had also to deal with the viewers' occluded view as they mounted the stairs (fig. 4.20). Here we can see Tiepolo's genius, making it a teasing game as bits appear and then disappear. In fact it is not the view of the whole, which the visitor cannot capture, or even the view of one entire enormous wall at a time, that pleases, but those snippets full of life and energy that emerge. Unlike Le Brun, who did not want to compromise the seriousness of his images of the glorious Louis, Tiepolo projects his view di sotto in sù and exploits the sometimes-bizarre elision of forms it produces to puzzle and hold viewers' attention.

His fresco technique was adapted to contemporary taste. An oil sketch, such as the one that survives for the Four Continents (fig. 4.21), served multiple uses: it could be shown to the patron as a modello, and it was used as the guide for laying out the composition on the wall. What is extraordinary about Tiepolo's procedure in fresco is that essentially he painted it twice. First he transferred the design, working from the oil sketch and perhaps drawings on a gridded wall. He did not use the traditional sinopia underdrawing, and it seems unlikely that he used cartoons (none survives), except possibly for the occasional difficult passage. Instead, he incised outlines in the wet plaster to aid in the placement of principal figures. The absence of giornata seams between one day's work and the next suggests that he used a plaster mix that stayed wet for longer than was usual.[69] He worked at great speed, reportedly covering five square meters in a day when painting a ceiling.[70] This first layer was executed using earth colors in true fresco and largely, we assume, by the master himself. There followed a period in which he studied the result of this first campaign and then made additional drawings that would guide his assistants in the second painting in

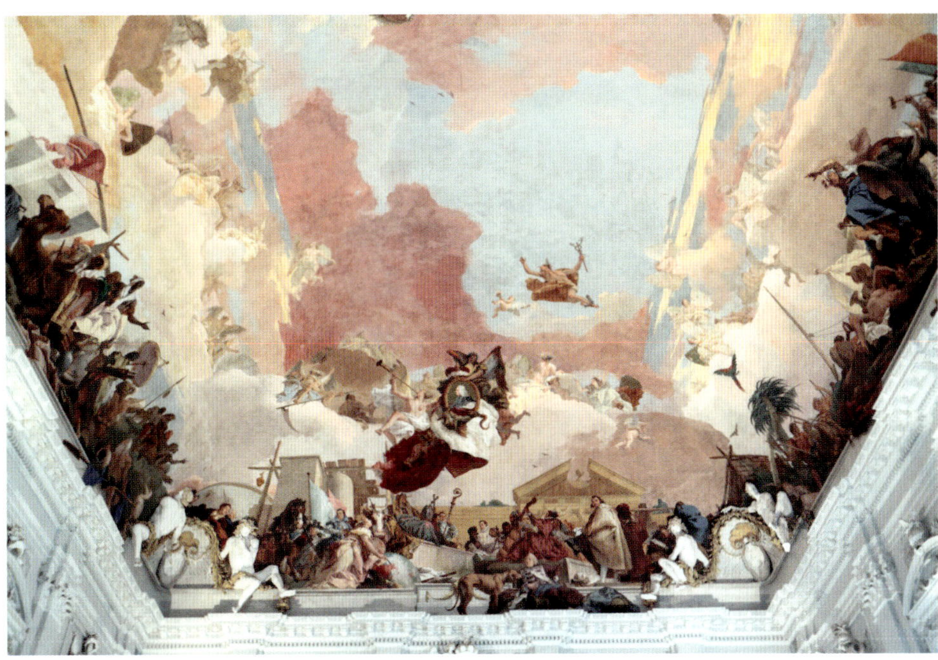

FIG. 4.20. Giovanni Battista Tiepolo, *Ceiling*, 1751–53. Fresco. Würzburg Residenz.

secco.[71] This was more than just retouching. At this stage came the addition of the darks that were darker than fresco allows—and there is a lot of such chiaroscuro— and the bright colors with the pigments that could only be used on dry plaster because they are antipathetic to the lime in fresco. The key to his designs is the dynamic of chiaroscuro on the macroscale. He might color the principal group in pale tones against a light sky, then at the frame show repoussoir figures barely decipherable in their obscurity. No one used the dramatic contrast of a vast expanse of sky broken by a band of clouds better than Tiepolo. Consider how uninteresting his depiction of *America* would be without the black cloud that sweeps obliquely across the sky (fig. 4.22). He shares the dramatic use of cloud with the Dutch landscapists, but unlike them his purpose was narrative and rhetorical, not descriptive.

Tiepolo knew how to make the allure of color coincide with thematic importance. The eye is drawn to the most important actors, lesser figures have less decorative allure, and those that are linked in the narrative are coloristically connected. As was the case with Veronese before him, some critics dismissed Tiepolo as a mere decorator, but those were critics who could not appreciate the genius of his unorthodox design and facture.

We barely considered the native painters of Italy in our exploration of the seventeenth century, but we took note of how important Italy and the Renaissance were

to Rubens and Poussin, and through Poussin to the academic classicism of Le Brun and his school, and we noted that fashionable collectors in Amsterdam, for example, specialized in Italian Renaissance paintings. By the eighteenth century it was de rigueur for young aristocrats of Europe and even America to complete their education by making the Grand Tour of Italy—a kind of secular pilgrimage—to enjoy and to acquire pictures and antiquities, and perhaps to have their portraits made by some eminent painter in Rome such as Pompeo Batoni. If they were English, when they stopped in Venice they might acquire one of Canaletto's *vedute* of the Grand Canal through the offices of his self-appointed agent, the art lover and wealthy businessman known as Consul Joseph Smith, some of whose own Canalettos found their way into the Royal Collection at Windsor.[72]

Rome was of course the goal of the Grand Tour, but the beautiful bay of Naples was often the last stop. From the 1730s, at the excavations of Herculaneum the adventurous traveler could enjoy a tour through the tunnels exploring the newly unearthed artifacts of the Roman patrician town buried in the eruption of Vesuvius. By the 1760s, on a day trip from Naples, the more staid visitors could remain above ground and take in the newly discovered wonders of the neighboring town of Pompeii. The learning that cultured young men acquired on their Grand Tour contributed to the taste for Neoclassicism that blossomed at that time.

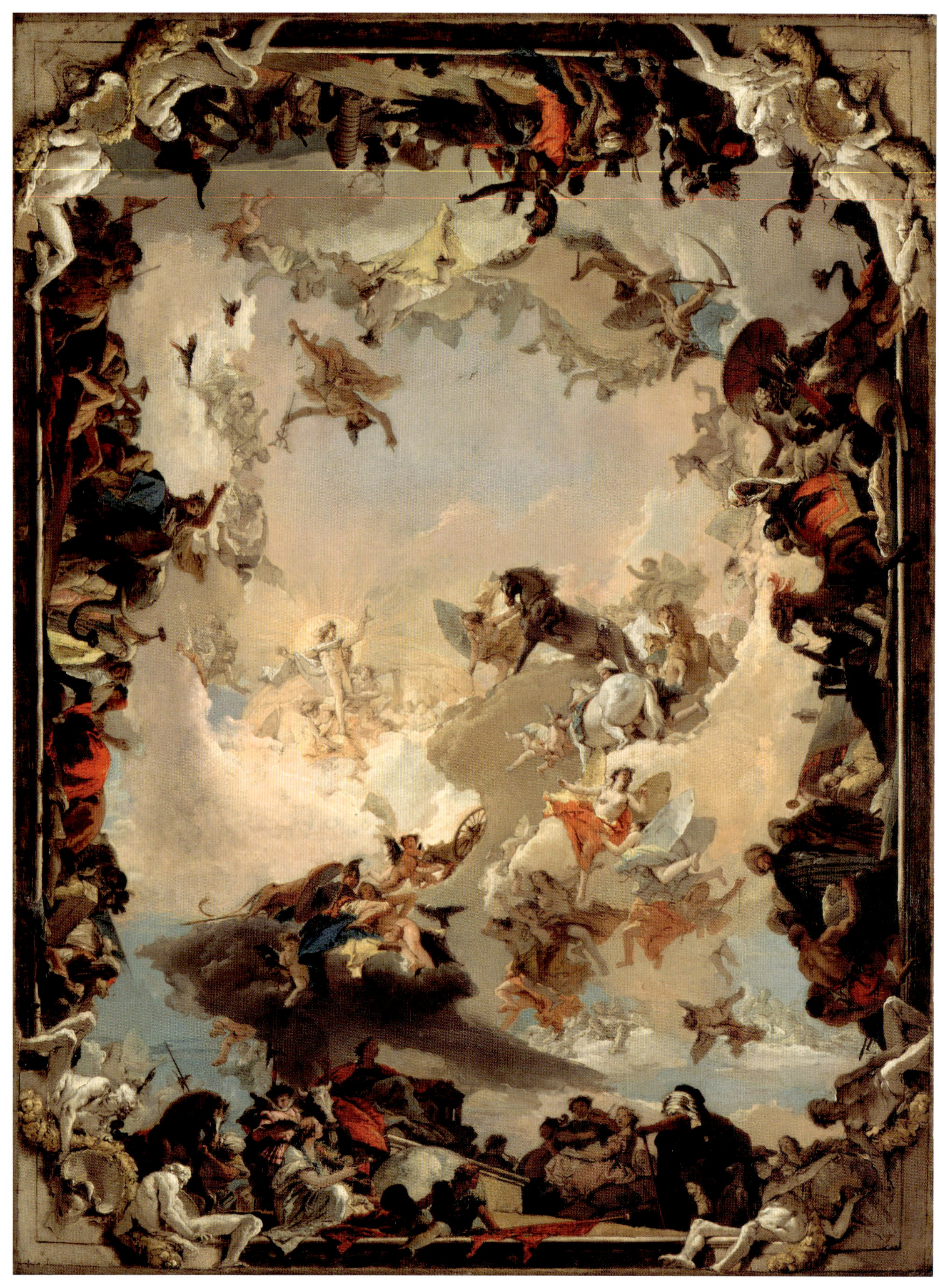

FIG. 4.21. Giovanni Battista Tiepolo, *Allegory of the Planets and Continents*, 1752. Oil on canvas, 73 × 54⅞ in. (185.4 × 139.4 cm). Metropolitan Museum of Art, New York.

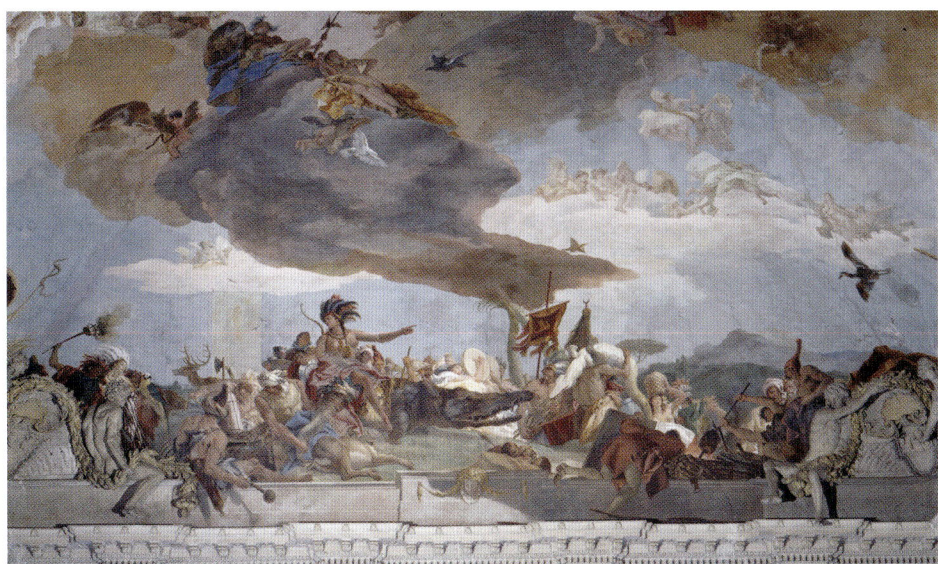

THE SHIFT IN TASTE FROM ROCOCO TO NEOCLASSICISM IN FRANCE

When Boucher was finally appointed First Painter to the King in 1765, his star was waning. In fact his slightly younger rival, Carle van Loo, had been awarded the honor in 1762, and Boucher only succeeded upon his death, more a reward for past achievement than for present prominence. Boucher died five years later. Madame de Pompadour's death in 1764 marked the end of an era, although establishing a new style to suit new times would prove to be a slow process.[73]

The winners of the Prix de Rome from 1745 to 1765 provide an index to the dominant taste. Not surprisingly, during the 1740s and 1750s the followers of Boucher dominated: a pupil of his won the prize in 1747 (Pierre-Charles Le Mettay); in 1752 Fragonard, another of his pupils, was the winner. The winner in 1751, Jean-Baptiste Deshays de Colleville, married Boucher's daughter upon his return to Paris. In Rome, the director of the French Academy from 1751 to 1775 was the very successful Rococo painter Charles-Joseph Natoire. Natoire was the same kind of Rococo painter as Boucher, and like him a favorite of the royal family. In 1750 he was chosen to represent an allegory on the birth of the daughter of the dauphin, the son of Louis XV (fig. 4.23). This very male view of childbirth shows the newborn presented to his mother in charming pastels by an angel on a billowing cloud, overseen by Juno and applauded by putti and sensuous allegories. The next year, when he was appointed to Rome, the mood at

the Académie was antithetical to classicism. As director he would have had a restraining influence on the winners of the Prix de Rome under his guidance, reining in the sway of classical Italy and antiquity. But in the mid-1760s, about a decade before his retirement, Natoire found himself out of sympathy with the pensionnaires who were being sent from Paris because they were more inclined to the classical than to the Rococo. In Paris the view was beginning to prevail that history painting was degraded in such works as Boucher's *Rising* and *Setting of the Sun* (see fig. 4.13). Subjects chosen from history or classical literature and not erotic myth could restore the premier genre to its former seriousness as exemplars of moral virtue. Winners of the Prix de Rome such as Jean Bardin (1765), one of the teachers of David, and François-Guillaume Ménageot (1766), who would be the director of the French Academy in Rome at the outbreak of the Revolution, were not to Natoire's taste. The winner in 1764 was Jacques-Philip-Joseph de Saint-Quentin, with his *Death of Socrates* (fig. 4.24), which anticipates Jacques-Louis David's epochal treatment of the same subject in 1787 (see fig. 4.36). One can imagine that Natoire would have found its grave subject—the philosopher choosing death over a compromise of his moral convictions—pompous, and its style pretentious, with its rhetorical gestures, its theatrical coloring and chiaroscuro, and its figures clad in sculpture-like draperies. Like the winning entries of Bardin and Ménageot, it is rather more Baroque in its oblique design than Neoclassical, but it

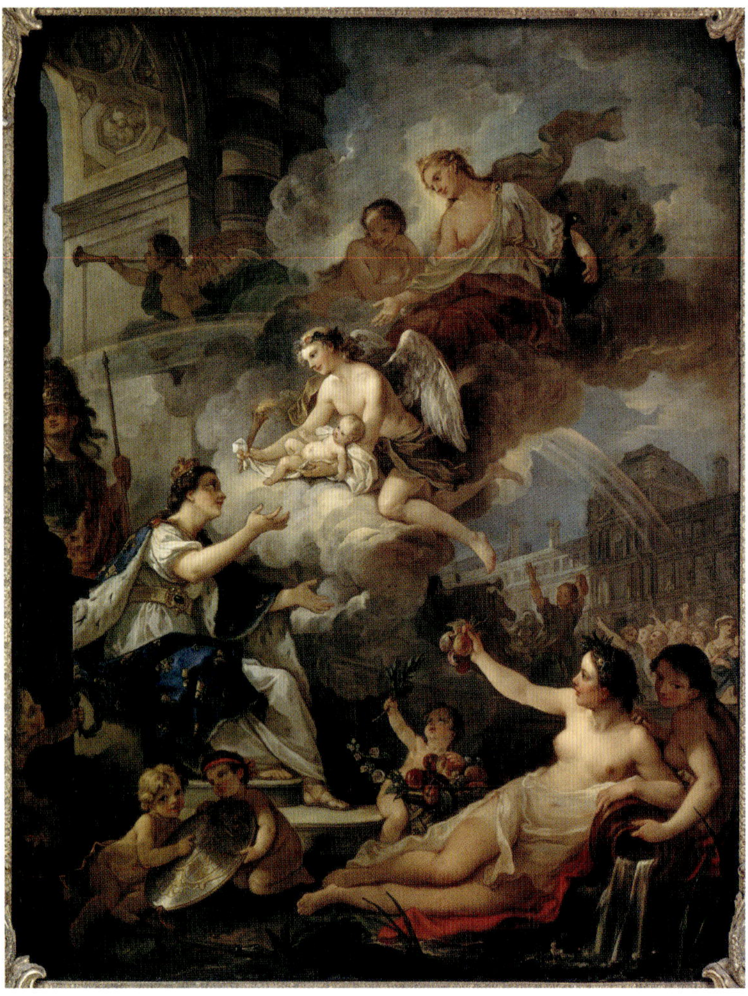

FIG. 4.23. Charles-Joseph Natoire, *Allegory on the Birth of Marie-Zéphirine of France in 1750*, 1750. Oil on canvas, 87 13/16 × 59 1/8 in. (223 × 150 cm). Château de Versailles.

is certainly not Rococo. Perhaps because of this friction Natoire was forced to retire in 1775, and he chose not to return to France but settled in Italy.

In the 1760s and 1770s there was a lack of consensus about the direction French art should be taking. For those who still favored the Rococo, Fragonard was available to continue the tradition of Boucher with capricious renderings of amorous encounters. The patron who commissioned the delightfully naughty *Happy Accidents of the Swing* suggested to the painter, "You will place me in such a way that I would be able to see the legs of the lovely girl, and better still, if you want to enliven your picture a little more" (fig. 4.25).[74] The girl, like a rose in a bower, all in lace and frills, flies over the head of her admirer, a fanciful mirage lifted out of time and space—and suggestively loses her shoe.

By contrast, at about the same time in 1764, the secretary Charles-Nicholas Cochin, in charge of decorating the royal Château de Choisy, commissioned four

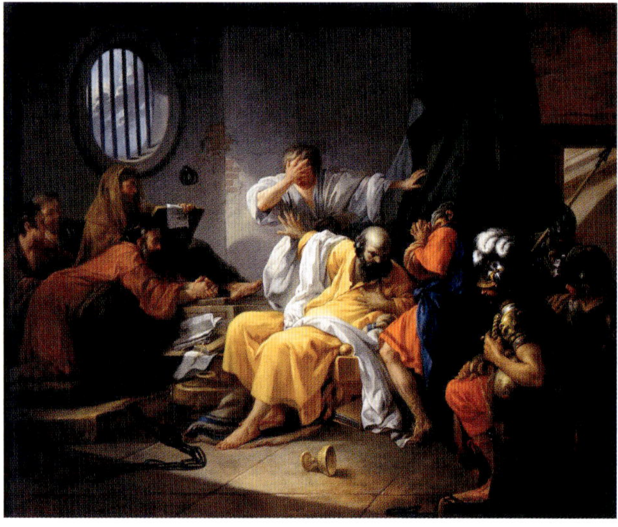

FIG. 4.24. Jacques-Philip-Joseph de Saint-Quentin, *Death of Socrates*, 1762. Oil on canvas, 43 15/16 × 54 1/2 in. (111.5 × 138.5 cm). École nationale supérieure des Beaux-Arts, Paris.

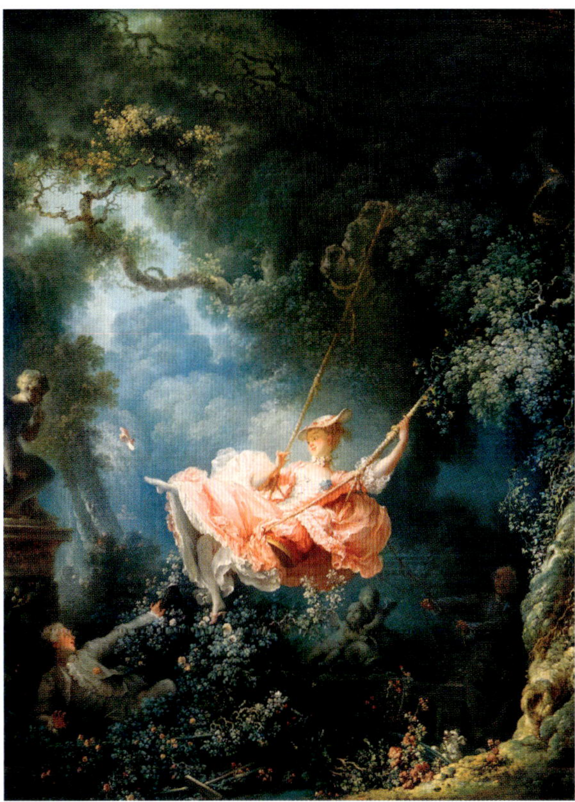

FIG. 4.25. Jean-Honoré Fragonard, *Happy Accidents of the Swing*, c. 1767–68. Oil on canvas, 31 ⅞ × 25 ¼ in. (81 × 64.2 cm). Wallace Collection, London.

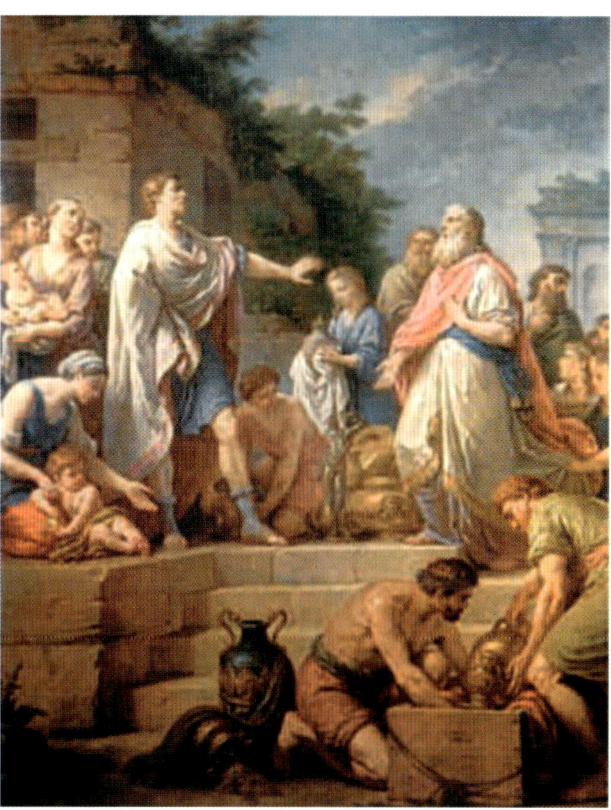

FIG. 4.26. Louis-Jean-François Lagrenée, *Fabricius Refuses the Presents the Ambassadors from Pyrrhus Had Been Ordered to Offer Him*, 1777. Oil on canvas. Musée René Princeteau, Libourne.

paintings depicting generous and humane deeds by the rulers Augustus, Trajan, Titus, and Marcus Aurelius. His intention was to put before the king scenes that could inspire him to noble action, but Louis XV greeted the new decorations with a yawn, and Cochin was compelled to replace them with works by Boucher.[75] Although the subjects of history paintings were nudged from mythological to historical in the mid-1760s, as we have seen, an anonymous critic of the 1769 Salon called for artists to choose interesting national themes instead of obscure and unfamiliar stories from classical history, whose chief virtue was that they provided the painter with the excuse to animate his oversized canvas with theatrical violence.[76] Certainly the subjects chosen by the Prix de Rome winner in 1765 and 1766 answered this description: Bardin presented *Tullius's Daughter Driving Her Chariot over the Body of Her Dead Father* (Mainz, Landesmuseum), and Ménageot, *Tomyris Plunging the Head of Cyrus in a Bowl of Blood* (today at Paris, École Nationale Supérieure des Beaux-Arts).

The commitment on the part of state officials to morally uplifting and didactic subjects continued. Louis XV

appointed Count d'Angiviller as minister of fine arts in 1775. As part of his policy to restore the grand manner, he commissioned for every Salon from 1777 until the Revolution big canvases (to be used also as cartoons for Gobelins tapestries), illustrating the most ennobling qualities of man in general and of the prince in particular.[77] Each painter was assigned a picture with a general moral that he was required to illustrate: (1) Act of Religious Piety among the Greeks; (2) Act of Religious Piety among the Romans; (3) Act of Unselfishness among the Greeks; (4) Act of Unselfishness among the Romans; (5) Act of Incentive to Work among the Romans; (6) Act of Heroic Resolve among the Romans. For the two subjects from French history the painters were to depict: (1) Act of Respect for Virtue; (2) Act of Respect for Morality.[78]

Louis-Jean-François Lagrenée's canvas for category 4 (Act of Unselfishness Among the Romans), *Fabricius Refuses the Presents the Ambassadors from Pyrrhus Had Been Ordered to Offer Him* (1777), has survived (fig. 4.26). The composition is indeed conceived in the grand style, but despite its edifying message, like everything else in this period until David finally consolidated his style, it

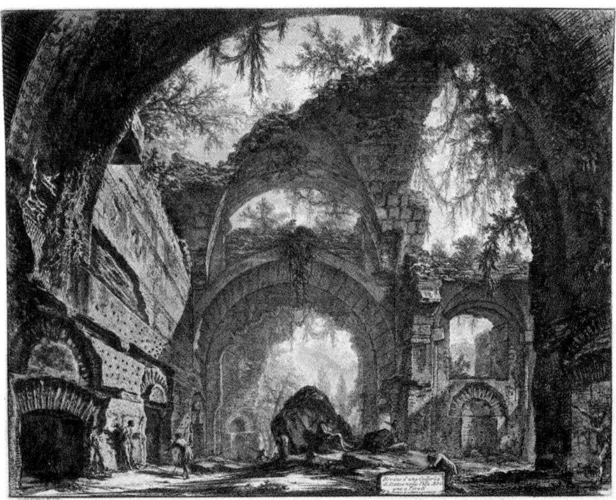

FIG. 4.27. Giovanni Battista Piranesi, *Ruins at Hadrian's Villa, Tivoli,* 1748–74. Etching, 21 1/2 × 31 1/8 in. (54.7 × 79 cm).

disappoints, above all in its coloring. It follows the rules. The whites are deployed somewhat mechanically to pick out the protagonists, with pale reds and blues balancing one another on the secondary figures. The laborers in the foreground are shadowed to show their role as staffage. The drapery folds are small and fussy, refined and elegant rather than grand—the same problem that would plague David himself in his early works.

Merely attempting to reinvigorate the grand style did not constitute creating a new artistic idiom. The Neoclassical would emerge as an answer to the exhaustion with the frivolity and hedonism of the Rococo, but its inspiration would arise, logically enough, from Italy. Since the 1730s visitors to Rome had found an excursion to Naples indispensable, as we have seen, but almost equally exciting and nearer to hand for the members of the French Academy were the excavations near Rome at Ostia and Hadrian's villa, and the opening of the Museo Pio-Clementino in 1772 by Pope Clement XIV. Giovanni Paolo Panini's painted reconstructions of ancient Rome stirred enthusiasm for the antique, and Giovanni Battista Piranesi's etchings stimulated the imagination with his romantic ruins (fig. 4.27). Most significant, Johann Joachim Winckelmann, arriving in Rome in 1755, published his *Thoughts on the Imitation of Greek Works in Painting and Sculpture,* in which he declared that the road to greatness was through imitation of antiquity. His classification of Greek art into the periods we recognize today, separating out and elevating the classic phase of the fifth century to the pinnacle of all art, gave new life to the study of antiquity and inspired many artists to

take up a new classicism. The German painter Anton Raphael Mengs met Winckelmann in Rome and became a celebrity there with his revival of Renaissance classicism in *Parnassus,* the ceiling fresco of the Villa Albani based closely on Raphael's fresco in the Stanza della Segnatura (fig. 4.28; see fig. 2.5). Mengs's version simplifies Raphael's composition, eliminating overlaps between figures and turning it into something more like a frieze than the space-embracing arc that binds Raphael's scene together. The sense of a conversation, which Raphael achieved not only through his groupings but also his coloring, is lost. Mengs deploys his hues more for contrast or balance than in friendly groups, with an eye on identifiable quotations from antiquity, such as Apollo as the Apollo Belvedere in reverse. Nevertheless it was highly acclaimed and influential. Mengs became a man to know on the Roman scene, especially after Winckelmann's murder in 1768, when he became a conduit through whom Winckelmann's ideas were made known. David would meet him when he arrived as a pensionnaire at the French Academy in the late 1770s and would be introduced to Winckelmann's theories through him.

THE DECORUM OF COLOR

Decorum was never far from the minds of the French. The system of correct behavior at the French court, adapted from Baldassare Castiglione's book *The Courtier,* was rearticulated by Nicolas Faret in his *L'honneste homme ou l'art de plaire à la cour* of 1630. Faret in many places copied Castiglione word for word, only omitting the Italian's requirement that the courtier be a scholar; the French courtier from the start was focused on manners, fashion, and ornamental skills.[79] Criticism of Rococo art was often couched in terms of Horace's decorum, either explicitly or by implication. "Decorum" means "appropriate" at its center, as Horace made clear:

> " . . . painters and poets
> Have always shared the right to dare anything."
> I know it: I claim that licence, and grant it in turn:
> But not so the wild and tame should ever mate,
> Or snakes couple with birds, or lambs with tigers.
> . . . Let it be what you wish, but whole and natural.[80]

Because decorum for Horace means matching nature, he rejected hybrid creatures because they are not natural.

When the Abbé Le Blanc wrote his famous letter, presumably to the Comte de Caylus, deploring the

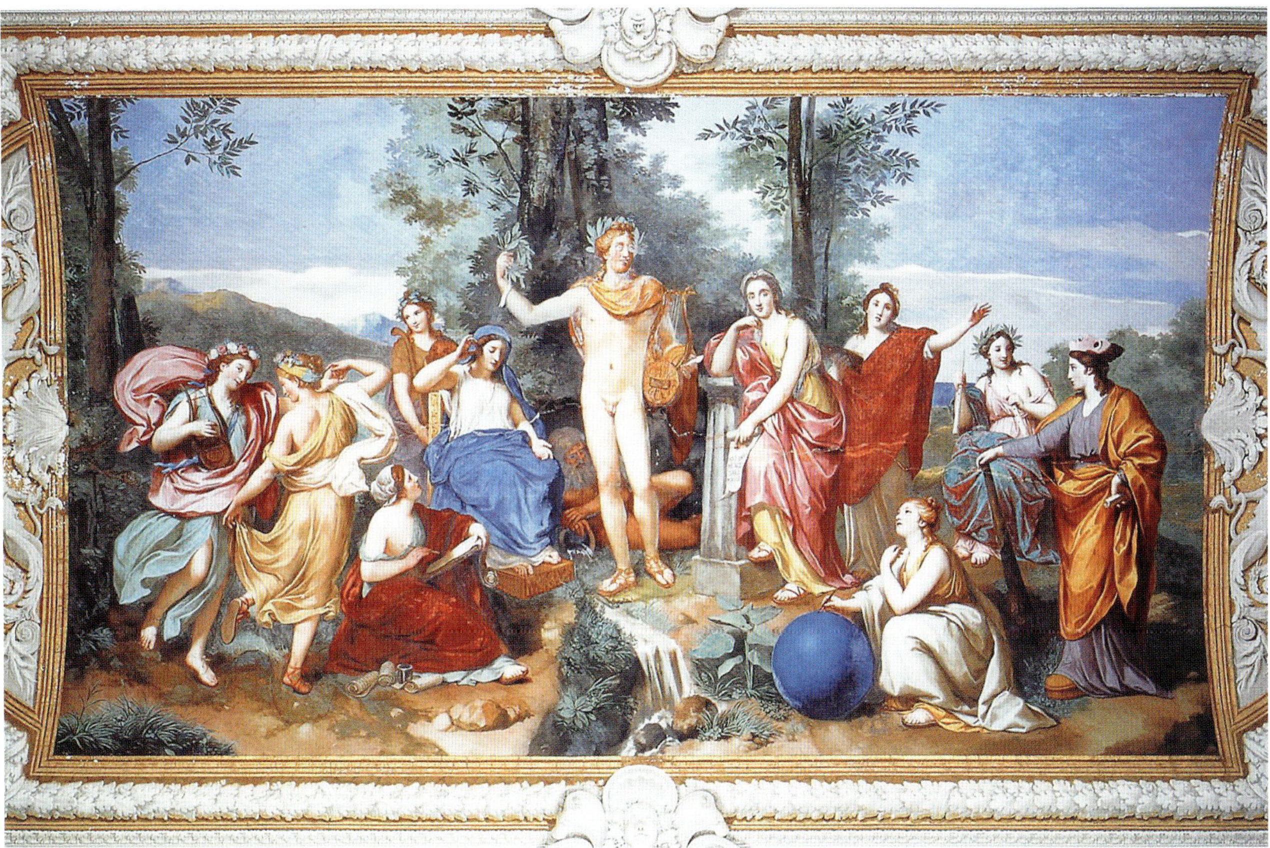

FIG. 4.28. Anton Raphael Mengs, *Parnassus*, 1761. Fresco. Villa Albani, Rome.

abandonment of the taste of Louis XIV—"the golden age for letters and fine arts in France"—he was explicit about the lack of decorum in the Rococo:

> Nothing is more monstrous, as Horace observes, than to couple together beings of different natures; yet 'tis what many of our artists at this time glory in doing. A cupid is the contrast of a dragon; and a shell, of a bat's wing; they no longer observe any order, any probability, in their productions.[81]

When Cochin, another Neoclassicist who deplored the Rococo taste, surreptitiously wrote his satiric letter to the newspaper *Le Mercure* pretending to be a Rococo architect defending the practices of his day, he addressed recent church decoration in terms of the decorum of genres:

> In the good old days it was believed that churches ought to present a grave, even a severe aspect. The most dissipated persons could hardly enter them without finding themselves impressed by serious ideas. We have quite changed all that. Now there is no lady's dressing-room prettier than the chapels we decorate. If some tombs are still put into them we curve their outlines prettily, we gild them all over, in fact we take from them anything lugubrious they might otherwise have. Even our confessionals have an air of gallantry.[82]

Cochin's parodic remarks imply that Rococo color is indecorous in church decoration. This is as close as critics come to discussing the appropriateness of color directly. In fact Rococo color is a perfect match for the amorous fantasies that were intended for the boudoir or for portraits of ladies in their exquisite dresses. Its failure to satisfy in other genres, not just church decoration but the politically important genre to the Académie of history painting, helped hasten the demise of the style.

There have been many moments in the period we have been studying in which the coloring system was happily consonant with the style and the message, or to put it another way, color was decorously matched to the message. The Cennini-style coloring of Fra Angelico and Lorenzo Monaco in the early fifteenth century made possible representing the natural world penetrated by the supernatural. Caravaggio's dark chiaroscuro enabled him to eradicate setting and therefore time, so that his narratives can take place in the past and the present simultaneously. Poussin's Raphaelesque coloring of his maturity suited his rational approach better than the Titianesque coloring of his early career, but his coloring would not have been appropriate at all to depict the Dutch landscape as it looked to contemporaries, for which genre the painters created a wholly different coloring system. Rubens's luscious surfaces and flesh and high-value tonality celebrate life, so that even a gory martyrdom incites contemplation of life eternal. Rembrandt's warm, glowing golden tones invite us to linger pensively to take in his compassionately revealed humanity.

There have been times when the painter deliberately chose a dissonant mode of coloring. Pontormo's unnatural cangiantismo in his *Entombment* transports the scene from this world to the next, invoking resurrection more than death (see fig. 2.19). His pupil, Bronzino, invented his own version of Pontormo's ironic coloring in his *Pietà*, where the splendidly arrayed participants seem better suited to celebrating than to mourning, as indeed they are actually doing in evoking redemption through the Eucharist (see fig. 2.25).

Rococo coloring is as artificial and fantastic as are the scenes depicted. Boucher's coloring had a decorum of its own, well suited to the Rococo architectural style, which substituted, for the large expanses of wall covered with dark fabric of the Louis XIV era, bright, intimate rooms with white walls and floor-to-ceiling windows. The decorum of color for the grand style called for dark pictures with highly dramatic chiaroscuro that would convey the seriousness of the message to the viewer. Boucher created a blond tonality using a pale ground, sometimes rosy in tint but never the double imprimatura of strong reddish brown under gray used in the previous century, which had lent itself to emphatic contrasts of light and shade. On top of his pale ground Boucher rendered his forms with colors tinted with admixtures of white and, most significantly, with almost no down modeling. His shadows, delicately modulated beiges and pearly grays, remain as light and translucent as are his weightless figures supported on clouds. We can actually see Boucher modeling with pinkish red under Venus's arm and on her hand, as Rubens had done, and the palest beige where her left arm casts a shadow on her hip (see fig. 4.14). It is a coloring system tailored to depict some other realm than the

natural world, resembling the supernatural so successfully rendered by Fra Angelico and Lorenzo Monaco and their contemporaries in the absence of down-modeling and with clean, brilliant colors. But Boucher's world is not a supernatural one; rather it is one of an exquisite sensuality. As Melissa Hyde put it, the Rococo is "a period when the arts become the theoretical province of the goddess of love, rather than the goddess of wisdom."[83] When Minerva again took charge, a new decorum of coloring had to be invented.

Color was a major hurdle in the transition from Rococo to Neoclassicism. While it was relatively easy to deduce a compositional model from antique reliefs, there existed no satisfactory model for a coloring system. The frescoes of Herculaneum and Pompeii were damaged and faded, and because they were fresco they tended to be pale. When Joseph-Marie Vien undertook a version of the *Cupid Seller,* copied from Herculaneum, he presented the three women in relief-like composition, parallel to the plane, in a strictly classical salon with antique objects and furnishings (fig. 4.29). Although his composition moves decisively toward Neoclassical, his coloring is not substantially different from the prevailing Rococo. His delicate pastels suit the erotic content well enough, but the whole falls short of laying the ground for a conversion in style.

When in the 1760s the Académie endorsed a return to history painting in the manner of the grand style, the painters to whom they awarded the Prix de Rome, such as Saint-Quentin, Bardin, and Ménageot, recognized that Rococo coloring did not suit their theatrical subjects. Like Vien, however, they failed to invent a new system, and in fact their pictures were essentially revivals of Le Brun and the grand style. If we compare Corneille's *Hercules Punishing Busiris* of 1675 (see fig. 4.2) with Saint-Quentin's *Death of Socrates* of a century later (1762; see fig. 4.24), we find a similar Baroque composition and strongly contrasted chiaroscuro. The protagonists are pulled out of the dark shadows, with the light focused on their high-value flesh or garments in yellow and white. To be sure, Saint-Quentin has moved toward the kind of didactic subject capable of teaching a moral lesson that critics of the Rococo were calling for, but in other respects there is nothing new here. Neither does Mengs contribute anything new in terms of coloring. Even as late as 1777, when Lagrenée is creating a state commission in his *Fabricius,* it is colored in Rococo pastels (see

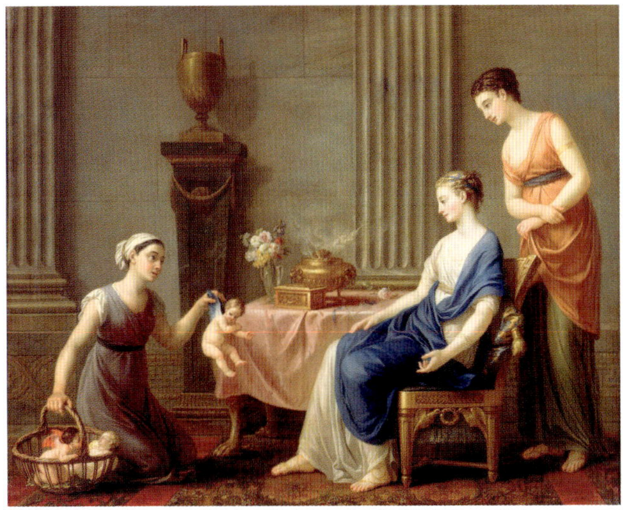

FIG. 4.29. Joseph-Marie Vien, *The Cupid Seller*, 1763. Oil on canvas, 46 × 55⅛ in. (117 × 140 cm). Musée National du Château de Fontainebleau.

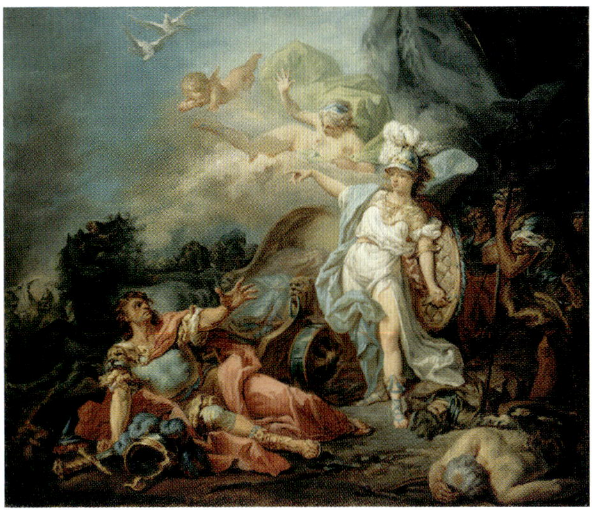

FIG. 4.30. Jacques-Louis David, *Combat between Minerva and Mars*, 1771. Oil on canvas, 44⅞ × 55⅛ in. (114 × 140 cm). Louvre, Paris.

fig. 4.26). It was David's incomparable contribution to discover a color style that matched the seriousness and severity of the message.

DAVID

The eighteenth-century engagement with politicized art culminated in Jacques-Louis David and the Revolution. No artist before him had been so deeply immersed in politics, and no political movement had had an artist as talented or as committed to its cause. But David did not develop early, nor did he find without struggle his groundbreaking solution to the call for a style that could convey moral conviction. He competed for the Prix de Rome three consecutive years, first in 1771, losing each year. After his second loss in 1772 he went on a hunger strike until he was persuaded by members of the Académie to continue to paint. Then, to his chagrin, he lost again in 1773. By 1774, when he finally won at the age of twenty-six, he had developed a deep resentment toward the academic system.[84] His first entry, *Combat between Minerva and Mars* (fig. 4.30), shows how surprisingly close he was to Boucher, his first teacher, despite the fact that Boucher had turned him over to Vien for instruction. The composition is constructed on oblique lines; billowing clouds, from which Minerva in her chariot seems just to have alighted, define the space. Rosy pinks and pale azure blues dominate the colors. By the time of his winning piece, *Antiochus and Stratonice*, he has moved from Rococo closer to Neoclassical in composition, but not in coloring or light

(fig. 4.31). Antiochus, laid out on his bed, suffers from an illness that the doctor, seated in the foreground, has diagnosed as love for his stepmother. When the doctor persuades the king, the crowned man at center, to give his young wife to his son, Antiochus recovers. The scene is set amid classical architecture and furniture, with the figures firmly planted and more nearly parallel to the plane. David has overcome for the most part his tendency to clutter, moving toward greater economy and restraint, but his draperies are still convoluted. His overtly dramatic chiaroscuro feels contrived and his coloring, still tinged with Rococo pastels,

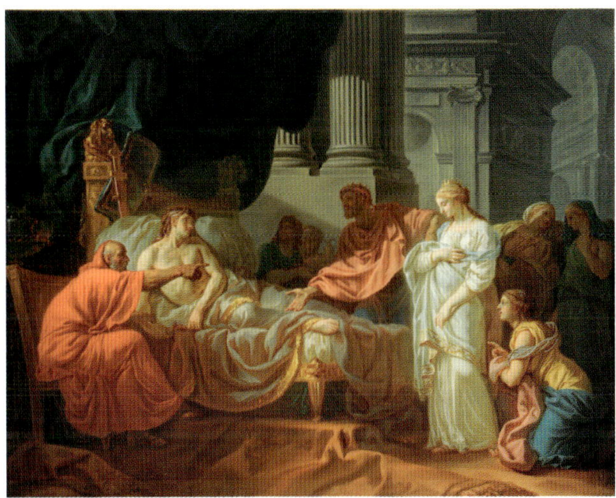

FIG. 4.31. Jacques-Louis David, *Antiochus and Stratonice*, 1774. Oil on canvas, 47¼ × 61 in. (120 × 155 cm). École nationale supérieure des Beaux-Arts, Paris.

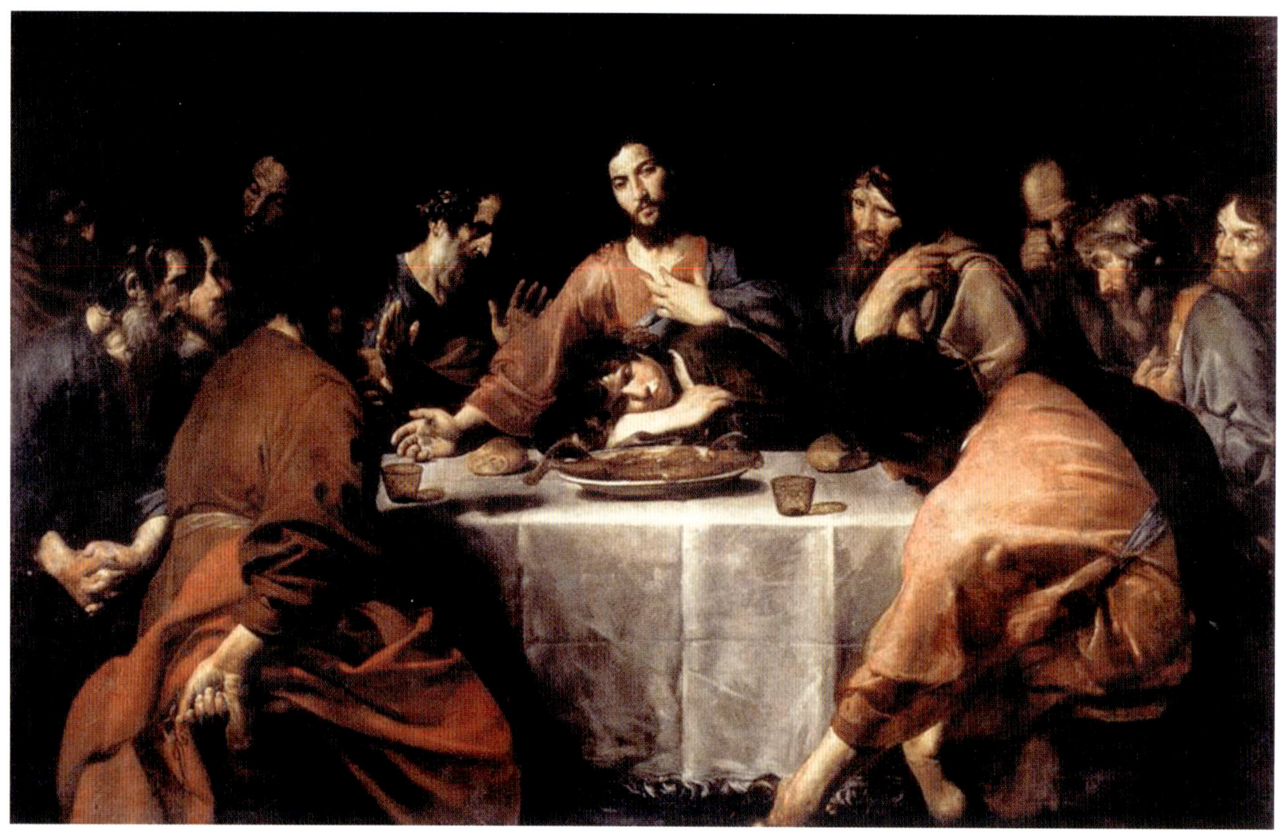

FIG. 4.32. Valentin de Boulogne, *Last Supper*, c. 1625–26. Oil on canvas, 54 ¾ × 90 ½ in. (139 × 230 cm). Galleria Nazionale d'Arte Antica, Rome.

FIG. 4.33. Jacques-Louis David, *Belisarius Begging for Alms*, 1781. Oil on canvas, 9 ft. 5 in. × 10 ft. 3 in. (288 × 312 cm). Palais des Beaux-Arts, Lille.

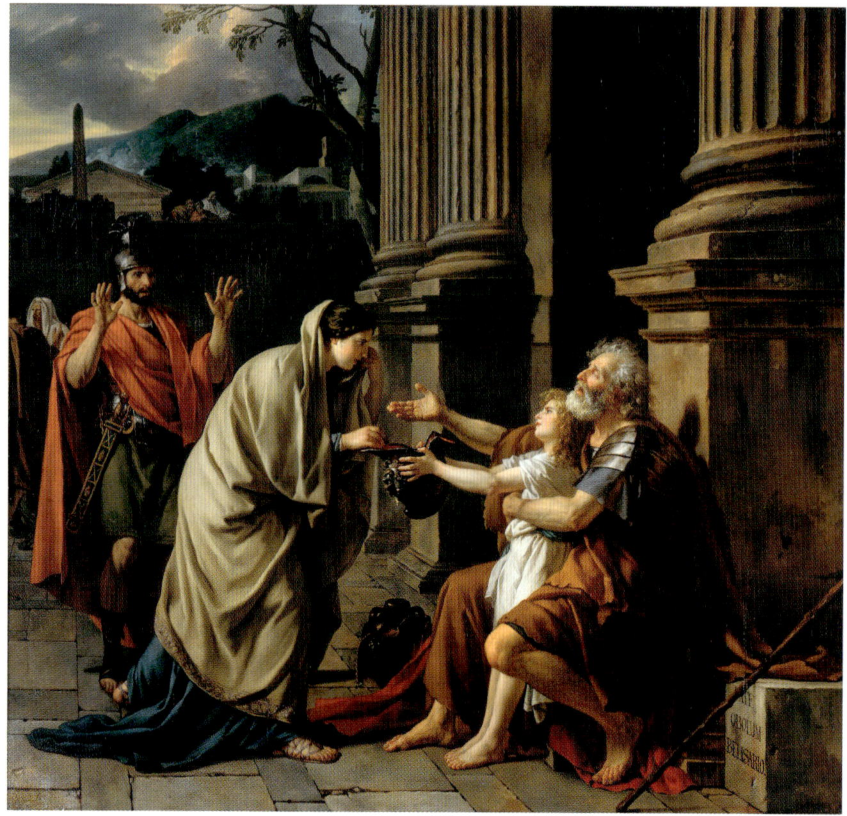

reminds us of his teacher, Vien. He could be said at this point to have achieved an acceptable re-evocation of the grand manner, but not yet to have arrived at his mature Neoclassicism.

In 1775 he traveled to Rome with Vien, who had just been appointed the new director of the French Academy, replacing Natoire. Although David announced that he was determined to resist the allure of antiquity, he was captivated by Caravaggio instead. His pupil Étienne-Jean Delécluze later recalled what David told him he learned in Rome. It was about color, with David believing:

> When we think of French painting, from the ceilings by Lemoine to those painted even today [1805] by Berthélemy, including such works as Natoire's, Vanloo,'s, etc, we are shocked, not so much by the weakness of their style or the lack of taste as by their insipidness and terrible drabness of their coloring. Color is what matters most in art, for it is color that makes the first impact on our senses.

He went on to recount his first experience upon arriving in Rome:

> When I arrived in Italy with M. Vien, the first thing that struck me in the Italian paintings I saw was the power of the tones and shades. In this they differed most radically from French painting, and this new relationship of light and shade, the impressive vividness of the relief which I had never known before struck me so forcibly that in the early days of my Italian stay I thought the whole secret of art consisted of reproducing—as some late sixteenth-century Italian colorists have done—the clear, positive relief almost always found in nature.

He allows that he had to work his way around to the more "delicate" colorists:

> I must admit that at the time my vision was so callow that I was quite unable to benefit from looking at anything so delicate as a painting by Andrea del Sarto, Titian, or any of the most skillful colorists; I could only appreciate and truly understand such brutal works—though they were also excellent—as a Caravaggio, a Ribera, and Valentin, their pupil . . . Raphael was far too delicate a dish for my coarse mind; I had to develop my taste gradually, through a diet, and my first ration was copying the Last Supper by Valentin.[85]

Valentin de Boulogne was a Frenchman who moved to Italy, where he was a pupil of Simon Vouet and, like Vouet, fell under the spell of Caravaggio.[86] His *Last Supper* provided an example to David of severe composition, uncluttered with only the essentials included, where the light picks out the expressions and gestures that make the narrative vivid (fig. 4.32). The color scheme, restricted to earthy browns against a blackish background, contributes to the focus. Caravaggio's own pictures allow a broader range of color, but it's evident that David found in Caravaggio's light and coloring the means to discipline his style, and at the same time to energize the staid Neoclassicism of his master, Vien.

By the time David had returned to Paris, he was able to imbue his *Belisarius Begging for Alms* with the urgency of his political and moral message (fig. 4.33). A woman and a soldier who had served under him recognize the aged, blind, and neglected war hero Belisarius. Belisarius had been a popular subject for recent history painting because his story resonated with a scandalous miscarriage of justice in which a French general had been falsely denounced and executed.[87] The austere columns and bases behind the general reinforce his dignity. David has learned from Caravaggio to substitute a heavy fabric that falls in ponderous folds, in the place of the thin, fine silks he had wrapped around his figures in *Antiochus and Stratonice.* Caravaggio's clean, simple draperies, with their strong relief, replace his earlier tangled and intricate folds, betokening a gravity suitable to his message. From Poussin he has taken spare, eloquent gestures, and from classical relief a strict planarity. His simplified lighting focuses on his coloring: strong, pure, allowing no distraction, modeled only as much as required to direct the viewer's attention.

Diderot had been seeking in Neoclassicism a return to the *grand goût.* He understood that it entailed more than the imitation of antique forms, and he had criticized the lack of true sentiment and the empty rhetorical gestures, rendered without conviction, that he saw in the history paintings that the Salons offered. When David exhibited *Belisarius* in 1781, Diderot recognized that it embodied the *grande manière* that he had been seeking: it had soul, the heads were expressive without affectation, and the figures were noble but at the same time natural. He remarked about the color interestingly, saying that it was beautiful without being brilliant.[88]

David received a commission to paint an episode from

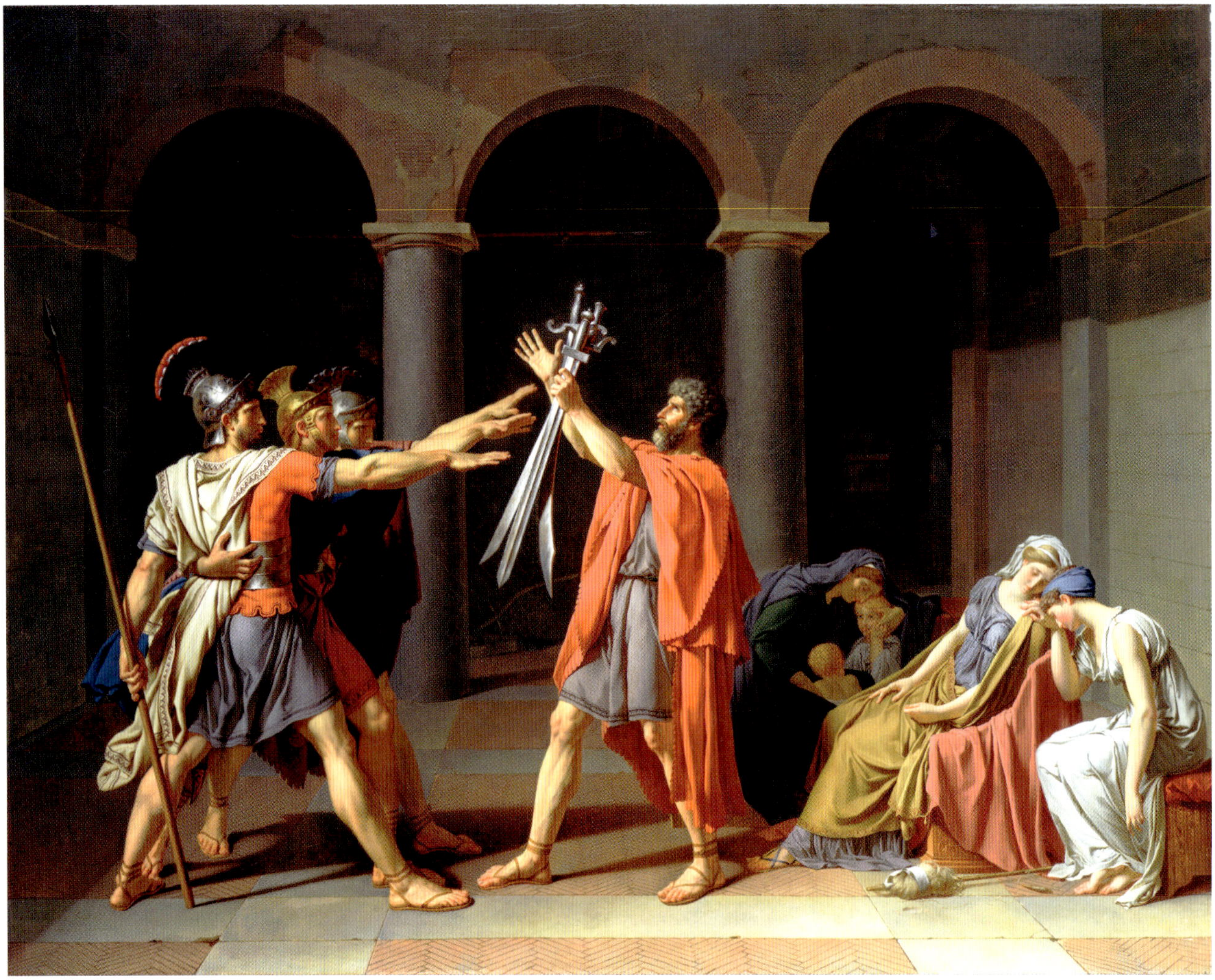

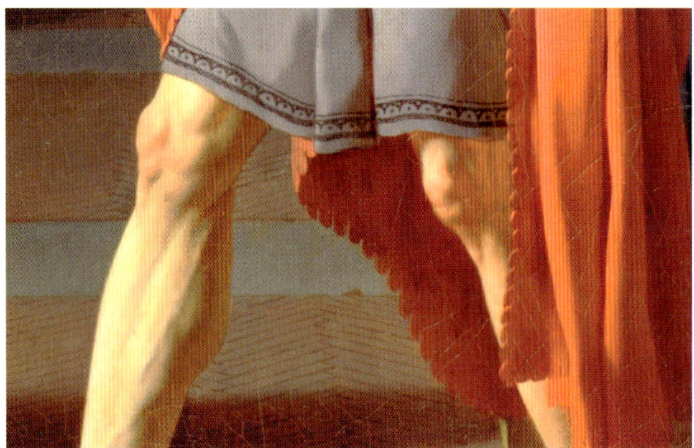

FIG. 4.34. Jacques-Louis David, *Oath of the Horatii*, 1784. Oil on canvas, 10 ft. 9 ⁴⁄₅ in. × 14 ft. (330 × 425 cm). Louvre, Paris.

the story of Horatius from Roman history for the king in 1782, which was intended for display at the Salon of 1783. He decided to complete his reception piece (*Andromache Mourning Hector*, Paris, Louvre) first in order to become a full member of the Académie, so he put off the project until the following Salon. He modified the topic to represent a moment that he invented: the father giving weapons to his three sons, who swear to fight to the death to defend Rome (the *Oath of the Horatii*, fig. 4.34). The story is complicated by intermarriage with a family of the enemy. The collapsing women at the right are made distraught not just by this commitment to warfare but also by conflicting loyalty. David's composition is as disciplined as the soldiers he depicts. An austere triple arcade with baseless columns parallels the three groups of figures. The courtyard is bare, laid out with receding

FIG. 4.35. Jacques-Louis David, *Oath of the Horatii* (detail; see fig. 4.34).

paving stones in perspective; Leon Battista Alberti might have drawn the space as a demonstration of Renaissance perspective. Even Poussin looks complicated in comparison to David here. The stronger colors are allotted to the men, with duller mixed tones to the women, to express both their feminine frailty and to place them deeper in space. The poses and gestures are ritually dramatic but as spare as the costumes and setting. The lighting sets it apart from his contemporaries. David avoids contrived melodramatic spotlighting. There is nothing mysterious about the light that enters from the left front, but there is a plausibility and correctness to it.

David gives weight and substance to his forms with his darkish modeling, but what is surprising when peering closely into his shadows is how much less dark than Caravaggio's they are (fig. 4.35). He has leavened what he learned from the Caravaggisti with what one might imagine was a very close look at Rubens. Note the blues and yellows on the flesh and the attention to reflections. David does not make use of Rubens's agitated brushstroke. His finish is smooth and impersonal, but the sensuous appeal is there, carefully hidden beneath a somber appearance.

Modern critics have debated whether the picture was intended to have revolutionary content. Simon Lee points out that although it was taken up in the 1790s as a symbol of the French Revolution, in 1785 "republicanism was not yet a force in France, and the overthrow and removal of the monarchy was unthinkable."[89] Michael Levey, on the other hand, opined that although "nothing has been discovered to prove David was a revolutionary *avant la Bastille* . . . nothing suggests that he was ever pro-royal, and it would be astonishing if, at the age of forty-one, he became a committed revolutionary which he undoubtedly did without ever having previously reflected on events in the uneasy years which preceded the Revolution itself."[90]

The painting was shown first in Rome to international acclaim, which whetted the appetite of the Salon audience when it was exhibited there in 1785. It was universally applauded, but the radicals of the younger generation were so extravagant in their praise that it spurred the conservatives to moderate theirs. They recognized vaguely and imprecisely that in the spareness of its style, David's painting was subversively revolutionary. The subject was a perfect exemplum of the kind of patriotic self-sacrifice that the Académie and the state were calling for—and yet what it depicts is the passing of power to the next generation.

Thomas Crow has analyzed the reviews by the younger generation with brilliant subtlety and recognized there was an undercurrent to them.[91] This group of intellectuals, which included Antoine-Joseph Gorsas, Jean-Paul Marat, Jacques-Pierre Brissot, and Jean-Louis Carra, wrote political pamphlets that attacked the elite, associating fine dress and a gracious manner, for example, with depravity and despotism; their very elegance of style concealed their duplicity. They used rules to bolster their position as the arbiters of culture. The establishment conservatives complained about David's breaches of the rules. The young radicals found in the *Horatii* a perfect expression of the values they promoted. The sparseness of his style is akin to their call for true nobility stripped of embellishment.

The *Death of Socrates* was displayed at the Salon of 1787 (fig. 4.36). The subject of the execution of the philosopher condemned by the state for false teaching and corrupting the morals of Athenian youth was a favorite in the copious eighteenth-century repertory of death scenes. When Saint-Quentin represented it, he chose the more piteous moment after Socrates has drunk the hemlock (see fig. 4.24). The empty cup is dashed to the floor, picked out in a pool of light, and Socrates clutches his heart. David has chosen what is identified as the "classic moment," just before the climax. Socrates reaches for the cup as he continues to teach his pupils gathered around him. Filled with dignity, he accepts his sentence stoically, bodying forth his belief in the immortality of the soul.

David displays the lessons he has learned in Rome. He has perfected his distillation of Caravaggio by separating Caravaggio's relief from his chiaroscuro. Retaining the heavy fabrics that fall in ponderous folds, lending dignity to the wearer, he allows more light to penetrate the shadows and he softens and smooths the modeling. He does away with the murky obscurity surrounding the principal figures favored by many of his contemporaries and predecessors. His rival, Pierre Peyron, also exhibited a *Death of Socrates,* commissioned by the king's minister of culture, at the same Salon (fig. 4.37). Peyron had beaten David in the Prix de Rome competition in 1773 and preceded him to Rome, but they were colleagues there after David joined him in 1775. There are many similarities between their two versions: Peyron uses a similar

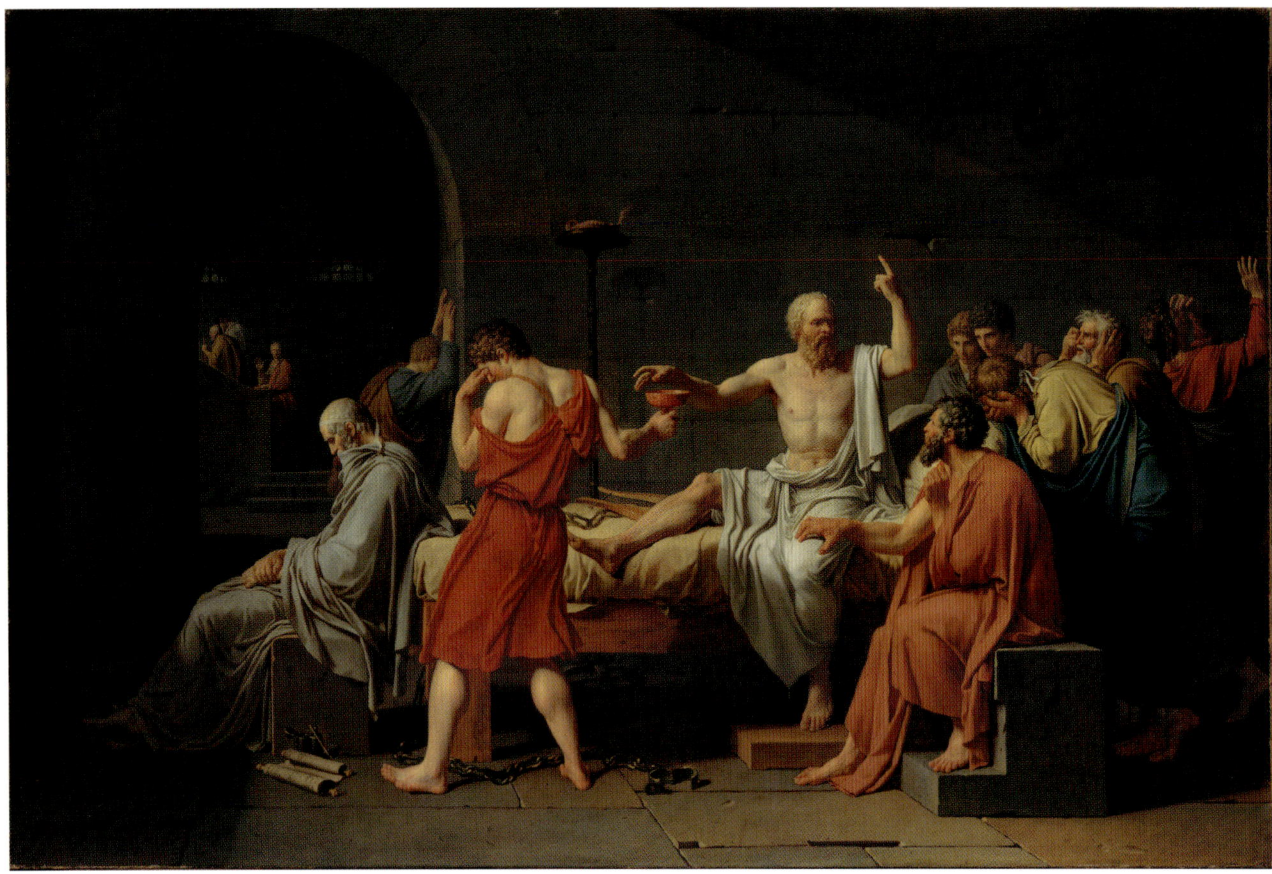

FIG. 4.36. Jacques-Louis David, *Death of Socrates*, 1787. Oil on canvas, 51 × 77¼ in. (129.5 × 196.2 cm). Metropolitan Museum of Art, New York.

spatial box with rear wall parallel to the picture plane and orthogonals indicated in the pavement, as well as a similar number of figures, as prescribed for the academic history painting, and similar rhetorical gestures.[92] Both painters have studied antique classical precedents, but they have chosen different models: the proportions of Peyron's figures are those of the Hellenistic, taller with smaller heads, like those of Vien or Mengs, whereas David has emulated the more robust fifth-century figures, as he had done in the *Horatii*.

David has absorbed the lessons in coloring from the more "delicate dishes" of Renaissance colorists, such as Andrea del Sarto and Raphael, as he called them. His colors do not compete or clash, nor do they try too hard to move the viewer's eye around, as Peyron's bright blue, yellow, and red do. What David learned from his Cinquecento mentors, probably via Poussin, is to reduce the saturation of each tone in equal measure—in other words, to emulate Raphael's unione. The logic and clarity of Socrates's thinking is given visual equivalence

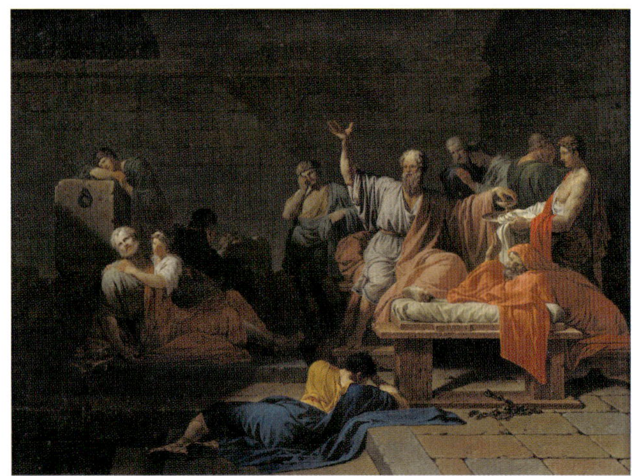

FIG. 4.37. Jean-François Pierre Peyron, *Death of Socrates*, 1787. Oil on canvas, 38 ⁹⁄₁₆ × 52½ in. (98 × 133.5 cm). Statens Museum for Kunst, Copenhagen.

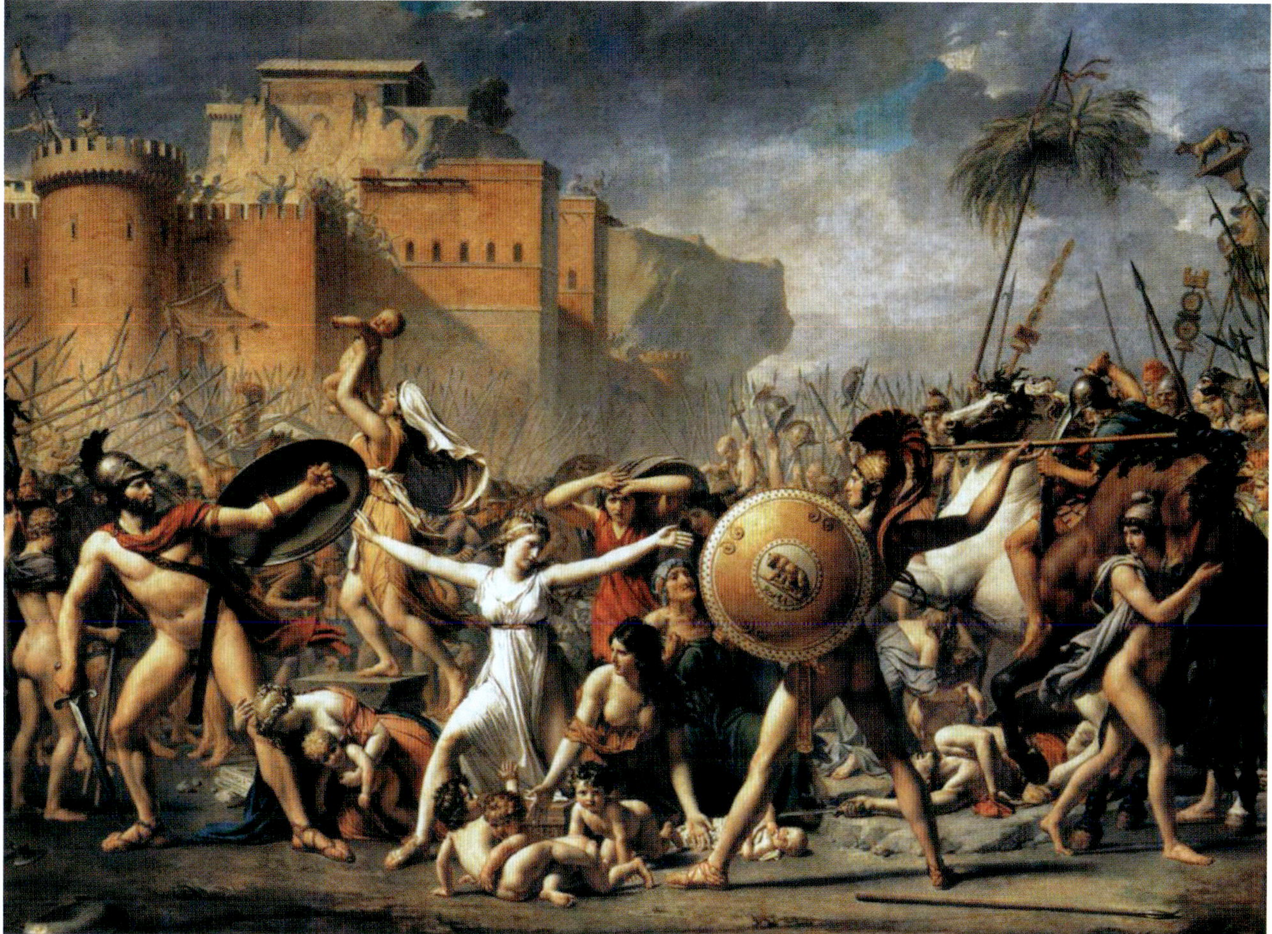

in David's pellucid rendering, where nothing is lost in obscure shadows and where the colors combine in melodious amity. The lighting is plausible, dramatic without being contrived. His stoic philosophy is mirrored in the spare, unadorned surroundings.

David conceived the *Intervention of the Sabine Women* in 1794, while he was in prison for his support of Maximilien Robespierre (fig. 4.38). He worked on it after he was released the following year, until 1799. He intended the huge canvas (twelve and a half by seventeen feet) to be a sequel to Poussin's famous *Abduction of the Sabine Women* (Paris, Louvre), which shows when the Romans stole the Sabine women as their wives. David's episode takes place several years later, after the Sabines have regrouped their forces. They attack Rome with the intention of recovering their wives and daughters, but Hersilia hurls herself between her father, Tatius, the king of the Sabines, and her husband, Romulus, the Roman

king on the right, to prevent further bloodshed. The theme of reconciliation must have appealed to the nation worn out by a tumultuous decade of political crisis and violence. David declared his intention to do something new, to recapture "pure Greekness." The warriors are represented nude, embodying the Greek ideal. As if to compensate for those limp women in the *Horatii*, Hersilia takes center stage in a heroic pose. Women had played crucial roles in the Revolution, en masse and singly, from marching on Versailles to confront the king, to assassinating Marat. Clad in white, with her children at her feet, she separates the antagonists who align themselves as in a bas-relief, with battling men and wailing women behind them. The outdoor setting does not permit the painter to use his usual chiaroscuro and focused lighting, but this picture anticipates the monumental canvases he would undertake after the turn of the century at the behest of Napoleon.

The state replaced the Church in France as the primary patron of the arts when Colbert preempted the Académie Royale after its founding in the mid-seventeenth century. Politics governed French art throughout the period culminating in the Revolution, and art was an integral part of the social evolution that led up to the Revolution. The Salon, opened to the public for the first time in 1737, would ultimately lead to the development of a new critical voice, an alternative to the Académie, which would empower the middle class and give them a stake in high culture. Often-anonymous pamphleteers put their judgments up against officialdom and eventually made a difference.

Colbert put all culture in the service of Louis XIV and the state. His ambition was that France would assimilate Italian accomplishment and surpass it. That the Paris Académie was modeled on those of Rome and Florence makes clear that Italy was the exemplar of what Colbert was pursuing. The founding of the branch in Rome, the French Academy, brought aspirant artists into direct contact with the inspirational font of classicism, both ancient and modern. Until well into the nineteenth century, an artist could not consider himself prepared for his profession until he had sojourned in Italy. The Prix de Rome was the award coveted by all would-be artists, and the entrée to membership in the Académie and a successful career. The program of Conférences organized by Le Brun offered presentations by members followed by discussion centered on works in the royal collection; all those paintings discussed were by Italian Renaissance masters, with Poussin as the only Frenchman included. The paradigms for the grand style Le Brun practiced and had taught at the Académie were Renaissance classicism and Poussin's classicism.

Colbert, Le Brun, and eventually Louis himself died, and the grand style came to look grandiose. Everyone longed for more informality, less bombast, and less control. The Rococo, embodied first in the charming pastoral scenes of Watteau, was a reaction to the high seriousness of the preceding century. Chiaroscuro yielded to delicate pastels. When Louis XV came of age and then took as his mistress Madame de Pompadour, she turned official taste toward lighthearted amorous, even erotic, decorations for intimate spaces. It was a feminine regime, dominated by cosmetic colors, which roused the indignation of many, both in government and among the public.

Diderot, the principal voice of the new public criticism, vociferously denounced Pompadour's favorite painter, Boucher, and his pink-bottomed women, and called for a return to art celebrating family and morality.

By the mid-1760s, when Madame de Pompadour died, the calls for a return to an art that would celebrate the state and promote virtue became widely based. Despite the control that the king's ministers and the Académie exercised, there was a rising tide of bourgeois art and taste, reflecting the rise of the middle class in commerce and wealth that was taking place. Ironically Pompadour herself was a bourgeoisie—which fueled the resentment in the establishment against her and the power she wielded. Chardin and Greuze, both approved by Diderot, appealed to this middle class and to those who favored art that depicted life realistically. A signal that the tide had turned: in 1770 Chardin replaced Boucher as First Painter to the King.

Meanwhile in Venice, Tiepolo practiced his version of the Rococo in his decorations of the palaces of patrician families nostalgic for fading glory, mostly in fresco. As in France, his palette was pale and washed with sun, the natural tonality of fresco. Tiepolo revised the traditional technique to bring his coloring in line with the contemporary taste for greater drama, using secco to create stronger shadows and darker tints than fresco permits. In both France and Italy, Rococo coloring enabled an escape into fantasy, a realm of pleasure where nearly weightless confections of rosy flesh, either allegorical or mythological, are supported on billowy clouds.

Coloring systems changed along with these politically motivated permutations. No one would have considered the pastels of the Rococo appropriate to the grand style, nor the theatrical chiaroscuro of the grand style suitable to the boudoir ornaments of the Rococo. The middle-class clients, now holding considerable buying power, were not attracted to the Rococo and preferred the earth tones of Greuze and the subtle realism of Chardin's domestic interiors. Finding a color style that was both fresh and fitting to the new classicism that was emerging in the last quarter of the century proved to be elusive, and simply imitating Poussin yet again did not satisfy. It was David's creative amalgam of Caravaggio, Poussin, and Rubens, honed by his own sensibility, that ultimately provided a powerful new interpretive instrument.

The 1770s saw sobriety prevail. The Académie rewarded history painters who strove to glorify the

nation with patriotic subjects in the grand manner of
Louis XIV. The king's minister commissioned pictures
for the royal collection and to be exhibited at the biennial Salon. The fruit of the steady stream of painters
sent to Rome on the Prix de Rome for a stay of three to
five years was an ever-increasing enthusiasm for classicism, energized by the new archeological discoveries at
Herculaneum and Pompeii near Naples, and Hadrian's
Villa and Ostia near Rome, and by the cult that developed
around Winckelmann and his books codifying and extol-
ing Greek art. Neoclassicism jelled when David brought
together the patriotic subject, a compositional style
based on classical bas-relief, and a system of coloring
and lighting that stripped away artifice and embellishment and concealed its appeal to the senses and emotions,
beneath an austere exterior of idealized verisimilitude.

David's reformulated Neoclassicism proved the
perfect vehicle for the Revolution, which replaced the
decadent monarchy with a republic directed by the Third
Estate. The public discourse unleashed when the Salon
was opened to the public found its voice at the time of
the Revolution, with strident objection to the whole
academic system. Seen as corrupt, entrenched, and sus-
taining mediocrity, it was suspended by the National
Convention and reinstated only in 1816 as the Académie
des Beaux-Arts.

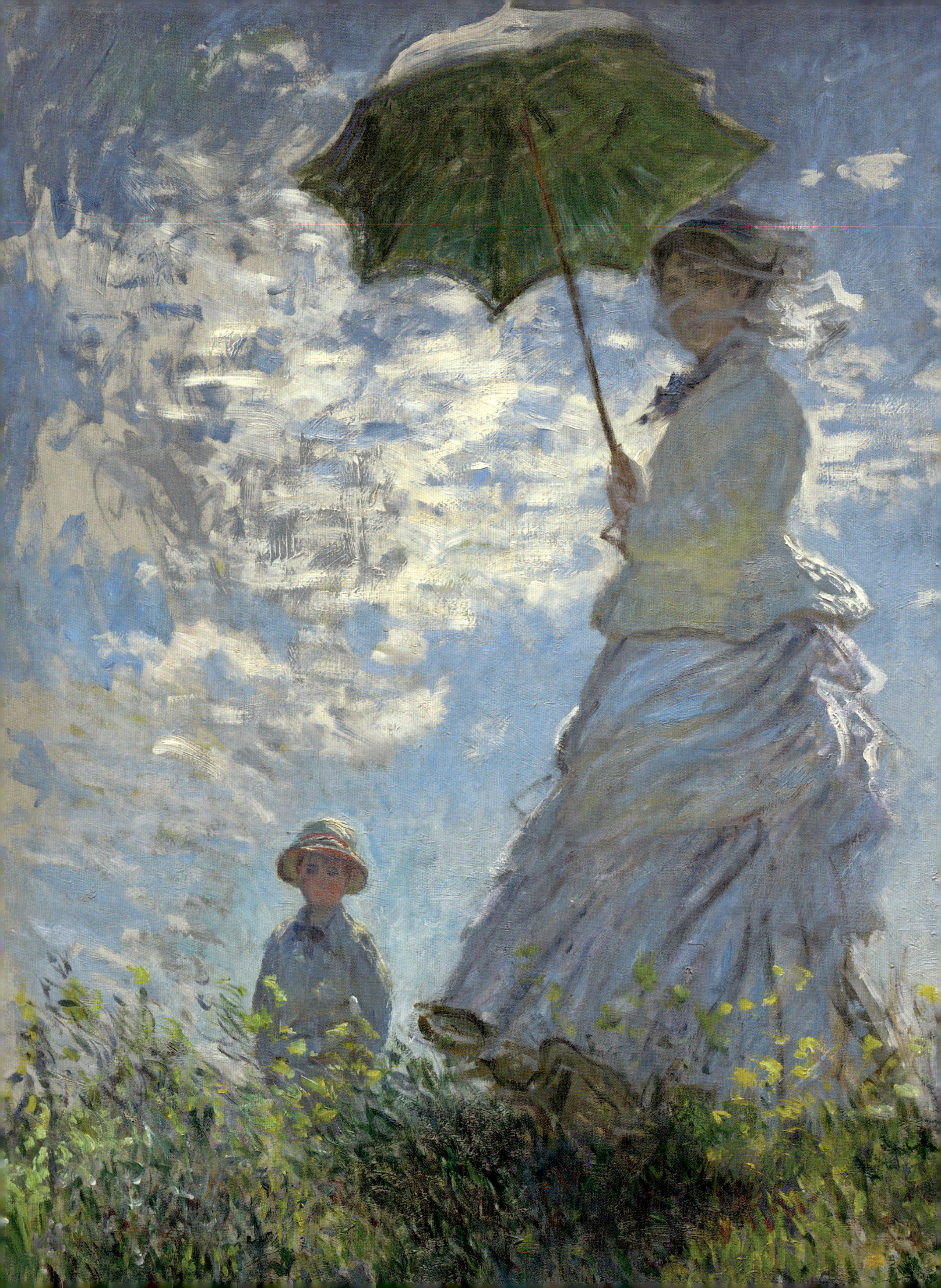

5 The Nineteenth Century

Industrialization and Globalization of Art

After playing a role in visualizing the French Revolution, color was subject to its own upheaval in the nineteenth century, first in materials, then in making. By the time of the Industrial Revolution, chemistry had replaced alchemy. Building on the classification of the elements and using modern experimental scientific methods, chemists discovered materials that could be used to synthesize and manufacture colorants superior to the natural products painters had always used. They invented new pigments and dyes that filled gaps in the palette—oranges and purples—and pigments of a brilliance never before available, above all greens and yellows. Commercial packaging of these pigments in metal tubes did away with the need for time-consuming preparations in the studio, and they could be easily packed up for on-site painting. Brushes clamped with a metal ferule expanded the range of size and shape, making possible a whole new repertory of brushstrokes.

The nineteenth century is famously when the Académie ceased to control the training and credentialing of artists in France, and when the Salon was replaced by commercial exhibitions. It is also when Paris became the indisputable art capital of the world. Several factors converged to bring about these momentous changes. The decline of the state and the aristocracy as patrons was balanced by the increased empowerment of a wealthy middle class, eager to buy art. Governmental efforts to support independents resulted in an enlarged army of artists who needed to make a living selling their art, far more than the system was designed to accommodate. The rise of dealers and critics marked the shift to the kind of art market we know today.

The nineteenth-century Académie was caught between the pressure of the government to open opportunities to non-academic painters and its commitment to a time-honored system. It became more rigid than it had ever been, even as the culture moved toward freedom of personal expression and buyers sought works that reflected the world around them. The system of training still required the painters to labor for years perfecting their drawing technique, working first from prints, then copying plaster casts of antiquities, then finally achieving access to the live model. The student would be enrolled in the atelier of a master, a member of the Académie, who would visit once or maybe twice a week and criticize the pupil's work. The system ran on a sequence of competitions, offering advancement to the winners. Thus the atmosphere within the studios was brutally competitive, to the point that it was life-threatening. Paul Delaroche ran the most popular and successful atelier in Paris, numbering over one hundred pupils at any given time, until 1843 when he closed it after a pupil died as a result of hazing.[1]

ACADEMIC PAINTING: DELAROCHE

Delaroche was catapulted to the forefront of painters, earning an international reputation with the success of his 1834 Salon presentation, *The Execution of Lady Jane Grey* (fig. 5.1). He was given the medal of the Legion of Honor. In 1837 he was commissioned to decorate the awards theater of the École des Beaux-Arts, known as the *Hémicycle,* with a mural more than eighty-eight feet long. In the academic tradition, he chose to portray a Raphael-inspired assembly of great architects, sculptors, and painters gathered around the masters of the Parthenon, the architect Phidias, sculptor Ictinus, and painter Apelles (fig. 5.2). Yet it is a measure of how swiftly taste changed that following his death only twenty years later, in 1857, he was regarded as a remnant of the past. And by the end of the century, former admirers such as Henry James and Théophile Gautier used him to signify,

as Stephen Bann noted, "the furthest point in the scale from what good modern painting may be taken to be."[2]

We can see what the best and most lauded of academic paintings looked like and how they were made by examining Delaroche and his perfectly orthodox facture. He had already scored a success with his *Joan of Arc in Prison Interrogated by the Bishop of Winchester* (Rouen) at the Salon of 1824, where there were no fewer than 1,152 artists represented.[3] In 1832 that recognition was parlayed into an appointment to the Institut, where he was the youngest member, and soon thereafter he was named professor at the École des Beaux-Arts. Like his other successful history paintings, the story of Lady Jane Grey, queen for nine days, is an affecting story from English history. The seventeen-year-old Jane, named by Edward VI as his successor, became a pawn in the duel between Edward's half-sisters, Catholic Mary and Protestant Elizabeth; she was convicted of high treason and beheaded in the Tower of London. Delaroche shows her attended by her distraught ladies-in-waiting, one of whom holds her cloak, in a brilliant white satin dress, betokening her innocence, kneeling blindfolded at the block, groping for it. Sir John Brydges, the lieutenant of the Tower, gently guides her hand while the axman watches.

Scrutiny of Delaroche's preparation and execution

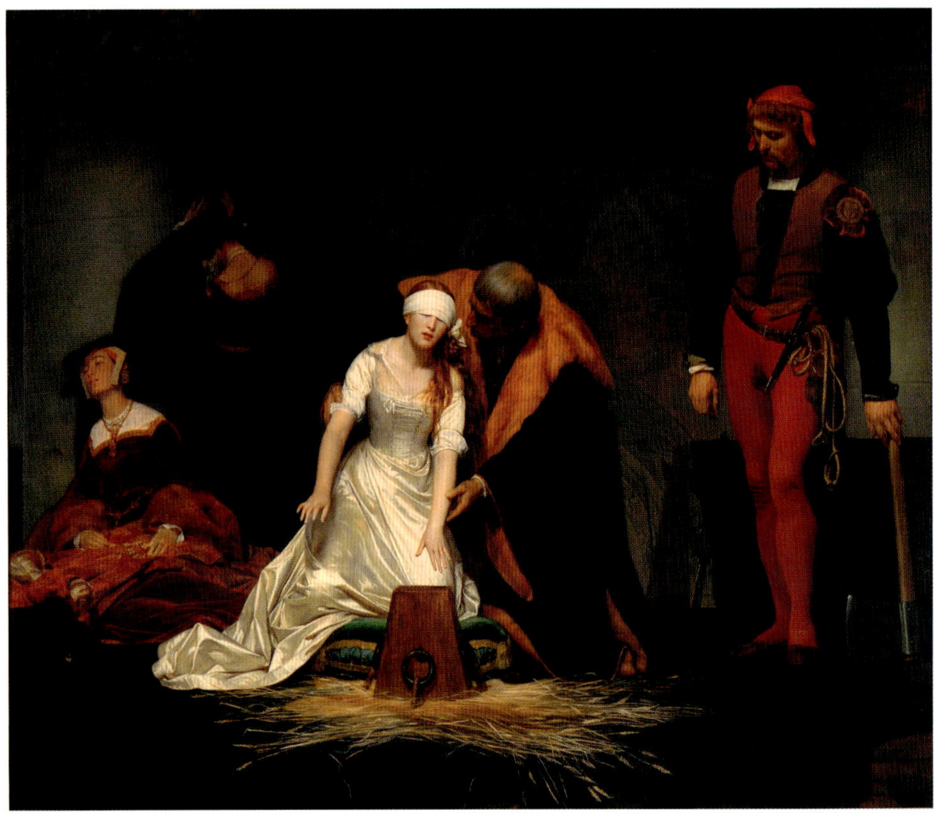

FIG. 5.1. Paul Delaroche, *The Execution of Lady Jane Grey,* 1833. Oil on canvas, 8 ft. × 9 ft. 9 in. (246 × 297 cm). National Gallery, London.

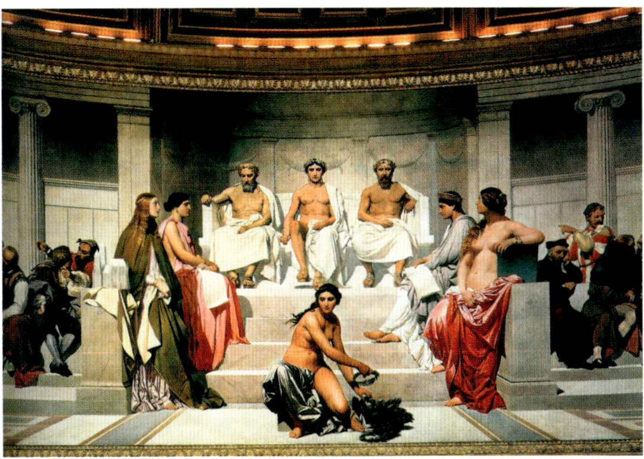

FIG. 5.2. Paul Delaroche, *Hémicycle* (detail), 1836–41. Encaustic wall painting. École nationale supérieure des Beaux-Arts, Paris.

reveals just how scrupulous the academic method was.[4] A watercolor and two drawings survive of what was doubtless a large number of studies. Delaroche was said often to prepare a composition by making wax or plaster models of the figures, putting them in a box, and studying the light, a procedure we have seen employed by Tintoretto and later Poussin, and also used by many of his contemporaries. Already by the time of the little watercolor (about seven by five and a half inches; fig. 5.3) he had worked out the composition: the only significant change was to the executioner, who would later be revised from the gawking churl here to the sensitive observer whose evident sympathy for Lady Jane deepens the pathos of the scene. In the drawings, Delaroche worked out the

poses and lighting (fig. 5.4). Because of the large size of the canvas—almost eight by ten feet—it would have been stretched-to-order and delivered with a priming of lead white in linseed oil. It was primed again in the studio, this time with lead white in walnut oil, a task that would have been carried out by one of his pupils. The drawings were enlarged onto the canvas to create a full underdrawing, to which many alterations would be made in the course of painting.

The next stage was the underpainting. The figures and the background were laid in with brownish or grayish paint made of lead white and primarily earth pigments. The tonality of this underpainting bears some relationship to the color that would be applied on top. It is not a uniform imprimatura such as was commonly used in the seventeenth and eighteenth centuries, but more like an undermodeling. It has been remarked that at this stage it resembled a grisaille version of the final painting. In the final painting, Delaroche would continue to make changes. The application of the local color was done so as to create a perfectly smooth surface, without visible brushstroke. Premixed, graduated middle tones applied side by side were then blended. The final layer is typically thin, but a mixture; passages of pure color are rare indeed. This systematic procedure of the accepted academic system, from preparatory studies, to underdrawing, to underpainting, to final painting, puts into relief just how unorthodox the Impressionist spontaneity that developed in the 1860s really was.

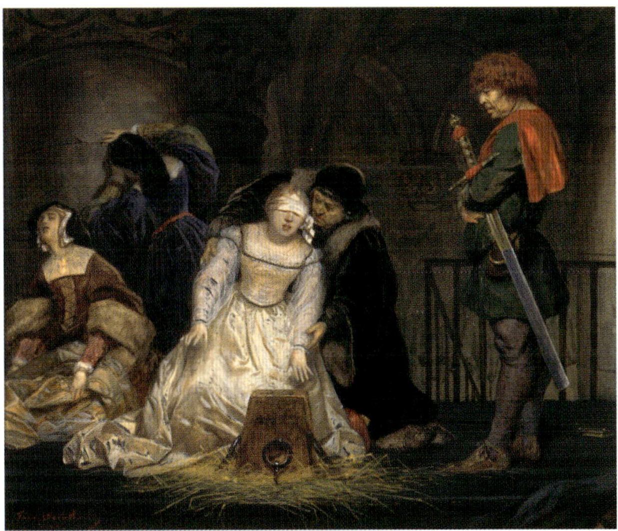

FIG. 5.3. Paul Delaroche, *The Execution of Lady Jane Grey* (study), c. 1833. Watercolor over pencil with varnish on paper, 5½ × 7¼ in. (14.3 × 18.4 cm). University of Manchester, Whitworth Art Gallery.

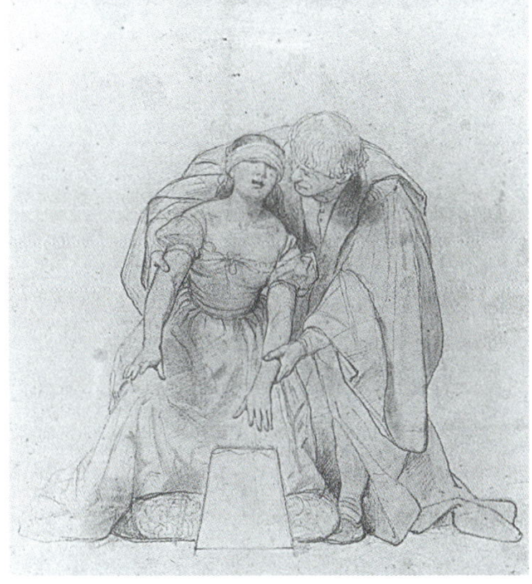

FIG. 5.4. Paul Delaroche, *The Execution of Lady Jane Grey* (drawing), 1832–33. Graphite on paper, 6 × 5⅓ in. (15 × 13.5 cm). British Museum, London.

The control of the chiaroscuro received a lot of attention, as it had from those painters in the later eighteenth century who were struggling to revive the grand style in their history paintings. The legacy of David was to lighten those brown shadows. Frequently in academic paintings of Delaroche's time one finds a semitransparent brown paint, known in the studio argot as "sauce," used, among other things, to deepen shadows. Its ubiquity accounts for the generally brown tonality of much academic painting. Apparently Delaroche wisely adjured its use, at least in *Lady Jane Grey*, where the pleasing but subdued coloring is perfectly calculated to stimulate the viewers' sentiments without *appearing* to appeal to the emotions.

The response of the viewer is calculated. The violence of the scene is all in the future, left to the imagination; what we are shown is the poignant prelude. The actors' feelings are calibrated to elicit the desired response: Lady Jane's pathetic groping for the block where she must place her head; the unbridled weeping of the lady-in-waiting; the sympathetic guiding hand of Sir John; the reluctance of the executioner. Nothing is undeliberated. The picture was a great success with the public and in fact still is, although Delaroche would later be blamed for the demise of history painting. The critic Ernest Chesneau wrote in 1868: "He substituted the historical anecdote for history."[5]

Like most history paintings of the nineteenth-century Académie, Delaroche's painting later fell into disrepute and was hidden away, in this case quite literally. When it was damaged in a flood at the Tate in 1928, it was rolled up, consigned to the basement, and recorded as "destroyed." When, almost fifty years later, the then-director of the National Gallery, Michael Levey, examined it, he found the damage rather minor. It was restored and exhibited at the National Gallery—somewhat apologetically, as an exemplar of Salon history painting. No one was prepared for its popularity with modern audiences. It is said that the wooden floor in front of where it hangs must be polished far more often than any other spot in the gallery.[6]

Delaroche's finish was precisely what the Académie preached. As the great master Jean-Auguste-Dominique Ingres declared: "All signs of facture should be eliminated. It is the result not the means that must appear."[7] But this was not universally agreed. There were advocates of the sketchy, painterly finish: most prominent in

Paris, Eugène Delacroix, and across the channel, Joseph Mallord William Turner.

An outcome of the Revolution was that teaching responsibilities were turned over to the École des Beaux-Arts, and the Académie became largely honorary. The number of academicians was fixed and membership was for life. This meant that it was no longer appointment to the Académie that launched an artist's career, as had been the case for David, who became a member after he returned from his tenure of the Prix de Rome and submitted his reception piece. In the nineteenth century the average age of admission to the Académie was fifty-three—in other words, it was a reward for a successful career. Unsurprisingly, these old men were conservative and unsympathetic to new developments. Under the leadership of Quatremère de Quincy, who believed that academies existed not to create new traditions but to preserve old ones, the classical style of David and his followers was promoted and Romanticism denounced.[8] The old curriculum and the competitions remained in place. An important innovation in 1816 was the establishment of a Prix de Rome for historical landscape, a recognition of the growing popularity of this formerly disdained genre.

The desire to find a middle way between the dogmatic classicism of the Académie and the Romantic insistence on originality and a rough finish resulted in the development of what came to be called the *juste milieu* in the 1830s. Delaroche's combination of academic technique with Romantic subject is an example. The Académie, by adhering to traditions associated with the *ancien régime* of the eighteenth century, associated itself with traditional authority and antagonized advocates of individuality and personal expression. The efforts of King Louis-Philippe to ratify public taste resulted in what Albert Boime identified as a split between academic and official art: "French art in the nineteenth century evolved in continual tension between Academy and State. Contrary to general thought, these terms are not synonymous nor mutually reinforcing. In fact they stand for clearly distinguishable entities."[9] The state professed democratic principles and so it patronized the juste milieu, the independents, or those opposed to the Académie, and so did much of the public. Under the July Monarchy, funds were made available to buy their works in recognition of an obligation to public taste—a quite new attitude in authoritarian France.

Delacroix and Delaroche were contemporaries. They both exhibited in the Salon of 1824, where Delaroche's *Joan of Arc in Prison* won acclaim. Delacroix also attracted attention with a very different kind of history painting, his *Scenes from the Chios Massacres,* which pictured Greeks captured and awaiting either death or slavery at the hands of the conquering Turks (fig. 5.5). The atrocities had taken place over a period of two months, hence Delacroix's title. A census taken at the end of that period showed nine hundred remaining inhabitants out of a population of nearly ninety-nine thousand.[10] The Greek

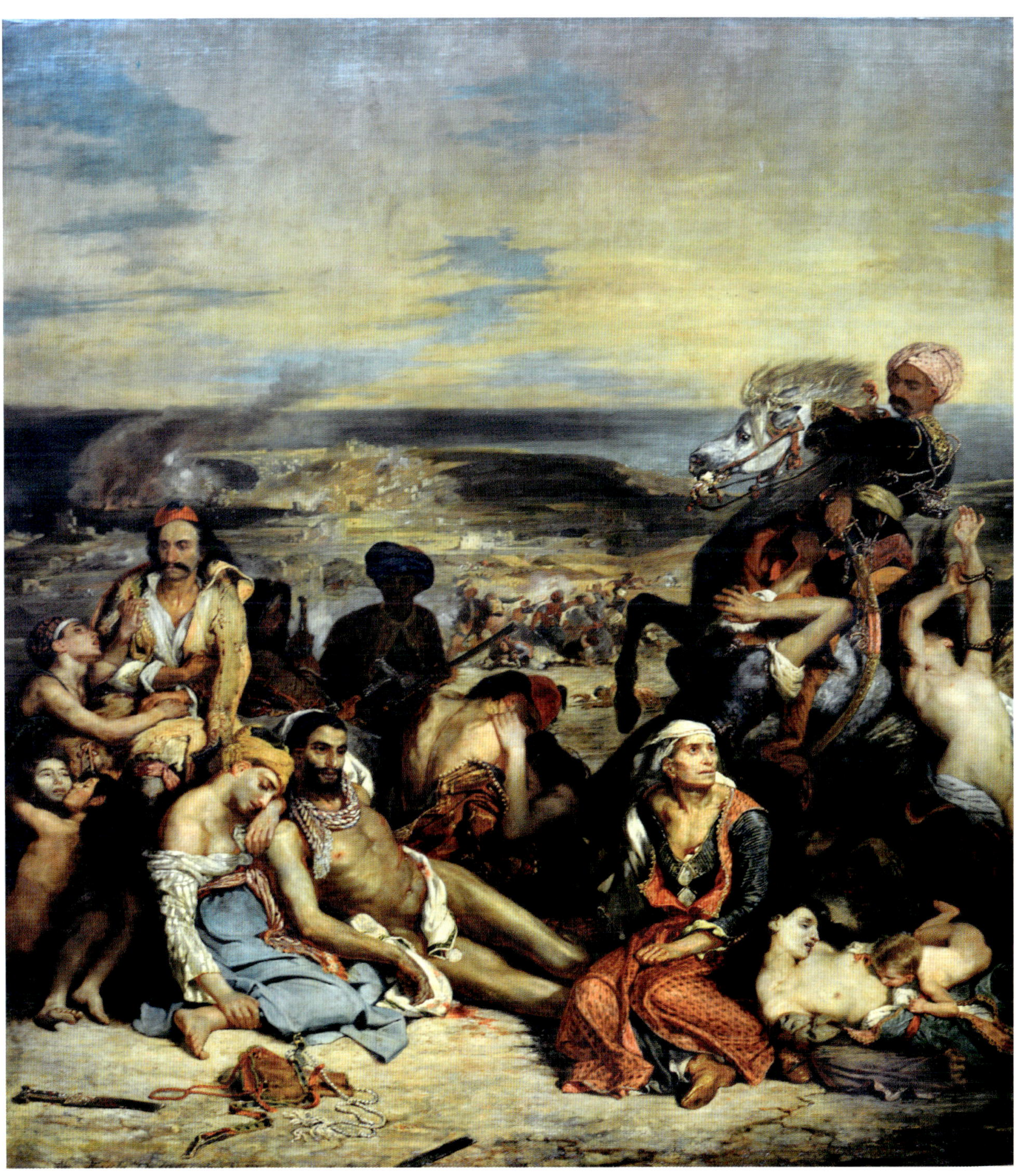

FIG. 5.5. Eugène Delacroix, *Scenes from the Chios Massacres,* 1824. Oil on canvas, 13 ft. 8 in. × 11 ft. 7 in. (419 × 354 cm). Louvre, Paris.

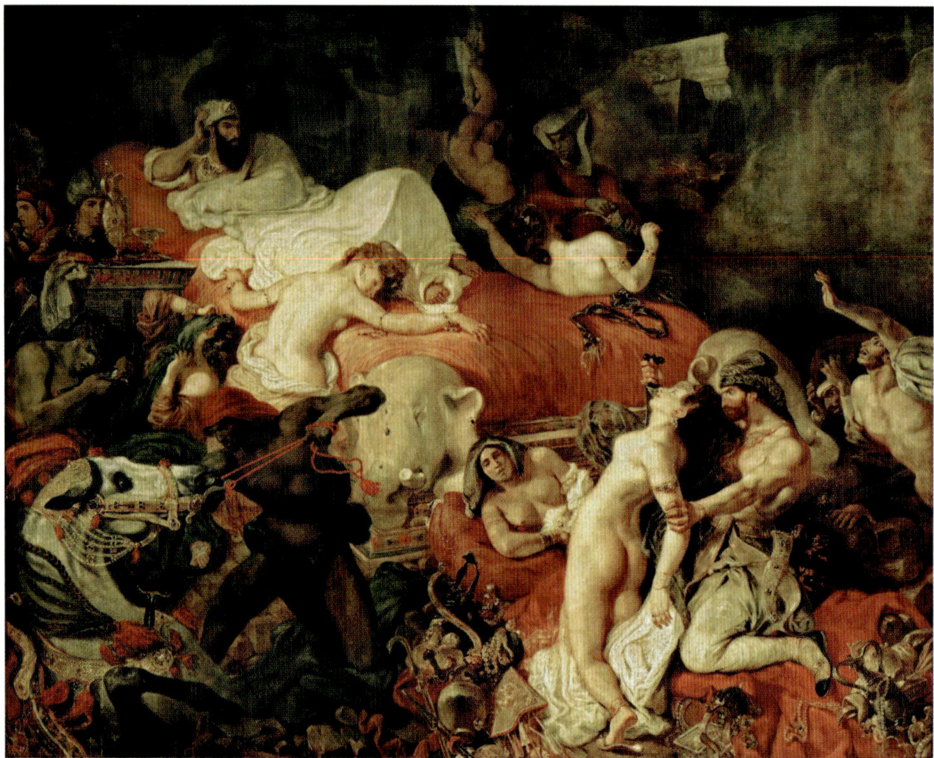

war of independence from the Ottomans had galvanized European sentiment, caught up as it was in the grip of Neoclassical Graecophilia in the wake of the writings of Winckelmann and his followers. A few months earlier the famous and flamboyant English poet Lord Byron had died of a fever at age thirty-six at Missolunghi while commanding a Greek rebel army—the quintessential Romantic adventure.

Delacroix has in this work disdained the classical rules of composition and the expectation of a focused climactic moment. It was from the moment of the presentation of this picture at the Salon that Delacroix was marked as a threat to the Neoclassical school.[11] The dazed and lethargic Greeks are spread in a disordered frieze across the front, flanked by the towering Turk on rearing horse, the only figure to break across the oppressive horizon. Each figure or pair is studied independently, their hopelessness expressed in their psychic isolation and by the vast plain opening behind them, where the battle continues. The very lack of ordering design tells the story of their lonely despair. The light flits arbitrarily across the surfaces; the color, applied in quick strokes of unmixed pigment, jumps and quivers without fully articulating forms. Although Delaroche, in his *Lady Jane Grey,* describes a scene as touching as Delacroix's, their

painting techniques are diametrically opposed, but each is well matched to his subject. Delaroche's meticulous finish is a perfectly suited facture for this planned and ritualized act of political violence; Delacroix's apparently chaotic presentation makes vivid the human toll of rebellion and warfare. Both subjects call for an emotional response, but Delaroche's historical reconstruction of an event nearly three hundred years past distances it, whereas Delacroix's drawing upon contemporary headlines is raw and undigested. What is missing from this description is acknowledgment of Delacroix's hidden artistry in holding the scene together: the geometry of the inverted pyramidal composition and the invisible discipline of the coloring, which maintains a balance among all the tones. He departed from academic procedure, but he had drawn upon his training in it.

How carefully he constructed his pictures is evident in Delacroix's next Salon offering in 1827, the explosive *Death of Sardanapalus* (fig. 5.6). Here again Lord Byron lurks behind the subject. He wrote a play in 1821 that told the story of the Assyrian monarch who, just as the walls of his palace were collapsing under attack, called for the destruction of all his possessions and had his throne torched. Delacroix makes Sardanapalus's king-sized bed serve as throne and pyre, filling the huge canvas (twelve by sixteen feet). Crowding around it are his servants, who bring his favorite horses, concubines, jewels, and ornaments. One wife lies dead on the bed; another is being knifed as we look on.

The chaos is choreographed, as can be seen by following the sequence of preparatory studies in pen, chalk, and oil.[12] The painter maximized the orgiastic violence by minimizing the ordering effect of perspective; substituting the rapidly receding oblique diagonal of the bed for stabilizing verticals and horizontals; and using sinuous S-shaped forms everywhere. The monarch reclines languidly half in shadow, unmoved by the spectacle he is staging. And yet despite the pandemonium, note again the painter's discipline, here in his limited range of colors. Delacroix has learned from his model, Rubens, and restricted his palette to red, black, gold, flesh, and, visually related to it, the expanse of Sardanapalus's white robe. The recurrent bright red, also sinuous like the shapes, weaves its way throughout and binds the whole together. Despite the extensive graphic preparation, there is not a clear contour to be seen.[13]

It will not surprise the reader to hear that this picture caused something of a sensation for its subject, its execution, and its unabashed appeal to the emotions. The familiar opposition of reason and emotion is sounded. Louis Vitet, a political journalist and critic, admonished sternly: "It is not enough to dazzle the eyes, it is still necessary that the intellect be able to understand that by which the eyes are amused. If you see only half a horse, women thrown pell-mell here and there."[14] But this is precisely Delacroix's point: the spectator does not need more than half a horse to understand. The painter's refusal to resolve, which maddened the classicists, was his strategy to engage the spectator. The critic who suggested that the painter would do better if he tried "to distinguish between a painting and a sketch" touches precisely upon the node of antagonism between the Romantics, whom Delacroix would come to head up, and the established academic classicists epitomized by Ingres.[15]

For the same Salon of 1827, Ingres presented his painting the *Apotheosis of Homer*, commissioned by the government to decorate the ceiling of the Musée Charles X, a museum of Egyptian art in the former Louvre palace (fig. 5.7). It represented Ingres's ultimate homage to classicism, containing portraits of philosophers, poets, and artists gathered around the original Greek poet, Homer, on the model of Raphael's famous frescoes of *Parnassus*

(see fig. 2.5) and the *School of Athens*. Raphael himself is present, holding hands with Apelles, as is Poussin and indeed Ingres himself. The symmetrical composition unfolds on an enormous scale (seventeen feet long), with every figure holding his pose as in the final tableau of a theatrical presentation. It has been suggested that Delacroix conceived his *Sardanapalus* deliberately to confront Ingres at the Salon after having been given the opportunity by one of Ingres's pupils to see the *Apotheosis* before it was presented to the public.[16] This is probably one of those anecdotes invented to dramatize the opposition of Ingres and Delacroix, an opposition that did not actually take shape until the 1840s.[17] Nevertheless, Delacroix's sixteen-foot canvas has the air of a manifesto about it, embracing as it does Rubens, violence, sensuality, feverish movement, and sumptuous coloring, presented in the format of an orthodox academic history painting. His vibrating energy underscores, by contrast, the contrived and glacial perfection of Ingres.[18]

Delacroix and Ingres are always depicted as antagonists, with Ingres representing the proponents of line and Delacroix as the champion of color and emotion. As we have seen, their opposition is the nineteenth-century reenactment of the Poussinistes–Rubénistes quarrel. In fact Delacroix had studied and continued to practice academic composition, and Ingres was one of the greatest colorists of all time, as a visit with any one of his exquisitely clad women painted late in his career makes clear—for example, *Princesse de Broglie* in the Lehmann Collection (New York, Metropolitan Museum), or *Louise*

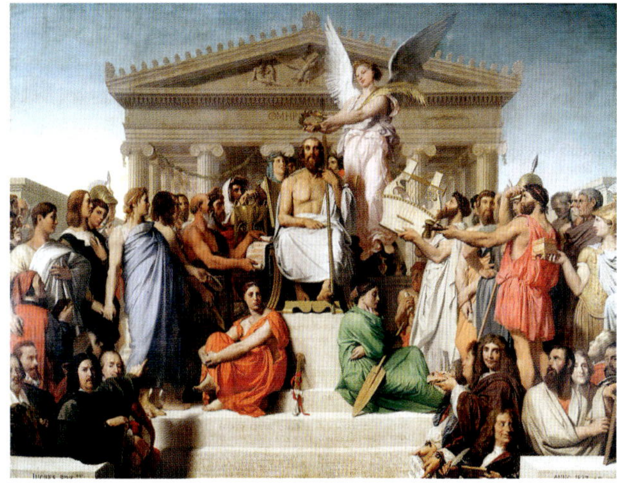

FIG. 5.7. Jean-Auguste-Dominique Ingres, *Apotheosis of Homer*, 1827. Oil on canvas, 12 ft. 8 in. × 16 ft. 9½ in. (386 × 512 cm). Louvre, Paris.

de Broglie, Countess d'Haussonville in the Frick Collection. Meticulously painted, these gentlewomen cannot fail to enchant, with their perfectly turned arms and their tenderly plump wrists and fingers adorned with exquisite bracelets and rings, gifts of their indulgent consorts. Despite the intellectual accomplishments of the Broglie women, they are depicted as arm candy, but perfect specimens. Ingres's choice of models from the Old Masters was not just the usual Raphael or Titian, but importantly also Agnolo Bronzino. Like their Renaissance mothers, these ladies display their husbands' wealth to the world, and those jewels and dresses are portrayed in as scrupulous detail as the lady herself. *Madame Moitessier* fixes us with her riveting poise (fig. 5.8). She appears to present herself openly to her viewer, but she is subtly aloof, abstracted almost imperceptibly, like her Renaissance predecessors. Ingres has imitated the exaggerated slope of the shoulders that Raphael used to create a graceful line—*Maddalena Doni* and the *Donna Velata* (where it is disguised beneath the veil), both in the Pitti Gallery in Florence, are examples—but as noted by Robert Rosenblum, Ingres has abstracted her shoulders so that they are slightly unalike.[19] Ingres's line is as inaccurate in its anatomy as Raphael's, but as graceful; her shoulders and décolletage echo the symmetry of her face, shaped by her dark hair parted in the middle. Bronzino certainly lurks behind this image, even in the slight cast of her right eye, a favorite device of Bronzino's to distance his sitter from the viewer.[20] Both Ingres and Delacroix were masterful colorists, but they used their coloring for opposite effects: Ingres to fix his forms in their perfection, Delacroix to incite his viewer to engage emotionally and sensuously with his scene. These differences were taken up in the popular press to turn an artistic debate into political hostility.[21]

The sketchy finish was criticized because it was held that it was not professional to present it to the public—it's like going out on the street in your underwear. According to some critics, one's thoughts and inner feelings should not be put on display. Not only does it lack dignity, but also, it can be argued, these inner feelings are not of interest.[22] No one cares what you feel; what people care about is your skillful composing of those feelings into a beautiful, properly thought-through and finished work of art. What the nineteenth-century critic did not at first understand is that the freshness and verve that is appealing in the sketch depends upon rough execution; turning

it into a polished, finished work vitiates the energy. Under debate was the degree to which the finished painting might be permitted to resemble the preliminary small-scale record of the design-in-progress (*esquisse*), rather than the *ébauche,* or laying-in of color. Delacroix himself did not at first understand this about his own sketchy style. He finally got it in the 1840s. In an entry in his *Journal* we see him defining for himself the difference between a sketch (esquisse) and a modello (ébauche):

> My ébauche is very good. It has lost some of its mystery; that is the drawback of the methodical ébauche. With a good drawing for the lines of the composition and the placing of the figures, one can do away with the esquisse, which represents a needless repetition of the work. One obtains the qualities of the esquisse in the picture itself, by means of the vagueness in which one leaves the details.[23]

Just how seriously committed Delacroix was to his coloring is demonstrated by a description by his studio assistant, Pierre Andrieu, of his procedure:

> Delacroix before starting on his large decorative pictures spent whole weeks combining on his palette the tonal relationships, which he transferred to bits of canvas pinned to the wall of his studio. On each of these tones he carefully noted the composition and the destination (reflection, shadow, half-tone and light, name of the figure, the feeling to be expressed, impasto, or glaze etc).

He was apparently making these numbered painting strips as early as 1827, but appreciation for the value of sketchy finish only dawned slowly in the face of adamant opposition from the Académie.[24] By the time of the Salon of 1845, Baudelaire could declare that "A work of genius . . . is always well executed so long as it is sufficiently executed." He added that "There is a world of difference between a 'completed' subject and a 'finished' subject and that in general, what is 'completed' is not finished and that a thing that is 'finished' in detail may well lack the unity of the 'completed' thing, that the value of an amusing, significant and well-placed touch of colour is enormous."[25] Finally in the 1850s Delécluze, who had criticized Delacroix over the decades for his sketchy finish, understood that in the landscapes of Camille Corot or Charles-François Daubigny the sketch conveyed imagination and feeling, and that Delacroix did

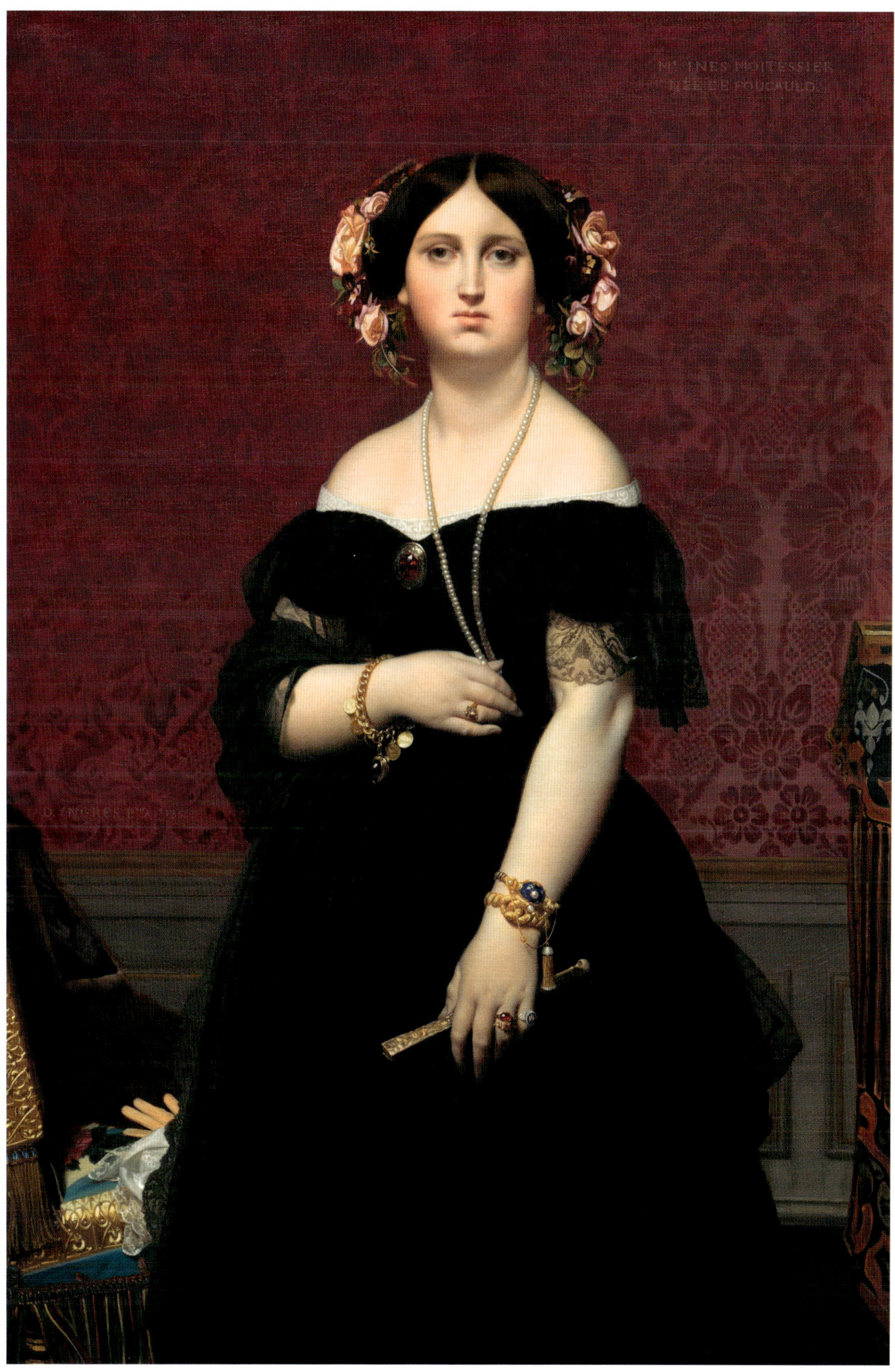

FIG. 5.8. Jean-Auguste-Dominique Ingres, *Madame Moitessier*, 1856. Oil on canvas, 57⅞ × 39⅜ in. (147 × 100 cm). National Gallery of Art, Washington, D.C.

not paint loosely in order to outrage, but in order to express his personal emotion.[26] The sketch was coming to embody a quality newly revered by the public: sincerity. Its apparent spontaneity reflected the painter's first impression. Whereas the Académie honored the conception, the new taste saw the artist's genius in his facture, his mark-making.[27]

MANUFACTURING PIGMENTS AND DYES

In the early nineteenth century, advances in chemistry brought about a revolution in colorants with the invention of synthetics that were then industrially manufactured. The repertory of colors expanded dramatically, and many of the traditional natural colorants, which in many cases were not bright enough, were replaced. The greens had always been dull and were usually produced by mixing blues and yellows; yellows were also dull, or subject to fading. The only blues that were really desirable, ultramarine and azurite, were expensive. Vermilion, although brilliant with excellent hiding power, was subject to blackening under certain conditions. Orange and purple had always been achieved only with mixtures.

Whereas the Renaissance painter was trained in the workshop to prepare his own pigments, little by little, middlemen took over some of this laborious work, beginning with the vendicolori in Venice in the late fifteenth century. Pigments could be bought already ground from a trusted supplier. The preparation of ultramarine in Florence, however, became a specialty of the convent of San Giusto alle Mura, where the Gesuati supplied many of the painters with their blue (and some other pigments as well). Perhaps patrons and painters felt they could trust the monks to sell it unadulterated and at a fair, if high, price. Research is under way to discover whether, or rather when, pigments already prepared became available in other parts of Italy and elsewhere. In Paris by the seventeenth century, it was possible to buy pigments already ground, although not in the provinces. By the mid-eighteenth century there were specialist color merchants selling artists' materials in Paris.[28] Steam-powered grinding of pigments began to appear in the 1830s, but at first they were too coarse to be used in the fine arts. When the manufacturers became able to produce fine grinds, painters sometimes rejected them because they produced an undesirable homogeneity.[29]

Pigments and dyes used by painters changed surprisingly little from the Renaissance to the nineteenth century, although their popularity could depend upon supply and cost. An important part of good business was obtaining and using materials economically. Beginning in the Age of Discovery, materials might be obtained from distant sources more cheaply by sea than the traditional overland routes. By the seventeenth century both materials and paintings were being exchanged through the Dutch East India Company and other trading companies. Global trade changed the supply and prices of certain colorants.

The story of indigo is a particularly intriguing one, spanning the period from 1600 up to the invention of a synthetic substitute on the brink of the twentieth century.[30] Useful as a versatile blue in fresco, it was not often used by painters in oil after the seventeenth century, but it continues to be used as a dye even today—for example, for denim. The blue dye had been produced in India for millennia. It is first mentioned by Vitruvius, and also by Pliny, but it was little used in Europe, where woad served as the basic blue dye. It is woad that Julius Caesar said the Britons used to paint themselves blue for battle, which gave them a terrifying appearance. It derived from the same plant as indigo, but because it had lower pigment content, it was weaker and duller. The livelihood of the woad farmers, especially in Germany and France, was threatened when sixteenth-century dyers, now able to import indigo directly from India, recognized how much superior it was. The woad producers instituted a successful smear campaign, calling indigo everything from "fugitive," meaning that it was not fast and would fade, to "corrosive," meaning it would eat the cloth or canvas. As a result laws were enacted prohibiting it in Europe throughout much of the seventeenth century.[31] By the mid-eighteenth century these laws had finally been repealed. To answer increased demand, indigo was then cultivated in their colonies by the British, Dutch, Portuguese, French, and Spanish. Spanish indigo from Guatemala and French from Santo Domingo (Haiti) then surpassed Indian in quality and efficiency of production. The British introduced the "Santo Domingo method" to India in the late eighteenth century. It became an enormously lucrative product and dominated the market for a hundred years until the invention of synthetic indigo in the late nineteenth century, when the market dried up.[32]

Another dye obtained from the Americas supplanted a European product not because it was cheaper but because it was superior. Cochineal, an insect that grows on the

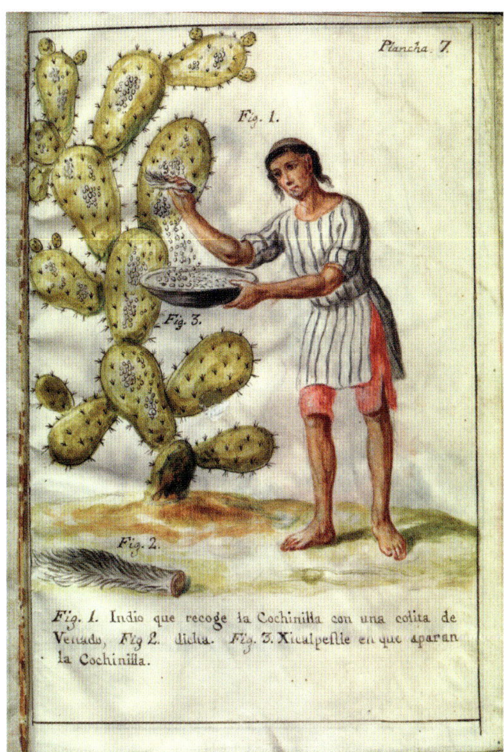

FIG. 5.9. José Antonio de Alzate y Ramírez, *Indian Collecting Cochineal with a Deer Tail,* from *Memoria sobre la naturaleza, cultivo, y beneficio de la grana,* 1777. Colored pigment on vellum. Newberry Library, Chicago.

nopal cactus, was brought back from the New World by the Spanish, who had been astonished to see the Aztec coloring their garments and painting their bodies with a red dye more brilliant than any available in Europe. It quickly replaced the formerly prized kermes, obtained from insects living on certain species of oaks, the evergreen kermes oak, which looked dull by comparison. For a brief period in the second half of the eighteenth century, domesticated cochineal was cultivated in Oaxaca in Mexico as a cottage industry sponsored by the state, involving perhaps a third of the peasant families in Oaxaca (fig. 5.9). Until demand in Europe declined after 1790, when war diverted attention and resources, cochineal was second only to silver in Mexican exports.[33]

There was even some reverse traffic in pigments. The North American Indians painted their bodies and faces with native red ochre until they discovered that vermilion was vastly more brilliant. Small amounts of vermilion imported from Europe would be traded for heaps of furs that were shipped back to Europe.[34]

Prussian blue is one of the few pigments synthesized before the nineteenth century and has therefore been called the first modern pigment. It was discovered by accident by a chemist in 1704 and made available on a small scale before it was manufactured widely in the 1720s. It has been found already in works of Watteau, who died in 1721.[35] The other blues available in the eighteenth century, azurite and ultramarine, were expensive, and the dye indigo was more suitable for watercolor, fresco, or tempera. A deep, blackish blue with a slight undertone of purple, Prussian blue is closer to indigo than to ultramarine, with good hiding power and a relatively cheap price. Until recently it was widely used and extremely popular. It has been found in works by Canaletto and Tiepolo and many of the Impressionists and Post-Impressionists—for example, in Claude Monet's *Bathers at La Grenouillère* (fig. 5.10), and in paintings by Edgar Degas and Paul Gauguin, though not by Paul Cézanne or Georges Seurat.[36]

Despite the popularity of Prussian blue, it did not replace ultramarine. Cobalt blue came much closer to doing that. It was discovered in 1802 and manufactured in France since 1807, but it was costly, though less so than ultramarine. Smalt, essentially ground glass containing cobalt, had been used since the fifteenth century, and even in the Trecento, but as we have seen, it deteriorates in oil and can become a yellowish beige. The new cobalt pigment was stable and lightfast and therefore a great improvement over smalt. The French government, recognizing the need for a synthetic ultramarine, offered a 6,000-franc prize in 1824 to anyone who could produce one, and in 1828 Jean-Baptiste Guimet claimed the prize. Guimet's synthetic pigment sold for 400 francs a pound, while the natural pigment from lapis lazuli cost between 3,000 and 5,000 francs a pound.[37] We can see synthetic ultramarine side by side with cobalt in Pierre-Auguste Renoir's *Umbrellas,* where the painter switched from cobalt, visible on the young woman and child at the right, painted in the first campaign, to synthetic ultramarine in the more severely costumed women, painted in the second campaign about six years later (fig. 5.11).

For yellow, frescoists relied on ochre, while oil painters used lead-tin yellow until the mid-eighteenth century, when it was replaced by Naples yellow. Chrome yellow, explored in the first decade of the nineteenth century in France, came into wide use after deposits of chromium were discovered near Baltimore in 1827. Compared to earlier yellow pigments, chrome had a welcome brilliance. Turner adopted it very early for his sun-drenched

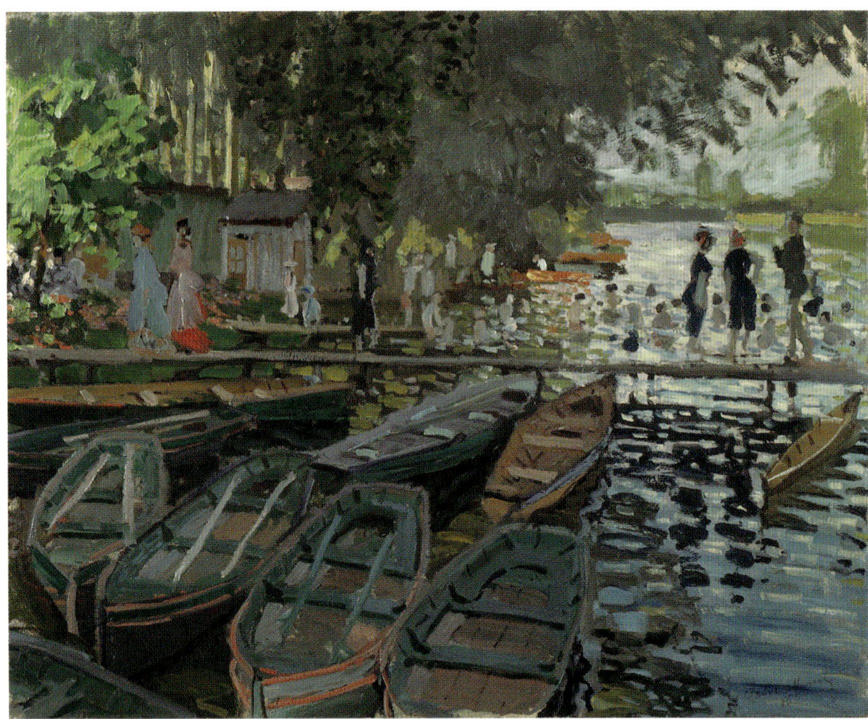

FIG. 5.10. Claude Monet, *Bathers at La Grenouillère*, 1869. Oil on canvas, 28 ¾ × 36 ¼ in. (73 × 92 cm). National Gallery, London.

scenes and continued to use it throughout his career (see fig. 5.17). It proved to have serious defects unknown to Turner, however, that have affected many of his canvases. Although it has good covering power, it darkens when exposed to light. Nevertheless it was popular with the Impressionists. Chrome orange became available in the 1830s and 1840s. Until then there had been no true orange on the painters' palette. Realgar served during and after the Renaissance as a gold tone, even though it was recognized that its arsenic base made it poisonous; it was frequently paired with the more golden orpiment, also arsenic based. They were difficult to use because they are incompatible with lead, including, of course, the indispensable lead white. Chrome orange was the first opaque orange pigment to become available to painters.[38]

A new metal, cadmium, was discovered in 1817, and the yellows, oranges, and reds made from it have become staples of the modern palette and an excellent alternative to the chromes, but the scarcity of the metal and limited production until the twentieth century drove the price up, so that it was not the preferred choice in the nineteenth century.[39]

Green was perhaps the greatest gap in the preindustrial arsenal of colorants. We have seen that so-called copper resinate (actually a glaze of verdigris in oil) was frequently glazed over verdigris or in a mixture in

landscape from the fifteenth to the seventeenth century, but it tends to brown and turn the look of originally lush fields parched. Malachite, another copper-based pigment, was used in the Renaissance, but its dull tone made it less satisfactory for landscape. For that purpose, mixtures, usually of blue and yellow, were used. No truly vivid green was available until the invention of emerald green in 1814.[40] It was the first green able to hold its own with traditional vermilion and ultramarine, and now with the new cobalt blue, chrome yellow, chrome orange, and cobalt violet. Cézanne loved *vert Véronèse*, as it was called in France, for his landscapes (fig. 5.12). It was cheap and therefore manufactured on a large scale for wallpapers and also as a dye for fabrics. Unfortunately it was another arsenic derivative and thus highly toxic. If the wallpaper became damp—which, of course, it did in England—it released a poisonous gas.[41] Its use as a dye was eventually abandoned when it became generally known that people who wore clothes dyed with it tended to die early.

Another green, known today as viridian, was based on chromium and was as widely used by the Impressionists as emerald green. Because it is somewhat transparent, it was useful as a glaze. It was stable and did not have the health hazard of emerald green. It was frequently mixed with other pigments in landscapes and with emerald green.

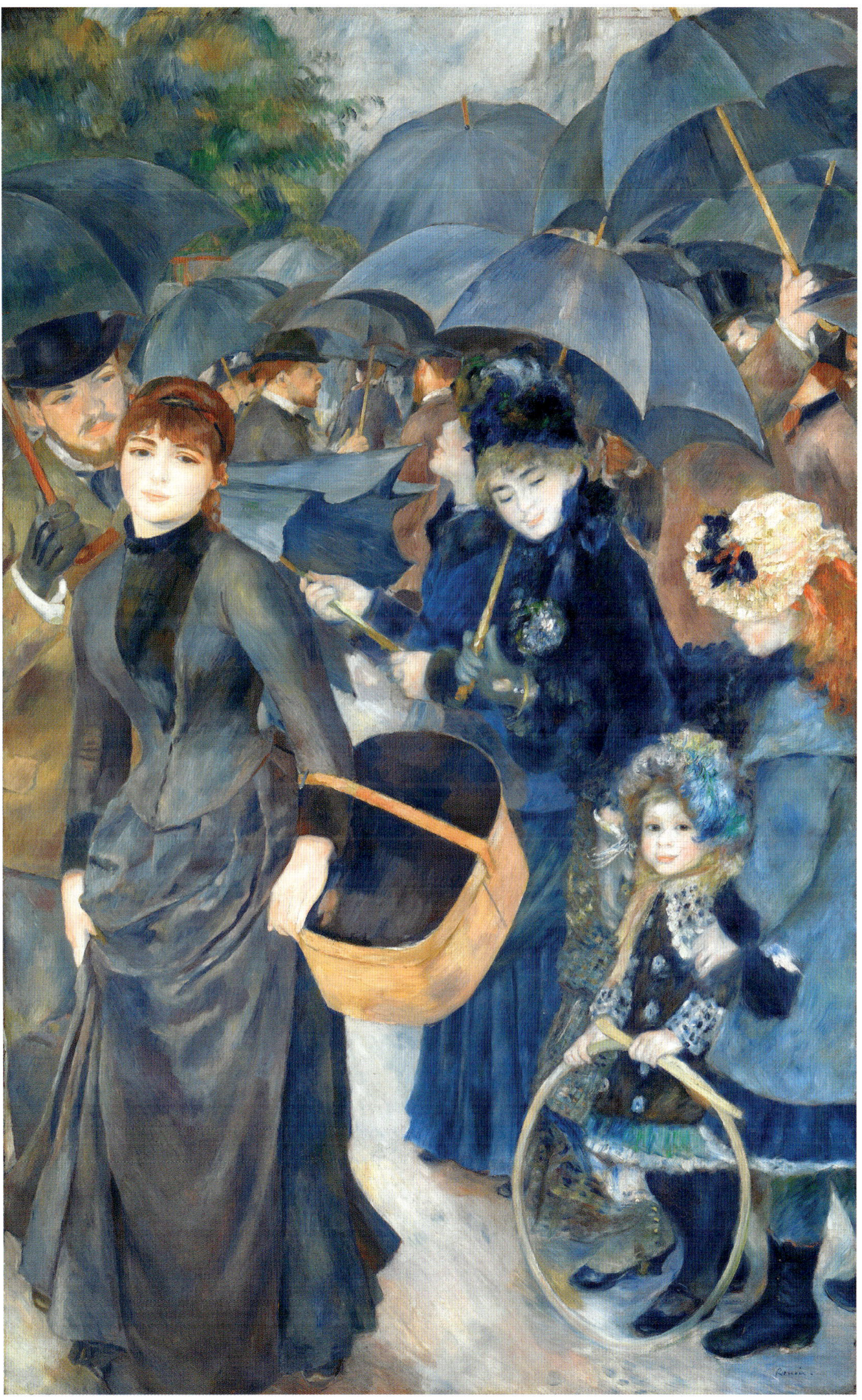

FIG. 5.11. Pierre-Auguste Renoir, *Umbrellas*, c. 1881–86. Oil on canvas, 71 × 45¼ in. (180.3 × 114.9 cm). National Gallery, London.

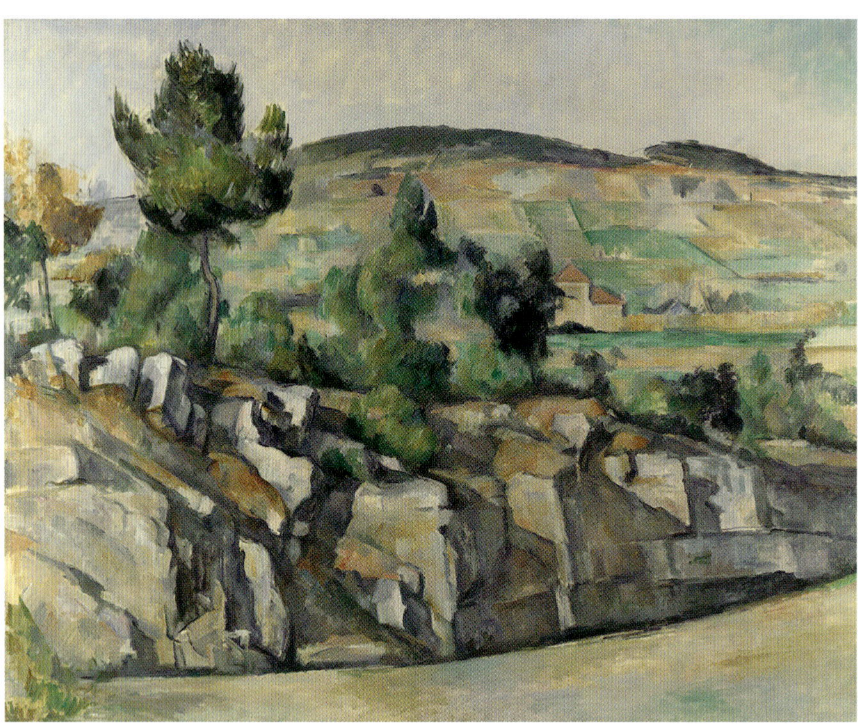

FIG. 5.12. Paul Cézanne, *Hillside in Provence*, 1890–92. Oil on canvas, 25 × 31¼ in. (63.5 × 79.4 cm). National Gallery, London.

Among the reds, vermilion continued in use until cadmium red largely replaced it in the early twentieth century because of its only defect: it blackens when exposed to hydrogen sulfides in the air.[42] Vermilion has excellent tinting strength and it is stable. It is also a favorite component of flesh coloring. Cadmium red is similarly vivid. Henri Matisse became enthralled with it when it was first manufactured: it is the pigment used in his *Harmony in Red* (see fig. 6.12). The innovations in the reds were in the organic dyes—for example, the importing of cochineal from America. Madder lake had been a mainstay of the palette since the Renaissance, and it was used under lakes containing kermes or cochineal or lac. Its delicate transparency also lent it to glazing, often over the strong opaque red earths and vermilion. Its principal fault was that it bleached in the light, so that today many crimson lakes are very pale records of the original.[43] Madder was synthesized as alizarin in 1868. Alizarin does not fade and could be manufactured in a wide range of hues, so the madder-growing industry declined rapidly and the synthetic colorant replaced the natural material.[44]

Among the most striking additions to the palette was the discovery of a true purple. Since the Renaissance, mixing blues and reds, either by glazing one over the other or making physical mixtures, had been the only way to achieve purple, and most were dull or somber.

The discovery of mauveine is a classic tale of an experiment gone wrong that produced a bonanza. The teenaged William Henry Perkin was trying to figure out something to do with aniline, a by-product of the great quantities of coal tar being generated by the coal burned for heating. His teacher at the Royal College of Chemistry, August Wilhelm von Hofmann, had published a paper hypothesizing the synthesizing of quinine, the malaria drug, from coal tar, so his assistant, Perkin, undertook some experiments. They failed, but in the process he discovered a residue that turned out with some further processing to produce a beautiful purple. It became available after 1859, and mauve-dyed fabric became the rage in Paris and London. Queen Victoria, who famously wore only black for fifty years after the death of her consort, Albert, wore a mauve dress to her daughter's wedding in 1862. Another purple, cobalt violet, a derivative of arsenic, was discovered in Germany. Monet was enamored of the light variety and used it unmixed in his flower gardens (fig. 5.13).[45]

Not surprisingly, younger painters took up the new pigments, while those who had been trained in the academic system continued to use what they had been taught. Delaroche, for example, who mixed virtually every tone in *Lady Jane Grey*, added only cobalt blue and synthetic ultramarine to the conventional palette of the

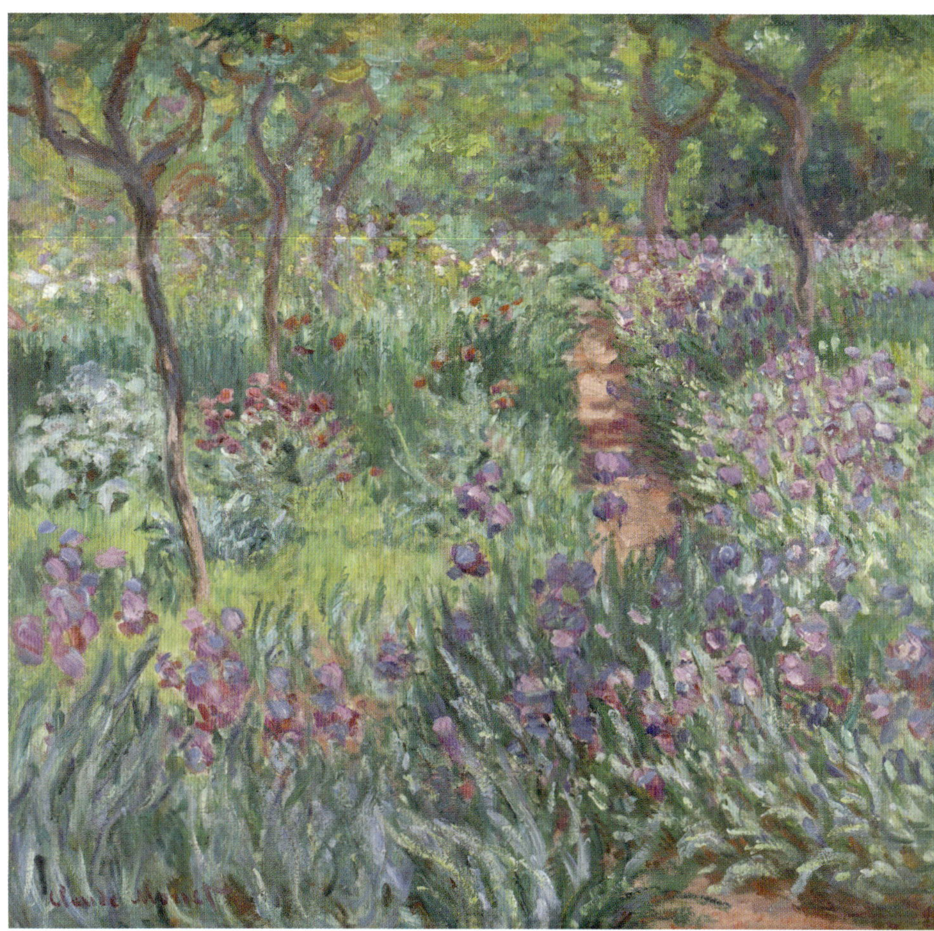

eighteenth century, which did include Prussian blue and the red lake glaze from cochineal. Delacroix, as innovative as he was in his application of paint, was conservative in his choice of colorants. Among his preserved letters from the 1820s are several in which he ordered pigments from his color merchant. They included a number of earths, including Cassel earth, peach black, Italian burnt umber, and yellow ochre. He also required Naples yellow and yellow lake. The only one of the new synthetics he ordered is cobalt blue.[46] Turner was quick to try out chrome yellow and other synthetics, although he had his father grind and prepare his paints, even the synthetics.

The Impressionists, born between 1834 and 1844, who in general did not undergo a full regimen of traditional training in an atelier, took up the new synthetics and used them, often unmixed, relishing their vivacity. This is not to say that they abandoned the traditional palette: vermilion and Prussian blue continued as favorites to which the new synthetics were added, but the earths were largely banished. They had been mainstays of the palette, not only in fresco but also in tempera and oil, essential

both to the Dutch landscapists and to the academic tradition that sought a subdued tonality, and Delacroix had been using them extensively in the late 1820s. He apparently changed his mind later, however, for he banned them in his *Journal* in 1857.[47] Like his rethinking of the sketch, he came to reject aspects of his academic training.

MANUFACTURING AND MARKETING MATERIALS

The new manufactured paints were initially sold in pigs' bladders, which were about the size of a walnut when filled (fig. 5.14). The painter would pierce the bladder, squeeze out the paint, and then plug the incision. Because the bladders were not impermeable, the paint could dry out quickly and become unusable. The tin tube, invented in 1841 and made available by about 1850 in France, was therefore a major breakthrough. The paints were preserved from moisture, air, and light because they could be resealed, eventually with the kind of screw top we are accustomed to today. These tubes were easily portable, making it possible for the painter to pack them up and go outdoors to paint.[48] Renoir was recorded as

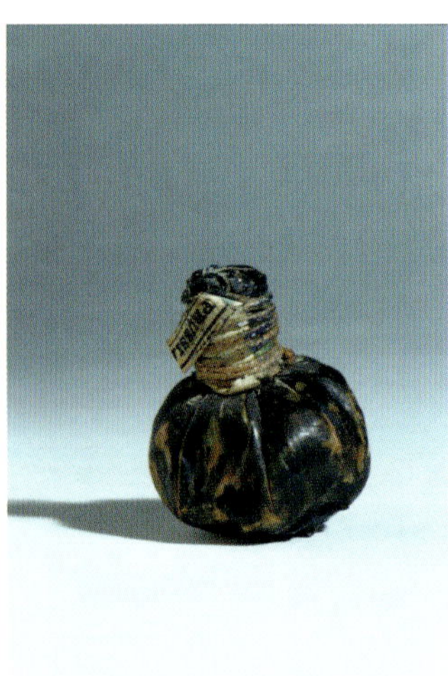

FIG. 5.14. Pig's bladder for oil paint, 19th century.

saying, "Without paint in tubes, there would have been no Cézanne, no Monet, no Sisley or Pissarro, nothing of what the journalists were later to call Impressionism."[49]

The artist was now freed from the tedious procedure of preparing his pigments and canvases. To be sure, prepared pigments had been available from color merchants in the previous century, but the taste for smaller pictures of standard sizes and the preference for white rather than tinted priming simplified the painter's whole process of preparation. He needed no assistants. His studio need be only as large as he required for himself. This development spelled an end to the workshop tradition and had far-reaching implications for the education of painters. They would no longer spend years in the workshop of a master who would teach them how to draw, how to design a painting, how to use the materials. Amateurs

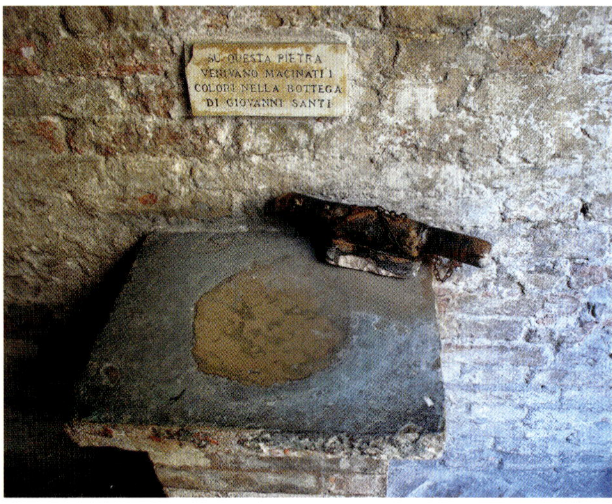

FIG. 5.15. Grinding stone for preparing pigments, Raphael's house, Urbino.

and untrained would-be artists could create without oversight and try to sell their products, a situation that accelerated the collapse of the Salon, because it could not accommodate the increased population of artists. Turner, though much older than the Impressionists, would show them the way to several of these innovations, as we shall see.

There were complaints, however, that the factory-made colors were ground either too coarsely or too finely or too much oil was added. As Cennino Cennini knew, every pigment requires a different fineness: some are most brilliant when the particles are left large, others could not be ground too fine. With hand grinding on a stone slab, just the right amount of oil could be added. Raphael's porphyry grinding stone is still preserved in the courtyard of his house in Urbino (fig. 5.15). Painters were sometimes advised in the new handbooks to remove excess oil by putting the tube paint on blotting paper. Manufacturers would also add extenders to economize and for easier handling: the pigments were "more buttery" and would go on smoothly. Additives such as wax would extend the shelf life. By the 1860s factory-made pigments had been available for a generation. The Impressionist painters generally preferred to have their pigments, including the synthetics, hand-ground by their colormen to their personal specifications.[50]

An important feature of marketing was that manufacturers created mixtures and sold them with new names. Because every manufacturer sold his product under its own newly minted name, it became difficult to know what was in a tube. Whereas the artists of the past had been trained to know their materials, painters were now dependent upon middlemen for guidance. Handbooks suddenly appeared in great numbers describing the properties, advantages, and defects such as incompatibilities of the new synthetics, and information on how to test in the studio for adulterants.[51]

Painters depended upon retailers for advice. A new class of middlemen appeared who handled artists' materials. The task of grinding and preparing the paints was increasingly turned over to specialists who did not deal with the large-scale production of colors for the decorator and carriage trade, but only with artists' pigments. Some colormen took over from the factories the grinding and preparation, but some others dealt only in sales. The painters would discuss their materials with their colormen, receiving advice and complaining in turn. If they were lucky they found a retailer whom they trusted and developed a relationship with him, as Van Gogh did. Julien Tanguy was a paint grinder who sold art supplies at his shop in Montmartre, which was frequented by several of the painters who became his friends, including Camille Pissarro and Cézanne. He took paintings in exchange for paint, so he became something of a dealer as well, although his wife was less affable and wanted to be paid for materials sold. Van Gogh painted his portrait three times in his Paris years, 1886–87 (fig. 5.16).

TURNER

J. M. W. Turner began his career as a topographical draughtsman making illustrations of antiquarian interest for popular magazines. He was accepted into the Royal Academy at the tender age of fifteen, and his first watercolor was exhibited there that summer of 1790. He worked and exhibited watercolors for ten years before he exhibited his oil paintings; this gave him unique experience that he could adapt to his needs in oil.[52] He learned from watercolor, for instance, to work from a light ground and to use paint with some transparency (fig. 5.17). The Impressionists would follow in his footsteps in abandoning the time-honored use of dark or mid-tone colored priming, and they must have been inspired by Turner's works to appreciate the fresh look of strong, unmixed pigment.

As a largely self-taught painter, Turner was experimental, both in techniques and with his materials. He

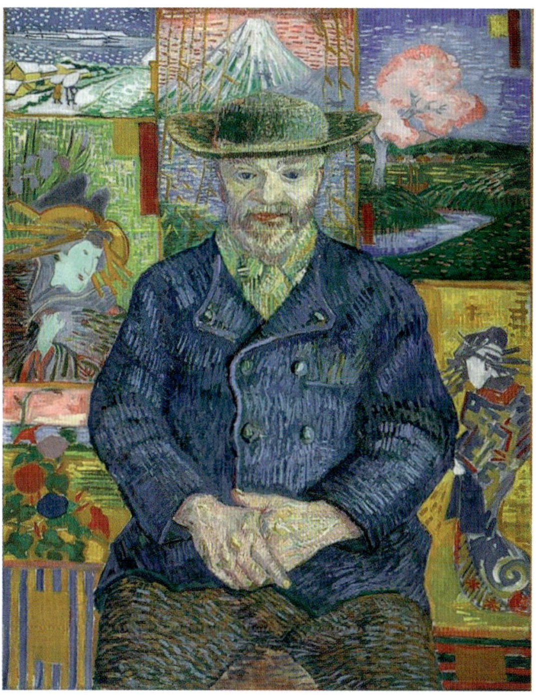

FIG. 5.16. Vincent van Gogh, *Portrait of Père Tanguy*, 1887. Oil on canvas, 36¼ × 29½ in. (92 × 75 cm). Musée Rodin, Paris.

was eager to try some of the new synthetic pigments. Cobalt blue was available in France in 1802; Turner was using it in oil painting by 1806–7. Chrome yellow was only available from 1814–15, but Turner had used it in a painting he exhibited in 1814. He was quick to try pale lemon chrome and chrome orange, both in 1822 or 1823. He used emerald green in the 1830s, which was only

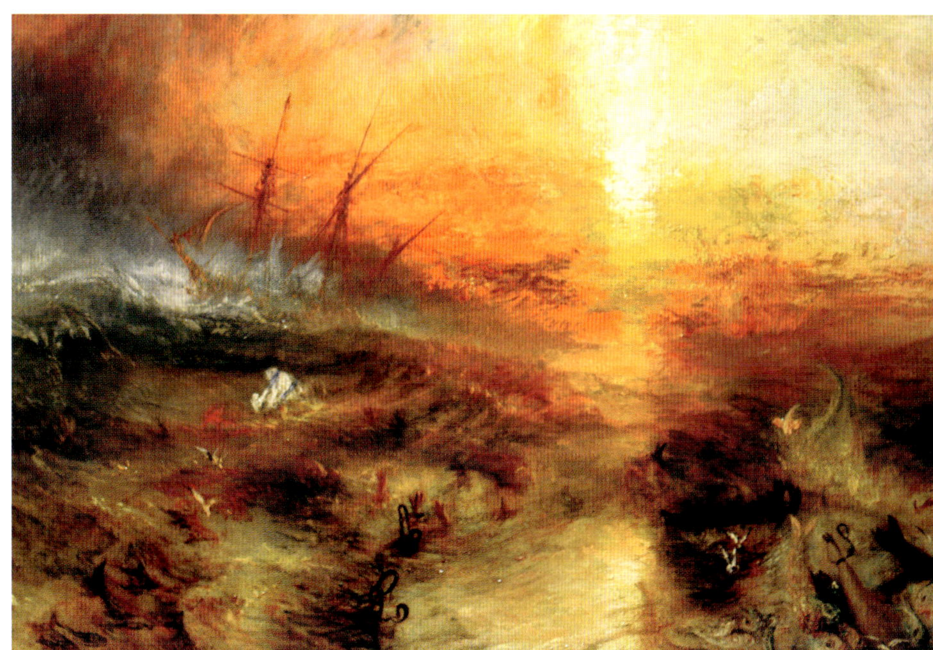

FIG. 5.17. Joseph Mallord William Turner, *Slave Ship*, 1840. Oil on canvas, 35¾ × 48¼ in. (90.8 × 122.6 cm). Museum of Fine Arts, Boston.

discovered in 1814, and he tried out synthetic ultramarine in watercolor within a couple of years of its marketing in 1826–27.[53] Unfortunately some of the deleterious characteristics of these new pigments and his procedures were not yet known and have only been revealed in recent times. For example, like some of his predecessors and contemporaries, including Sir Joshua Reynolds, he used megilp, which is a prepared mixture of mastic varnish with linseed oil, used for quicker drying. Turner worked rapidly and spontaneously, so it is easy to understand his impatience with slow-drying materials. What Turner didn't know was that when a conservator tried to remove a discolored varnish coating, the varnish in the paint would be soluble, making it impossible to clean his pictures. His favorite yellow, the new chrome yellow, which he loved both for its brilliance and its fast-drying nature, we now know can turn brown over time. Like many of his contemporaries, he sometimes used bitumen for his shadows. Because it does not dry, it eventually causes often severe darkening and cracking of the paint.

Because Turner had his father prepare his canvases and grind his paints, he had a rare control over his materials. His father primed his canvases at a time when commercial priming was in general use, and he appears to have had them prepared to suit his rapid execution, without size, so that some of the oil would be absorbed. The shorter working time because of the absorbent ground was not a problem for him—in fact it was an advantage, because he worked so rapidly. There is a canvas at the Clark Art Institute the back of which is entirely soaked with oil. After his father died in 1829, he used commercially primed canvas.

Turner always took a sketchbook with him and he often made watercolor sketches on-site. Although many of his sketches have survived and are valued today, he made his paintings for exhibition in his studio. He did not prepare an underdrawing; instead he blocked in the composition with washes of thinned oil paint. Even his earliest paintings revealed him to be interested in dramatic landscape quite at odds with the usual serene scenery preferred by most landscapists of the day. He varied the textures of his paint, from the thinnest glazes to thick impastos, applied even with the palette knife, and to achieve the variations he boldly incorporated a variety of additives such as beeswax, many of them untried before.

Turner is the first painter we have examined here who worked on his own. As he had his father's help, he did not need to run a workshop with a platoon of assistants and pupils for whom he had to model the correct procedures. Unlike the master who ran a workshop that had to maintain a reputation for quality and durability of its production for the sake of those who depended upon him, he was free to experiment. He was trying things no one had ever done before. In this freedom he was a model to the Impressionists, who also shed the obligations of running an atelier and worked solo.

Turner's works are the scourge of the conservator today because they have deteriorated as a result of his choices and use of materials. Working on his own, he would do whatever it took to achieve the effect he wanted. Disregard for the permanence of materials is an attitude that contemporary artists sometimes adopt. The fast pace of life and the rapid obsolescence of so much around us no doubt contributes to this cavalier attitude. Turner was one of its founders.

Turner painted light. Claude Lorrain was one his favorite painters, whose work he studied closely. Like Claude, he recorded atmosphere, haze, smoke, fog. When Turner bequeathed the contents of his studio to the government, he stipulated that his *Decline of the Carthaginian Empire* be hung beside Claude's *Embarkation of the Queen of Sheba* (see fig. 3.16), where it can be seen at the National Gallery today. Also like Claude he constructed landscapes around a narrative, sometimes historical, sometimes mythological, but sometimes based on contemporary events, such as disasters at sea. His interest is not in re-creating the event so much as evoking the mood or offering a meditation upon the fragility of human life or fame.

Napoleon was again on people's minds in 1842 when Turner painted *War. The Exile and the Rock Limpet* and exhibited it (fig. 5.18). In December 1840, nineteen years after the British had buried him on the island of his exile and death, Napoleon's ashes had been returned to Paris upon the request of King Louis Philippe and he was given a state funeral. In the work the emperor—instantly recognizable by his uniform, even if the painter has made his short and stolid figure tall and slim—is a lonely figure. His loneliness is amplified by the stiff echo far behind him of a solitary armed British guard. Turner needs no details, no facial features to tell Napoleon's story, only the gesture of his arms crossed in resignation, a gesture so contrary to his familiar cocky one of hand tucked inside his vest. Napoleon contemplates a limpet in the pool of

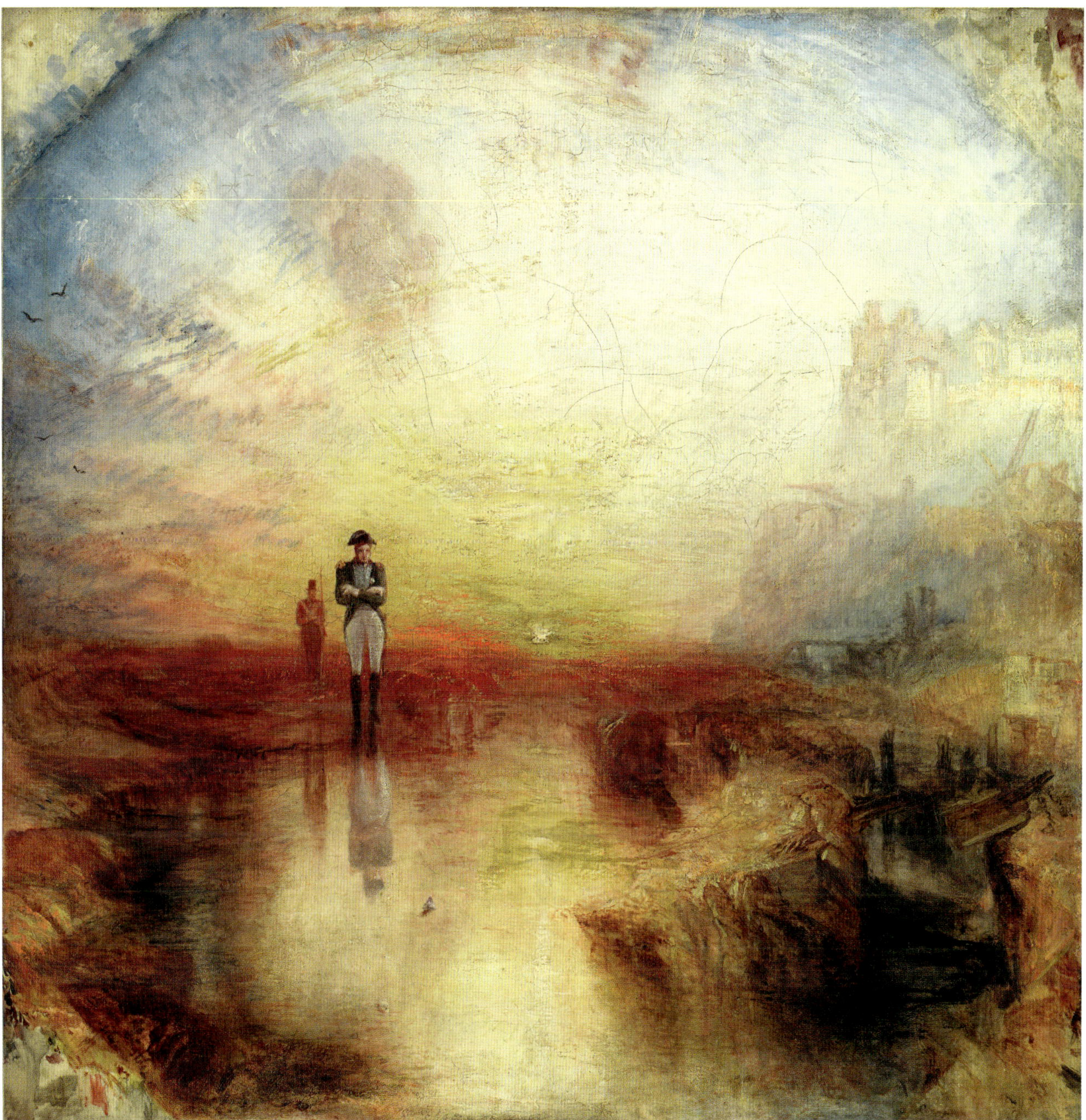

FIG. 5.18. Joseph Mallord William Turner, *War. The Exile and the Rock Limpet*, 1842. Oil on canvas, 31¼ × 31¼ in. (79.4 × 79.4 cm). Tate, London.

water, a kind of mollusk or barnacle that clings to a rocky surface with a ferocity like Napoleon's stubborn grip on power. Turner himself called the fiery sunset sky a sea of blood. On the right are broken structures, contrastingly dark and difficult to decipher but evocative of the ruins of war; behind are vague structures suggestive of conquest made and lost. Turner was fond of creating sets and pairs. This Romantic subject of the disgraced hero he paired with a painting called *Peace. Burial at Sea* of the same

year. Turner's friend the painter David Wilkie had died while returning by ship from Constantinople. Opposing not just the subjects but also the color schemes, Turner depicts serenity achieved with a cool pearly palette and saturated blacks.

At the end of his life he created a set of four paintings on Dido and Aeneas, which he exhibited in 1850. In *Departure of the Fleet*, looking into the setting sun, as in one of Claude's golden harbors, we are blinded and

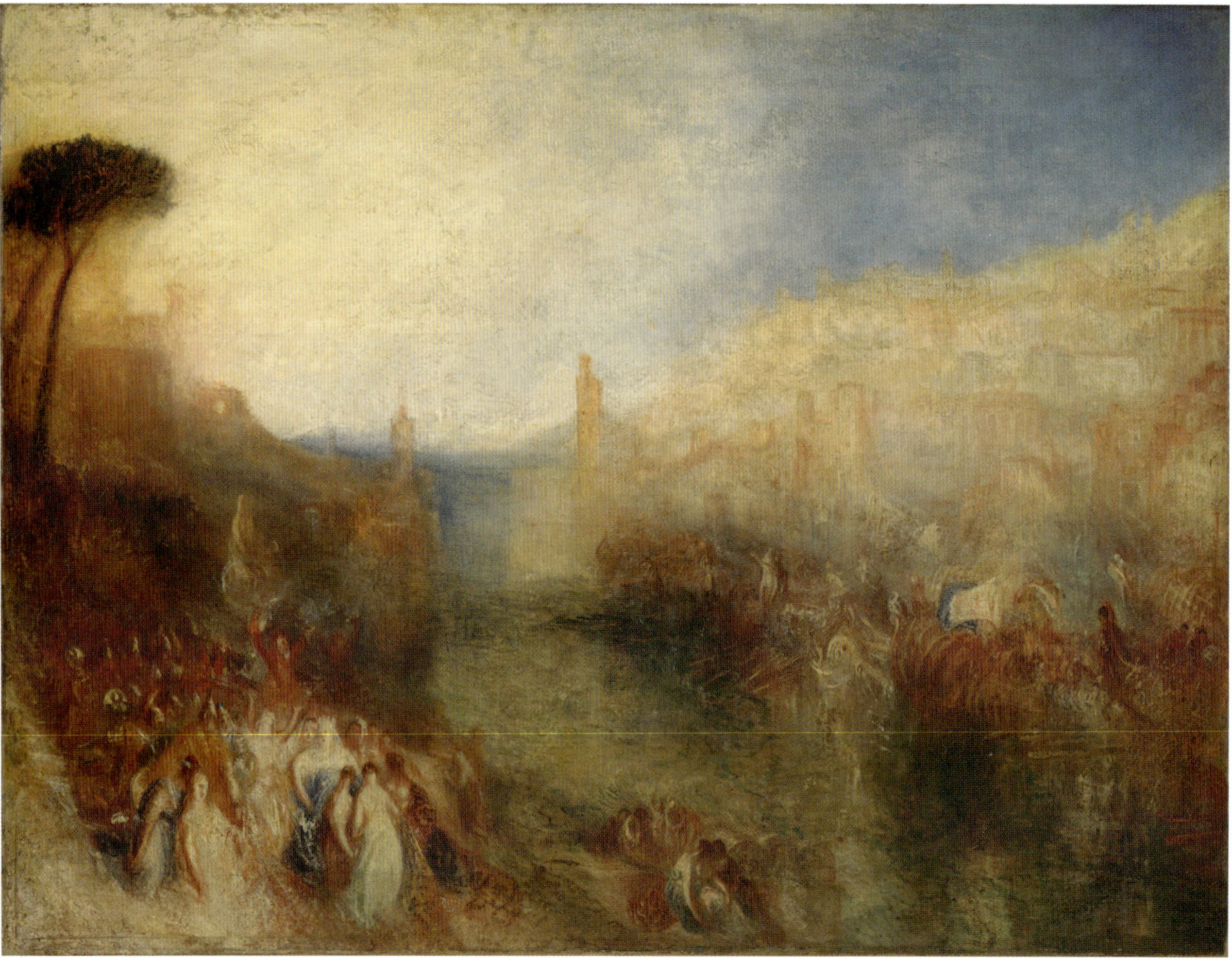

forms evanesce, losing their definition (fig. 5.19). The figures at the left are faceless and barely discernible, even less legible than Napoleon. We now have to guess from the title that they are Dido and Aeneas saying their last farewell. At right the walls of Carthage, painted in the thinnest of glazes, dissolve; at center the bold impasto of the sun roughens the canvas. As always with Turner, the figures are small and insignificant compared to nature. He had become bolder as he matured, now considering finished what he had previously regarded as a sketch. As in watercolor, which does not favor sharply delineated forms, there are no contours here. On varnishing days at the Royal Academy, when painters were given three days to add final touches to their works before the exhibition opened, Turner seemed to enjoy putting on a show of his virtuosity. Others gathered round as he painted or repainted whole sections of his exhibit.

When Monet was in London, having fled the Franco-Prussian War, he experienced Turner's paintings, bequeathed to the nation and hanging in the Tate. When he went home to Paris in 1872 he painted a scene like Turner's celebrations of light, *Impression: Sunrise* (fig. 5.20), the picture that gave its name to the movement when shown at the first Impressionist exhibition in 1874.[54]

COROT AND THE BARBIZON SCHOOL

As landscape gained popularity and manufactured colorants became available as portable products, painters moved out-of-doors with their easels, at first making colored sketches that they completed in the studio. The new bright colors were applied to canvases commercially primed in white or off-white. The Barbizon painters preceded the Impressionists by a generation in devoting themselves to landscape and painting *en plein air*, particularly in the forest of Fontainebleau outside Paris. They

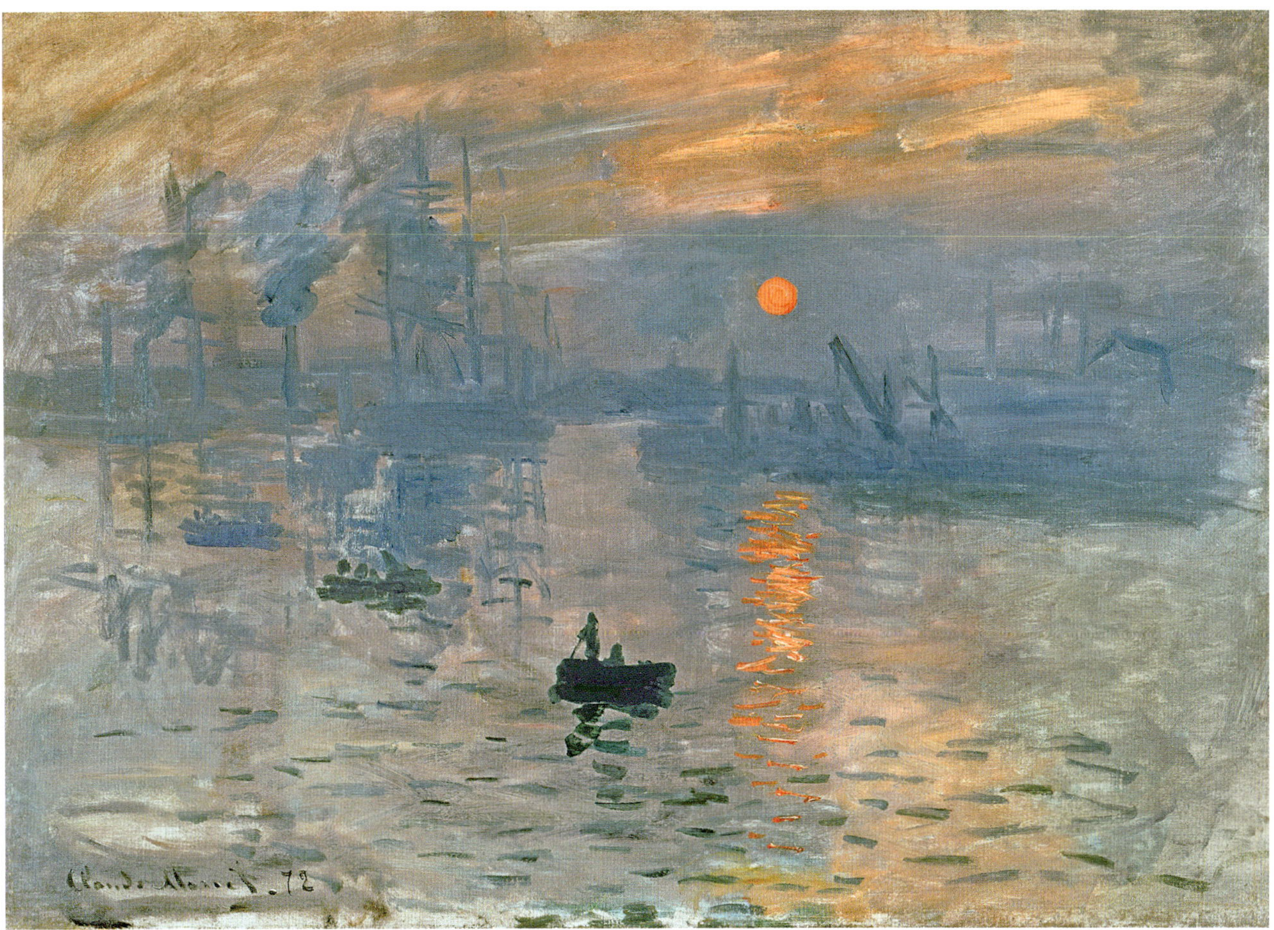

FIG. 5.20. Claude Monet, *Impression: Sunrise*, 1872. Oil on canvas, 18 7/8 × 24 4/5 in. (48 × 63 cm). Musée Marmottan Monet, Paris.

made use of some of the new pigments, but willingness to abandon traditional procedures did not come easily. Camille Corot, for example, despite his adoption of new synthetics such as viridian and even for a while emerald green, used them alongside traditional pigments to mix his greens. He preferred Prussian blue with yellows: Naples yellow or yellow lake or sometimes chrome yellow. His mixtures could be very complex: up to nine different-colored pigments have been found in his muted greens.[55] In *Peasants under the Trees at Dawn,* Corot shows a man sawing a tree and a woman gathering twigs (fig. 5.21). We are looking into the light, which makes forms dissolve and colors turn pale and grayish. The foliage of the tree is one of those complex greens, made from a tube green (a mixture of chrome yellow and Prussian blue) to which he has added red lake, yellow, vermilion, and cobalt blue.[56] Corot's conservatism is revealed by his retention of the academic ébauche, a thin black/brown layer under the landscape. It is not present in his skies,

which he painted last, so it was not an overall toning layer that we would call an imprimatura. Numerous corrections and overpaintings make clear that Corot worked up his canvases over time in the studio.

DEALERS

By the mid-nineteenth century the government had long since cut its official funding to commission or buy art for the state, thereby thrusting the artist into the world of commerce. The Salon was overburdened with submissions. Into the gap stepped the commercial dealers, who offered exhibition opportunities to artists and sometimes a kind of protection that resembled that of the old-time patron.[57] Like a Renaissance prince, Paul Durand-Ruel took the Impressionists under his wing, buying their paintings and sometimes advancing them money on future production.

Dealers in the modern mold had been around since the 1820s, migrating from trades such as framing,

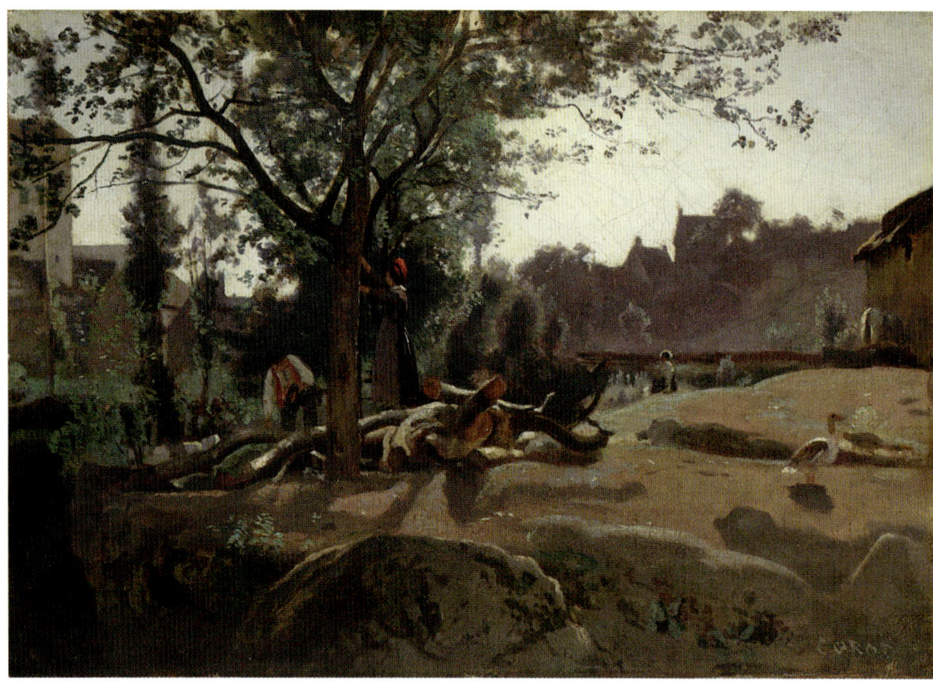

FIG. 5.21. Jean-Baptiste-Camille Corot, *Peasants under the Trees at Dawn*, c. 1840–45. Oil on canvas, 10 ¾ × 15 ¼ in. (27.3 × 38.8 cm). National Gallery, London.

restoring, and selling prints, and then selling some pictures alongside other luxury items and hiring out pictures to clients for an evening event or a month, as was the fashion. Paul Durand-Ruel's father, Jean, was such a dealer. He had purchased a stationery shop, and in 1825 he added artists' materials, sometimes exchanging supplies for work.[58] He began showing works by Delacroix, Antoine-Louis Bayre, and the Barbizon landscapists. His shop gradually became a gallery where art could be viewed, purchased, or rented. By the 1860s dealers were springing up everywhere, but not for contemporary art. Goupil, with branches on Broadway and in Brussels, specialized in prints to appeal to middle-class clients with a taste for domestic decoration. Vincent van Gogh's uncle, also named Vincent, entered Goupil in 1868 and persuaded the firm to include drawings and paintings. In London, Agnew moved to Old Bond Street in 1861, specializing in Old Masters. Nathan Wildenstein set up his gallery in Paris at the beginning of the 1870s, dealing at first in eighteenth-century French painting and sculpture and later expanding to Italian, Spanish, Dutch, and Flemish art. Durand-Ruel was unique because he supported contemporary painters.

Paul Durand-Ruel first met Monet and Pissarro in London, where they had all fled in 1870 to avoid the Franco-Prussian War. He opened a gallery on New Bond Street and even sold a Monet.[59] When all three returned

to Paris, Durand visited Édouard Manet's studio and bought the entire contents of twenty-one paintings for 35,000 francs. Manet was not a marketable artist at the time, so it is clear that Durand-Ruel was counting on the future market for his work. It appears that Monet and Pissarro introduced their friends Alfred Sisley, Renoir, and Degas to the dealer. In 1872 Monet received 9,000 francs, and in 1873, 19,000 francs, from Durand-Ruel.[60] Although it is sometimes claimed that the dealer was paying Monet and some others a stipend, he was actually buying whatever the prolific Monet produced, and Monet was painting faster than Durand was paying. He promoted the work of these young artists, choosing to include their paintings among those he sent to exhibit in London in 1875 of older and established artists, for example. He published a three-volume catalogue of engravings of works in his possession, including work by Manet, Pissarro, Monet, Sisley, and Degas alongside Delacroix, Courbet, Corot, and the like.[61]

THE SALON DES REFUSÉS

The Salon was first instituted in 1667 at the insistence of Jean-Baptiste Colbert, who wanted the public to have the opportunity to admire the art he was commissioning to glorify the state and Louis XIV. The academicians resisted because in founding the Académie they had just liberated themselves from the guild and from the stigma of being mere artisans, and they wanted nothing to do with commerce and marketing. This early Salon went forward because it was for viewing only and nothing was for sale. It was intended to be biennial—but there were gaps—and was a semi-private event where the public could see the work of members of the Académie.[62] There was no jury until 1748. Later, during the Revolution, open admission to exhibit had been imposed, but that was quickly abandoned. In the nineteenth century the Salon was removed from the control of the Académie, and the number of entries grew steadily from 350 in 1789: by 1810 it had passed 1,000; by 1831 there were 3,211. When that number passed 4,000 in 1861, the reaction of the next jury in 1863 was to severely restrict the entries by accepting only 2,923 and refusing over 4,000.[63] The rejected included even artists who had been admitted to earlier exhibitions—for example, Manet, whose *Spanish Guitar Player* had attracted the attention of younger artists and had been awarded an Honorable Mention in 1861.[64] By this time there were so many artists competing for the attention and the patronage of the public that they were dependent on the Salon for exposure. Without it they could not make a living. Addresses of artists were published in the catalogue. As early as 1827 the critic Auguste Jal remarked that "There are very many artists who exhibit in the Salon solely to earn a living; they want their address in the catalogue even more than they want admission of their pictures."[65] Louis Philippe's unsatisfactory compromise at the time was to make the Salon annual, but the Académie was its jury, which began rejecting artists as prominent as Delacroix.

Harrison White and Cynthia White summarized the Salon, calling it "the central event in the French painting world of the nineteenth century. . . . Significant historical changes in its structure brought out different, conflicting purposes and meanings. What was it? An exhibition of and for a professional group? A show put on by a benevolent state? Or an enormous picture shop? No one was quite sure."[66] Or even a great bazaar. Whatever the case, the Salon had evolved from a venue to see to *the* place to sell.

The rejection of so many works in 1863 precipitated a crisis. In response to the uproar, Louis Napoleon announced that the rejected works would be displayed in another venue. Of course some artists withdrew, not wishing to be identified in this company, but thus was born the famous, and infamous, Salon des Refusés. The Académie recognized that its authority had been dismissed, and it heard it clearly stated in the emperor's declaration that he wished the public to be the judge.[67] The Salon des Refusés consolidated the independents and isolated the classicists and Romantics, who were then recognized as simply two possible options, the ones sponsored by the Académie. Boime has commented on the political importance of the Refusés:

> This event may well represent the most decisive institutional development in the progress of modern art, serving as the model for all subsequent independent and counter-Establishment shows. It marked the official sanction of the artist's right to demonstrate freely the fruits of his or her labor without regard to stylistic classification. It further implied that freedom to exhibit was inextricably linked to freedom of pictorial expression. The *refusés*—especially as represented by Manet and Whistler and the future impressionists—celebrated qualities of spontaneity and originality that critics perceive as incompleteness.[68]

The revolution in modeling and chiaroscuro and tinted priming, already anticipated by Turner and Corot, complemented the revolution brought about by the industrialization of artists' materials.

LIGHTING AND COLORING: MODELING, CHIAROSCURO, AND TINTED IMPRIMATURA

We have seen that first modeling and then chiaroscuro had been invented in the Renaissance, then varied and refined with each new generation. Together with perspective they were the essential tools in creating a simulacrum of light in the visual world. Taste for high contrast chiaroscuro came and went: it was out of favor for Rococo mythological fantasies, but indispensable for academic history paintings. David's adaptation of Caravaggesque chiaroscuro bequeathed to the nineteenth-century Académie a disciplined lighting that purged and clarified colors. The nineteenth-century procedure, as we saw in Delaroche, required multiple stages, from preliminary drawings, to sketches that might be in watercolor (see fig. 5.4), through underpainting in a thin brown that laid-in the darks and created a monochrome first version. The perfectly modulated shading of the final product was achieved by applying mixed colors thinly and smoothly.

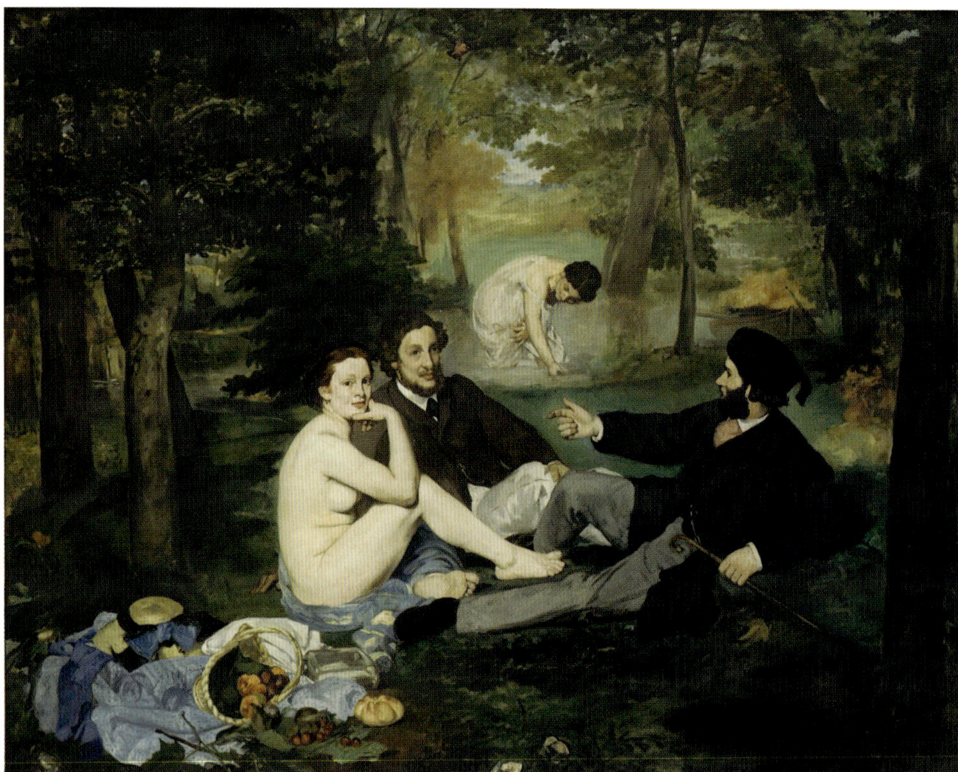

Continuous modeling had been the practice since the Renaissance. To be sure, Titian's pittura di macchia ("blob painting") modified the system by juxtaposing unblended brushstrokes in a technique that many seventeenth- and eighteenth-century painters would imitate. In the nineteenth century, Corot abbreviated the modeling sequence. Manet also omitted the nuances between light and dark, summarizing what he saw with starkly juxtaposed strokes of light and dark. For the Impressionists, the brilliant light of the out-of-doors bleached shadows; Monet saw color in shadows and green reflections from the grass. There is no chiaroscuro and no down-modeling in his pictures, no dark browns or neutral grays. Renoir generally used dark blue instead of black in his outdoor scenes. It was above all Cézanne, however, who invented an alternative to traditional modeling with his patches of juxtaposed color.

The Impressionists also abolished the mid-tone or dark imprimatura. After it was invented in the Renaissance, each painter thereafter practiced his own version according to his needs and the mood he wished to create. Although the tint varied from middle gray to rosy to deep reddish brown and shades between, it was almost universal—unless an undermodeling was used instead—until the Impressionists. Their return to using the white of the prepared canvas or a very pale tint was a shift fundamental to giving their paintings their new look.[69] The newly synthesized pigments could produce brilliant tones, but as Corot and others showed, a tinted priming could be used to reduce their brilliance to something barely distinguishable from the traditional palette. At the technical level, the freshness of Impressionist painting resulted from the use of the new pigments on a white or off-white canvas, and the rejection of continuous modeling.

MANET

Young artists rallied around the Realist Manet, and he was adopted as the leader of the independents. Among the paintings that were hung with the Refusés was Manet's confrontational *Luncheon on the Grass* (fig. 5.22), an evocation of Giorgione's *Pastoral Concert* (today usually regarded as a collaboration of Giorgione with Titian; fig. 5.23). Manet was provocative in his choice of subject, of course, in showing contemporary students on a picnic with ladies in stages of undress, but the fact that he parodied Giorgione's beloved icon in the Louvre rankled even more. Giorgione was admired for his proto-Romantic idyll, in which the dreamy, soft-edged sfumatesque execution created the aura of an Eden where nymphs and

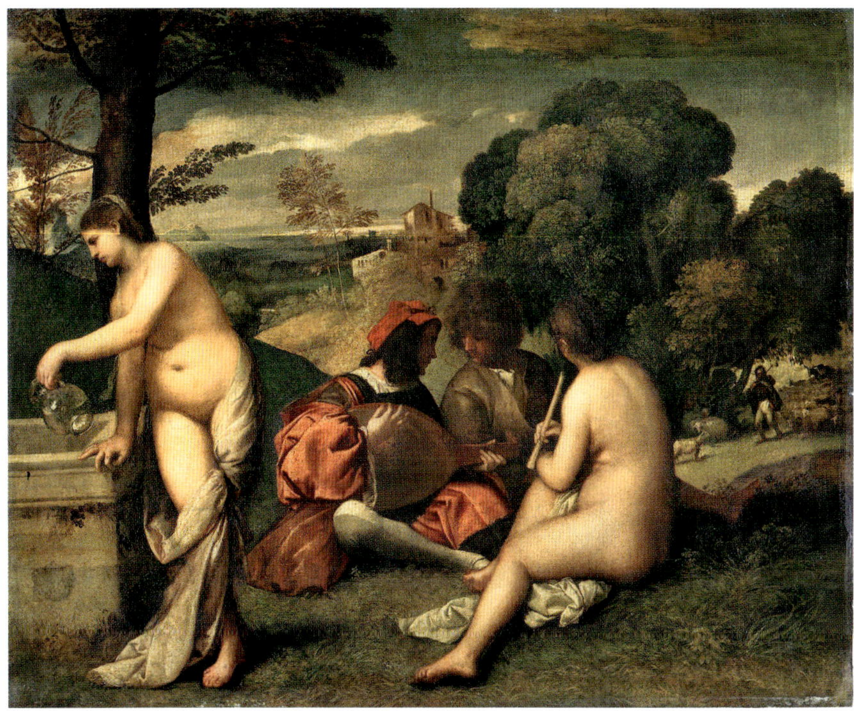

mortals mingle, and their behavior falls outside the realm where rules of decorum apply. Manet, with his abrupt brushwork and harsh juxtaposition of colors, banished Eden and brought the scene all too brazenly into the Parisian viewer's space. Where Giorgione had averted the faces, Manet turns them to stare down the spectator eye to eye. Where the golden varnish softens the flesh tones of Giorgione's work, Manet's nude body is starkly white, of pasty complexion, and harshly contrasted with the dark suits of her companions. Suggesting an ironical attitude, the painter has preserved studio lighting, making it all the harder to believe.[70] Above all, it was the patchy texture and unblended brushstrokes that gave offense to an audience schooled in the slick finish of academic painting.

The great draw of the Salon was Alexandre Cabanel's history painting, the *Birth of Venus*, which was immediately purchased by the emperor (fig. 5.24). Recalling Boucher, Venus is surrounded by cupids and supported on the waves. Apparently asleep, her eroticism is heightened by her coyly half-opened eyes beneath her arm.[71] Manet responded with his own version of history painting, the nude *Olympia* (fig. 5.25), based on Titian's masterpiece the *Venus of Urbino* (Florence, Uffizi). Shown in the Salon of 1865, Olympia, whose jewelry, slippers, and maid with bouquet from an admirer mark her as a

prostitute, does not allure the viewer but confronts him and defiantly blocks her crotch with her hand. Manet has replaced Titian's dog, symbolic of marital fidelity, with a black cat. Critics reacted to the substitution of soft, appealing flesh with what was seen as "dirty"-colored, its jaundiced yellow set off against the white bedclothes.[72] Equally adversarial is again Manet's facture, which replaces Cabanel's academic polish with bold, blunt brushstrokes.

Manet had displayed his technique earlier in 1862 in his *Concert in the Tuileries,* which had been exhibited at Galerie Martinet and attracted considerable notice (fig. 5.26). While the public identified him as an Impressionist, Manet could not even be called a reluctant Impressionist: he never exhibited with them and continued to submit his pictures to the Salon. In fact his *Concert* is very different in its coloring from the Impressionists' palette, as it was developed in the 1870s. Manet's is dominated by the earth colors—the blacks, browns, and grays of the men's costumes—that the Impressionists would banish. His use of black, which appears so prominently here in the men's hats, set him apart from both sides: the Impressionists avoided it and preferred Prussian blue; academic painters steered clear of black because it disrupted their delicate harmonies.[73] Manet's neutral tones serve as a foil for touches of bright color in the women's

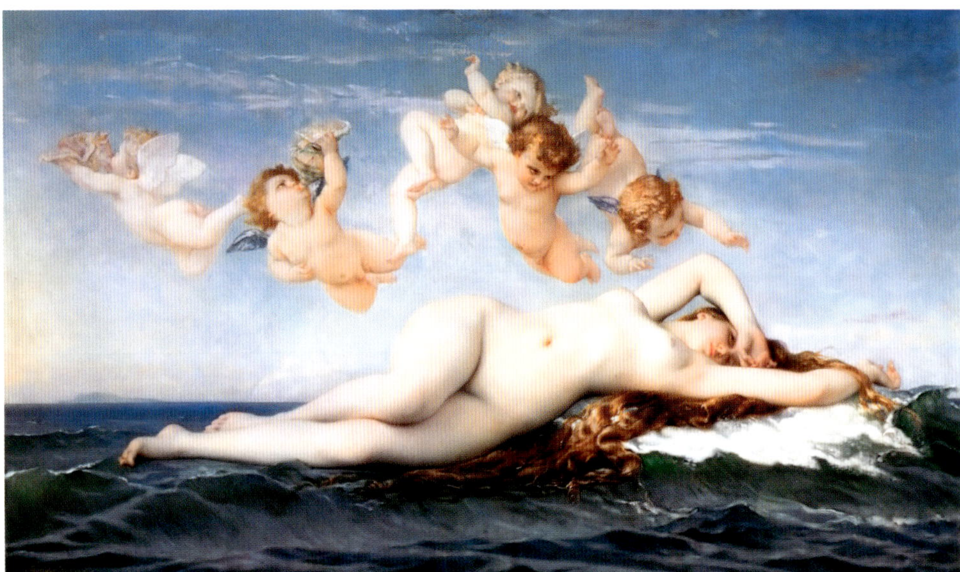

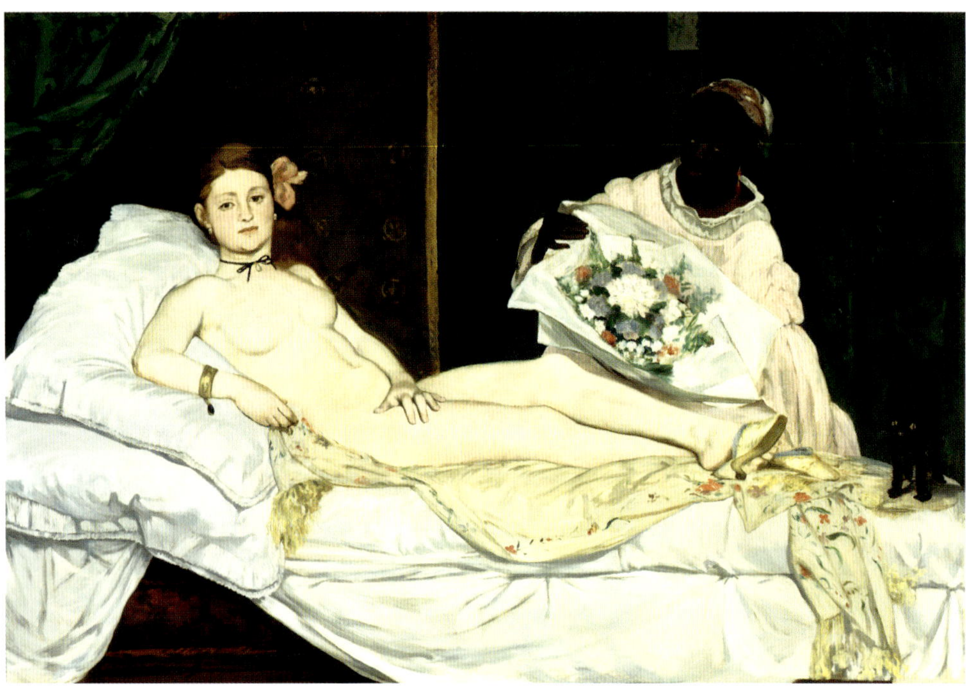

bonnets, which are painted with the new synthetics, cobalt blue and chrome yellow.[74] *Concert* is aggressively innovative also in the way it is painted. Monet noted Manet's "bold modeling which suppressed intermediate tints and sharply articulated the highlights"—that is to say, he gives up continuous modeling and juxtaposes *taches* ("blobs").[75] At the very center he has left the figures of the seated women in nothing more than underpaint, asserting the power of sketchy rendering. The Impressionists would embrace the facture of the sketch, but as we recall, Delacroix had already proclaimed it. In places Manet has glazed in a traditional manner, but used

new pigments to do so. It is as though he is tentatively exploring how to use the new bright pigments as a critique of traditional techniques and values. Since Manet intended the painting to be a manifesto for daily life and thus the appropriate subject for the "new painting," in line with his friend Baudelaire's proclamation regarding literature, this marriage of old and new is appropriate.

The system in which the state controlled and managed artistic production had failed. One of the principal functions of the medieval guild had been to limit supply. When the government, supporting the juste milieu and wanting to offer these painters exposure to the public,

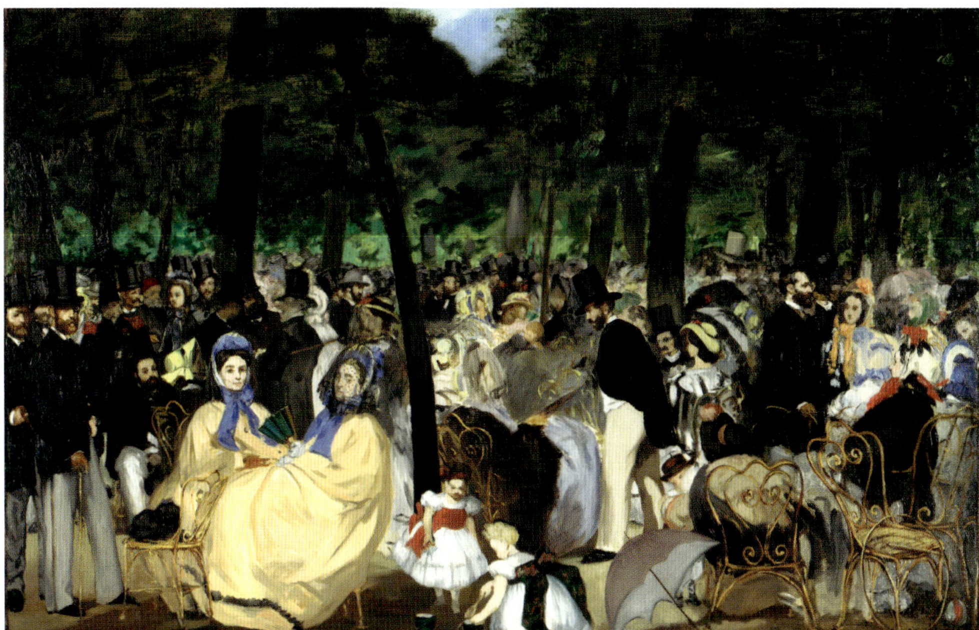

ceased to control the numbers, the system broke down. What the Refusés made clear was that the Salon was no longer able to handle the task of exhibiting the work of all the artists of France. Alternative exhibition opportunities had already appeared, and they would multiply. The disparate artists, who valued independence and personal expression above the sanction of the authorities, were brought together by the Refusés and empowered to organize themselves. Although a second Salon des Refusés in 1864 was successfully manipulated by the administration to make the participants look bad, a decade later the Impressionists converted the energy first generated in 1863 to found their first independent exhibit. Nevertheless it is important to note that while there were 450,000 attendees of the Salon of 1874, visitors to the Impressionist exhibition at the same time numbered 3,500.

PAINTERS OF MODERN LIFE

Paris was in a state of upheaval beginning in 1853, when Emperor Louis Napoleon hired Baron Haussmann to modernize the city. Medieval districts with their dark, airless, squalid streets were eviscerated as new broad boulevards, averaging eighty feet wide, were cut through to create straight roads and give access to the center. Haussmann turned the streets into places where people could promenade, lining them with trees and supplying street furniture such as benches, lanterns, and columns for advertisements. New apartment buildings lined these avenues, while shops and cafés, taking advantage of the sidewalks, invited pedestrians. People could now saunter through the streets out of the mud and filth that previously had made walking for pleasure impossible. Desperately needed new infrastructure, including water supply and sewers, gas lighting and bridges across the Seine, required tearing up streets everywhere. About twenty-seven thousand buildings were knocked down between 1852 and 1870. The *grands travaux* forced three hundred and fifty thousand people, or 20 percent of the population, to move.[76]

The Impressionist painters recorded not just the landscape of the suburbs and the spots where day-trippers, making use of the new railways, sought recreation. They recorded the life of the streets of Paris, though curiously enough, not the turmoil of the tearing down and rebuilding that was transforming the city. The *flâneur* is depicted by Gustave Caillebotte, among others, as he strolls across the bridge at the Gare Saint-Lazare with a well-dressed lady carrying a parasol (fig. 5.27). The painter uses perspective to call our attention to the vista and the openness of the space, and he captures the quality of urbane leisure that makes Paris so attractive still today. Caillebotte, Manet, and Monet all lived nearby and they all painted the train station. Monet made a series of eleven paintings of the station, delighting in its steam and smoke, using his rough impastoed brushstroke to depict the atmosphere and the energy.

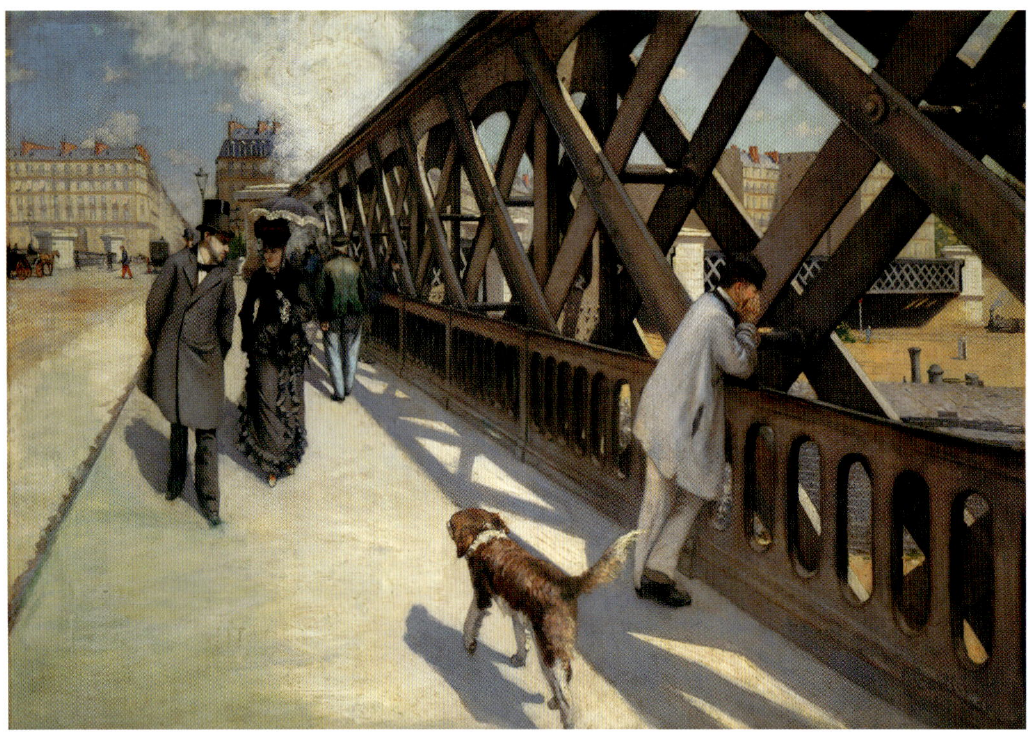

DEGAS

Edgar Degas had little use for the suburbs and relished
instead the places of entertainment and business on
the busy streets. His work exemplifies this other side of
Impressionism, the depiction of modern urban life. It
was a more innovative subject, really, by the 1860s, than
landscape. Degas was enamored of café life, theaters,
the opera, and particularly the ballet, where he became
a familiar, almost invisible observer, not only at perfor-
mances, but backstage and at rehearsals, where he could
capture the less glamorous side of the life of the hard-
working girls. The city subjects he chose were obscure
and offbeat—for example, scenes of women visiting the
new millinery shops and trying on hats, or laborers such
as laundresses at work. He depicted interiors for the most
part and was never drawn to landscape, although the
racetrack was a lifelong preoccupation. This was as close
as he came to plein-air painting, and these scenes were
executed in his studio from sketches.

Degas came from a well-off family, so he was not
dependent on selling his art for a living. He wanted to
succeed with the establishment and admired Ingres
extravagantly. Assiduously copying Old Masters at the
Louvre, he repeatedly sent pictures to the Salon, where
he wanted to make his mark as a history painter, even
though the jury at the Universal Exposition of 1867

decided not to make any awards in history painting,
thus sounding the death knell of the genre.[77] Degas's
bid for recognition from the establishment failed, so he
showed with the Impressionists, despite his differences
from them, and he supported them, especially Mary
Cassatt, in difficult times.[78]

Degas resembled the Impressionists, not in their
delight in nature or in natural light, nor in revealing
color in natural light, but in his experimental nature,
above all with his materials. He must be one of the most
technically curious and experimental artists who ever
lived. He famously remarked that if he ever found his
manner, he would be bored.[79] He was intrigued by process in everything; how dancers moved, how horses ran,
how businessmen bought and sold cotton. Any kind of
professionalism fascinated him, and scientific procedures
were no less absorbing. He used gouache, tempera, casein,
and pastel. He discovered monotype printing, a printmaking process in which a drawing is made in black ink
on a copper plate. He sometimes added pastel to these
prints after they were dry. He collected recipes, some
from Old Masters, and shared them with his colleagues.
He experimented with the texture of his paint, sometimes
oiling the paper so that the brush would slide more easily. He invented a technique for the opposite effect, which
can be seen in his *Dancers at the Barre* (fig. 5.28). Seeking a

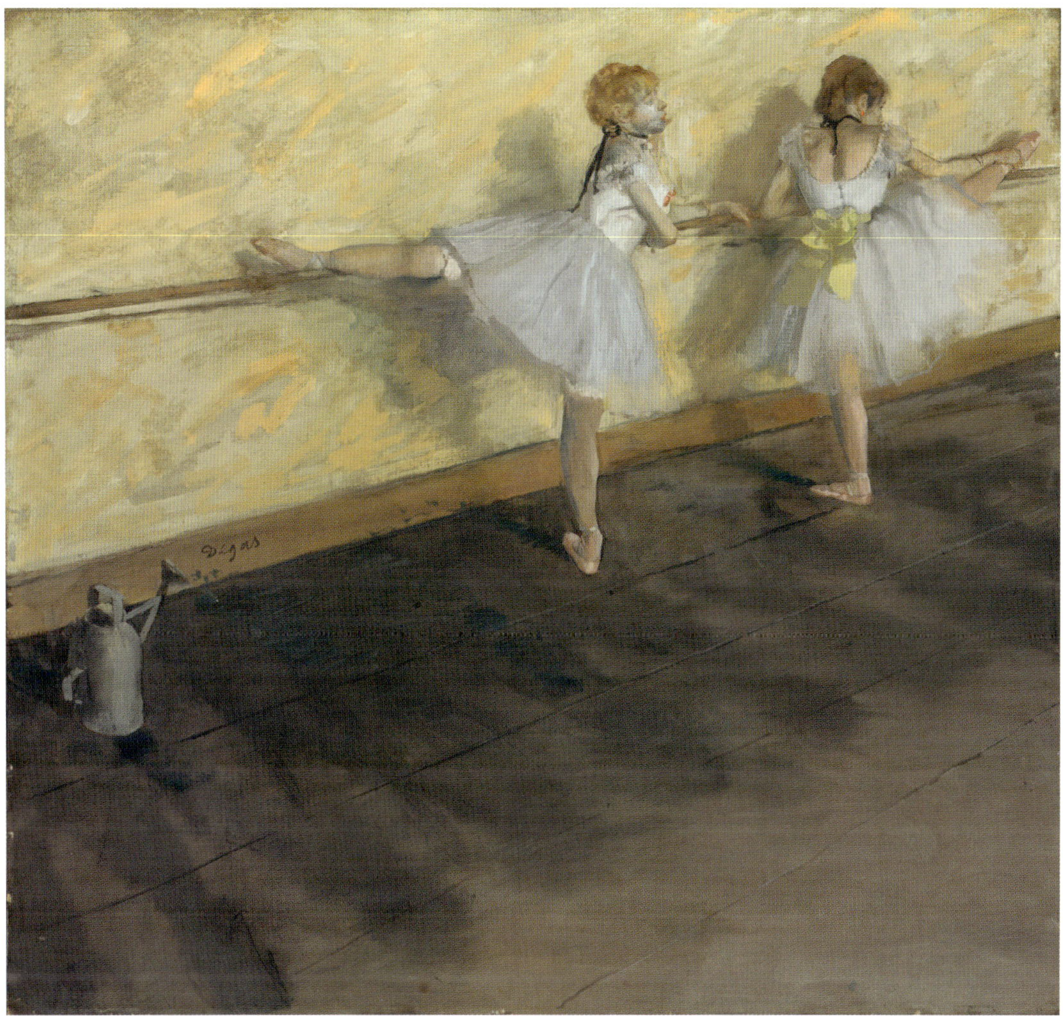

FIG. 5.28. Edgar Degas, *Dancers at the Barre*, 1877. Oil on canvas, 29 ¾ × 32 in. (75.6 × 81.3 cm). Metropolitan Museum of Art, New York.

dry and chalky matte finish, he soaked the oil out of the pigment, using blotting paper, then diluted it with turpentine.[80] This technique, called *peinture à l'essence,* was thought to describe the technique of the *Dancers,* until it was examined more closely. It was found that indeed the floor is painted à l'essence, but above the diagonal where floor and wall meet Degas has painted with egg yolk tempera. It is likely that Degas was dissatisfied and repainted it at a later date, as he often did, using a homemade concoction of ground pastels and egg.[81]

His subjects were largely indoor life, backstage scenes, people caught in moments when they don't know they are observed, in a café, emerging from the bath, at work, shopping. Among the most affecting is the *Absinthe Drinker,* originally called *In a Café* (fig. 5.29), which seems to carry a tinge of social comment on the drink that would eventually be banned in France, the United States,

and much of Europe. Degas's painting coincides roughly with the publication of Émile Zola's *L'Assommoir* of 1877, the novel that tracks the decline into drunkenness of a working-class family in Paris, hooked on absinthe. Degas's ill-matched man and woman are sitting side by side at separate tables at the Nouvelle Athènes café, a favorite of the painters, sunk in their private worlds. The man smokes, his pipe cut off casually by the frame; the woman stares vacantly at nothing, slumping awkwardly with her feet apart. Degas had studied Japanese prints, as had several of his contemporaries, and was intrigued by their unfamiliar ways of composing. He makes an ordinary scene arresting because of his unexpected asymmetric compositions. Here a table bars our entry, and we are distanced yet captured by the swift movement of perspective on an oblique line moving out of the picture to the right. Ominous shadows of the drinkers' heads are

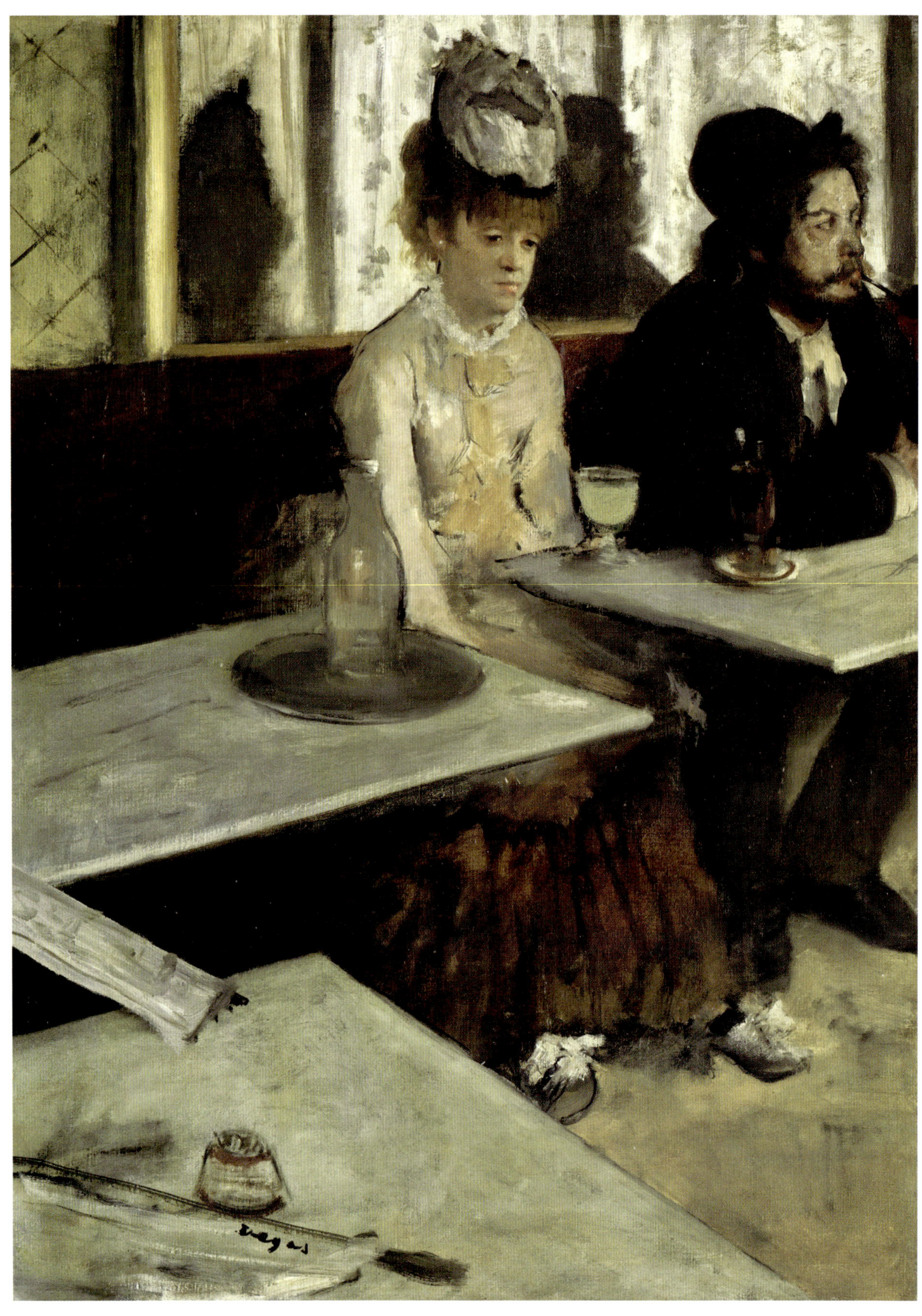

FIG. 5.29. Edgar Degas, *In a Café* (*Absinthe Drinker*), 1875–76. Oil on canvas, 36 ¼ × 27 in. (92 × 68.5 cm). Musée d'Orsay, Paris.

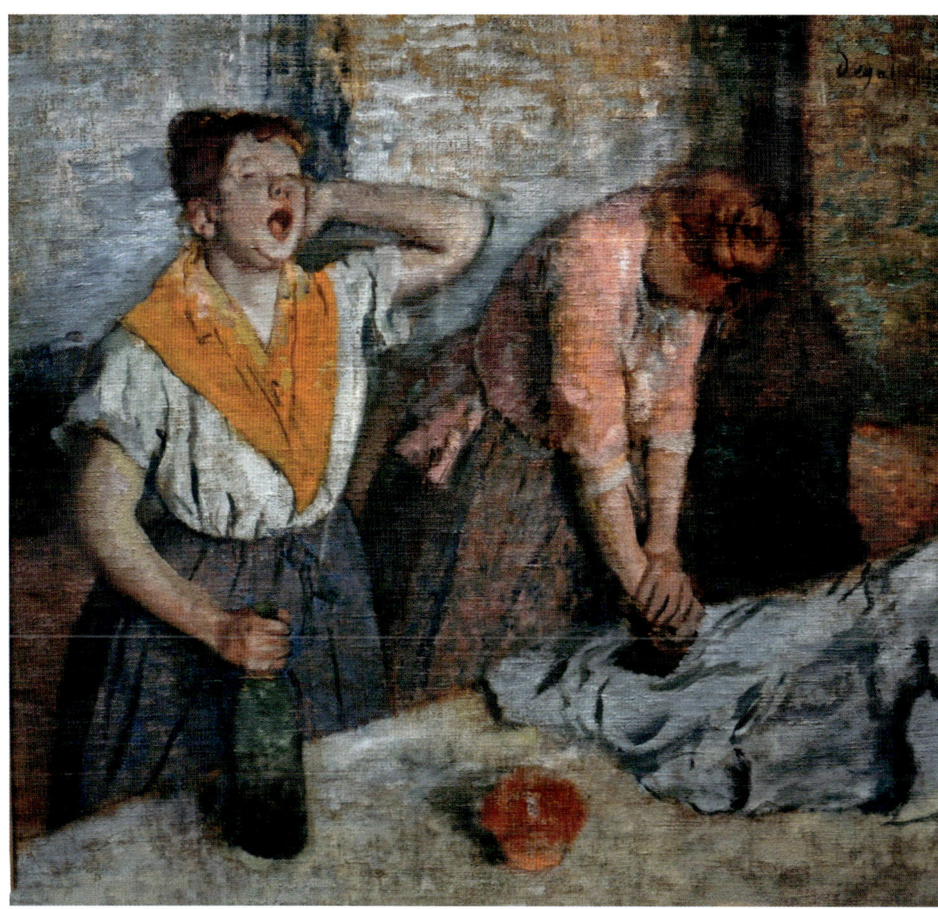

FIG. 5.30. Edgar Degas, *Women Ironing*, c. 1884–86. Oil on canvas, 29 7/8 × 32 in. (76 × 81.5 cm). Musée d'Orsay, Paris.

projected on the wall behind them. The colors are blacks, browns, off-whites, the pale green of the absinthe, and a straw yellow brushed roughly on the woman's bodice. Many of Degas's scenes are of people enjoying themselves, so this rare and poignant portrayal of the underside of café life stands out by contrast.

Women Ironing shows a subject he returned to several times (fig. 5.30). Seen close-up and half-length, they are absorbed in their work, even if that means yawning in boredom. The painter neither glamorizes nor patronizes them, but he conveys empathy. Their rough work is analogized in the rough paint, which is laid directly on an unprimed, rough canvas. By dragging his brush across the coarse weave he makes the paint skip along the top of the raised threads, leaving gaps that reveal the linen support. We see here, as in the *Absinthe Drinker,* oblique perspective leading off to the right and colors with no particular appeal in themselves but drawing the eye nonetheless. Like the other Impressionists, Degas catches the viewer's attention with his unprecedented subjects and fresh view, raising the ordinary to something worthy of commemorating in paint.

MONET

Claude Monet, the quintessential Impressionist, was rejected three of the six times he offered paintings to the Salon. It was of course his *Impression: Sunrise* (see fig. 5.20) that provided the derisive critic Louis Leroy with the name of the movement that stuck. Even before his escape to London and fortuitous meeting with Durand-Ruel, Monet was committed to painting the plein-air landscapes for which he is best known, following in the footsteps of the Barbizon painters. What the new materials made possible, Monet was quick to exploit. No longer needing to prepare his canvas and paints in the workshop, or even worry about them drying out in a pig's bladder, he packed up his paint box and set out. Renoir showed Monet standing at his easel, painting in his garden (fig. 5.31). A whole new line of equipment had appeared for the painter, who needed a portable easel and stool, equipment to keep wet paintings separated on the return to the studio, and possibly a parasol to keep the sun out of his eyes. Monet, interested in the ever-shifting effects of light and weather, would invent series in the 1890s—*Haystacks, Poplars, Rouen Cathedral*—perhaps on

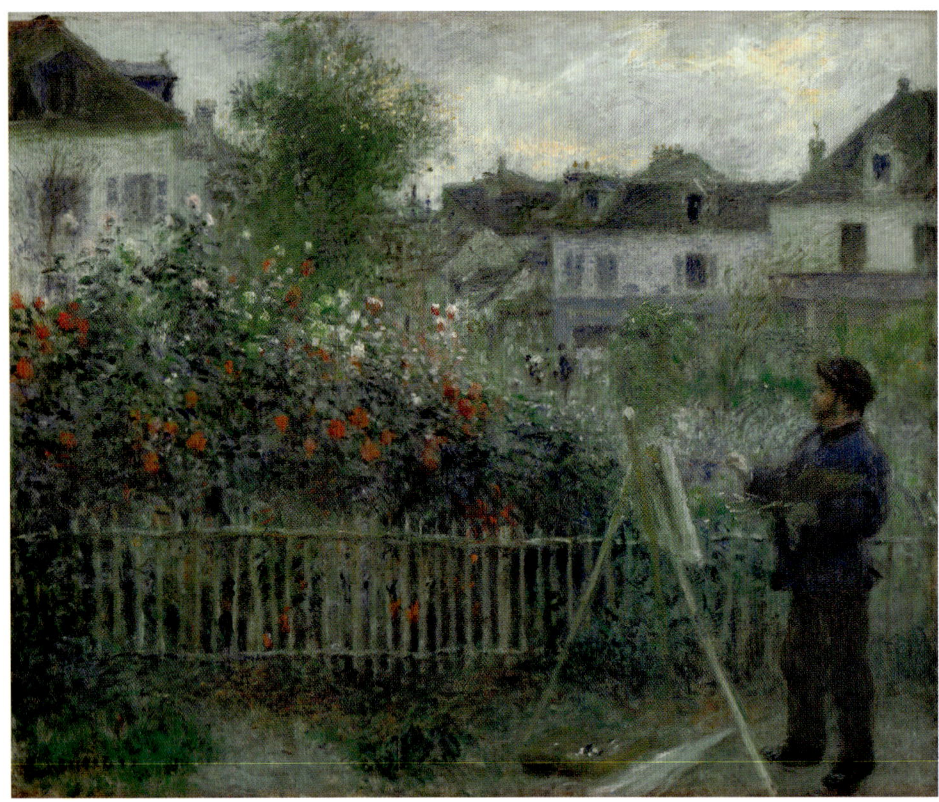

FIG. 5.31. Pierre-Auguste Renoir, *Monet Painting in His Garden*, 1873. Oil on canvas, 18 ⅜ × 23 ½ in. (46.7 × 59.7 cm). Wadsworth Atheneum Museum of Art, Hartford, Conn.

the model of Japanese prints such as Hokusai's *Thirty-Six Views of Mount Fuji*. For the last, he rented a room in Rouen opposite the western façade of the cathedral in 1892 and 1893 and worked on multiple canvases, moving from one to another as the light changed. Like Turner's late work, Monet's surfaces, even stone surfaces such as the cathedral façade, evanesce in the light. He paints, in the words of George Hamilton, "the impalpable atmosphere rather than the substantial objects within it."[82]

For two months in the summer of 1869, Monet went to La Grenouillère, a popular place for Parisians to enjoy an outing of boating and bathing, and he was joined there by Renoir. Monet made a group of sketches on-site that, as he wrote to artist Frédéric Bazille, were preparatory to an ambitious picture he intended to develop for the Salon. The *Bathers at La Grenouillère* (see fig. 5.10), often described as an early example of Monet's technique, is actually only one of those rough sketches, but it nevertheless reveals him working out techniques he would develop more systematically in the following decade. At this time he was using some elaborate mixtures of pigments that he would later abandon for more pure applications. He used a pre-primed canvas of an off-white color and a surprising range of at least fifteen pigments (there

are perhaps more that have escaped identification in the laboratory). Most of these pigments are inexpensive, and Monet indicates some uncertainty at this point about which would serve him best in his plein-air projects. He mixed highly colored pigments for drab passages. For instance, for the dull tones of the foreground boats in the shade, he mixed emerald green, viridian, and cobalt blue, but there are touches of brilliant vermilion for the foreground flowers and chrome yellow for the highlight on one of the distant boats.[83] Most interesting is the way he is exploring a varied brushstroke: for the foliage, directional strokes, some dense, some thin, give the effect of dappled sunlight. For the rippling water he uses rapid strokes of opaque, fluid Prussian blue applied with wide square brushes. This will become that signature brushstroke of the Impressionists, the tache, or blob. It replaces traditional blending of colors, with artists instead applying thick strokes with an evenly loaded brush. It was enabled by another invention of the Industrial Revolution, the metal ferule, a circular metal clamp that made it possible to manufacture flat brushes, instead of the round brushes that could be made by hand and had always been used (fig. 5.32).[84]

For the second Impressionist exhibition in 1876,

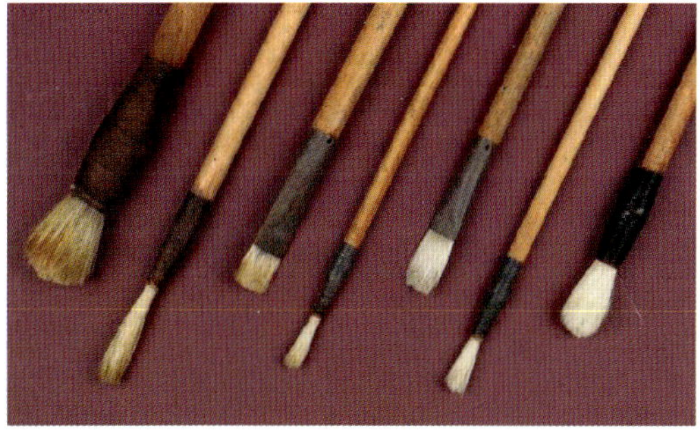

FIG. 5.32. Manufactured brushes with metal ferule.

Monet prepared *Woman with a Parasol—Madame Monet and Her Son* (fig. 5.33). He is more sure of his technique now, showing off his skill at painting both figures and nature in one apparently effortless *aperçu*. He has disciplined his varied brushstroke. In the foreground we have quick strokes of unmixed color juxtaposed to give the effect of tall grass in motion. Madame Monet is seen from below, set against the sky on a windy spring day. The breeze whips her veil and her dress, and longer strokes describe its swirl. Wispy clouds scud across the bright sky, painted with thick impasto in a flurry of overlapping strokes going every which way. The cast shadow on the grass is full of color, the new mauve tone now taking the place of the more somber Prussian blue he had used earlier.[85] The underside of Madame Monet's parasol reflects the green beneath her feet.

It is worth considering how adeptly Monet conveys perspective without the usual techniques of receding orthogonals, three-dimensional modeling, or diminishing focus. Here, with everything in motion, there is nothing in focus. Madame Monet's features, though at the center, are indicated with the vaguest touch, and their son Jean's face is shaded by his hat. His small size, standing on the far side of a rise and shown only from the waist up, exaggerates the difference of scale and dramatically conveys depth.

We should recall Monet's later instructions to Lilla Cabot Perry: "When you go out to paint, try to forget what object you have before you, a tree, a house, a field or whatever. Merely think, here is a little square of blue, here an oblong of pink, here a streak of yellow, and paint it just as it looks to you, the exact color and shape, until it gives you your own naïve impression of the scene before you."[86] Monet thought in terms of color, not of contoured shapes or concrete objects.

RENOIR

Pierre-Auguste Renoir was an enthusiastic Impressionist in the 1870s. He was not included with other Impressionists in Durand-Ruel's catalogue of works in his possession. His record at the Salon was checkered, with five acceptances and four rejections between 1864 and 1873.[87] He decided to join the Impressionists in their first group exhibit in 1874, where Louis Leroy mocked him along with others in his review. Leroy's dialogue partner remarks about Renoir's *Dancer* (now in Washington, D.C., National Gallery of Art): "What a pity that the painter, who has a certain understanding of color, doesn't draw better; his dancer's legs are as cottony as the gauze of the skirts."[88] Two years later, when Durand-Ruel hosted the second Impressionist exhibit, the press was even more jeering. Albert Wolff wrote of Renoir: "Try to explain to M. Renoir that a woman's torso is not a mass of flesh in the process of decomposition with green and violet spots which denote the state of complete putrefaction of a corpse."[89] *Study: Torso, Sunlight Effect* was bought by Caillebotte and bequeathed to the state and is now on view at the Musée d'Orsay (fig. 5.34).[90] Part of what the critic saw as "putrefaction," the breakdown of the substance, was Renoir's use of varied focus to simulate the effect of outdoor light coming from all directions at once, which served also to concentrate the viewer's attention.[91]

A particularly favored venue for Renoir was the theater. In paintings such as *La Loge* (fig. 5.35) and *At the Theatre* (London, National Gallery) the people may look like portraits, but in fact they are exemplary of their company at the entertainment, showing their pleasure at seeing and being seen.[92] Renoir, and Monet too, were successful portraitists, although as their careers proceeded Monet would paint them less frequently and Renoir more frequently. *La Loge,* painted in 1874, shows his typical brushstroke of the mid-1870s, which he abandoned later: tache strokes made with a broad, square brush loaded with paint. The flesh is painted thinly using little lead white and allowing the white ground to show through and serve as the mid-tone.

Renoir's pigments have been studied and, like his Impressionist colleagues, he combined new pigments with the standard traditional ones. Jean Renoir described his father's palette from 1877–78: besides white lead and bone black, traditional pigments included Naples yellow, madder lake, vermilion, and the earths, ochre and raw sienna. Of the new synthetics, at this time he was using

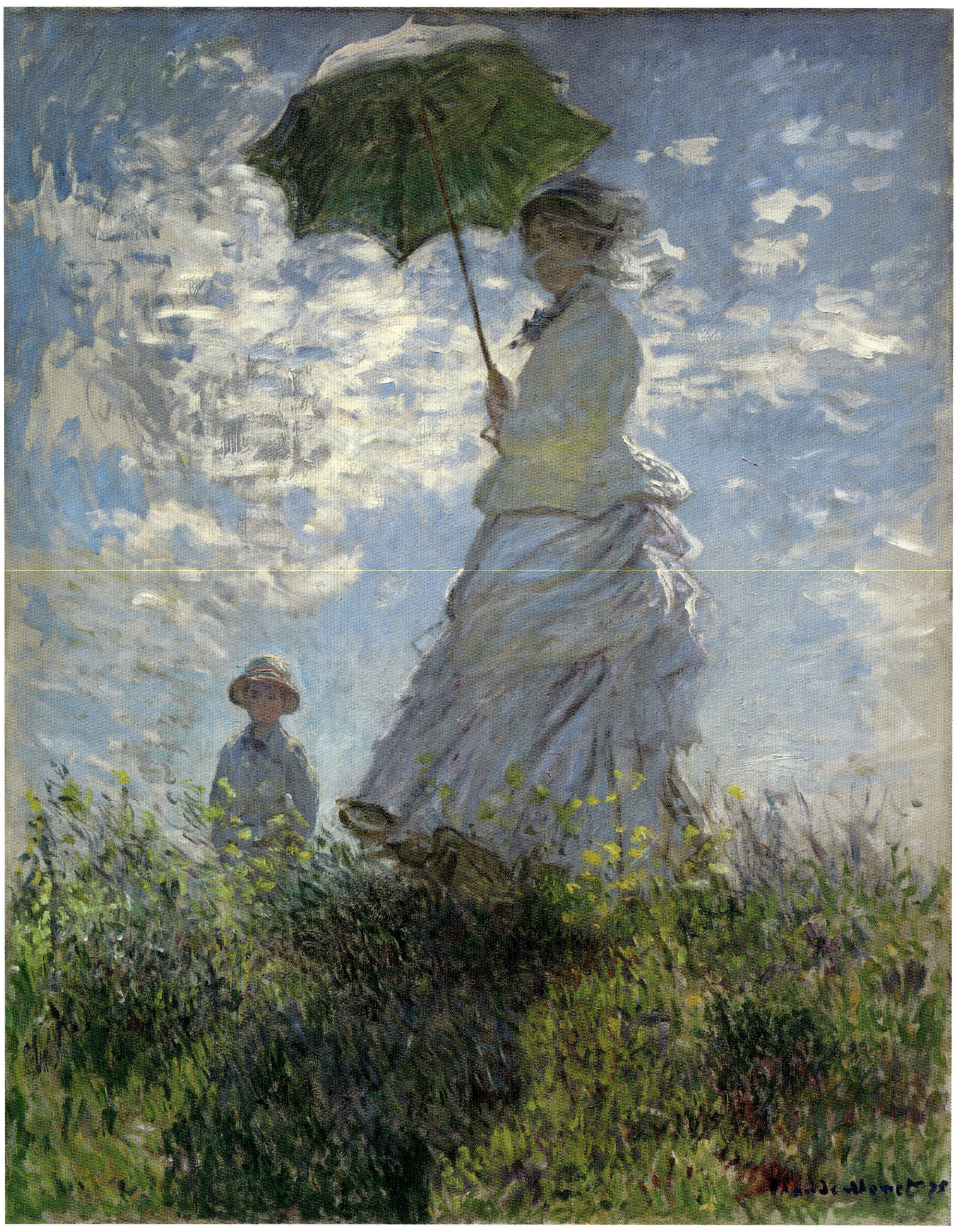

FIG. 5.33. Claude Monet, *Woman with a Parasol—Madame Monet and Her Son,* 1875. Oil on canvas, 39 ⅜ × 31 ⅞ in. (100 × 81 cm). National Gallery of Art, Washington, D.C.

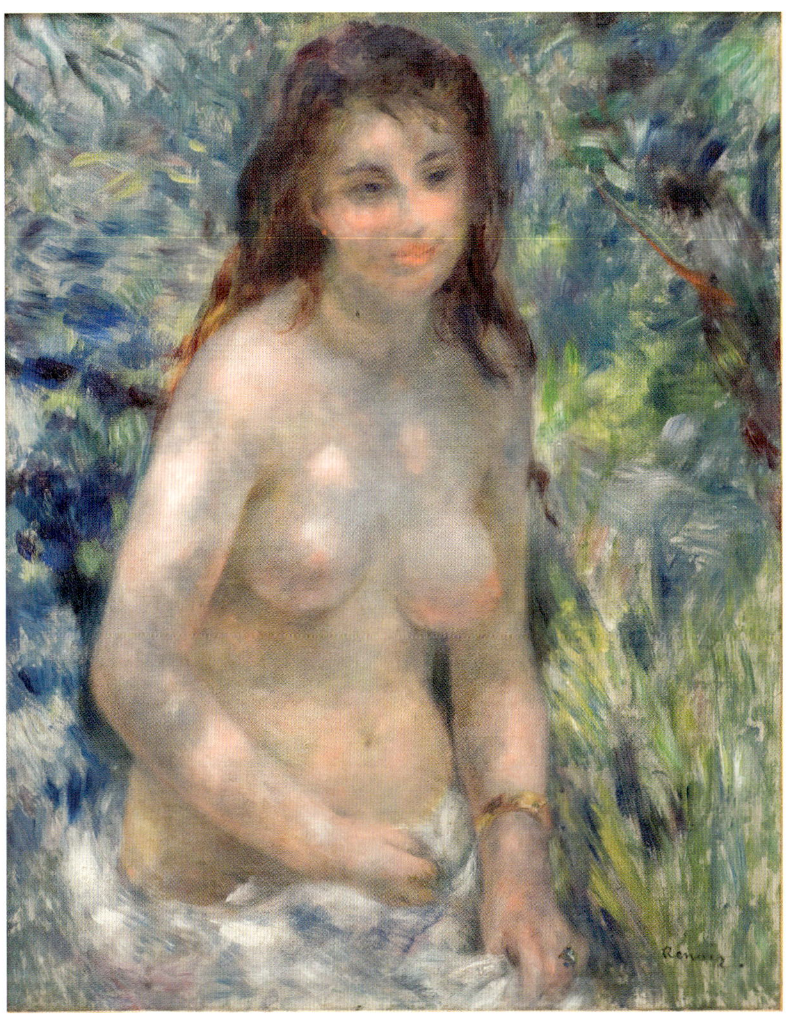

FIG. 5.34. Pierre-Auguste Renoir, *Study: Torso, Sunlight Effect*, c. 1876. Oil on canvas, 31 15/16 × 25 5/8 in. (81 × 65 cm). Musée d'Orsay, Paris.

chrome yellow, viridian, vert Véronèse (emerald) green, cobalt blue, and ultramarine blue. Analysis of three paintings at the center of his Impressionist period, *La Loge* (1874), *At the Theatre*, and *Lady at the Piano* (Art Institute of Chicago), the last two both painted in 1876, showed him using a closely similar palette. The Impressionists reportedly substituted blue for black in their shadows, and Renoir did at certain periods, but he was not consistent. Blue shadows are conspicuous in *La Loge* and *Boating on the Seine* (London, National Gallery, 1878–79), but in *La Loge* the dark passages of the lady's dress are achieved with bone black and white applied over a sienna-colored underpaint. It is often the case, not only with Renoir but also with other Impressionists, that what looks like cool, bluish tints are actually created with a light tone over black.[93]

In the 1880s, Renoir, like Monet, began to have doubts about Impressionism, and he revised his procedure. He became uncomfortable with the Impressionist obsession with devouring light, as the *Umbrellas* clearly demonstrates (see fig. 5.11). He painted it in two campaigns six years apart and left visible the change in his style and technique. When he began to paint it in 1880–81, he was still using the typically loose brushwork and bright, pure colors of the Impressionists, although he had already begun to worry that his paintings lacked solidity and structure. He had refused to exhibit in the fourth Impressionist exhibition in 1878. When he traveled to Italy in the autumn of 1881 he became enamored of Raphael and the frescoes at Pompeii. Upon his return he stopped off to visit Cézanne in Provence. In response to these experiences, he tightened his technique, painting in a crisper and more solid manner. When he returned to the *Umbrellas* in 1885–86 he used a more muted palette, renouncing his earlier iridescence, and substituted synthetic ultramarine for cobalt blue, and zinc yellow for Naples yellow. Evidently he wanted his viewer to be aware of his conversion, because he didn't attempt to

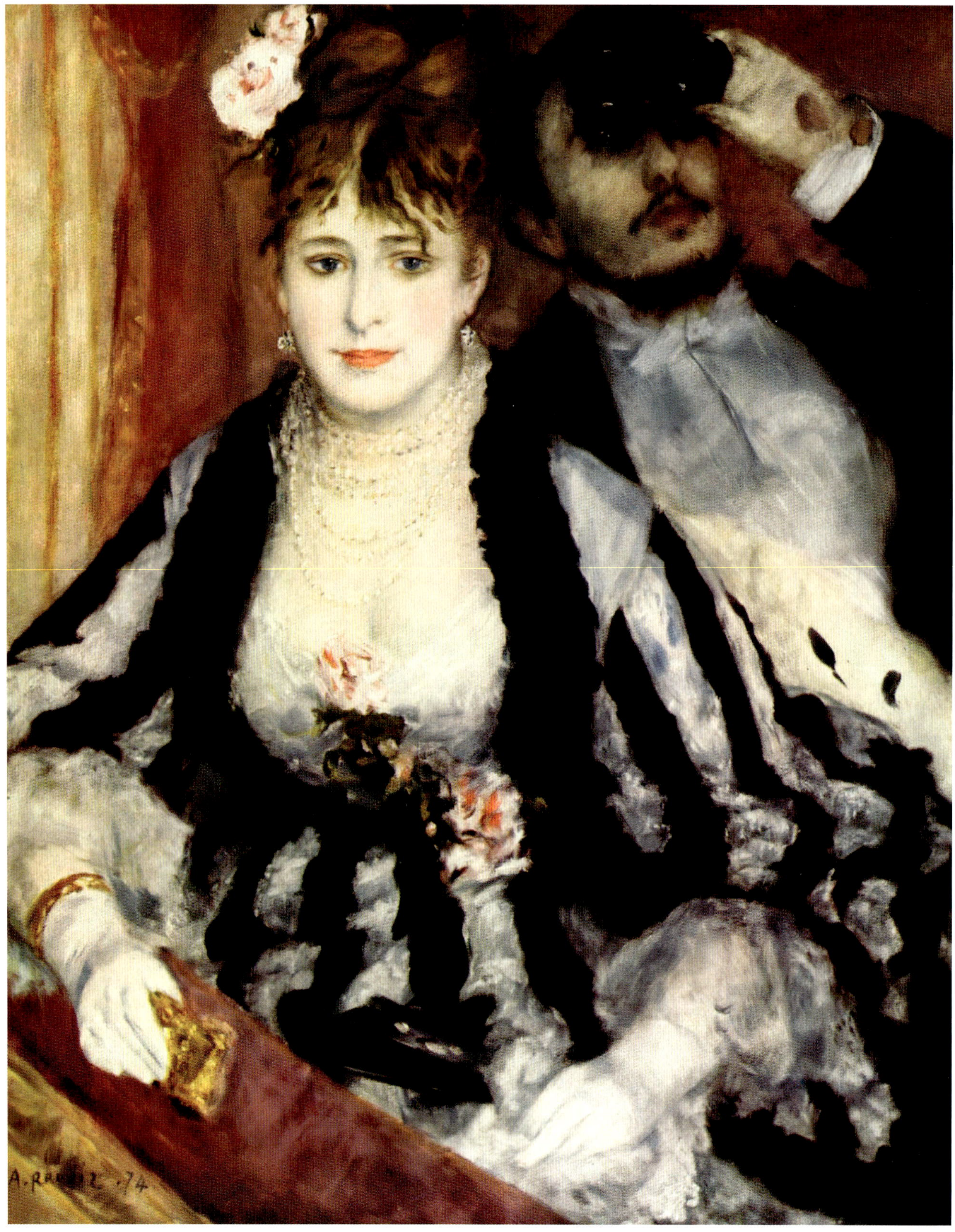

FIG. 5.35. Pierre-Auguste Renoir, *La Loge*, 1874. Oil on canvas, 31½ × 25 in. (80 × 63.5 cm). Courtauld Institute of Art, London.

blend the two manners. The children and their mother
at the right display the softer and frillier manner and
brighter blue of his earlier style. The severely painted and
dressed woman with the market basket in the foreground
is in the new style, colored with ultramarine mixed with
other pigments to mute and gray it; in the x-ray it can be
seen that she was originally dressed in the earlier fashion
with lace collar and cuffs, and cross-sections show that
she was painted in a bright cobalt blue.[94] The umbrellas,
too, must have been added, for they are in synthetic ultramarine and there is no evidence that they were intended
in the earlier version.[95] Perhaps Renoir turned the scene
into a cloudy day as an excuse to mute his colors and
avoid the sharp contrasts of bright sunshine.[96]

Renoir painted *Two Sisters*, also called *On the Terrace*
(fig. 5.36), in 1881 on an island in the Seine in Chatou,
a suburb of Paris, where he had just completed his
masterful *Luncheon of the Boating Party* (Washington,
D.C., Phillips Collection). Like Monet's *Bathers at La
Grenouillère,* it shows Parisians enjoying their leisure
in the country. Durand-Ruel bought it as soon as it was
finished in July 1881 for 1,500 francs, and it was exhibited
the next year at the seventh Impressionist exhibition. The
girls here are not in fact related, and though it looks like
a portrait, it is not. Renoir has painted his models as a
kind of genre picture, where the real subject is the season
and the pleasure these people are taking in their surroundings. The background of *On the Terrace* is painted
with very light strokes of thin glaze, recording the effect
of light on the water. The figures, however, are solidly
painted, giving them a firmer appearance, different from
Monet's reflective, almost transparent Madame Monet.
We can see how different this is from *La Loge,* where
he used the same brushstroke for everything and did
not distinguish between spatial planes, as he did here
where the spatial recession is conveyed by the contrasted
brushstroke. The faces are modeled in blended strokes.
The older sister's red hat and blue jacket are densely and
smoothly painted. Loose, unblended impasto strokes
are reserved for the flowers on the little girl's hat and
the pure colors of the balls of yarn in the basket. As he
evolved his style, he used thinner paint and smoother textures and translucent thin washes. In this his technique
resembled Cézanne's, and it may be that Renoir borrowed
from his friend during this period when he was searching
for a new technique.

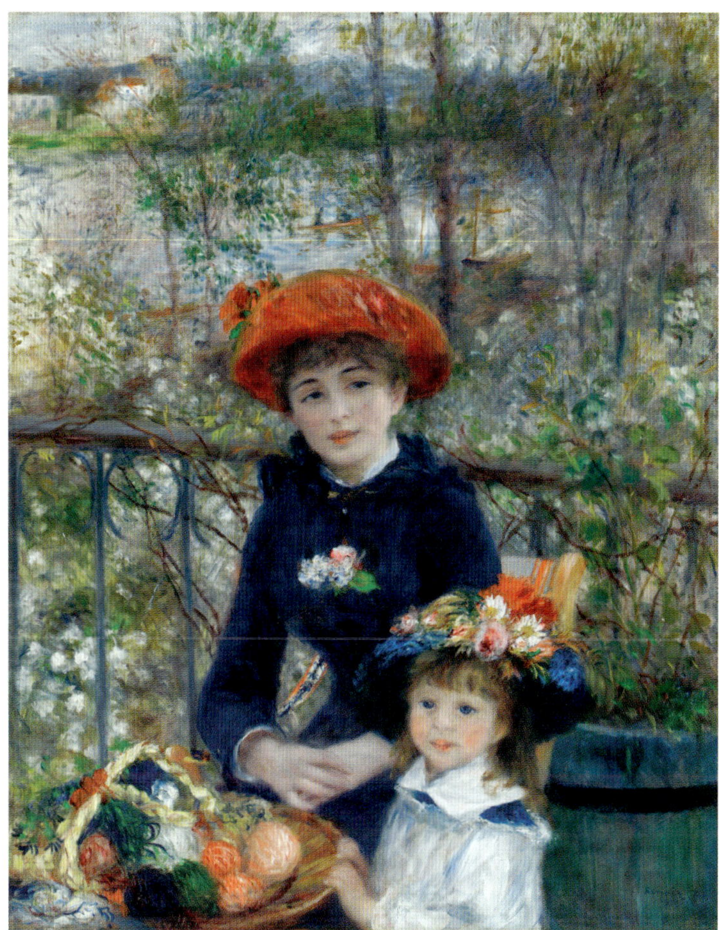

FIG. 5.36. Pierre-Auguste Renoir, *On the Terrace*, 1881. Oil on canvas,
39½ × 31⅞ in. (100.4 × 80.9 cm). Art Institute of Chicago.

CÉZANNE

It is difficult to classify Paul Cézanne either as a Post-
Impressionist, as is often done, or as an Impressionist,
with whom he fits chronologically. Unlike Gauguin or
Van Gogh or Seurat, he never used nonrepresentational
colors, but like them he sought something deeper and
more permanent than fleeting appearance. He is often
seen as a precursor of Modernism: supposedly both
Picasso and Matisse called him "the father of us all,"
and his square brushstroke influenced the invention of
Cubism. Born in Aix-en-Provence, he had come to Paris
in 1861, exhibited at the Salon des Refusés in 1863, and
was rejected at each Salon from 1864 to 1869. He exhibited with the Impressionists in their first show in 1874
and again in the third in 1877, even after he returned to
his native South of France in the early 1870s. There he
slowly abandoned his early, heavy, dark manner under

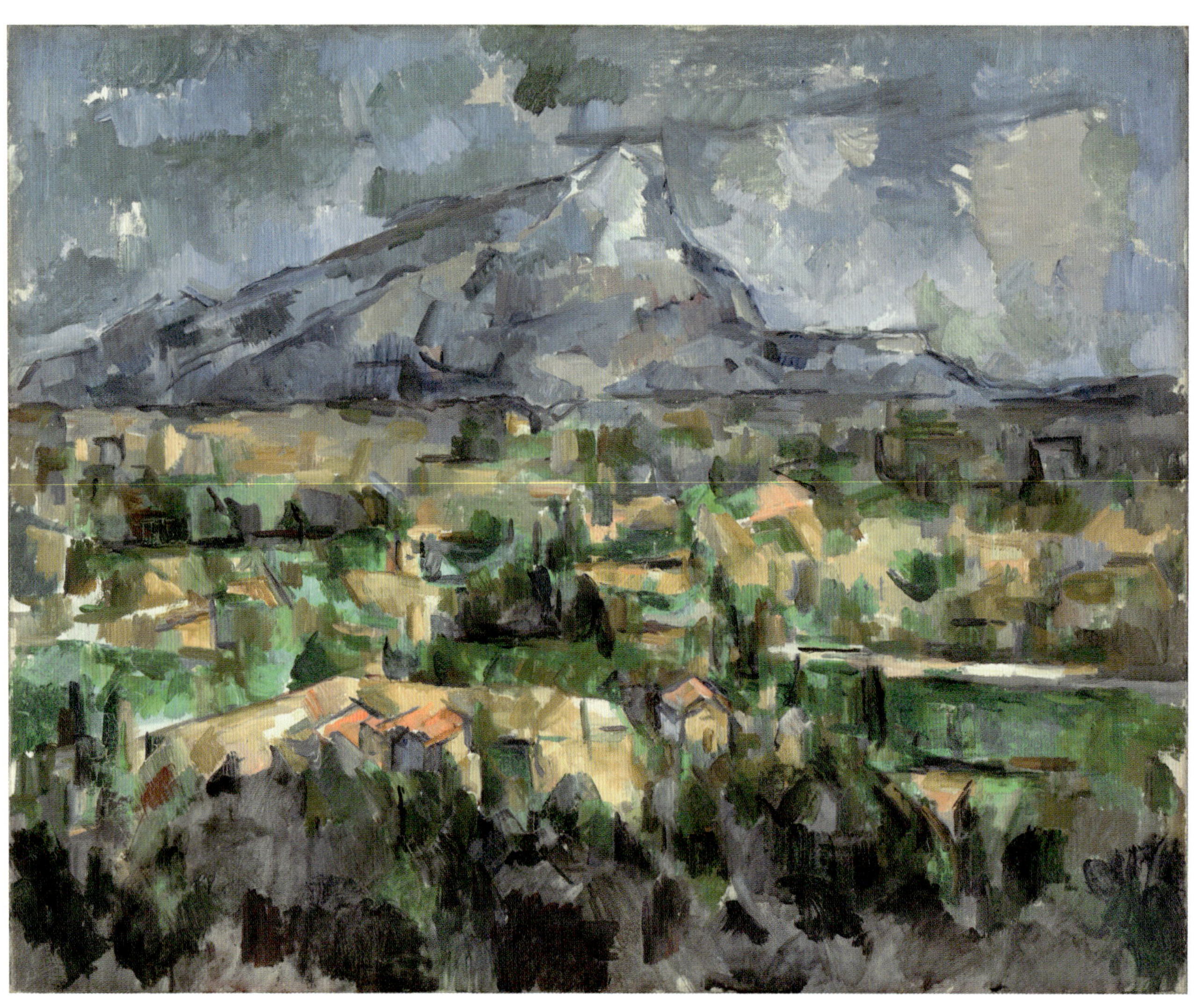

FIG. 5.37. Paul Cézanne, *Mont Sainte-Victoire,* 1902–4. Oil on canvas,
28 ¾ × 36 ³⁄₁₆ in. (73 × 91.9 cm). Philadelphia Museum of Art.

the influence of Pissarro, and his palette lightened. He was not a rapid or spontaneous painter by nature. As he matured he was increasingly interested in discovering an underlying structure and in building solid recession rather than in capturing the fugitive moment. In this he differed from Monet and other Impressionists, but like them he painted directly on the white or off-white canvas, depending on the new synthetics, especially for his greens. In *Hillside in Provence* of 1890–92, he was painting with his characteristic harmonious palette (see fig. 5.12). The vibrant greens here he achieved with emerald green mixed with a little viridian. The complementary oranges are made up of yellow and brown ochres. Consistent with Cézanne's more deliberate approach, he often, as here, planned out his composition in pencil on the canvas before beginning to paint. He then outlined with grayish-blue paint containing ultramarine, which he also used in the shadows on the foreground rocks. Unlike the Impressionists, he often chose side-lit scenes: here the rays fall at a forty-five degree angle.[97] He painted thinly so that the lightly colored ground imparted luminosity, some of which remained unpainted.

Cézanne shared with the Impressionists the search for new means to paint without traditional modeling or chiaroscuro or linear perspective. Perspective became his consuming concern, and he experimented with the means to imply recession without resorting to a winding road or diminished scale or other devices such as those Monet and Pissarro employed. Varying his brushwork, he was able to differentiate textures and distance: for example, in this work the trees are rendered with thicker paint in curved strokes that suggest their shape. Those new square brushes clamped with a metal ferule allowed him to apply paint in squarish patches of a single hue, overlapping the adjacent patch and blending the edges wet-in-wet. Modeling he replaced as well with his patches of color.

In conversations recorded by his fellow painter Émile Bernard, Cézanne referred to what he did not as modeling but as "modulation." Instead of the traditional system, he used simultaneous contrast of complementary colors and juxtapositions of warm and cool colors to create volume and recession. Bernard believed that Cézanne determined these modulations in advance, and some scholars have agreed. However, Elisabeth Reissner, in her recent study of Cézanne's paintings in the National Gallery,

London, concludes that his method allowed him to improvise as he patiently studied the subject and painted it. In his efforts to capture the look of nature without copying it, he intuitively placed his color patches, using a very limited palette that he didn't change over the course of his mature career.[98]

For Cézanne, color replaced drawing as the foundation of composition. Working up his canvas in patches, he did not move from back to front as was traditional, nor in any other prescribed order. As Richard Shiff has described it: "By working from part to part with patches of color, the artist could avoid the sense of a preconceived compositional hierarchy and would seem to respond only to immediate sensation." Cézanne wished to supplant the classical system with his original manner of proceeding, substituting juxtapositions of color for chiaroscuro, and leaving behind perspective, both central-point and aerial.[99] He does not differentiate light and dark to create a center of focus, but distributes light and hues evenly across the whole.[100] Specific times of day or conditions of light are not what he records—and here he differs fundamentally from the Impressionists—as he was seeking instead a more substantial and permanent record. Cézanne told Maurice Denis that his intention was to "represent" rather than "imitate" nature, creating "a harmony parallel with nature."[101]

Perhaps to hone and perfect his technique, he chose to paint the same motif over and over again. Mont Sainte-Victoire became his favorite. He built a studio in 1902 from which he could walk a mile or so to find a place where he could set up his easel. In his late pictures, his brushstroke becomes more eloquent (fig. 5.37). Contradicting traditional practice of making objects blurry as they recede, he used bolder and broader strokes: he appears to have used a quarter-inch brush for the foreground and a half-inch brush for the distant mountain and sky.[102] The color is a little stronger now, the blue not ultramarine but cobalt. To a traditionalist it might seem that Cézanne was trying to prove how little descriptive information the viewer actually needs to be able to make sense of a scene and comprehend the space. There is play, if not even tension, between the illusion of depth and awareness of the surface to which he calls attention with his rough facture and the bare canvas, which he allowed to show through more and more as he matured and gained experience. Perhaps more important for the future than his contribution to the brushstroke of analytic Cubism was Cézanne's elevation of color to primacy above drawing.

CONCLUSION

We have seen that the Académie remained committed to tradition; the government, on the other hand, feeling itself vulnerable to the perception that it was elitist, supported the juste milieu and the independents. This rift widened as the century progressed. When the Provisional Republic made the Salon of 1848 open to all contributions, it set a precedent and opened the door to the opponents of the Académie. The establishment of the Salon des Refusés in 1863 by Emperor Louis Napoleon was one more in a line of concessions that served to undermine the authority of the Académie. Within two decades, the Salon had been abolished. The International Expositions of 1855 and 1867, sponsored by the government to showcase French science, industry, technology, and culture, offered opportunities for artists outside the academic establishment to receive patronage and exposure. In 1881 the government withdrew official sponsorship from the annual Salon, and a group of artists organized the Société des Artistes Français to take responsibility for the show. Thus ended government involvement in the choice of which art would be exhibited. At this point the state resigned as the arbiter of taste, effectively putting an end to the system put in place with the founding of the Académie. In the words of Albert Boime, "The proclivity to compromise became the hallmark of French official art" in the nineteenth century.[103] It was thanks to that proclivity to compromise that the avant-garde finally overcame the stultifying influence of conservative classical tradition and became itself the mainstream.

The climate of controversy energized the dissidents and encouraged critical debate. The growing power of the bourgeoisie and its shift of taste away from academic art to genres such as landscape or scenes from daily life eroded the government's confidence in the Académie. The inadequacy of the system to handle the large numbers of artists vying for the public's attention fostered the rise of alternatives. The pressure to provide exhibition opportunities encouraged dealers to expand their role by offering galleries for viewing and sale. The growing popular press provided an opportune venue for critics to review art on offer outside the annual Salon.

A global market fostered exchange among artists, and better communication across national boundaries meant not only that a painter might find an audience outside his or her own country, but also have access to what was being done elsewhere. Durand-Ruel, when he found the French market saturated with Impressionist paintings, took these works to New York and sold them to a generation of newly rich American industrialists and bankers such as Andrew Carnegie, Henry Clay Frick, George Widener, Paul Mellon, Chester Dale, and Sterling Clark. The resistance of the French national museums to the Impressionists cost dearly. In the mid-1890s it was recognized that nearly all of Monet's *Rouen Cathedral* series, for example, had found homes abroad. It was only in 1911, through the bequest of Isaac de Camondo, that four of the *Cathedrals* entered the national collection of the Musée de Luxembourg, predecessor to the Musée d'Orsay. As successful as the Impressionists were abroad, we should not underestimate how slow to die the conservative taste was in France.

The story of the Caillebotte bequest is indicative of how long it took for the Impressionists to be fully accepted by the state. Caillebotte, who inherited a fortune from his father, had bought from his fellow painters during his lifetime as a way of helping out needy friends. When he died in 1894 he left his collection of sixty-eight Impressionist works to the state to be hung in the Musée de Luxembourg, but with the stipulation that they must all be exhibited, not placed in the storeroom. After a year of negotiating, Renoir and Caillebotte's younger brother Martial were informed that the state would accept forty, but the other twenty-eight were rejected. Until his death in 1919, Renoir continued to press, offering the remaining paintings on at least two more occasions. Then in 1928, after three rejections, the museum finally solicited the work, but Martial's son's widow this time refused. They were sold on the open market to such collectors abroad as Albert Barnes, H. O. Havemeyer, Louisine Havemeyer, and Sterling and Francine Clark.[104]

Industrialization brought about a revolution in artistic practice. Newly invented pigments opened up the painter's palette with a range of bright greens and yellows/oranges, purple, and superior, less costly blues, colors never before available. Once pigments were packaged in portable tubes, a new experimental generation of painters took them along and set up their easels out-of-doors. No longer needing to prepare either their canvases or their paints in the studio, they could do away with the cumbersome system of a workshop of pupils and assistants. Because they did not need to set an example or model correct technique, they felt freer to experiment. If they didn't like the result, they could paint over it. Once freed of pupils and assistants looking over their shoulders, they were more daring. They did away with traditional modeling, chiaroscuro, and perspective in the search for the appearance of spontaneity and the record of changing light. The ephemeral interested them more than the eternal, and daily life rather than the lives of saints, martyrs, or pagan deities.

The economic cost of being a painter was reduced to materials and studio rent, but this freedom came at a price. There was no safety net in the form of a system that ensured progress through a succession of steps to the final reward, prestigious membership among an acknowledged elite in the Académie. Many artists struggled to earn a living and many failed; but if they succeeded in finding support, they were free as never before to paint only what pleased them. Thus personal expression replaced traditional subjects, and it was now the painter, not a patron, who determined what would be painted. The nineteenth-century art-buying public was not interested in exploring the painter's psyche as exposed on a canvas, but it was open to seeing through his or her fresh and sensitive eyes.

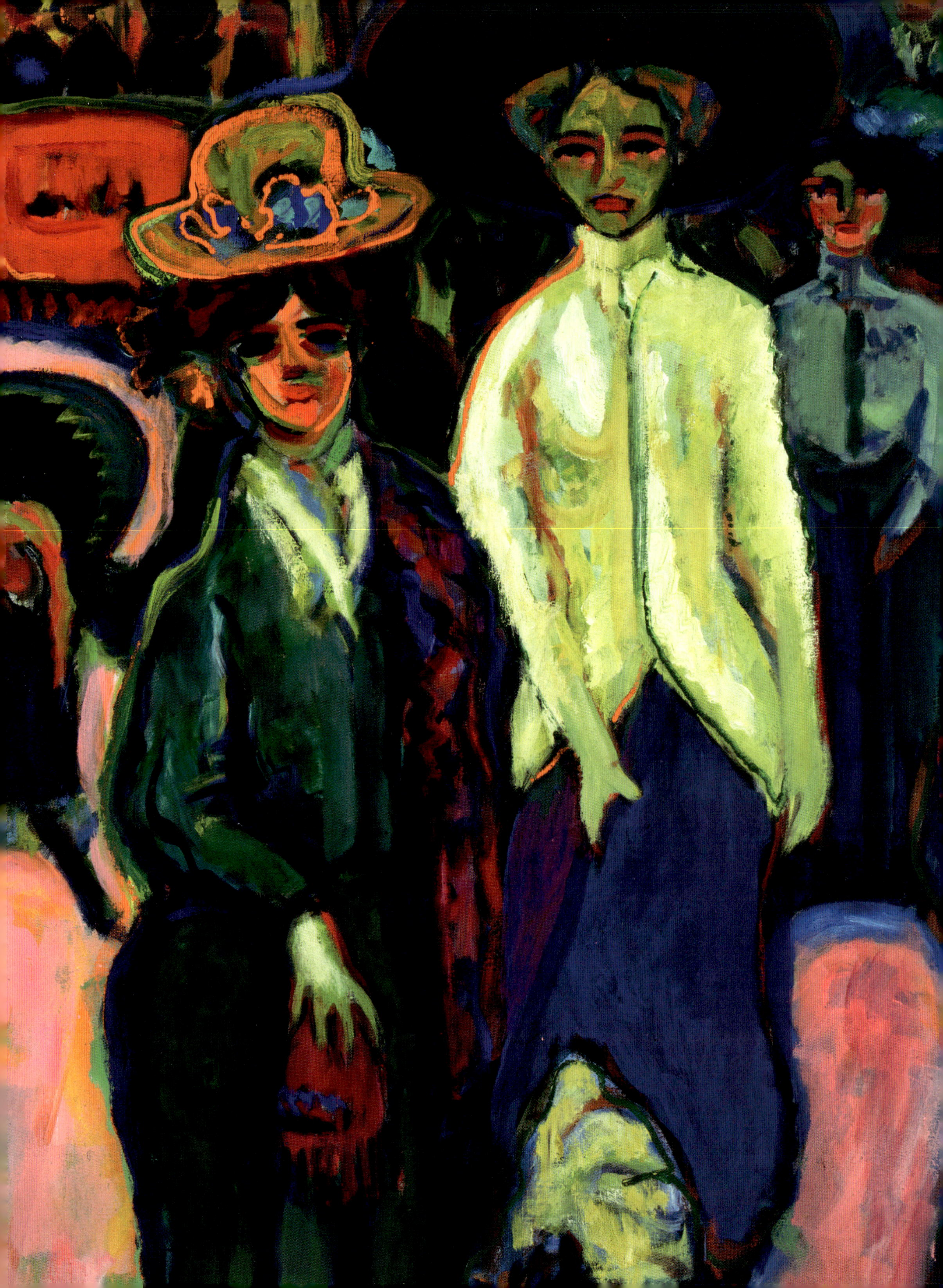

6 Color as the Expression of the Immaterial

Beginning in the 1880s, painters introduced color that did not represent visual reality. Turning away from materialism and what they often described as decadent urban society, these painters delved inside themselves for ways to express the values they held dear. Although disassociated from institutional religion, Paul Gauguin and Vincent van Gogh sought to express spiritual realities. For Gauguin, escape to an exotic, "primitive" society provided the environment where he could explore alternatives to Western civilization and his personal expression in nonrepresentational color. The brilliant light of Provence led Van Gogh to a color palette that unleashed his emotional responses to his subjects. Henri Matisse dissociated his world of art from the mundane with an elegant calligraphy and colors determined by aesthetic, not representational, concerns. In Germany the discovery of nonrepresentational color came only around 1905, but in Ernst Ludwig Kirchner it was the means to express his disaffection with modern life and his sense of the alienation of urban society. Vasily Kandinsky, like Gauguin, came to trust his unconscious to guide him out of the material and into the spiritual realm. He found in the inherent expressive properties of color the means to transcend the material.

By 1880 official support for the annual Salon dissolved and its organization was turned over to the artists themselves. In its place the state proposed an exhibition every three years of "more elevated art" on the model of the old Salon, for which the jury would select no more than eight hundred works. For the first exposition, the Nationale Triennale, in 1883 they were able to gather only 717, nearly all history painting, more by Cabanel than anyone else. No one in the public was really interested, and the attempt to repeat it in 1886 was scuttled by the artists, who were engaged in their own commercial Salon. The Triennale, Patricia Mainardi noted, which was "attacked by artists, unvisited by the public, ignored by the critics, and abandoned by the government," marked the collapse of the academic system that had been in place since the mid-seventeenth century, and the passing of the baton to the artists and the marketplace.[1]

Along with being liberated from any kind of state control, artists lost the prestige that was associated with official support—the purpose and goal, after all,

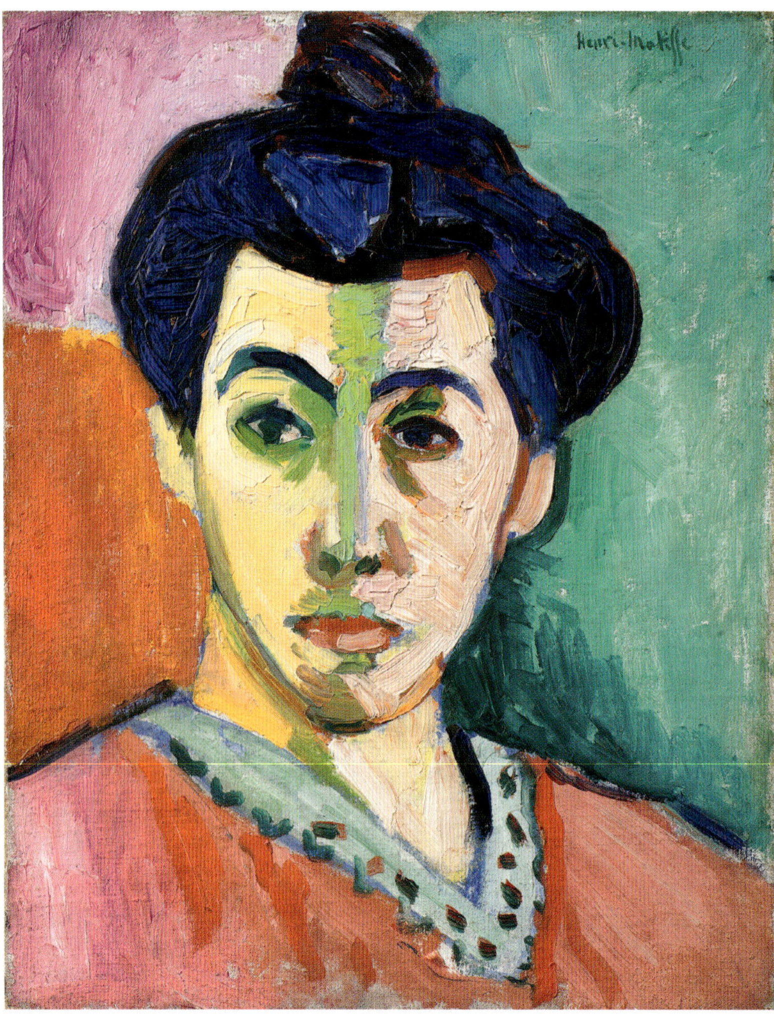

FIG. 6.1. Henri Matisse, *Portrait of Madame Matisse: The Green Line*, 1905. Oil on canvas, 16 × 12 ⅝ in. (40.5 × 32.5 cm). National Gallery of Denmark, Copenhagen.

of the original Académie. In the culture overseen by the Académie, shared societal concerns had been assumed to be the collective interest of public art, but now the artists were on their own. No longer representatives of the institution that symbolized and curated French culture, they spoke for no one but themselves. The extreme individualism that characterizes contemporary artists was born at this moment when they were thrown on their own resources, not just to support themselves but also to justify themselves and their art.

Dealers had by now become not just financial go-betweens but interpreters to the buying public, and they became arbiters of what was worth vending. It was the dealers who exhibited to the public. For the artist, finding a sympathetic dealer was as important now as having an interested and indulgent patron, or a reputation for reliable quality and prompt delivery, was to the Renaissance artist, or winning the Prix de Rome from the Académie jury had been to French artists. Gauguin

was rescued from his years of penury when finally in 1901 a young Parisian art dealer by the name of Ambroise Vollard signed a contract with him, assuring him a regular income, sufficient to live on without further worries. In exchange for all the works he produced, Van Gogh was supported by his brother, Theo, who was a dealer working for Goupil, to whom Vincent sent his pictures as he completed them.

The role the painter assumed in society was changing. Even the Impressionists were for the most part responding to the taste of their public for landscape and for images of life in the exciting modern city of Paris. Now the painter began to see himself as the critic of modern life. Certainly it is true that Manet had pioneered such a position, with his catalogue of paintings of social misfits: the homeless, the drinker, the prostitute, the traveling actor, the beggar.[2] And certainly before him William Hogarth in England, Francisco Goya in Spain, and Honoré Daumier in France, for example, had put social criticism in the domain of the artist. Now such contentiousness increasingly characterized the artists' stance. The pugnacious painters began to see themselves as prophets, like their Old Testament prototypes situated outside society, where they could view it critically and objectively. Once the art establishment broke down, they were no longer insiders. The oldest among the painters who will concern us in this final chapter, Gauguin, Van Gogh, and Georges Seurat, all saw themselves as geniuses charged with redeeming a decadent culture. (A group that formed around Gauguin called themselves Les Nabis, Hebrew for "prophet.")

They celebrated their personal vision and opened the way for Les Fauves and the Expressionists in the twentieth century. If Matisse saw the shadow on his wife's nose as green, he painted her that way, without regard for whether that was how anyone else saw her (fig. 6.1). He no longer felt constrained to depict normalcy or the universal—what was generally regarded as the way people perceive the visible world. His subjective vision, however distorted it might be, was a valid subject for a painting. Delacroix said it clearly in his *Dictionary of the Fine Arts:* "Oh! Young artist, you want a subject? Everything is a subject; the subject is yourself; it is your impressions, your emotions before nature. You must look within yourself and not around yourself."[3]

The painters who will concern us in this chapter were born between 1848 (Gauguin) and 1880 (Kirchner). While Van Gogh and Gauguin were largely self-taught, Seurat, Matisse, Kirchner, and Kandinsky all received some kind of traditional academic training. Matisse studied at the Académie Julien in Paris, Seurat attended the École, Kirchner studied architecture in Dresden, and Kandinsky went to art school in Munich.

The definitive abandonment of the classical tradition took place with Post-Impressionism. Even if it had included angels and nymphs, the classical tradition rendered the illusion of the visible world; and even though the Impressionists had rejected chiaroscuro, continuous modeling, and perspective—the essential tools of illusionism—they were still representing what they saw as they chose to see it. The Impressionists admitted the camel's nose in the tent, to be sure, in reifying appearance. By not claiming objective truth for what they painted, they authorized the artist's personal apprehension as a legitimate subject. Since the artist was viewer and maker, he or she introduced subjectivity. Gauguin

and Van Gogh plunged further into the realm of the painter's private vision and denied that painting should be about representing the merely material. As painters were no longer supported or constrained by state or religious institutions, they were freed to explore their own personal vision. The way things look could be better recorded by photography, but in their view no photograph could capture the spiritual, which lies behind appearance and is the proper subject of art.

GAUGUIN

Paul Gauguin was searching for an alternative religion to replace his own faltering faith. Rejecting the idealism honored by the Salon and the naturalism sought by the Impressionists, he employed his colors in arbitrary patterns with an eye to decorative effect. Within the classical tradition, the decorative was regarded as the opposite of the art of reason. It was mindless, its purpose merely aesthetic, not narrative.[4] Gauguin embraced "decorative" as a moniker for his painting because he wanted to get beyond and beneath narrative, beyond and beneath reason, to the underlying spiritual essence. He wrote: "People will feel the sacredness of it [what I paint] and take off their hats as though they were in church."[5]

After sailing the world for three years as a merchant seaman, Gauguin married a Danish woman in 1873, had five children, and became a successful stockbroker in Paris. He began his art career late in life by the usual standards, but by 1882, when the stock market crashed, he had decided to devote himself full-time to his art. He had exhibited with the Impressionists in 1881 and 1882. In 1886 he showed no fewer than nineteen pictures at the last Impressionist show. Urged by his wife and family, he tried half-heartedly to find a job, but without success. He was becoming more and more alienated from what he saw as decadent and materialist European society. Attracted by "primitivism," he hoped to find more direct access to spiritual values and a model for his own painting.[6] He found appealing the naïve piety of the people in nearby Brittany, where he was able to live cheaply, with other painters, who admired him and were similarly attracted to the "primitive," gathered around him. There in late summer 1888 he painted his *Vision after the Sermon* (fig. 6.2).

What turned out to be Gauguin's breakthrough painting, in which he discovered how to render what was in the minds of his actors, shows a group of Breton women

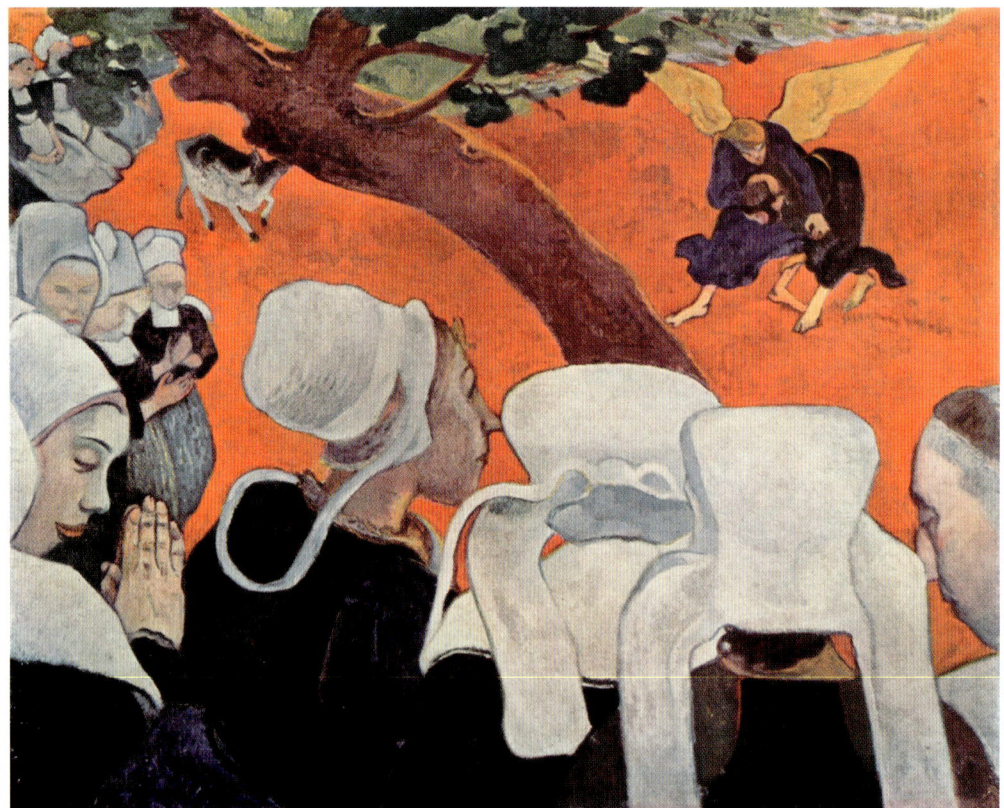

FIG. 6.2. Paul Gauguin,
Vision after the Sermon (Jacob Wrestling with the Angel),
1888. Oil on canvas, 28 3/8 ×
35 6/8 in. (72.2 × 91 cm).
National Galleries of
Scotland, Edinburgh.

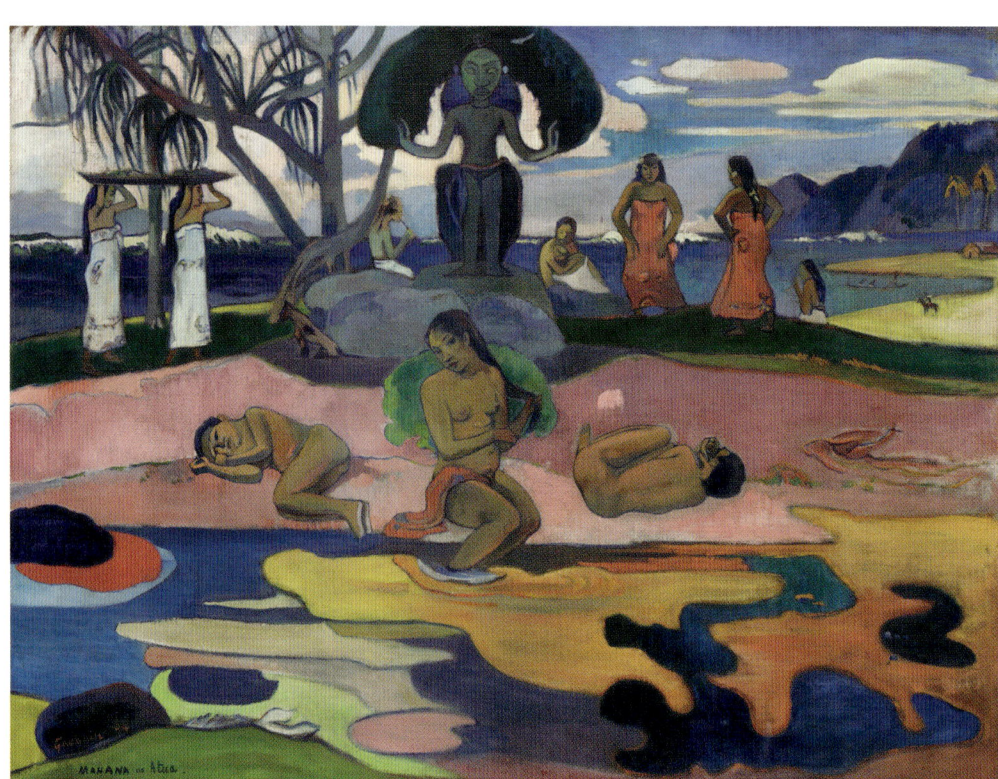

FIG. 6.3. Paul Gauguin, *Day of the God* (*Mahana No Atua*), 1894. Oil on canvas,
26 7/8 × 36 in. (68.3 × 91.5 cm).
Art Institute of Chicago.

praying after the priest has preached a sermon on Jacob wrestling with the angel. Drawing upon techniques he had seen in Japanese prints, Gauguin played with proportion, recession, and viewpoint.[7] A large apple tree with a cow beneath it bisects a large field of bright vermilion, on which the vision takes place. In the foreground the heads of the women in their caps loom. Perhaps understanding how important this piece was, he described it in a letter to Van Gogh: "The landscape and the fight exist only in the imagination of the people who pray after the sermon—that's why there is a contrast between the life-sized people and the unnatural and disproportionate fight in the landscape."[8] Abandoning the landscapes with Impressionist-style space with which he had been recently dabbling in his Breton works, he understood that to signal he is going inside the mind, he has to violate the semblance of naturalistic spatial recession and modeling. His modeling is as innovative as the treatment of space. If the vermilion field or the white caps were truly flat, the painting would read like a cartoon. Vojtěch Jirat-Wasiutyński and H. Travers Newton, a team of art historian and conservator, have examined the surfaces and described the subtlety with which Gauguin built them:

> Areas of paint are carefully built up, in most cases over thin wash, in sequence [as he had done previously]. . . . But here he used the procedure with great inventiveness to create effects of light, modeling, and texture in a less descriptive, more abstract manner. The red field is modulated by application of a higher-key and more intense red in parallel vertical strokes over a darker, more muted lay-in of red. As a result, light appears to flicker over the surface and suggests stubble illuminated by the oblique rays of the sun.

In the headdresses, particularly the two seen from the back,

> Gauguin produced subtly differentiated paint surfaces that catch the light in varied ways to suggest starched cloth and three-dimensional form. In areas of thin white washes the paint conforms to the fine texture of the canvas weave; where there is a thin lay-in underneath, a smooth and luminous surface is created; and where the top layer is thick and built up, a suggestion of relief is produced.[9]

Gauguin's brushstroke here is not used for modeling, as it was in Impressionism and his own earlier work. In this painting Gauguin has left behind the remnants of traditional illusionism in color, upon which Impressionism, with its commitment to depicting visual reality, had continued to rely. Hereafter, he would freely and creatively use his colors arbitrarily, guided by expressive need and aesthetic preference, not naturalism.

He began his search, which famously took him to Tahiti and the South Seas, with visits to Panama, the island of Martinique in the Caribbean, and Arles with Van Gogh. In 1891 he departed on his first trip to Tahiti. In an interview given to the *Echo de Paris* on February 23, 1891, some months before his departure, he explained his reason for leaving for the French colony: "I wish to live in peace and to avoid being influenced by our civilization. I only desire to create a simple art. In order to achieve this, it is necessary for me to steep myself in virgin nature, to see no one but savages, to share their life and have as my sole occupation to render, just as children would do, the images of my own brain, using exclusively the means offered by primitive art, which are the only true and valid ones." Gauguin eagerly explored Tahitian religion and mythology. There was very little remaining of sacred imagery since the arrival of the missionaries, so he often had to rely on photographs and descriptions of primitive art in other locations. *Day of the God,* painted after Gauguin had returned to France in 1893, is a kind of compendium of his experience in Tahiti and an expression of his nostalgia for the pastoral Eden he thought he had found there (fig. 6.3). It combines people going about the chores of daily life in the uppermost zone against the backdrop of tropical vegetation and the ocean. A dark idol looms at the center, based on descriptions of Easter Island statues in Jacques-Antoine Moerenhout's *Travels to the Islands of the Pacific Ocean*, and photos of figures from the temple complex at Borobudur.[10] The lowest zone slips into the zone of the visionary. On a pink sand beach are placed three enigmatic figures; the woman at the middle, dipping her feet in the pool, is flanked by reclining ones, perhaps sleeping, perhaps resting. The pool slides into an exuberant display of psychedelic color, anchored by the emerald-green hillock at the lower left with the painter's signature and held in check only by the suggestion that these are reflections on its surface: orange and blue, yellow, vermilion, and tones in between. Gauguin comes as close here as he will ever come to purely nonrepresentational color.

Gauguin selected and used his materials to enhance

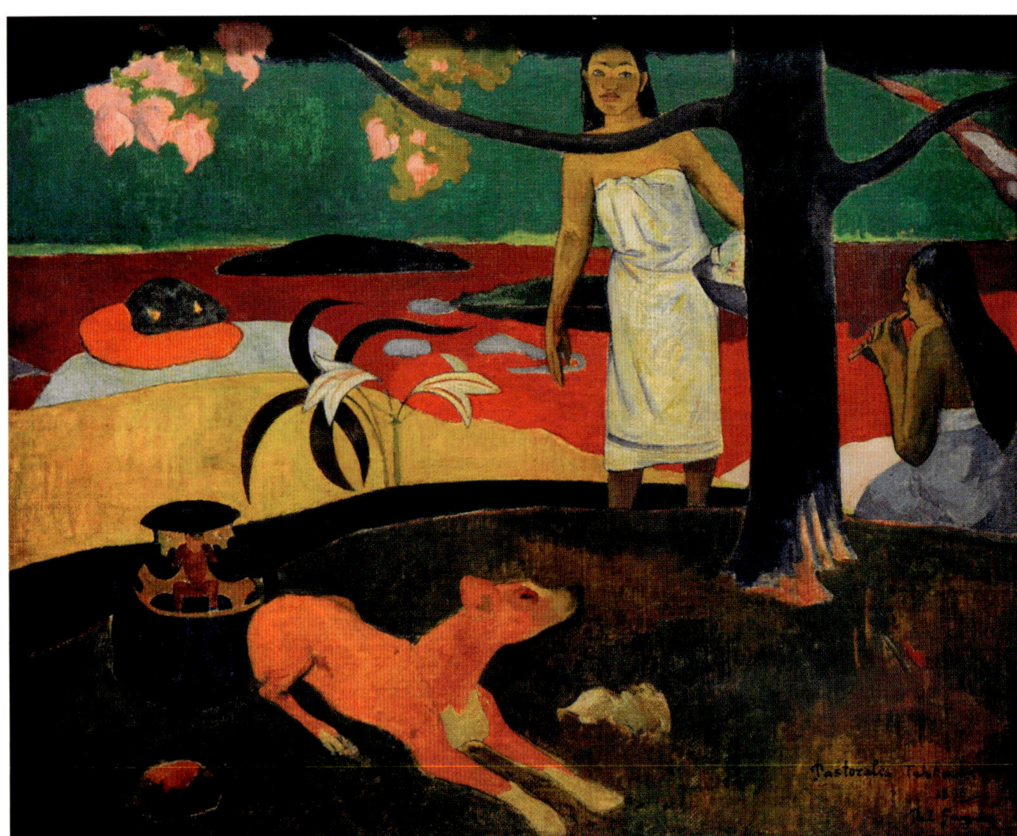

FIG. 6.4. Paul Gauguin, *Tahitian Pastoral*, 1892. Oil on canvas, 34 ⅖ × 44 ¾ in. (87.5 × 113.7 cm). Hermitage, Saint Petersburg.

his message. He painted on a coarse, burlap-like canvas to suggest that beautiful and spiritually enriching images can be made with commonplace materials. He used an absorbent chalk ground to avoid the richness of an oily look, and he applied his paints thinly, sometimes even with a watery look, to eliminate all texture except that of the coarse support. He wanted no sheen, so he used no varnish. He wanted a sensuous but not a luxurious effect. There is no beautiful texture even to his gloriously colored and sometimes patterned native fabrics. His paradise is abundant with vegetation, but not with the stuff of European civilization.

He took care to keep the look of his paint thin and matte. Like Degas he painted à l'essence, the process in which oil is drained from the paint and then remixed with turpentine to thin it.[11] He may have added wax to his paint, in part to stretch his supplies, when he had to depend upon shipments to Tahiti from Europe, but its presence has not been proved. He did instruct that paintings be coated with wax after they arrived in France.[12] He also washed his paintings when he finished them to minimize surface gloss.[13] He abhorred the glossy natural resin varnish in common use, and he wrote that he "always

worried that his pictures will be ruined with this dirty disgusting varnish which picture dealers use."[14]

We know about Gauguin's pigments from the requests he sent by letter for supplies, and through technical analysis. His choice of pigments did not change in the course of his mature career. His palette centered on vermilion and emerald green, Prussian blue and yellow ochre; he often used ultramarine and cobalt blues, viridian, chrome yellow 1, and cadmium citron. His colors become brighter in the South Seas mainly because he mixed less white and fewer complementary colors into his tone after he began painting there. There are no requests in his letters for dark earth pigments such as umbers and siennas, or for black, and they were not found in the pigment analyses.[15] He outlined his forms often with Prussian blue, but never with black.

Flesh tones therefore were made without browns; they were simply mixed with more ochre and less white pigment than is traditionally used. He enhanced his glowing palette by juxtaposing the dark ochre-colored skin with very light, bright colors in the middle ground and background. These bright colors are often reflected in the highlights of the figures' skin, recalling an effect

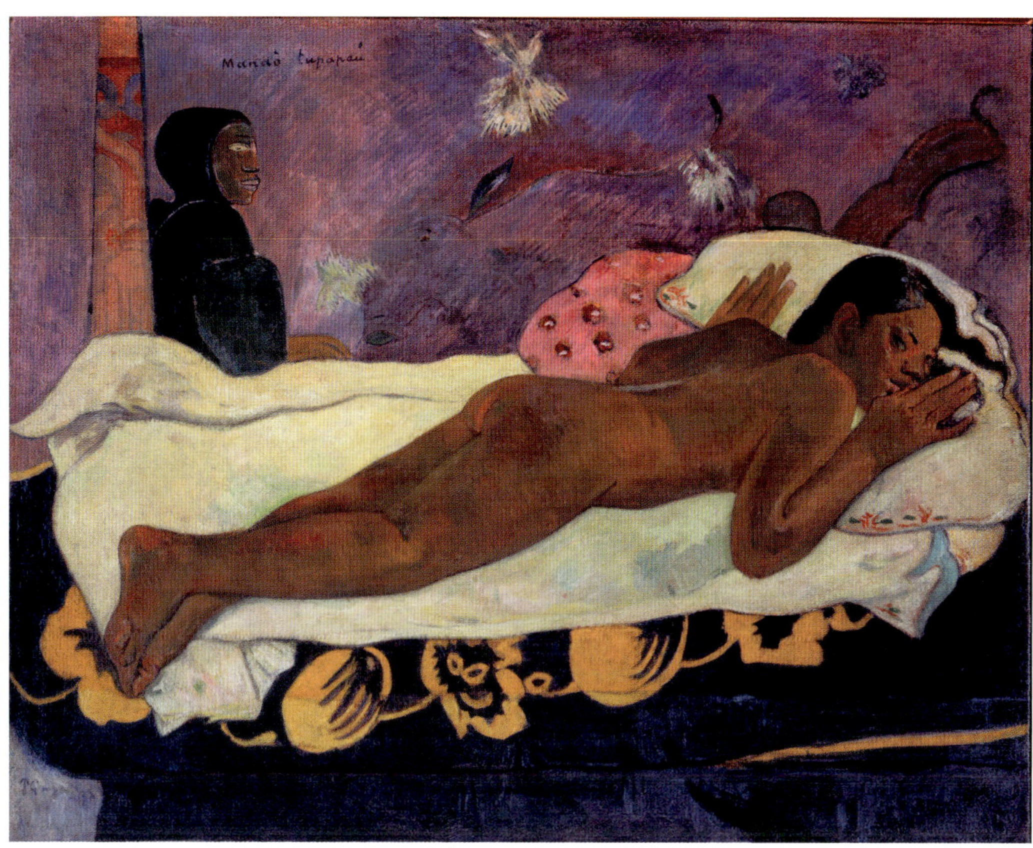

FIG. 6.5. Paul Gauguin, *Spirit of the Dead Keeps Watch (Manaò Tupapaú)*, 1892. Oil on jute mounted on canvas, 28 3/4 × 36 3/8 in. (73 × 92.4 cm). Albright-Knox Art Gallery, Buffalo.

of reflected tropical light.[16] Gauguin also increased the vibrancy of his palette by juxtaposing complementary colors, vermilion and emerald green in *Tahitian Pastoral* (fig. 6.4), or purple and yellow in *Woman of the Mango* (Baltimore Museum of Art), where the upper layer of the purple dress is laid in over a pink underpaint.[17]

Gauguin makes clear that it is the relationship of his tones that most concerned him in his description of the *Spirit of the Dead Keeps Watch* (fig. 6.5): "Overall harmony; somber sad blue violet and chrome-1—the sheets [on the bed] are chrome 2 because this color suggests the night without explicitly describing it and also serves as a transition between the yellow-orange and the green which completes the musical accord."[18] The relationship between visual and auditory harmonies, often alluded to by artists since the Renaissance, comes to fruition in the nineteenth-century and twentieth-century painters—for example, Seurat and especially Kandinsky.[19] Gauguin seldom used pigment straight from the tube, except ultramarine and Prussian blue. This painting is also, not incidentally, Gauguin's riposte to Manet's *Olympia* (see fig. 5.25): the figure in dark skin tones is lying prone, but still eyes the viewer directly.[20]

Unlike Van Gogh, whose impasto surfaces and unblended brushstroke express urgency, Gauguin's ascetic use of materials promotes the silence and stillness of his dream-like atmosphere. Gauguin wrote to Émile Bernard from Arles: "As to pigment he [Van Gogh] appreciates thick paint . . . while I detest any form of tampering by brushstroke."[21] His statuary and immobile figures stare without seeing, or turn the spectator's gaze back on him; they are engaged in no business, but are enfolded in their surroundings. The colors work in consonance with those around them to make us feel that the actors live in harmony with their environment.

Gauguin did not intend or wish to paint what he saw, as he frequently stated. He believed that the image coalesced in the mind and then emerged without conscious thought. Nevertheless he prepared the "spontaneous" image with quick pencil sketches, which he might transfer either by squaring up or more rarely by pounced cartoon, as in *Words of the Devil* (Washington, D.C., National Gallery of Art). He wished to create the impression that he worked directly on the canvas. He wrote to Georges-Daniel de Monfreid that he had created his very large mural *Where Do We Come From?* (Boston, Museum of Fine Arts, 1897–98) in a burst of creative energy, sketched directly on the canvas, but in fact there exists a squared drawing on tracing paper, colored with watercolor.[22] Admitting to careful preparation would suggest a more ratiocinated process, like that of the Académie that he professed to abhor, rather than the outpouring of his subconscious mind.

VAN GOGH

Vincent van Gogh grew up the son of a Dutch rural pastor who was responsible for fifty-six indigent farmers. The family was pious and strict, but deeply committed to helping others in need. Vincent himself spent a year studying theology in Amsterdam before he made his decision to follow a career as a painter. Although he separated himself from the Church and advised his brother, Theo, that he should flee "the whitewashed wall, which meant hypocrisy and Pharisaism," that dedication to helping others never left him and underlies his art.[23] He and Gauguin shared the belief that art was not the description of visual reality, but the means to spiritual awareness. From Arles he wrote to Theo: "In a painting I'd like to say something consoling, like a piece of music. I'd like to paint men or women with that *je ne sais quoi* of the eternal, of which the halo used to be the symbol, and which we try to achieve through the radiance itself, through the vibrancy of our colorations."[24]

Van Gogh left the Netherlands in 1886 for Paris, where he encountered Impressionism and became friends with many of the artists living there. His style evolved away from the brownish pictures he had been making to embrace bright color and expressive brushstroke. His colorman, Julien Tanguy, was given the portrait Van Gogh made of him (see fig. 5.16), in exchange for materials. It shows not only Van Gogh's emerging style, but a display on the wall behind him of the Japanese prints Tanguy stocked. Van Gogh was particularly taken with the prints of Hiroshige and Hokusai, from whom he learned, like many of his peers, arbitrary perspective and expressive distortion, and alternatives to traditional Western viewpoint and composition.

In Arles, where he settled in February 1888, Van Gogh found his style, based on the rapid and impassioned application of paint in colors reflecting the sun-drenched light of Provence. That light and those colors were Van Gogh's means to express the joy or admonition or consolation he wanted his viewer to receive. The *Night Café*, painted before Gauguin arrived, is an admonition (fig. 6.6).

Van Gogh makes clear in the descriptions of his paintings in his letters to Theo that he thought in terms of color. Although the space in the *Night Café* recedes in an alarming way, he talks only about his use of color to create a nightmarish scene—"one of the ugliest I have made," he said.

> I've tried to express the terrible human passions with the red and the green. The room is blood-red and dull yellow, a green billiard table in the centre, lemon yellow lamps with an orange and green glow. Everywhere it's a battle and an antithesis of the most different greens and reds; in the characters of the sleeping ruffians, small in the empty, high room, some purple and blue. The blood-red and the yellow-green of the billiard table, for example, contrast with the little bit of delicate Louis XV green of the counter, where there's a pink bouquet.[25]

The next day in another letter to Theo he wrote, "I've tried to express the idea that the café is a place where you can ruin yourself, go mad, commit crimes. . . . All of that in an ambience of a hellish furnace, in pale sulphur."[26]

Red and green are not necessarily antagonistic; he used them as friendly complementaries in other contexts—for example, in the warm maternal portrait *La Berceuse* (*The Lullaby*), which he called "a lullaby in colours" and with which he intended to convey consolation (fig. 6.7).[27] It's the juxtaposition of this red and this green with the sulfur-yellow that creates the "hellish furnace." The "tender" green of the counter sets off the green of the billiard table, alienating it. Van Gogh is not equating a pigment with a particular feeling or symbolic value; it is the selection of a particular tone in combination with others that achieves the atmosphere he wants.

Earlier that summer he had painted the *Sower* (fig. 6.8). In accord with his own upbringing, he sees peasant labor as having a certain sanctity, and nature as the reflection of God's infinite creation. When he described it to his friend and fellow painter Bernard in a letter, he again talked about the colors—purple, chrome yellow 1 and 2, yellow ochre with a little carmine—and said, "The Sower's smock is blue, and his trousers white." But he went on to make clear that imitating the phenomenal world was not what interested him. The picture is

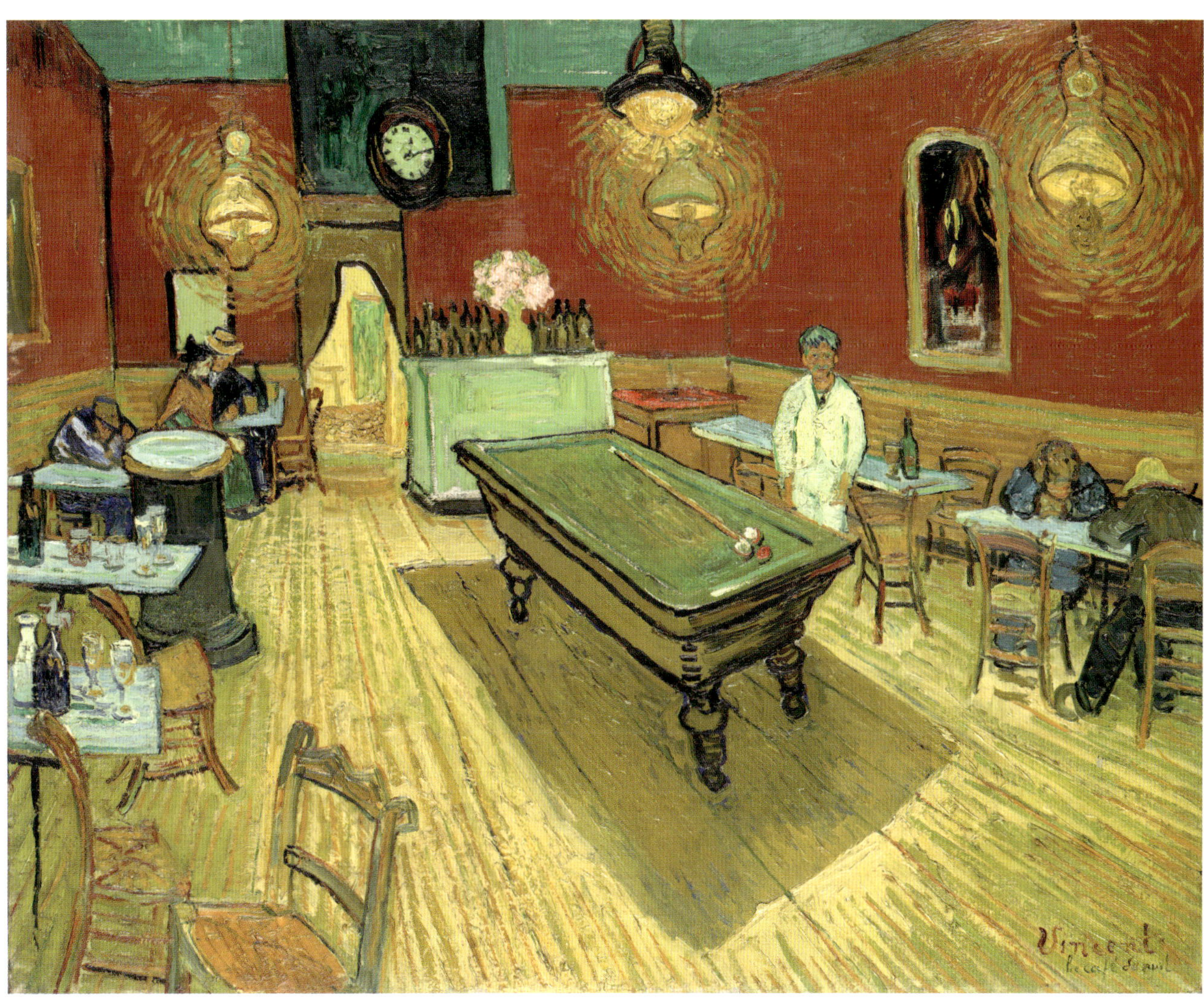

FIG. 6.6. Vincent van Gogh, *Night Café,* 1888. Oil on canvas, 28 1/2 × 36 1/4 in. (72.4 × 92.1 cm). Yale University Art Gallery, New Haven.

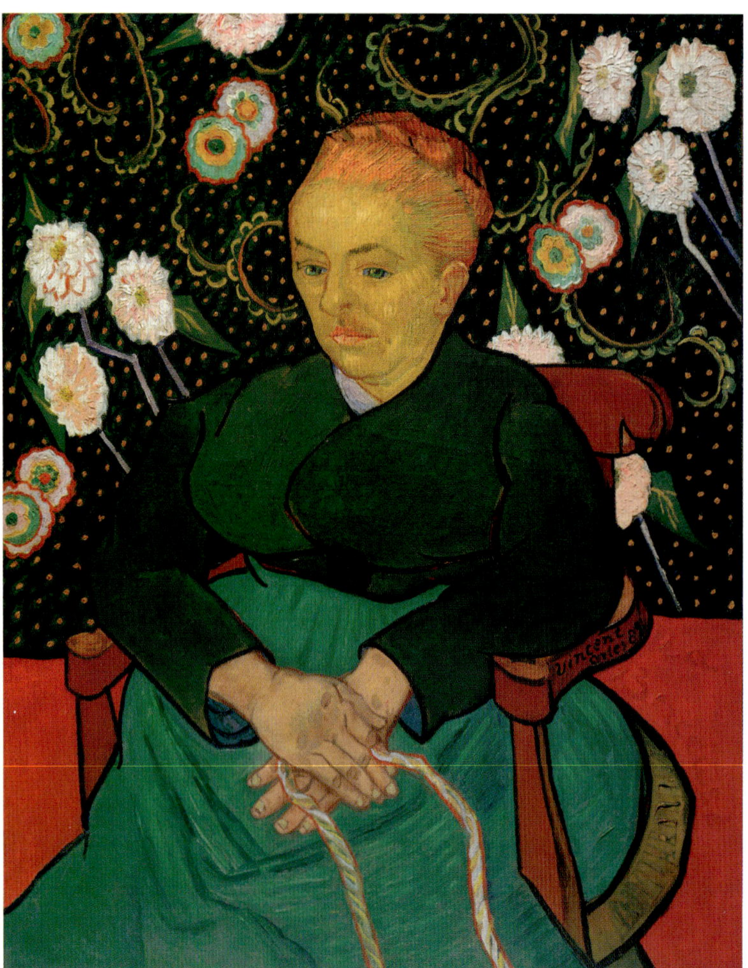

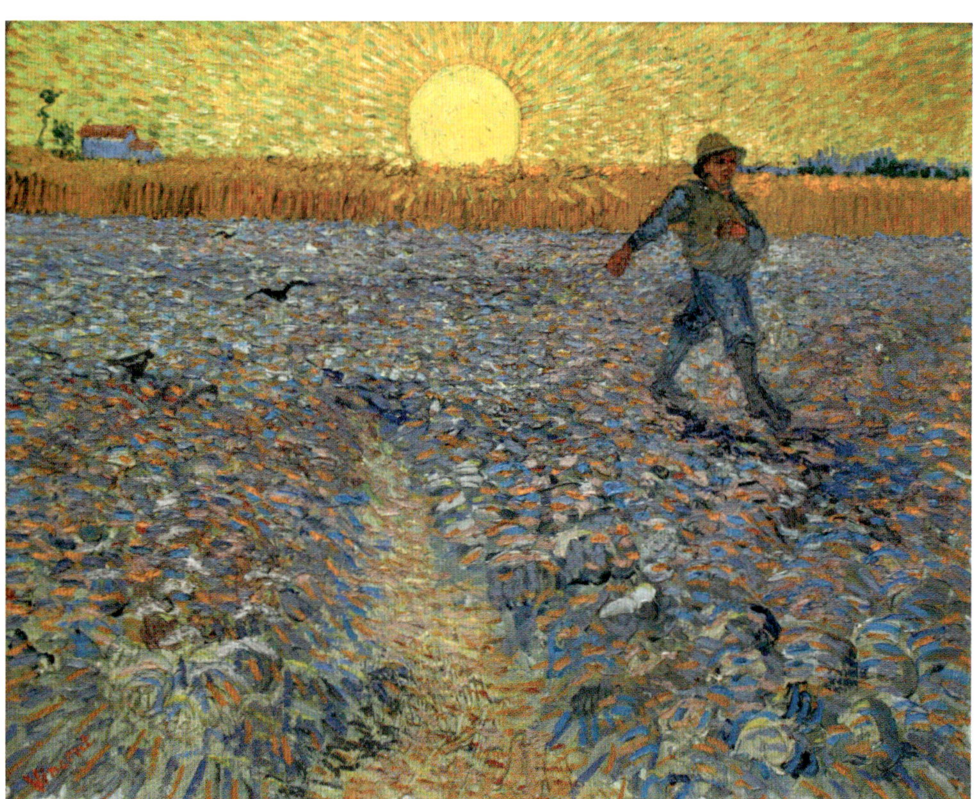

FIG. 6.7. Vincent van Gogh, *La Berceuse* (*The Lullaby*), 1889. Oil on canvas, 36 1/2 × 29 in. (92.8 × 73.8 cm). Metropolitan Museum of Art, New York.

FIG. 6.8. Vincent van Gogh, *Sower*, 1888. Oil on canvas, 25 1/2 × 31 5/8 in. (64.2 × 80.3 cm). Kröller-Müller Museum, Otterlo, Netherlands.

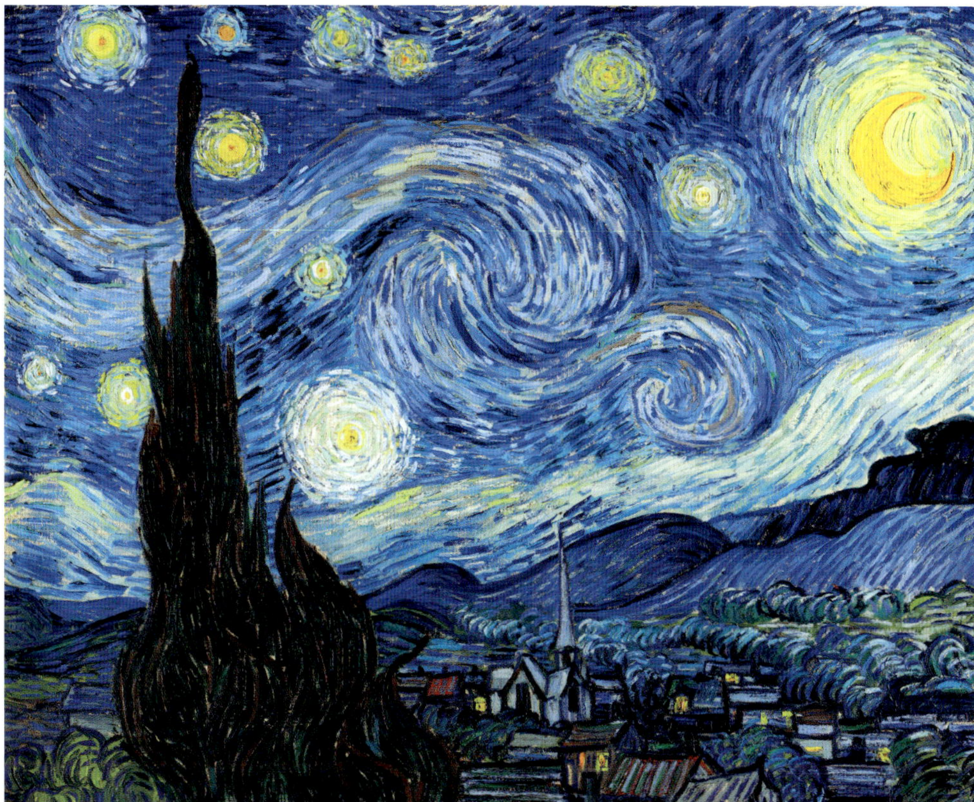

FIG. 6.9. Vincent van Gogh, *Starry Night*, 1889. Oil on canvas, 29 × 36¼ in. (73.75 × 92.1 cm). Museum of Modern Art, New York.

symbolic and certainly recalls the sower of Jesus's parable, where God casts the seed and it is up to us to either accept the seed, which represents salvation, or reject it. "There are many repetitions of yellow in the earth, neutral tones, resulting from the mixing of violet with yellow, but I could hardly give a damn about the *veracity* of the colour. . . . [I] have yearnings for that infinite of which the Sower, the sheaf, are the symbols."[28]

The tragic events surrounding the tumultuous sojourn of Gauguin in the autumn of 1888, which had come to an abrupt end when Vincent cut off part of his ear and culminated in his admitting himself to the asylum at Arles, where he died in July 1890, are as well known as his iconic *Starry Night* (fig. 6.9).[29] The painter's view from the barred window of his room in the asylum can be reconstructed, as can the night sky that he saw that early morning when he rose before dawn to paint it. He wrote to Theo: "This morning I saw the country from my window a long time before sunrise, with nothing but the morning star, which looked very big."[30] The changes he made to what he could actually see are significant. He exaggerated the presence of the three celestial bodies that were visible, and he reversed the moon from gibbous to crescent. He imported from nearby the church

of Saint-Martin, so its presence is telling, but he buried it and its steeple below the horizon, whereas the cypress that he could see has instead been grown to touch the heavens.[31] It is not the institutional church but the wonder of creation that inspires. The cypress is a traditional symbol of death, often used to ornament graveyards. Van Gogh wrote: "Looking at the stars always makes me dream. Why, I ask myself, shouldn't the shining dots of the sky be as accessible as the black dots on the map of France? Just as we take the train to get to Tarascon or Rouen, we take death to reach a star."[32] In the midst of his own mental anguish he created, in Albert Boime's words, "a visionary image he hoped could liberate others from fear of the unknown."[33]

The materials Van Gogh used are not the extraordinary feature here. The pigments are the ones we would expect: the sky is made up of ultramarine blue and cobalt blue; emerald green was used in the light bluish-green strokes around the moon.[34] What is extraordinary is the application of the paint in bold impasto strokes that are not blended, creating the roiling and swirling sky, as if capturing the aura of the heavenly bodies. The energy in the landscape is contained with strong, dark contours; the serpentine cypress convulses toward the stars. The

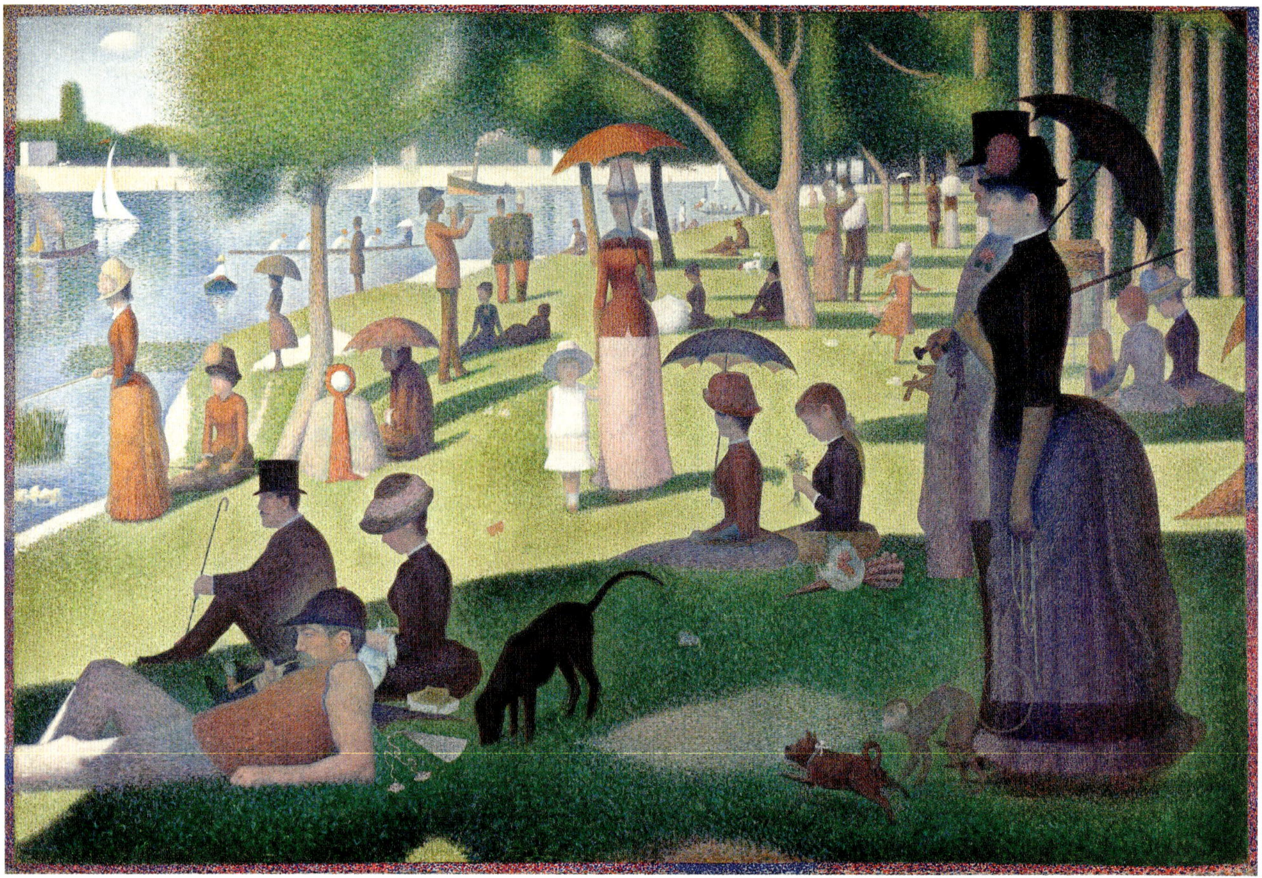

urgency of the brushstroke transmits the painter's passion. This is Titian's open brushwork pushed to the ultimate degree of expressivity.

Gauguin and Van Gogh were seeking to express a spiritual content that they both felt required going beyond visual reality. For Van Gogh, although he had liberated himself from institutional religion, the source of creativity was his Christian conviction of an eternal divinity present in the material world.[35] Gauguin, equally indoctrinated in Christian orthodoxy and likewise severed from the Church, was vitalized to give shape to his dreamed reality by denying the stuff of the civilized world and the rule of reason. For each of them, the more important reality of the spiritual had to be signaled with the colors and textures they intuited rather than saw.

SEURAT

Georges Seurat, born nearly thirty years after the first of the Impressionists, came of age artistically just as that movement was breaking up. He defies categorization. As interested in color as any painter of the century, Seurat hoped to apply science where the Impressionists relied on subjective observation. Rejecting the imaginative nonobjective coloring of Gauguin and Van Gogh, he dissected the experience of color and reconstructed it to stamp it with an order beyond that of the natural world. After attending the École until he was twenty, he set out to reform Impressionism by submitting its use of color to more ordered procedures. Seurat devoted an entire year to drawing in monochrome in 1883. He had studied the color theorists Michael Eugéne Chevreul, Ogden Rood, and Charles Blanc, and was persuaded that he could use color scientifically to create harmony in a way analogous to the way composers create harmony in music.[36] Chevreul had observed that two juxtaposed colors, when perceived by the eye, create a third color that is more intense and pleasing than if the pigments were physically mixed. Seurat's divisionist technique was demonstrated on a monumental scale in his *A Sunday on La Grande Jatte*, a ten-foot canvas that he worked on over a period of five years (fig. 6.10).

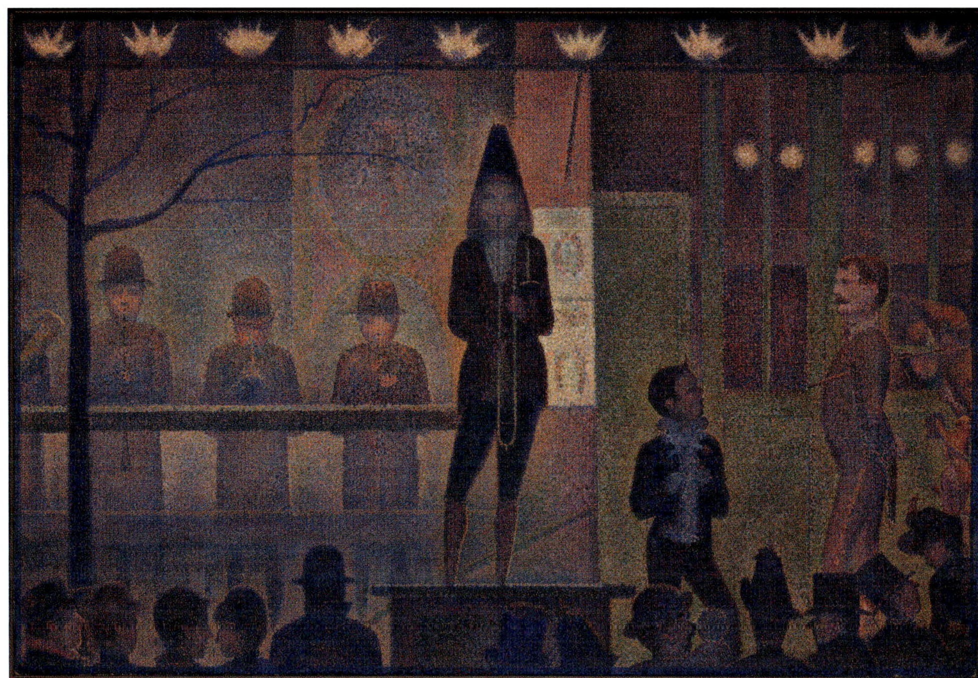

FIG. 6.11. Georges Seurat, *Circus Sideshow*, 1887–88. Oil on canvas, 39 ¼ × 59 in. (99.7 × 149.9 cm). Metropolitan Museum of Art, New York.

His process was characteristically systematic, making use of a grid of twenty-four squares to aid in the transfer of designs developed first in a series of color sketches and then drawings. The first painted version of 1884 was worked in a style similar to the Impressionists, but with brushwork somewhat more ordered and regular. He also used some earth colors that he later abandoned. The second painting campaign, beginning in October 1885, reflects his growing interest in the theories of Chevreul and Blanc, especially simultaneous contrast and successive contrast. He used a new technique for applying paint: small and varied brushstrokes in dabs, dashes, dots, and lines.[37]

Small points of color are applied without blending, creating a powerful clarity and precision of form. As Robert Herbert insists, however, Seurat's technique is more creative and experimental than is acknowledged. Herbert draws a more appealing portrayal of the painter than the usual characterization of him and his painting as coldly "scientific." He points out that optical mixing does not really work here, although the colors do vibrate in the eye. In the shade on the grass, Seurat broadly brushed in several tints of green and blue green, then enlivened the surface with touches of orange, yellow, blue purple, and red.[38] There is somewhat less vibrancy in certain passages than there was originally, an example of the kind of loss caused by the instability of some of the new

synthetic pigments. It has now been discovered that zinc yellow, used in the second campaign, is the culprit that has caused the darkening and discoloration.[39]

Critics recognized the irony in the picture when it was exhibited in 1886. It is at the same time an image of the Parisian middle class enjoying a leisurely Sunday afternoon in the suburbs and a satire of fashion and manners. One critic pointed out the stiffness of the people, their cookie-cutter forms, their cramped clothing.[40] The entertainments of the Parisian bourgeoisie are also the subject of *Circus Sideshow,* in which Seurat pictures performers working to lure visitors to buy tickets to the main act inside the tent (fig. 6.11). It was a popular subject, especially in prints and cartoons, where it was often given political or social overtones. Instead of the usual raucous scene, however, Seurat's is eerily silent, despite the trombonist at the center and the band at the left. Although interpretations of it in political and social terms have been offered, the work remains enigmatic and mysteriously dignified.

Preparatory studies reveal how carefully the mathematics and the proportions were worked out. Unlike *La Grande Jatte, Circus Sideshow* is frieze-like, with overlapping providing the clues to recession. Forms are aligned along vertical and horizontal grid lines, with strategic diagonals such as the balcony railing at the feet of the trombonist and the walking stick under the arm of the circus master. This stern geometry gives the scene a solemnity that's unexpected. Some critics have found its mood melancholy, pointing to the coloring and the downward-facing instruments, for instance; even as early as 1891, when Seurat was still alive, Gustave Kahn, a critic friendly to the painter, perhaps attempting to head off misinterpretations, described the composition as "deliberately wan and mournful."[41]

Certainly Seurat was inspired by the challenge of representing the light effects of an outdoor nighttime setting illumined by gaslight. We see the line of gas lamps running across the top. The trombonist is a dark, backlit silhouette, like the foreground spectators, while the other musicians closer to the light take on a hazy glow. Seurat worked on what was probably a custom-made canvas, pre-primed in pale gray. The colors are applied in stages, beginning with large, widely shaped dots and dashes in the dominant color, then proceeding with more dots and dashes of diminishing size. In places where he needed to mimic the effect of the gaslight he added tiny dots of orange, a mixture of vermilion and chrome yellow, as on the trombonist's calves. The boundaries are the most highly worked, to create shading and form. Theoretically the colors mix in the eye, but in fact the divisionist technique here captures the softened contours and foggy appearance of night vision.[42]

Like the Post-Impressionists, Seurat used a kind of nonrepresentational color, but not to signal spiritual values so much as to give an ordered image corresponding to visual reality. He declared that the purpose of a painting was to create harmony.[43] The cosmic dimension of this ambition suggests that he was seeking something akin to Gauguin and Van Gogh. Seurat died at the age of only thirty-one. His divisionist technique was pursued by its co-inventor, Paul Signac, who wrote about it in a book published in 1899, *From Eugène Delacroix to Neo-Impressionism,* which Henri Matisse would read and be drawn to.

MATISSE

With Matisse we enter a world where color reigns supreme. Van Gogh and Gauguin prepared the way: Van Gogh conceived his pictures in terms of color, and Gauguin used nonrepresentational colors, but they always refer to something particular for which he has transposed the color he uses. With Matisse, color becomes truly abstract, not only arbitrary but sometimes not conforming to the boundaries of the objects

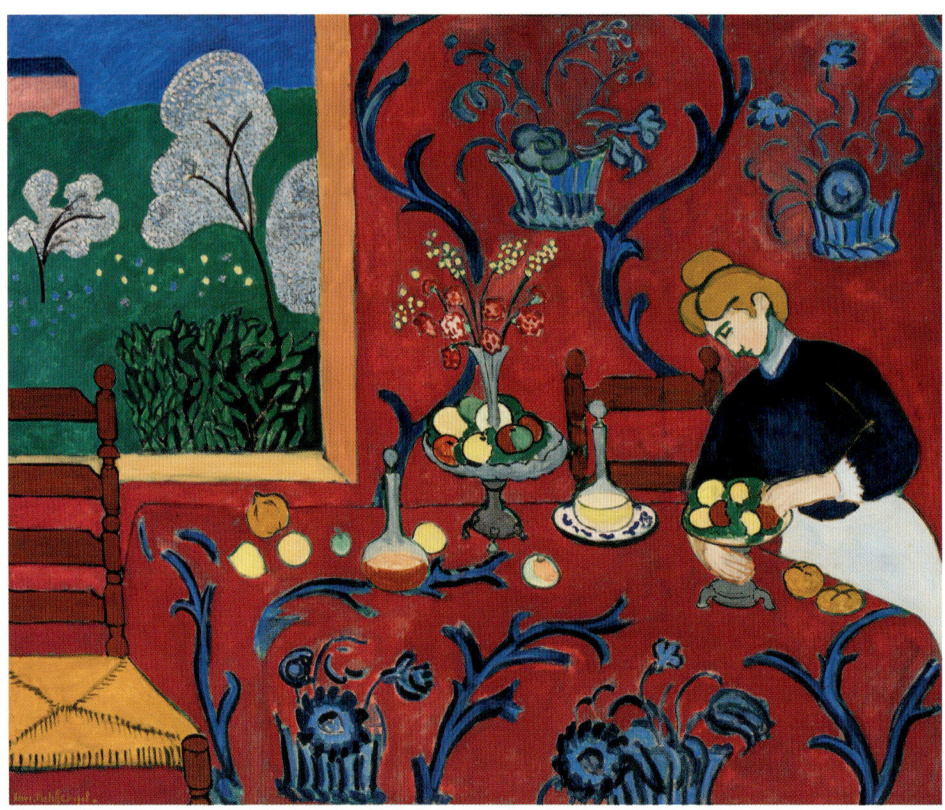

FIG. 6.12. Henri Matisse, *Harmony in Red,* 1908. Oil on canvas, 71 × 87 in. (180.5 × 221 cm). Hermitage, Saint Petersburg.

depicted. *Harmony in Red* (fig. 6.12) and the *Red Studio* are
the extreme expression of this tendency. Whereas the
Post-Impressionists, especially Van Gogh, associated an
emotional expression with the colors chosen, Matisse did
not necessarily link his color with the subject. He originally painted the *Harmony in Red* blue, based on a blue
textile that he owned. He sold it to a Russian client, then
a year later, before delivering it, he repainted it in red.
When someone objected that the change made it a completely different picture, he denied it. What was important to him was not whether the room was blue, therefore
perhaps sad or peaceful, or red, making it exciting or
threatening or something else. What interested him was
the abstracting and space-effacing effect of the merging
of wallpaper and tablecloth. Color, for Matisse, is not
"expressive" in the way we use that term for Gauguin and
Van Gogh, nor for the Expressionists. He creates an experience for his viewer with the ensemble of his coloring.

Matisse, in his long life, never embraced a style and
stuck to it. He was constantly evolving, much like his
younger contemporary Pablo Picasso. Matisse had read
Signac's book and was drawn to the methodical treatment of color with divisionist brushstrokes that was
meant to reconstruct perceived reality as closely as possible. In 1904, together with his colleague André Derain,
Matisse was taken to see de Monfreid's collection of
Gauguin. At this time Matisse was still using chiaroscuro
and modeling, but the impact of Gauguin's works seen
together must have persuaded him to abandon them. He
then spent the summer at Saint-Tropez with the Neo-
Impressionists Paul Signac and Henri-Edmond Cross.
There he painted *Luxe, Calme, et Volupté* using the divisionist brushstroke (fig. 6.13). The title was taken from a
couplet in Baudelaire's "L'Invitation au Voyage":

> Là, tout n'est qu'ordre et beauté,
>   Luxe, calme et volupté
>
> There, all is order and beauty,
>   Abundance, peace and sensuous delight

Like Gauguin, Matisse gives us a tranquil escape
from daily life in the city, but it is not like Gauguin's
escape to a "primitive," savage world. This is a civilized excursion with his wife and son, complete with
pique-nique and a sailboat ready for the return trip. It is
more like Watteau's Cythera (see fig. 4.10) than Tahiti.
He once said: "What I dream of is an art of balance, of

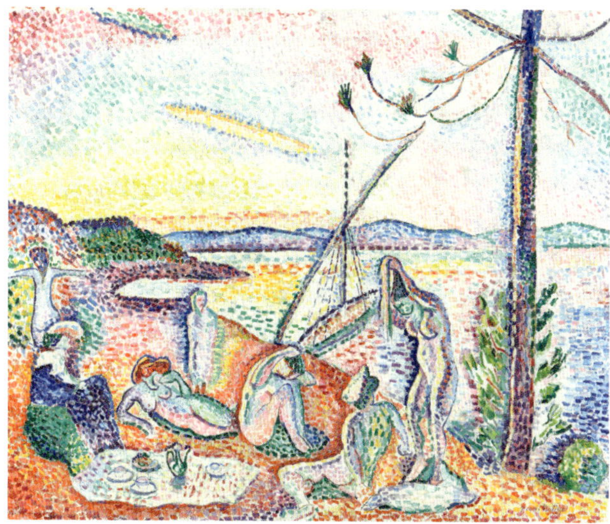

FIG. 6.13. Henri Matisse, *Luxe, Calme, et Volupté*, 1904. Oil on canvas,
38 ⅗ × 46 ⅗ in. (98 × 118.5 cm). Musée d'Orsay, Paris.

purity and serenity, devoid of troubling or depressing
subject matter."[44] He is like Gauguin in understanding
art as the expression of intuited sensations, but not raw,
undigested sensation. He reworked paintings day after
day, seeking what he called "that state of condensation of
sensations which makes a painting." Recalling Cézanne's
search for permanence, he remarked: "A rapid rendering
of a landscape represents only one moment of its exis-
tence. I prefer, by insisting upon its essential character, to
risk losing charm in order to obtain greater stability."[45]

Matisse applied pure, bright colors in bold, unblended
daubs, like mosaic tesserae, which roughly follow the
shapes with their direction. The brushstrokes are more
widely placed than Signac's, so that more of the white
ground shows through, giving his forms a less solid,
evanescent quality. Signac loved *Luxe, Calme, et Volupté*
and bought it when it was exhibited in 1905. There is a
remarkable economy here, as if Matisse is discovering
how little it takes to define form and create mood. He will
apply this economy, though not the divisionist stroke,
when he takes up *Le Bonheur de Vivre* the following year,
a large and ambitious painting akin in spirit (fig. 6.14).

In *Le Bonheur de Vivre* Matisse extended the use of
arbitrary color that Gauguin introduced. He applied
color without boundaries in blotches, as if it were watercolor. Color here does not correspond to specific visual
experience. It has been cut loose to wander wherever
the painter wants it, because the work of art is a creation
independent of visual experience. Note the aureoles of
color around certain figures, in particular the reclining

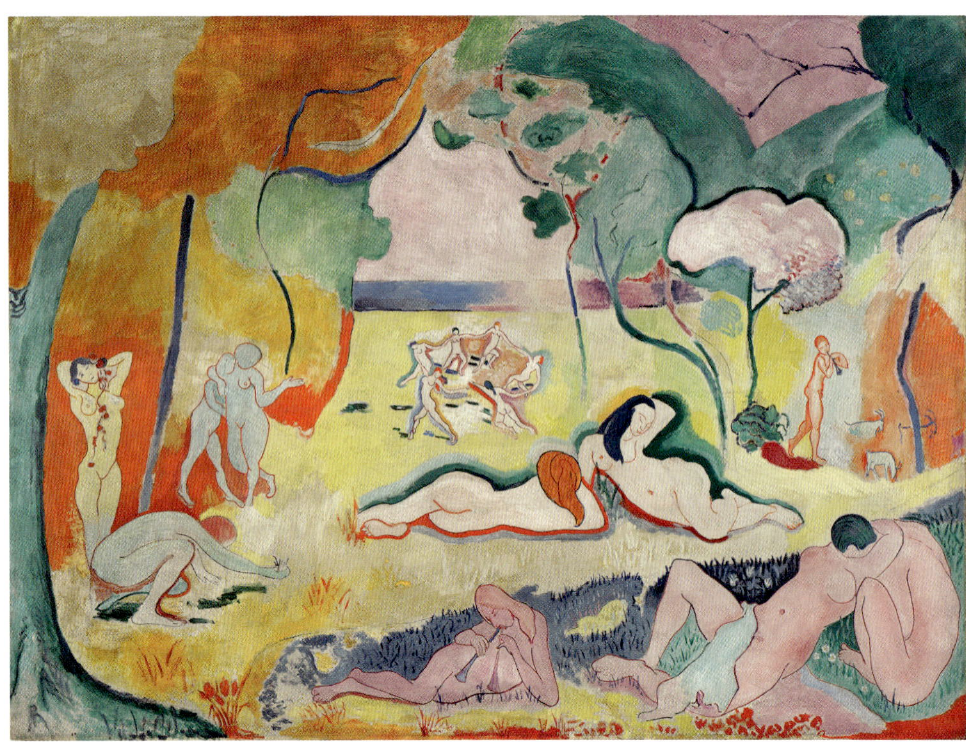

nudes. The spatial construction of the picture is taken over by the organization of the color.[46] The picture has literally taken on a life of its own. Its purpose is to give the viewer an experience, in this case an experience of happiness.[47] This is not an erotic experience; it is not titillating. Though the nudes' poses are taken from the stock *Playboy*-type repertory, they are not specific enough to arouse. It is their roundness, the arabesque of their shapes that pleases. There is no moral lesson embedded here, nor is it an invitation to debauchery.[48] It is a celebration of life, using the cues that incite a warm sense of well-being: nature, love, music, dance, pure, bright color, sensuous line. It conjures a sense of release, of escape, a Cythera without the corsets and the etiquette of proper behavior.

The tradition of the pastoral is presupposed. Beginning with Giorgione, fugitives from the city enjoying the pleasures of the countryside has been a subject of painting (see fig. 5.23). Giorgione's fantasy placed musicians in the company of two nudes, usually described as nymphs. Partaking of the same spirit is his *Sleeping Venus* (Dresden, Gemäldegalerie), who with an enviable abandon has settled herself on a bed of her own sumptuous garments for a nap in the countryside, assured that she is unobserved and oblivious to our intrusion. In Giorgione

and later, escaping the regulation of society is a key component of the pastoral.

When Watteau took up the theme, his well-dressed excursionists have sailed off to Cythera, an idyllic island overseen by Venus, who was born there (see fig. 4.10). Men and women paired as in a dance make their way to the boat that awaits them. The eighteenth-century Académie would permit no nudity in such company, but the implication of amorous dalliance is clear. Manet, in his *Luncheon on the Grass* (see fig. 5.22), by reviving Giorgione's double date with unclad ladies, had mocked both the prissiness of his viewers and the tradition itself, and Gauguin (see fig. 6.4) had dreamed it as some distant, unattainable Eden, but in both there is the same nostalgia for an untrammelled life. Matisse reasserts the delight of the pastoral, perhaps as a state of mind.

In *Le Bonheur de Vivre* there is no particularity of place or of social class or order. Here Matisse departs from the tradition and remakes it. Giorgione's musicians were Venetian aristocrats dressed in fine velvet. Watteau's excursionists were courtiers day-tripping to escape the confines and rigors of life at the palace of Versailles. Manet's students were properly attired bourgeoisie picnicking in the Bois de Boulogne. Matisse creates a place where there are no reminders of the urban or of urbanity. No clothing intrudes to establish hierarchical order. There is no nostalgia, no sense of the unattainable because there is no contrast, no memory of what has been escaped or excluded. Matisse has made his pastoral unlike any other because it is present and within reach, based in fact on a landscape in the coastal town of Collioure.

Among the pigments used here—lead white, synthetic ultramarine, vermilion, a madder lake, cobalt violet, chrome yellow, cadmium yellow, cadmium orange, viridian, a carbon black—the red and green dominate, together with the yellows. Unfortunately the cadmium yellow has degraded to tan in patches across the center and conspicuously in the upper left.[49] The scholar Lawrence Gowing, who was himself a painter, recognized that beginning in 1905 Matisse created many of his works around the polarity of red and green. After Matisse gave up divisionism, which carefully constructs the illusion of space with controlled tonal juxtapositions, he became increasingly interested in the picture surface. Red and green rise to the surface and emphasize the plane. As Gowing explained it: "Where red and green meet something happens; there is a continuous, fluorescent palpitation as between no other colours . . . the extremity of the contrast in hue between equivalent tones sets up a dazzling vibration."[50]

Among the pairs of complements, red and green behave differently because colors have inherent value: there can be no such thing as a dark yellow. When pure colors are charted in terms of their intrinsic value, yellow and orange are at the top (highest in value, lightest) and blue and purple are at the bottom. Thus when yellow is combined with its complement, purple, or orange with its complement, blue, there is a natural contrast in value that enables the depiction of light and shade or recession. Red and green on the chart, on the contrary, are equivalent in value, thus the "palpitation" and "dazzling vibration" that Gowing speaks of. In the traditional pairing of red and blue for the garments of Mary and Christ, for example, the hues behave differently. Because red is intrinsically higher in value than blue, it advances and the tones harmonize rather than vibrate.

The Impressionists, who also worked with Chevreul's theory, often depended on the contrasting complementary pairs of yellow/purple and orange/blue to create the illusion of space. In his iconic *Impression: Sunrise* Monet puts the bright spot of orange sun against blue sky and water, then daubs in orange reflections (see fig. 5.20). It shimmers, but it is also spatially convincing. In *Water Lilies, Setting Sun* the yellow reflections are set against the purple and mauve at the left, so that this otherwise virtually abstract composition takes on spatial connotations (fig. 6.15).

Van Gogh and Gauguin exploited the red/green tension, Van Gogh for the positive emotion of *La Berceuse* (see fig. 6.7) or for the negative threatening atmosphere of the *Night Café* (see fig. 6.6). Gauguin used bands of red and green to press the image forward toward the plane in *Tahitian Pastoral,* for example (see fig. 6.4). Titian, although he did not have a scientific basis yet in the sixteenth century, knew intuitively to use the red/green pair,

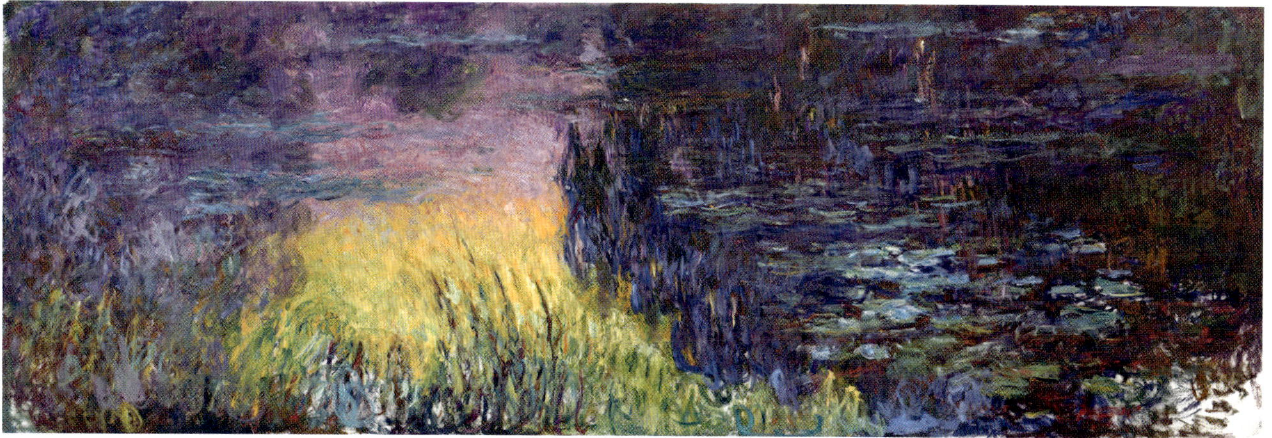

FIG. 6.15. Claude Monet, *Water Lilies, Setting Sun,* c. 1918. Oil on canvas, 6 ft. 6¾ in. × 19 ft. 8¼ in. (200 × 600 cm). Musée de l'Orangerie, Paris.

as he did often in his landscapes such as the *Bacchanal of the Andrians* (see fig. 2.28), to add sparkle to the dancing light. It also dominates the Giorgione/Titian *Pastoral Concert,* although the effect is diminished today because the green is dimmed by varnish and discoloration of the pigment (see fig. 5.23).[51] Poussin, after his Titianesque phase in the 1620s, learned to favor red/blue and yellow/blue combinations to enhance his all-important illusion of recession (see fig. 3.26).

Michelangelo, in his bold cangiante on the drapery of Daniel, makes use both of the equivalence of red and green and of the space-creating effect of yellow and purple: the yellow advances and purple violet recedes to model the knee, while the red and green scintillate, enhancing the power of the prophet's presence (see fig. 2.10). Michelangelo complicates the visual impact still more using green to shade the yellow, and then contrary to nature, red, which refuses to recede, as shadow to the violet. Matisse, if he had been able to see this tour de force after its restoration, would surely have lauded Michelangelo as an intuitive colorist.

Matisse explored the red-green dyad in *Le Bonheur de Vivre* in 1906, then again at the end of the same year in *Still Life with Vegetables* (New York, Metropolitan Museum of Art); in *Girl Reading* in 1906 (New York, Museum of Modern Art); and the following year in *The Bank* (Basel, Kunstmuseum), where both the blue and the red have been shifted toward a purplish tone, but the resonance of the colors is very spirited. The red/green couplet served his purpose of flattening as he became increasingly interested in the pattern on the surface and less and less interested in spatial recession. With the *Green Line* (see fig. 6.1) he gave us a manifesto of his view of what his painting is about. The title does not identify his wife as the sitter, but focuses instead on a formal trait and on color. The head is placed against aggressive patches of red, green, and mauve. The mauve resonates with the yellow skin of half the face, creating another vibrant duo of complementary colors. The green stripe apes the effect of chiaroscuro in traditional portraiture, where the face is divided into a lighted and a shaded side, but here both sides are equal in value, differentiated by color: one side yellowish and the other pinkish. The green stripe, furthermore, is not a highlight on the nose, as would be conventional: it is lower in value and extends all the way up the forehead to the hairline. Matisse gives us an entirely recognizable portrait head while violating all the rules. Rather than characterizing Madame Matisse, as a portrait would normally do, he gives us a study of color, giving new meaning to art for art's sake. There is nothing here of Post-Impressionist concern with expression, and he has swept beyond Impressionism's concern with rendering the world as the painter sees it. He said: "I simply put down colours that render my sensation. . . . The expressive aspect of colours imposes itself on me in a purely instinctive way."[52] This is not a record of particular conditions of weather or light and there is nothing spiritual about it. It is an experience, beautiful, pleasing, and complete, invented by the painter for the viewer.

PICASSO

Matisse is the final link in the Titian–Rubens–Delacroix chain in which color takes precedence, and Picasso was set up against him as the proponent of drawing or form. Color rises and falls in importance in the career of Picasso; throughout much of the period that concerns us here, before World War I, it is unimportant. To be sure, color was used expressively in his Blue and Rose periods. In his Blue period, when he suffered from a depression, he turned his attention to the miserable and discarded of society: paupers, outcasts, prostitutes. The silence and solitude of his forlorn and emaciated figures could not be more poignantly conveyed than with the dilute Prussian blue that is the sole colorant he used.[53] Though many painters would call blue an uplifting or inspiring color, Prussian blue is dull and lacks luminosity: Kandinsky called it "a dully sonorous, cold color."[54] It is so dark it could be substituted for black, as Gauguin regularly did. It was the perfect choice for Picasso's purpose. In a sense, it was not functioning as a hue so much as a range of value, a substance to provide a scale of light to dark for relief, as Linda Nochlin pointed out.[55]

Once he and Georges Braque embarked on the challenge of Cubism, Picasso seems to have forgotten about color, or intentionally excluded it, if Nochlin is correct: "His rejection of color in this phase should be read as a conscious repudiation of the recent vanguard past, especially of the four great Post-Impressionist masters— Cézanne, van Gogh, Gauguin and Seurat."[56] In Cubism the problems of space and texture were worked out in neutral tones of brown, gray, and black. He sometimes introduced colored passages in these years, but then painted them out.[57] After this purge, when color re-

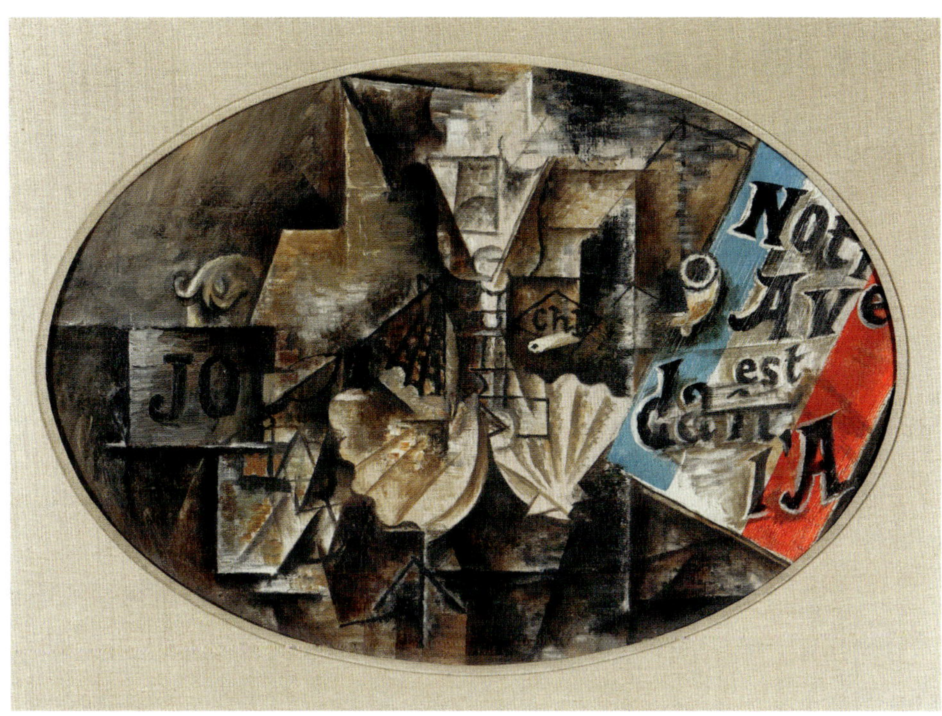

FIG. 6.16. Pablo Picasso, *Scallop Shell: Notre Avenir est dans l'Air*, 1912. Enamel and oil on canvas, 15 × 21 ¾ in. (38.1 × 55.2 cm). Metropolitan Museum of Art, New York.

appears around 1912, it is of a very different sort, "totally metamorphosed," in Nochlin's words, from that of the Post-Impressionists (fig. 6.16).[58] The Cubists wished above all to dissociate color from modeling and chiaroscuro, and to use it as a purely abstract compositional structure, but they also wished to alienate color from expression. When Picasso included the red, white, and blue reference to the French flag with the slogan "Notre Avenir est dans l'Air" ("Our Future Is in the Air") in this otherwise Cubist composition, it is not the power of the colors but its symbolism that is paramount. Copied from a brochure supporting French military aviation, it's also a cheeky response to the Italian Futurists who had exhibited in Paris in February, claiming the future for their style that celebrated the modern world of speed and motion. Picasso and Braque, who privately thought of themselves as the Wright brothers of painting, co-opted the flying machine to replace Futurism's bicycles, automobiles, and steam engines. "Picasso's color often seems to *mean* rather than, like Matisse's, simply *be*," in Nochlin's well-turned phrase.[59] The colors of the tricolor may be an indignant response to the bright colors of Futurism, but their function is not to arouse emotion. Even though the painter used a material, enamel, that would be shiny and attractive, its purpose is semiotic. The color here interrupts the Cubist composition with multilayered references.

KIRCHNER

The purpose of the art of Ernst Ludwig Kirchner is the antithesis of Matisse's. Whereas Matisse intended his world of painting to be an escape from reality, Kirchner created a painfully intensified experience of this world. Both used high-key color liberated from description, but for opposite effect. Matisse created joyous and jubilant harmonies. Kirchner explored dissonance to express his sense of the alienation and angst of modern urban society.

Kirchner was the founder in 1905 of the movement that called itself Die Brücke, with three other architecture students from the Dresden technical university: Fritz Bleyl, Karl Schmidt-Rottluff, and Erich Heckel. They were joined in 1906 by Max Pechstein and Emil Nolde. The name, meaning "The Bridge," was chosen to express their intention to bridge the old and the new, the past and the future, and to move art away from established academic practices and decadent society to a radical involvement with twentieth-century modernity. Strident color and summary drawing were the intentionally crude means they chose to make their statement. Kirchner moved to Berlin in 1911 to found an art school, which failed, and the group dissolved itself in 1913.

Street, Dresden (fig. 6.17) reflects Kirchner's admiration for Edvard Munch, whose street scenes of the 1890s captured the isolation of urban life and its anxieties (fig. 6.18).

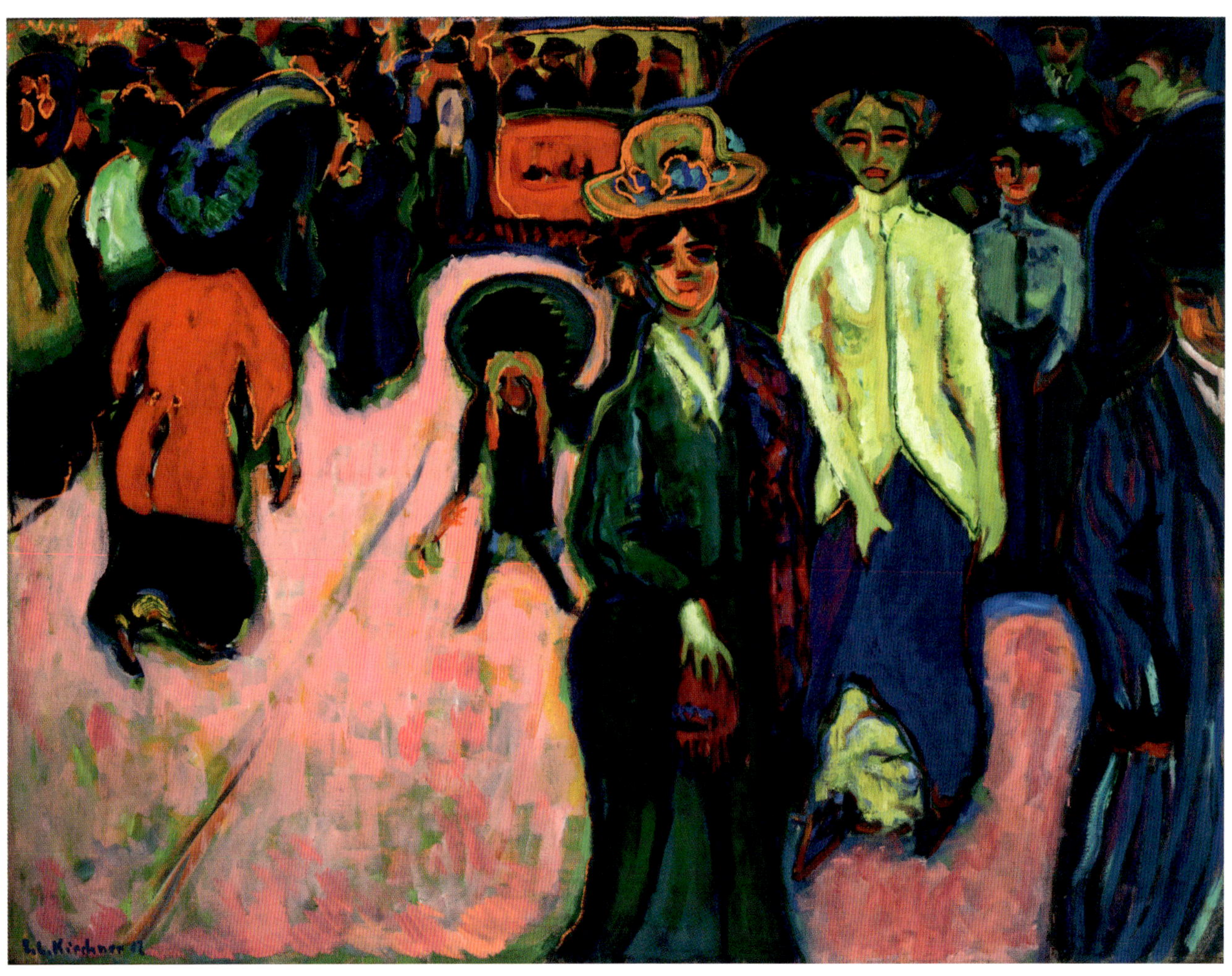

FIG. 6.17. Ernst Ludwig Kirchner, *Street, Dresden*, 1907 (reworked 1919). Oil on canvas, 59¼ × 78⅞ in. (150.5 × 200.4 cm). Museum of Modern Art, New York.

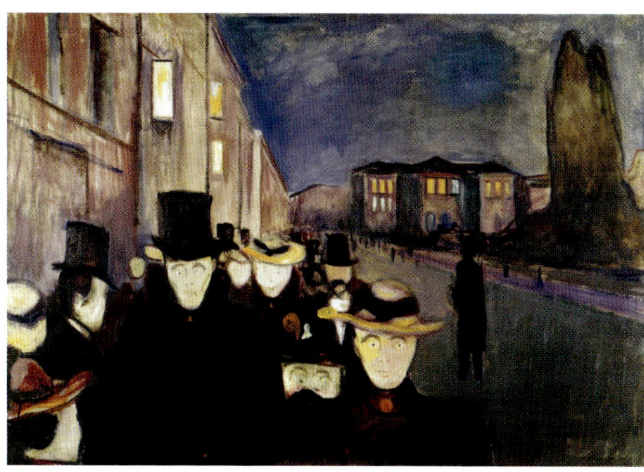

Kirchner loosens his pack of pedestrians compared to Munch's, giving them more space, only to heighten the tension by compressing that space. The alarming tilt of the street upward is accomplished by color working with accelerated perspective, indicated by the single track rising precipitously toward the red tram stopped at the top. The pink of the street is made to vibrate with daubs of green and blue. The crowd here is shoved to the sides, cut through callously by the frame, and the tilt of the street propels them forward. The space is collapsed not by traditional overlapping, as in Munch, but by the active force of color: reds reverberate in identical patches on the woman seen from behind and the tramcar, closing the interval between them. The tram moves forward visually, threatening the little girl who stands defiantly in its path—her hat nearly touches the wheels. The electrified tram was introduced in Dresden in 1901, so it was still a novelty in 1908. Youth here is as resistant to technological advances as the elders, it would seem.

Munch's black-clad automatons wear whitened masks. Kirchner lets loose a cacophony of warring orange and green (see fig. 6.17) in the face of the woman in white, echoed in the adjacent woman's hat. The woman behind to the right has a green stripe, perhaps intentionally recalling Matisse. What had been stifling Victorian social repression in Munch bursts out in aggressive self-assertion in Kirchner's twentieth-century version. Conformity, expressed by Munch in the uniform black they all wear, becomes indignant irascibility in

Kirchner's people, expressed in the disharmony of their colors and their need for space. Kirchner noted in his journal in 1919 that he had restored the painting and was pleased with it. We don't know what changes he made, but *Street, Dresden* remains a masterwork of his Die Brücke period.[60]

Kirchner wrote: "Movement is my point of departure. . . . I believe that I can capture the real, the actual quality of the objects and beings better when I observe them without their knowing." Instead of posing their models, Die Brücke artists had them walk around the studio while the painters sketched them. Kirchner went on to say: "All of the human being's visual and sensory experiences arise very much more from this state of movement, and for that reason a form that has been derived from movement speaks much more to people than the other [form], which I refer to as the academic."[61]

Kirchner took great interest in his materials and prided himself on being innovative, especially in color intensity. He related that he never modeled down with black to darken his color; if he wanted a darker red, for example, he used madder lake. He used his colors pure with only white added, either zinc white or lead white.[62] To achieve the desired intensity, he used absorbent primer and added benzene and wax to his pigments, which intensified their luminosity. Gauguin is recorded as having used these techniques. Also like Gauguin, Kirchner was opposed to the use of varnish as a protective coating. According to the museum curator in Essen in 1930, Kirchner came to the museum every two years to wash and dry his pictures to retain their matte surface.[63] We recall that Gauguin washed his paintings when he finished them. Die Brücke espoused primitivism and Gauguin was one of their admired models, so it seems likely that Kirchner was imitating Gauguin's means of eliminating gloss from his surfaces.

His interest in materials included attending to the durability and lightfastness of his pigments. He wrote a detailed letter to the manufacturer of one of his pigments reporting on a problem he had with its qualities. By the time he was painting, aniline dyes had made their way into painters' materials. They were regarded with suspicion and much discussed in terms of their lightfastness. Kirchner used them, and they have survived very well, which indicates that they were more reliable than the contemporary debate suggests.[64]

Kirchner and Vasily Kandinsky were the leaders of the two movements that constituted Expressionism. Kandinsky had studied and taught law in Moscow before he moved to Munich in 1896 and decided to pursue art at the age of thirty. In the first years of the new century, he was painting landscapes and towns; if there were figures in them, which was rare, they were highly schematized. His brushstroke was inspired by Signac's divisionism. His colors were brilliant and arbitrary. He would later write in *Concerning the Spiritual in Art* (1912): "Colours are used not because they are true to nature, but because they are necessary to the particular picture."[65]

Like Matisse and Kirchner, Kandinsky found in color the means to express what was essential, which for him was the spiritual. In his writing he established an opposition between the material and the spiritual, and attempted to show how in the various arts and spheres of life there was a turning away from nineteenth-century materialism to a more spiritual worldview.[66] Art, he believed, had to deny the material: "It is an unconscious protest against materialism, against the demand that everything should have a use and practical value."[67] For Kandinsky, the unconscious played a crucial role in his creative process. He gradually discovered that colors have intrinsic expressive qualities and intuition, and that the unconscious mind could guide him in employing them to evoke the spiritual realities. By dissolving material objects in his paintings he could move toward abstraction, toward the purification of art and spiritual expression. He worked his way gradually away from material realism: "Modelling was abandoned. In this way the material object was made more abstract and an important step forward was achieved."[68] He came to the recognition that "objects harmed my pictures."[69] By 1914 he had achieved his goal of total abstraction. In a lecture that year, accompanying an exhibition of his paintings in Cologne, he looked back: "Objects began to dissolve more and more in my pictures. This can be seen in nearly all the pictures of 1910."[70]

For Kandinsky, colors have symbolic value. Deploring the competition, vanity, and greed of the world and the striving for material gain and fame in the art world, he invested in color the power to overcome materialism with spiritualism. Blue in particular inspires inwardness: "The power of profound meaning is found in blue, and first in its physical movements (1) of retreat from the spectator, (2) of turning in upon its own centre. The inclination of blue to depth is so strong that its inner appeal is stronger when its shade is deeper."[71] He equates colors with feelings and also with the sound of particular musical instruments: "Light warm red has a certain similarity to medium yellow, alike in texture and appeal, and gives a feeling of strength, vigour, determination, triumph. In music, it is a sound of trumpets, strong, harsh, and ringing."[72]

Like many of his contemporaries and predecessors such as Van Gogh, Kandinsky believed that painting should resemble music, the most abstract of the arts, and through color it could achieve a harmony similar to music. He initially admired Richard Wagner, and then came under the spell of Arnold Schoenberg.[73] For the titles of his paintings he used terms borrowed from music—"Impression," "Improvisation," "Composition"—and in defining them he emphasized the unconscious nature of his creating. When he called a painting *Improvisation,* he meant that it was "a largely unconscious, spontaneous expression of inner character, the non-material nature."[74]

In 1911 Kandinsky formed the group called Der Blaue Reiter (The Blue Rider), together with Franz Marc, August Macke, and others, which espoused Kandinsky's ideas promoting modern art; the relationship of art to music; the spiritual associations of color; and an intuitive approach to painting. Although it was short-lived because Marc and Macke were killed in World War I, and Kandinsky and other members who were Russian émigrés were forced to return to Russia, it was important in providing exhibition opportunities and in the formulation of German Expressionism, along with Die Brücke.

When he began *Painting with White Border,* Kandinsky had just returned from a trip home, visiting family in Odessa and friends in Moscow (fig. 6.19). He was attempting to record his feeling about Russia and his conviction about its messianic role in leading the way to the triumph of the spiritual. He embedded two specifically Russian motifs, abstracted beyond recognition, that he had used in earlier paintings and that appear in the numerous preparatory studies he made. The troika, that Russian vehicle pulled by a team of three horses abreast, appears in upper-left center as three brownish humps surrounded with gold. In nineteenth-century literature the troika had become a symbol of Russia as the deliverer of spiritual salvation and renewal. A pencil drawing

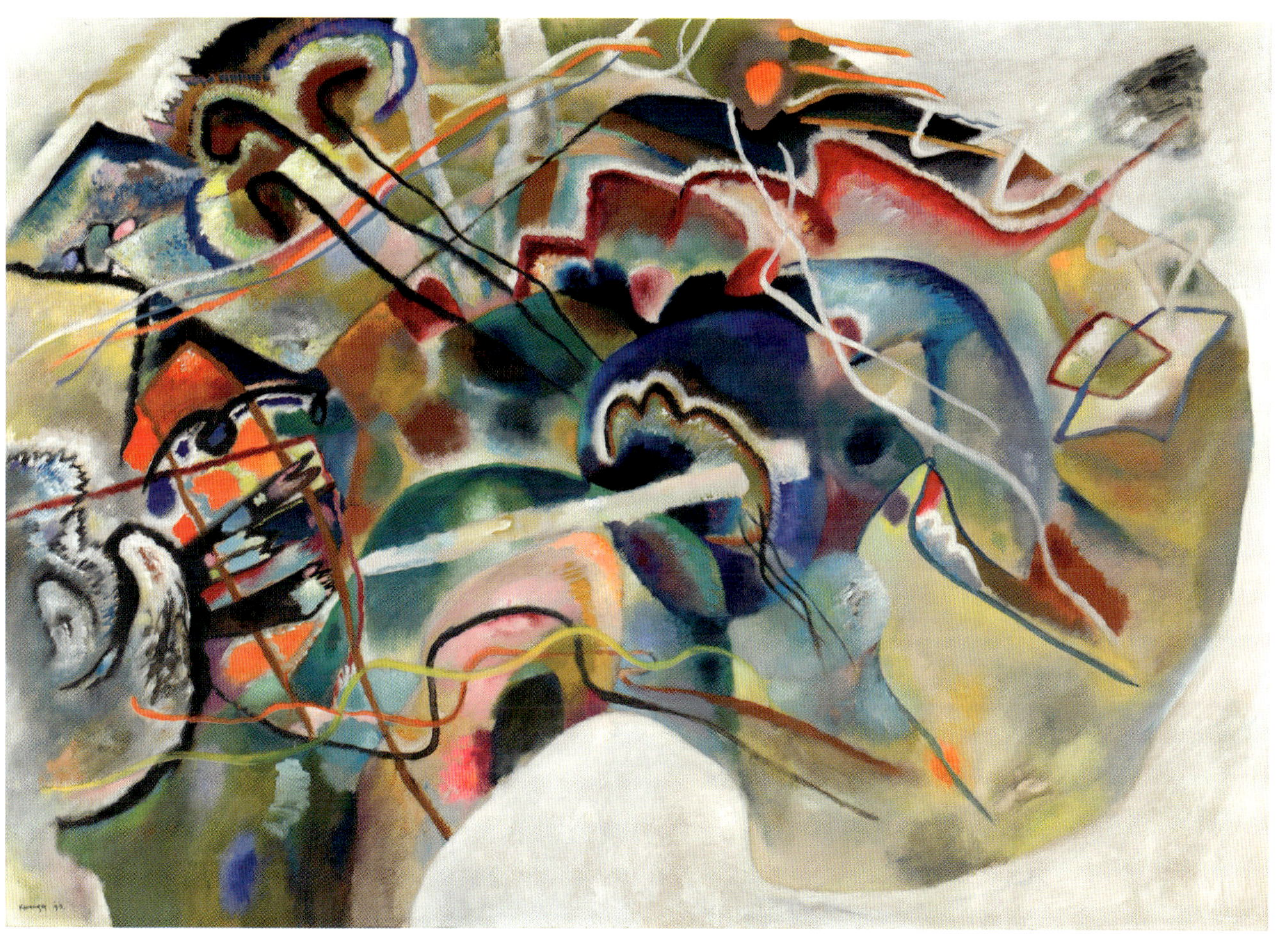

FIG. 6.19. Vasily Kandinsky, *Painting with White Border,* 1913. Oil on canvas, 55¼ × 78⅞ in. (140.3 × 200.3 cm). Solomon R. Guggenheim Museum, New York.

shows the painter practicing the radical reduction to a three-humped line. At the center is a white diagonal that represents the lance of Saint George slaying the dragon. Kandinsky had painted Saint George, the patron saint of Russia, repeatedly in works on glass and in oil in preceding years, so that by 1912 he was able to dissolve the form into this pictograph. The lance is aimed at a black claw with pink fingers that emerges from the densely colored mass at the left, the remnant of the dragon.[75]

Despite his trust in intuition and the unconscious, Kandinsky prepared his paintings with the greatest care. He struggled for five months with the preparatory stage of *Painting with White Border.* He made at least fifteen studies, but he wasn't satisfied. He came to the idea of the white border only after months of working on preparatory studies: "It was only after nearly five months . . . when it suddenly dawned on me what was missing—the white edge."[76] When he finally began painting, he was very sure of how he wanted to proceed. Although he was accustomed to using darker grounds, sometimes even black, here he applied a white ground, which he used as a luminous element, glowing through thinly applied washes and giving an overall radiance. He worked from light to dark, sometimes adding thinly painted highlights over areas already painted in dark colors.[77]

He laid in outlines of the composition with a wide, soft graphite pencil, drawing directly on the white ground, and he made no changes at the drawing stage. Conservators have found a great range in his construction of the colors, from only one or two pigments to complex mixtures. An opaque green in the lower left is composed of two very thin layers: the darker green contains ten different pigments, the lighter green layer on top contains six or more pigments. He must have created this mixture himself for a carefully considered visual effect, because no manufactured product would be so complex.[78] He wrote about his use of green in this painting:

> It was quite unconsciously—and, as I see now, purposefully—that I used so much green: I had no desire to introduce into this admittedly stormy picture too great unrest. Rather, I wanted, as I noticed later, to use turmoil to repress repose. I even used too much green, and especially too much Paris [Prussian] blue (a dully sonorous, cold color), with the result that it was only with exertion and difficulty that I was able to balance and correct the excess of these colors.[79]

The white border was drawn in pencil, then painted with zinc white. It is Kandinsky's genius that none of this care in preparation and execution diminishes the spontaneity of the image.

CONCLUSION

With the collapse of the state system of control and sponsorship of art, artists were thrown to their own devices to find a market. With their subjects and their styles no longer subject to institutional approval, they were free to express what was important to them in their personal idiom. Impressionism turned out to be the last style that represented appearances. Whereas the Impressionists had engaged with and celebrated bourgeois life in the renewed city of Paris, the Post-Impressionists, disillusioned with what they regarded as the materialism of a sullied world, escaped like Gauguin to a distant, "primitive" culture, or at least to the provinces, like Cézanne and Van Gogh. Matisse sojourned in Morocco and eventually resided in Nice, but wherever he located himself he divorced the world of his art from ordinary life, creating an aesthetic harmony complete in itself. Color for him had no symbolic value, only decorative. Kirchner expressed his attitude toward technology and modern life by deforming color, space, and human form.

These painters rejected the classic academic tools of illusionism—chiaroscuro, modeling, and perspective—and explored the expressive power of distortion, exaggeration, and outright anti-naturalism. They discovered how little it takes to depict form and convey content. For Kandinsky, objects themselves became unwanted tethers to materiality, from which he gradually freed himself. Color, he said, "is a power that directly influences the soul."[80]

As long as the goal of art remained the imitation of nature, drawing was generally more highly regarded than color. When the painters liberated themselves from the traditional role, that hierarchy was reversed. No longer the recorders of visual reality, they had become the champions of higher spiritual values. Each of them sought release from material reality, and each found in nonrepresentational color the means to transcend it. Violating the rules of nature by painting a field red or a face green signals that we are in another realm. Beauty can be separated from nature, and aesthetic harmony can become a manifestation of the spiritual. In times past, when the superiority of drawing versus color was being deliberated in the various iterations we have traced of the disegno–colore or Poussinistes–Rubénistes or Ingres–Delacroix debate, color was often despised because it was held to be subversive of reason. Its virtue now became its very lack of contamination with reason. Freed from the responsibility of representing the external phenomenal world, these painters delved inside themselves. They trusted the promptings of intuition to access the spiritual, and they called upon the unconscious mind as a guide. The inherent expressive properties of color were the means to escape the dominance of conscious, rational thought. Both Gauguin and Kandinsky gave voice to these discoveries, which would be seminal to the art of the twentieth century as it developed. Color has arrived.

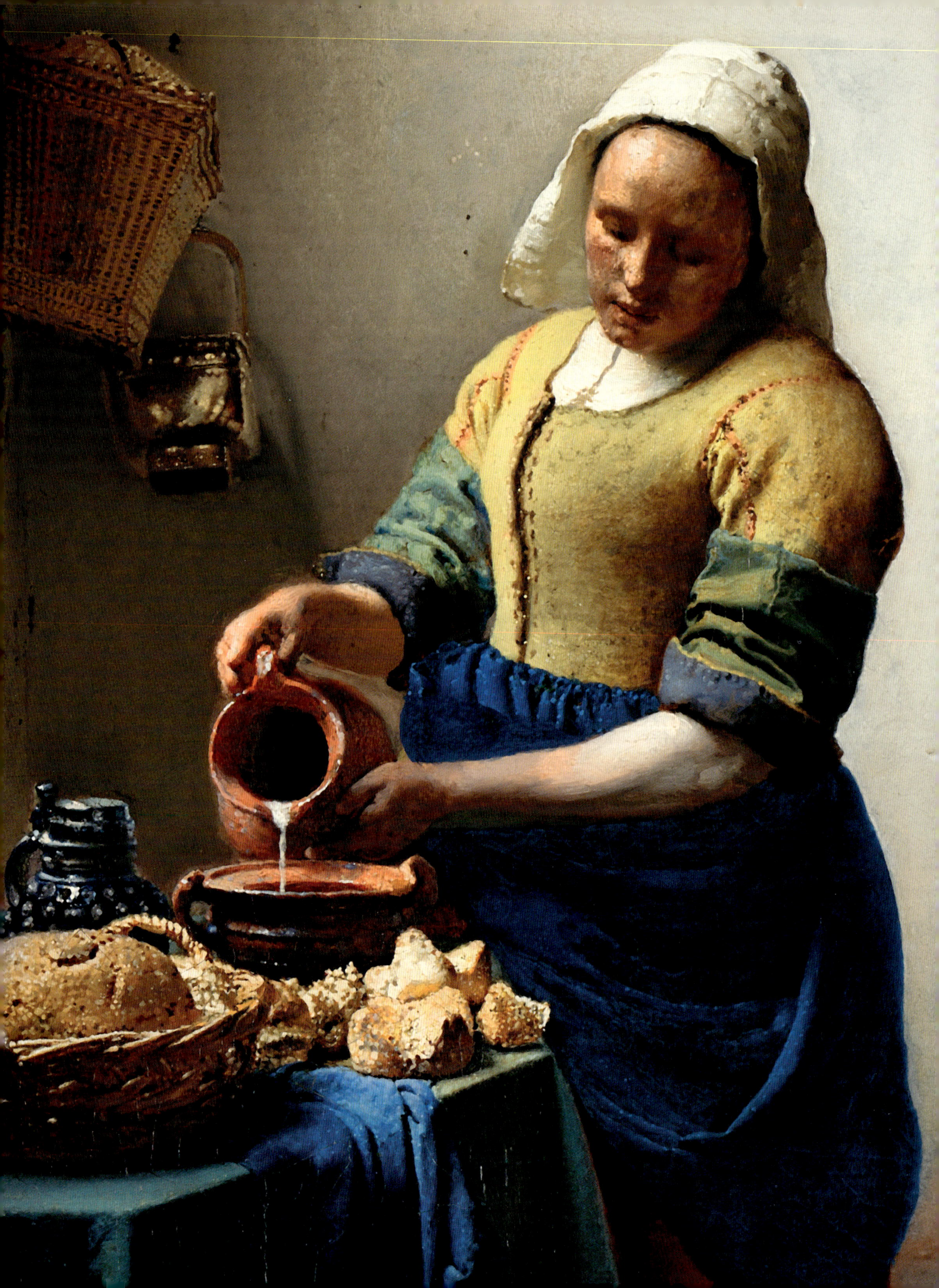

Postscript

Across the five centuries we have traversed, we have seen color evolve in ways that mirror the shift from reliance on a Christian worldview to an inner, personal search for meaning. The quest for spiritual values has moved from external and universal to internal and individual, but throughout, the painters have been seeking to express them in their art. From a system of symbols that were understood across the culture, through stages of naturalism that were based on shared experience, we arrive in the modern world at colors used to express the feelings of the creator, without regard for their representational value.

The spiritual reality to which the coloring of Lorenzo Monaco and Fra Angelico bore witness was universally acknowledged at their time and place. As coloring became increasingly naturalistic, it made the world the painter depicted recognizable to the viewing community. Even when the artists' subjects were imaginative fantasies such as those of the Rococo painters, their resemblance to (if not their exact identity with) experienced reality opened them to the viewers' access. The preference for recording the transitory that emerged in the nineteenth century can be seen as reflecting agnostic doubt about permanence and the knowability of universal truths. Much the same movement could be traced, of course, in music and the literary arts, or other spheres of human endeavor, but isn't nonrepresentational color the quintessential emblem for our replacement of external authority with steadfast confidence in the individual to deal with questions of ultimate reality?

We have observed a constant seesaw between new opportunities for painters and new forms of circumscription on their freedom. While technical innovation, broadened markets, and newly available materials expanded their options, they had constantly to respond to the demands to glorify religion or the state, and answer the needs of the patron or the taste of unknown clients. Above all, the need to make a living hovered. What we observe is the boundless inventiveness with which artists have met these demands and exploited their options.

The history of *materials* begins here with painters working in the late medieval system, described by Cennini, in which the palette was limited to about a dozen pigments applied meticulously in the medium of egg tempera. Although the finite choice of pigments, which were available to everyone, enforced a certain

Fig. 0.2 detail

uniformity, these masters found ways to distinguish their production from the competition by manipulating the grind of the pigments and utilizing other trade secrets. Within these seemingly highly restrictive bounds, they gave life to visions of otherworldly splendor that brightened the lives of the worshippers paying homage to the deity and saints represented in them.

Oil opened up a new world of naturalism that expanded over the centuries as painters explored its luminosity, its transparency, its viscosity, its variable texture. Improved transportation and communication made materials from distant places available or cheaper. We have traced the story of indigo, for instance, from India as part of the spice trade to the Caribbean, then back to India, then finally to the synthetic replacement manufactured in Europe at considerable reduction in cost. The much-prized ultramarine had always come from Afghanistan, but the supply could fluctuate; there were times when, because the trade routes were disrupted, it became unavailable and painters had to rely on stored caches or generate substitutes—as in expanding the uses of the difficult to handle smalt. There were times when ultramarine simply became prohibitively expensive, a situation the French government finally addressed in the 1820s with its competition to find a synthetic substitute. In those infrequent instances before the modern era when new pigments became available, either through trade or invention, painters were quick to make use of them, as they were when chemists synthesized and factories mass-produced a wide range of new colors in the nineteenth century. Soon the look of paintings was revolutionized because painters could individualize their palettes in ways not possible before. With so many pigments and pigment combinations now available in tubes, artists developed their own personal preferences, and thus their styles diverged from one another to create a stunningly abundant buffet for the buyer to choose from.

As with materials, *making* was hampered in the early workshops by the need for diversified skills, which the master had to delegate, and for apprentices and assistants to do these tasks, which he had to oversee. He was required to be an effective manager as well as an expert craftsman. He needed a keen awareness of what was being produced in the other workshops and of innovations that his shop would need to adapt and hopefully surpass. He was the one who conceived the designs. His judgment determined how far to push the accepted template to catch the eye of the prospective patron, but not violate his sense of decorum. When that patron was the Church or the state, he walked a fine line between supplying the expected and proffering creative innovation. If he misjudged, it could cost him future patronage.

When materials such as ground pigments and primed canvas became available in shops, the workshop could be consolidated. The master had to be vigilant to assure he was getting only the best quality from his supplier, but his assistants could focus more on art than on craft, and he could limit the number of assistants according to his needs. He might prefer to work alone, allowing him to experiment, until it became the norm to have no one around except whatever students he might choose to instruct. For the enforced camaraderie of the workshop, painters working alone sought companionship and professional conversation in common meeting places, often cafés. But they also sought more desirable or exotic homes, such as in the South of France or, in the case of Gauguin, the French colonies of the South Seas, where his making was solitary indeed. What artists created could depend more on their inner vision, but it had always to be in touch with their culture. The painter who tried to paint just what he wanted often found that he was the only person who wanted it. Before the nineteenth century the idiosyncratic genius was rarely rewarded in the marketplace, but as the artist's personal vision gradually became the subject of art, clients aligned themselves with artists whose aesthetic expression appealed to them—and to their pocketbooks—even if the creator was working half a world away.

The *market*, in the form of the patron, the client, or a distant anonymous buyer, always shaped what painters could make. Painters had always to be businesspeople, proficient at determining the balance point between the cost of materials and labor and the price the work could bring, and adept at selling their products. The on spec market of the seventeenth century that largely replaced the patronage system of the Renaissance freed painters to work without direction, but they no longer had a guarantee that what they produced would be paid for. Efficient working procedures and prudent choice of materials could make the difference between success and bankruptcy. A change in the taste of the public could spell disaster if the painter did not respond to it, as Rembrandt sadly would learn.

With the development of marketplaces, first in the North, dealers could assume the burden of selling, but at the cost to the painters of their percentage. They could advise about what would sell and how much the buyer would pay. But painters pushed the buyer to accept what they envisioned as often as the other way around. Though their vision usually reflected the worldview of their times, we rejoice in those moments when an innovative genius created something quite out of step and succeeded in selling it. One thinks of Titian, Caravaggio, Rembrandt, or even Chardin and Greuze.

Meaning, at the beginning of our period, was inherent in the narrative represented and admitted little interpretation by the maker. Nevertheless those Renaissance artists found ways to individualize their images in the way they used their materials. The story we have told here is of how in increments that interpretation became increasingly individualized, reflecting and revealing the view of the maker through the deployment of materials. At the same time that the community dictates through its willingness to buy, artists seek to direct the taste of a now global community with their version of their shared experience of the human condition. It is obvious that the painters project their vision in the choice of subject, but we have seen that their materials and how they use them is how they make that vision visible.

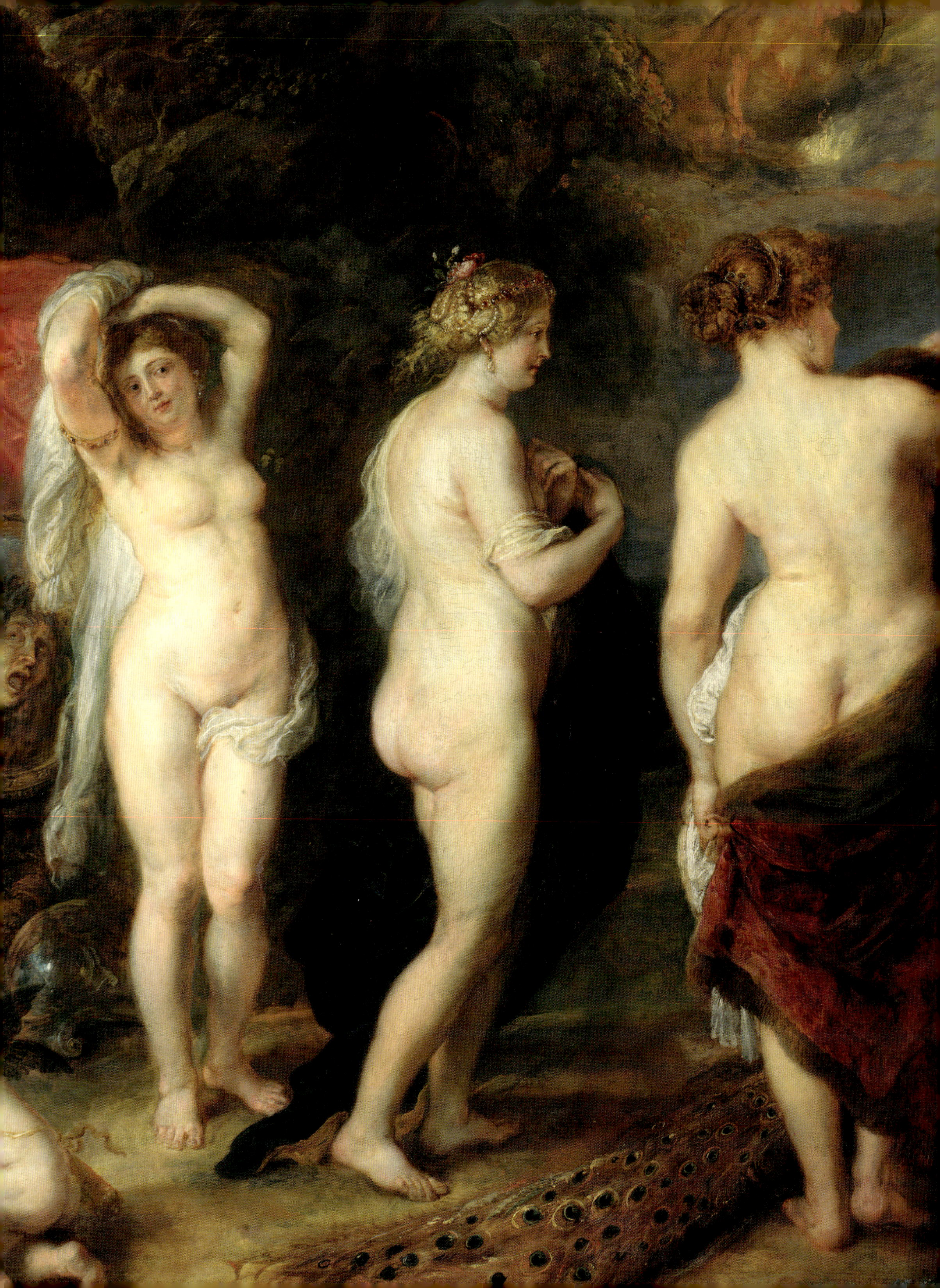

Notes

1. Beck [1988]. Beck extended his argument in book form in Beck and Daley [1996].
2. The lunette of the ancestors of Christ, Mathan and Eleazar, on the entrance wall was the trial piece cleaned in the spring of 1980. Pietrangeli [1994].
3. Samples are still needed to understand the unexpected or the unusual or the details of lead tin yellows or yellow lakes, or antimony grays, for example.
4. The groundbreaking study of Jill Dunkerton and Marika Spring [1998] tabulating the imprimatura of 140 paintings, primarily in the National Gallery, London, is now being expanded to a database with the collaboration of other key collections.
5. Falomir [2006], 147: "A good copy cost more than many originals, and many painters in Madrid, especially those who worked for the king, found in the production of copies from originals in the royal collection an efficient means of supplementing their income."
6. See the creative use of infrared and x-ray images of Giovanni Bellini images by Keith Christiansen [2004] and by George Goldner [2004], both in Humfrey [2008].
7. McTighe [2014], 11.
8. New imaging technologies are making us increasingly aware of inky washes that underlie the strokes of opaque tempera, which slowed the laborious process even more. An example, with excellent images, is the study of Giotto in Berrie et al. [2015].
9. Cennini [2015], chaps. 64–65, 95–97, explains how to make these brushes. Cennini warns that the bristles should be taken from a white pig because they are better than the black ones, "but make sure they are from a domestic pig."
10. Henri Delavallée remembered Gauguin's conversation in 1886. Christensen [1993], 87.
11. See Galassi and Walmsley [2009]. On the "penello mozzetto," see 118–19.
12. Bois [1990], 22, quoting Louis Aragon, *Henri Matisse: A Novel* (1972), 2:308, dubbed this Matisse's "quantity-quality equation."
13. For a discussion of the implications of the x-rays and cross-sections of *The Tempest*, see Settis [1990].
14. I explored this aspect of Titian's facture, especially its role in his Counter-Reformation altarpieces, in Hall [2011].
15. Reff [1960] discussed the painters whom Cézanne referred to or whose work he had in reproductions in his studio.
16. Boime [1965].
17. Shiff [1984], xiv.

CHAPTER 1. THE FIFTEENTH CENTURY

1. Bent [2000] transcribed and translated the inscription and suggested Domenico di Zanobi as the patron who dedicated the altar to his forebear.
2. O'Malley [2005] has studied surviving contracts in detail and drawn conclusions that have informed us richly about Trecento and Quattrocento practice. Almost all the surviving contracts are either for altarpieces to adorn the patron's chapel, or frescoes for an ecclesiastical setting or a palace.
3. O'Malley [2005], 42–44.
4. These punches were made in the workshop and handed down from generation to generation. They were sufficiently distinctive to make possible the identification of a workshop in which a painting originated. See Skaug [1983].
5. O'Malley [2005], table 2B and 49–57.
6. Cennini advises painters always to "buy solid vermilion, and not crushed or ground. The reason? Because more often than not you are cheated either with red lead or crushed brick." Cennini [2015], 64.
7. The earliest documented vendecolori so far is from 1493, according to Louisa Matthew (oral communication with the author).
8. Chambers [1971], in his collection of 127 contracts, transcribed and translated the contract between the painter and the Company of the Purification, nos. 27, 53–55.
9. O'Malley [2005], 70.
10. The technical analysis of the *Coronation* confirms that the technique follows the procedure described by Cennini: the pigments were used pure with only the addition of white, and no black was found in the shadows. It was noted that the quality and quantity of ultramarine and of other precious materials used indicate that it was made for a very rich patron. Ciatti, Frosinini, and Riitano [1998], 89–98, esp. 95.
11. Isochromatism: from "iso- (equal) color." Shearman [1987], 151.
12. I described the Cennini coloring system first in Hall [1992], 14–29.
13. Burnstock [1988], 58–65. There is no mention in the literature I have found of a similar alternation in the Uffizi *Coronation*.
14. Vermilion (mercuric sulfide) and lead-tin yellow were not incompatible with lime, but they are rarely found in frescoes.
15. Gage [1993], 30–31, discussed the prohibitions against mixing in ancient texts and the reasons for the assumption that "mixtures were not common in ancient times."

See the discussion in chaps. 2 and 3 here of broken color.

16. Cennini [2015], 190: "How to paint faces."

17. Cennini [2015], 117.

18. Cennini [2015], 190: "The faces of young people with fresh flesh tone, should be bound . . . with egg from city hens because they are whiter yolks than those that country or farm hens produce: those are good, because of their ruddiness, for binding flesh tones of old or brown-skinned people."

19. O'Malley [2005], 90–96, provides a very helpful discussion of subcontracting and the legal implication of the *sua mano* ("his hand") clause.

20. "[Where] you modify a color with a very little white, there you will also add black in the same way, on the opposite side, in an appropriate place. In fact, he who allows that prominent [features] emerge through this distribution, so to speak of black and white, becomes more discerning. Follow then, with equal parsimony in the additions until you perceive you have achieved what is sufficient." Alberti [2013], 69, para. 46.

21. Borsook [1980], 89. The method actually used in this case was stacco, an older version of the now preferred strappo. With stacco some of the accompanying plaster was removed, but strappo is accomplished by removing only the skin with the colors.

22. Colalucci [1994], 35.

23. Vasari [1960], 222: "Therefore let those who desire to work on the wall work boldly in fresco and not retouch in the dry, because, besides being a very poor thing in itself, it renders the life of the pictures short."

24. Minoan scholars found that the sinopia showed through the plaster on top when it was wet. I am grateful to Maria Pareja for this information. See P. Angelicas et al., "The Preliminary Designs of the Theran Wall-Paintings," in *Paintbrushes: Wall-Painting and Vase-Painting of the 2nd millennium BC in Dialogue*, ed. A. Vlachopoulos (Athens: Society for the Promotion of Theran Studies, 2013), 140–43.

25. The most dramatic case of sinopie being revealed occurred in the Campo Santo in Pisa. During World War II the roof was bombed and the lead melted, stripping the frescoes off the walls and revealing the underlying sinopie.

26. Bambach [1999a], 209; Borsook [1980], 88. At almost the same time, Domenico Veneziano frescoed *John the Baptist and Saint Francis* for the Cavalcanti Chapel on the tramezzo in Santa Croce. (The wall with this fresco was moved by Vasari and is now in the Museo Santa Croce.) Domenico's spolveri are clearly visible on close inspection, particularly in the face of Saint John.

27. Alberti [2013].

28. The sky at the top of the wall is a pale blue. The pigment has not been identified, but we can rule out azurite because it would have turned greenish on the damp wall. Indigo, or a pale wash of ultramarine, which Cennini described as "ashen" and was not expensive, seem the most likely possibilities. Cennini [2015], 90: "But bear in mind that the first two drainings, if you have got good lapis lazuli, are worth, this same blue, eight ducats per ounce; the last two drainings are worse than ash."

29. Zuffi [1991], 53.

30. On Neri di Bicci and the operation of his workshop, see Thomas [1995].

31. Ruda [1984], 210–36; Rowlands [1989], 53–83.

32. Bambach [1999a], 233.

33. Bambach [1999a], 239, summarized: "By the last quarter of the fifteenth century, a greater variety of painters, from diverse regions of Italy, more or less routinely employed cartoons, transferring them by means of both *spolvero* and *calco* (stylus tracing or *incisione indiretta*). Notable examples of cartoon use arise in the works of Melozzo da Forlì, Andrea Mantegna, Andrea Verrocchio, Antonio and Piero Pollaiuolo, Pietro Perugino, Bernardino Pinturicchio, Francesco di Giorgio, Domenico Ghirlandaio, Filippino Lippi, Vittorio Carpaccio, Luca Signorelli, Bartolomeo della Gatta, Girolamo Genga, and Leonardo."

34. A pricked cartoon for *Faith* in the series of allegorical virtues survives in the Uffizi. See Bambach [1999a], pl. II.

35. The purchase of paper for cartoons for his frescoes in the Gianfigliazzi Chapel is recorded in Baldovinetti's account book on April 28, 1471, in Bambach [1999b], 42–43.

36. Vasari [1963], 2:97.

37. Ames-Lewis [1981], 108.

38. O'Malley [2013], 87. Filippino had a second workshop in Florence besides this one attached to his house, which surely had other work, but the inventory has not been found. For the inventory, see Carl [1987], 384–90.

39. The *Adoration of the Magi* has recently been studied and restored, and much was learned about Leonardo's procedure. See Bellucci [2017].

40. The *Mona Lisa* and the *Madonna and Child with Saint Anne* as well as the original version of the *Madonna of the Rocks* were still in his possession when he died in France in 1519, and they therefore became the property of the king and eventually of the Louvre.

41. Bambach [1999b], 116–18; Bambach [1999a], 105–33.

42. Bambach [1999a], 283–95, esp. 286. "As can be deduced, 'substitute cartoons' were blank sheets of paper, placed underneath the '*ben finite cartone*' (or any other drawing, print, or pattern to be transferred), that were either pricked or stylus-incised simultaneously with the design on top."

43. Reiss [2005], 54–55. The appreciation of cartoons and drawings that began in the Cinquecento is evidence for the rising status of the artist. As he came to be acknowledged as an inventor more than an artisan, collectors became interested in the creative process.

44. The earliest use of oil in an Italian painting that the laboratory has found to date is in the 1420s in Masolino; see Strehlke [2007], 14. We now know that oil had been in use for centuries; see Roy [2000].

45. Nuttall [2004], 254–60, appen. 1 and 2.

46. Tura is documented as working in the studiolo at the villa of Belfiore from 1459–63. Dunkerton [1994], 115 and 198–99.

47. Dunkerton, Foister, and Gordon [1994], 198. The *Baptism of Christ* in the National Gallery, London, has been examined and found to be in tempera, though it is possible that there is a little oil in the glazes in the landscape.

48. The contract, dated 20 December 1466, originally published by Gaetano Milanesi, *Sulla storia dell'arte Toscana, scritti varj* (Soest, Neth.: Davaco, 1973), 299–301, was cited by Glasser [1977] and Hall [1992], 247n12.

49. As reported by the National Gallery, London, study of Van Eyck's *Portrait of Arnolfini and His Wife* and *Man in a Turban*; see Billinge et al. [1997], 38. On imprimatura, they remark: "Painting on a light surface is regarded as a fundamental characteristic of Early Netherlandish painting technique" (23).

50. White [2000], 101–5, esp. 104.

51. The following is based upon the analysis described by Gifford, Metzger, and Delaney [2013]. I am indebted to Melanie Gifford for clarifying some points in personal correspondence.

52. Bouts, for example, was found to have used lead white with ultramarine for the

Virgin's robe in the *Virgin and Child* in the National Gallery, London. Bomford, Roy, and Smith [1986], 56.

53. Filarete, trans. in Eastlake [1960], 66; Nuttall [2004], 162.

54. Hartt, Corti, and Kennedy [1964], 27–46.

55. Cecchi [1999], 82–83. Baldovinetti's *Annunciation* in the chapel is also on oak.

56. Dunkerton, Foister, and Gordon [1994], 201–3.

57. Dunkerton and Roy [1996] found that all the artists in their study, which included Filippino, Ghirlandaio, and Michelangelo, used a drying oil for darker and more transparent shades of red, green, and blue. They noted that it can be difficult to distinguish by analysis whether egg and oil have been employed in distinct layers or combined to make tempera grassa (30).

58. Tongiorgi Tomasi and Hirschauer [2002], 108–17, 24. The plants along the lower edge can be identified as acacia, bulrush, mallow or hollyhock, dandelion, iris, poppy, strawberry and violet, various symbols of suffering, death, and redemption.

59. Fra Bartolomeo, *Madonna and Child with the Infant Baptist* (New York, Metropolitan Museum of Art, c. 1497). See Nuttall [2004], 133–35. For technical analysis of Memling, see Campbell [1993].

60. Dunkerton, Foister, and Gordon [1994], 203.

61. Baldini and Casazza [1986], 49.

62. Kline [2011].

63. Dunkerton and Roy's Table of Results shows that the dark-green carpet was painted in "artificial malachite in egg with some walnut oil." Elsewhere a red lake is bound in egg with a little oil. Dunkerton and Roy [1996], 24.

64. In the same Table of Results, Ghirlandaio also used walnut oil for a dark green, and in a red lake glaze. Dunkerton and Roy [1996], 25.

65. This was pointed out to me by Barbara Berrie.

66. He worked from his Florentine workshop until 1501, when demand in Perugia made it good business to open a second workshop there, which he operated for a decade. O'Malley [2007], 112.

67. Letter from Agostino Chigi to Mariano Chigi, 1500, quoted in Crowe and Cavalcaselle [1871], 49.

68. Vasari [1963], 2:125.

69. Summarized by the authors of the study of Perugino's works in French collections, Martin and Rioux [2004], 49–50. For example, his reds were built up as we see in Flanders: the bottom layer is an opaque vermilion, followed by a middle layer of mixed vermilion and red lake, finished with a red lake glaze. For his greens he applied a thick layer of what is probably verdigris mixed with lead-tin yellow and some white lead, glazed with a thinner layer of a mixture of copper green and lead-tin yellow. He would typically use azurite under lapis lazuli, presumably to economize. They also reported finding tinted imprimatura in his *Marriage of the Virgin* at Caen, dated 1504. Vasari says that Perugino was a member of Verrocchio's workshop, where oil was explored early by Leonardo and also by Lorenzo di Credi.

70. Smyth [1979], 230–34.

71. For the history and context, see Hall [1992], 85–91.

72. See, for example, Roy, Spring, and Plazzotta [2004]. Raphael has been found to use an imprimatura tinged with yellow like that described in the following note, which was typical of Perugino.

73. A slightly yellowish imprimatura has been found on the Pavia Altarpiece in the National Gallery, London, dated sometime between 1496 and 1500; see Roy [2003]. For other paintings by Perugino, see Mottin, Laval, and Martin [2007].

Van Hout [1998], 200, gives this definition of "imprimatura": "By *imprimatura* most often a coloured isolation layer is understood. It consists of pigments bound in an oil medium. Applied onto chalk or gesso grounds, this layer prevents the medium in the subsequent paint layers from being absorbed by the ground. The *imprimatura* can be either opaque or transparent. It covers the surface of the painting completely. If the chalk or gesso layer has been omitted and only one pigmented isolation layer is applied, this layer can be called 'ground.'"

74. Dunkerton [2004], 200–201, on the *Transfiguration* and *Pietà with Two Angels* (both in the Museo Correr, Venice): "The palette and general tonal range . . . are little different from Bellini's works known to have been painted in egg. Transitions between tones may be more smoothly blended, but the forms have usually been built up in the same way as in tempera. Passages of hatched application are visible, especially in the highlights, and the modeling of drapery folds is achieved by the admixture of white or by *cangiante* effects. . . . Moreover, it should not be thought that the tempera paintings necessarily predate those in oil. In common with many Italian painters of his generation, Bellini kept both media in his repertoire throughout his career."

75. Poldi and Villa [2011], 30–31.

76. See Christiansen [1998], 39–61; Aikema, Brown, and Scirè [2000]; and Lucco [2004], 75–94.

77. For example, there is no azurite under the lapis lazuli, and the green on the central angel is modeled with white lead added to malachite, very different from the elaborate glazing in green in the Pesaro Altarpiece. See Dunkerton [2004]. This is an exemplary article by a conservator explaining technique to art historians. See also Volpin and Lazzarini [1994]; and Volpin and Stevanato [1994].

78. Dunkerton [2004], 201.

79. Galassi [1998], 65–68. Dunkerton [2004], 202–3, has cited cases where underdrawing does not show through the paint layers. On underdrawing versus undermodeling, see Galassi [2001].

80. Dunkerton [2004], 205.

81. Dunkerton [2004], 218n69, lists examples as: San Zaccaria Altarpiece, *Pietà* (Venice, Accademia), *Virgin and Child with the Baptist and a Female Saint* (Venice, Accademia), *Virgin in Glory with Saints* (Murano, San Pietro Martire); all in Goffen and Nepi Scirè [2000].

82. Hills [1999], 140–46.

83. Bagarotto et al. [2000], 193.

84. DeLancey [2010], 74, found a reference to orpiment in a document of a shipment from Venice in 1394, for instance. Its use may have been medicinal or other (78).

85. Cennini [2015], 73–74. Cennini adds the warning: "Look out for yourself."

86. Vasari [1963], 2:54.

87. Baxandall [1972], 14–23.

88. O'Malley [2013], 86.

89. O'Malley [2013], 102. See her table of documented works on panel by Botticelli, Filippino Lippi, Ghirlandaio, Perugino, and Cosimo Rosselli (120–23).

90. See O'Malley [2007], 127. She notes as additional bibliography: "On the development of techniques for transferring designs, the uses of copying, and Perugino's re-use of designs, see [Bambach (1999a)], 12–32 and 83–126. On Verrocchio's inventiveness and his workshop organization, see [Rubin and Wright (1999)], 93–7; and [Mazzati (2004)], 95–103; Gaertringen [1998], 53–69."

91. O'Malley [2013], 204.

92. Holmes [2004], 62–63. For technical evidence she cites Bambach [1999a], 233; and Giordana Benizzi and Paolo Virilli, *Filippo Lippi nel duomo di Spoleto, 1467–1469: Notizie*

dopo il restauro (Spoleto: Il Messagero, 1990), 13–17.

93. Christiansen [2004], 24.

94. Gregori, Paolucci, and Acidini Luchinat [1992], 37. The frame of the altarpiece is lost, so it is shown without the predella in photographs, as here.

95. O'Malley [2005], 90–96.

96. See Ames-Lewis [1981], 63–84.

97. Covi [2005], 155. He must have commuted between Florence and Venice between 1483, when he began work on the project, and 1486, when he moved to Venice.

CHAPTER 2. THE SIXTEENTH CENTURY

1. The concept of unione comes from Vasari, who defined it thus: "Unity [unione] in painting is a discord of different colours harmonized together, which in the diversity of the most divided show the parts of the figures as distinct from one another, like the flesh from the hair, and one garment different in colour from another. When these colours are applied brightly and vividly in a disagreeable disharmony so that they are tinted and loaded with body—as was formerly the practice with some painters—the design becomes marred so that the figures remain painted less by the brush, which makes the light and shade seem natural and in relief, than by the colour. All pictures, then, whether in oil or in fresco or tempera, should be made so united in their colours that the principal figures in the stories are brought out with utmost clarity, the draperies of those in front being kept so light that the figures which stand behind are kept darker than the first, and so little by little as the figures retire inward, they become also in equal measure gradually lower in tone in the colour both of the flesh tints and the garments." From Vasari's Introduction, repr. in Vasari [1960], trans. in Kern [2016], 196–97.

2. The best biography of Michelangelo is Wallace [2010].

3. On the four modes of coloring, see Hall [1992], chap. 3.

4. Seven paintings from Raphael's pre-Roman period in the National Gallery, London, were examined. All but one, which was not sampled, were found to have a similar off-white imprimatura consisting of lead white with powdered glass and a small proportion of lead-tin yellow. Roy, Spring, and Plazzotta [2004], 12, 15, 18, 20, 25, 26, 31. For technical studies on Raphael, see also Shearman and Hall [1990]; and Spring [2007].

5. Berrie and Walmsley [2007], 105: "A thin layer of paint corresponding to the final colour was laid down, it was covered by a layer of gesso, and the granular yellow-color layer was applied over this. It is covered by a more complex sequence of paint layers used to build up a dark fold in the bodice of the robe."

6. Dunkerton and Spring [1998]. Imprimatura has been little studied by art historians or scientists, but this technical study from the National Gallery, London, is of fundamental importance because it gives us a detailed comparison based on 140 paintings. Because samples of paintings taken in the course of modern conservation studies have been carefully saved, there is now a sufficient archive to make possible the categorization of findings on a large sample of paintings mainly in the National Gallery, London. The authors arranged their findings in four tables, separating schools or geographical regions, and ordered them from lightest to darkest. This table is now being expanded in an international collaboration into a database.

7. Stibnite (antimonite, antimony trisulfide) was found in the priming layer of Correggio's *Madonna of the Basket:* see Spring and Grout [2003], 102. Guidi et al. [1991] first noted its presence in several of Correggio's paintings, and additional instances were recently reported by Cauzzi, Moioli, and Seccaroni [2015], 44—for example, in the *Danae* in the Borghese Gallery.

8. Baxandall [1972], 15.

9. Gombrich [1972].

10. Vasari, quoted by Colalucci in Pietrangeli [1994], 30.

11. Angelini [1985], 165: "Besides this intonaco applied directly to the wall, Sebastiano introduced in Rome a color effect never before used in fresco in central Italy: a brilliant blue applied directly to the intonaco without preparation." For the most recent technical analysis of the Polyphemus, see Santopadre et al. [2012].

12. Bonito and Silver [1984], 71–72: "Raphael also chose not to employ an *intonachino* often utilized in preceding centuries to provide a very fine white ground on which to paint. Instead he frescoed directly on a unique gray *intonaco*. Microscopic examination of this *intonaco* revealed a distinctive composition, including burned organic matter. Consequently, Raphael's choice of a gray *intonaco* suggests an aesthetic decision as well."

13. Berrie and Walmsley [2007], 106: "Coloured underpainting has been

observed in some other works by Raphael. It has been noted in *Saint Cecilia* and in *The Transfiguration*. In these works, the underpainting is not necessarily the same colour as the intended final colour. In several later paintings, including *Saint Cecilia*, Raphael chose to use pink under the blue of the sky. . . . However, he did not use this in the Alba Madonna." See Rossi-Manaresi [1990] on the *Saint Cecilia*.

14. Dunkerton [2009], 35, described the priming of the *Pietà:* "The upper part has a white or very pale preparation and the lower part, comprising the foreground and the dead Christ, has a mid-grey underlayer."

15. Dunkerton and Spring [2013], 14.

16. Vasari [1963], 3:113. For the imprimatura layer, see Bruno Marocchini, "La Pietà di Viterbo: la tecnica di esecuzione," in Barbieri [2004], 89–93.

17. Dunkerton [2009] reported that in the 1770s it was transferred to canvas.

18. Over the gray imprimatura he painted a pale pink mixture of red lake and lead white. Dunkerton [2009], 36. Because lapis in oil has poor covering power, the pink layer lends a purplish cast to the lapis. This is the only area of the painting where ultramarine is used in its fully saturated form (43). Sebastiano adhered to the tradition of reserving the most precious pigments for the most important figure and using them in their pure form (44).

19. Shearman [1986], 32–33, discusses the problem with the foundations of the chapel.

20. The original plan was to paint it in the fashionable *all'antica* manner of the vaults that had been recently discovered in the Domus Aurea, the Golden House of the notorious Emperor Nero, which would have been a much less demanding project. See Hall [1999], 33. Julius would have a similar all'antica vault, divided into compartments with interstices filled with *grotteschi*, painted by Pinturicchio in the chancel of Santa Maria del Popolo in 1509.

21. Vasari [1963], 3:119.

22. For example, he made a cartoon of *Venus and Cupid* for his friend Bartomeo Bettini that was executed by Pontormo (Florence, Accademia). Michelangelo's cartoon, or a copy of it, is in Naples, at the Museo di Capodimonte.

23. Mancinelli [1997], 162, referred to the intonachino in the Sistine vault. Tiffany Hunt pointed out this reference to me.

24. Lodovico Dolce called his painting "licentious," by which he meant he took

excessive license with nature. Roskill [1968], 178–79.

25. Letter from Raphael to Alfonso d'Este, 21 September 1518, cited in Shearman [2003], 1518/66, 371–72. The painting is in the Louvre.

26. The earliest mention of the cartoon in 1544 identified it as by Raphael. Shearman [2003], 1544/2, 933.

27. Henry and Joannides [2013], 167–77.

28. Ana González Mozo, "Raphael's Painting Technique in Rome," in Henry and Joannides [2013], 342.

29. On Sebastiano's Borgherini Chapel, see Strinati [2009], cat. 33, 172–76; Hirst [1981], 49–65; and Marocchini [2008].

30. See Vasari's description of the technique in his life of Sebastiano: Vasari [1963], 2:117. Vasari described his own method: Vasari [1960], 232–35.

31. Rona Goffen made this competition vivid; Goffen [2002].

32. Letter from Sebastiano to Michelangelo, 7 September 1520, Goffen [2002], 258; Barocchi and Ristori [1988], *carteggio* 2:242–43, CDLXXI.

33. See my extended analysis of the Sala di Costantino, in Hall [1999], 42–49.

34. Despite its technical success, oil mural did not have much of a future. There were two disadvantages: it was a slow process, and the result was a dark wall. Although it works well in the small Borgherini Chapel, enlarged to a full wall it would have been overwhelming.

35. See the discussion of Andrea del Sarto's use of imprimatura, monochrome underpaint, and mixtures of tempera and oil in Yvonne Szafran and Sue Ann Chui, "A Perfectionist Revealed," in Brooks [2015], 13–19.

36. Cox-Rearick [1964], no. 259, discussed and reproduced the drawing for the lost *God the Father* (Uffizi) (254).

37. See the discussion of Giulio's paintings in Rome after Raphael's death in Henry and Joannides [2013], 81–84. They credit Arnold Nesselrath with identifying the background architecture as Trajan's Market.

38. Reported in the conservation study, Guiducci, Francescone, and Valente [1994], 80.

39. Cennini described the training the apprentice underwent in the opening chapters of his handbook; see Cennini [2015].

40. On the training of the artist in the Quattrocento and particularly drawing, see Ames-Lewis [1981 and 2000].

41. Talvacchia [2005 and 2007] has led the way in the new assessment of Raphael's late practice where, instead of assuming that he was too busy to properly control his workshop, it is now understood that his method allowed greater freedom for his assistants to express their own styles in interpreting the master's designs.

42. Armenini [1977], 86. See Williams [1995].

43. Dacos [2001], 195–213. Dacos identified the hand of Tibaldi in *The Destruction of the Idols and the Temples.*

44. Tibaldi is often credited with executing the faux bronze scenes of Alexander in the Sala Paolina on Perino's designs; see figs. 2–20.

45. Marciari [2009], 201, noted the dearth of workshops in Rome at mid-century.

46. Cavazzini [2008], 57.

47. Cavazzini [2008], 59.

48. Lorizzo [2006], 352ff.

49. Barzman [2000].

50. Marciari [2009].

51. Marciari [2009], 206–7, argues that even the leading painter in Rome in the 1570s and 1580s, Girolamo Muziano, who would persuade Pope Gregory in 1577 to found the precursor of the Accademia di San Luca, did not draw from a model but rather from his imagination. As a result there is a sameness to his figures and a patterned fall of his draperies that becomes monotonous.

52. On the guild and marketing in Venice in the seventeenth century, see Cecchini [2006].

53. On Venetian paintings, see Humfrey [1993 and 1995]. On Venetian color, see Hills [1999].

54. Dunkerton and Spring [2013], 4–31. Thirteen of Titian's paintings in the National Gallery, London, were examined in a recent comprehensive study. The technical observations reported here are based on it.

55. Elke Oberthaler and Elizabeth Walmsley, "Technical Studies of Painting Methods," in Brown [2006]; see particularly Giorgione, *Three Philosophers* (293) and *Adoration of the Shepherds* (*Allendale Nativity*) (297). Titian drew with a brush and black paint, so his underdrawings are usually visible in reflectographs; see *Madonna and Child* (*Gypsy Madonna*) (296–98).

56. Sometimes he would redraw on top of the paint layer, probably in the same black paint he had used originally for the underdrawing; Oberthaler and Walmsley, "Technical Studies," 19.

57. De Piles, *Conversations sur la connaissance de la peinture* (1677), cited in Delapierre, Gilles, and Portiglia [2004], 150.

58. Letter from Pietro Aretino to Duke Cosimo, n.d., cited in Hall [2011], 160.

59. Described by Dunkerton, Foister, and Penny [2002], 268; Dunkerton, "Titian at Work: Titian's Painting Technique," in Hope et al. [2003], 52. Dunkerton calls this technique "broken brushwork." I prefer "open brushwork," to avoid confusion with "broken color."

60. From Vasari's life of Giulio Romano: "Giulio always expressed his conceptions better in drawings than in his workmanship or in his paintings, since in the former one sees more vivacity, pride, and emotion; and this could come about because he made a drawing in an hour, all proud and on fire with the work, where in the paintings he consumed months and even years." Trans. in Hartt [1958], 1:17–18.

61. Sohm [1991], 146, described what Boschini was doing: he "transported the artist's experience of creation onto the viewer so the viewer, like the artist, experiences the thrilling metamorphosis of primordeal disorder into meaningful form. The viewer who approaches the canvas and deciphers the markings becomes a participant in the creation of order." See Hall [2011], 124, for further discussion.

62. Lank [1982], 400–406, reproduces an x-ray.

63. Gautier, quoted in Gowing and Laclotte [1987], 262.

64. Roger de Piles, *L'abrégé de la vie des peintres* (1699; repr., London: Printed for T. Payne, 1754), 176.

65. Gisolfi [2017], 224. Technical studies from the mid-1990s of paintings in the National Gallery, London, found that in the instances where he chose to use a priming, it was pale. Penny, Roy, Spring [1996]. Gisolfi [2017], 224, notes that sometimes, especially in his allegorical paintings, he created a pale pink imprimatura by adding a little red to the lead white. Exceptionally, for the night scene of his *Christ in the Garden of Gethsemane* (Milan, Brera, c. 1584), the abraded surface reveals a dark ground applied over the gesso (226).

66. The yellow sleeve is painted in lead-tin yellow type II. Penny, Roy, Spring [1996], table, pl. 5, 41.

67. Kern [2016], 199–200.

68. Kern [2016].

69. Vasari in his description of unione, quoted above in n1.

70. Giovanni Paolo Lomazzo, *Idea of the Temple of Painting* (1590; repr., University Park, Pa.: Pennsylvania State University Press, 2013), 167.

71. André Félibien, *Des principes de l'architecture, de la sculpture, de la peinture et des autres arts qui en dependent* (1676), as trans. in Kern [2016], 208.

72. On Barocci and his relationship to the Counter-Reformation, see Hall [2011], chap. 8.

73. See Lingo [2008] for explication of Barocci's vaghezza.

74. Barbieri [2013], 207, cites the evidence given at the trial for Neri's canonization.

75. Bellori [2010], 171–72.

76. See Joyce Plesters and Lorenzo Lazzarini, "The Examination of the Tintorettos," in Clarke and Rylands [1977]. See also the results of the examination of *Finding the Body of Saint Mark* (Milan, Brera) in Tardito [1990], 25.

77. Dunkerton [2007], 139, points out that Tintoretto himself contributed to the legend of his bravura execution. See her excellent analysis of his painting technique here.

78. Armenini [1977], 169, tells us about Michelangelo's use of wax figurines. Lomazzo, *Idea of the Temple of Painting*, appears to be the earliest source to describe Tintoretto's stage (1590). It is also discussed in Carlo Ridolfi, *The Life of Tintoretto* (1642; repr., Philadelphia: Pennsylvania State University, 1984), 17 (although he mistakenly attributed it to Titian), and Marco Boschini, *Le Ricche Minere della Pittvra Veneziana* (Venice: Nicolini, 1674), 730–31. Bellori [2010], 171–72, described Barocci's use of figurines as part of his elaborate preparatory practice. A number of wax or clay dolls were inventoried in El Greco's studio after his death; see Susanna Griswold, "Two Paintings by El Greco: Saint Martin and the Beggar—Analysis and Comparison," *Studies in the History of Art: Conservation Research* 41 (1993): 150n30.

79. Dunkerton [2007] points out repeatedly that the contrasts of light and dark have been exaggerated by the increased transparency of Tintoretto's thin paint over time and sometimes also by damage from light; Plesters and Lazzarini [1978].

80. Robert Wald, "Tintoretto's Vienna Susanna and the Elders: History, Technique and Restoration," in Falomir and Aikema [2009], 183.

81. Dunkerton [2007], 151.

82. Jonckheere [2012], 269–70, points out Matthew's hitherto unnoticed dirty fingernail and states that "a quarter of a century before Caravaggio some Antwerp painters had already given the initial impetus to the desacralization of sainthood" (85).

Jonckheere does not enter the debate over which figure is Matthew and assumes it is the money collector at the end of the table. The dirty feet of the pilgrims kneeling in the *Madonna di Loreto* (Rome, Sant'Agostino) could be cited as another example of Caravaggio taking inspiration from Adriaen Thomasz Key and Frans Pourbus and others working in Antwerp after the Iconoclast outbreak.

83. Bell [1995], 144.

84. Quoted in Bell [1995], 144. See Bellori [2010], 184.

85. In a letter dated 2 May 1548, he scolded his nephew Leonardo for addressing him as "Michelagniolo scultore": "I was never a painter or a sculptor like those who run workshops." Barocchi [1965], 4:299.

86. For a summary of El Greco's bad treatment in Spain, see Hall [2011], 228–29. See also Carlos Mas Gonzáles, ed., *El Greco: Su vida, su obra* (Madrid: Millennium Liber, 2014).

87. Letter from Isabella d'Este to Fra Pietro da Novellara, 27 March 1501, cited in Chambers [1971], 144.

CHAPTER 3. THE SEVENTEENTH CENTURY

1. Letter from Andrea Mantegna to Marquis Ludovico Gonzaga, 13 May 1478, cited in Chambers [1971], 118–19. Italian text in Paul Kristeller and S. Arthur Strong, *Andrea Mantegna* (London: Longmans, Green, 1901), appen. 4, 478n30.

2. Hatfield [2002], 229. His lifetime earnings after taxes came to at least L44,646, and he left an estate worth at least L24,064: "All of these figures compared favorably with those for the wealthiest patricians of Michelangelo's day; they were unheard-of for artists."

3. The economics of art in the Netherlands has been pioneered in the past generation by John Montias [1987, 1988, 1991], Michael North [1997], and Neil de Marchi [2006, with Van Miegroet], among other scholars, producing the body of literature upon which much of this chapter is based.

4. North [1997], 74, notes that "an incredible number of artists were successful and prosperous in the middle of their careers but became impoverished later on."

5. Crenshaw [2006], 24–25.

6. Crenshaw [2006], 23.

7. Documents 1654/15, cited by Crenshaw [2006], 42. Huygens's description in his autobiography is quoted in full in Bomford et al. [2006], 56. In part he wrote: "Summon all Italy, summon whatever remains from remotest antiquity that is

beautiful and wonderful, the portrayal of the despairing Judas alone . . . I set against all the elegances of the ages."

8. On Rembrandt's collaboration with Van Uylenburgh in the years 1631–38, see Lammertse and Van der Veen [2006], chap. 3.

9. For the details of Rembrandt's financial affairs, I am depending here on Crenshaw [2006].

10. Alan Chong, "The Market for Landscape Painting," in Sutton [1987], 109.

11. Clark [1966], 33. He illustrates, with the *Ganymede* (Dresden, 1635), Rembrandt's rejecting response both to the style and the morality of Michelangelo's larger-than-life version, which Rembrandt could have known through an engraving. Clark drew the illuminating distinction between "nude" and "naked" in his book *The Nude: A Study in Ideal Form* (New York: MJF, 1956).

12. Documents 1662/11, cited in Crenshaw [2006], 128–30.

13. When the painting was cleaned, it was established that it had been cut into two paintings and then sewn back together: Gordenker [2015a and 2015b].

14. Vermeylen [2003], 82.

15. Leeflang and Ainsworth [2015]; Leeflang [2006], 21–22.

16. Infrared reflectography was performed with a Grundig 70 H television camera outfitted with a Hamamatsu N 214 IR vidicon (1981), a TV macromar 1:2.8/36mm lens, and Kodak wratten 87 A filter cutting on at 0.9 micron placed behind the lens, with a Grundig BG 12 monitor set at 875 lines. Any photographic documentation is done with a Canon A-1 35mm camera, a 50mm macrolens, and Kodak Plus X film and/or Ilford film, ASA 125. The IRR-assembly/assemblies reproduced here consists of images that were scanned from photo negatives belonging to the archive of Professor Molly Faries at the RKD.

17. Wilson [1998] has studied the social and visual culture of Bruges.

18. Brown [1995], 153.

19. Cecchini [2006], 125–34.

20. Cavazzini [2008], 4.

21. Cavazzini [2008], 5.

22. Loredana Lorizzo, "Dispelling Negative Perceptions: Dealers Promoting Artists in Seventeenth-Century Naples," in DeMarchi and Van Miegroet [2006], 352ff. See above, chap. 2.

23. The causes for this boom in picture-buying have been much discussed. One factor was the migration of Flemish

painters from the Southern Netherlands following the fall of Antwerp to the Spanish in 1585. It has been estimated that 225 fully trained painters settled in the Northern Netherlands in the period 1580–95. Martin Jan Bok, "Fine and Decorative Arts: Amsterdam," in O'Brien [2001], 194.

24. Prak [2003], 238n15, cites Jan de Vries, "Art History," in *Art in History/History in Art: Studies in Seventeenth-Century Dutch Culture,* ed. David Freedberg and Jan de Vries (Santa Monica: Getty, 1991), 273n9, table 2, cols. 5 and 6.

25. De Parivial, quoted in Prak [2003], 238.

26. The emergence, first in Antwerp in the sixteenth century, of the new genre of secular landscape from earlier scenes of religious narrative taking place in the countryside is studied by Silver [2006].

27. On the creation of the ideal landscape, see Lagerlöf [1990].

28. Sutton [1987], 23.

29. Gifford [1995], 142.

30. The classic study of Dutch seventeenth-century landscape painting is Stechow [1966].

31. Gifford [1996], 70: "His palette was chosen from the most muted tones available, dominated by white lead, black, and red yellow and brown ochres. For foliage he used yellow ochre or the brighter lead tin yellow, often mixed with a blue: either smalt, made from blue glass, or the mineral azurite." I am indebted to Melanie Gifford for the English version of her chapter published in Dutch (see Vogelaar, Van Goyen, and Buijsen [1996]).

32. Brouwer was Flemish-born, but he lived and worked part of his life in Holland and his pictures were popular there.

33. Montias [1991], 334, reported that in the Amsterdam inventories he studied, landscapes were more frequently found than any other kind of painting by 50 percent.

34. The average price for 37 paintings, 16.8 guilders, was well below the average price of 21.77 guilders for landscapes during this period. Compare to Savery, whose paintings that were sold between 1600–50 averaged 72 guilders. Chong, "Market for Landscape Painting," 113; table 1, 116; table 3, 117–18. The average price for Van Goyen's paintings reported by Montias [1991], 366, table 10b, in the period 1651–79 was 12 guilders.

35. During his working life between 1651–75, Van Ruisdael's paintings averaged 42 guilders; Chong, "Market for Landscape Painting," table 3, 118; Montias's [1991]

findings for the same period concur (table 10b, 366).

36. Walford [1991]. Slive [2001] was averse to interpretation; Bruyn [1987] saw religious symbolism everywhere. Alpers [1983] characterized Dutch painting in general as engaged in the task of describing, not allegorizing.

37. Kern [2014], 71. The author quotes Gérard de Lairesse on landscape in his *Groot Schilderboek:* "[Landscape painting] consists principally in a proper arrangement of light and shape against one another. This causes a good *reddering* which insensibly deceives our sight, and depicts, although it is a flat panel, a natural prospect—indeed nature itself" (76).

38. See Ann Adams, "Competing Communities in the 'great bog of Europe': Identity and Seventeenth-Century Dutch Landscape Painting," in Mitchell [1994], esp. 48–49; and Schama [1987], 37ff.

39. Adams, "Competing Communities," 51–57.

40. For his graduated tones, Claude needed the scales that Zaccolini laid out in his treatise. See Conisbee [1979]; and Gage [1993], 167.

41. Joyce Plesters, "Possible Causes of Blanching Involving Changes in Pigments or Interaction of Pigment and Medium," in Wyld, Mills, and Plesters [1980], 63. It is also possible that he bought a pigment that was a mixture of smalt and ultramarine. Ultramarine was prohibitively expensive in the seventeenth century outside of Italy.

42. Conisbee [1979].

43. Büttner [2006], 74.

44. Landau and Parshall [1994] discuss the issue of reproductive prints in chap. 4.

45. Wetering [2009], 21–22. This document dates from 1676, but the author points out that primers are mentioned in the Haarlem guild archives already in 1631, and that by the time of the Leiden document, apparently "doing one's own priming had disappeared from workshop practice."

46. "Van Dyck seems to have been content to use the priming method in common currency in the country in which he was painting, and perhaps this indicates also the habitual use of ready-primed canvases from local sources of supply." Roy [1999], 50.

47. Other painters in Paris at the time using the red ground included Philippe de Champaigne, the brothers Le Nain, and Simon Vouet. McTighe [2014], 12.

48. As noted by Foulke [2014], 92, in the Harvard *Holy Family,* particularly the Virgin's face.

49. Cadogan, Kornhausen, and Garland [2015]. Other paintings by Poussin have been similarly but not so drastically affected.

50. Wetering [2009], 22, explains the difference between painting on white ground or colored ground: "While on a white ground all tonal shades have to be deliberately applied, a tinted ground acts as a middle tone by itself. It opens up the possibility to select the position of the highlights and their intensity with greater precision. With a white ground every unsufficiently covered part of the ground would function as a highlight, while with the tinted ground it can remain partly uncovered without the tonal cohesion being distorted."

51. The term is no longer used, but one finds it in Dutch (*"doodverf"*), in French (*"couleur morte"*), and in English ("dead color"). It is used here in its historical context.

52. Wetering [2009], 30ff. The underpainting might be done in color as well: it is called the *maniera lavata* or washed manner in one source, described as filling in the area within the outline with only one color. Thomas Marshall, who compiled an English manuscript, the Commonplace-book (c. 1640–50), describes a method of dead coloring connected to Van Dyck "in which for each individual area the final colour is approximated in a flat tint."

53. Wetering [2009], 27.

54. Gifford [1996], 76–77.

55. Gifford [1996], 70, described each phase of Van Goyen's technique as he evolved.

56. Haskell [1980], 15. Haskell describes how a certain Fabrizio Valguarnera, "a Sicilian adventurer and diamond smuggler," found in Lanfranco's studio sketched-in canvases of the *Crucifixion* and of the *Magdalen,* which he asked the painter to complete, and in Poussin's studio he ordered that the preliminary sketch of the *Plague at Ashdod* be completed for him. Cited in Wetering [2009], 30n46.

57. Gifford [1996], 77.

58. Wetering [2009], 42–43. The unfinished painting, *Henry IV in the Battle of Paris* (fig. 3-25), is adduced by Wetering as proof (201).

59. Kern [2014], 70.

60. Willem Goeree, *Inleyding tot d'Algemeene Teykenkonst* (1670). In his full explanation, houding is "that which binds everything together in a drawing or painting, which makes things move to the front or back, and which causes everything from the foreground to the middle ground and thence to the background to stand in its

proper place without appearing further away or closer, and without seeming lighter or darker than its distance warrants; so that everything stands out, without confusion, from the things that adjoin and surround it, and has an unambiguous position through the proper use of size and colour, and light and shadow, and so that the eye can naturally perceive the intervening space, that distance between the bodies which is left open and empty, both near and far, as though one might go there on foot, and everything stands in its proper place therein." Trans. in Taylor [1992], 211.

61. Vasari writes in his life of Raphael that his *Marriage of the Virgin* (Milan, Brera) was "adorned with a perspective." See Stumpel [1990], 169–72, who contrasts the Renaissance with the modern view: "That a perspective could have no other purpose than to enrich the 'ground' of a painting is also considered improbable by modern critics."

62. See Wetering [2009], 162–69, for a brilliant discussion of Rembrandt's relationship to Titian and his use of impasto.

63. Wetering [2009], 150: "This observation has in addition been confirmed by studies of paint samples from Rembrandt's paintings, which time and again reveal that only a limited number of pigments were used in a given passage. The mixtures found usually consist of two to four different pigments."

64. Kern [2016], 190, found the term used first in Dutch treatises in Samuel van Hoogstraten, *Inleyding tot de hooge schoole der schilderkonst, anders de zichtbaere werelt* (Rotterdam, 1678).

65. Kern [2016], 196.

66. Blunt [1967], 6.

67. Blunt [1967], 116–17.

68. Bellini's altered original is in Washington, D.C., National Gallery of Art. Poussin's copy is in Edinburgh, National Gallery of Scotland.

69. On the Carraccis' practice, see Feigenbaum [1993].

70. De Grazia and Steele [1999], 64, from a contemporary description of Poussin's working procedure. Poussin may have been unique among seventeenth-century painters in using the theatrical stage.

71. Hibbard [1974], 84.

72. De Grazia and Steele [1999], 123, diag., 127, fig. 73. The version in the National Gallery of Art, Washington, D.C., was believed to be the original until recently. Badt [1969], 361, for example, analyzed the coloring of the Washington, D.C., version, not the one in Cleveland, and Blunt [1967], 181ff, discussed it and not the Cleveland version.

73. Gage [1993], 153, said of this picture that "it is as much an exposition of the notion of the three primaries and the three secondaries, laid out across the foreground of the painting, as it is a demonstration of perspectival construction."

74. It was discovered by Carlo Pedretti in the Laurentian Library in Florence. See Bell [1993]; Cropper and Dempsey [1996], chap. 4; Bellori [2010].

75. Bell [1993], 97.

76. On Poussin's debt to Leonardo da Vinci and Zaccolino for aerial perspective, see Glanville [2001 and 2014].

77. His technique is described as being atypical of seventeenth-century and earlier practice in that he superimposed opaque layers without transparent glazes. Plender and Burnstock [2014], 57.

78. Sawyer and Steele [1999], 121.

79. Letter from Nicolas Poussin to M. de Lisle, 22 December 1647.

80. For the sketch for the *Image of the Virgin Glorified by Angels* for the high altar, Chiesa Nuova in the Gemäldegalerie der Akademie der bildenden Künste, Vienna, see Held [1980], cat. 397. Bellori reported that Barocci made "*cartoncini per i colori*" (small colored cartoons). Because Barocci was working from his studio in Urbino, he must have submitted designs to the Oratorians in advance. We know they closely supervised the decoration of their church—for example, they required a drawing from Scipione Pulzone for his *Crucifixion* in 1585–90; Hall [2011], 128. Barocci painted his *Visitation* in 1585 and completed the *Presentation in the Temple* in 1603. His other painting for the right transept was delivered after Rubens had returned to Antwerp. No colored cartoons have survived for these paintings. Mann, Bohn, and Plazzotta [2012], 60–61, doubt that Barocci made such cartoons and believe that those accepted by scholars were made as *ricordi* or for sale to private collectors.

81. See Plesters [1983] for the technical examination.

82. One version for the *Assumption of the Virgin* for the Antwerp Cathedral (painting finally executed 1624–26) has been preserved in Saint Petersburg, in the Hermitage; the other is lost but may be preserved in a drawing in Budapest. Sutton, Wieseman, and Van Hout [2004], 23.

83. Vasari [1960], 209.

84. See Van Hout's detailed reconstruction of Rubens's procedure preparing and using the oil sketch in Sutton, Wieseman, and Van Hout [2004], 74–81.

85. See the discussion in Held [1980], 1:68–69. When the twelve oil sketches for the Constantine tapestries were inventoried in 1627, they were valued at more than twice what Rubens had been paid for the twelve large cartoons.

86. Martin [1968], 82–83; Held [1980], 1, cat. 20; Sutton, Wieseman, and Van Hout [2004], 122–25, cat. 10.

87. Letter from Peter Paul Rubens to William Trumbull, 13 September 1621, cited in Magurn [1991], 77, letter 46.

88. Oliver et al. [2005], 6–7, fig. 1.

89. The Dresden version is discussed here in chap. 4. Its underdrawing is in a different hand from that of the London original; Oliver et al. [2005], 10n7. The National Gallery authors use the term "underdrawing" rather than "dead coloring," used by Van Hout [2000], to describe the two unfinished paintings by Rubens.

90. Letter from Rubens to Fabri, Sieur de Valavez (brother of Nicolas-Claude Fabri de Peiresc), 26 December 1624, cited in Magurn [1991], 99, letter 59.

91. Letter from Rubens to Valavez, 10 January 1625, cited in Magurn [1991], 101, letter 60.

92. Roger de Piles (*L'Abrégé* [1699]) criticized Rubens harshly for the practice of turning over the execution to his assistants and only retouching himself: "He had skilled disciples make a great number of pictures after his coloured sketches, which he then retouched with fresh eyes, a lively intelligence and a quick hand that poured in his entire spirit, and this acquired him a lot of wealth in a short time. But the difference between these sorts of paintings, which were thought to be by him, with those which were truly by his hand, brought ill to his reputation, since they were mostly badly drawn and poorly painted." Trans. in Hélène Dubois, "The Master's Own Hand? Contribution to the Study of Rubens' Retouching of Monumental Formats," in Hermens and Townsend [2009], 87.

93. On Rubens's Munich *Lion Hunt,* see Rosand [1969].

94. Letter from Lord Henry Danvers to Sir Dudley Carleton, 27 May 1621, cited in Magurn [1991], 446, letter 46n1.

95. Letter from Rubens to Trumbull, 26 January 1621, cited in Magurn [1991], 76, letter 45.

96. Tummers and Jonckheere [2008].

97. Letter from Rubens to Trumbull, 26 January 1621, cited in Magurn [1991], 76, letter 45.

98. Letter from Peter Paul Rubens to Sir Dudley Carleton, 28 April 1618, cited in Magurn [1991], 60–61, letter 28; Tummers and Jonckheere [2008], 43.

99. Montias [1988], 246.

100. Held [1980], 1:11.

CHAPTER 4. THE EIGHTEENTH CENTURY

1. Parliament registered the privileges of the new Académie in 1648. Pevsner [1940], 86.

2. Boime [1971], 3.

3. The Florentine Accademia del Disegno was founded in 1563; the Roman Accademia di San Luca in 1593. On the Florentine Accademia, see Barzman [2000]; on the Roman Academy, see Lukehart [2009].

4. It has been doubted that much instruction was actually going on in the early years of the Seicento; Cavazzini [2008,] 72 and n171.

5. Lukehart [2018].

6. On Vouet, see Thuillier, Brejon De Lavergnée, and Lavalle [1990].

7. See Lukehart [2018].

8. Gail S. Davidson, "Nicholas Poussin, Jacques Stella, and the Classical Style in 1640: The Altar Paintings for the Chapel of Saint-Germain-en-Laye," in Hargrove [1990], 37–67.

9. Letter from Jean-Baptiste Colbert, 6 September 1669, in Anatole de Montaiglon, *Correspondance des Directeurs de l'Academie de France à Rome avec les Surintendants des Bâtiments* (Paris, 1887–1912), 1:27, quoted in Haskell and Penny [1981], 37.

10. See Hall [1999], 120, 126; Cox-Rearick [1996] catalogued and discussed the king's collection.

11. Pevsner [1940], 99, notes that the plan for the Academy in Rome dates back to 1664. On Colbert and the formulation of the program for the Académie, see Antoine Schnapper, "The Debut of the Royal Academy of Painting and Sculpture," in Hargrove [1990], 27–34.

12. See Romano Alberti, *Origine, et progresso dell'Academia del disegno de' pittori, scultori, e architetti di Roma* (Bologna: Forni, 1978).

13. Félibien [1987]. For an analysis of Le Brun's Conférence on Poussin's *Israelites Gathering Manna*, see Badt [1969], 329–40.

14. Corneille was a friend of Roger de Piles and co-authored *Les Premiers Elémens de la Peinture Pratique*, which he illustrated for publication in 1684. Gage [1993], 178. There is not much published about Corneille; see Marandet [2009] for a preparatory drawing for the *Hercules.*

15. Louis was represented allegorically as Hercules in one of the temporary decorations for his entry with Marie-Thérèse into Paris in August 1660, as described in the *Gazette de France;* see Berger [1999], 94. "Hercules Punishing Busiris" was the subject of a *discours* at the Académie by Georges Guillet de Saint-Georges, first historian of the Académie, in 1685 and a second time on November 7, 1699.

16. Posner [1959], 241.

17. Kern [2016], 201.

18. Félibien [1663]. Kern [2016], 206–8, gives a detailed analysis keyed to a diagram of Félibien's description.

19. On Le Brun's procedures, see Burchard [2016].

20. Lichtenstein [1993], 209.

21. On the adoption of Venetian-style mirrors at Versailles, see Chaimovich [2008].

22. Gilding was added to the vault of the Sala Paolina in 1723 under Pope Innocent XIII, probably in rival response to the Hall of Mirrors. See Colalucci's description of the restoration in Gaudioso [1981], 1:51.

23. Minor [1999], 333. To what extent painters in seventeenth-century France used di sotto in sù has not been studied. Peter Lukehart pointed out to me that for one of the chapels at Versailles, c. 1675–77, *Dieu dans sa Gloire* (Burchard [2016], cat. 172), there is a modello viewed partially di sotto in sù.

24. On de La Fosse, see the recent exhibition catalogue, Sarrazin, Collange-Perugi, and Gustin-Gomez [2015].

25. Piles [1708].

26. Vasari's words are: "Disegno . . . procedendo dall'intelletto cava di molte cose un giudizio universale simile a una forma overo idea di tutte le cose della natura." Giorgio Vasari and Gaetano Milanesi, *Le opere di Giorgio Vasari: Con nuove annotazioni e commenti di Gaetano Milanesi* (Florence: Casa Editrice le Lettere, 1998), 1:168. Williams [1997], 32–37, has pointed out the Aristotelian origin of Vasari's definition and the debt to the philosopher Benedetto Varchi. Puttfarken [1991], 78.

27. Puttfarken [1991], 79.

28. Roskill [1968], 155.

29. Lichtenstein and Michel [2009], 44–51.

30. Teyssedre [1957], 142–44. Jean Nocret delivered his lecture on December 6, 1670; Le Brun delivered his remarks on January 10, 1671.

31. Bryson [1981], 60, citing Louis Hourticq, *De Poussin à Watteau* (Paris: Hachette, 1921), 49. In Blunt's summary: "Drawing is to colour as the soul is to the body." Anthony Blunt, *Art and Architecture in France: 1500–1700* (Harmondsworth, UK: Penguin, 1973), 220.

32. De Piles, quoted in Puttfarken [1985], 63. I am depending on Puttfarken's exegesis for what follows.

33. "So the artist must not imitate all the colours which indifferently present themselves to the eye; but chuse the most proper for his purpose; adding others, if he think fit, in order to fetch out the effect and beauty of his work." Puttfarken [1985], 70.

34. Shelton [2000], 737.

35. Gersaint's life of Watteau: Quentin de Lorangere and Edme François Gersaint, *Catalogue raisonné des diverses curiosités du cabinet de feu M. Quentin de Lorangere . . . Par E. F. Gersaint* (Paris, 1744); Rosenberg [1984], 30–31.

36. Gaehtgens [1990], 208.

37. Bryson [1981], 82, pointed out that the long-shot consistently preferred by Watteau may have been chosen because it makes facial expression unreadable.

38. For the later version called *Embarkation for Cythera* in Berlin he used a rosy imprimatura with a touch of ochre added. Martin and Sindaco-Domas [2010].

39. This was the conclusion reached by Fisher [1984], who studied the *Italian Comedians* in the National Gallery, Washington, D.C. See also Vogtherr, Preti, and Faroult [2014], 35.

40. Healy [1997] makes the point that in all eight of his versions of the subject, Rubens put the focus on the serious problem of making a choice, to which she plausibly attributes political significance. As a diplomat he was deeply concerned with the decisions made by his Flemish government, especially over issues of relations with the Spanish crown.

41. Oliver et al. [2005], 19.

42. Berger [1999], chaps. 5 and 6.

43. On the first anniversary of the king's decapitation, August 10, 1793, the Musée de Louvre put on display 537 paintings and 184 objects of art confiscated from the Church and the royal collection. The Prado first opened to the public in 1819; the building of the National Gallery in London was not built until 1838, although the kernel of its picture collection had been on display since the mid-1820s. The Vatican collections were not opened to the public until 1929.

44. Crow [1985], intro.

45. Hyde [2000 and 2006].

46. Étienne La Font de Saint-Yenne, quoted in Démoris [2006], 203.

47. Friedrich Melchior Grimm, quoted in Démoris [2006], 204.

48. Guillaume-Thomas Raynal, quoted in Démoris [2006], 204.

49. When it was moved in 1764 to the Hotel d'Evreux after her death, it was probably displayed as an oval mounted on the wall. Conisbee, Rand, and Baillio [2009], technical notes, 19.

50. Bryson [1981], 92: "For its erotic content to be fully yielded up, the body must be presented to the viewer as though uniquely made to gratify and to be consumed in the moment of the glance." Bryson makes the case for the rejection of perspective in the Rococo in his opening chapter.

51. Domenichino also painted *Diana and Her Nymphs* (Rome, Borghese Gallery), and while some of the nymphs are observed bathing, Diana herself is clothed.

52. Diderot, Salon of 1765, quoted in Hyde [2006], 14.

53. Diderot, Salon of 1765, quoted in Schieder [2006], 61.

54. Brookner [1972], 38. Brookner quotes the Marquis d'Argens: "Today, to the enduring shame of the arts, one sees so-called lovers of painting forming large collections of little Dutch pictures which they buy at exorbitant prices, although the only merit such pictures have is a servile imitation of the lowest form of nature, offering the spirit images incapable of inspiring those virile and sublime ideas that the great history painters provide for those who examine their works with attention" (39).

55. Abbé de la Porte, 1761, quoted in Brookner [1972], 63.

56. Gaehtgens, cited in Hargrove [1990], 210.

57. Quoted in Démoris [2006], 202–3.

58. Diderot, Salon of 1761, quoted in Brookner [1972], 62.

59. Démoris [2006], 202.

60. Gaehtgens, cited in Hargrove [1990], 208–9.

61. Rosenberg [1979], 252–57.

62. Merrill [1981]. Chalk was found in the period 1730–66, but no further studies were made.

63. François de Salignac de la Mothe-Fénelon, *De l'education des filles* (1687), cited in Edizel [1995], 182.

64. Chardin is the master of what Fried [1980], esp. 46–51, has identified as the absorptive tradition, figures engrossed in what they are doing, producing examples like this in a secular, domestic setting.

65. On Boucher's *Return from the Market*, see Zafran and Resendez [1998].

66. Alpers and Baxandall [1994], 84, 88.

67. Barcham [1989], 71, discusses the reference to the influence of Veronese in contemporary literature.

68. See my discussion of the device of "making strange" in Hall [2011], 8–15.

69. Alpers and Baxandall [1994], 76.

70. Pasquale Rotondi in Molajoli, Scattolin, and Rotondi [1970], 115: "The central medallion was painted by Tiepolo in four days, three of which were devoted to covering very large spaces—each space corresponds to about a third of the whole—while the fourth day saw the artist engaged only on the drapery at the edge of the medallion, below the figure of Time."

71. Alpers and Baxandall [1994], 76. Tiepolo may have used another "cheater" technique called *mezzo-fresco*—that is, painting on nearly dry intonaco so that the pigment only penetrates slightly into the plaster. It is a way of extending the window of time in which the fresco can be executed.

72. On Canaletto, see Constable and Links [1989].

73. Rosenblum [1967b] is fundamental to our understanding of the emergence of the Neoclassical, especially his chap. 2, "The *exemplum virtutis.*"

74. Quoted in Honour and Fleming [2011], 628.

75. Schnapper [1982], 11; Leith [1965], 74–75.

76. Leith [1965], 74–76.

77. Schnapper [1982], 65.

78. Crow [1985], 189.

79. Plax [2000], 112–13.

80. Horace, *Ars Poetica.*

81. Abbé le Blanc, "Letter to le Comte de C**, 1737–44, about Architecture in England, etc.," cited in Eriksen [1974], 231. Le Blanc was selected by Madame de Pompadour to lead the study tour to Italy of her younger brother, the future Marquis de Marigny, who would be the virtual dictator of official art from 1751 to 1773. Le Blanc saw to it that he was indoctrinated in Neoclassicism.

82. C.-N. Cochin, "Letter to M. l'Abbe R** about a Very Poor Pleasantry from the Society of Architects, 1754," cited in Eriksen [1974], 245. Cochin accompanied Pompadour's brother along with Le Blanc on his Italian tour.

83. Hyde [2006], 21.

84. Schnapper [1982], 22–26.

85. Delécluze, quoted in Schnapper [1982], 42.

86. On Valentin, see the exhibition catalogue, Lemoine et al. [2016].

87. David's colleague and rival Pierre Peyron, who had beaten him for the Prix de Rome in 1773, presented *Belisarius Receiving Hospitality from a Peasant* (Toulouse) in 1779.

88. Else Marie Bukdahl traced Diderot's growing understanding of what was required for modern history painting to fulfill the ambition that it attain the qualities of classicism. See her essay, "Diderot's Conception of Classical Art and Its Theoretical Foundation," in Hargrove [1990], 91–115.

89. Lee [1999], 94.

90. Levey [1993], 293.

91. Crow [1985], 214–23.

92. Thomas Crow compares the David and Peyron versions in Crow [1985], 243–44.

CHAPTER 5. THE NINETEENTH CENTURY

1. Boime [1971], 58.

2. Bann [1997], 25–26. Henry James had been infatuated with Delaroche when he was a teenager, but in 1873 he wrote: "He was the idol of our youth, and we wonder we can judge him so coldly. But, in truth, Delaroche is fatally cold himself. . . . [His last paintings] exhibit a singular union of vigorous pictorial arrangement and flatness and vulgarity of execution."

3. Bann [1997], 35. At the Salon of 1834, where *Lady Jane Grey* was presented, Delaroche was one of 2,314 artists (36).

4. I am drawing upon the technical examination of Kirby and Roy [1995].

5. Chesneau, in *Les Nations rivales dans l'art* (1868), quoted in Mainardi [1989], 158.

6. Reported in Richard Dorment, "Painting History: Delaroche and Lady Jane Grey at the National Gallery," *Telegraph*, February 23, 2010.

7. Ingres [1947], 14.

8. Boime [1971], 4–7.

9. Boime [1971], 15.

10. Johnson [1981], 1:86.

11. As Delacroix himself later recognized; Johnson [1981], 1:87.

12. Spector [1974] reconstructed the development of the composition. See also Johnson [1969].

13. Delacroix was trained in the academic tradition and did not find it easy to put its precepts aside. He castigated himself in his early career for his weak contours; Boime [1971], 90.

14. Spector [1974], 81. Louis Vitet writing in the *Globe*, March 28, 1828. Délécluze had criticized Delacroix's first Salon exhibit, the *Barque of Dante*, as "a sketch composed and painted with verve." Baschet [1942], 282, quoted in Boime [1971], 89.

15. Spector [1974], 81. An oil sketch, like those of Rubens, is conserved at the Louvre.

16. Johnson [1969], 299. A letter dated 1827 from Delacroix to an unknown recipient

thanks him for letting him see the painting of M. Ingres.

17. Shelton [2000], 728.

18. Rosenblum [1967a], 130, remarked: "Always respected but seldom loved, *The Apotheosis of Homer* has come to symbolize Ingres's most doctrinaire statement of his belief of timeless values that are based on classical precedent."

19. Rosenblum [1967a], 156.

20. Bronzino used the wall-eye repeatedly in his portraits: the *Young Man* in New York at the Metropolitan Museum of Art and also in *Lodovico Capponi* in the Frick Collection; *Cosimo I as Orpheus* (Philadelphia Museum of Art); and *Duke Cosimo in Armor* (Florence, Uffizi) are also among the examples. See Hall [1999], 216.

21. See the discussion in chap. 4, based on the discovery of Shelton [2000]; Mainardi [1985].

22. Boime [1971], chap. 4, is on "The Academic Sketch."

23. Delacroix [1932b], 1:187, quoted in Boime [1971], 90.

24. Described by Piot [1931], quoted in Gage [1993], 187.

25. Baudelaire [1970], Salon of 1845, 45.

26. Boime [1971], 91.

27. Callen [2000], 2.

28. Bomford et al. [1990], 32–33.

29. Callen [2000], 98–99.

30. Helmut Schweppe, "Indigo and Woad," in FitzHugh, Berrie, and Feller [1997], 81–87.

31. Just how strong the resistance to indigo was is indicated by the fact that during the reign of Henri IV in France, in 1609, its use became a capital offense and persons using indigo were liable to the death sentence. Padmini Tolat Balaram, "Indian Indigo," in Feeser, Goggin, and Tobin [2012], 143.

32. The company today known as BASF, which had been the first to produce Perkin's aniline purple, known as mauve, made synthetic indigo available commercially in 1897.

33. Jeremy Baskes, "Seeking Red: The Production and Trade of Cochineal Dye in Oaxaca, Mexico, 1750–1821," in Feeser, Goggin, and Tobin [2012], 101–17. See also Phipps [2010].

34. Jean-François Lozier, "Red Ochre, Vermilion, and the Transatlantic Cosmetic Encounter," in Feeser, Goggin, and Tobin [2012], 119–37.

35. Fisher [1984], 465–67, cited by Barbara Berrie, "Prussian Blue," in FitzHugh, Berrie, and Feller [1997], 191–217.

36. Berrie, "Prussian Blue," in FitzHugh, Berrie, and Feller [1997].

37. Pigments through the Ages, "Ultramarine."

38. Bomford et al. [1990], 62.

39. Bomford et al. [1990], 63–64.

40. Bomford et al. [1990], 58–59.

41. On emerald green and vert Véronèse, see Bomford et al. [1990], 60.

42. See the study on the blackening of vermilion by Spring and Grout [2002].

43. A great deal of work has been done on these organic red pigments. See Kirby, Spring, and Higgitt [2007], which summarizes earlier literature.

44. Pigments through the Ages, "Madder Lake."

45. See Roy [2007] for a discussion of Monet's palette in his late paintings, which includes light cobalt violet.

46. Letters from Eugène Delacroix to M. Haro, 29 October 1827; 16 December 1827, and 20 September 1830, in Delacroix [1936], 1:200, 207.

47. Bomford et al. [1990], 81.

48. Bomford et al. [1990], 39.

49. Jean Renoir quoted his father; see Bomford et al. [1990], 41.

50. Callen [2000], 98–99.

51. Carlyle [2001] has brought together a comprehensive and valuable study of such handbooks and instruction manuals in nineteenth-century Britain. Townsend [2002] gives a valuable supplement to Carlyle, including information on French painters.

52. Townsend [1993], 38.

53. Townsend [1993], 41.

54. Dominique Lobstein in Pickeral and Robinson [2005], 40.

55. Kate Stonor, "Further Observations on Corot's Late Painting Technique," in Wrapson et al. [2012], 126.

56. Herring [2009], 96.

57. Galenson and Jensen [2007] argued that White and White [1965] exaggerated the role of dealers and pointed out that it was the painters themselves, not the dealer Durand-Ruel, who organized the first Impressionist exhibition in 1874. They insist on what Mainardi [1993], 147, made clear—that it continued to be a Salon-led culture: "Until the 1870s, however, there was effectively only one prestigious publisher for fine art. A painter's work could not be widely reviewed by critics, or considered for purchase by important dealers and collectors until the painter had proven himself by being admitted to the Salon, and had received at last some degree of recognition from the jury. The Salon's effective monopoly of the legitimate presentation of new art to the public gave its jury the power to determine whether an aspiring artist could have a successful career as a professional painter."

58. Patry et al. [2015], 35. I am following this source for what follows.

59. *Breakwater at Trouville, Low Tide,* now in Budapest. Patry et al. [2015], 86.

60. Patry et al. [2015], 88.

61. Rewald [1946], 250.

62. Mainardi [1993], 11. Berger [1999], chap 5.

63. These numbers are from Mainardi [1993], 18–19, table 1.

64. Rewald [1946], 44.

65. Jal, quoted in Mainardi [1993], 17.

66. White and White [1965], 27.

67. "Laisser le public juge de la légitimité de ces reclamations"; quoted in Boime [1969], 413.

68. Boime [2008], 685.

69. Callen [2000], 70, describes the Impressionist use of pale tinted ground in ecru or grays, even mauvish, to break the stark white of the commercial ground.

70. Herbert [1988], 177.

71. Despite its success, the critics did not find in Cabanel a replacement for the recently deceased Ingres. Chesneau commented: "Are we saying that this painter, whose success has been so fortunate and swift, might be the master who could make us forget those we mourn, the Ingres and the Delacroix? I don't believe it, M. Cabanel himself doesn't believe it." Ernest Chesneau, *Les Nations rivales dans l'art* (1868), quoted in Mainardi [1987], 157.

72. Théophile Gautier, in his review of June 24, 1865, complained that "le ton des chairs est sale." Quoted in Clark [1999], 285n24.

73. Callen [1982], 44.

74. Bomford et al. [1990], 117.

75. House [1986], 75, quoting Philippe Burty, *Salon de 1883: Cent vingt planches en photogravure par Goupil et cie; trente dessins d'après les originaux des artistes* (Paris: L. Baschet, 1973).

76. Kirkland [2014], 133–34. The author's quote from Haussmann, *Memoire du Baron Haussmann* (1854–58), reveals the reforming zeal with which Haussmann tackled the task: "I would be able to begin ripping open the neighborhoods of the center of the city with their tangle of streets almost impossible to navigate by carriage and their crowded, sordid, and unhealthy houses; these neighborhoods that are for the most part a seat of misery and disease and a subject of shame for a great country such as France" (90).

77. Mainardi [1987], 154.

78. The exhibition catalogue Jones and Davis [2014] documents many instances of Degas helping and advising Mary Cassatt.

79. "Fortunately for me, I have not found my method; that would only bore me." Quoted by Reff [1976], 270, from A. Vollard, *Degas* (1924).

80. Reff [1976], 277; Bomford et al. [2004], 25.

81. Fletcher and Desantis [1989], 263; Bomford et al. [2004], 36.

82. Hamilton [1967], 16.

83. See the catalogue entry for details of the technique analysis; Bomford et al. [1990], 120–25.

84. Evidence has been found that as early as the sixteenth century "brushes in small metal tubes" were being sold by artists' brush makers; see Haller [2010], esp. 332. The industrial production of brushes clamped with metal of course made them more widely available and affordable.

85. The pigment here has not been identified. Monet used cobalt violet light in his late paintings (see Roy [2007], cited above), but this could also be a cheaper mixture.

86. Dating from around 1890; House [1986], 75, quoting Lilla Cabot Perry.

87. He had been accepted at the Salons of 1864 and 1865, then rejected in 1866 and 1867, then accepted to the next three (1868–70), and rejected again in 1872 and 1873. White and White [1965], 142, table 12.

88. Leroy, quoted in Rewald [1946], 256.

89. Wolff, quoted in Rewald [1946], 299.

90. Patry et al. [2015], 264.

91. Quoted in Callen [2000], 125.

92. See Bomford et al. [1990], 152–57, for technical analysis of *At the Theatre*.

93. Burnstock, Van der Berg, and House [2005], 57.

94. Bomford et al. [1990], 191.

95. Bomford et al. [1990], 188–95. See fig. 90 for the x-ray. Further study in 2012 showed that the man at the left leering at the woman with basket was added in the second stage. Roy, Billinge, and Riopelle [2012], 73–81.

96. Renoir's paintings in Chicago, spanning much of his career, were sampled and the following pigments were found: lead white, chrome yellow, Naples yellow, yellow earth, red lead, vermilion, crimson lake (unidentified organic dye), emerald green, viridian, malachite, cobalt blue, ultramarine, bone black. Marigene Butler, "Technical Note," in Maxon [1973], 210.

97. Bomford et al. [1990], 116.

98. Reissner [2008].

99. Shiff [1984], 116. I am following Shiff's analysis here.

100. Butler [1984], 31, noted: "His consuming interest in capturing the light is revealed by the high value of his hues: percentages of lead white mixed with other pigments run between 45–70%, and this preference for whitened hues remains consistent in his landscapes throughout his mature career."

101. Quoted from P. M. Doran, Emile Bernard, and Paul Cézanne, *Conversations avec Cézanne* (Angers: Macula, 1978), 173, in Bomford et al. [1990], 199.

102. Butler [1984], 26.

103. Boime [1971], 16.

104. Walsh [2013].

CHAPTER 6. COLOR AS THE EXPRESSION OF THE IMMATERIAL

1. Mainardi [1989], 26.

2. Locke [2012], 9–27.

3. Delacroix [1923], 1:76, quoted in Noon and Riopelle [2015], 32.

4. On the opposition of the classical tradition and the decorative, see Connelly [1995].

5. Gauguin, quoted in Hamilton [1967], 74.

6. "Primitive" for Gauguin expressed what he sought: a rural and unsophisticated culture rooted in nature. The term has been rejected in more recent times as demeaning.

7. Welten [2015], 12: "All the typical Japanese ukiyo-e features are present: flat areas of unmodulated color, simplified forms, arbitrary perspective, high viewpoint, asymmetric composition, high viewpoint."

8. Letter from Paul Gauguin to Vincent Van Gogh, 22 September 1888, Brittany, www .webexhibits.org/vangogh/letter/19/etc -Gauguin-2.htm.

   Gauguin described the pigments he used: vermilion, chrome yellow 1 for the angel's wings; chrome yellow 2 for the hair; viridian for the foliage of the apple tree; ultramarine for the robe. These are pigments he had discovered from Pissarro in 1879, when he was learning Impressionist technique, so the materials are unchanged, and he was still using all of them in Tahiti. In Christensen [1993], appen. 3, see the table of pigments found in technical analysis. Zinc yellow and organic red lake were also identified in the most recent examination; Lesley Stevenson, "Gauguin's Vision: A Discussion of Materials and Technique," in Fowle, Stevenson, and Thomson [2005], 115.

9. Jirat-Wasiutyński and Newton [2000], 96–97. The painting underwent a thorough technical examination in 2005, reported by Lesley Stevenson and Belinda Thomson, "*Vision of the Sermon* by Paul Gauguin: An Exploration of Making and Meaning," in Saunders, Townsend, and Woodcock [2006], 34–40.

10. Gauguin studied Jacques-Antoine Moerenhout's 1837 descriptions, especially his reconstruction of Tahitian religion; see Moerenhout [1993]. Brettell [1988], 363–65, cat. 205. On Gauguin in Tahiti, see Danielsson [1966 and 1969].

11. Christensen [1993], 80.

12. Letter from Paul Gauguin to Georges-Daniel de Monfreid, 8 December 1892, cited in Christensen [1993], 81.

13. Letter from Gauguin to de Monfreid, 8 December 1892, instructing him to wash the paintings sent from Tahiti when they arrived and then wax them, cited in Christensen [1993], 82.

14. Letter from Gauguin to de Monfreid, 27 February 1901, cited in Christensen [1993], 92.

15. See Christensen [1993], 86, 83, and appen. 2–3.

16. Christensen [1993].

17. Christensen [1993], 85, citing an examination report by Mary Sebera from 1987, Baltimore Museum of Art.

18. Letter from Gauguin to de Monfreid, 8 December 1892, cited in Christensen [1993], 83.

19. On the Renaissance, see Lingo [2008] on Barocci painting musical harmonies, esp. chap. 9, "Ut Pictura Musica."

20. The relationship was pointed out to me by Gerald Silk.

21. Christensen [1993], 71, quoting an undated letter from Paul Gauguin to Émile Bernard from the third or fourth week of November 1888; Gauguin and Merlhès [1984], no. 182.

22. Brettell [1988], 114–15.

23. Letter from Vincent to Theo van Gogh, 27 July 1883, cited in Boime [2008], 23.

24. Letter from Vincent to Theo van Gogh, 3 September 1888, http://vangoghletters .org/vg/letters/let673/letter.html.

25. Letter from Vincent to Theo van Gogh, 8 September 1888, http://vangoghletters .org/vg/letters/let676/letter.html.

26. Letter from Vincent to Theo van Gogh, 9 September 1888, http://vangoghletters .org/vg/letters/let677/letter.html.

27. Letter from Vincent van Gogh to A. H. Koning, 22 or 23 January 1889, Arles, http://vangoghletters.org/vg/letters /let740/letter.html.

28. Letter from Vincent van Gogh to Émile Bernard, c. 19 June 1888, Arles, http://

vangoghletters.org/vg/letters/let628
/letter.html.

29. Gauguin related his version of these events
in his *Intimate Journals,* written years later
in Tahiti and published posthumously.
Gauguin [1952].

30. Letter from Vincent to Theo van Gogh,
between about Friday, 31 May, and about
Thursday, 6 June 1889, http://vangogh
letters.org/vg/letters/let777/letter.html.

31. Boime [2008], 20.

32. Quote given on Museum of Modern Art,
"Vincent van Gogh: Starry Night," www
.moma.org.

33. Boime [2008], 50.

34. Zhao [2008].

35. Silverman [2000], 163.

36. This topic was explored in the papers of
a conference, *Musica e Arti figurative:
Rinascimento e Novecento;* see Ruffini
and Wolf [2008].

37. Zuccari [2006], 67–75, reported on the
technical examination of 2005. The
same discoloration was observed in
the National Gallery, London, *Bathers*
and reported by Kirby et al. [2003], esp.
24–25.

38. Herbert [1991], 173.

39. Zuccari [2006], 73.

40. See Herbert [1991], 177, quoting the contemporary critic Paul Adams, May 1886.

41. Zimmermann [1991], 354, citing Robert L.
Herbert, "'Parade de cirque' de Seurat
et l'esthétique scientifique de Charles
Henry," *Revue de l'art* 50 (1980): 19.

42. Hale and Centano [2017].

43. Herbert [1991], 177: "Seurat created in *La
Grande Jatte* a harmonic middle-class society, an ideal of peaceful leisure signaled by
the Sunday of the painting's title."

44. Matisse, "Notes of a Painter, 1908," in Flam
[1973], 38. He goes on to say, "An art that
could be for every mental worker, for the
businessman as well as the man of letters,
for example, a soothing calming influence
on the mind, something like a good
armchair that provides relaxation from
fatigue" (36).

45. Matisse, "Notes of a Painter, 1908," quoted
in Flam [1973], 37.

46. Bois [1990], 28, discussed how Matisse
replaced relief and perspective with color
as the organizing principle.

47. The title is sometimes given as *Joie de
Vivre,* but Elderfield argues that "it is not
the joy of life.... Rather it is happiness,
the contentment of living; something
slower, dreamier, far more deeply interior." Quoted in Bois, Butler, and Grammont [2015], 2:64.

48. A contrary view was put forward by Werth
[1990].

49. Technical analysis in Bois, Butler, and
Grammont [2015], 86–97, where the areas
of discoloration have been mapped and
color corrected photographs are offered.
Degradation of cadmium yellow has been
found in works by Van Gogh, Mondrian,
Munch, and others. A layer of gray grime
has been observed both above and below
a layer of varnish, indicating that it was
varnished some time after it left the painter's studio.

50. Gowing [1979], 50.

51. The browning of "copper resinate," an
indispensable pigment for green landscape in the Renaissance, was discussed
in chap. 1.

52. Matisse, "Notes of a Painter, 1908," quoted
in Flam [1973], 38.

53. Belloli [2005] identifies Picasso's blue of
this period as Prussian blue. On Picasso,
see Baldassari [2014].

54. "Picture with the White Edge," in Kandinsky [1982], 390–91.

55. Golding [1988], 115.

56. Nochlin [1980], 106.

57. Golding [1988], 115. He quotes Braque: "I
sensed that colour could produce sensations which would interfere a bit with
space, and it is because of that I abandoned it."

58. Nochlin [1980], 106.

59. Nochlin [1980], 107. The quote continues:
"It always seems to be inserted in context
of such complexity or lack of self-evident
raison d'être that we tend to impose
meaning upon it."

60. Journal entry of October 6, 1919, in Lothar
Grisebach, *Ernst Ludwig Kirchners Davoser
Tagebuch* (Ostfildern: G. Hatje, 1997), 54.
Cited in Schick [2012], 49. The Museum of
Modern Art displays the date of the paint-
ing as 1919.

61. Kirchner, quoted in Nerina Santo-
rius, "The Expressionist in Dresden,"
in Krämer [2010], 71, from Eberhard
W. Kornfeld, *Ernst Ludwig Kirchner:
Nachzeichnung seines Lebens* (Bern: Kornfeld, 1979), 341.

62. From Kirchner's journal entry of
April 15, 1927, in Grisebach, *Ernst Ludwig
Kirchners,* 150–52. Cited in Schick [2012],
45.

63. Kurt Wehlte, *The Materials and Techniques
of Painting* (New York: Van Nostrand
Reinhold, 1975), 536; German ed. cited in
Schick [2012], 48.

64. Schick [2012], 46.

65. Kandinsky and Sadler [1977], 53.

66. Short [2010]. Short distills the essence
of *Concerning the Spiritual in Art*
while pointing out its inconsistencies
and contradictions.

67. Kandinsky [1977], 54.

68. Kandinsky [1977], 44.

69. "Reminiscences/Three Pictures," in Kandinsky [1982], 370.

70. Cologne lecture, 1914, in Kandinsky [1982],
396.

71. Kandinsky [1977], 38.

72. Kandinsky [1977], 40.

73. Short [2010], chaps. 3 and 4.

74. Kandinsky [1977], 57.

75. Smithgall [2011], 17–30.

76. "Picture with the White Edge," in Kandinsky [1982], 391.

77. Narayan Khandekar, Gillian McMillan,
Erin Mysak, and Elizabeth Steele, "Side
by Side: The Technical Investigation of
Sketch I for Painting with White Border and
Painting with White Border," in Smithgall
[2011], 111.

78. "Side by Side," 118–19.

79. "Picture with the White Edge," in Kandinsky [1982], 390–91.

80. Kandinsky [1977], 25.

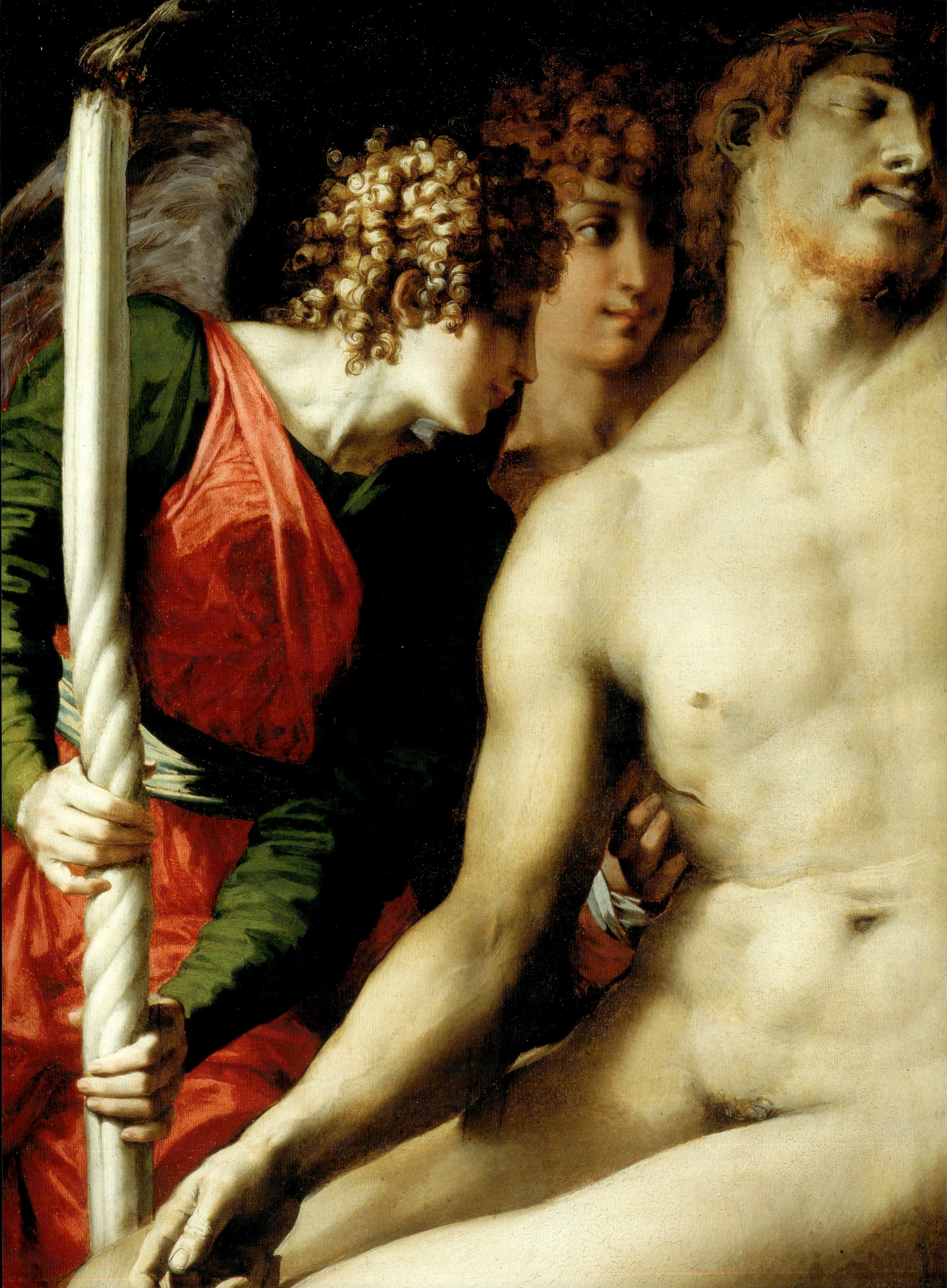

Glossary

à l'essence A technique to achieve a matte, chalky look in painting by draining the oil from the paint onto blotting paper and then diluting it with turpentine.

aerial perspective A method of creating the illusion of distance by modulating color and blurring contours to mimic the effect of the atmosphere on colors.

Alberti coloring system A system of modeling described by Leon Battista Alberti in *On Painting* (Della pittura, 1435), in which shadows were created by adding black or a dark monochrome. It provided a more naturalistic alternative to the Cennini system.

antimony *See* **stibnite**.

arriccio In fresco, the layer of rough plaster on which the *sinopia* was drawn and over which the *intonaco* was applied.

atmospheric perspective *See* **aerial perspective**.

bole A reddish (or brownish) clay used as the preparatory base under gold leaf on panel painting.

bottega (plural *botteghe*) The workshop of an artist.

broken color *See* **couleur rompue**.

buon fresco From the Italian for "good" or "true" fresco; it describes fresco in which the pigment was applied in water to damp plaster. In drying, it bonds chemically to the calcium carbonate in the plaster to form a durable surface; it was usable in regions where the climate was not damp.

cangiantismo One of the four modes of coloring in Cinquecento central Italy, characterized by its frankly ornamental and artificial manner, in which contrasting colors are juxtaposed for modeling; hue-shifting. (*See also* **chiaroscuro, sfumato mode,** and *unione*.)

cartoon A full-scale preliminary drawing used as a guide to the final work, which could be pounced or incised to transfer the design to the support.

Cennini coloring system A system of modeling practiced by Giotto and painters following him and described by Cennino Cennini in his *Craftsman's Handbook* (Libro dell'arte, c. 1390–1400). Pure color was used in the shadows, with gradations of white added for the mid-tones and lights.

central-point perspective A method of producing the illusion of three dimensions on a two-dimensional surface. In central-point perspective, all parallel lines in the composition converge on the vanishing point, typically on the horizon line at the eye level of the viewer.

chiaroscuro Contrast of light and shade. One of the four modes of coloring used in Cinquecento Italy that created harsh contrasts of light and shade, usually with saturated colors for theatrical effect. (*See also cangiantismo,* **sfumato mode,** and *unione*.)

colorire from the Italian for "to color"; refers to composing with colors rather than to the coloring materials themselves.

couleur rompue Refers to the medieval concept of "corrupted color"; using a physical mixture of "friendly colors" to produce a clean tertiary color.

dead color In oil painting, the monochrome or reduced color underpainting added on top of the ground layer or underdrawing, which, because it soaked up some of the oil, gave a matte or dead effect.

decorum Principle of appropriateness for a chosen subject, location, or function.

disegno–colore **debate** The debate in sixteenth-century Italy, associated with Florence/Rome versus Venice, between the advocates of *disegno* (design, conception), which appeals to the intellect, and *colore*, which appeals to the senses and the emotions. This takes the form of the *Poussinistes–Rubénistes* quarrel in the seventeenth century.

down-modeling *See* **Alberti coloring system**.

ébauche A *modello* or rough sketch in oil, sometimes the first layer of the underpainting.

egg tempera Paint medium in which ground pigment is suspended in a mixture of raw egg (yolk, white, or whole) and water. It was popular in the Renaissance for painting panels until it was superseded by oil.

esquisse A compositional sketch representing the design in progress in preparation for the finished work.

ferule The metal band that holds the bristles or hair of a brush to its handle.

gesso Surface preparation for panel or canvas made of plaster or chalk mixed with glue. Its hard white surface can be sanded smooth and is absorbent.

giornata From the Italian for "day"; in fresco, the patch of *intonaco* applied for a day's work.

glazing In oil painting, the application of a thin, translucent film of color over a dried layer to alter the color.

grisaille A method of painting in shades of monochrome gray or another neutral color.

houding A term coined by Dutch theorists to describe a perspective technique for the manipulation of chiaroscuro, color, and overall composition to create a convincing sense of space.

impasto Paint that is thickly applied so that it stands in relief and retains the marks of the brush or palette knife.

imprimatura A layer of priming that functions to isolate the oil paint from the absorbent ground; if tinted, it can provide a homogeneous base tone for the colors painted on top.

intonachino In Roman fresco painting, a very thin layer of white plaster applied over the *intonaco* to mask the tint of the *pozzolana* and restore its brilliant whiteness.

intonaco In fresco, the final layer of smoothed plaster applied over the rough *arriccio*, which the painter works while it is damp.

isochromatism A compositional device in which identical or nearly identical tones are balanced to create a pattern on the surface of the painting.

local color An object's "true color" when seen in daylight, unmodified by such things as aerial perspective.

macchia (plural *macchie*) From the Italian for "blob"; "*pittura di macchie*" is Giorgio Vasari's term for open brushwork. It was called *tache* painting in nineteenth-century France.

maniera From the Italian for "hand"; *see* **mannerism**.

mannerism Refers to a style of late Renaissance art that emphasized artifice over naturalism; it can also be used as a period designation for mid-sixteenth-century painting in central Italy.

modeling The process of creating the illusion of three dimensionality on a two-dimensional surface by the use of light and shade.

modello A preparatory study or model for a painting, usually at a smaller scale.

naturalism A style of art seeking to represent objects as they appear in nature.

one-point perspective *See* **central-point perspective**.

open brushwork A technique of leaving brushstrokes unblended so they create a lively effect on the viewer's eye.

orthogonal In a perspective construction, a line imagined to be behind and perpendicular to the picture plane. The orthogonals in a painting appear to converge as they recede toward the vanishing point on the horizon.

patina In painting, refers to the changes in the surface resulting from the passage of time or interventions, such as crackle, discoloration of varnish, or accumulation of dust and grime.

pentimento From the Italian for "repentance"; a change in composition during the working process.

plein air From the French for "open air"; the practice adopted in the nineteenth century of painting out-of-doors rather than in the studio or workshop.

pouncing The method of transferring a design from a pricked cartoon to another surface by forcing black chalk through the holes, to leave little dotted lines on the receptive surface.

pozzolana A volcanic ash added to the plaster of fresco, particularly in Rome, where the climate was damper than in Florence; it varied in color from brownish to grayish to slightly purple.

Realism A style of art seeking to create objective representations of the external world based on the impartial observation of everyday life.

reddering Used by Dutch painters, a means of creating the illusion of space by alternating bands of light and shade.

relief In painting, the degree in which figures appear to project from the background, obtained by modeling colors.

secco From the Italian for "dry"; the technique of painting on dry plaster, rather than damp (fresco).

sfumato mode One of four modes of coloring used in Cinquecento central Italy in which transitions between color fields are softened and blurred, as if engulfed in a smoky mist. The range of tones tends to be restricted to mid-tone and low color values. (*See also* **cangiantismo**, **chiaroscuro**, and **unione**.)

sinopia In fresco, the brush underdrawing applied to the wall before the *intonaco*, the final layer of wet plaster; it was replaced after the mid-Quattrocento by pounced cartoons.

size A thin layer, often made of dilute hide glue, applied during priming to reduce the porous, absorbent nature of the ground.

spolvero (plural *spolveri*) The dots made by pouncing a pricked cartoon.

stacco A technique for detaching fresco from the wall in which some of the plaster is removed together with the paint layer. *See also* *strappo*.

stibnite A rare grayish pigment used notably by Correggio in his tinted *imprimatura*.

strappo From the Italian for "to rip off"; a method for transferring fresco from its original support by gluing cloth to the surface and pulling the paint layer away from the plaster. *See also* *stacco*.

support The solid substance on which a painting is executed: for example, wood panel, canvas, plastered wall.

tache painting *See macchia.*

tempera *See* egg tempera.

tempera grassa From the Italian for "fat tempera"; a mixture of
oil and egg tempera that produces more blended effects and a
deeper tonality akin to the oil medium, but retains the more rapid
drying effects of egg tempera. A favorite medium of late Quattrocento painters.

tenebrism Very intense chiaroscuro. It describes a strong contrast of
light and dark and referred originally to the work of Caravaggio.

tinted *imprimatura* *See* imprimatura.

underdrawing The drawing or transferred design under a painting
on the ground or *imprimatura.* For fresco, *see* sinopia.

unione One of the four modes of coloring used in Cinquecento Italy
that aimed to achieve tonal unity by equalizing the range of value
and intensity of pigments. (*See also* **cangiantismo,** **chiaroscuro,** and
sfumato mode.)

up-modeling *See* Cennini coloring system.

value The degree of a color's lightness or darkness. In gray scale,
white is high value and black is low value.

vendecolori Venetian specialist shops that supplied artists and other
craftsmen with already prepared pigments.

verdaccio From the Italian for "dirty green"; a mixture of green with
such pigments as ochre, burnt sienna, and lampblack, used especially to undermodel flesh tones in egg tempera.

wet-in-wet painting The technique of brushing fresh oil paint into
a layer while it is still wet, resulting in partial or complete mixing
on the support.

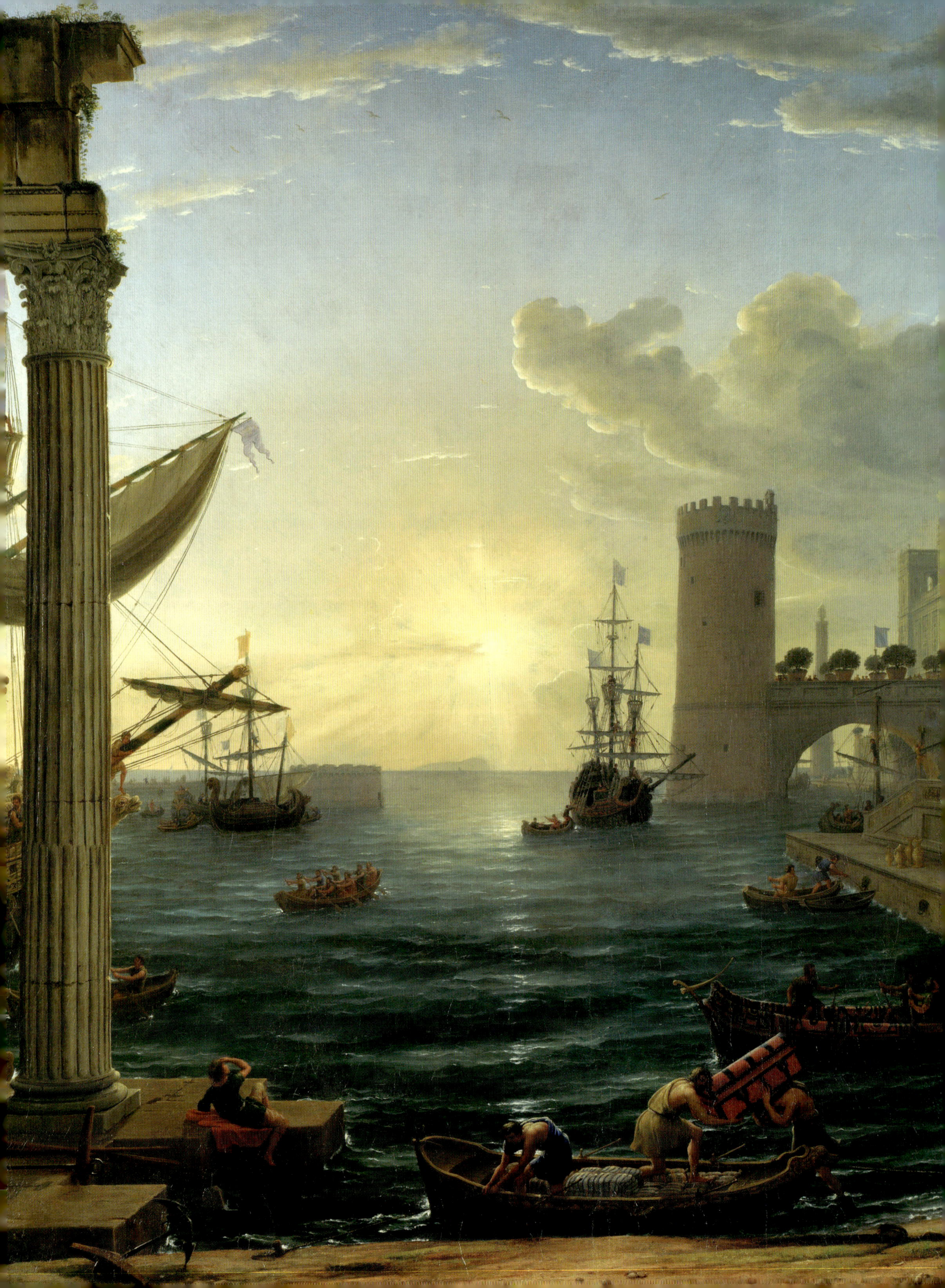

Bibliography

Aikema, Bernard, Beverly Louise Brown, and Giovanna Nepi Scirè. 2000. *Renaissance Venice and the North: Crosscurrents in the Time of Bellini, Dürer, and Titian.* New York: Rizzoli.

Ainsworth, Maryan W. 1998. *From Van Eyck to Bruegel: Early Netherlandish Painting in the Metropolitan Museum of Art.* New York: Metropolitan Museum of Art.

Alberti, Leon Battista. 2013. *On Painting: A New Translation and Critical Edition.* Translated and edited by Rocco Sinisgalli. Cambridge: Cambridge University Press.

Alpers, Svetlana. 1983. *The Art of Describing: Dutch Art in the Seventeenth Century.* Chicago: University of Chicago Press.

Alpers, Svetlana, and Michael Baxandall. 1994. *Tiepolo and the Pictorial Intelligence.* New Haven: Yale University Press.

Ames-Lewis, Francis. 1981. *Drawing in Early Renaissance Italy.* New Haven: Yale University Press.

———. 2000. *The Intellectual Life of the Early Renaissance Artist.* New Haven: Yale University Press.

Angelini, Aldo. 1985. "Sulla tecnica della pittura murale nella villa Farnesina." *Racar Société pour Promouvoir la Publication en Histoire de l'Art au Canada Département d'Histoire, Université Laval.*

Armenini, Giovanni Battista. 1977. *On the True Precepts of the Art of Painting.* Translated and edited by Edward J. Olszewski. New York: B. Franklin.

Badt, Kurt. 1969. *Die Kunst des Nicolas Poussin.* Cologne: M. Du Mont Schauberg.

Bagarotti, Rosella, Rossella Cavigli, Luisa Gusmeroli, Maria Chiara Maida, Alfeo Michielotto, Gloria Tranquilli, Antonella Casoli, and Stefano Volpin. 2000. "La tecnica pittorica di Giovanni Bellini." In *Il Colore Ritrovato: Bellini a Venezia,* edited by Rona Goffen and Giovanna Nepi Scirè, 184–202. Milan: Electa.

Baldassari, Anne. 2014. *Picasso's Masterpieces: The Musée Picasso Paris Collection.* Paris: Flammarion.

Baldini, Umberto, and Ornella Casazza. 1986. *Primavera: The Restoration of Botticelli's Masterpiece.* New York: Abrams.

Bambach, Carmen. 1999a. *Drawing and Painting in the Italian Renaissance Workshop: Theory and Practice, 1300–1600.* Cambridge: Cambridge University Press.

———. 1999b. "The Purchases of Cartoon Paper for Leonardo's 'Battle of Anghiari' and Michelangelo's 'Battle of Cascina.'" In *I Tatti Studies in the Italian Renaissance,* 105–33. Florence: L. S. Olschki.

Bann, Stephen. 1997. *Paul Delaroche: History Painted.* Princeton: Princeton University Press.

Barbieri, Costanza. 2004. *Notturno Sublime: Sebastiano e Michelangelo nella Pietà di Viterbo.* Rome: Viviani.

———. 2013. "'To Be in Heaven': St. Philip Neri between Aesthetic Emotion and Mystical Ecstasy." In *The Sensuous in the Counter-Reformation,* edited by Marcia B. Hall and Tracy E. Cooper, 206–29. New York: Cambridge University Press.

Barcham, William L. 1989. *The Religious Paintings of Giambattista Tiepolo: Piety and Tradition in Eighteenth-Century Venice.* Oxford: Clarendon.

Barocchi, Paola. 1965. *Il Carteggio di Michelangelo.* Florence: Sansoni.

Barocchi, Paola, and Renzo Ristori. 1988. *Il carteggio indiretto di Michelangelo.* Florence: SPES.

Barzman, Karen-edis. 2000. *The Florentine Academy and the Early Modern State: The Discipline of Disegno.* New York: Cambridge University Press.

Baschet, Robert. 1942. *E.-J. Delécluze, Témoin de Son Temps, 1781–1863.* Paris: Boivin.

Baudelaire, Charles. 1970. *Art in Paris, 1845–1862.* New York: Phaidon.

Baxandall, Michael. 1972. *Painting and Experience in Fifteenth-Century Italy: A Primer in the Social History of Pictorial Style.* Oxford: Oxford University Press.

Beck, James. 1988. "The Final Layer; 'l'Ultima Mano' on Michelangelo's Sistine Ceiling." *Art Bulletin* 70: 502–3.

Beck, James H., and Michael Daley. 1996. *Art Restoration: The Culture, the Business and the Scandal.* New York: W. W. Norton.

Bell, Janis. 1993. "Zaccolini's Theory of Color Perspective." *Art Bulletin* 75: 91–112.

———. 1995. "Light and Color in Caravaggio's Supper at Emmaus." *Artibus et Historiae* 16: 139–70.

Belloli, Lucy. 2005. "Lost Paintings beneath Picasso's La Coiffure." *Metropolitan Museum Journal* 40: 151–61.

Bellori, Giovanni Pietro. 2010. *The Lives of the Modern Painters, Sculptors and Architects.* Translated by Alice Sedgwick Wohl. Cambridge: Cambridge University Press.

Bellucci, Roberto, and Cecilia Frosinini. 2017. "L'Adorazione dei Magi di Leonardo da Vinci: Il restauro di un dipinto non finite." In *Il cosmo magico di Leonardo: L'Adorazione dei Magi restaurata,* edited by Eike D. Schmidt, Marco Ciatti, and Daniela Parenti. Florence: Giunti.

Bent, George R. 2000. "A Patron for Lorenzo Monaco's Uffizi Coronation of the Virgin." *Art Bulletin* 82: 348–54.

Berger, Robert W. 1999. *Public Access to Art in Paris: A Documentary History from the Middle Ages to 1800.* University Park: Pennsylvania State University Press.

Berrie, Barbara H., John K. Delaney, Joanna R. Dunn, and Lisha Deming Glinsman. 2015. "The Creation of Giotto's 'Madonna and Child': New Insights." *Facture/National Gallery of Art* 2: 2–17.

Berrie, Barbara, and Elizabeth Walmsley. 2007. "Raphael's *Alba Madonna.*" In *Raphael's Painting Technique: Working Practice before Rome,* proceedings of the Eu-ARTECH workshop, edited by Ashok Roy and Marika Spring. Florence: Nardini.

Billinge, Rachel, Lorne Campbell, Jill Dunkerton, Susan Foister, Jo Kirby, Jennie Pilc, Ashok Roy, Marika Spring, and Raymond White. 1997. "Methods and Materials of Northern European Painting." *National Gallery Technical Bulletin* 18: 6–55.

Blunt, Anthony. 1967. *Nicolas Poussin.* New York: Pantheon.

Boime, Albert. 1965. "Seurat and Piero della Francesca." *Art Bulletin* 47: 265–71.

——. 1969. "The Salon des Refusés and the Evolution of Modern Art." *Art Quarterly* 30: 411–26.

——. 1971. *The Academy and French Painting in the Nineteenth Century.* London: Phaidon.

——. 2008. *Art in an Age of Civil Struggle, 1848–1871.* Chicago: University of Chicago Press.

Bois, Yve-Alain. 1990. "Matisse and the Arche-Drawing." In *Painting as Model,* 3–63. Cambridge, Mass.: MIT Press.

Bois, Yve-Alain, Karen K. Butler, and Claudine Grammont. 2015. *Matisse in the Barnes Collection.* Vol. 2. Philadelphia: Barnes Foundation.

Bomford, David, Sarah Herring, Jo Kirby, Christopher Riopelle, and Ashok Roy. 2004. *Art in the Making: Degas.* London: National Gallery.

Bomford, David, Jo Kirby, John Leighton, and Ashok Roy. 1990. *Art in the Making: Impressionism.* London: National Gallery.

Bomford, David, Jo Kirby, Ashok Roy, Axel Ruger, and Raymond White. 2006. *Art in the Making: Rembrandt.* London: National Gallery.

Bomford, David, Ashok Roy, and Alistair Smith. 1986. "The Technique of Dieric Bouts: Two Paintings Contrasted." *National Gallery Technical Bulletin* 10: 39–57.

Bonito, Virginia, and Constance Silver. 1984. "Some Technical Observations on Raphael's 'Isaiah' and the Accademia San Luca 'Putto.'" *Source* 3: 68–80.

Borsook, Eve. 1980. *The Mural Painters of Tuscany: From Cimabue to Andrea Del Sarto.* Oxford: Clarendon.

Brettell, Richard R. 1988. *The Art of Paul Gauguin.* Washington, D.C.: National Gallery of Art.

Brinkman, Pim. 1984. "Het Lam Godsretabel van Van Eyck: Een Heronderzoek Naar de Materialen En Schildermethoden 1: De Plamuur, de Isolatielaag, de Tekening En de Grondtonen." *Bulletin de l'Institut Royal du Patrimoine* 20: 137–66.

Brookner, Anita. 1972. *Greuze: The Rise and Fall of an Eighteenth-Century Phenomenon.* Greenwich: Graphic Society.

Brooks, Julian. 2015. *Andrea del Sarto: The Renaissance Workshop in Action.* Los Angeles: J. Paul Getty Museum.

Brown, David Alan, and Sylvia Pagden Ferino. 2006. *Bellini, Giorgione, Titian, and the Renaissance of Venetian Painting.* Washington, D.C.: National Gallery of Art.

Brown, Jonathan. 1995. *Kings and Connoisseurs: Collecting Art in Seventeenth-Century Europe.* Princeton: Princeton University Press.

Bruyn, J. 1987. "Toward a Scriptural Reading of 17th-Century Dutch Landscape Paintings." In *Masters of 17th-Century Dutch Landscape Painting,* edited by Peter Sutton. Boston: Museum of Fine Arts.

Bryson, Norman. 1981. *Word and Image: French Painting of the Ancien Régime.* Cambridge: Cambridge University Press.

Burchard, Wolf. 2016. *The Sovereign Artist: Charles Le Brun and the Image of Louis XIV.* London: Paul Holberton.

Burnstock, Aviva. 1988. "The Fading of the Virgin's Robe in Lorenzo Monaco's 'Coronation of the Virgin.'" *National Gallery Technical Bulletin* 12: 58–65.

Burnstock, Aviva, Klaas van der Berg, and John House. 2005. "Painting Techniques of Pierre-Auguste Renoir: 1868–1919." *ArtMatters: Netherlands Technical Studies in Art* 3: 47–65.

Butler, Marigene H. 1984. "An Investigation of the Materials and Technique Used by Paul Cézanne." In *American Institute for Conservation Preprints of Papers Presented at the Twelfth Annual Meeting.* Washington, D.C.: The Institute.

Büttner, Nils. 2006. "Aristocracy and Noble Business: Some Remarks on Rubens's Financial Affairs." *Munuscula Amicorum* 1: 67–78.

Cadogan, Jean K., Stephen Kornhausen, and Patricia Sherwin Garland. 2015. "'The Crucifixion' by Nicolas Poussin in the Wadsworth Atheneum Museum of Art, Hartford, Connecticut." *Kermes: Arte e Tecnica del Restauro* 94/95: 84–88.

Callen, Anthea. 1982. *Techniques of the Impressionists.* Secaucus, N.J.: Chartwell.

——. 2000. *The Art of Impressionism: Painting Technique and the Making of Modernity.* New Haven: Yale University Press.

Campbell, Lorne. 1993. "Memling's Creative Process as Seen in His Paintings in the National Gallery, London." In *Le Dessin Sous-Jacent dans la Peinture. Colloque X: Le Dessin Sous-Jacent dans le Processus de Creation; Université Catholique de Louvain, 5–7 Septembre 1993,* edited by Helen Verougstraete-Marcq and Roger van Schoute, 149–52. Louvain-la-Neuve: Collège Érasme.

Carl, Doris. 1987. "Das Inventar der Werkstatt von Filippino Lippi Aus Dem Jahr 1504." *Mitteilungen Des Kunsthistorischen Institutes in Florenz* 35: 373–91.

Carlyle, Leslie. 2001. *The Artist's Assistant: Oil Painting Instruction Manuals and Handbooks in Britain, 1800–1900, with Reference to Selected Eighteenth-Century Sources.* London: Archetype.

Cauzzi, Diego, Pietro Moioli, and Claudio Seccaroni. 2015. "Materiali e tecnica in alcuni dipinti del Correggio." *Bollettino ICR* 30: 39–50.

Cavazzini, Patrizia. 2008. *Painting as Business in Early Seventeenth-Century Rome.* University Park: Pennsylvania State University Press.

Cecchi, Alessandro. 1999. "The Conservation of Antonio and Piero del Pollaiuolo's Altar-Piece for the Cardinal of Portugal's Chapel with a Conservation Report by Sandra Freschi and Nicola MacGregor." *Burlington Magazine* 141: 81–88.

Cecchini, Isabella. 2006. "Troublesome Business: Dealing in Venice, 1600–1750." In *Mapping Markets for Paintings in Europe, 1450–1750,* edited by Neil De Marchi and Hans J. Van Miegroet, 125–34. Turnhout, Belg.: Brehols.

Cennini, Cennino. 2015. *Cennino Cennini's il libro dell'arte: A New English Language Translation and Commentary with Italian*

Transcription. Translated and transcribed by Lara Broecke. London: Archetype.

CHAIMOVICH, FELIPE. 2008. "Mirrors of Society: Versailles and the Use of Flat Reflected Images." *Visual Resources* 24, no. 4: 353–67.

CHAMBERS, DAVID. 1971. *Patrons and Artists in the Italian Renaissance.* Columbia: University of South Carolina Press.

CHRISTENSEN, CAROL. 1993. "The Painting Materials and Technique of Paul Gauguin." *Studies in the History of Art* 41: 62–103.

CHRISTIANSEN, KEITH. 1998. "The View from Italy." In *From Van Eyck to Bruegel: Early Netherlandish Painting in the Metropolitan Museum of Art,* edited by Maryan W. Ainsworth and Keith Christiansen. New York: Metropolitan Museum of Art.

———. 2004. "Bellini and Mantegna." In *Cambridge Companion to Giovanni Bellini,* edited by Peter Humfrey, 48–74. Cambridge: Cambridge University Press.

CIATTI, MARCO, CECILIA FROSININI, AND PATRIZIA RIITANO. 1998. *Lorenzo Monaco, Tecnica e Restauro: l'Incoronazione della Vergine degli Uffizi, l'Annunciazione Di Santa Trinita a Firenze.* Florence: Edifir.

CLARK, KENNETH. 1966. *Rembrandt and the Italian Renaissance.* New York: New York University Press.

CLARK, T. J. 1999. *The Painting of Modern Life: Paris in the Art of Manet and His Followers.* Princeton: Princeton University Press.

CLARKE, ASHLEY, AND PHILIP RYLANDS. 1977. *The Church of the Madonna dell'Orto: Restoring Venice.* London: Elek.

COLALUCCI, GIANLUIGI. 1994. "The Technique of the Sistine Chapel Frescoes." In *The Sistine Chapel: A Glorious Restoration,* edited by Loren Partridge, Gianluigi Colalucci, and Fabrizio Mancinelli. New York: Abrams.

CONISBEE, PHILIP. 1979. "Pre-Romantic Plein-Air Painting." *Art History* 2: 413–28.

CONISBEE, PHILIP, RICHARD RAND, AND JOSEPH BAILLIO. 2009. *French Paintings of the Fifteenth through the Eighteenth Century.* Washington, D.C.: National Gallery of Art.

CONNELLY, FRANCES S. 1995. *The Sleep of Reason: Primitivism in Modern European Art and Aesthetics, 1725–1907.* University Park: Pennsylvania State University Press.

CONSTABLE, W. G., AND J. G. LINKS. 1989. *Canaletto: Giovanni Antonio Canal, 1697–1768.* 2nd ed. Oxford: Clarendon.

COVI, DARIO. 2005. *Andrea del Verrocchio: Life and Work.* Florence: Leo S. Olschki.

COX-REARICK, JANET. 1964. *The Drawings of Pontormo.* Cambridge, Mass.: Harvard University Press.

———. 1996. *The Collection of Francis I: Royal Treasures.* New York: Abrams.

CRENSHAW, PAUL. 2006. *Rembrandt's Bankruptcy: The Artist, His Patrons, and the Art Market in Seventeenth-Century Netherlands.* New York: Cambridge University Press.

CROPPER, ELIZABETH. 1980. "Poussin and Leonardo: Evidence from the Zaccolini MSS." *Art Bulletin* 62: 570–83.

CROPPER, ELIZABETH, AND CHARLES DEMPSEY. 1996. *Nicolas Poussin: Friendship and the Love of Painting.* Princeton: Princeton University Press.

CROW, THOMAS. 1985. *Painters and Public Life in Eighteenth-Century Paris.* New Haven: Yale University Press.

CROWE, J. A., AND G. B. CAVALCASELLE. 1871. *A History of Painting in Italy: Umbria, Florence and Siena, from the Second to the Sixteenth Century.* London: Murray.

DACOS, NICOLE. 2001. "Italiens et Espagnols dans l'atelier de Salviati: La chapelle du Pallio à la Chancellerie." In *Francesco Salviati et la bella maniera: Actes des colloques de Rome et de Paris, 1998,* edited by Catherine Monbeig Goguel, Philippe Costamagna, and Michel Hochmann. Rome: École française de Rome.

DANIELSSON, BENGT. 1966. *Gauguin in the South Seas.* Garden City, N.Y.: Doubleday.

———. 1969. "The Exotic Sources of Gauguin's Art." *Expedition* 11: 16–26.

DEGRAZIA, DIANE, AND MARCIA STEELE. 1999. *Cleveland Studies in the History of Art 4.*

DELACROIX, EUGÈNE. 1923. *Oeuvres Littéraires.* Paris: G. Crès.

———. 1932a. *Journal.* New ed. Paris: Plon.

———. 1932b. *Journal de Eugène Delacroix.* Edited by André Joubin. Paris: Plon.

———. 1936. *Correspondance Générale d'Eugène Delacroix.* Edited by André Joubin. Paris: Plon.

DELANCEY, JULIA A. 2010. "Shipping Colour: Value, Pigments, Trade and Francesco di Marco Datini." In *Trade in Artists' Materials: Market and Commerce in Europe to 1700,* edited by Jo Kirby, Susie Nash, and Joanna Cannon. London: Archetype.

DELAPIERRE, EMMANUELLE, MATTHIEU GILLES, AND HÉLÈNE PORTIGLIA. 2004. *Rubens contre Poussin: La querelle du coloris dans la peinture française à la fin du XVIIe siècle.* Ghent: Ludion.

DE MARCHI, NEIL, AND HANS J. VAN MIEGROET. 2006. *Mapping Markets for Paintings in Europe, 1450–1750.* Turnhout, Belg.: Brepols.

DÉMORIS, RENÉ. 2006. "Boucher, Diderot, Rousseau." In *Rethinking Boucher,* edited by Melissa Hyde and Mark Ledbury. Los Angeles: Getty Research Institute.

DOLAN, THERESE. 2012. *Perspectives on Manet.* Farnham, UK: Ashgate.

DUNKERTON, JILL. 2004. "Bellini's Technique." In *The Cambridge Companion to Giovanni Bellini,* edited by Peter Humfrey, 195–225. New York: Cambridge University Press.

———. 2007. "Tintoretto's Painting Technique." In *Tintoretto,* edited by Miguel Falomir, 139–58. Madrid: Museo Nacional del Prado.

———. 2009. "Sebastiano Del Piombo's 'Raising of Lazarus': A History of Change." *National Gallery Technical Bulletin* 30: 29–51.

DUNKERTON, JILL, SUSAN FOISTER, AND DILLIAN GORDON. 1994. *Giotto to Dürer: Early Renaissance Painting in the National Gallery.* New Haven: Yale University Press.

DUNKERTON, JILL, SUSAN FOISTER, AND NICHOLAS PENNY. 2002. *Dürer to Veronese: Sixteenth-Century Painting in the National Gallery.* New Haven: Yale University Press.

DUNKERTON, JILL, AND ASHOK ROY. 1996. "The Materials of a Group of Late Fifteenth-Century Florentine Panel Paintings." *National Gallery Technical Bulletin* 17: 20–31.

DUNKERTON, JILL, AND MARIKA SPRING. 1998. "The Development of Paintings on Coloured Surfaces in Sixteenth Century Italy." In *Painting Techniques: History, Materials and Studio Practice,* edited by Ashok Roy, 120–30. London: International Institute of Conservation of Historic and Artistic Works.

———. 2013. "Titian's Painting Technique before 1540." *National Gallery Technical Bulletin* 34: 4–31.

EASTLAKE, CHARLES LOCK. 1960. *Methods and Materials of Painting of the Great Schools and Masters.* New York: Dover.

EDIZEL, GERAR. 1995. "Jean-Siméon Chardin: Seeing, Playing, Forgetting, and the Practice of Modern Imitation." PhD diss., Cornell University.

ERIKSEN, SVEND. 1974. *Early Neo-Classicism in France: The Creation of the Louis Seize Style in Architectural Decoration, Furniture and Ormolu, Gold and Silver, and Sèvres Porcelain in the Mid-Eighteenth Century.* London: Faber.

ERTZ, KLAUS, AND HEINZ ALTHÖFER. 1976. *Fälschung und Forschung.* Essen: Museum Folkwang.

Ewing, Dan. 1990. "Marketing Art in Antwerp, 1460–1560, Our Lady's Pand." *Art Bulletin* 72: 558–84.

Falomir, Miguel. 2006. "Artists' Responses to the Emergence of Markets for Paintings in Spain, c. 1600." In *Mapping Markets for Paintings in Europe, 1450–1750*, edited by Neil De Marchi and Hans J. Van Miegroet. Turnhout, Belg.: Brehols.

Falomir, Miguel, and Bernard Aikema. 2009. *Jacopo Tintoretto*. Madrid: Museo del Prado.

Feeser, Andrea, Maureen Daly Goggin, and Beth Fowkes Tobin. 2012. *The Materiality of Color: The Production, Circulation, and Application of Dyes and Pigments, 1400–1800*. Aldershot, UK: Ashgate.

Feigenbaum, Gail. 1993. "Practice in the Carracci Academy." *Studies in the History of Art* 38: 59–76.

Félibien, André. 1663. *Les Reines de Perse aux pieds d'Alexandre: Peinture du Cabinet du Roy*. Paris: Pierre Le Petit.

———. 1987. *Entretiens sur les Vies et sur les Ouvrages des plus Excellents Peintres Anciens et Modernes: Entretiens I et II*. Paris: Société d'édition "Les Belles Lettres."

Ferretti, Marco. 1990. "The Presence of Antimony in Some Grey Colours of Three Paintings by Correggio." *Studies in Conservation* 30: 235–39.

Fisher, Sarah. 1984. "The Examination and Treatment of Watteau's Italian Comedians." In *Watteau 1684–1721*, edited by Margaret Morgan Grasselli and François Moureau. Washington, D.C.: National Gallery of Art.

FitzHugh, Elisabeth West, Barbara H. Berrie, and Robert L. Feller. 1997. *Artists' Pigments: A Handbook of Their History and Characteristics*. Vol. 3. 3rd ed. Washington, D.C.: National Gallery of Art.

Flam, Jack D. 1973. *Matisse on Art*. New York: Phaidon.

Fletcher, Shelley, and Pia Desantis. 1989. "Degas: The Search for His Technique Continues." *Burlington Magazine* 131: 256–65.

Foulke, Rikke. 2014. "'The Holy Family with the Infant Saint John the Baptist and Saint Elizabeth.'" *Kermes: Arte e Tecnica del Restauro* 27: 89–96.

Fowle, Frances, Lesley Stevenson, and Belinda Thomson. 2005. *Gauguin's Vision*. Edinburgh: National Galleries of Scotland.

Fried, Michael. 1980. *Absorption and Theatricality: Painting and Beholder in the Age of Diderot*. Berkeley: University of California Press.

Gaehtgens, Thomas. 1990. "The Tradition of Antiacademism in Eighteenth-Century French Art." In *The French Academy: Classicism and Its Antagonists*, edited by June Ellen Hargrove. Newark: University of Delaware Press.

Gaertringen, Rudolf Freiherr Hiller von. 1998. "L'uso ed il reuso del cartoni nell'opera del Perugino: La ripetizione della formula perfetta." In *The Ascension of Christ: by Pietro Perugino*, edited by Stefano Casciu. Milan: Silvana.

Gage, John. 1993. *Color and Culture: Practice and Meaning from Antiquity to Abstraction*. Boston: Little, Brown.

Galassi, Maria Clelia. 1998. *Il disegno svelato: Progetto e immagine nella pittura italiana del primo Rinascimento*. Nuoro, Italy: Ilisso.

———. 2001. "Underdrawing vs. Undermodelling: Form Construction in Tuscan Painting during the First Half of the 15th Century." In *La Peinture et Le Laboratoire*, edited by Roger Van Schoute and Hélène Verougstraete, 131–41. Paris: Peeters.

Galassi, Maria Clelia, and Elizabeth Walmsley. 2009. "Painting Technique in the Late Works of Giotto: Infrared Examination of Seven Panels from Altarpieces Painted for Santa Croce." In *The Quest for the Original*, edited by Hélène Verougstraete and Colombe Janssens De Bisthoven, with Jacqueline Couvert and Anne Dubois, 116–22. Leuven: Peeters.

Galenson, David W., and Robert Jensen. 2007. "Careers and Canvases: The Rise of the Market for Modern Art in Nineteenth-Century Paris." *Van Gogh Studies* 1: 136–66.

Gaudioso, Filippa Maria. 1981. *Gli affreschi di Paolo III a Castel Sant'Angelo: Progetto ed esecuzione, 1543–1548*. Rome: De Luca.

Gauguin, Paul. 1950. *Lettres à Daniel de Monfreid*. Paris: Falaize.

———. 1952. *The Intimate Journals of Paul Gauguin*. Translated by Van Wyck Brooks. London: William Heinemann.

———. 1984. *Correspondance de Paul Gauguin: Documents, Témoignages*. Edited by Victor Merlhès. Paris: Fondation Singer-Polignac.

Gibson, Walter S. 1989. *Mirror of the Earth: The World Landscape in Sixteenth-Century Flemish Painting*. Princeton: Princeton University Press.

Gifford, E. Melanie. 1995. "Style and Technique in Dutch Landscape Painting." In *Historical Painting Techniques, Materials, and Studio Practice*, edited by Arie Wallert and Erma Hermens. Marina Del Rey: Getty Conservation Institute.

———. 1996. "Jan van Goyen en de techniek van het naturalistische landschap," translated as "Jan van Goyen and the Practice of Naturalistic Landscape." In *Jan van Goyen*, edited by Christiaan Vogelaar, Edwin Buijsen, Sabine Giepmans, and Jaap Engelsman. Zwolle, Neth.: Waanders.

Gifford, E. Melanie, Catherine A. Metzger, and John K. Delaney. 2013. "Jan van Eyck's Washington Annunciation: Painting Materials and Techniques." *Facture* 1: 128–53.

Gisolfi, Diana. 2017. *Paolo Veronese and the Practice of Painting in Late Renaissance Venice*. New Haven: Yale University Press.

Glanville, Helen. 2001. "Veracity, Verisimilitude, and Optics in Painting in Italy at the Turn of the Seventeenth Century." *Italian Studies* 56: 30–56.

———. 2014. "Nicolas Poussin: Creation and Perception." *Kermes: Arte e Tecnica del Restauro* 27: 16–30.

Glasser, Hannelore. 1977. *Artists' Contracts of the Early Renaissance*. New York: Garland.

Goffen, Rona. 2002. *Renaissance Rivals: Michelangelo, Leonardo, Raphael, Titian*. New Haven: Yale University Press.

Goffen, Rona, and Giovanna Nepi Scirè. 2000. *Il Colore Ritrovato: Bellini a Venezia*. Milan: Electa.

Golding, John. 1988. *Cubism: A History and an Analysis, 1907–1914*. Cambridge, Mass.: Harvard University Press.

Goldner, George. 2004. "Bellini's Drawings." In *The Cambridge Companion to Bellini*, edited by Peter Humfrey, 226–55. Cambridge: Cambridge University Press.

Gombrich, Ernst H. 1972. "Raphael's *Stanza della Segnatura* and the Nature of Its Symbolism." In *Symbolic Images*, 85–101. London: Phaidon.

Gordenker, Emilie. 2015a. "Saul and David Reconsidered—Part 1." *Mauritshuis in Focus* 28, no. 2: 6–10.

———. 2015b. "Saul and David Reconsidered—Part 2," *Mauritshuis in Focus* 28, no. 2: 12–22.

Gowing, Lawrence. 1979. *Matisse*. London: Thames and Hudson.

Gowing, Lawrence, and Michel Laclotte. 1987. *Paintings in the Louvre*. New York: Stewart, Tabori and Chang.

Grasselli, Margaret Morgan, Pierre Rosenberg, and Nicole Parmantier. 1984. *Watteau, 1684–1721*. Washington, D.C.: National Gallery of Art.

Gregori, Mina, Antonio Paolucci, and Cristina Acidini

Luchinat. 1992. *Maestri e botteghe: Pittura a Firenze alla fine del Quattrocento*. Milan: Silvana.

Guidi, Giolj, Pietro Moioli, Raffaele Scafè, Claudio Seccaroni, and Marco Ferretti. 1991. "The Presence of Antimony in Some Grey Colours of Three Paintings by Correggio." *Studies in Conservation* 36, no. 4: 235–39.

Guiducci, Elisabetta, Loredana Francescone, and Elisabetta Diana Valente. 1994. "L'istituto centrale del restauro per Palazzo Te." *Bollettino d'arte*. Rome: Istituto poligrafico e Zecca dello Stato, Libreria dello Stato.

Hale, Charlotte, and Silvia A. Centano. 2017. "Materials, Technique, Evolution." In *Seurat's Circus Sideshow*, edited by Richard Thomson, 112–16. New York: Metropolitan Museum of Art.

Hall, Marcia B. 1992. *Color and Meaning: Practice and Theory in Renaissance Painting*. New York: Cambridge University Press.

———. 1999. *After Raphael: Painting in Central Italy in the Sixteenth Century*. New York: Cambridge University Press.

———. 2011. *The Sacred Image in the Age of Art: Titian, Tintoretto, Barocci, El Greco, Caravaggio*. New Haven: Yale University Press.

Haller, Ursula. 2010. "'Administrator of Painting': The Purchase and Distribution Book of Wolf Pronner (1586–1590) as a Source for the History of Painting Materials." In *Trade in Artists' Materials*, edited by Jo Kirby, Susie Nash, and Joanna Cannon, 325–35. London: Archetype.

Hamilton, George. 1967. *Painting and Sculpture in Europe, 1880–1940*. Baltimore: Penguin.

Hargrove, June Ellen. 1990. *The French Academy: Classicism and Its Antagonists*. Newark: University of Delaware Press.

Hartt, Frederick. 1958. *Giulio Romano*. New Haven: Yale University Press.

Hartt, Frederick, Gino Corti, and Clarence Kennedy. 1964. *The Chapel of the Cardinal of Portugal, 1434–1459, at San Miniato in Florence*. Philadelphia: University of Pennsylvania Press.

Haskell, Francis. 1980. *Patrons and Painters: A Study in the Relations between Italian Art and Society in the Age of the Baroque*. New Haven: Yale University Press.

Haskell, Francis, and Nicholas Penny. 1981. *Taste and the Antique: The Lure of Classical Sculpture, 1500–1900*. New Haven: Yale University Press.

Hatfield, Rab. 2002. *The Wealth of Michelangelo*. Rome: Edizioni di storia e letteratura.

Healy, Fiona. 1997. *Rubens and the Judgement of Paris: A Question of Choice*. Turnhout, Belg.: Brepols.

Held, Julius S. 1980. *The Oil Sketches of Peter Paul Rubens: A Critical Catalogue*. Princeton: Princeton University Press.

Henry, Tom, and Paul Joannides. 2013. *Late Raphael*. London: Thames and Hudson.

Herbert, Robert L. 1988. *Impressionism: Art, Leisure, and Parisian Society*. New Haven: Yale University Press.

———. 1991. *Georges Seurat, 1859–1891*. New York: Metropolitan Museum of Art.

———. 2004. *Seurat and the Making of La Grande Jatte*. Chicago: Art Institute of Chicago.

Hermens, Erma, and Joyce Townsend. 2009. *Sources and Serendipity: Testimonies of Artists' Practice: Proceedings of the Third Symposium of the Art Technological Source Research Working Group*. London: Archetype.

Herring, Sarah. 2009. "Six Paintings by Corot: Methods, Materials and Sources." *National Gallery Technical Bulletin* 30: 86–111.

Hibbard, Howard. 1966. *Bernini*. Baltimore: Penguin.

———. 1974. *Poussin: The Holy Family on the Steps*. New York: Viking.

Hills, Paul. 1999. *Venetian Color*. New Haven: Yale University Press.

Hirst, Michael. 1981. *Sebastiano del Piombo*. Oxford: Clarendon.

Holmes, Megan. 2004. "Copying Practices and Marketing Strategies in a Fifteenth-Century Florentine Painter's Workshop." In *Artistic Exchange and Cultural Translation in the Italian Renaissance City*, edited by Stephen Campbell and Stephen Milner. Cambridge: Cambridge University Press.

Honour, Hugh, and John Fleming. 2011. *The Visual Arts: A History*. Harlow, UK: Pearson.

Hope, Charles, and David Jaffé. 2003. *Titian*. London: National Gallery.

Horace. "Ars Poetica." Translated by A. S. Kline. www.poetryintranslation.com.

House, John. 1986. *Monet, Nature into Art*. New Haven: Yale University Press.

Humfrey, Peter. 1993. *The Altarpiece in Renaissance Venice*. New Haven: Yale University Press.

———. 1995. *Painting in Renaissance Venice*. New Haven: Yale University Press.

———. 2008. *The Cambridge Companion to Giovanni Bellini*. Cambridge: Cambridge University Press.

Hyde, Melissa. 2000. "The 'Makeup' of the Marquise: Boucher's Portrait of Pompadour at Her Toilette." *Art Bulletin* 82: 453–75.

———. 2006. "Getting into the Picture: Boucher's Self-Portraits of Others." In *Rethinking Boucher*, edited by Melissa Hyde and Mark Ledbury. Los Angeles: Getty Research Institute.

Ingres, Jean. 1947. *Ecrits sur l'art: Textes recueillis dans les Carnets et dans la Correspondance de Ingres*. Paris: Jeune Parque.

Jacobs, Lynn. 1989. "The Marketing and Standardization of South Netherlandish Carved Altarpieces: Limits on the Role of the Patron." *Art Bulletin* 71: 208–29.

Jirat-Wasiutyński, Vojtěch, and H. Travers Newton. 2000. *Technique and Meaning in the Paintings of Paul Gauguin*. New York: Cambridge University Press.

Johnson, Lee. 1969. "An Early Study for Delacroix's 'Death of Sardanapalus.'" *Burlington Magazine* 111: 296–99.

———. 1981. *The Paintings of Eugène Delacroix: A Critical Catalogue*. Oxford: Clarendon.

Jonckheere, Koenraad. 2012. *Antwerp Art after Iconoclasm: Experiments in Decorum: 1566–1585*. Antwerp: Mercatorfonds.

Jones, Kimberly A., and Elliot Bostwick Davis. 2014. *Degas–Cassatt*. Munich: Prestel.

Kandinsky, Wassily. 1977. *Concerning the Spiritual in Art*. Translated by Michael Sadleir. New York: Dover.

———. 1982. *Kandinsky, Complete Writings on Art*. Edited by Kenneth Clement Lindsay and Peter Vergo. Boston: G. K. Hall.

Kern, Ulrike. 2014. *Light and Shade in Dutch and Flemish Art*. Turnhout, Belg.: Brepols.

———. 2016. "The Origins of Broken Colours." *Journal of the Warburg and Courtauld Institutes* 79: 183–210.

Kirby, Jo, and Ashok Roy. 1995. "Paul Delaroche: A Case Study of Academic Painting." In *Historical Painting Techniques, Materials, and Studio Practice: Preprints of a Symposium Held at the University of Leiden, the Netherlands, 26–29 June, 1995*, 166–75. Marina Del Rey: Getty Conservation Institute.

Kirby, Jo, Marika Spring, and Catherine Higgitt. 2007. "The Technology of Eighteenth- and Nineteenth-Century Red Lake Pigments." *National Gallery Technical Bulletin* 28: 69–95.

Kirby, Jo, Kate Stonor, Ashok Roy, Aviva Burnstock, Rachel Grout, and Raymond White. 2003. "Seurat's Painting Practice: Theory, Development and Technology." *National Gallery Technical Bulletin* 24: 4–37.

Kirkland, Stephane. 2014. *Paris Reborn: Napoléon III, Baron Haussmann, and the Quest to Build a Modern City.* New York: Picador.

Kline, Jonathan. 2011. "Botticelli's Return of Persephone: On the Source and Subject of the Primavera." *Sixteenth Century Journal* 42: 665–88.

Krämer, Felix. 2010. *Ernst Ludwig Kirchner: Retrospective.* Ostfildern, Ger.: Hatje Cantz.

Lagerlöf, Margaretha Rossholm. 1990. *Ideal Landscape: Annibale Carracci, Nicolas Poussin, and Claude Lorrain.* New Haven: Yale University Press.

Lammertse, Friso, and Jaap van der Veen. 2006. *Uylenburg and Son: Art and Commerce from Rembrandt to de Lairesse: 1625–1675.* Zwolle, Neth.: Waanders.

Landau, David, and Peter W. Parshall. 1994. *The Renaissance Print, 1470–1550.* New Haven: Yale University Press.

Lank, Herbert. 1982. "Titian's 'Perseus and Andromeda': Restoration and Technique." *Burlington Magazine* 124: 400–406.

Lee, Simon. 1999. *David.* London: Phaidon.

Leeflang, Micha. 2006. "The 'Saint Reinhold Altarpiece' by Joos van Cleve and His Workshop: New Insights into the Influence of Albrecht Dürer on the Working Process." In *Making and Marketing,* edited by Molly Faries. Turnhout, Belg.: Brepols.

Leeflang, Micha, and Maryan W. Ainsworth. 2015. *Joos van Cleve: A Sixteenth-Century Antwerp Artist and His Workshop.* Turnhout, Belg.: Brepols.

Leith, James A. 1965. *The Idea of Art as Propaganda in France, 1750–1799: A Study in the History of Ideas.* Toronto: University of Toronto Press.

Lemoine, Annick, Keith Christiansen, Patrizia Cavazzini, Jean-Pierre Cuzin, and Gianni Papi. 2016. *Valentin de Boulogne Beyond Caravaggio.* New York: Metropolitan Museum of Art.

Levey, Michael. 1993. *Painting and Sculpture in France, 1700–1789.* New Haven: Yale University Press.

Lichtenstein, Jacqueline. 1993. *The Eloquence of Color: Rhetoric and Painting in the French Classical Age.* Berkeley: University of California Press.

Lichtenstein, Jacqueline, and Christian Michel. 2009. *Les Conférences au Temps de Guillet de Saint-Georges 1682–1699.* Paris: Beaux-Arts de Paris.

Lingo, Stuart. 2008. *Federico Barocci: Allure and Devotion in Late Renaissance Painting.* New Haven: Yale University Press.

Locke, Nancy. 2012. "Manet and the Ethics of Realism." In *Perspectives on Manet,* edited by Therese Dolan, 9–27. Farnham, UK: Ashgate.

Lorizzo, Loredana. 2006. "People and Practices in the Paintings Trade of Seventeenth-Century Rome." In *Mapping Markets for Paintings in Europe, 1450–1750,* edited by Neil De Marchi and Hans J. Van Miegroet, 343–62. Turnhout, Belg.: Brehols.

Lucco, Mauro. 2004. "Bellini and Flemish Painting." In *Cambridge Companion to Giovanni Bellini,* edited by Peter Humfrey. Cambridge: Cambridge University Press.

Lukehart, Peter. 2009. *The Accademia Seminars: The Accademia di San Luca in Rome, c. 1590–1635.* Washington, D.C.: National Gallery of Art.

——. 2018. "The Roman Connection: The Accademia di San Luca as an *Exemplum* for the Académie royale de peinture et de sculpture."

In *Accademia Artistiche tra eredità e dibattiti contemporanei, Conference Proceedings of the Académie de France à Rome-Accademia di Belle Arti-Accademia di San Luca,* edited by Jérome Delaplanche, Sarah E. Linford, and Francesco Moschini. Rome: Presses of the Accademia di San Luca.

Magurn, Ruth Saunders. 1991. *The Letters of Peter Paul Rubens.* Evanston, Ill.: Northwestern University Press.

Mainardi, Patricia. 1985. "The Political Origins of Modernism." *Art Journal* 45: 11–17.

——. 1987. *Art and Politics of the Second Empire: The Universal Expositions of 1855 and 1867.* New Haven: Yale University Press.

——. 1989. "The Double Exhibition in Nineteenth-Century France." *Art Journal* 48: 23–28.

——. 1993. *The End of the Salon: Art and the State in the Early Third Republic.* New York: Cambridge University Press.

Mancinelli, Fabrizio. 1997. "The Painting of the Last Judgment: History, Technique, and Restoration." In *Michelangelo—The Last Judgment: A Glorious Restoration,* edited by Loren Partridge, Gianluigi Colalucci, and Fabrizio Mancinelli, 155–86. New York: Abrams.

Mann, Judith Walker, Babette Bohn, and Carol Plazzotta. 2012. *Federico Barocci: Renaissance Master of Color and Line.* St. Louis: Saint Louis Art Museum.

Marandet, François. 2010. "A Preparatory Study for the Reception Piece of Jean-Baptiste Corneille." *Master Drawings* 48: 348–52.

Marciari, John. 2009. "Artistic Practice in Late Cinquecento Rome and Girolamo Muziano's Accademia di San Luca." In *The Accademia Seminars,* edited by Peter M. Lukehart, 197–223. New Haven: Yale University Press.

Marocchini, Bruno. 2008. "S. Pietro in Montoria a Roma: Sebastiano del Piombo e Michelangelo nella Cappella Borgherini." *Kermes: Arte e Tecnica del Restauro* 21, no. 70: 45–53.

Martin, Elisabeth, and Claudia Sindaco-Domas. 2010. "La technique picturale des peintures de fêtes galantes dans le context du XVIIIe siècle." *Techne* 30/31: 25–36.

Martin, Elisabeth, and Jean Paul Rioux. 2004. "Comments on the Technique and the Materials Used by Perugino, through the Study of a Few Paintings in French Collections." In *The Painting Technique of Pietro Vannucci, Called Il Perugino,* edited by Brunetto Giovanni Brunetti and Claudio Seccaroni, 43–56. Florence: Nardini.

Martin, John R. 1968. *The Ceiling Paintings for the Jesuit Church in Antwerp.* New York: Phaidon.

Maxon, John. 1973. *Paintings by Renoir.* Chicago: Art Institute of Chicago.

Mazzati, Tommaso. 2004. "Produzioni in serie, derivazioni e modelli: Perugino e la bottega di Andrea del Verrocchio." In *Perugino: Il divin pittore,* edited by Vittoria Garibaldi and Francesco Federico Mancini. Cinisello Balsamo, Italy: Silvana.

McTighe, Sheila. 2014. "Poussin's Practice: A New Plea for Poussin as a Painter." *Kermes: Arte e Tecnica del Restauro* 94/95: 11–15.

Merrill, Ross. 1981. "A Step Toward Revising Our Perception of Chardin." In *Preprints of Papers Presented at the Ninth Annual Meeting: Philadelphia, Pennsylvania, 27–31 May 1981,* 123–28. Washington, D.C.: American Institute for Conservation of Historic and Artistic Works.

Minor, Vernon Hyde. 1999. *Baroque and Rococo: Art and Culture.* New York: Abrams.

Mitchell, William John Thomas. 1994. *Landscape and Power.* Chicago: University of Chicago Press.

Moerenhout, Jacques-Antoine. 1993. *Travels to the Islands of the Pacific Ocean.* Lanham, Md.: University Press of America.

Molajoli, Bruno, Angelo Scattolin, and Pasquale Rotondi. 1970. *Palazzo Labia, oggi.* Torino: ERI.

Montagu, Jennifer. 1994. *The Expression of the Passions: The Origin and Influence of Charles Le Brun's Conférence sur L'expression Générale et Particulière.* New Haven: Yale University Press.

Montias, John. 1987. "Cost and Value in Seventeenth-Century Dutch Art." *Art History* 10: 455–66.

——. 1988. "Art Dealers in the Seventeenth Century Netherlands." *Simiolus* 18: 244–56.

——. 1991. "Works of Art in Seventeenth-Century Amsterdam: An Analysis of Subjects and Attributions." In *Art in History/History in Art: Studies in Seventeenth-Century Dutch Scales,* edited by David Freedberg and Jan de Vries. Santa Monica: Getty Center.

Mottin, Bruno, Eric Laval, and Élisabeth Martin. 2007. "Raphael's Paintings in French Museums: Some New Results from Recent Technical Investigations." In *Raphael's Painting Technique,* edited by Ashok Roy and Marika Spring, 13–24. Florence: Nardini.

Neidhardt, Uta. 2000. "Jan van Eyck's Dresden Triptych." In *Investigating Jan van Eyck,* edited by Susan Foister, Sue Jones, and Delphine Cool. Turnhout, Belg.: Brepols.

Nochlin, Linda. 1980. "Picasso's Color: Schemes and Gambits." *Art in America* 68, no. 10: 105–23; 177–83.

Noon, Patrick J., and Christopher Riopelle. 2015. *Delacroix and the Rise of Modern Art.* New Haven: Yale University Press.

North, Michael. 1997. *Art and Commerce in the Dutch Golden Age.* New Haven: Yale University Press.

Nuttall, Paula. 2004. *From Flanders to Florence: The Impact of Netherlandish Painting, 1400–1500.* New Haven: Yale University Press.

O'Brien, Patrick. 2001. *Urban Achievement in Early Modern Europe: Golden Ages in Antwerp, Amsterdam, and London.* New York: Cambridge University Press.

Oliver, Lois, Fiona Healy, Ashok Roy, and Rachel Billinge. 2005. "The Evolution of Rubens's Judgement of Paris (NG 194)." *National Gallery Technical Bulletin* 26: 4–22.

O'Malley, Michelle. 2005. *The Business of Art: Contracts and the Commissioning Process in Renaissance Italy.* New Haven: Yale University Press.

——. 2007. "Pietro Perugino and the Contingency of Value." In *The Material Renaissance,* edited by Michelle O'Malley and Evelyn Welch. Manchester: Manchester University Press.

——. 2013. *Painting under Pressure.* New Haven: Yale University Press.

Patry, Sylvie, Anne Robbins, Christopher Riopelle, Joseph J. Rishel, and Jennifer A. Thompson. 2015. *Inventing Impressionism: Paul Durand-Ruel and the Modern Art Market.* London: National Gallery.

Penny, Nicholas, Ashok Roy, and Marika Spring. 1996. "Veronese's Paintings in the National Gallery, Technique and Materials: Part II." *National Gallery Technical Bulletin* 17: 33–55.

Pevsner, Nikolaus. 1940. *Academies of Art, Past and Present.* Cambridge: Cambridge University Press.

Phipps, Elena. 2010. *Cochineal Red: The Art History of a Color.* New York: Metropolitan Museum of Art.

Pickeral, Tamsin, and Michael Robinson. 2005. *Turner, Whistler, Monet.* London: Flame Tree.

Pietrangeli, Carlo. 1994. "Introduction, An Account of the Restoration." In *The Sistine Chapel: A Glorious Restoration,* edited by Loren Partridge, Gianluigi Colalucci, and Fabrizio Mancinelli. New York: Abrams.

Pigments through the Ages. "Madder Lake." www.webexhibits .org.

Pigments through the Ages. "Ultramarine." www.webexhibits.org.

Piles, Roger de. 1708. *Cours de Peinture par Principes.* Paris: Jacques Estienne.

Piot, René. 1931. *Les Palettes de Delacroix.* Paris: Librairie de France.

Plax, Julie Anne. 2000. *Watteau and the Cultural Politics of Eighteenth-Century France.* London: Cambridge University Press.

Plender, Sophia, and Aviva Burnstock. 2014. "Technical Examination and Conservation of 'The Triumph of David' by Nicolas Poussin." *Kermes: Arte e Tecnica del Restauro* 94/95: 55–60.

Plesters, Joyce. 1983. "'Samson and Delilah': Rubens and the Art and Craft of Painting on Panel." *National Gallery Technical Bulletin* 7: 30–49.

Plesters, Joyce, and Lorenzo Lazzarini. 1978. "Preliminary Observations on the Technique and Materials of Tintoretto." In *Conservation and Restoration of Pictorial Art,* edited by Norman Bromelle and Perry Smith, 7–26. London: Butterworths.

Poldi, Gianluca, and Giovanni Carlo Federico Villa. 2011. "A New Examination of Giovanni Bellini's 'Pesaro Altarpiece': Recent Findings and Comparisons with Other Works by Bellini." In *Studying Old Master Paintings. Technology and Practice. The National Gallery Technical Bulletin 30th Anniversary Conference Postprints,* edited by Marika Spring, 28–36. London: Archetype.

Posner, Donald. 1959. "Charles Lebrun's Triumphs of Alexander." *Art Bulletin* 41: 237–48.

Prak, Maarten. 2003. "Guilds and the Development of the Art Market during the Dutch Golden Age." *Simiolus* 30: 236–51.

——. 2005. *The Dutch Republic in the Seventeenth Century: The Golden Age.* Cambridge: Cambridge University Press.

Puttfarken, Thomas. 1985. *Roger de Piles' Theory of Art.* New Haven: Yale University Press.

——. 1991. "The Dispute about Disegno and Colorito in Venice: Paolo Pino, Lodovico Dolce and Titian." In *Kunst und Kunsttheorie 1400–1900,* edited by Peter Ganz and Martin Gosebruch, 75–99. Wiesbaden, Ger.: Harrassowitz.

Reff, Theodore. 1960. "Cézanne and Poussin." *Journal of the Warburg and Courtauld Institutes* 23: 150–74.

——. 1976. *Degas, the Artist's Mind.* New York: Metropolitan Museum of Art.

Reiss, Sheryl. 2005. "From the Court of Urbino to the Curia and Rome: Raphael and His Patrons, 1500–1508." In *The Cambridge Companion to Raphael,* edited by Marcia B. Hall, 36–58. New York: Cambridge University Press.

Reissner, Elisabeth. 2008. "Ways of Making: Practice and Innovation in Cézanne's Paintings in the National Gallery." *National Gallery Technical Bulletin* 29: 4–30.

Rewald, John. 1946. *The History of Impressionism.* New York: Museum of Modern Art.

Rosand, David. 1969. "Rubens' Munich Lion Hunt: Its Sources and Significance." *Art Bulletin* 51: 29–40.

Rosenberg, Pierre. 1979. *Chardin, 1699–1779.* Paris: Ministère de la culture et de la communication, Réunion des musées nationaux.

——. 1984. *Vies anciennes de Watteau.* Paris: Hermann.

Rosenblum, Robert. 1967a. *Jean-Auguste-Dominique Ingres.* New York: Abrams.

——. 1967b. *Transformations in Late Eighteenth Century Art.* Princeton: Princeton University Press.

Roskill, Mark. 1968. *Dolce's "Aretino" and Venetian Art Theory of the Cinquecento.* New York: New York University Press.

Rossi-Manaresi, Raffaella. 1990. "A Technical Examination of Raphael's Santa Cecilia with Reference to the Transfiguration and the Madonna di Foligno." In *The Princeton Raphael Symposium,* edited by John Shearman and Marcia B. Hall, 125–34. Princeton: Princeton University Press.

Rowlands, Eliot. 1989. "Filippo Lippi and His Experience of Painting in the Veneto Region." *Artibus et Historiae* 10: 53–83.

Roy, Ashok. 1999. "The National Gallery Van Dycks: Technique and Development." *National Gallery Technical Bulletin* 20: 50–83.

——. 2000. "Van Eyck's Technique: The Myth and the Reality." In *Investigating Jan van Eyck,* edited by Susan Foister, Sue Jones, and Delphine Cool, 97–100. Turnhout, Belg.: Brepols.

——. 2003. "Perugino's Certosa di Pavia Altarpiece: New Technical Perspectives." In *The Painting Technique of Pietro Vannucci, called Il Perugino,* edited by Brunetto Giovanni Brunetti and Claudio Seccaroni, 13–20. Florence: Nardini.

——. 2007. "Monet's Palette in the Twentieth Century: 'Water-lilies' and 'Irises.'" *National Gallery Technical Bulletin* 28: 58–68.

Roy, Ashok, Rachel Billinge, and Christopher Riopelle. 2012. "Renoir's Umbrellas Unfurled Again." *National Gallery Technical Bulletin* 33: 73–81.

Roy, Ashok, Marika Spring, and Carol Plazzotta. 2004. "Raphael's Early Work in the National Gallery: Paintings before Rome." *National Gallery Technical Bulletin* 25: 4–35.

Rubin, Patricia Lee, and Alison Wright. 1999. *Renaissance Florence: The Art of the 1470s.* London: National Gallery.

Ruda, Jeffrey. 1984. "Flemish Painting and the Early Renaissance in Florence: Questions of Influence." *Zeitschrift für Kunstgeschichte* 47: 210–36.

Ruffini, Mario, and Gerhard Wolf. 2008. *Musica e Arti Figurative: Rinascimento e Novecento.* Venice: Marsilio.

Santopadre, Paola. 2012. "Il Polifemo di Sebastiano del Piombo e La Galatea di Raffaello: Nuove Acquisizioni Tecniche." *Bolletino ICR* 24–25: 15–25.

Sarrazin, Béatrice, Adeline Collange-Perugi, and Clémentine Gustin-Gomez. 2015. *Charles de La Fosse (1636–1716): Le triomphe de la couleur.* Paris: Somogy.

Saunders, David, Joyce H. Townsend, and Sally Woodcock. 2006. *The Object in Context: Crossing Conservation Boundaries; Contributions to the Munich Congress, 28 August–1 September 2006.* London: International Institute for Conservation of Historic and Artistic Works.

Sawyer, Carol, and Marcia Steele. 1999. "Poussin's 'Holy Family on the Steps': New Technical Discoveries, Comparisons, and the Washington Copy." *Cleveland Studies in the History of Art* 4: 112–60.

Schama, Simon. 1987. *The Embarrassment of Riches: An Interpretation of Dutch Culture in the Golden Age.* New York: Alfred A. Knopf.

Schick, Karin. 2012. *"No One Else Has These Colors"; Kirchner's Painting.* Ostfildern, Ger.: Hatje Cantz.

Schieder, Martin. 2006. "Between 'Grâce and Volupté': Boucher and Religious Painting." In *Rethinking Boucher,* edited by Melissa Hyde and Mark Ledbury. Los Angeles: Getty Research Institute.

Schnapper, Antoine. 1982. *David.* New York: Alpine Fine Arts Collection.

Settis, Salvatore. 1990. *Giorgione's Tempest: Interpreting the Hidden Subject.* Cambridge: Polity.

Shearman, John. 1986. "The Chapel of Sixtus IV: The Fresco Decoration of Sixtus IV: Raphael's Tapestries." In *The Sistine Chapel: The Art, the History, and the Restoration,* by Carlo Pietrangeli. New York: Harmony.

——. 1987. "Isochromatic Color Compositions in the Italian Renaissance." In *Color and Technique in Renaissance Painting,* edited by Marcia B. Hall. Locust Valley, N.Y.: J. J. Augustin.

——. 2003. *Raphael in Early Modern Sources (1483–1602).* New Haven: Yale University Press.

Shearman, John, and Marcia B. Hall. 1990. *The Princeton Raphael Symposium: Science in the Service of Art History.* Princeton: Princeton University Press.

Shelton, Andrew. 2000. "Ingres versus Delacroix." *Art History* 23: 726–42.

Shiff, Richard. 1984. *Cézanne and the End of Impressionism: A Study of the Theory, Technique, and Critical Evaluation of Modern Art.* Chicago: University of Chicago Press.

Short, Christopher. 2010. *The Art Theory of Wassily Kandinsky, 1909–1928: The Quest for Synthesis.* Oxford: Peter Lang.

Silver, Larry. 2006. *Peasant Scenes and Landscapes: The Rise of Pictorial Genres in the Antwerp Art Market.* Philadelphia: University of Pennsylvania Press.

Silverman, Debora. 2000. *Van Gogh and Gauguin: The Search for Sacred Art.* New York: Farrar, Straus and Giroux.

Skaug, Erling. 1983. "Punch Marks—What Are They Worth? Problems in Tuscan Workshop Relationships in the Mid-Fourteenth Century: The Ovile Master and Giovanni da Milano." In *La pittura nel XIV e XV secolo—il contributo dell'analisi tecnica della storia dell'arte,* edited by H. W. van Os and J. R. J. van Asperen de Boer, 253–82. Atti del XXIV congresso internazionale di storia dell'arte, 3. Bologna: CLUEB.

Slive, Seymour. 2001. *Jacob van Ruisdael: A Complete Catalogue of His Paintings, Drawings, and Etchings.* New Haven: Yale University Press.

Smithgall, Elsa. 2011. *Kandinsky and the Harmony of Silence: Painting with White Border.* New Haven: Yale University Press.

Smyth, Craig. 1979. "Venice and the Emergence of the High Renaissance in Florence: Observations and Questions." In *Florence and Venice: Comparison and Relations,* edited by Sergio Bertelli, Nicolai Rubinstein, and Craig Smyth. Florence: La Nuova Italia.

Sohm, Philip. 1991. *Pittoresco: Marco Boschini, His Critics, and Their Critiques of Painterly Brushwork in Seventeenth and Eighteenth Century Italy.* Cambridge: Cambridge University Press.

Spector, Jack J. 1974. *Delacroix: The Death of Sardanapalus.* New York: Viking.

Spring, Marika. 2007. "Raphael's Materials: Some New Discoveries and Their Context within Early Sixteenth-Century Painting." In *Raphael's Painting Technique,* edited by Ashok Roy and Marika Spring, 77–86. Florence: Nardini.

Spring, Marika, and Rachel Grout. 2002. "The Blackening of Vermilion: An Analytical Study of the Process in Paintings." *National Gallery Technical Bulletin* 23: 50–61.

Spring, Marika, Rachel Grout, and Raymond White. 2003. "'Black Earths': A Study of Unusual Black and Dark Grey Pigments Used by Artists in the Sixteenth Century." *National Gallery Technical Bulletin* 24: 6–114.

Stechow, Wolfgang. 1966. *Dutch Landscape Painting of the Seventeenth Century.* London: Phaidon.

Strehlke, Carl. 2007. "The Brancacci Style and the Carmine Style." In *The Brancacci Chapel: Form, Function and Setting: Acts of an International Conference, Florence, Villa I Tatti, June 6, 2003,* edited by Nicholas Eckstein. Florence: Olschki.

Strinati, Claudio, 2009. *Sebastiano del Piombo: 1485–1547.* Milan: Motta.

Stumpel, Jeroen. 1990. "The Province of Painting: Theories of Italian Renaissance Art." PhD diss., Rijksuniversiteit, Utrecht.

Sutton, Peter. 1987. *Masters of 17th-Century Dutch Landscape Painting.* Boston: Museum of Fine Arts.

Sutton, Peter, Marjorie E. Wieseman, and Nico van Hout. 2004. *Drawn by the Brush: Oil Sketches by Peter Paul Rubens.* New Haven: Yale University Press.

Talvacchia, Bette. 2005. "Raphael's Workshop and the Development of a Managerial Style." In *The Cambridge Companion to Raphael,* edited by Marcia B. Hall, 167–85. New York: Cambridge University Press.

———. 2007. *Raphael.* London: Phaidon.

Tardito, Rosalba. 1990. "La Scuola Grande di San Marco: Le pitture." In *Il Ritrovamento del Corpo di San Marco Del Tintoretto,* 9–18. Milan: Ministero per i Beni Culturali e Ambientali, Soprintendenza per i Beni Artistici e Storici Di Milano.

Taylor, Paul. 1992. "The Concept of Houding in Dutch Art Theory." *Journal of the Warburg and Courtauld Institutes* 55: 210–32.

Teyssedre, Bernard. 1957. *Roger de Piles et les debats sur le coloris au siecle de Louis XIV.* Paris: Bibliothèque des arts.

Thomas, Anabel. 1995. *The Painter's Practice in Renaissance Tuscany.* New York: Cambridge University Press.

Thomson, Richard, Susan Alyson Stein, Charlotte Hale, and Silvia A. Centeno. 2017. *Seurat's Circus Sideshow.* New York: Metropolitan Museum of Art.

Thuillier, Jacques, Barbara Brejon De Lavergnée, and Denis Lavalle. 1990. *Simon Vouet.* Paris: Éditions de la Réunion des Musees Nationaux.

Tongiorgi Tomasi, Lucia, and Gretchen A. Hirschauer. 2002. *The Flowering of Florence: Botanical Art for the Medici.* Washington, D.C.: National Gallery of Art.

Townsend, Joyce. 1993. *Turner's Painting Techniques.* London: Tate Gallery.

———. 2002. "The Materials Used by British Oil Painters throughout the Nineteenth Century." *Studies in Conservation* 47: supp.-1.

Tummers, Anna, and Koenraad Jonckheere. 2008. *Art Market and Connoisseurship: A Closer Look at Paintings by Rembrandt, Rubens and Their Contemporaries.* Amsterdam: Amsterdam University Press.

Van Gogh, Vincent. "Van Gogh's Letters." www.webexhibits.org.

Van Hout, Nico. 1998. "Meaning and Development of the Ground Layer in Seventeenth-Century Painting." *Leids Kunsthistorisch Jaarboek* 11: 199–225.

———. 2000. "Rubens and Dead Colouring: Some Remarks on Two Unfinished Paintings." In *Concept, Design and Execution in Flemish Painting (1550–1700), Rubenianum,* edited by Hans Vlieghe and Arnout Balis. Turnhout, Belg.: Brepols.

Vasari, Giorgio. 1960. *Vasari on Technique: Being the Introduction to the Three Arts of Design, Architecture, Sculpture and Painting, Prefixed to the Lives of the Most Excellent Painters, Sculptors, and Architects.* Edited by G. Baldwin Brown. Translated by Louisa S. Maclehose. New York: Dover.

———. 1963. *The Lives of the Painters, Sculptors and Architects.* Translated by A. B. Hinds. Introduction by William Gaunt. New York: Dutton.

Vermeylen, Filip. 2003. *Painting for the Market: Commercialization of Art in Antwerp's Golden Age.* Turnhout, Belg.: Brepols.

Vogelaar, Christiaan, Jan van Goyen, and Edwin Buijsen. 1996. *Jan van Goyen.* Leiden: Waanders.

Vogtherr, Christoph Martin, Monica Preti, and Guillaume Faroult. 2014. *Delicious Decadence: The Rediscovery of French Eighteenth-Century Painting in the Nineteenth Century.* Farnham, UK: Ashgate.

Volpin, Stefano, and Lorenzo Lazzarini. 1994. "Il colore e la tecnica pittorica della pala di San Giobbe di Giovanni Bellini." *Quaderni della Soprintendenza ai Beni Artistici e Storici di Venezia Ministero per i Beni Culturali e Ambientali* 19: 29–37.

Volpin, Stefano, and Roberto Sevanato. 1994. "Studio dei leganti pittorici della pala di San Giobbe Di Giovanni Bellini." *Quaderni della Soprintendenza ai Beni Artistici e Storici di Venezia Ministero per i Beni Culturali e Ambientali* 19: 39–43.

Walford, E. John. 1991. *Jacob van Ruisdael and the Perception of Landscape.* New Haven: Yale University Press.

Wallace, William. 2010. *Michelangelo: The Artist, the Man, and His Times.* New York: Cambridge University Press.

Walsh, John P. 2013. "The 'Tricky Business' of the Caillebotte Bequest." johnpwalshblog.com.

Welten, Ruud. 2015. "Paul Gauguin and the Complexity of the Primitivist Gaze." *Journal of Art Historiography* 12: 1–13.

Werth, Margaret. 1990. "Engendering Imaginary Modernism: Henri Matisse's 'Bonheur de vivre.'" *Genders* 9: 49–74.

Wetering, Ernst van de. 2009. *Rembrandt: The Painter at Work.* Amsterdam: Amsterdam University Press.

White, Harrison, and Cynthia White. 1965. *Canvases and Careers: Institutional Change in the French Painting World.* New York: Wiley.

White, Raymond. 2000. "Van Eyck's Technique: The Myth and the Reality II." In *Investigating Jan van Eyck,* edited by Susan Foister, Sue Jones, and Delphine Cool. Turnhout, Belg.: Brepols.

Williams, Robert. 1995. *The Vocation of the Artist as Seen by Giovanni Battista Armenini.* Oxford: Blackwell.

———. 1997. *Art, Theory, and Culture in Sixteenth-Century Italy: From Techne to Metatechne.* New York: Cambridge University Press.

Wilson, Jean C. 1998. *Painting in Bruges at the Close of the Middle Ages: Studies in Society and Visual Culture.* University Park: Pennsylvania State University Press.

Wrapson, Lucy, Jenny Rose, Rose Miller, and Spike Bucklow. 2012. "Further Observations on Corot's Late Painting Technique." In *In Artists' Footsteps: The Reconstruction of Pigments and Paintings, Studies in Honour of Renate Woudhuysen-Keller.* London: Archetype.

Wyld, Martin, John Mills, and Joyce Plesters. 1980. "Some Observations on Blanching (with Special Reference to the Paintings of Claude)." *National Gallery Technical Bulletin* 4: 49–63.

Zafran, Eric, and Sydney Resendez. 1998. *French Paintings in the Museum of Fine Arts, Boston.* Boston: Museum of Fine Arts.

Zhao, Y., R. S. Berns, L. A. Taplin, and J. Coddington. 2008. "An Investigation of Multispectral Imaging for the Mapping of Pigments in Paintings." *Proceedings SPIE, the International Society for Optical Engineering* 6810.

Zimmermann, Michael. 1991. *Seurat and the Art Theory of His Time.* Antwerp: Fonds Mercator.

Zuccari, Frank. 2006. "Seurat and the Making of *La Grande Jatte.*" *Postprints American Institute for Conservation of Historic and Artistic Works: Paintings Specialty Group* 18: 67–75.

Zuffi, Stefano. 1991. *Giotto.* Milan: Arnoldo Mondadori Arte.

cartoon: full, 35, 65; pieced (partial), 33, 45, 57; pricked (pounced), 26, 33, *64*, 260nn33–34, 260n42

Cassatt, Mary, 214

Castagno, Andrea del, 25–27, 32–33; *Resurrection (sinopia)*, 26, *26*; *Sant'Apollonia (Last Supper* and *Resurrection)*, *24*, 25, 26

Castiglione, Baldassare, 87, 145, 174

Cavazzini, Patrizia, 86

Cellini, Benvenuto: *Saltcellar*, 147

Cennini-style coloring, 19, 22–23

Cennini, Cennino, 5, 21, 27, 51, 68, 85, 202, 259n9, 259n6, 259n10, 260n28, 261n85. *See also* Cennini-style coloring

central point perspective. *See* perspective

Cézanne, Paul, 15, 198, 202–3, 210, 223–26; *Hillside in Provence*, 198, *200*, 225; *Mont Sant-Victoire*, *224*, 225

Champaigne, Philippe de, 93

Chardin, Jean-Baptiste-Siméon, 13, 163–67, 184; *The House of Cards*, 166, *166*; *Servant Returning from Market*, 165, *165*, 167

Chesneau, Ernest, 190, 269

chiaroscuro, 12; Leonardo da Vinci, 33, 34, 59, 66–70; lighting and coloring, 209–10; Roger de Piles, 156; Raphael, 70; Rembrandt, 106; Romano, 83–84; Rubens, 137; Sebastiano Sebastiano del Piombo, 73; Tiepolo, 169

cochineal. *See* pigments, red

Christus, Petrus, 36

chrome orange. *See* pigments, orange

chrome yellow. *See* pigments, yellow

chromophobia, 5

Cima da Conegliano, 88

cobalt violet. *See* pigments, purple

Cochin, Charles-Nicholas, 172–73, 175, 268n82

Colbert, Jean-Baptiste, 146–47, 148, 151–53, 184, 208

collectors, American, 226

Colleoni, Bartolomeo, 57

color, 176–77; anti-naturalism, 252; Kandinsky, 250–52; as symbolic, Le Brun, 154–55

color notations, 114

coloring mode, 5, 11–12, 73. *See also*

cangiantismo, chiaroscuro, sfumato, tenebrism, unione

colormen, 202

Concerning the Spiritual in Art. See Kandinsky, Vassily

conservation studies, 1–5, 262n6

continuous modeling, 210

contracts, 9, 17–19, 22, 55–56, 138

copies, 4, 9, 50, 112–16, 123–24, 141, 259n5, 261n90

copyright, 123

Corneille, Jean-Baptiste, 176, 267; *Hercules Punishing Busiris*, 147, *148*, 176

Corot, Jean-Baptiste-Camille, 194, 209; and the Barbizon School, 206–7; *Peasants Under the Trees at Dawn*, 207, *208*

Correggio, 60–62, 95, 262n7; *Madonna of the Basket*, 60, *62*; *Venus, Cupid, and Mercury*, 101, *102*

couleur rompue, 94–95, 130, 149. *See also* broken color

Courtier, The. See Castiglione, Baldassare

Count d'Angivillier, 173

Courbet, Gustave, 13, 208; *Burial at Ornans*, 13, *14*

Crow, Thomas, 181

Cubism, 223, 226, 247

da sua mano, 22

Dacos, Nicole, 86

Daniele da Volterra, 86

Daubigny, Charles-François, 194

David, Jacques-Louis, 13, 171, 173–74, 177–85, 190, 209; *Andromache Mourning Hector*, 180; *Antiochus and Stratonice*, 177, *177*; *Belisarius Begging for Alms*, 178, 179; *Combat between Minerva and Mars*, 177, *177*; *Death of Socrates*, 171, 181, *182*; *Intervention of the Sabine Women*, 183, *183*; *Oath of the Horatii*, 180, *180*, 181

de Hooch, Pieter: *The Bedroom*, 118, 119, 121

dealers, 12, 87, 106; guilds and, 114–15; nineteenth century, 207–8; Rococo, 159; twentieth century, 230, 269n57

decorum, 13, 23, 174–77

Degas, Edgar, 91–92, 197, 208, 214–17; *Dancers at the Barre*, 214, *215*; *In a*

Café (Absinthe Drinker), 215, *216*; *Women Ironing*, 217, *217*

Delacroix, Eugène, 156, 190, 191–96, 201, 208, 231, 268nn13–14, 268n16, 269n71; *Scenes from the Chios Massacres*, 191, *191*; *Death of Sardanapalus*, 192, *192*

Delaroche, Paul, 188–90, 191, 192, 200, 209, 268n2; *The Execution of Lady Jane Grey*, 188, *188*; *The Execution of Lady Jane Grey* (study), 189, *189*; *The Execution of Lady Jane Grey* (drawing), 189, *189*; *Hémicycle*, 189, *189*; *Joan of Arc in Prison Interrogated by the Bishop of Winchester*, 188, 192

Delécluze, Étienne-Jean, 179, 194–96

de Piles, Roger, 89, 92, 94, 153, 156–57, 159, 266n92

Derain, André, 243

di sotto in sù, 151, 168

Diderot, Denis, 159, 163–64, 179, 184, 268

Die Brücke, 247

disegno–colore debate, 153–56

Dolce, Ludovico, 154, 262–63

Donatello, 57

Dou, Gerard, 127

down modeling. *See* Alberti-style coloring

drawing, absence of preparatory: Caravaggio, 98–99; Chardin, 165–66; facture, 124; Gauguin, 235–36; Rembrandt, 129; Titian, 90

Drouais, François-Hubert, 160

Dunkerton, Jill, 68, 260–64

Durand-Ruel, Paul, 207–8, 217, 219, 223, 226, 269

Dürer, Albrecht, 37, 123

Dutch East India Company, 106, 196

Dutch Republic, 116, 117

ébauche, 194, 207. *See also* esquisse; modello; oil, sketch

education of the artist, 59–60, 84–87, 145–48, 187–88, 202

efficiency, 112–4

egg tempera, 21, 22, 37, 44, 260n18, 260n47, 261n74

El Greco, 97, 101, 264n78

emerald green. *See* pigments, green

en plein air, 206

esquisse, 194. See also ébauche; modello; oil, sketch

Expressionism, 250

Faret, Nicolas, 174

Fauvism, 231

Félibien, André, 94–95, 149

ferule. *See* brushes

Filarete, Antonio, 39

Flanders, 116, 123

Flemish oil technique, 9, 41, 49, 50

Flinck, Govert: *Portrait of Susanna van Baerle*, 111, *111*

Florence, 27, 39–48, 51, 54–55

Fouquet, Nicolas, 148

Fra Angelico, 22–23, 28, 32–33, 255; *Coronation of the Virgin*, 9, *10*, 15

Fragonard, Jean-Honoré, 164; *Happy Accidents of the Swing*, 172, *173*

freelance artists, 11, 55

fresco, 6, 25–27, 32, 65–66, 74, 168–69, 260n23, 260nn25–26, 35, 262nn11–12, 268n71; arriccio, 25, 26; mezzo fresco, 25

Gaehtgens, Thomas, 157

Gauguin, Paul, 5, 13, 15, 229, 230, 231, 231–36, 259n10, 270n6, 270n8, 270n10, 270n13, 271n29; *Day of the God (Mahana No Atua)*, 232, 233; Kirchner, 249; Matisse, 243, 244, 245; Picasso, 246; Seurat, 240, 242; *Spirit of the Dead Keeps Watch (Manaò Tupapaú)*, 235, *235*; *Tahitian Pastoral*, 234, *234*, 244, 245; Van Gogh, 236–40; *Vision after the Sermon (Jacob Wrestling with the Angel)*, 231, *232*; *Words of the Devil*, 235

Gautier, Théophile, 92, 188, 269n72

Gerard de Lairesse, 127, 265

Gérôme, Jean-Léon, 13

Gersaint, Edme-François, 157

gesso, 5, 17, 46–48, 88, 92, 261n73

Ghiberti, Lorenzo, 22

Ghirlandaio, Domenico, 33, 260n33; *Adoration of the Magi*, 34, *35*, 45, 55; *Adoration of the Shepherds*, 40; workshop and marketing, 54–55

gilding, 23, 28, 44

Giorgione, 101, 210–11, 244; Giorgione and Titian, *Pastoral Concert*, 210, *211*; *Sleeping Venus*, 244; *The Tempest*, 8, 11, 88

glazing: Antonio Filarete, 39;

and, *Stoning of Saint Stephen*, 70, *71*, 125; *Sala dei Giganti*, 84, *84*, 138
Rome, 74, 78–80, 85–87
Rosselli, Cosimo, 41, 45, 54
Rosso Fiorentino, 74–78, 90; *Dead Christ in the Tomb*, 75, *75*, 90, 272; *Deposition*, 75, *75*, 127; *Marriage of the Virgin*, 75
Rubens, Peter Paul, 135–41, 127, 266n80, 266n85, 266n89, 266n92, 267n40; *Arrival in Marseilles*, 138, *139*; *Arrival in Marseilles* (sketch), 138, *139*; dead coloring, 124–25; Delacroix, 193; disegno-colore, *Henry IV in the Battle of Paris*, 125, *125*; *Judgment of Paris*, 138, 140, *140*, 258 (x-ray), 156, *157*; *Judgment of Paris* (and workshop), *157*, *158*; *Last Supper*, 138, *138*; Le Brun, 150; *Life of Constantine*, 137; *Lion Hunt*, 141; marketing, 123–24; originality, 141–42, 95–96, 97; Poussinistes-Rubénistes, 153, 156; *Samson and Delilah*, 135, *136*; *Samson and Delilah* (sketch), 135, *137*; Tiepolo, 167–68; Watteau, 157–58, 161

Saint-Quentin, Jacques-Philip-Joseph de: *Death of Socrates*, 171, *172*, 176, 181
Sala di Costantino, 72–74, 84. *See also* Raphael, workshop
Salon des Refusés, 208–9, 213, 223
Salviati, Francesco, 78, 86; *Death of Saul*, *80*, 86; *Trumpeting Allegory*, *80*, 81
Sandrart, Joachim von, 121, 130
Sant'Apollonia, 25–26, 32
Santa Maria degli Angeli, 17
Sarto, Andrea del, 75, 179, 182, 263n35; *Sacrifice of Isaac*, 127, *127*
Savery, Roelandt, 116–17, 265n34; *Landscape with the Flight into Egypt*, 117, *117*, 132
Scuola di San Rocco, *98*, 159
Sebastiano del Piombo, 59, 65, 66–68, 72–74, 262n11, 262n18; *Flagellation*, 72, *73*; *Pietà*, 66, *66*; *Polyphemus*, 65; *Raising of Lazarus*, 66, *67*; *Salome with the Head of John the Baptist*, 66
secco, 25, 274
Seurat, Georges, 15, 231, 240–42;

Circus Sideshow, 241, *241*; *A Sunday on La Grand Jatte*, 240, *240*
sfumato: coloring modes, 59–60; Leonardo da Vinci, 33–34; Veronese, 95
Shearman, John, 21
Shiff, Richard, 18
Signac, Paul, 242
sinopia, 5, 25–26. *See also* fresco
Sisley, Alfred, 202, 208
Sistine Chapel: ceiling, 68–70, *69*; ceiling plaster, 65; cleaning, 1–2; response to, 77–78; sidewalls, 54
smalt. *See* pigments, blue
Smyth, Craig Hugh, 46
Snyders, Frans, 124
Société des Artistes Français, 226
Sodoma, 63
Some Thoughts Concerning Education (Locke), 166
speculation, 55, 106, 112, 115, 119
spolvero, 26, 33, 260
Stalbemt, Adriaen van: *Gallery Picture (The Sciences and the Arts)*, 115, *115*
Stanza della Segnatura, 63–66, *64*, 68, 174. *See also* Raphael
Stanza di Eliodoro, 66. *See also* Raphael
Steen, Jan, 119
stibnite. *See* pigments, gray
strappo, 25–26, 260. *See also* fresco

tache. *See* macchia
Tanguy, Julien, 203, 236
technical studies. *See* conservation studies
Technical Bulletin, National Gallery, 4
tempera grassa, 39–48, 50. *See also* oil
tenebrism, 103, 106
terra verde. *See* pigments, green
The Blue Rider, 250
Thoughts on the Imitation of Greek Works in Painting and Sculpture. See Winckelmann, Johannes Joachim
Tiepolo, Giovanni Battista, 167–69, 184, 168n70–71; *Allegory of the Planets and Continents*, 168, *170*; *America*, 169, *171*; *Crucifixion*, 168; *Institution of the Rosary*, 168; Würzburg Residenz *Ceiling*, 168, *169*
Tintoretto, 60, 97–101, 131, 189, 264nn77–79; *Crucifixion*, 97,

98; *Institution of the Eucharist*, 97, *98*; *Susanna and the Elders*, 97, *98*
Titian: aerial perspective, 127–29; *Bacchanal of the Andrians*, 88, 89, 101, 130, 154, 246; cartoons, 55; *Crucifixion*, 90, *90*; *Danaë and the Shower of Gold*, 89, *89*, 128, *129*; *Diana and Actaeon*, 163, *163*; disegno-colore debate, 154; *Entombment*, 93; Manet and, 211; and open brushwork, 87–91; *Pastoral Concert*, 210, 211, 244, 246; Poussin, 130, 135; and the Rococo, 163; Spain, 4; *Venus of Urbino*, 211, 263nn54–55, 263n59
tonal painters, 119
training of the artist. *See* education of the artist
Tummers, Anna, 141
Tura, Cosimo: *Allegory*, 36, *37*, 260n46
Turner, Joseph Mallord William, 190, 197–98, 201–6, 209, 218; *Decline of the Carthaginian Empire*, 204; *Departure of the Fleet*, 205–6, *206*; *The Exile and the Rock Limpet*, 204, *205*; *Peace. Burial at Sea*, 205; *Slave Ship*, 198, *203*

Uccello, Paolo, 32
ultramarine. *See* pigments, blue
underdrawing, 4, 33, 112–14; van Eyck, 37; Bellini, 49–51; Venetian painting, 88, 263n55
undermodeling, 33, 59, 124, 127
unione, 11–12, 60–63; Barocci, 97; Raphael, 70; Stanze frescos, 65–66, 262n1
up modeling. *See* Cennini-style coloring

Vaga, Perino del, 70, 74, 85, 86, 150; *Alexander Cutting the Gordion Knot*, 78, *79*, 138; *The Muses Erato and Thalia and the Blinding of Elymas*, 78, *79*, 139; *Nativity*, 74
vaghezza, 95
Valentin de Boulogne: *Last Supper*, 178, *179*
van Cleve, Joos, 112–14; *Reinhold Altarpiece*, 112, *113*, 114
van der Wetering, Ernst, 126, 265n45, 265n50, 265n52, 265n56, 265n58, 166n62–63

van der Weyden, Rogier, 36, 37
van Dyck, Anthony, 108, 109, 124, 265n46, 265n52
van Eyck, Jan, 37–39; *Annunciation*, 37, *38*; Florence, 36; *Saint Jerome in His Study*, 36, 260n49
van Gogh, Vincent, 236–40; *La Berceuse (The Lullaby)*, 236, *238*, 245; dealers, 208, 230; Gauguin, 233, 235; Tanguy, 203; Matisse, 242–43, 245; *The Night Café*, 236, *237*, 245; *Portrait of Père Tanguy*, 203, *203*; *Sower*, 236, *238*; *Starry Night*, 238, *239*, 270n8, 271n49
van Goyen, Jan, 106, 117, 119, 126–27, 265n31, 265n34; *View of Dordrecht*, 117, *118*, 121, 126; *View on the Oude Maas near Dordrecht*, 126, *126*
van Loo, Carle, 171
van Loo, Jacob, 111
van Mander, Karel, 129
van Ruisdael, Jacob, 119–20, 265n35; *Forest Scene*, 119, *120*
varnish, 2, 5, 271n49; Gauguin, 234; Munch, 249; Turner, 204
Vasari, Giorgio, 25, 33, 36, 45, 48–49, 260n23, 260n26, 262n1, 263n61, 266n61, 267n26; cangiantismo, 77–78; coloring, 137; composition, 129; Sebastiano del Piombo, 66; disegno, 154; marketing, 54–55; perspective, 127; status of the artist, 91, 101; training of the painter, 85; workshop management, 86, 87, 89, 90, 93
Velázquez, Diego: *Juan de Pareja*, 159
vendecolori, 19, 48
Veneziano, Domenico, 32, 260n26; *Saint Lucy Altarpiece*, 28, *30*
Venice, 48–51, 115, 167–69
verdaccio, 21. *See also* pigments
verdigris. *See* pigments, green
Vermeer, Jan, 12, 106, 119; *The Milkmaid*, 6, *7*, 15
vermilion. *See* pigments, red
Veronese, Paolo, 149; *Allegory of Love, Happy Union*, 56, 92, *93*, 168; and broken color, 91–95; *Dream of Saint Helena*, 92; *Feast in the House of Levi*, 91–92; *The Marriage at Cana*, 93; *Mars, Venus, and Cupid*, 92, *95*; *Mystical Marriage of Saint*